W9-AQG-431

5, 140n, 27C-78   LOG 10

THE IRWIN SERIES IN ECONOMICS

CONSULTING EDITOR

LLOYD G. REYNOLDS
YALE UNIVERSITY

BOOKS IN THE IRWIN SERIES IN ECONOMICS

Economic Theory in Retrospect

ECONOMIC THEORY
IN RETROSPECT

by

M. BLAUG
Assistant Professor of Economics
Yale University

1962

RICHARD D. IRWIN, INC.

HOMEWOOD, ILLINOIS

to my son,

DAVID RICARDO

Someone said: "The dead writers are remote from us because we know so much more than they did." Precisely, and they are that which we know.

T. S. ELIOT

We hold that for the mastery of a speculative and controversial science a certain multiplication of authorities is desirable. The false tendency of teachers to inculcate, and pupils to learn by rote, the very phrases and metaphors of a favourite author can only be corrected by dividing the allegiance of those who, like the Roman of old, "rush to slavery." Hence the history of theory is particularly instructive in political economy as in philosophy. History and literature, dialectics, and all that the Greeks comprehensively called 'words,' seem the best correction of the narrow prejudices and deceptive associations which are sure to be contracted by those who have been confined to a single school or system.

F. Y. EDGEWORTH

PREFACE

THIS BOOK is a study of the logical coherence and explanatory value of what has come to be known as orthodox economic theory. The history of this body of received doctrine goes back at least as far as Adam Smith. I am not concerned, however, with historical antecedents for their own sake. My purpose is to teach contemporary economic theory. But contemporary theory wears the scars of yesterday's problems now resolved, yesterday's blunders now corrected, and cannot be fully understood except as a legacy handed down from the past. It is for this reason that I have adopted a historical presentation. Nevertheless, the focus is on theoretical analysis, undiluted by entertaining historical digressions or biographical coloring.

Students are often told of the inspiration to be derived from the study of the history of economics. They are not so often reminded of the inspiration which the historian of economic thought derives from a study of contemporary economic theory. In truth, one should no more study modern price theory without knowing Adam Smith than one should read Adam Smith without having learned modern price theory. There is a mutual interaction between past and present economic thinking for, whether we set it down in so many words or not, the history of economic thought is being rewritten every generation.

The study of the history of economics must derive its *raison d'être* from the extent to which it encourages a student to become acquainted at first hand with some of the great works of the subject. It is for this reason that I have included Reader's Guides to the works of Smith, Ricardo, Mill, Marx, Marshall, Wicksteed, and Wicksell. The importance of reading original sources in a subject such as economics cannot be overemphasized. We must all have had the experience, after reading a commentary on some great book, of going back to the text itself and finding how much more there is in it than we had been led to expect. Commentaries are tidy and consistent, great books are not. This is why great books are worth reading.

I wish to express my gratitude to H. Barkai, B. Belassa, W. Fellner, T. W. Hutchison, R. L. Meek, and G. Shepherd who read parts of the manuscript and made many helpful suggestions. I am also grateful to my graduate students, too numerous to mention, who from time to time argued me off some of my pet hobbyhorses. Further, I must thank

Miss Margaret Lord for her stylistic improvements and Mrs. A. Granger for the efficient typing of the manuscript.

I am indebted to the following publishers for permission to quote from works published by them: Harper and Brothers—J. Viner, *Studies in the Theory of International Trade,* copyright 1937; University of Chicago Press—*Adam Smith, 1776–1926,* ed. J. M. Clark, and others, copyright 1928 by the University of Chicago, and G. J. Stigler, "The Development of Utility Theory, II," *Journal of Political Economy,* October, 1950; Harcourt, Brace and World—J. M. Keynes, *The Economic Consequences of the Peace,* copyright 1919; Review of Economic Studies—O. Lange, "Marxian Economics and Modern Economic Theory," *Review of Economic Studies,* June, 1935; The Macmillan Company—A. Marshall, *The Principles of Economics,* copyright 1930, and K. Wicksell, *Lectures in Political Economy,* copyright 1934; and Routledge and Kegan Paul—P. Wicksteed, *The Common Sense of Political Economy,* copyright 1934.

M. BLAUG

New Haven, Conn.
November, 1961

ABBREVIATIONS

AER	—	*American Economic Review*
BJPS	—	*British Journal for the Philosophy of Science*
CJEP	—	*Canadian Journal of Economics and Political Science*
DET	—	*The Development of Economic Thought,* ed. H. W. Spiegel (1952)
EA	—	*Economie Appliqué*
Ec	—	*Economica*
Ecom	—	*Econometrica*
EET	—	*Essays in Economic Theory,* ed. J. J. Spengler, W. R. Allen (1960)
EH	—	*Economic History*
EHR	—	*Economic History Review*
EJ	—	*Economic Journal*
ER	—	*Economic Record*
ESS	—	*Encyclopaedia of the Social Sciences*
ET	—	*Economisk Tidskrift*
IEP	—	*International Economic Papers*
JEH	—	*Journal of Economic History*
JHI	—	*Journal of the History of Ideas*
JPE	—	*Journal of Political Economy*
KYK	—	*Kyklos*
MeEc	—	*Metroeconomica*
MS	—	*Manchester School*
OEP	—	*Oxford Economic Papers*
PDPE	—	*Dictionary of Political Economy,* ed. R. I. Palgrave
PAPS	—	*Proceedings of the American Philosophical Society*
PS	—	*Population Studies*
QJE	—	*Quarterly Journal of Economics*
REA	—	*Readings in Economic Analysis,* II, ed. R. V. Clemence (1950)
REStud	—	*Review of Economic Studies*
REStat	—	*Review of Economics and Statistics*
SAJE	—	*South African Journal of Economics*
SEHR	—	*Scandinavian Economic History Review*
SJE	—	*Southern Journal of Economics*
SR	—	*Social Research*
SJPE	—	*Scottish Journal of Political Economy*
SZV	—	*Schweizerische Zeitschrift für Volkswirtschaft*
WA	—	*Weltwirtschaftliches Archiv*
WP	—	*World Politics*
ZN	—	*Zeitschrift für Nationalökonomie*

TABLE OF CONTENTS

xiii

Introduction | # HAS ECONOMIC THEORY PROGRESSED?

THIS IS a study of the theories of the past, not of theorists and their times. It concentrates on the theoretical analysis of leading economists, neglecting their lives, their own intellectual development, their precursors, and their propagators. Criticism implies standards of judgment and my standards are those of modern economic theory. This would hardly be worth saying were it not for the fact that some students of the history of economic thought have held out the prospect of judging a theory of the past on its own terms. Literally speaking, this is an impossible accomplishment. What they have meant to say, however, is that ideas should be weighed sympathetically in the context of their times, lest the history of economic thought degenerate into a boring exercise in omniscience. The danger of arrogance toward the writers of the past is certainly a real one—but so is ancestor worship. Indeed, there are always two sorts of dangers in evaluating the work of earlier writers: on the one hand, to see only their mistakes and defects without appreciating the limitations of the analysis they inherited and the period in which they wrote; and, on the other hand, to expand their merits in the eagerness to discover an idea in advance of their times, and frequently their own intentions. To put it somewhat differently: there is the anthropomorphic sin of judging older writers by the canons of modern theory, but there is also what Samuelson once called "the sophisticated-anthropomorphic sin of not recognizing the equivalent content in older writers; because they do not use the terminology and symbols of the present."

The conflict between those who regard earlier economic doctrine as consisting of little more than elementary blunders and fallacies and those who view it as the repository of a series of remarkable insights, goes deeper than economics. It is a fundamental division of attitude toward intellectual history as such. With a little training in German philosophy it is possible to represent the conflict in terms of two polar

1

opposites: relativism and absolutism. The relativist regards every single theory put forward in the past as an expression and reflection of contemporary conditions, each theory being in principle equally justified; the absolutist has eyes only for the strictly intellectual development of the subject regarded as a steady progression from error to truth. Now, of course, few people have ever held either of these positions in its extreme form, but almost every commentator on the history of economic thought can be placed well toward right or left of center on what is in fact a continuum.

Each of the two positions is capable of further subdivision. One version of the relativist position, for example, is that the ideas of economists are nothing more than the rationalizations of class or group interests, or, to go one step further, the motivated pleadings of people with a political axe to grind. This is the doctrine of "ideology" or "false consciousness" which in its Marxist form is forever equating ideological bias with apologetic intent, though the two are by no means equivalent. E. Roll's *History of Economic Thought* (1939) exemplifies this approach despite the fact that the author only claims that changes in the economic structure and institutions are "major influences"—a question-begging phrase!—on economic thinking. Relativism is driven to extremes in W. Stark's *History of Economics in Its Relation to Social Development* (1944) which views theories as little more than a mirror reflection of the contemporary world; we are asked to believe, to open the book at random, that Ricardo was justified in accepting the labor theory of value in 1817 because fixed capital was little used at the time, but when he qualified the theory three years later he simply "yielded to the victorious march of mechanization."[1] A singularly untenable version of the relativist interpretation is to be found in L. Rogin's posthumous study *The Meaning and Validity of Economic Theory* (1956). In appraising the validity of an economic theory the relativist is likely to ignore its internal coherence and explanatory scope and to fix his attention solely upon its congruence with the historical and political currents of the time. But Rogin goes further and argues that the objective meaning of a particular economic theory lies in its practical policy recommendations; what is worse, he does not seem to mean by this the logical implications of the theory for policy as that theory was understood at the time, but the policy implications as they appear to a twentieth century theorist writing under the influence of the Great Depression. The trouble with the general thesis, however, is that economic

[1] Stark's recent book *The Sociology of Knowledge* (1959), a really stimulating work, suggests he no longer adheres to this extreme position.

theories are seldom devised to reach specific policy conclusions: time and time again, economists have recommended diametrically opposed policies while appealing to the same theory for authority.

In its moderate versions the relativist interpretation may result in a really valuable fusion of the history of economic thought with the history of political and moral philosophy against the background of economic and political history. One of the best examples of this broad approach is W. C. Mitchell's *Lectures: Notes on Types of Economic Theory* (1949) which deliberately plays down "the passing of ideas from one to another and the development of these ideas by successive generations as an intellectual stunt." The same viewpoint is upheld in A. Gray's delightful introductory survey, *The Development of Economic Doctrine* (1931): "Economic science, if it be a science, differs from other sciences in this, that there is no inevitable advance from less to greater certainty; there is no ruthless tracking down of truth which, once unbared, shall be truth to all times to the complete confusion of any contrary doctrine." A glance at the latter portions of Mitchell's or Gray's book, dealing with the period after 1870, shows immediately what is wrong with the argument. Economics became an academic subject in the 1880's and, for the first time perhaps, "the passing on of ideas from one generation to another" thoroughly dominated the development of the subject. No relativist has been able to carry the institutional or historical interpretation beyond the classical era and so, like Mitchell and Gray, they either neglect the modern period, or like Roll and Rogin, shift grounds in their treatment of economic ideas after 1870.

Speaking generally, it is really absurd to think that economic and social history alone can furnish the key to intellectual variations in a discipline like economics. Many relativists claim only that economists write always *sub specie temporis* and that a knowledge of the prevailing historical circumstance "illuminates" the theories of the past. This is obviously true but one wonders why it is necessary to argue this so insistently unless it is subtly designed to make us forget that ideas have a momentum of their own. As Jacob Viner observed, relativism frequently amounts to a kind of whitewashing with historical necessity:

The economic historians seem to derive from their valid doctrine, that if sufficient information were available the prevalence in any period of a particular theory could be *explained* in the light of the circumstances then prevailing, the curious corollary that they can also be *justified* by appeal to these special circumstances. There are some obvious obstacles to acceptance of this point of view. It would lead to the conclusion that no age, except apparently the present one, is capable of serious doctrinal error. It overlooks the fact that one of the historical circumstances which has been undergoing an evolution has been the capacity for economic analysis.

No assumptions about economic behavior are absolutely true and no theoretical conclusions are valid for all times and places, but would anyone seriously deny that in the matter of tools and analytical constructs there has been progress in economics? Adam Smith, for example, had a glimpse of the manner in which the market mechanism co-ordinates the independent decisions of buyers and sellers with maximum result and at minimum cost, but anything so fundamental as the functional relationship of demand and price escaped him. It never occurred to him that it was possible to demonstrate precisely in what sense a decentralized economy produces optimum results, and it took a hundred years before Walras, Marshall, Pigou, and Pareto worked out the logic of Smith's convictions about the workings of "the invisible hand." Thoughts such as these produce the absolutist who, looking down from present heights at the errors of the ancients, cannot help but conclude that truth is concentrated in the marginal increment to economic knowledge.

It is very likely that absolutists are created by their reading of too many relativists. It is difficult nowadays to appreciate how fresh was Cannan's iconoclastic approach in his famous book *The History of the Theories of Production and Distribution* (1893) to a generation nurtured on the relativist texts of Blanqui, Roscher, Ingram, and Cossa. But recognizing that economic theory has indeed progressed should not be allowed to obscure the highly uneven rate of improvement which has typified the history of analytical progress in economics. General insights into the pure logic of the price system make their appearance embedded in a particular theoretical framework associated with conditions and problems peculiar to the times. As the body of ideas gives way under criticism, much of what is still valuable gets discarded in the enthusiasm over the latest novelty. As a result, the history of economics is not so much the chronicle of a continuous accumulation of theoretical achievements as the story of exaggerated intellectual revolutions, in which truths already known are neglected in favor of new revelations. Indeed, sometimes it seems as if economics has been propelled forward by a sense of symmetry which demands that every new theory should always be the exact reverse of the old.

In the first half of the nineteenth century economics itself was regarded as an investigation of "the nature and causes of the wealth of nations," "the laws which regulate the distribution of the produce of the earth," or simply "the laws of motion of capitalism." After 1870, however, it came to be regarded as a science that analyzed "human behavior as a relationship between given ends and scarce means which have alternative uses"—a definition which, if taken strictly, would exclude much of what had gone before as being economics. After two centuries of being concerned with the growth of resources and the rise of wants it became largely a study of the problem of efficient allocation of resources given once and for all.

Classical economic theory was almost wholly macroeconomics; neoclassical theory was nothing but microeconomics. It is doubtful whether such dramatic shifts in the focus of attention can be explained solely in terms of intellectual forces. In the final analysis, even pure economic theory is framed for the purpose of throwing light upon the actual workings of the economic system. A change of emphasis as drastic as "the marginal revolution" must surely have been associated with changes in the institutional structure of society and with the emergence of new practical problems.

One possibility, which many relativists have urged, is that such shifts in emphasis within economics are due to changes in philosophical attitudes. It was in opposition to this interpretation that Schumpeter insisted upon the strictly autonomous nature of scientific economics. The political preference and philosophical value judgments of economists impinge upon the development of economics, he declared, but leave it fundamentally unaffected: "economic analysis has not been shaped at any time by the philosophical opinions that economists happen to have." This piece of dogmatic "positivism," put forward in the introduction to his erudite *History of Economic Analysis* (1954), is not in fact sustained in the body of the text, half of which is given over to narrative history, political theory, and philosophical climates of opinion, presumably because of their relevance to economic theory. Upon close inspection it turns out that Schumpeter did not mean that economic analysis is logically independent of philosophy but rather that the philosophical beliefs of economists are not relevant to its validity. The latter point is only too well taken. Witness the numerous pseudo-explanations that treat the history of economic thought in terms of a struggle between contending philosophical principles: "individualism" versus "universalism"—O. Spann, *The History of Economics* (1930); the biological view of the economic system as an organism versus the mechanical view of the system as a machine—E. Heimann, *History of Economic Doctrines* (1945); or, for that matter, there is G. Myrdal's brilliant *Political Element in the Development of Eco-*

nomic Thought (1953), which pursues the chimera of *wertfrei* theory and deprecates every analytical insight found to be associated with philosophical or political preconceptions.

Indeed, why stop at philosophical or political bias? W. Weiskopf in a recent book, *The Psychology of Economics* (1955), gets the great economists to lie down on the couch, discovering, for example, a new significance in Petty's famous remark that "land is the mother and labor the father of value." For Ricardo and Malthus the fecundity of the human female and the niggardliness of Mother Earth are the roots of all economic ills, while the only source of value is the "male" factor of labor. But this is just how we would expect people to think in a patriarchal civilization, the author concludes triumphantly. Certainly it is conceivable that a knowledge of the psychological quirks of great economists might throw some light on their theories, but to infer the theories from the psychological association of words is to ignore the systematic character and empirical content of economic analysis.

Economic theory, even in its purest form, has implications for policy and in that sense makes political propaganda of one kind or another. This element of propaganda is inherent in the subject and, even when a thinker studiously maintains a sense of olympian detachment, philosophical and political preferences enter at the very beginning in forming his "vision," the preanalytical act of selecting certain features of reality for examination. The problem is not that of denying the propaganda which is always there, but that of separating the scientific ideas from the ideology in which they are embedded and to submit these ideas to scientific tests of validity. Moreover, propaganda is not the same thing as lying: to say that Karl Marx wanted to discredit capitalism and began with preconceptions about its defects is not to imply that his analysis is for that reason worthless. Political prejudices may even assist scientific analysis: a critic of capitalism is likely to pay more attention to the real blemishes of the system.

It is surely no accident that Marx's comments on the business cycle were fifty years ahead of his time. The task of the historian of economic thought is to show how definite preconceptions lead to definite kinds of analysis and then to ask whether the analysis stands up when it is freed from its ideological foundation. It is doubtful whether Ricardo would have developed his theory of international trade without a strong animus against the landed classes; but this theory survives the removal of his prejudices. When it came to proving that landlords would have no interest in making agricultural improvements, however, ideological bias prevented him from arriving at the correct result, correct, that is, in terms of his own assumptions. The history of economic thought is full of such examples and nothing is gained by laying down flat generalizations about the relationship between the value judgments of individual economists and the quality of their theoretical work. Propaganda and ideology are always there, but so is the discipline exerted by rules of scientific procedure built into economics by generations of practitioners: economics is forever catching up with the biases of yesterday.

Has there been progress in economic theory? Clearly, the answer is yes: analytical tools have been continuously improved and augmented; empirical data have been increasingly marshaled to verify economic hypotheses; extrascientific biases have been repeatedly exposed and separated from the core of testable propositions which they enmesh; the operations of the economic system are better understood than ever before. And yet the relativists do have a point. Economic thought has not taken the form of a linear progression towards absolute truth. It has progressed despite the detours conditioned by the exigencies of time and place. Whether we adopt a relativist or absolutist interpretation, therefore, depends entirely upon the questions that one is raising. If a commentator is interested in explaining why certain people held certain ideas at certain times, he must look outside the sphere of intellectual debate for a complete answer. But if he wants to know why some economists in the past held a labor theory of value while others taught that value is determined by utility, and this not only at the same time and in the same country, but also in different countries generations apart, he is forced to concentrate on the internal logic of theory.

If, in the chapters that follow, there is little about *Zeitgeist,* social milieu, economic institutions, and philosophical movements, it is not because these things are unimportant but because they fall outside the scope of our inquiry. What do economists know? How much does economics explain? What are the principles upon which economic theories have been accepted or rejected? What features have characterized endurable economic ideas? These are the questions to which this book is addressed.

Chapter 1   PRE-ADAMITE ECONOMICS

1. MERCANTILISM

THE TERM "mercantilism" first acquired significance at the hands of
Adam Smith. "The different progress of opulence in different ages and
nations has given occasion to two different systems of political economy,
with regard to enriching the people," he noted: "the system of commerce" or "mercantile system" and "the system of agriculture." These
two systems, however, were not quite on the same footing. Quesnay
and his band of disciples, whom posterity has agreed to call the Physiocrats—*les économistes* was their own designation—presented a common front and formed a definite school of opinion. But the English
pamphlet writers of the seventeenth and eighteenth centuries showed
no awareness of contributing to any definite stream of ideas, much less
to a tradition Adam Smith attacked under the rubric of mercantilism.
They had neither agreed principles nor common analytical tools. Nevertheless, throughout the three hundred years of unco-ordinated intellectual effort, full of controversy and reflecting a great variety of practical circumstances, certain doctrinal threads appear again and again. It is
these threads that we knit together into something called "mercantilism," thereby imposing a far greater sense of unity and logical coherence upon the literature than it in fact possessed. In recent times, mercantilism, as a label for a phase in the history of economic policy, has
been called a "cumbersome portmanteau," "a red-herring of histori-
ography," and "a gigantic theoretical balloon." But as a description of
a central tendency in economic thought from the close of the sixteenth
to the middle of the eighteenth century the label retains general validity. Certainly, for our purposes there is great convenience in looking
comprehensively at the predecessors of Adam Smith, much in the same
way as he did.

8

The Balance-of-Trade Doctrine. The leading features of the mercantilist outlook are well known: bullion and treasure as the essence of wealth; regulation of foreign trade to produce specie inflow; promotion of industry by inducing cheap raw-material imports; protective duties on imported manufactured goods; encouragement of exports, particularly finished goods; and an emphasis upon increasing population and low wages. The core of it, of course, is the doctrine that a favorable balance of trade is desirable because it is somehow productive of national prosperity. The question that immediately arises is how such a notion ever came to be held. Adam Smith gave the first and still the simplest answer: mercantilism is nothing but a tissue of protectionist fallacies foisted upon a venal Parliament by "our merchants and manufacturers," grounded upon "the popular notion that wealth consists in money." As must an individual, a country must spend less than its income so that its wealth will increase. What tangible form does this surplus take? The mercantilist authors identified it with the acquisition of hard money or "treasure"; money was identified with capital, and the favorable balance of trade with the annual balance of income over consumption. This is the gist of Adam Smith's critique of mercantilism.

Since his day commentators have never ceased to debate this question. Did the mercantilists really identify money and capital, or, to use the old-fashioned words, bullion and wealth? Considering the extraordinary looseness with which writers in those days used such common, everyday words, it is hardly surprising that the literature admits of more than one interpretation. "Some of the best English writers on commerce," Smith conceded, citing Thomas Mun and John Locke, do warn their readers of the folly of thinking that wealth consists of specie instead of the things that specie buys, but "in the course of their reasonings, the lands, houses, and consumable goods seem to slip out of their memory, and the strain of their argument frequently supposes that all wealth consists of gold and silver." In estimating the value of property in England at the close of the seventeenth century, William Petty concluded that the amount of money was less than 3 per cent of the total, and in his *Taxes and Contributions* (1662) he opposed the indefinite accumulation of bullion by appealing to what we call the "needs-of-trade doctrine" of the quantity of money: "There is a certain measure and due proportion requisite to drive the trade of a Nation, more or less than which would prejudice the same." Nevertheless, this did not stop later writers from making the quantity of money synonymous with national wealth or from calling for a permanently favorable balance of trade.

It is easy to cite moderate mercantilists who did not identify money with capital and who followed Aristotle in emphasizing the purely conventional nature of money, but it is also true that almost all mercantilist writers entertained the illusion that money is somehow *nervi rerum.* Money is "the life of commerce," "the vital spirit of trade," "like muck," as Bacon put it, "not good except it be spread." Such anthropomorphic language found its rationalization in the eighteenth-century doctrine that "money stimulates trade," but it was current for centuries without any apparent theoretical justification. In the final analysis, it is pointless to argue the question because the absence of a professional jargon in the literature of the day makes it almost impossible to distinguish between the axiomatic identification of money and wealth and the loose suggestion that an increase of one causes an increase of the other.

The Specie-Flow Mechanism. If mercantilism in its more sophisticated formulations does not involve the identification of money with capital, why the universal concern over a favorable balance of trade? What advantages was an excess of exports over imports supposed to confer upon a country? Once again, the lack of a common terminology and the preanalytic character of the literature makes it difficult to know what was meant when a writer gave expression to the desirability of an export surplus. Does it imply something as silly as that a favorable balance of trade is the only source of wealth for a nation, or that it is the sole advantage a nation derives from foreign trade, or is it merely a way of speaking to justify measures which are regarded as advantageous on other grounds? Whatever the precise interpretation, the idea that an export surplus is the index of economic welfare may be described as the basic fallacy that runs through the whole of the mercantilist literature. The title of Thomas Mun's book puts it nicely: *England's Treasure by Forraign Trade, or the Ballance, of our Forraign Trade Is the Rule of Our Treasure* (1664). But even this has been denied. One student of English mercantilism, E. A. J. Johnson, declared that "the ultimate concern of the mercantilists was the creation of effective factors of production. Not ten per cent of English mercantilist literature is devoted to the ill-fated doctrine of the balance of trade." To which J. Viner has retorted that "on the basis of my turning of the pages of English mercantilist literature I venture the conclusion that not ten per cent of it was free from concern, expressed or clearly implied, in the state of the balance of trade and in the means whereby it could be improved." It is, of course, no fallacy to be concerned with the balance of trade. What distinguishes mercantilist theory is a fixation on the balance of trade and the desire to maintain an imbalance even in the long run.

The balance of *payments* must always be balanced, for it is merely a bookkeeping identity of credits and debits. But the balance of trade of commodity exports and imports need not be in balance. A country earns foreign exchange by either (1) visible commodity exports, (2) invisible exports of services, (3) export of precious metals, or (4) *im*ports of capital, either in the form of investments or in the form of loans granted by foreigners. A country spends foreign exchange by (1) visible imports, (2) invisible imports, (3) imports of gold and silver, and (4) *ex*ports of capital in the general form of acquiring claims on foreigners. The four items always balance because, if the first three do not, the difference appears as a capital export or import. When mercantilist authors speak of a surplus in the balance of trade, they mean an excess of exports, both visible and invisible, over imports, calling either for an inflow of gold or for the acquisition of credits from foreign countries (capital exports).

The classical economists never doubted that the arguments of their predecessors in favor of a chronic export surplus were based, from start to finish, on an intellectual confusion. Whatever the mercantilists hoped to achieve with a favorable balance of trade was bound to be short lived. Thomas Mun, writing as early as 1630, had realized that an inflow of bullion raises domestic prices and that "selling dear and buying cheap" tends to turn the balance of trade against a country. It was only the failure of later writers to take this into account that made the Cantillon-Hume statement of the specie-flow mechanism in the eighteenth century appear as a refutation of mercantilist principles. Purely automatic forces, the argument ran, tend to establish a "natural distribution of specie" between the trading countries of the world and such levels of domestic prices that each country's exports equal imports. Any additional mining of gold in one country will raise its price level relative to those of other countries; the resulting import surplus must be financed by a specie outflow; this engenders the same reaction in the gold-receiving country, and the process continues until all trading nations have established a new equilibrium between exports and imports corresponding to the higher supply of gold. Since external trade and gold are akin to water in two connected vessels, constantly seeking a common level, a policy aiming at a favorable balance of trade is simply self-defeating.

All the elements forming such a theory of the self-regulatory mechanism of specie distribution were already at hand in the seventeenth century. Thomas Mun had shown that any net deficit or surplus in the balance on current account, the visible plus invisible items, must be paid in specie and that the volume of exports and imports depends upon relative price levels in different countries. John Locke, writing in the 1690's, made it perfectly clear that the quantity of money in circulation is a determinant of the price level. All that was required was to put these ideas together and it would follow that concern over the long-run state of the balance of trade was unnecessary. Although Adam Smith does not refer to the specie-flow mechanism in *The Wealth of Nations*—one of the great mysteries of the history of economic thought, as Viner observes, because he had discussed it in his earlier *Lectures*—it is this kind of reasoning that prompted the classical economists to dismiss the writings of the mercantilists as confused and self-contradictory.

They might have added that the hearty protectionist sentiments of the time caused many mercantilist writers to employ the balance-of-work argument in favor of import restrictions without any reference to the balance of trade, or else invoking the latter only to reinforce the former. For it was widely held that imports should consist of raw materials, semifabricated goods, and exports of finished goods on the grounds that a net outflow of labor services sustains domestic employment and increases "foreign-paid incomes." To this familiar protectionist argument were added the military, the strategic, and the infant-industry argument. To an age that had discovered the Law of Comparative Cost as well as the Automatic Specie-Flow Mechanism, this seemed like error compounded upon error.

The Defense of Mercantilism. The stern condemnation visited upon mercantilist errors by classical theory went unchallenged for a hundred years. The relativist interpretation had to wait upon the revival of protectionism in Europe and the rise of the German Historical School. First, Roscher, Schmoller, and then their English disciples, Cunningham and Ashley, rose to defend mercantilist policies as perfectly rational, meaning that they were appropriate in promoting certain desired ends; the ends were national autarchy and the expansion of state power, and these too were now regarded as reasonable in and for their time. This interpretation came to be widely accepted by economic historians. When Adam Smith at one point commented carelessly that "defence is more important than opulence," he was stating a position that mercantilist writers are said to have held seriously. This viewpoint helps to throw light on one of the central beliefs of the mercantilist age. The goal of state-building can be achieved just as well, if not better, by weakening the economic powers of neighbors as by strengthening one's own. As Locke expressed it, "riches" means, not just more gold and silver, but more in proportion to other countries. Indeed, most mercantilist writers subscribed to the view that the economic interests of nations are mutually antagonistic, as if there were a fixed quantity of resources in the world that one country could acquire only at the expense of another. This explains why the mercantilists were not embarrassed to advocate beggar-my-neighbor policies or to deprecate domestic consumption.

But, even if we grant that state power was the sole end of mercantilist policies, with wealth valued solely as a means thereto—an interpretation that Viner has called into question—little has been said to remove the stigma of intellectual error in mercantilist theory. For a full-blown defense we must go to Keynes's provocative "Notes on Mercantilism" in *The General Theory* (1936). As soon as it is realized that an economic system does not automatically tend toward a state of full employment, Keynes argued, the whole of the classical case against protectionist policies, based upon the advantages of the international division of labor, loses much of its force: "As a contribution to statecraft, which is concerned with the economic system as a whole and with securing the optimum employment of the system's entire resources, the methods of the early pioneers of economic thinking in the sixteenth and seventeenth centuries may have attained to fragments of practical wisdom which the unrealistic abstractions of Ricardo first forgot and then obliterated." The preoccupation of the mercantilists with gold inflows was no "puerile obsession" but an intuitive recognition of the connection between plenty of money and low interest rates. There has been a "chronic tendency throughout human history for the propensity to save to be stronger than the inducement to invest," and the mercantilists must be praised for recognizing that the weakness of the inducement to invest is the key to the economic problem. In a society in which direct public investment or monetary policy is out of the question, the best that could be done was to encourage inflation through a favorable balance of trade: the export surplus would serve to keep up prices and the inflow of gold would lower interest rates, stimulating investment and employment by boosting the money supply. This, Keynes felt, was "the element of scientific truth in mercantilist doctrine."

Precursors of Keynes? No doubt the English economists of the seventeenth and eighteenth centuries often sound like precursors of

Keynes. They railed against "locking up money," converting it into "dead stock"; they urged spending on luxury goods and proposed public works programs to relieve "supernumeraries"; and the frequency with which statements concerning the desirability of bullion were associated with a belief in its employment-producing effect is indeed striking. But this is not to say that the writers of the period had a pre-Keynesian appreciation of the problem of aggregate effective demand. Keynes's defense of mercantilism seems to rest in part on the notion that a permanently favorable balance of trade involves the export of capital, thus absorbing excess savings at home. But foreign investment plays no role in mercantilist analysis, and there are no instances of arguments in favor of permanent foreign investment before James Steuart, writing in the 1760's. The basic flaw in Keynes's interpretation, however, as Heckscher points out in his critique of Keynes's "Notes," is the belief that unemployment in the mercantilist era was similar in character to technological and cyclical unemployment recurrent in industrialized economies. Unemployment caused by a fall in fixed investment was virtually unknown before the Industrial Revolution. In seventeenth-century England, a predominantly rural economy, most unemployment was due to the seasonality of agriculture or the incidence of poor harvests. Even in industry, much unemployment was seasonal, as winter ice or spring floods interrupted the functioning of the water-powered mills. A trade crisis might produce cyclical unemployment that called for special remedial measures, but the kind of unemployment that attracted most attention was voluntary unemployment in the sense of a sheer disinclination to work or a marked preference for leisure instead of higher earnings: not involuntary unemployment but "an idle and debauched populace" was the problem.

This brings up a distinction that will recur again in the course of our analysis: the distinction between what, for obvious reasons, has been called Keynesian and Marxian unemployment. Keynesian unemployment denotes a situation in which the flow of investment is insufficient to mop up the savings that would be forthcoming at full-employment levels of income. Because of relative overabundance of capital, rates of return are too low to call forth the investment required to produce full employment. Marxian unemployment, on the other hand, is the result of scarcity of capital relative to the labor supply: inappropriate resource endowments and the limited technical possibilities of substituting labor for capital make it impossible to absorb idle labor even when the capital stock is used to capacity. Marxian unemployment is the result either of excessive population growth or of income levels too low to produce an adequate flow of savings. Too little thrift, not insufficient effective demand, impedes the expansion of output. Unemployment is a structural, not a cyclical, problem and for that reason public investment or expansionary monetary policy, so effective in curing Keynesian unemployment, will merely produce inflation without leading to full employment. The symptom is the same in either case, but the successful cure is not, for the nature of the illness is quite different. It follows that the analogy to the problem of unemployment as it appears in the mercantilist literature is not underemployment in a mature capitalist economy but unemployment in the now overpopulated underdeveloped countries of Asia and Africa. Keynes's interpretation of mercantilism is merely another example of his penchant to appraise all previous theories in terms of his own and to generalize the problems of his own day and age throughout human history.

When writers in the seventeenth and eighteenth centuries praised luxury spending on the part of the rich, their rationale was the belief that "high living" on the part of the well-to-do generates wants and stimulates pecuniary incentives all round. An underdeveloped economy with rudimentary markets is very likely, as we know from modern experience, to develop the idea that the upper classes have an obligation to provide work by maintaining a large retinue of "menial servants." Dr. Johnson expressed orthodox eighteenth-century opinion when he told Boswell: "You cannot spend money in luxury without doing good to the poor. Nay, you do more good by spending it in luxury than by giving it; for by spending it you make them exert industry, whereas by giving it you keep them idle." As for approval of public works, that was frequently based on nothing more than the typical mercantilist belief in the magical efficacy of state action simply because it is action undertaken in the public interest. Sometimes a trade depression caused a contemporary writer to advocate public works, and, in the careless manner of the day, a recommendation designed to alleviate an immediate problem might get itself expressed as permanent advice. There is very little in the literature to suggest that concern over employment-promoting schemes stemmed from a recognition that underemployment was due to a failure of effective demand. Worse than that, schemes were recommended without any attention to the necessity of stimulating saving or of providing appropriate institutions to transmit such funds as were saved to long-term investors.

Rational Elements in Mercantilist Theory. Despite Heckscher's cogent criticism of Keynes's unhistorical interpretation, his own analysis of mercantilism displays an almost absurd irritation with anything that smacks of economic determinism. He not only attributes every mercantilist proposition to the powerful hold of fallacious economic ideas but goes so far as to assert that "there are no grounds whatever for supposing that the mercantilist writers constructed their system . . . out of any knowledge of reality however derived"—a perfect example of the absolutist position. Now it is true that the mercantilists had indeed little interest in the practical use of precious metals for war chests or for final export. Nor did they desire bullion to overcome a deficiency of currency. "Scarcity of money" was, of course, a frequent complaint at the time, but even contemporary writers realized that a genuine shortage of coin could be remedied by clipping or by paper money and that such complaints often rested on a confusion between a mismanaged currency—scarcity of coins of particular denomination—and stringent credit or slack trade. But recently a British historian has submitted evidence to show that the desire for hard money in the mercantilist era had merits under the then prevailing circumstances that it later lost: the conditions of British trade with the Baltics and the East Indies were such as to make it necessary to achieve international liquidity through acquisition of stocks of precious metals. England produced virtually nothing that could have been exported to these areas, and they in turn would not accept sterling exchange owing to the then underdeveloped international money market. To obtain Baltic wheat and Indian "spices"—and "spices" at that time meant not merely seasonings but all Oriental wares such as textiles, dyes, sugar, coffee, tea, and saltpeter, items for which no adequate substitutes could be produced in Europe— Britain had to squeeze her colonial trade to yield precious metals. Thus the economic setting of the mercantilist world made free multilateral trade unworkable and required a system of bilateral controls. In his reply to this argument, Heckscher maintained that foreign exchange markets in the sixteenth and seventeenth centuries were sufficiently developed to permit currency exchange but admitted that the mercantilists had good reasons to be concerned about the Indian drain on bullion supplies. Be that as it may, this debate does suggest hitherto unsuspected elements of rationality in mercantilist thought.

One may wonder why the mercantilists themselves never drew attention to the peculiarities of trade with the Baltics and the East Indies. The answer, of course, is that they never recognized it as particularly unusual. As a matter of fact, the whole body of mercantilist theory involves unspoken assumptions about the real world that may have been obvious to observers at the time. The static conception of economic activity as a zero-sum game, so that one man's or one country's gain was

another's loss; the tacit acceptance of limited wants; a prevailing inelastic demand; weak pecuniary incentives—these were all notions that
one would expect to be held in a preindustrialized economy, accustomed to a growth of output and population so slow as to be barely discernible. At a time when foreign trade was notable for windfall gains
—those were the days of buccaneering imperialism—and when domestic trade was backward, what was more natural than to think that only
beggar-my-neighbor policies could enrich a nation? What more natural
than to regard a favorable trade balance as a net addition to sales on
what was regarded as a more or less limited home market or to suppose that higher wages would only decrease the supply of labor when
regularity of employment and consistency of effort was virtually unknown? Such general attitudes to economic life are so firmly rooted in
reality as hardly to need stating, but they alone explain why reasonable
men could have held the doctrines that were advanced in that age.

This does not mean that misconceptions and even downright fallacies played no role. After all, the balance-of-trade doctrine was already current in the fifteenth century and was espoused at various times
as early as the fourteenth. The notion that bullion supplied "the sinews
of war" had genuine appeal in the days of Henry VIII, and when Henry
squandered the state treasure this idea persisted, fed by the rational fear
of illiquidity in an era when credit institutions were little developed.
Protectionist sentiment, popular in any age, but particularly in one that
took state regulation of foreign trade for granted, clung easily to the
innocent identification of money and capital born out of the analogy
from personal finance, that oldest fallacy of composition. The undisci-
plined pamphleteers, swept along on the tide of public belief, found
striking and sometimes cogent reasons for defending the mercantilist
economics of the man in the street and, in grappling with the logical
consequences of premises, displayed economic theory in its infancy.
There is plenty of room here for the relativist and the absolutist interpretation: a mercantilist "vision" of reality, on the one hand, and, on
the other, an essentially crude analysis, erring more often by omission
than by commission.

2. THE EIGHTEENTH-CENTURY PREDECESSORS

Since the days of Hume, students of English mercantilism have
been puzzled by the failure of mercantilist writers to realize that their
objectives were self-contradictory. Thomas Mun could write that "all
men do consent that plenty of money in a Kingdom doth make the na-

tive commodities dearer" and that "as plenty of money makes wares dearer, so dear wares decline in their use and consumption," yet did not hesitate to advocate the indefinite accumulation of hard money. One might be tempted to argue that Mun did not grasp the full meaning of the quantity theory of money. But in that case how was it that mercantilist ideas survived into the eighteenth century once Locke had demonstrated that the value of money varies inversely with its quantity? The mystery deepens when it is realized that very few mercantilists made the mistake of advocating a favorable balance of trade as a method of price inflation; Heckscher found more evidence of inflationary sentiments in the literature than did Viner, but the fact remains that even the eighteenth-century advocates of paper money and note-issuing banks did not really want higher prices.

The Mercantilist Dilemma and the Quantity Theory. The resolution of the dilemma lies in the characteristic mercantilist doctrine that money "quickens" trade by increasing the velocity of circulation of goods. According to the familiar Equation of Exchange $MV \equiv PT$: the quantity of money in circulation is identically equal to the total volume of trade multiplied by the average prices of these goods. The quantity *theory* of money is nowadays understood as a doctrine linking M to P, with T determined by "real" forces and V given by the payment habits and financial institutions of the economy. But the mercantilists emphasized the effect of M on T rather than on P. The quantity theory in the seventeenth and eighteenth centuries had at its center the proposition that "money stimulates trade," a doctrine that lived on in the nineteenth century in the forced-saving thesis. An increase of money was thought to be attended by a rise in the demand for money, and hence neither prices nor the balance of trade need be directly affected by a specie inflow. The mercantilists did not conceive of Hume's self-regulating mechanism because they did not interpret the quantity theory of money as he did.

The Quantity Theory of Money. As first formulated by Locke, the quantity theory stated simply that average prices are always in proportion to the quantity of money, the quantity of money being understood to include "the quickness of its circulation." This is nothing but a truism, but a useful truism, because it emphasizes the function of money as a medium of exchange. It compares the total quantity of money with the total volume of goods and thus demonstrates that the absolute size of the money supply is of no significance to the wealth of a nation. Money is peculiar in that, as a means of exchange, it has no "intrinsic" value. The thesis is obviously destructive of mercantilist principles, but

Locke remained a mercantilist, nevertheless, by stressing the importance of the relative quantity of money with respect to other trading nations.

Hume, failing to recognize that the quantity theory as Locke stated it presupposes a *different* amount of money, not an *increase* in the money supply, introduced the notion of causality and laid down the commonly accepted version: T and V being insensitive to monetary changes, M and P will vary proportionately. As long as money is merely a standard of value and a medium of exchange, this proposition is a tautology. But, as soon as we consider the demand for money to hold as a store of value, M and P will not necessarily vary proportionately. It was understood at the time, however, as a verifiable statement about the real world. If nothing else, the price revolution of the sixteenth century was taken as overwhelming evidence of a direct causal relationship between variations in M and in P.

The Theory of Beneficial Inflation. It is clear that by 1700 no writer could ignore the fact that a permanent inflow of specie involved a contradiction in terms. Indeed, all eighteenth-century writers justify a permanently favorable balance of trade on the grounds that prices need not rise when the extra bullion is used to finance a greater volume of trade. Although the *amount* of money itself had no economic importance whatever, the *process* of increasing the amount of money in circulation might have a significant effect in promoting demand. What they held was not so much a quantity theory of the value of money as a monetary theory of the volume of trade and employment.

Perhaps the best exponent of the doctrine that "money stimulates trade" was the so-called "paper-money mercantilist" John Law. The argument in his *Money and Trade Considered* (1705), as in Jacob Vanderlint's *Money Answers all Things* (1734) and in Bishop Berkeley's *Querist* (1737), is based in essence on profit inflation and the premise that "an addition to the money will employ the people that are now idle." It utilizes the needs-of-trade doctrine to show that extra specie or paper money will be taken up by borrowers owing to abundant profit opportunities, while income payments to the previously unemployed gives rise to new consumers' demand. As money is cheaper to borrow, realized profits and sales rise without leading to a rise in prices; indeed, Law thought that prices might actually fall. It is evident that Law's argument supposes that the supply of commodities is highly elastic, a small increase in price leading to large increases in the amount of goods offered. Law himself realized the necessity of making some such assumption. In the case of perishable goods, he explicitly assumes a horizontal supply curve so that "as the demand for them increases or decreases their value continues equal or near the same," whereas for durable goods he assumes a negative elasticity of supply: they become "less valuable" as the demand rises.

Law's doctrine, while apparently contradictory to the quantity theory of money, is of course perfectly compatible with it. For he stresses the necessity of a gradual increase in the money supply so as not to disrupt the level of wages and prices that had come about through the prevailing international distribution of specie; the doctrine that "money stimulates trade" may be interpreted in Irving Fisher's language to apply to "transitional periods." The demand for a continual inflow of precious metals amounts to a demand for a continuous series of transitional periods. Even Hume allows for this possibility in his dynamic version of Locke's comparative static argument, a version that minimizes but does not deny the proposition that creeping inflation may promote economic growth. An inflow of gold, Hume observed, has a gradual effect on prices: "at first, no alteration is perceived; by degrees the price rises, first of one commodity, then of another; till the whole at last reaches a just proportion with the new quantity of specie which is in the Kingdom. In my opinion, it is only in this interval or intermediate situation between the acquisition of money and the rise in prices, that the enhancing quantity of gold and silver is favorable to industry." It was this passage that prompted Keynes's remark that Hume was "still enough of a mercantilist not to overlook the fact that it is in the transition that we actually have our being."

Cantillon's Essays. A very different resolution of the mercantilist dilemma is to be found in Cantillon's *Essays on the Nature of Commerce,* written in the 1720's but published in 1755, which is the most systematic, the most lucid, and at the same time the most original of all the statements of economic principles before the *Wealth of Nations.* Cantillon is the first to leave absolutely no doubt that the effect of an increase in V is equivalent to an increase in M alone, and he put monetary analysis on its feet by showing that the effect of an increase in the quantity of money upon prices and incomes depends upon the path by which cash is injected into the economy. "Mr. Locke has clearly seen that the abundance of money makes everything dear," Cantillon declared, "but he has not considered how it does so. The great difficulty of this question consists in knowing in what way and in what proportion the increase of money raises prices." In an oft-quoted passage Cantillon describes how an increase in the output of gold mines first affects incomes in that industry, then spending on consumer goods, then the price of foodstuffs, causing farming profits to rise and real wages to fall; this leads to an upward pressure on money wages and further cycles of increased expenditures and rising prices. He stresses the fact that P rises in proportion to M *and* T when M increases and that not only will the level of prices rise but the structure of prices will alter depending upon the initial recipients of the new cash and their relative demand for goods. The differential effect of a cash injection, as governed by the nature of the injection, will hereafter be called the "Cantillon Effect"; it was reproduced *in toto* by Hume in his essay "On Money" and in this way was handed down to the classical economists.

Cantillon also gave an excellent account of the specie-flow mechanism and a sound critique of Law's doctrine that "money stimulates trade," which, he noted, is much more likely to be true when the increase in specie is due to an export-surplus than to increased production in gold mines. In the latter case, it is likely to raise prices directly without promoting an expansion of output. Still, Cantillon was a mercantilist who did not hesitate to say that "the comparative power and wealth of states consists, other things being equal, in the greater or less abundance of money circulating in them" and that "every state which has more money in circulation than its neighbor has an advantage over them so long as it maintains this abundance of money." A specie inflow will indeed raise domestic prices to some extent, but this is all to the good. Selling dear and buying cheap means not only favorable barter terms of trade—a high ratio of export to import prices—but a favorable balance of payment as well, implying that the foreign demand for domestic goods and the domestic demand for foreign goods is highly inelastic. He did not, however, propose to let the inflationary process run its natural course if demand should prove to be elastic. Following Petty, he recommended the policy of preventing imported specie from going into active circulation by lending it abroad or by melting it down in the form of plate and ornaments. Thus, on both theoretical and practical grounds, he saw no reason why a country should not continue indefinitely to import precious metals.

Cantillon's argument ignores the fact that the fall in the price level of the foreign countries drained of bullion would in and of itself turn the balance of trade in their favor. Nevertheless, it is theoretically correct to say that a rise in domestic prices will produce a favorable, not an unfavorable, balance of trade if the elasticity of demand for imports at home and that for exports abroad is less than unity. Whether Cantillon was empirically justified in making this extreme assumption is another question. At any rate, Hume, writing only twenty years after him, treated demand as relatively elastic and hence produced a full-blown specie-flow argument that rang the death knell of mercantilism. Jogging backward, this created something we have labeled "the mercantilist dilemma." But, as we have seen, this was no real dilemma to the predecessors of Hume.

Monetary Analysis. Enough has been said to show that monetary theory in the eighteenth century consisted of dynamic process analysis of a crude kind, which was gradually extended to imply "a theory of the economic process in its entirety." In demonstrating that an increase in the supply of money generates additional purchasing power, which stimulates output, the inflationists of the eighteenth century finally provided the theoretical justification for the notion that more gold and silver is the avenue by which wealth and power are to be attained, a notion that had been mouthed for over two hundred years without any explanation of what it really meant. Nevertheless, despite the remarkable advances in monetary theory in the eighteenth century, one may well doubt whether the belief in the benefits of gradual inflation was justified in the light of contemporary conditions. There is insufficient recognition in the writings of Law and Berkeley of the real problems of a dominantly agrarian economy that cannot be cured simply by cranking the monetary pump. Adam Smith and Ricardo may have overemphasized thrift and enterprise, but their skepticism over monetary panaceas was well taken in the circumstances of an economy suffering from scarcity of capital and chronic structural unemployment.

The gradual emergence of real analysis in the eighteenth century and its victory over the monetary analysis of the early mercantilists is nowhere better expressed than in the development of the theory of interest. By "monetary analysis" is meant any analysis that introduces the element of money at the outset of the argument and denies that the essential features of economic life can be represented by a barter model. By "real analysis" is meant analysis that explains economic activity in terms of decisions about goods and services and relations between them; money is a veil because a well-functioning monetary system permits analysis of trade as if it were barter. With these distinctions in mind, we can make short shrift of the so-called "monetary theory of interest" of the mercantilists.

The idea that the rate of interest varies inversely with the quantity of money is found in Locke, Petty, and Law, among others; it rested on the common-sense idea that, since interest is the price paid for the hire of money, borrowing is easier and interest lower when there is more money about, just as a commodity falls in price when it is less scarce. Adam Smith accused Locke and Law of believing that, as the quantity of money increases and prices rise, the rate of interest must fall because any given sum of money will buy fewer goods for the borrowers. This error, Smith pointed out, has been "fully exposed by Mr. Hume": given that the only effect of an increased supply of money is to raise the level of prices, it is obvious that interest as a ratio of two sums of money will not be affected. However, it is unlikely that anyone ever held that point of view. Rather, as Cantillon put it, it is the "common idea, received of all those who have written on trade, that the increased quantity of currency in a State brings down the price of Interest there, because when Money is plentiful it is more easy to find some to borrow." It is important to remember that the relationship between the quantity of money and the rate of interest was never considered in isolation from the normal course of economic progress. An increase in M leads to a reduction in the rate of interest because it is normally accompanied by an increase in real national wealth. Casual empiricism sufficed to establish this argument: everyone knew that the general level of the market rate of interest—the rate on first-class commercial loans—tended downward in the seventeenth century, and it was also a familiar fact that interest in such poor countries as Spain, Scotland, and Ireland was almost twice as high as in Holland and England.

This is all there is to the mercantilist theory of interest, and it is extraordinary indeed that Keynes saw merit in it or, for that matter, in any *purely* monetary theory of interest. It is often forgotten, not least by Keynes himself, that the rate of interest in the complete Keynesian system is not determined merely by the quantity of money and the state of liquidity preferences but also by "real" forces expressed in the investment-demand schedule and the consumption function. The Hicks-Hansen LM-IS diagram, found in most modern textbooks on Keynesian economics, brings out clearly how monetary and real forces together determine the rate of interest.

The Real Rate of Interest.   Real theories of interest came to the fore with Cantillon, Hume, and Turgot. All three criticized the monetary theories of interest of their predecessors but admitted that an increase in the supply of money could depress the rate of interest temporarily. If prices rose in proportion to the increase in money, however, equilibrium was impossible unless the rate of interest resumed its former height: at higher prices more money would have to be borrowed to finance any project; hence, the demand for money loans would be increased, and equilibrium implied that it would be increased in the same proportion as supply. Generally speaking, however, the rate of interest was not thought to be uniquely related to the supply of money. The repercussions of an increase in the money supply could be traced by means of the Cantillon Effect: for example, if the new money flowed into the hands of entrepreneurs to be saved and invested, the rate of interest would probably fall, but if it came first into the hands of landowners, it would be spent on consumption, and the rise in consumers' demand would make entrepreneurs more willing and able to pay higher interest charges.

This contrast between the frugal merchant and the prodigal landlord is characteristic of all eighteenth-century theory, including that of Adam Smith. The rate of real saving and of net investment is not made a function of the rate of interest or even of the merchant's expectation of profits but is, rather, connected with the preponderance of certain classes in the community imbued with the philosophy of thrift. The rate of interest depends on the supply of and demand for loanable funds, with the profitability of investment and the prodigality of landlords governing the demand side and the wealth of the country and the distribution of that wealth governing the supply side. The old doctrine that advanced countries would have low interest rates was maintained, but the forces causing variations in demand and supply were now analyzed in detail. Economic expansion would increase the importance of the "moneyed interests" and thereby augment the supply of loanable capital; agriculture would decline in importance and hence consumption loans to landlords would dwindle away. Moreover, capital accumulation per se would reduce profit margins by increasing competition for an essentially limited number of available investment outlets. Since interest was a derived income, a deduction from business profits, this alone would reduce the yield on money loans. The changing proportions between lenders and borrowers would do the rest.

3. PHYSIOCRACY

Adam Smith praised the physiocratic system "with all its imperfections" as "perhaps the nearest approximation to the truth that has yet been published upon the subject of Political Economy." The physiocrats' attack on mercantilism and its free trade proposals roused his admiration; from them he drew the theme of wealth as "the consumable goods annually reproduced by the labor of society," the doctrine of productive labor, and the emphasis on the essential circularity of the process of production and distribution. It comes as something of a shock, however, to realize that he refers only obliquely to the most notorious of physiocratic concepts, *l'impôt unique,* and does not mention it at all in the chapter specifically devoted to the physiocrats. Moreover, he misrepresents the no less infamous notion of *la classe stérile* by condemning Quesnay for seeking "to degrade the artificers, manufacturers, and merchants by the humiliating appellation of the barren or unproductive classes." The physiocrats did not regard industry as useless but simply as a sector that produces no net additions to income: Turgot's *classe stipendiée* is indeed a happier expression than Quesnay's *classe stérile.* Ironically enough, Adam Smith found difficulty in upsetting the physiocratic viewpoint; in the end he was forced to argue that manufacturing *is* productive because its receipts are sufficient to pay wages and to replace worn-out capital, but that agriculture is *more* productive because it yields rent over and above wages and depreciation. But apart from a quibble on words, this concedes the whole of the physiocratic argument.

The Meaning of Physiocracy. Physiocracy, as Adam Smith suggests, should be understood as a reaction to the mercantilist policies of Colbert during the reign of Louis XIV. The glory of the age of *Le Roi Soleil* was the growth of industry, and agriculture was consistently neglected. The war of the Spanish succession and the magnificence of the Versailles court placed a severe burden upon taxable capacity, and the land tax, or *taille,* being the chief source of revenue, was steadily increased. By the death of Louis XIV in 1715 the plight of French agriculture had produced a wave of reaction against *Colbertisme,* fanned by the religious struggle against the Huguenots. Louis XV, instead of recouping losses at home, threw himself into the Seven Years' War with England, from which France emerged defeated, deprived of Canada and her Oriental possessions, and reduced to a second-rate power in Europe. The stage was set for a back-to-nature movement, a return to rustic simplicity, of which the writings of Rousseau and the paintings of Boucher and Fragonard are familiar witnesses.

Inclined to emphasize agriculture, the physiocrats could hardly resist casting envious glances at England. The combination of small holdings, antiquated methods, and a maze of feudal obligations made it difficult for France to adopt the improvements affected by the much admired "agricultural revolution" in England. The program of the physiocrats was to eliminate the vestiges of medieval particularism in the countryside, to rationalize the fiscal system by reducing all taxes to a single levy on rent, to replace *petite* with *grande culture,* and to free the corn trade of all mercantilist restraint; in short, to emulate English agriculture. Placed in context, there is nothing very surprising about all this. It was only the effort to reduce agrarian reform to a watertight theoretical argument that produced conclusions that even at the time struck many contemporaries as slightly absurd.

The Tableau Economique. Quesnay's "Tableau Economique," published three years after Cantillon's *Essay,* was regarded in its day as the crowning achievement of the physiocratic school. Mentioned but not explained by Adam Smith, it soon fell into oblivion and had to be rediscovered by Marx in the middle of the nineteenth century. Since that time it has never ceased to fascinate commentators, and yet, despite its importance, it should not be regarded as the centerpiece of the physiocratic system. What it achieved was a vivid graphic picture of general interdependence by means of a drastic simplification of the economic system into three interacting sectors. Out of this emerged a conception of the closed "stationary state" as a circular flow that in each period repeats itself, a conception that has ever since maintained a powerful grip upon the imagination of economists. But the conclusions of physiocratic theory are not deducible from the Tableau; on the contrary, they form the premises upon which the zigzag diagram of the stationary process is constructed. A discussion of the Tableau, however, serves to bring out the principal analytical weakness of Quesnay's system: not so much that it attributed the net return to economic activity to land alone but rather that it failed in any way to prove that land is productive of *value*. The Tableau most frequently reproduced is that printed at Versailles in 1759; long thought to be destroyed, a copy of it was discovered in 1894. This zigzag diagram, however, is not a macroeconomic table but rather an illustration of the circular flow involving the expenditure of one landlord. Later editions of the Tableau simplify the argument by giving the total annual receipts and expenditures of three classes. This is the form of the table presented in Quesnay's *Analyse* (1766), to which Marx first drew attention (see accompanying diagram).

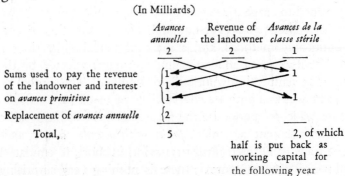

(In Milliards)

	Avances annuelles	Revenue of the landowner	Avances de la classe stérile
	2	2	1
Sums used to pay the revenue of the landowner and interest on *avances primitives*	1 1 1		1 1 1
Replacement of *avances annuelle*	2		
Total,	5		2, of which half is put back as working capital for the following year

Quesnay inaugurated the tradition of regarding capital as consisting of a series of "advances." First, there is fixed capital in the form of *avances primitives*—livestock, buildings, and implements—the interest of which at 10 per cent is included as depreciation in the table. Second, there is fixed capital in the form of *avances foncières*—drainage, fencing, and other permanent land improvements—which do not figure in the table as such. Last, there is working capital under the title of *avances annuelles*—the wages of agricultural labor, seeds, and other recurring annual costs. The process of circulation is as follows: the gross value added by agriculture is 5 milliards, 3 milliards of which constitute *reprises,* costs of production incurred in cultivation. Farmers use two fifths of their own output for working capital; one fifth is sold to artisans in exchange for goods required to replace worn-out fixed capital. Since farmers receive only "wages of management"—it is land that is productive, not their labor—the remainder goes to the proprietors as rent. The landowners in turn exchange half of that for manufactured articles, while the artisans purchase 2 milliards worth of raw materials and foodstuffs from the agricultural sector. The whole process may be conceived of in real terms, with three fifths of output entering into circulation, or, as Quesnay suggested, it may equally well be pictured in money terms. At the beginning of the process, the farmers are in possession of the entire money stock of the economy (2 m.). They pay this to landowners to purchase "rental services," who in turn spend it on foodstuffs and fabricated commodities; the farmers now spend the 1 milliard just received to replace fixed capital, and the artisans spend their total receipts of 2 milliards on agricultural products. At the end, the farmers have received 3 milliards and spent 1; they are back to where they started. The net effect for the sterile sector is nil, and the 2 milliards of money is paid out once more to landowners as a new cycle of production begins.

The Tableau as conceived by Quesnay involves a one-period income-spending lag; landowners spend the previous period's rent, while the artisans always retain 1 milliard of the last period's receipts for spending in the following period. Presumably, Quesnay was thinking of output as identical with the annual harvest, the whole of which is consumed in the following twelve months. The Tableau, however, can also be pictured with leads as well as lag, each sector simply spending in each income period the receipts of the same period. In this case, the whole argument can be represented by a two-way transaction diagram in the manner of a Leontief input-output table: as in Leontief's system, all factors required to produce a good are used in fixed proportions and the value of an industry's output is entirely exhausted by the industry's total payments to other industries (see accompanying table).

PRODUCING INDUSTRY	PURCHASING INDUSTRY			TOTAL OUTPUT
	I	II	III	
I. Farmers................	2	1	2	5
II. Proprietors..............	2	0	0	2
III. Artisans................	1	1	0	2
Total purchases..........	5	2	2	9

A three-industry closed Leontief model can be represented by three simultaneous equations:

$$(1 - a_{11})X_1 \qquad - a_{12}X_2 \qquad - a_{13}X_3 = 0,$$
$$- a_{21}X_1 \quad + (1 - a_{22})X_2 \qquad - a_{23}X_3 = 0,$$
$$- a_{31}X_1 \qquad - a_{32}X_2 \quad + (1 - a_{33})X_3 = 0,$$

where the X's stand for the rates of output of the three industries and the a_{ij} coefficients for the input-output relations: the ith industry's product is used as input to produce a unit of the jth industry's output. The equations state simply that if $(1 - a_{ii})X_i$ stands for the amount of output an industry does not retain, this must be equal to the amounts purchased from it by other industries $(a_{ij}X_j)$. So, for example, reading across the first row, the total output of agriculture equals the amount retained by farmers $(a_{11}X_1)$ plus the amount sold to landowners and artisans $(a_{12}X_2 + a_{13}X_3)$. The input-output coefficients of the table are quickly computed in our simple case and, when substituted into the equations given above, yield:

$$0.6(5) - 0.5(2) - 1(2) = 0,$$
$$- 0.4(5) + 1(2) \qquad = 0,$$
$$- 0.2(5) - 0.5(2) + 1(2) = 0.$$

This set of equations provides a scale model of the economy, given the final demand for output (the X's). The practical purpose of the construction is limited to evaluating the effects of small changes in the final bill of goods, small enough to leave the input coefficients unchanged. This is a limitation inherent in the Tableau itself, which has no other purpose than to illustrate the phenomenon of mutual interdependence between industries.

L'impôt unique. There are obvious formal defects in the Tableau. The sterile sector is simply assumed to possess fixed capital, but no provision is made for its replacement. Competition is supposed to reduce the value of output of this sector to the sum of the wages of workers and managers, but no argument is supplied here or elsewhere to show why competition of the farmers for the use of land does not reduce rents to zero. Quesnay does not succeed either in showing that manufacturing is sterile or in demonstrating that agriculture necessarily yields a *produit net.*

The physiocrats regarded rents as a perfectly legitimate income, a payment for costs incurred in clearing the land and for keeping up *avances fonciéres.* The bulk of receipts, however, were admittedly *disposable,* ready to provide the revenue of the state. And, indeed, since rent is at least in part a return for the use of a nonreproducible natural agent, the incidence of any tax will always fall upon landlords; the returns of all other classes consist of *reprises* or necessary expenses of production. Thus, the physiocratic demand for a single tax aims at minimizing collection costs by taxing directly those incomes that ultimately bear taxes. Note that *l'impôt unique* is not a tax on land values, much less a tax on "the unearned increment" of rental values in response to rising population à la Henry George, but a levy on pure rent, which Quesnay estimated to be about one-third of the *produit net.*

Say's Law. The notion subsequently popularized by J. B. Say as the Law of Markets formed an integral part of the physiocratic critique of mercantilism. Mercier de la Rivère, whose *L'Ordre naturel et essentiel* (1767) was cited by Smith as giving "the most distinct and best connected account of physiocracy," remarks that "personne n'est acheteur qu'autant qu' il est vendeur," and it is a short step from Quesnay's "que tout achat est vente, et que toute vente est achat" to Say's "supply creates its own demand." The central lesson of the Tableau is, after all, that money is merely a medium of exchange, that trade reduces essentially to barter exchange, and that the creation of output automatically generates the income whose disbursement makes it possible to enter upon another cycle of production. But, strangely enough, Say directed the Law of Markets against his physiocratic predecessors because they had argued that income received is not automatically restored to the income stream. The landlord's income, as Cantillon had stressed, is not necessarily balanced by a cost item and hence can be withheld, breaking the income stream. Here is the origin of the idea developed by Malthus that the balanced spending of landlords on luxury goods is the factor that maintains the circular flow and therefore economic prosperity. Here, too, is the origin of the underconsumptionist thesis, which passed from Quesnay to such English physiocrats as Thomas Spence and via Malthus to the Ricardian socialists to issue into a full-scale attack upon capitalism with Marx.

4. SCHOLASTIC INFLUENCES: AN AFTERTHOUGHT

The prehistory of economics, some commentators have insisted, starts in the thirteenth century with the scholastic pioneers in market analysis rather than with the mercantilists. Schumpeter has even put forth the claim that the skeleton of Adam Smith's analysis hails from the Schoolmen and the natural-law philosophers, not from the British free-trade writers of the eighteenth century and the physiocrats. This is not a question to be settled here, but it may be worth while to touch upon it to round out the picture of pre-Adamite economics.

There can be no doubt that scholastic doctrines were transmitted to Adam Smith by way of the seventeenth-century natural-law philosophers, Hugo Grotius and Samuel von Pufendorf. Moreover, the writings of the physiocrats with which he was acquainted are replete with scholastic influences; Quesnay often sounds like an eighteenth-century version of Thomas Aquinas. For our purposes, the distinctive contributions of scholastic economics may be broken down into three elements: an emphasis on utility as the principal source of value, the notion of the just price, and the proposition that money capital is sterile. On the first score, it is generally agreed now that the Doctors did develop a utility-cum-scarcity doctrine of value. This would have been denied a hundred years ago because of the interpretation given to the scholastic concept of the *justum pretium*. Aristotle, in the fifth book of the *Nicomachean Ethics,* had argued that commutative or contractual justice requires an "exchange of equivalents"; Aquinas commented upon this passage, suggesting that "equivalence" be interpreted in terms of cost, chiefly labor costs. It was this commentary that led to the view that the scholastics held a labor theory of value, ignoring Aquinas' insistence that all goods are valued only in relation to human wants. Scholastic economics based value squarely on wants and their satisfaction and in its later versions related utility to the relative scarcity of a good. How much we should make of this is another question. A utility theory of value without a concept of diminishing utility to explain why demand at a given price is satiable hardly amounts to a theory of relative price. Next, there is the scholastic concept of the just price, which is often thought to reflect an underlying notion of the just wage. This seems to be a historical myth. There is no suggestion in the scholastic literature of a just price that corresponds to cost of production as determined by the producer's social status. The Schoolmen did not distinguish between short-run and long-run equilibrium and had no conception of how competition produces a long-run normal price that just covers costs. They seldom gave much attention to what constituted a just price, but usually they identified it with the current market price, the price given to an individual that he cannot himself affect. They did not question the right of civil authorities to set and regulate prices on any grounds whatever, so the just price is simply the price ruling at the moment, whether produced by competition or not.

Clearly, Adam Smith was in no way indebted to his scholastic predecessors in developing the fundamental distinction between the "natural" and the "market" price, and in deliberately rejecting the explanation of value along the lines of utility he completely ignored scholastic thinking. It is hardly necessary to add that he also discarded the standard doctrine of the church that interest is "a breed of barren metal" and probably had read little of the scholastic literature dealing with the question of interest. It is difficult to believe that he missed anything in neglecting it, for the bulk of scholastic writing on the subject dealt with the legal distinction between a loan and a partnership; a loan was a gratuitous contract, and interest could be demanded only for reasons extraneous to a loan. Two of the reasons were a loss on the part of the lender as a result of the loan (*damnum emergens*) and a gain forgone on an alternative investment (*lucrum cessans*); this equates interest to the opportunity cost of liquid funds, which, however fatal to the prohibition of usury, must be put down as a genuine analytical insight. Ingenious apologists have found other nuggets in the literature, but, on the whole, it is analytically sterile.[1]

The scholastic writers always handle economic questions within the compass of the different types of contracts concerned in the transaction. This juristic approach in the tradition of Roman Law is a distinctive feature of scholasticism and sets it apart from the mercantilist tradition. And, indeed, it was the mercantilists who, long before Adam Smith, broke with the canonical conception of market behavior as a moral problem and fashioned the concept of the economic man. The pamphleteers of the seventeenth century assumed as a matter of course that the profit motive was a controlling motive in economic conduct. Although they had a qualified notion of spontaneous harmony, they believed in the directive power of self-interest and in domestic matters came near to advocating laissez faire. Adam Smith was not alone in having confidence in the workings of "the invisible hand." Nor is it

---

[1] Once again we have a bizarre interpretation by Keynes that regards the disquisitions of the Schoolmen as directed toward raising the marginal efficiency of capital, while using moral suasion to lower the rate of interest. But scholastic doctrine regards all interest on borrowed money as "usury" and therefore unjustified, and variations in the rate of interest play no part in their analysis.

necessary to appeal to scholastic influences to account for his grasp of the determination of prices by supply and demand. One of the oldest British mercantilist tracts, John Hales's *Discourse of the Common Weal of This Realm of England,* written in 1549, already shows a fairly sophisticated understanding of the price mechanism as an efficient method of allocating resources. Only a few writers prior to Adam Smith were free traders, but all the basic elements of the classical approach to economic activity are embedded in the mercantilist literature.

One may doubt, therefore, whether recent work on scholastic economics requires a revision of the history of economic thought prior to Adam Smith. The Schoolmen may have contributed ideas that passed through Grotius, Locke, and Pufendorf to Francis Hutcheson and Adam Smith, but we are hardly justified for that reason in following Schumpeter, who reduces mercantilism to a mere by-current.

NOTES ON FURTHER READING

1. *Mercantilism.* J. R. McCulloch's *Early English Tracts on Commerce,* reprinted for the Royal Economic Society in 1954, contains Mun's *England's Treasure,* North's *Discourses upon Trade,* and Martin's *Considerations on the East-India Trade,* to which must be added I. Gervaise, *The System or Theory of the Trade of the World,* ed. J. Viner (1954), the most brilliant statement of the liberal elements in English mercantilism.

All critical study of mercantilism begins with Adam Smith, *The Wealth of Nations,* Book IV, chaps. 1–8. If a student had to confine himself to a single secondary source, the choice would naturally fall on the first two chapters of J. Viner, *Studies in the Theory of International Trade* (1937); this incisive survey of mercantilist theory and policy proposals is profoundly critical in tone. By way of contrast, see Schumpeter's subtle defense of mercantilism: J. A. Schumpeter, *History of Economic Analysis* (1954), Part II, chap. 7. C. Y. Wu, *An Outline of International Price Theory* (1939), chap. 2, complements Viner and Schumpeter in its treatment of mercantilist monetary theory.

The outstanding historical study of mercantilism in all its phases is E. F. Heckscher, *Mercantilism,* ed. E. F. Söderland (1955). An appendix in the new edition criticizes Keynes's views on mercantilism. For a quick summary of the book's general argument see Heckscher's article on "Mercantilism," *ESS,* reprinted in *DET.* A reading of Heckscher's book should be supplemented by H. Heaton's masterful review article (*JPE,* June, 1937) and D. C. Coleman's recent criticism of Heckscher's fundamental approach: "Eli Heckscher and the Idea of Mercantilism," *SEHR,* V (1937), 1, which contains references to the Wilson-Heckscher debate on the nature of British trade with the Baltics and the Indies. J. Viner, "Power versus Plenty as Objectives of Foreign Policy in the Seventeenth and Eighteenth Centuries," *WP,* 1948, reprinted in *The Long View and the Short* (1958), attacks the stereotype that views mercantilism as a system that aimed exclusively at national power as an end in itself.

Those grown weary of reading about *the* mercantilist system will find support in E. A. J. Johnson, *Predecessors of Adam Smith* (1937), which denies any common designation to the economic doctrines of the seventeenth and eighteenth centuries. Johnson presents an intellectual portrait gallery of ten leading writers and reconstructs the primitive theory of production that they held.

The *locus classicus* of English mercantilism is Mun's *England's Treasure by Forraign Trade.* For evidence that a substantial part of this book represents the fruits of reflection on the events of the depression of 1620–24 see R. W. K. Hinton, "The Mercantile System in the Time of Thomas Mun, *EHR,* April, 1955, and J. D. Gould, "The Trade Crisis of the Early 1620's and English Economic Thought," *JEH,* August, 1955. W. D. Grampp shows that the mercantilists anticipated almost every classical idea but that, unlike the classical authors, their economic objective was primarily to secure full employment: "The Liberal Element in English Mercantilism," *QJE,* November, 1952, reprinted in *EET.* J. M. Letiche, "Isaac Gervaise on the International Mechanism of Adjustment," *JPE,* February, 1952, does justice to an early example of the income approach to international economic equilibrium. J. M. Low presents a fascinating discussion of Scottish mercantilism in the early years of the eighteenth century: "A Regional Example of the Mercantilist Theory of Economic Policy," *MS,* January, 1953. A valuable book on the trading practices of the sixteenth and seventeenth centuries is R. de Roover, *Gresham on Foreign Exchange: An Essay on Early English Mercantilism* (1949).

For those who wish to compare English with Continental mercantilism, admittedly less interesting from a theoretical standpoint, see C. W. Cole, *French Mercantilist Doctrines before Colbert* (1931) and *Colbert and a Century of French Mercantilism 1683–1700* (1939); A. V. Castillo, *Spanish Mercantilism: Gerónimo de Uztáriz—Economist* (1930), and an article on the same author by E. J. Hamilton in *Economics, Sociology and the Modern World,* ed. N. E. Himes (1935); R. S. Smith, "Spanish Antimercantilism of the Seventeenth Century," *JPE,* June, 1940; M. Grice-Hutchinson's little book of readings in sixteenth-century Spanish monetary theory, with an excellent accompanying text: *The School of Salamanca* (1953); and L. Sommer, "Cameralism," *ESS.* Heckscher has nothing to say about Dutch mercantilism, and the last full-length study of the Dutch school is now a century old. Some recent monographic work is unfortunately available only in Dutch; a good English study is badly needed.

2. *Eighteenth-Century Predecessors.* Of the treatises published before *The Wealth of Nations,* Cantillon's *Essai sur la nature du commerce en général* —a French-English version was published for the Royal Economic Society in 1931—and Turgot's *Reflections on the Formation and the Distribution of Riches* (1898)—now out of print—can still be read with pleasure, and occasional surprise. Hume's scintillating essays on economics are brought together for the first time in *David Hume: Writings on Economics,* ed. E. Rotwein (1955); for a bird's-eye review of their content see M. Arkin, "The

Economic Writings of David Hume—A Reassessment," *SAJE,* September, 1956, reprinted in *EET.*

On Cantillon see F. A. v. Hayek's introduction to the German edition of Cantillon's *Essai* (1931) and the prolix but comprehensive discussion of the whole of the contents of the *Essai* by J. J. Spengler, "Richard Cantillon: First of the Moderns," *JPE,* 1954, reprinted in *EET.* The recent French edition of Cantillon's book by A. Sauvy (1952) contains some important accompanying studies and commentaries. C. H. Hull's introduction to *The Economic Writings of Sir William Petty* (1899) is still useful. T. W. Hutchison gives an excellent précis of Berkeley's *Querist* and concludes with some controversial comments on the Keynesian aspect of pre-Adamite economics (*BJPS,* May, 1953). I. D. S. Ward takes exception to Hutchison's interpretation in an article whose title is self-explanatory: "George Berkeley: Precursor of Keynes or Moral Economist on Underdevelopment?" *JPE,* February, 1959; see also the revealing exchange between Hutchison and Ward, *JPE,* June, 1960. D. Vickers, *Studies in the Theory of Money, 1690–1776* (1959), emphasizes the preoccupation of eighteenth-century authors with employment-generating schemes and lends support to Keynes's enthusiastic endorsement of mercantilist theory. J. M. Low's brilliant paper, "The Rate of Interest: British Opinion in the Eighteenth Century," *MS,* May, 1954, provides a healthy antidote to Keynesian exuberance, as do the first two chapters of G. S. L. Tucker, *Progress and Profits in British Economic Thought, 1650–1850* (1960). D. C. Coleman, "Labour in the English Economy of the Seventeenth Century," *EHR,* April, 1956, argues that the employment theme in the literature of the period must be understood in the context of an underdeveloped food-producing economy. E. S. Furniss, *The Position of the Laborer in a System of Economic Nationalism* (1920), the classic book on mercantilist labor policy, makes interesting reading in this connection. Sir James Steuart, a contemporary of Adam Smith, is rescued from the oblivion to which his mercantilist confusions and unreadable style have consigned him by S. R. Sen, *The Economics of Sir James Steuart* (1957). Sen treats Steuart as a pioneer theorist of economic planning, bearing a family resemblance to Keynes. A debate among Hume's personal friends on his ideas about economic development in relation to foreign trade is the subject of another splendid article by J. M. Low, "An Eighteenth Century Controversy in the Theory of Economic Progress," *MS,* September, 1952.

On the emergence of the quantity theory of money see the standard work by A. E. Monroe, *Monetary Theory before Adam Smith* (1923), and the incisive treatment of H. Hegaland, *The Quantity Theory of Money* (1951). Schumpeter deals brilliantly with the struggle between monetary and real analysis in the eighteenth century: *History,* Part II, chap. 6.

3. *Physiocracy. Œuvres économiques et philosophiques de F. Quesnay* were edited by A. Oncken in 1888 but remain untranslated in English. Oncken wrote an excellent account of Quesnay's system, *Geschichte der Nationaloekonomie die Zeit vor Adam Smith* (1902), which was soon superseded, however, by the authoritative works of G. Weulérsse, *Le mouvement physiocratique en France de 1756 à 1770* (1910) and *La physiocratie sous les minestères de Turgot et de Necker, 1775–1781* (1950). In opposition to Weulérsse, N. J. Ware denies that the physiocrats were consistent economic liberals: "The

Physiocrats: A Study in Economic Rationalization," *AER*, December, 1931. Ware views physiocratic ideas as expressive of the interests of a new class of bourgeois landowners emerging from the French bureaucracy; this neo-Marxist interpretation makes an interesting contrast with Marx's own more subtle explanation in *Theories of Surplus-Value* (1951). M. Beer's stimulating but questionable book, *An Inquiry into Physiocracy* (1939), traces the parallels between scholastic and physiocratic doctrine.

A good brief treatment of physiocracy can be found in C. Gide and C. Rist, *A History of Economic Doctrines* (1948), chap. 1. L. Rogin in *The Meaning and Validity of Economic Theory* (1956), chap. 2, treats the physio-crats as agrarian reformers. Schumpeter, *History*, Part II, chap. 4, deals not only with the physiocrats but also with Petty and Cantillon. The contrast between the conditions of French and English agriculture, so important for grasping Smith's reaction to physiocracy, is well brought out by S. J. Brandenburg, "The Place of Agriculture in British National Economy Prior to Adam Smith," *JPE*, June, 1931. A. I. Bloomfield shows how meager were the contributions of the physiocrats to the classical theory of the nature and gains of foreign trade: "The Foreign Trade Doctrines of the Physiocrats," *AER*, December, 1938, reprinted in *EET*. On Quesnay's zigzag diagrams see A. Phillips, "The Tableau d'Econo-mique as a Simple Leontief Model," *QJE*, February, 1955; R. L. Meek, "The Interpretation of the 'Tableau Economique,'" *Ec.*, November, 1960.

T. P. Neill, "Quesnay and Physiocracy," *JHI*, April, 1958, and "The Physiocratic Concept of Economics," *QJE*, November, 1949, provide a useful reminder that the physiocrats had no notion of economics as an autonomous science; they regarded their system as an all-embracing normative social science. For an acute analysis of the natural-law foundation of physiocratic thinking see M. Albaum, "Moral Defenses of Physiocrat's Laissez-Faire," *JHI*, April, 1955. Adam Smith's strange notions of Chinese economic development (*Wealth of Nations*, Book IV, chap. 9) were apparently derived from Quesnay, who believed that China practiced Mandarin despotism, esteemed agriculture, and allowed the natural order to prevail: see the fascinating study of L. A. Maverick, "Chinese Influences upon Quesnay and Turgot," *Claremont Oriental Studies*, No. 4, 1942. Physiocratic ideas survived in England well into the nineteenth century and were taken up by English underconsumptionists. Say's Law of Markets grew out of the debate between "Physiocracy and Classicism in England"; see the article by that title by R. L. Meek, *EJ*, March, 1951, and J. J. Spengler, "The Physiocrats and Say's Law of Markets," *JPE*, 1945, reprinted in *EET*.

4. Scholastic Economics. My comments on scholastic economics lean heavily on a series of articles by Raymond de Roover: "Monopoly Theory Prior to Adam Smith: A Revision," *QJE*, November, 1951; "Scholastic Economics: Survivals and Lasting Influence from the 16th Century to Adam Smith," *QJE*, May, 1955; "Joseph A. Schumpeter and Scholastic Economics," *KYK* 2, 1957; and "The Concept of the Just Price: Theory of Economic Policy," *JEH*, December, 1958. J. T. Noonan, Jr., *The Scholastic Analysis of Usury* (1957), is also useful in dispelling the many misconceptions about scholastic doctrine that still prevail. For a succinct but excessively laudatory discussion of the subject see Schumpeter's *History*, Part II, chap. 2, pp. 73-107. M. Beer, *Early British Economics* (1938), is valuable for its emphasis upon the continuity of scholastic ideas. Scholastic economics forms part of the broad stream of premarginal utility theory that runs back to Aristotle and forward through Galiani, Condillac, and Say to Gossen, Jevons, and Menger: see J. Soudek, "Aristotle's Theory of Exchange," *PAPS,* February, 1952; E. Kauder, "Genesis of Marginal Utility Theory," *EJ,* 1953, reprinted in *EET;* L. Einaudi, "Ferdinando Galiani," *SZV,* 1945, reprinted in *DET;* and H. R. Sewall, *The Theory of Value before Adam Smith* (1901), which is still the standard reference work on the subject, covering a long list of writers from Plato to Steuart and tracing in detail the fluctuations of opinion that stressed now demand, now supply.

On the natural-law philosophers see O. H. Taylor's well-known articles: "Economics and the Idea of Natural Laws," *QJE,* 1929–30, reprinted in *Economics and Liberalism* (1955). The first of these discusses the influence of natural-law doctrine in fostering analysis of the operation of a free market; the second deals in detail with the physiocrats and Adam Smith. British natural-law doctrine is treated by A. F. Chalk, "Natural Law and the Rise of Economic Individualism," *JPE,* August, 1951.

Chapter 2 ADAM SMITH

THE PRACTICE of reading the expansive tomes of the eighteenth century from cover to cover seems to have almost wholly died out. Nowadays we read selections of Gibbon and Hume and confine ourselves to the first ten chapters of the *Wealth of Nations*. But one participant at the sesquicentennial commemoration of Smith's book told of someone who actually read the whole volume:

Once upon a time there was a man who read the *Wealth of Nations;* not a summary, nor a volume of selected passages, but the *Wealth of Nations* itself. He began with the Introduction, he read the famous first chapter on the division of labor, the chapters on the origin and use of money, the prices of commodities, the wages of labor, the profits of stock, the rent of land, and all the other well-known economic portions of the first book, not omitting the long digression on the fluctuation in the value of silver during the last four centuries, and the statistical tables at the end. Having completed the first book he went on to the second, not deterred by the fact that it is supposed to contain an erroneous theory of capital and an untenable distinction between productive and unproductive labor. In Book III he found an account of the economic development of Europe since the fall of the Roman Empire, with digressions upon the various phases of medieval life and civilization. In the fourth book he came upon extended analyses and criticisms of the commercial and colonial policies of European nations, and a whole battery of free trade arguments. Finally, he attacked the long concluding book on the revenue of the sovereign. Here he found even more varied and unexpected matters: an account of the different methods of defense and of administering justice in primitive societies, and of the origin and growth of standing armies in Europe; a history of education in the Middle Ages and a criticism of eighteenth-century universities; a history of the temporal power of the church, of the growth of public debts in modern nations, of the mode of electing bishops in the ancient church; reflections as to the disadvantages of the division of labor, and—what is the main purpose of the book—an examination of principles of taxation and of systems of public revenue. Time is too short to enumerate all that he found here before he finally came to the concluding paragraphs, written during the opening events of the American Revolution, concerning the duty of colonies to contribute towards the expenses of the mother country.

Now, of course I may have exaggerated somewhat. There probably never was any such man.

Adam Smith and the Industrial Revolution. Let us assume, in a triumph of hope over experience, that such people are not as rare as is sometimes believed. Before presenting a reader's guide to the *Wealth of Nations,* however, there is one point that must be cleared up at the outset. In his Introduction to the book, Adam Smith makes it clear that his leading theme is economic development: the long-term forces that govern the growth of the wealth of nations. It is evident that by "wealth" he really means, not the community's capital at a given moment of time—a stock—but the community's income produced during a *period* of time—a flow—although he did not always adhere consistently to this conception. The growth of income is made dependent, in the first place, upon the scope of the division of labor in a society, with division of labor so broadly defined as to include everything we would nowadays call technological progress. No sooner has he described division of labor in "a very trifling manufacture" in the opening pages of the work than he notes that industry generally affords greater scope for specialization than does agriculture and that rich countries usually excel in manufacturing. "The prophet of the Industrial Revolution," "the spokesman of manufacturing interests," we are likely to mutter to ourselves. But this is all wrong! The whole book is directed against "the mean rapacity, the monopolizing spirit of merchants and manufacturers, who neither are, nor ought to be, the rulers of mankind." The merchants and master-manufacturers are the architects of the hated Mercantile System, and there is no indication in the *Wealth of Nations* that these same men were even then launching England upon a new industrial age. Indeed, there is nothing in the book to suggest that Adam Smith was aware that he was living in times of unusual economic change.

He speaks of "the invention of all those machines which facilitate and abridge labor" but gives concrete examples of innovations dating back to the Middle Ages. He talks of iron ore smelted with charcoal, although it was generally smelted with coke by his time. And, despite the fact that the last revised edition of the *Wealth of Nations* appeared in 1784, he nowhere mentions Kay's fly-shuttle, Hargreaves' spinning jenny, Crompton's mule, or Arkwright's water frame, inventions that revolutionized the textile industry in the 1780's. James Watt, the inventor of the steam engine, was a personal friend; the Boulton-Watt partnership was formed in 1775; yet Smith never refers to the successful commercial application of the steam engine to coal mining in the late 1770's. As a matter of fact, he took a dim view generally of the speculative trading of "projectors" and in Book II of the *Wealth of Nations* condemned Scottish banks for extending credit too liberally to the "spirited undertakings" that were being carried on at the time in Scotland. Is this the language of a prophet of the Industrial Revolution?

When Toynbee gave currency to the term "Industrial Revolution" over 75 years ago, he dated the onset of the movement at 1760. But, as Ashton has argued, if by an industrial revolution we mean, not a stampede on the Patent Office, but a sudden acceleration in the rate of growth of output, we should move the date forward to 1790. It is only in the late 1780's that almost every statistical series of production begins to show a sharp upward trend. Of course, contemporaries were slow to recognize what was happening, and even by the turn of the century there were still many acute observers who were unimpressed by the recent "progress of the mechanical arts" in England. It is not surprising, therefore, that Adam Smith failed to anticipate the Industrial Revolution. We need to remember that, when the book appeared, the typical water-driven factory held 300–400 workers and there were only twenty or thirty such establishments in the whole of the British Isles. This helps to account for Adam Smith's neglect of fixed capital and for the conviction, which he never really abandoned, that agriculture was the principal source of Britain's wealth.

READER'S GUIDE TO THE WEALTH OF NATIONS

Division of Labor. Book I contains the core of Smith's theory of value and distribution; it opens with a discussion of the advantages of division of labor, understood in the sense of the specialization of tasks within an industry—later, in Book V, excessive specialization is admitted to have some disadvantages. But "division of labor" may also mean the separation of different trades and their concentration upon the production of single goods. This sense of the term soon comes to overshadow the earlier conception. Indeed, the whole of Book I is constructed upon the grand theme of the *social* division of labor: the economic system is in essence a vast network of interrelations among specialized producers held together by "the propensity to truck, barter, and exchange." The last magnificent paragraph of chapter 1—a beautiful example of eighteenth-century prose—makes this plain enough, and in the next chapter we are told that "the certainty of being able to exchange all that surplus part of the produce of his own labor, which is over and above his own consumption, for such parts of the produce of other men's labor as he may have occasion for, encourages every man to apply himself to a particular occupation, and to cultivate and to bring to perfection whatever talent or genius he may possess for that particular species of business." The characteristic eighteenth-century faith in the powerful influence of nurture as against nature explains why Smith neglects to cite the accommodation of different natural aptitudes as one of the advantages of the division of labor; but the territorial division of labor is ignored without any apparent reason, although the idea had been broached frequently by previous writers. Chapter 3 points out what is almost self-evident, that "the division of labor is limited by the extent of the market"; still, this chapter foreshadows all later discussions of the limits to increasing returns to scale. There is a striking emphasis in the chapter upon the economies brought by improved means of transportation and communication.

The Measure and Cause of Value. So far, exchange is considered solely as barter. In chapter 4 money is introduced and exchange value is distinguished from use value as illustrated by the water-diamond paradox; the chapter closes with an appeal to the reader's patience for the next three chapters, which investigate "the principles which regulate the exchangeable value of commodities." It is "a subject extremely abstracted," Smith concedes, and it "may perhaps, after the fullest explication which I am capable of giving it, appear still in some degree obscure." Most readers would put this remark down as the greatest understatement in the history of economic thought: chapter 5 in particular is difficult to follow and has attracted a bewildering variety of interpretations. The trouble lies in the fact that Smith himself was in two minds about the problem he was posing. "In order to investigate the conditions which regulate the exchangeable value of commodities," he declared, "I shall endeavor to show

"First, what is the real measure of this exchangeable value; or, wherein consists the real price of all commodities.

"Secondly, what are the different parts of which this real price is composed or made up.

"And, lastly, what are the different circumstances which sometimes raise some or all of these different parts of prices above, and sometimes sink them below their natural or ordinary rate; or what are the causes which sometimes hinder the market price, that is, the actual price of commodities, from coinciding exactly with what may be called their natural price."

This confuses two very different sorts of questions: what is the best measure of value and what is it that determines value? Chapter 5 takes up the first question and chapters 6 and 7 deal with the second question. For the sake of clarity, these two lines of inquiry ought to be kept strictly separate. Let us, therefore, pass over chapter 5 at this point and come back to it when we have dealt with the remainder of Book I.

Cost-of-Production Theory. Chapters 6 and 7 take up the traditional problem of value theory: Why are relative prices what they are? At any moment of time, of course, the "market price" is determined by supply and demand. But, as the forces of supply and demand work themselves out, the daily and even hourly fluctuations of the market price tend constantly to be reduced to a "normal" or, as Smith says, a "natural" level. What he calls "market price" and "natural price" is identical to what Marshall calls the short-period and the long-period price and, like Marshall, Smith is essentially interested in explaining how prices are determined in the long run. To motivate his ultimate explanation, Smith begins by constructing a simple model in which only one factor of production is used to produce commodities; this is his "early and rude state of society," where land is free and capital is nonexistent. In this one-factor world relative prices are obviously governed by relative labor costs, and even the premium that skilled labor receives over unskilled labor is no more than a payment for the labor cost of extra training: in a society of hunters—using their bare hands? —one beaver will exchange for two deers when it takes twice as much labor to kill a beaver as it does to kill a deer. But this argument is designed to show only that in the real world the exchange value of a commodity cannot be determined simply by the labor expended on its production. The value of a commodity is the sum of the normal amounts payable to all the factors used in making it; hence, in the real world the "natural price" of an article is determined by money costs of production as made up of wages, rents, and profits, themselves the "natural price" of labor, land, and capital.

A cost-of-production theory of the value of a commodity is obviously empty and meaningless if it does not include some explanation of how the prices of productive services are determined. But in fact Adam Smith had no consistent theory of wages and rents and no theory of profit or pure interest at all. But to say that the normal price of an article is the price that just covers costs is to explain prices by prices. In this sense, Adam Smith had no theory of value whatever. Be that as it may, it is clear that he had no labor theory of value, meaning by that the proposition that commodities exchange at ratios that are the reciprocals of the quantity of labor expended in their production, including the labor embodied in the participating capital goods. There is no suggestion in the *Wealth of Nations* that the different factors of production can be assimilated in terms of some common denominator other than money, and, in particular, there is no suggestion that the value of capital goods can be reduced to labor expended on their production in the past. Indeed, the construction of chapter 6 shows clearly that it was meant to be a refutation of the labor-cost theory of value hinted at by so many of Smith's predecessors; he shows that such a theory is valid only under the special and artificial conditions of an "early and rude state of society."

Supply-Determined Prices. Chapter 7, one of the high points of the book, is full of the kind of partial equilibrium analysis that has always been the bread and butter of economists. His reference to the effect of a public mourning on the price of black cloth is classic: a temporary shortage of black cloth raises the wages of tailors and the price of mourning cloth but does not affect the wages of weavers because the scarcity is temporary, while it reduces the price of substitutes like colored silk and the wages of workers producing the substitute. It is only when the producers of an article are neither gaining excess profits nor suffering actual losses that the price corresponds to its normal value. The constant adjustments of supply and demand are forever tending to produce the long-run "natural price," which just covers the cost of bringing the product to market. "Effectual demand," Smith points out, is the demand of those "who are willing to pay the natural price of a commodity"; it is the demand effective at the long-run equilibrium price. Now "the *quantity* of every commodity brought to the market naturally suits itself to the effectual demand," but the long-run *price* of a commodity is said to be governed solely by the outlays of producers on the supply side of the market. When it comes to the determination of natural price, demand is supposed to have no influence.

Smith did not justify his neglect of demand; he lacked the apparatus to do so. But it is possible to justify the argument with the aid of Marshallian reasoning. But notice first that his mention of "the paradox of value"—useful goods like water are free, whereas useless diamonds are expensive—is not an attempt to defend the neglect of demand. The passage begins with the remark that "the word value has two different meanings," and the statement of the paradox drives home the distinction between use value and exchange value; exchange value is the proper subject of investigation, Smith concludes. It is obvious to any modern reader that Smith means by "use value" the total utility of a whole class of commodities instead of the marginal utility of individual units: he is thinking of utility, not as the power to satisfy a want, but as the power to satisfy a biological or social need. He does not even trouble to say that use value is a prerequisite to exchange value, and, clearly, as he employs the word, it is not. Locke, Law, and Harris before him had contrasted the value of water with that of diamonds to show that relative scarcity governs value irrespective of the social usefulness of an article. And what governs relative scarcity? In the short run, supply and demand: this is exactly what Smith himself says later about the high price of precious stones (Book I, chap. 11, part 2). But in the long run, it was held, scarcity is governed solely by the cost of producing an article. This curious belief that only the short-run or market value of a commodity is the province of the forces of demand and supply is very characteristic of eighteenth-century economics, and it survived until the marginal revolution. It rests, of course, on a misunderstanding. When we say that value is determined by supply and demand, we mean merely that they are the channels through which ultimate factors like cost or utility operate: whatever regulates value does so via its effect upon supply and demand. But this is not how the matter was regarded in Smith's time. It is not that they rejected a utility theory of value because they thought utility was incapable of being quantitatively related to price but rather that they saw no relationship between utility, in their sense of the term, and demand and, moreover, dismissed demand and supply explanations of relative price as superficial.

If we look carefully at Smith's examples of price determination, we notice that he always assumes implicitly that the "natural price" of a commodity does not vary with its rate of output. In other words, he assumes that the industry in question produces under conditions of constant costs: to make two units of an article costs twice as much as to make one unit of it; cost per unit remains constant regardless of the level of output. This is the case in which the long-run supply curve of the industry is perfectly horizontal and in which the level of demand governs the quantity produced but has indeed no influence on price. Without realizing it, Adam Smith investigated a special case of the Marshallian theory of value, the case in which price is determined by supply alone. Under what conditions this case obtains we must leave until later.[1] Suffice it to say that a

[1] A somewhat different justification of Smith's approach will help to clarify the logic of the constant cost case. Recall the two-commodity one-factor society of hunters: let us express the rate at which deers can be turned into beavers through hunting by means of a production-transformation curve (Fig. 1). Since there is only one scarce resource, the transformation curve is in fact a straight line: the ratio of deers gained per beavers sacrificed is the same no matter what the amount of beavers or deers killed; when there is only one factor of production, the scale of operations cannot affect costs per unit of output because a

good argument could be made for it even now as the simplest general assumption. Still, the fact that we need Marshall to make sense of Smith affords an excellent illustration of what is meant by "analytical progress" in economics.

It may be useful to present Smith's argument graphically (Fig. 2). Consider the following passage:

"When the quantity of any commodity which is brought to market falls short of the effectual demand [the short-run supply curve S_1 shifts to S_2], all those who are willing to pay the whole value of the rent, wages, and profit, which must be paid in order to bring it thither, cannot be supplied with the quantity which they want [which is Q_1]. Rather than want it altogether, some of them will be willing to give more [to pay P_2]. A competition will immediately begin among them, and the market price will rise more or less above the natural price according as either the greatness of the deficiency, or the wealth and wanton luxury of the competitors, happen to animate more or less the eagerness of the competition. . . . When the quantity brought to market exceeds the effectual demand [S_1 shifts to S_3], it cannot be all sold to those who are willing to pay the whole value of the rent, wages, and profit, which must be paid in order to bring it thither. Some part must be sold to those who are willing to pay less, and the low price which they give for it must reduce the price of the whole. The market price will sink more or less below the natural price [fall to P_3], according as the greatness of the excess increases more or less the competition of the sellers, or according as it happens to be more or less important to them to get immediately rid of the commodity. . . . When the quantity brought to market is just sufficient to supply the effectual demand and no more, the market price naturally comes to be either exactly, or

---

factor of production is defined as consisting of units of equal efficiency. It takes two hours to kill a beaver as against one hour for a deer. Beavers should cost twice as much to buy as deers. But suppose that the rate of exchange is one deer per beaver instead of two. In that case, a beaver producer will give up producing *one* beaver in two hours and produce two deers instead, with which he can then buy *two* beavers. Deer hunting will increase and beaver hunting will decline until the rate of exchange is once again equal to the production-transformation ratio; the price is entirely determined by supply considerations. It would not matter if we imposed a pattern of demand in the form of a family of convex indifference curves. Equilibrium would be found at the tangency point with the transformation curve, and once again the market price ration would necessarily have the same slope as the transformation line. Under conditions of constant costs, relative prices are not influenced by demand.

If, however, as we approached the deer axis the beaver-cost of deers rose because hunters have to go farther afield for deers, while beavers can be obtained nearer home, the transformation curve would become concave. Now the structure of demand—the position of the indifference curves—does help to determine relative price. In the latter case we have introduced an additional factor of production, namely land, and land and labor cannot be combined with equal effi-

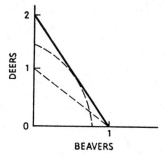

FIG. 1

ciency regardless of the absolute amount of each required. This means that the constant-cost case is analogous to the case of a single factor: although several factors are used, they are employed in fixed proportions, so that we can talk of a composite dose varying in amount but unchanged in composition.

as nearly as can be judged of, the same with the natural price. The whole quantity upon hand can be disposed of for this price, and cannot be disposed of for more. The competition of the different dealers obliges them all to accept of this price, but does not oblige them to accept of less."

It will be noticed that Smith thinks of demand and supply as referring to people's willingness to buy or sell at a particular price rather than at all possible prices; the former is expressed in actual amounts desired or offered, the latter in a schedule of amounts, each corresponding to a different price. Still, the whole of the passage given above has no real meaning unless demand at any rate is interpreted in the sense of a schedule, and a negatively inclined schedule at that. Here and elsewhere Smith intuitively gropes his way toward the right answer.

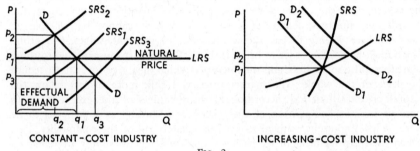

FIG. 2

The common usage of the term "competition" as denoting rivalry is reflected in his remark that a reduced supply leads to "competition" among buyers, which raises the price—a race to get limited supplies—while an excess supply leads to rivalry to get rid of the surplus, which causes the price to fall. He is aware of the fact that competition deprives the participants in the market process of the power to influence price and that the larger the number of sellers, the greater the obstacles to "combinations." In the course of chapter 7 he mentions not only these but also perfect information and perfect mobility of resources as prerequisites of competition; only homogeneity of the product is missing in a discussion that any modern textbook might envy. On the other hand, his brief treatment of monopoly at the end of the chapter is decidedly old-fashioned: monopoly prevails for any articles in fixed supply. Nonreproducible commodities, such as valuable paintings or "some vineyards in France," fall outside the scope of the theory of competitive price. But something like imperfect competition is hinted at when he remarks that "secrets of manufacture" induce monopoly, meaning presumably that they give the manufacturer some power over the price. He concludes that "the price of monopoly is upon every occasion the highest which can be squeezed out of the buyers," a misleading remark that nevertheless has the merit of recognizing that demand is responsive to price.

Wages. Chapters 8–11 contain Smith's theory of distribution. Chapter 8 is simply a compendium of wage theories. In the space of a half-dozen pages, we meet the wages fund theory, the subsistence theory, the bargaining theory, something like a productivity theory, and even a residual-claimant theory, without any recognition of the fact that these cannot all hold true on the same level of analysis. From the outset Smith adheres to the conception of capital or "stock" as consisting of "advances" to workmen to tide them over the period of production; hence, a connection is laid down between "the demand for those who live by wages" and "the funds which are destined for the payment of wages." This relationship is not explored but it is made the basis of the conviction that the growth of capital entails a constantly rising demand for labor. This short-run supply and demand theory—supply is given by the size of the labor force and demand by the size of the wages fund—is combined with a

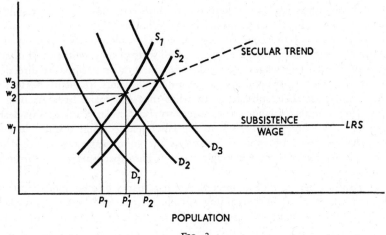

FIG. 3

long-run minimum-of-existence theory. Smith is not very clear as to how this adjustment takes place, but a Malthusian wages-population mechanism is implied.

The argument is perfectly analogous to the determination of the normal price of a commodity. (See Fig. 3.) The "natural price" of labor is the subsistence wage rate; labor is produced at a constant cost. Suppose the demand for labor increases from D_1 to D_2; wages rise to w_2 and, since "the demand for men, like that of any other commodity, necessarily regulates the production of men," this will in time induce population growth to p_1 (population = labor force), which causes wages to fall back to the subsistence level. But if demand is continuously rising, population growth will lag behind, and the secular trend in real wages along a third axis showing the passage of time may be upward, from w_2 to w_3, etc. The subsistence theory of wages, therefore, is perfectly compatible with a belief in the long-run tendency of wages to rise— and this quite apart from vertical upward shifts in the long-run supply curve as labor's notion of "subsistence" changes.

As a matter of fact, Smith does say that wages in Great Britain are in excess of subsistence. Britain and North America are examples of the "cheerful" progressive state where demand for labor outruns the supply. In "dull" stationary countries like China, however, wages have sunk to the subsistence level. At this point Smith makes an interesting slip in speaking of the minimum-of-existence wage as the lowest rate that "common humanity" allows; it has, of course, nothing to do with the benevolence of employers, being a function of the elasticity of supply of labor. In fact, Smith never adopts a consistent subsistence theory: it is only among "inferior ranks of people," he observes, that population varies with the supply of food. Moreover, he emphasizes the very remote application of the subsistence theory to practical problems of wage determination: (1) summer wages are invariably higher than winter wages, yet the cost of a worker's maintenance is lower in the summer than in the winter, and the reason for this is that the demand for agricultural labor falls off in cold weather; (2) while the price of "provisions" fluctuates continually, money wages vary little and sometimes remain constant for as much as a half-century, presumably because of the influence of custom in setting wages; (3) wages vary greatly in different parts of the country, but the price of food is almost everywhere uniform owing to the fact that "a man is of all sorts of luggage the most difficult to transport"; and (4) wages and food prices often move in opposite directions. In years of bumper crops and low wheat prices "servants frequently leave their masters, and trust their subsistence to what they can make by their own industry"; the shortage of labor causes wages to rise. Similarly, in years of dearth, wages fall as workmen flock back to the labor market. Adam Smith in effect makes the "mode of subsistence" a result of the going wage rate rather than a cause of it. Certainly there is enough material here that points away from the subsistence theory.

In the earlier part of chapter 8 Smith remarks briefly, and almost as a matter of course, that the bargaining advantage in a labor market always lies on the side of the employer, employers "being fewer in number" and able to "hold out much longer." Moreover, the law favors employers. Hence, "masters" are "always and everywhere in a sort of tacit, but constant and uniform combination, not to raise the wages of labor above their actual rate." Taken strictly, this argument sits uneasily next to remarks about "common humanity," and it flies in the face of the emphasis in the rest of the chapter upon the upward pull on demand for labor in a growing economy. But it has all the germs of the Marshallian thesis that there is indeterminacy in the labor market because it is by its nature a noncompetitive market. Marshall, too, drew attention to the significance of fewness on the buying side in the labor market and, as did Smith, noted that workers lack reserves for a protracted struggle with employers.

This chapter closes on an optimistic note. Wages have been rising in "the course of the present century," and higher wages have not reduced incentives. The mercantilist notion that the short-run supply of labor is backward sloping is strongly condemned: a rise in wages will bring about an increase in supply of labor services.

Profits. Chapter 9 deals with the "profits of stock" without saying very much about the nature of profit as income. Earlier, in chapter 6, Smith pointed out that profits are not to be confused with the wages of management, which vary with "the quantity, the hardship, or the ingenuity of this supposed labor of inspection and direction"; more than this we are never told. The burden of chapter 9 is that the rate of profits tends to fall in the course of economic progress owing to "mutual competition" as the "stocks of many rich merchants are turned into the same trade." But so long as output is growing, it is difficult to see why "mutual competition" alone should lead to falling profit margins. It is only later, in Book II, chapter 4, that a satisfactory reason is given, namely, the increasing difficulty of finding new profitable investment outlets. Throughout this chapter Smith speaks of profits as consisting of interest plus a risk premium. In such countries as Britain, he thinks, about one half of what is normally regarded as profits is pure interest on capital; the rest is a payment for superintendence and risk. The trend in the rate of profit, therefore, can be roughly inferred from movements in the market rate of interest. The rate of interest has been falling for centuries and seems everywhere inversely related to the degree of economic development of a country. Generally, wages rise and profits fall in the process of capital accumulation; a new colony, however, may experience both rising wages and a rising rate of profit.

Relative Wages. Chapter 10, part 1, digresses from the main theme to discuss the structure of wages. It is perhaps the best piece of economic analysis in the *Wealth of Nations,* and, although it leans heavily on Cantillon, a reading of the corresponding chapters in Cantillon's *Essai* (chaps. 7 and 8) is likely to raise one's respect for Adam Smith. Quite apart from its classic treatment of relative wage differences, this chapter has an important role to play in the general structure of Book I; indeed, without it the troublesome fifth chapter makes little sense. Smith traces all differences in wages rates in stationary equilibrium to differences in (1) the agreeableness of different occupations, (2) the cost of acquiring the skill to carry them on, (3) the degree of regularity of employment, (4) the trust and responsibility imposed upon those employed, and (5) the probability of success, given the great uncertainty of earnings in some lines of employment. The second reason would diminish in significance if we looked at lifetime earnings, and the third would disappear if we considered yearly instead of daily wages. One may also wonder whether the fourth reason is really tenable, assuming as it does either that responsibility is irksome or that high wages for those subject to temptations are a necessary insurance policy against theft and betrayal; one might argue about either assumption. The fifth reason is particularly interesting because it involves choice under uncertainty. Until recently, these pages in Smith and a few pages in Marshall's *Principles* exhausted the content of economic analysis of choices among unsure prospects. Smith uses casual evidence from lotteries and insurance to show that people tend to overvalue uncertain gains and to undervalue uncertain losses: apparently, there is something like "love of gambling" and "contempt for risk." He argues that all professions that hold out the prospect of high but uncertain incomes for the few will show a mean rate of reward below that of comparable occupations whose earnings can be predicted with perfect certainty. Men will overestimate their chances of success and so overcrowd the risky professions. This line of reasoning is then applied with some appropriate qualifications to differential rates of profit in different industries.

The general implication of the chapter is more important than matters of detail. Perfect competition, Adam Smith is saying, while it may not equalize the monetary return of different occupations, does equalize the "net advantages" of employments to individuals as a unit. The market tends to reduce the various types of labor to a common measure: equal units of labor in the sense of disutility are at any one time compensated by equal amounts of money wages. This assumes, of course, that the labor market is perfectly competitive and, in particular, that there is perfect mobility of labor between different occupations; this is so obvious that Smith hardly bothers to say it, but he does add that net advantages are equalized only when there is adequate information about the monetary and nonmonetary alternatives of different occupations and when they are the sole employ of those who occupy them.

Adam Smith's analysis of the wage structure, remarkable as it is, is inadequate. In the face of the imperfections that almost all labor markets exhibit, any analysis based on perfect competition is unlikely to explain the wage differentials that we observe. Moreover, Smith's stationary treatment leaves out of account such a significant dynamic influence as the mobility between socioeconomic classes. Even to this day, however, economics has not provided a satisfactory explanation of the perverse character of wage scales in most labor markets, perverse in the sense that wages seem to vary perfectly inversely to the disutility of labor.

Chapter 10, part 2, on the "Policy of Europe," may be passed over quickly but it does contain some excellent economic history. It condemns the exclusive privileges of trading companies, the apprenticeship laws, the Settlements Acts and the Poor Laws in general, for restricting the scope of competition and interfering with the mobility of labor. The threat of monopolistic practices is ever present: "people of the same trade seldom meet together but the conversation ends in a conspiracy to raise prices."

Rent. Chapter 11 deals formally with rent. Here rent is treated as a differential surplus and hence as price-determined: "high or low wages and profit, are the cause of high or low price; high or low rent is the effect of it." Moreover, this surplus is made a function of both differences in fertility and differences in situation. The whole treatment is suggestive of the later Ricardian theory of rent. Earlier in the book, however, rent is regarded as price-determining because land not receiving going rentals will be withdrawn from cultivation (chapter 9). Letting this contradiction stand for the moment, we turn to the conclusion of chapter 11. Parts 1–3 of chapter 11 can be skipped without too much loss, although part 2 contains a significant distinction between foodstuffs, the demand for which is highly inelastic, and luxury goods, the demand for which is generally elastic: "The desire for food is limited in every man by the narrow capacity of the human stomach." The concluding pages of chapter 11 declare without proof that economic progress entails rising money rents, rising real rents, and a rising rental share of national income. The interests of landowners, though they "reap where they never sowed," are therefore inseparably connected with the general interests of society, whereas the interests of merchants and manufacturers are always antisocial: since the rate of profits declines as wealth accumulates, their interest is always "to widen the market and to narrow the competition." Any notion that Smith is an apologist for the industrial classes is dispelled by a reading of the acid sentence that closes Book I; a similar acerbic sentiment appears at the end of Book IV, chapter 2.

A Social Unit of Accounting. We turn back now to chapter 5, entitled "Of the Real and Nominal Price of Commodities, or of Their Price in Labour, and Their Price in Money." This is concerned, not with value theory, but with welfare economics and, in particular, with the problem of index numbers. The real price of a thing is, of course, its purchasing power over all other goods; it is its nominal price corrected for changes in the value of money. Smith decides, however, to correct nominal values for changes in money wage rates rather than changes in the level of prices. This peculiar solution to the index-number problem reminds us immediately of Keynes, who adopted Smith's procedure, defining real income in terms of employment rather than of physical output. By using a wage unit as a deflator—the money wage rate paid for an hour of common labor —Keynes obtained a one-to-one relationship between income and employment, given a constant share of wages in total income.[2] In the short run it makes little difference whether one corrects for price changes or for wage changes, but in the long run the choice of a deflator is a serious matter, for, as the productivity of labor rises, prices will normally fall relative to wage rates. Unlike Keynes, Adam Smith did want to measure real income over long periods of time, and his choice of a labor standard was dictated, not by any conviction that money wages are less subject to variation than prices in general, but by his conception of the nature of economic welfare.

The purpose of an index number is that it enables us to estimate whether an individual or a society is better off over changes in time and place. Nowadays we assume that an increase in real income is tantamount to an improvement in welfare. But Adam Smith tried to go deeper, associating improvements in welfare with a reduction in the sacrifices required to obtain a slab of real income. Labor is irksome, and "toil and trouble" is the ultimate scarce factor of production. An individual's "wealth" is naturally measured by the ability to command other people's products, but the pursuit of wealth under a division of labor is motivated by the desire to save ourselves disagreeable labor and to impose it instead upon others; so a man values his wealth or a commodity that he possesses by the amount of other people's labor he can buy with it in the market. The "real value" of a commodity is its labor price, meaning by labor not a certain number of man-hours but units of disutility, the psychological cost of work to the individual, and meaning by value esteem value rather than exchange value.

With this much in mind, chapter 5 is plain sailing. In "that rude and original state of society" when "the whole produce of labor belongs to the laborer," the personal labor embodied in commodities coincides with their purchasing power over labor. A man is then rich or poor according to the value of his own labor services or his purchasing power over other men's labor, for the two are identical. With the rise of property income, this coincidence is broken: the value of a commodity measured in current wage units—the quantity of labor that it can command in exchange—now exceeds the value of the labor embodied in its production by the whole value of profits and rents. Nevertheless, the "real value," or effort price of a commodity, is still to be measured by the units of "toil and trouble" that it can purchase in the market at the going wage rate. But whose "toil and trouble" is to be the invariant standard of subjective welfare? Different types of labor are not all equally disagreeable.

[2] If Y = money income, N = employment, W = the money wage bill and w = the money wage rate, then real income = Y/w, labor's relative share = W/Y and $(Y/w)(W/Y) = N$, from which follows the statement above.

Smith dismisses this problem in chapter 5 with a curt reference to "the higgling and bargaining of the market," which will establish some "sort of rough equality" between the esteem value of labor of different skills. Strangely enough, he does not refer the reader to chapter 10, where he demonstrates, as we have seen, that competition equalizes the monetary return to units of disutility of labor. In principle, therefore, it should be possible to construct a representative wage unit.

A standard of measurement, as Smith points out, must itself be invariable in order accurately to reflect changes in the things being measured. But it is true that the disutility of an hour of labor remains the same to individuals with the passage of time? Yes, Smith postulates, appealing to our intuitive feeling of pain cost: "Equal quantities of labor, at all times and places, *may be said* to be of equal [esteem] value to the laborer," in that they represent "the same proportion of his ease, liberty, and happiness." Once this is granted, it can be argued that when a worker receives more wage goods per unit of effort "it is their [esteem] value which varies, not that of the labor which purchases them"; this remark, which has puzzled so many commentators, is perfectly logical in the context.

Having defended his labor standard of "real value," Smith directs attention to the problem of selecting a stable value coefficient to express the wage unit. For calendar periods of moderate lengths a nominal wage unit in terms of silver will prove satisfactory owing to the relative stability of the value of silver "from year to year" and even "for half a century or a century together." However, for longer periods a corn-wage unit is more suitable: the price of corn fluctuates sharply in the short run and rarely in the same direction or with the same amplitude as money wages, but "from century to century" corn prices are remarkably stable. As he explains in the "Digression concerning the Variations of the Value of Silver," appended to Book I, the reason for this is that cost-reducing improvements in agriculture are "more or less counterbalanced" by the rising price of cattle, "the principal instruments of agriculture." And, since corn is "the basic subsistence of the people," the money price of corn governs money wages in the long run. The argument is complete: the wage unit in real terms (the wages of common labor measured in corn) is invariant through time and reflects an invariant disutility of labor.

The burden of Smith's comments is that the labor-commanded standard provides a *positive* index of welfare: the higher the "real price" of a commodity measured in wage units, the better off we are for having it; a nation is "richer" the more labor the total product commands. This makes welfare a simple positive function of population: "the most decisive mark of prosperity in any country is the increase of the number of its inhabitants." But if money wages rise faster than the money value of output, that is, if labor's relative share rises, the total product will not yield a larger value expressed in terms of current wage units. This shows only that Smith's wage unit must be held constant at its base-year value. Let us not be deceived, Smith seems to say, by a rise in money wages associated with a rise in output. What we want to know is how many hours of toil and trouble the larger output really represents, for the esteem value of an hour of toil and trouble never alters.

As soon as we drop the idea of a constant real wage rate, expressing a constant disutility of labor, Smith's argument may produce a *negative* index of economic welfare. If real wages are rising or prices are falling because of a rise in the productivity of labor, the number of current wage units commanded by the total product year after year may tend downward: a glance at the last footnote will show that the necessary condition for a negative index is a rise in real wages in excess of output per man. Actually, the negative index makes much better sense because a fall in the amount of labor that a commodity commands in exchange is the reciprocal of labor's purchasing power over a commodity. As the total product commands less labor, labor's purchasing power over real income rises. So interpreted, Smith's standard of welfare would give the same answer as Ricardo's. Ricardo's standard makes improving welfare a negative function of human effort per unit of output. The practical difficulty of Smith's approach is the untenable assumption of constancy in real wages, and this in turn reflects the heroic assumption of a constant outlay of subjective sacrifice per unit of effort "at all times." Most of us would argue that a major element in the improvement of welfare in a growing economy is the falling effort-price of income: as the work sheet declines and real wages rise, the disutility of labor surely increases. An equal disutility of labor "at all places" is probably a no more defensible assumption, although that is what is often assumed in making international comparisons of economic welfare. For instance, Soviet living standards may be compared with American living standards by asking how many hours of work, rewarded at the going rate, would be required to buy specific articles at current prices in each of the two countries. This procedure assumes, among other things, that the disutility of labor in the U.S.S.R. is the same as in the U.S.A.

Adam Smith, it used to be said, tried to formulate a labor theory of value but got horribly confused between the "labor commanded" by a product and the "labor embodied" in its production. The origins of this legend are to be found in Ricardo's *Principles,* but the authorized version is by Marx. In a profit economy the labor equivalent of a commodity always exceeds the labor required to produce it; hence, Marx implies, different relative prices result from using one standard rather than the other. The fallacy here is obvious: if two commodities exchange at a ratio determined by the relative man-hours required to produce them, they will of course command the same labor, or apples, in the market. That Adam Smith could have confused two such different things as the labor price and the labor cost of a product is absurd. To speak of the exchange value of a thing as its purchasing power over other things, or as the rate at which it exchanges for other things, is to use two different expressions for the same meaning, and neither remark implies any theory of value. Smith did not try to formulate anything properly called a labor theory of value: chapter 5 presents a labor theory of subjective welfare, chapter 6 toys with a primitive theory of price determination in the special case in which labor is the only factor of production, and chapter 7 offers a cost-of-production theory of relative prices. It is perfectly true that the *Wealth of Nations* starts with the sentence: "the annual labor of every nation is the fund which originally supplies it with . . . produce," but it is obvious that this is designed to emphasize the fact that wealth consists of real resources and not of money. The phrase "labor is the foundation and essence of wealth" was among the shibboleths of the time, a convenient weapon against mercantilist thinking.

The Trend of Prices. The "Digression" on the value of silver (chap. 11) makes use of the labor standard in analyzing the history of prices. This is Smith the economic historian at his best. It begins with a study of the wheat price of silver between 1350 and 1750, an excellent example of the use of the quantity theory of money in its dynamic eighteenth-century version. After a brief and unimportant section on the relative value of gold and silver, he launches upon a lengthy and really masterful analysis of the price structure of wage goods. The general thesis is that agricultural products rise in price in the course of economic progress, while the price of manufactured articles tends naturally to fall. This is the origin of the famous classical notion that agriculture operates under conditions of diminishing returns, while industry enjoys increasing returns, returns being defined in a historical sense. The reader who skips this section because it is called a digression misses one of the most interesting sections of the *Wealth of Nations.*

Capital and Income. Book II deals with capital accumulation as the mainspring of economic progress. The introduction immediately lays down the conception that capital is in essence a stock of unfinished goods that permits the producer to span the time interval between the application of inputs and the emergence of final output. Chapter 1 distinguishes between fixed and circulating capital and emphasizes the different proportions of fixed and working capital in different industries. Circulating capital consists of those goods that yield a return to their owners by being sold, in contrast to fixed capital goods, which take part in the productive process without changing hands. It is an essential characteristic of circulating capital goods that they embody a quantity of purchasing power that perpetually returns to their owner as he disposes of them; this led later writers to think of circulating capital in money terms, with disastrous results for the understanding of problems of capital theory. But with Adam Smith, circulating capital is still conceived in real terms. Fixed capital he defined as including not only implements and buildings but also human capital, the capital value of "the acquired and useful habits of all the members of the society." This follows quite rightly from the fact that capital stands for "produced means of production": the acquired skills of workers is certainly "produced" by using up material resources.

Chapter 2 contains the bulk of Smith's theory of money and defines gross and net revenue. Gross revenue is apparently equal to what we now call gross national product; net revenue is equal to our net national product, or gross revenue minus depreciation on fixed capital. At first, Smith suggests deducting the expenses of maintaining both fixed and circulating capital, but in the end he does not go as far as Ricardo in confining net revenue to profits plus rent. But if the capital stock includes human capital, we ought to net out all payments necessary to keep human capital intact, consisting of physical maintenance charges in the form of subsistence wages plus a depreciation and replacement allowance in the form of expenditures on the rearing and training of new workers. All these represent "real costs" in the sense of necessary outlays to make production physically possible. The physiocrats were quite consistent in deducting the whole of wages paid out from the final product, treating workers' consumption as an intermediate product. Moreover, such a definition of net revenue is perfectly sensible in a society oriented to maximum capital accumulation.

Banking. The function of banking is to economize upon the stock of precious metals: paper money "never can exceed the value of the gold and silver, of which it supplies the place" because excess paper will go abroad or be presented to banks in payment for gold: this is the Law of Reflux, which received a thorough airing in the monetary controversies over the Bank Charter Act of 1844. But paper money has been issued to excess owing to speculative "over-trading of some bold projectors." This would not have happened if banks had only discounted "real bills of exchange"; here is the origin of the real-bills doctrine, which survived through the nineteenth century to be enshrined in the Federal Reserve Act of 1913. There follows a brief discussion of Law's scheme to establish land banks and a history of the Bank of England.

Productive and Unproductive Labor. Chapter 3 introduces the concept of productive labor, followed by a powerful eulogy of saving and a hint of Say's Law. Smith's distinction between productive and unproductive labor is probably the most maligned concept in the history of economic doctrines. But, unsatisfactory as is Smith's discussion, his meaning is perfectly clear and by no means nonsensical. The chapter is entitled "On the Accumulation of Capital, or of Productive and Unproductive Labor," and its subject matter cannot be understood independently of Smith's value judgment that the rate of net investment must be maximized. What he is driving at is the distinction between activity that results in capital accumulation and activity that services the needs of households. In a country poor in capital, the unproductive use of savings in service industries catering to the demand for luxuries may be as serious a block to economic development as insufficiency of saving itself. What Smith is saying is that saving should be used to create productive—income-generating and capacity-adding—equipment or to improve technical facilities. And, however unfashionable it has become to distinguish between productive and unproductive labor in this sense, the distinction is always revived during wartime, when it is made the basis of drafting some people and deferring others.

Smith offers two definitions of productive labor. First, the value versions: productive labor adds net value to the product, or, to use Smithian language, "the price of that subject, can afterwards, if necessary, put into motion a quantity of labor equal to [or greater than] that which had originally produced it." This is a very modern definition and would convey Smith's meaning if he had confined net revenue to profits plus rent. The second definition is the more famous storage version: productive labor "realizes itself in some particular subject or vendible commodity," while the services of unproductive labor "perish in the very instant of their performance." Hence, the greater the proportion of labor force that is productively employed, the greater the tangible stock of means of production and the greater the economy's capacity to produce in the following year. This latter version comes closer to catching the spirit of Smith's argument, but it is hardly foolproof even on his own grounds: labor engaged in transmitting technical knowledge is unproductive on this score, but knowledge, however intangible, can be accumulated and does affect a society's rate of economic growth. But this is quibbling. Despite much criticism, Smith's distinction was never abandoned by any of the leading classical economists and was handed down in the end to Marx to become the basis of present-day Soviet national income accounting.

Say's Law is suggested by Smith's paradoxical dictum that "what is annually saved is as regularly consumed as what is annually spent, and nearly in the same time too; but it is consumed by a different set of people." Now, what is saved is invested and hence is not consumed; but Smith implies that investment results in income payments, which in turn get spent on consumption. Smith's way of putting the matter, however, is positively misleading; nevertheless, these words were echoed and re-echoed by two generations of economists. Properly understood, the dictum attacks the popular fallacy that saving destroys purchasing power; this is why it appealed to Smith's followers. Saving is not a problem as such, the argument ran, for it generates purchasing power as much as luxury spending. The operative proposition hidden away in Smith's phraseology is that saving is tantamount to investment because "hoarding," the building-up of monetary holdings, is regarded as an exceptional occurrence. This is tied up in turn with the view, in evidence in this chapter, that the medium-of-exchange function of money is the monetary function par excellence. In Book I, chapter 4, Smith had conceded that people do have a demand for money-to-hold for liquidity reasons: "prudent men" will hold "a certain quantity of some one commodity such as they imagined few people would be likely to refuse in exchange for the produce of their industry." But typically he argued that money will be promptly spent because "it is not for its own sake that men desire money, but for the sake of what they can purchase with it" (Book IV, chap. 1). By ruling out hoarding, money is indeed reduced to serving as a medium of exchange and no more: in consequence, saving or nonconsumption is necessarily identical to investment. The saving-is-spending theorem, therefore, implies a definite theory of money, and vice versa.

Smith never suggests that saving is a function of the rate of interest or of the size of net revenue. Saving habits are thought to be institutionally and indeed ideologically determined. "The principle which prompts to save, is the desire of bettering our condition," which is said, on the whole, to overcome "the principle which prompts to expense, the passion for present enjoyment." Bank credit is used to finance working capital, but increases in fixed capital depend upon reinvested earnings; hence, the frugal man who is called a public benefactor is invariably identified as a manufacturer, just as landowners are constantly pictured as prodigals. Near the end of the chapter Smith observes that, contrary to popular opinion and the flood of pamphlets by "very candid and intelligent people," the national income of England has been rising since the Restoration; that it was necessary to assert this emphatically tells us much about the climate of opinion at the time.

An Optimum Investment Pattern. In chapter 4 we come back to interest, the theory of the declining rate of profit, and a vigorous critique of monetary theories of interest. Smith gives qualified approval to the existing Usury Laws, which limit the rate of interest to 5 per cent because only "prodigals and projectors" would give more than that and this would mean that "a great part of the capital of the country would thus be kept out of the hands which were more likely to make a profitable and advantageous use of it." Chapter 5 defends

middlemen and retailers as productive laborers and sketches of optimum investment policy for a country. The criterion invoked is net value added measured
in terms of wage units—the amount of labor "put in motion"—by equal
quantities of capital in equal periods of time. The so-called "hierarchy of productivity of industries" is headed by agriculture, on the grounds that the value
of the product of agriculture is sufficient to pay rent as well as wages and profits.
This argument is wrong if we adopt Ricardo's notion of rent as a differential
surplus; at the margin, agriculture no more yields rent than does manufacturing.
Next in the order of productivity comes manufacture, then inland trade, then
foreign trade, and, last, the carrying trade. The turnover rate of domestic capital
is greater in inland trade than in foreign trade because the inland trader reduces
the turnover period of two domestic industries, while foreign trade reduces the
turnover period of only one domestic producer. The carrying trade comes last
because it neither economizes domestic capital nor implements productivity.
The whole argument is employed against the mercantilist policy of favoring
foreign commerce and manufacturing, and the sense of it seems to be that the
natural stages in the evolution of a nation's industries are dictated by the practical
need to minimize the capital-labor ratio: agriculture is most productive because
here a unit of capital will set the maximum amount of labor in motion. An
environment of severe capital scarcity is implicit throughout the discussion.

Synoptic History. Book III discusses "the different progress of opulence
in different nations," with a wealth of historical illustrations. In effect, it is a
separate monograph on the development of agriculture in Europe since the fall
of the Roman Empire. Book IV, as we already know, is devoted to mercantilist
theory (chap. 1) and policy (chaps. 2–8), with two badly placed and rather
tedious monographs on "Banks of Deposits" and the "Corn Trade," concluding
with a final chapter on the physiocrats. The introduction to Book IV defines
political economy as a branch of statecraft, a definition in violent opposition
to the whole tenor of the *Wealth of Nations.*

The Invisible Hand. Book IV, chapter 2 presents a simple argument in
favor of free trade. It can never pay an individual to produce himself what he
can buy more cheaply from someone else, and "what is prudence in the conduct
of every private family, can scarce be folly in that of a great Kingdom"—a
fallacy of composition that Smith had earlier condemned in the mercantilists.
He enlists the powerful motive of self-interest to show that the general welfare
is best promoted by removing all restrictions on imports and exports. Intending
only their own good, men are led by "an invisible hand" to further social ends.
The underlying thesis is that the interest of the community is simply the sum
of the interests of the members who compose it: each man, if left alone, will
seek to maximize his own wealth; therefore, all men, if unimpeded, will maximize aggregate wealth. But a legend has grown up that the whole of the *Wealth
of Nations* rests on this kind of naïve reasoning, the so-called doctrine of the
spontaneous harmony of interests. But "the obvious and simple system of natural
liberty," which is said to reconcile private interests and economic efficiency, turns
out upon examination to be identical with the concept of perfect competition;
the "invisible hand" is nothing more than the automatic equilibrating mechanism
of the competitive market.

That perfect competition does have optimizing characteristics we cannot doubt, and, primitive as is Smith's argument, he had shown earlier in the book that competition, by equalizing rates of return and by eroding excess gains, leads to an optimum allocation of labor and capital between industries. This is only part of a complete proof that competition maximizes welfare, but it is enough to exonerate Adam Smith from the charge of having indulged in naïve philosophizing. Furthermore, if we draw up a list of the defects that Smith admits in the natural order—the conflicts of interests, the cases where the pursuit of private gain leads to socially undesirable results—we should have sufficient ammunition, as Viner said, for several socialist orations. For instance, in the chapter under discussion, given over to a plea for free trade, protectionist measures are justified in the case of infant industries and in retaliation against foreign tariffs, the Navigation Laws are defended because "defence is of more importance than opulence," and complete freedom of trade is regarded as a utopian dream, too much to hope for in view of the vested interests of manufacturers. And in chapter 9 he notes that the state has "three duties of great importance": the provision of military security, the administration of justice, and "the duty of erecting and maintaining certain public works and certain public institutions, which it can never be for the interest of any individual, or small number of individuals, to erect and maintain; because the profit could neither repay the expense to any individual or small number of individuals, though it may frequently do much more than repay it to a great society." As Pigou was to say later, the private costs of public works greatly exceed the social costs owing to the presence of external economies for which the private investors cannot charge. The presence of external effects in production and consumption constitutes the chief source of nonoptimality under perfect competition: the whole is no longer the mere arithmetic sum of the individual parts. Of course, Adam Smith did not look at matters this way, but, at the same time, he seems perfectly aware that laissez faire creates only a presumption of maximum social welfare not a complete program for its achievement.

Chapters 3 and 4 warm to the task of exposing mercantilist legislation. Chapter 5 notes that the influx of specie in a country tends to turn the balance of trade against it, but the argument stops short of Hume's specie-flow proposition. Chapter 6 comes back to a discussion of the Methuen Treaty and the mysteries of seignorage. Chapter 7, together with the closing remarks of Book V, spells out Smith's anticolonial position. Chapter 8 describes the prevailing system of customs and excises in England and concludes with a plea for consumers' sovereignty: "in the mercantile system, the interest of the consumer is almost constantly sacrificed to that of the producer."

Taxation and the Public Debt. Book V, covering one third of the total volume, is a self-contained treatise on public finance, composed of a historical analysis of state revenues and expenditures and an elementary theory of incidence. Chapter 1, part 1, provides a history of warfare since ancient times; part 2 presents a Marxist theory of the state; part 3 deals with public works, such as "good roads, bridges, navigable canals, harbors," followed by a typical Smithian digression on the education of the young. As one reads his analysis of the evolution of civil government, of justice, of standing armies, and of the human family, it becomes clear that he held definite views about the nature of the historical process. Like other Scottish writers of the time, such as Adam Ferguson,

John Millar, William Robertson, and even David Hume, he expounds a philosophy of history that attaches unique significance to the nature and distribution of property. It is no exaggeration to describe these men as forerunners of "the materialist conception of history."

Chapter 2 is devoted to taxes, beginning with the famous four canons of taxation—it would be better to say, beginning with the ability-to-pay theory and three administrative canons. The upshot of his theory of incidence is that all taxes fall ultimately on landlords because of their ownership of a fixed immobile resource. He mentions the "very ingenious theory" of the physiocrats and, without approving of *l'impôt unique,* nevertheless leans favorably in the direction of taxing ground rent. Taxes on wages raise wages by the full amount of the tax, except as disguised by a consequent fall in the demand for labor; this implies either that the demand for labor is perfectly inelastic—the crude wages fund doctrine—or that the long-run supply curve of labor is perfectly elastic— the subsistence theory of wages. The closing section of chapter 2, "Taxes upon Consumable Commodities," is rich with implicit suggestions about the demand-elasticities of different types of goods.

Chapter 3, on public debts, is strongly flavored by the classical prejudice against public expenditures and the "Treasury View" that public spending financed by the sale of government bonds necessarily diverts productive labor into unproductive employment.

Adam Smith as Economist. In appraising Adam Smith, or any other economist, we ought always to remember that brilliance in handling purely analytical concepts is a very different thing from a firm grasp of the essential logic of economic relationships. Superior technique does not necessarily imply superior economic insight, and vice versa. Judged by standards of analytical competence, Smith is not the greatest of eighteenth-century economists. But for acute insight into the nature of the economic process, it would be difficult to find Smith's equal.

The central theme that inspires the *Wealth of Nations* is the workings of "the invisible hand." It is not to the benevolence of the baker but to his self-interest that we owe our bread. Smith had caught sight of the pregnant consideration that under certain social arrangements, which we would describe as perfect competition, private interests are indeed harmonized with social interests. Without collective regulation or single design, a market economy nevertheless conforms to orderly rules of behavior. Each individual, being one among many, can exert only a negligible influence upon the total market situation. In effect, he takes prices as given and is free only to vary the quantity bought and sold at given prices, driven by the motive of maximizing his own gain. Yet the sum of all these separate actions determines prices; each person, viewed separately, is ruled by prices, and yet prices themselves are governed by the sum total of all individual reactions. The "invisible hand" of the market in this way assures a social result that is independent of individual will and intention.

Moreover, these automatic market results have definite optimizing characteristics. The prejudice that every action motivated by private gain must be antisocial by virtue of this fact alone was widely current in the eighteenth century. Even today, man-in-the-street socialism takes comfort in the idea that a free market economy cannot possibly promote public interests because it is a system motivated by private profit not by consciously designed social ends. It was Smith's task to shift the burden of proof and to create the presumption that a decentralized price system produces "maximum satisfactions." No doubt, his demonstration of this proposition was incomplete and unsatisfactory. It seems at times to rest upon nothing else than the notion of the arithmetic addibility of individual satisfactions: since everyone maximizes his own satisfactions when freely permitted to do so, laissez faire will maximize the satisfactions of the whole community. But in fact Smith's demonstration of the doctrine of "maximum satisfactions" went much deeper. In Book I, chapter 7, he had shown that free competition tends to equate prices to costs of production, tending to optimize the allocation of resources *within* industries. In chapter 10 he showed that free competition in factor markets would equalize the "net advantages" of factors in all industries and thus establish an optimum allocation of resources *between* industries. He did not show that the product sold would be optimally distributed among individual consumers or that the different factors would be combined in optimal proportions in production. But he did take the first step toward the theory of the optimum efficient allocation of *given* resources under perfect competition.

It is true to say, however, that his own faith in the benefits of "the invisible hand" rested very little upon static considerations of allocative efficiency. "Atomistic" competition was desirable because of its dynamic effects in widening the scope of the market and extending the advantages of the division of labor—in short, because of its tendency to foster the accumulation of capital and the growth of income. But he was no crass exponent of harmony doctrine. In his refreshingly cynical manner, he returned again and again to the theme of class conflict and to the weapons of "ideology"—false consciousness—which the classes wielded in the struggle for political supremacy. It is this quality, combined with his understanding of the "rule of law" provided by the price system, that makes the *Wealth of Nations* a masterpiece of *political* economy.

NOTES FOR FURTHER READING

The definitive edition of the *Wealth of Nations* by E. Cannan is reprinted in the Modern Library Series. The standard biography is by J. Rae, *Life of Adam Smith* (1895)—it has little on the man, but much on his times; new findings are reported in W. R. Scott, *Adam Smith as Student and Professor* (1937). The question of Smith's sources of influence has undergone serious modification since the turn of the last century; for a review of this development see W. R. Scott, *Studies Relating to Adam Smith during the Last Fifty Years* (1940).

For an interesting discussion of Smith's attitude to the innovators of his day see R. Koebner, "Adam Smith and the Industrial Revolution," *EHR*, April, 1959; additional materials on the factual background of the *Wealth of Nations* will be found in T. S. Ashton, *An Economic History of England: The Eighteenth Century* (1955). E. Cannan, *History of the Theories of Production and Distribution* (1953), chap. 1, secs. 5–7; chap. 3; chap. 4, secs. 1–3; chap. 6, secs. 1–3, calls for special notice as the classic discussion of Smith's confused treatment of the concepts of capital and income. For a useful but topheavy article on the same topic see H. Aujac, "En manière d'introduction l'emploi chez Adam Smith," *EA*, juillet-décembre, 1951. P. H. Douglas analyzes "Smith's Theory of Value and Distribution," *Adam Smith, 1776–1926* (1928), reprinted in *DET*. The Marxist interpretation of Smith's value theory is that Smith had two labor theories of value; this interpretation is open to question, but the reader should consult what is perhaps the best exposition of it: R. L. Meek, *Studies in the Labour Theory of Value* (1956), chap. 2. For counterarguments see Schumpeter, *History*, pp. 181–94, which incidentally ranks Smith below Petty, Cantillon, Quesnay, and Turgot in an effort to deflate the usual estimate. See also H. M. Robertson and W. L. Taylor, "Adam Smith's Approach to the Theory of Value," *EJ*, 1957, reprinted in *EET*, and D. F. Gordon, "What Was the Labor Theory of Value?" *AER*, May, 1959. Smith's doctrine of productive labor, and what his followers made of it, are sympathetically discussed by H. Myint in a stimulating book, *Theories of Welfare Economics* (1948), chap. 5. Myint emphasizes the classical preoccupation with problems of development. For a verbal description of Smith's model of economic growth see A. Lowe, "The Classical Theory of Economic Growth," *SR*, Summer, 1957.

J. Viner, "Adam Smith and Laissez Faire," *Adam Smith, 1776–1926*, reprinted in *The Long View and the Short* (1959), is an article no one can afford to neglect. It concludes that "the modern advocate of laissez faire who objects to government participation in business on the ground that it is an encroachment upon a field reserved by nature for private enterprise cannot find support for this argument in the *Wealth of Nations.*" The contrast between the rationalism of natural-law doctrine and Smith's own empirical and historical method is brought out by H. J. Bitterman, "Adam Smith's Empiricism and the Law of Nature," *JPE*, August, October, 1940. Those who see an obvious and rather simple ideological bias in Smith's book should read A. H. Cole, "Puzzles of the *Wealth of Nations,*" *CJEP*, February, 1958. Smith's concern with the appropriate institutional framework for a competitive market economy is clearly brought out by N. Rosenberg, "The Institutional Aspects of the *Wealth of Nations,*" *JPE*,

December, 1960. The influence of the Scottish Historical School, of which Smith was a member, upon classical economics is discussed by R. L. Meek, "The Scottish Contribution to Marxist Sociology," *Democracy and the Labour Movement,* ed. J. Saville (1954).

Reading Adam Smith, or Ricardo and Mill, for that matter, is a good deal more interesting when one is acquainted with the contemporary institutions that are being criticized, such as the Poor Laws, the Corn Laws, the Sinking Fund, and the like. The reader who knows little of British economic history in the period is urged to repair the deficiency by perusing A. Redford, *An Economic History of Great Britain, 1760–1850* (1960), a little book that manages to cram an unbelievable amount of information in 200 pages.

Chapter	POPULATION, DIMINISHING
3	RETURNS, AND RENT

1. THE THEORY OF POPULATION

ALTHOUGH Malthus was not the first to speculate on the problems of population growth, he was the first to succeed in systematizing a general theory of population. Ever since, his views have been the point of departure in every discussion of population problems. In his own day, however, the theory attracted attention, not so much as a scientific contribution to the study of demography, as a refutation of the optimism of Godwin, Condorcet, and Owen regarding the perfectibility of human society by means of social legislation. More important for our purposes, Malthus' theory had definite analytical consequences that made it an integral part of classical economics long after the "vision" that prompted Malthus had receded to the background. By emphasizing the rigid dependence of population growth upon the food supply, the Malthusian theory lent support to the subsistence theory of wages and prepared the way for the Ricardian preoccupation with the land-using bias of economic progress; by explaining poverty in terms of a simple race between population and the means of subsistence, it provided the touchstone for all classical thinking about economic policy. Any one of these would have been enough to make its influence significant. Put together, they fully account for Malthus' astonishing success.

It is hardly surprising, however, that the Malthusian doctrine met with violent resistance from social reformers and men of letters. Malthus went out of his way to antagonize all those who believed in the amelioration of social conditions. Every effort at the deliberate improvement of conditions was said to come to grief upon the irrepressible tide of human numbers. To relieve poverty directly by state subsidies or private charity was to remove the major check against an increase in population: the necessity of each to fend for himself and to bear the full burden of his own improvidence. These implications were

61

driven home in one purple passage after another almost as if to irritate the sensitive reader. Nevertheless, with hindsight it is plain to see that these were merely the ideological trappings of the theory, not its rigorous consequences. With a minor adjustment in outlook admitting the moral propriety of birth control, men like Francis Place and John Stuart Mill were able to use the Malthusian theory as a banner in a program of social reform.

The Population Explosion. The first edition of Malthus' *Essay on Population* was published in 1798. The first decennial census was taken three years later, and it suggested, contrary to the prevailing belief, that the population of England was rapidly increasing. We now know that the last decade of the eighteenth century witnessed a population explosion, and we have become accustomed to crediting Malthus with prophetic foresight in drawing attention to its dangers. But, as a matter of fact, history was kind to Malthus, for he shared the general belief of contemporaries that the population of England had increased little, if at all, since the revolution of 1680. In the second edition of the *Essay* in 1803 he took notice of the census of 1801 but barely examined its findings. Modern authorities are still not agreed upon whether the industrial revolution largely created its own labor force by a demand pull on births or whether improvements in sanitation, nutrition, and housing produced an additional supply of population through a fall in the death rate. But it is certain that the 1780's and 90's saw a significant decline in mortality. Malthus, however, emphasized birth and marriage rates, and even in the later editions of the *Essay* he seriously underestimated the significance of the fall in the death rate. It is paradoxically true that Malthus never clearly grasped, or took much interest in, the nature of the population explosion that gave such prominence to his views.

Malthus' Analytical Schema. Malthus' frame of reference was entirely in terms of a dualistic opposition between a biological capacity for procreation, attributed to natural instincts that man shares with animals, and a set of checks that limit this capacity (see accompanying tabulation). The checks themselves are classified into positive and pre-

Growth Capacity	Checks to Growth			
Instincts of reproduction	Preventive: all limitations on births		Positive: all causes of deaths	
	Moral restraint	Vice	Vice	Misery
Means of subsistence				

ventive checks, separating the forces that affect mortality and natality. Upon this "positive" dichotomous classification he superimposed a "normative" tripartite division of the checks into misery, vice, and moral restraint. As a master check behind all the others is the "means of subsistence," defined sometimes as a biological, sometimes as a cultural, minimum supply of provisions required for existence.

These are the categories Malthus employed to construct his theory. The theory itself consisted in essence of three propositions: (1) man's natural capacity to reproduce exceeds his capacity to increase the food supply, (2) either the preventive or the positive check is always in operation, and (3) the ultimate check to reproductive capacity lies in limitations on the food supply. The first proposition is obviously the crucial primitive axiom; the second and third propositions are really deductive corollaries of the first. Lack of subsistence is an "ultimate" check, not in the sense that it comes later in time, but in that all the other checks are analyzed as ways in which the scarcity of food manifests itself; this is true even of the preventive check because man, being naturally indolent, according to Malthus, all voluntary limitation of numbers must be impelled by fear of hunger.

The utter simplicity and familiarity of the ideas involved, calling for no new concept or factual discovery, was the essence of Malthus' immediate appeal. All he seemed to be doing was bringing together a few familiar facts of life and deducing the necessary consequences of these facts. Surely, it is true that population always multiplies up to the limits of the available food supply? And, surely, an unchecked multiplication of human beings must quickly lead to an impossible situation, whatever the plausible rates of increase that can be imagined for the means of subsistence. The contrast that Malthus drew between the two kinds of progressions, the geometrical and the arithmetical, carried the hypnotic persuasive power of an advertising slogan. It was easy to see—"a slight acquaintance with numbers will show," as Malthus said —that even the smallest finite sum growing at the smallest compound rate must eventually overwhelm the largest possible finite sum growing at the highest simple rate. It followed that, whatever the initial situation, there would soon be standing room only. The reader was likely to forget at such moments that unchecked populations do not exist in the real world and hence that all such hair-raising calculations still leave the fundamental hypothesis unverified.[1]

[1] An American physicist, Putnam, has calculated that if the human race had sprung from a couple living in 10,000 B.C. and had grown since then, not at the maximum biological rate, but only at a modest 1 per cent per annum, the earth would now be a sphere of flesh several thousand light-years in diameter with a surface advancing into space at a rate many times faster than the rate at which light travels.

The Empirical Content of the Theory. Malthus defended his theory partly by logic, partly by facts, but not rigorously by either. He had no doubt that what we have called his primitive axiom was factually true. From dubious American data that did not distinguish between fecundity and immigration he inferred that an unchecked population will double itself every twenty-five years, implying a growth rate of just under 3 per cent per annum—actually, rates of 5 per cent per annum seem to be biologically possible. He admitted that the standard of living had not declined in the American colonies, from which it followed that subsistence too had grown at a compound rate of 3 per cent. But this Malthus denied; there are "no cases on record," he insisted, of subsistence growing at a compound rate. But, if subsistence increased arithmetically, how is that population increased geometrically without producing starvation?

Identifying "means of subsistence" with foodstuffs, he tried to show, by logic this time, that a rapid increase of crops is out of the question, since the supply of land is limited and technical improvements do not come fast enough. The magic phrase that was subsequently used to sanction this assertion is the Law of Diminishing Returns. But Malthus argued, not that land was augmentable only at increased cost, but that capital accumulation and technical change could not offset limitations in natural resources. But there is no *law* of diminishing returns to technological progress. The law of diminishing returns, properly understood, is a static proposition about returns to varying factor proportions under given technical knowledge, having nothing to do with the dynamic problem of an actually growing population working a given land area under conditions of constantly improving technology. Malthus himself made no mention of a tendency to diminishing returns in agriculture until the second edition of the *Essay,* but throughout the six editions and even in the last published statement of his theory, the *Summary View on Population,* he showed a decided preference for a direct appeal to the reader's intuition.

The confusion as to which version of the law of diminishing returns is relevant to the comparative rapidity of the increase of population and subsistence is present in everything Malthus wrote. In the *Summary View* we are told, first, that the power to produce food is "obviously limited by the scarcity of land . . . by the decreasing proportion of the produce which must necessarily be obtained by the continual additions of capital applied to the land already in cultivation"— an incomplete statement of the static law framed characteristically in average rather than marginal terms. Then a dozen pages later we are asked to believe that "although the saving of labor and an improved system of husbandry may be the means of pushing cultivation upon much poorer lands than could otherwise be worked; yet the increased quantity of the necessities of life so obtained can never be such as to supersede, for any length of time the operation of the preventive and positive checks to population"—the questionable notion of diminishing returns to technical change so typical of all classical reasoning about the secular progress of agriculture.

In the nature of the case, Malthus was contrasting a hypothetical capacity of population to grow at a certain rate with an actual incapacity of food to grow at the same rate. At first glance there would seem to be no way of verifying such an assertion. But it was central to his argument that population is never restrained for nonfinancial motives, so the pressure of population upon the available food supply is ever present. As he said in his correspondence with Senior, "except in new colonies, favorably circumstanced, population was always pressing against food, and was always ready to start off at a faster rate than that at which the food was actually increasing." This has the clear verifiable implication that a steady rise of living standards can never be associated in "old" countries with a growing population. And, indeed, this is just what Malthus asserted in the first edition of the *Essay*. But by the second edition he added a new check to his argument: "the [moral] restraint from marriage which is not followed by irregular gratification." This rendered the theory perfectly general, and perfectly empty: rising living standards prove that moral restraint is checking population growth, falling living standards prove that the absence of prudential restraint results in misery or vice. Malthus' theory cannot be refuted because it can be applied to any actual or conceivable population movement; but a theory that is not falsifiable by any conceivable event is a tautology masquerading as a theory. Malthus' statistical investigations were inconclusive, not because good statistics were lacking, but because his theory was incapable of being confronted by empirical evidence. Keynes once praised Malthus' facts and figures as "inductive verification," and even Marshall paid tribute to what he regarded as "the first thorough application of the inductive method to social science." But Malthus himself was nearer the mark when he observed in the Preface to the second edition that "any errors in the facts and calculations which have been produced in the course of the work . . . will not materially affect the general scope of the reasoning."

Automatic Checks. Critics sometimes suggest that Malthus misled his readers by entertaining the biological possibility of a rate of population growth far in excess of rates usually observed in the real world. But there is no methodological bar on hypotheses that postulate the existence of abstract "tendencies" that in reality are never observed unaccompanied by disturbing influences. What is required is that the hypothesis entail predictable consequences; in practice this usually means showing that the "pure tendency" is truly independent of the counteracting factors so that the deviation caused by "frictions" can be quantified. Galileo's law of falling bodies in a perfect vacuum is an excellent example of this methodological rule. In the case of Malthus, however, the checks were themselves the product of population pressures, and moral restraint in particular was admitted to be an automatic check induced by population growth. It is not often realized that Malthus, in the later sections of the *Essay,* did in fact concede everything his contemporary critics from Godwin to Senior held out against him; yet, he could not afford it prominence at the center of his system without destroying it.

It was Senior who first divided consumer goods into "necessaries, decencies, and luxuries." As the economy developed, the luxuries of one generation became the decencies of its successors, and eventually the necessaries of subsequent generations. The desire to preserve one's standard, the hope of rising in the world, Senior stressed, are motives as strong as those leading to marriage and procreation. Thus, a rise in living standards provided an automatic preventive check to the growth of population. Malthus denied the practical importance of "the desire to better one's condition" among the working class and in particular denied Senior's claim that this principle supplied an automatic check. For Malthus, only an improvement of moral and religious habits could alleviate the problem. Yet in many places in the *Essay* he spoke of the prevalence in England of "a decided taste for the conveniences and comforts of life, a strong desire of bettering their condition (that master-spring of public prosperity)," in consequence of which "a most laudable spirit of industry and foresight are observed to prevail . . . throughout a very large class of people." And in the last chapter of the book, entitled "Of Our Rational Expectations respecting the Future Improvement of Society," he pinned all his hopes on the "apparently narrow principle of self-interest which prompts each individual to exert himself in bettering his condition." After a volume dedicated to showing that only prodigious efforts will stave off famine and disease, he then concluded that the powerful check of competitive emulation was operative and would be increasingly operative in all "civilised and populous" countries.

Granting the existence of automatically correcting influences, the Malthusian theory falls to the ground. No wonder then that Malthus himself never made it quite clear what he hoped to accomplish by recommending moral restraint. He strenuously condemned contraceptives because "improper arts to conceal the consequences of irregular connection" would encourage sloth by removing the stimulus of fear of hunger. But why moral restraint should not have the same effect it is difficult to see. On the one hand, he seems to have had no faith that the working class would ever exercise such restraint, but, on the other hand, he admitted that they already did so. In general, he displayed a startling lack of interest in the laws of population growth: he neglected to consider the time lag necessary for population to respond to changes in the means of subsistence and said nothing about the age and sex distribution of the population, particularly the proportion of women of childbearing age, making a substantial difference to a population's growth capacity. In all his writings he seemed to regard the birth rate as independent of the death rate and the checks to population growth as independent of the size of the population itself. He was aware, as was Adam Smith, of the finding that the size of the family in almost all societies is inversely related to the height of the income class; yet, he drew no important conclusions from this fact. Indeed, it is largely because of Malthus' own treatment that the growth of population came eventually to be regarded as peculiarly subject to nonpecuniary considerations lying outside the domain of economics.

The Optimum Theory and Subsistence Wages. One of the difficulties in interpreting Malthus is to give definite meaning to the concept of overpopulation. If we suppose that Malthus meant a population too large to be fed with domestic resources, then the possibility of foreign trade is enough to banish the Malthusian specter. But in places even Malthus, and certainly Senior and John Stuart Mill, suggested a more meaningful definition: a population too large for maximum efficiency of production such that a reduction in numbers would raise output per head. If the population of a particular area may be too small for maximum efficiency—"the division of labor is limited by the extent of the market"—as well as too large, it is obvious that there must be some point in between at which it is optimum. In other words, a population of optimum size is one that maximizes output per head. Combined with a subsistence theory of wages, this notion seems to imply overpopulation. If wages per man are equal to the subsistence rate, equilibrium requires that population be of size B (Fig. 4). For any smaller population, extra numbers produce more income than they cost to maintain, and hence population will increase; any increase beyond *B,* however, is choked off through the positive check. An improvement of technology or an expansion of foreign trade will raise the income curve and generate population growth until wages are once again equal to subsistence.

But, in fact, a subsistence wage rate does not prove that a country is at *B* rather than at *A,* that it is overpopulated rather than underpopulated. The wage rate might be at subsistence with population = *A;* nevertheless, technical progress is so rapid that population never has the chance to catch up. During the adjustment process workers get accustomed to higher living standards; the subsistence wage rate shifts up

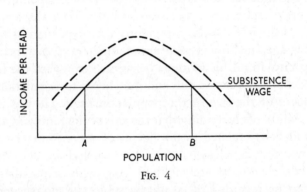

FIG. 4

and population growth slows down until technical change gives it a new jolt. If subsistence is a function of "habit and custom," as Ricardo said, and not just a biological minimum, the statement that wages are at subsistence has no specific implications for the desirable level of population.

This should dispel the notion, which is the small coin of potted social histories, that the classical economists were "pessimists" simply because they believed that wages tend to be held at subsistence. They might have been pessimists on other grounds, but without exception they did believe that it was possible to raise the standard of living of workers. The wages-population mechanism was used to demonstrate the perfect elasticity of the long-run supply curve of labor. In practice, however, it was admitted that the adjustment to rising wages might require a generation or more. In his *Principles* (1820), Malthus noted that "a sudden increase of capital cannot affect a proportionate supply of labor in less than sixteen or eighteen years," giving expression for the first time to a specific time lag between an increase in wages and an increase of population. This lag permits real wages to rise, which in turn alters the equilibrium subsistence wage rate. In this way, even without belief in moral restraint or birth control, it was possible to look forward to a rosy future while continuing to operate analytically with a subsistence theory of wages.

It is evident that the subsistence *theory* of wages is not a theory at all: it amounts to taking subsistence as a datum, given by the prevailing level of medical skills and the workers' attitude to procreation. It is only another example of the classical tendency to simplify analysis by reducing the number of variables to be determined. In any concrete case of wage determination, the subsistence theory is hopelessly ambiguous because we never know what time period is relevant to the particular problem. For instance, a subsistence wage rate implies that workers rear a replacement labor force; ignoring infant mortalities, each family has two children. Since population growth is normally positive, the market rate of wages must be currently in excess of the natural subsistence rate. What is the actual nature of the adjustment mechanism: will some children who would otherwise have perished reach working age, or will the extra income be spent on having more children? Or will mortalities be unaffected and births be allowed to increase so slowly that income per head rises permanently? There is nothing in the theory that helps us here, but these are the questions we want answered when we consider the future prospects of living standards.

Malthusianism Today. The concept of an optimum population is intellectually clarifying, but it is only fair to say that it is of little assistance in social action. In practice, the problem of overpopulation is, not that of closing a gap between a population's actual size and its optimum size, but that of confining the movement of a country's population through time to an optimum moving path. Even if it is possible to discover that a country is overpopulated, the process of moving to the optimum point may affect its locations; the theory has nothing to say about the nature of an optimum path of growth and does not even insure that the optimum, once reached, can be maintained. This is the familiar problem of dynamic stability in price theory, but it is particularly relevant here because a positive rate of population growth is probably one of the preconditions of maximizing output per head.

The chief advantage of the optimum population theory is that it provides an analytical framework that makes it possible to entertain under- as well as overpopulation. But it is like the Malthusian theory in being silent on the crucial question of the determinants of population growth. That behavior of mortality trends is affected by sanitary measures and medical improvements is reasonably well understood. It is fertility that is problematic. The Malthusian theory, however, does suggest the possibility of dealing with fertility rates in terms of conventional economic theory, and at first glance it is difficult to understand why later economists did not pursue the classical approach to birth-rate differentials. The outstanding feature of classical population theory is that it treats the production of children, not as a means of spending income on "consumer goods" to acquire satisfaction, but as a method of investment in "capital goods" for the sake of a future return. In the Malthusian theory, children were thought to be produced at constant cost so that any increase in the demand for labor generated a stream of expected returns in excess of costs. But it is more realistic to assume that children are produced at increasing cost in the sense of the current expenses of rearing a child as well as the opportunities forgone as the result of additional children: the growth of population is associated with urban crowding and, hence, an increase in the mother's earning potential, in the school-leaving age, and in required technical training. At the same time, the loosening of family ties associated with the process of industrialization reduces the expected returns from children in the form of old-age security. Given the steady rise in the cost of rearing children relative to the decline in expected returns, it is hardly surprising that fertility is a declining function of income in a developed society.

The reason economists have been reluctant to accept the idea that procreation is influenced by deliberate economic choice in terms of the balancing of returns over costs is that human beings cannot capitalize their earning capacity. In a nonslave society an individual cannot "alienate" his productive services, nor can his parents contract to deliver his services in the future. Hence, in national income accounting all expenditures on human beings, whether for want satisfaction or for growth of future earning capacity are always treated as final consumption. Nevertheless, the kinship of labor capacity with capital has been recognized ever since Adam Smith: although human beings are not property in the full sense that capital goods are, there is a tendency for capital invested in the process of training to yield a return roughly equal to the general market rate. Skill and experience, being a produced means of production, is a form of capital, and to that extent their creation involves a pecuniary calculation.

This line of thought was never pursued by economists after Malthus. The decline of fertility in the last half of the nineteenth century was explained by a change in the "taste for procreation." In practice, economists simply abandoned the field of population studies. The result has been to leave the profession unprepared to tackle the current problem of overpopulation in the underdeveloped countries of the world. The difficulty of most underdeveloped countries today is that of having both the high birth rates typical of agrarian economies and the low death rates characteristic of industrial Europe. Industrialization will in time cure these difficulties, but for the next few generations the alternative is either the Malthusian checks of famine and disease or the voluntary limitation of families. As always, there are lucid extremists on both sides: the neo-Malthusians hold that all efforts at economic improvement in the backward countries must be subordinated to, and in fact come after, the successful introduction of birth control; Marxists, on the other hand, hold that population control without industrialization will not work and, in practice, refuse to support efforts to promote birth control. The name of Malthus is still bandied about in the debate, but, if truth were told, the Malthusian theory of population has no longer any relevance to the discussion of population problems.

A theory is meaningless unless it can be falsified by a conceivable course of events. We ought always to ask: What would happen if the theory were not true? In Malthus' case, the answer is, or ought to be, that income per head would rise, not fall, with increasing population. The history of Western countries, therefore, disproves Malthus' theory. The defenders of Malthus reply: But what of India today? No one denies that India is overpopulated and poor. It is overpopulated because the death rate was lowered by the introduction of Western medicine, thus divorcing population growth from income levels. It follows that India would be better off if she could also "westernize" her birth rate. But all this has absolutely nothing to do with the Malthusian theory of population.

2. DIMINISHING RETURNS AND THE THEORY OF RENT

The year 1815 saw the appearance of four publications by West, Torrens, Malthus, and Ricardo, each of which independently formulated the theory of differential rent. Each tract was in its own way a reaction to committees appointed by both Lords and Commons to report on the recent fall in grain prices, and each took as its starting point the relationship between high grain prices and the extension of cultivation to less fertile and less accessible land during the years of the Napoleonic Wars. The underlying explanation, the four authors agreed, lay in the phenomenon of diminishing returns, "the principle," as West put it, "that in the progress of the improvement of cultivation the raising of rude produce becomes progressively more expensive." "Each equal additional quantity of work bestowed on agriculture," West went on to explain, "yields an actually diminished return. . . . Whereas it is obvious that an equal quantity of work will always fabricate the same quantity of manufactures." One would think from West's formulation that "the principle" holds only for a constant state of technology, but in fact, West thought, as did Torrens, Malthus, and Ricardo, that returns to agricultural activity do actually diminish in the course of history in spite of all technical progress. Of the four, he was the most explicit on this point: "the necessity of having recourse to land inferior to that already in tillage, or of cultivating the same land more expensively, tends to make labor in agriculture less productive in the progress of improvement . . . [which] more than counteracts the effect of machinery and the division of labor in agriculture." The gradual substitution of what Cannan called "a pseudo-scientific law of a 'tendency' to diminishing returns for the roughly general rule of diminishing returns rashly deduced from experience during the great war" came later with Ricardo's followers in the 1830's.

The Law of Diminishing Returns.   The vague reference to "an equal quantity of work" in West's statement of the "law" of diminishing returns is characteristic of rent theory in this period. As Ricardo was to make clear, West was really thinking of a single homogeneous dose of capital and labor combined in fixed proportions and applied to land in equal successive increments: despite references to a productive triad, the argument is really developed in terms of a two-factor model. Moreover, it is always the average rather than the marginal product of capital and labor that is said to be diminishing. For most purposes, however, this confusion between the proportional and the incremental law of diminishing returns is not very serious: a declining average product always implies a declining marginal product, although the converse does not necessarily hold true.[2] With each of the four authors,

[2] Holding one factor fixed and varying the other, we obtain a typical curve of total product (*TP*); the average product (*AP*) is equal to the slope of *TP* at each point on the *TP* curve, or tan α, and the marginal product (*MP*) is equal to the slope of a tangent drawn to each point on the *TP* curve. Rational factor-hire eliminates regions I and IV from consideration. Since *MP* reaches a maximum before *AP*, *AP* is still increasing in region II, whereas *MP* is already declining. Only in region III do both decline together.

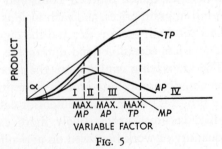

Fig. 5

the law of diminishing returns is supposed to be applicable only to agriculture, and the proof of its validity is either by way of an appeal to history, to show that the growth of population forces recourse to inferior soil, or through a logical deduction from the fact that different grades of soil are at any moment of time simultaneously cultivated. If it were possible to raise additional product at constant or diminishing expense from soil of given fertility, why resort to inferior soil? But the extension of cultivation to inferior soil is no proof of universally diminishing returns to equal amounts of labor on equal quantities of land at a constant state of technique; some plots of land may show increasing returns as long as these do not rise as fast as returns diminish on other land. The extension of cultivation, however, is a temporal process with techniques altering all the time; in that case, even when the fertility of all uncultivated land is known and correctly estimated, an improvement in technology may make profitable for cultivation land that had hitherto been regarded as unprofitable. At the new level of technical knowledge the acres taken last into cultivation might be more productive than previous acres.

Some minor writers in subsequent decades tried to prove diminishing returns by a *reductio ad absurdum*. If proportional increments of labor and land produced proportional or increasing increments of output, the country's wheat supply could be grown in a flowerpot: extension of cultivation, therefore, proved the existence of diminishing returns. But even with increasing returns, the wheat supply would not be grown in a flowerpot if returns in the flowerpot did not increase as rapidly as returns in actual production: the extension of cultivation *is* compatible with increasing returns.

Assuming without proof that the law of diminishing returns does at any rate pertain to *in*tensive cultivation, it follows that price is regulated by the least favorable circumstance under which production is carried on. All four authors shared this insight and inferred from it that rent is the excess of the product over the outlays of the intramarginal farmer for capital and labor. In modern language, price is determined by marginal cost, but the marginal cost of the intramarginal farmer exceeds his average cost, and this excess goes to the landlord as rent.

Differential Rent. Let us be more specific. The theory of differential rent is formally identical with the marginal productivity theory, though the marginal increments considered were enormously large instead of being negligibly small, as marginal analysis requires. Suppose we are given the accompanying schedule of the grain produced on five grades of land of equal acreage. From it we derive the table of incremental products resulting from the application of successive doses

CAPITAL-AND-LABOR	TOTAL PRODUCT FROM LAND					MARGINAL PRODUCT FROM LAND				
	A	B	C	D	E	A	B	C	D	E
0	0	0	0	0	0					
						180	170	160	150	140
1	180	170	160	150	140					
						170	160	150	140	
2	350	330	310	290						
						160	150	140		
3	510	480	450							
						150	140			
4	660	620								
						140				
5	800									

of "capital-and-labor" (Fig. 6). We will suppose that the price per bushel of corn is $1.00 so that the schedule of physical quantities can be translated into money values by writing dollar signs in front of each number. The price of homogeneous doses of "men-with-shovels" is given at $140. Each farmer on each grade of land will apply doses of the variable factor so long as it adds more to revenue than to cost.

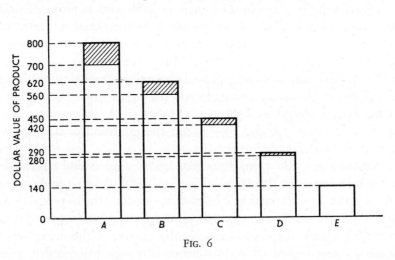

FIG. 6

Since the composite doses are indivisible, farmer E will find it profitable to apply one unit but no more. Competition will insure equalization of the marginal value productivity of capital-and-labor in all locations; hence, two units of capital-and-labor will be applied to land D, three to land C, and so forth. Grade A land will produce a product worth $800 with five units of capital-and-labor—the sum of their marginal products—whose total cost is $700. Thus, rent on A will be $100, rent on B $60, rent on C $30, rent on D $10, and rent on E zero.

Reading horizontally, E is the extensive margin of cultivation, being that quality of land which yields a product just equal to the cost of the capital and labor expended upon it. But if it pays at all to apply resources to E, it pays to apply them more intensively to A, B, C, and D until an intensive margin equal to the extensive margin is reached; reading vertically, the intensive margin is the last increment of the variable agent on superior land that adds only as much to receipts as to costs.

The fact that rent so determined is equal to the marginal productivity of land is easy to demonstrate. In Ricardian theory, the variable factor receives a reward equal to its marginal product, while the fixed factor land earns the intramarginal residual. Holding capital-and-labor constant and varying the amount of land until the value product of a marginal acre is equal to its cost should yield a rental per acre identical to rents calculated as an intramarginal surplus to a fixed amount of land. Suppose we withdraw a unit of land from use, say, grade B. The total product now falls by $620. The four units of capital-and-labor released are now employed at the intensive margins on A, C, D, and E where—ignoring the inappropriately large numbers in our example—they would produce $560 worth of product. Hence, the marginal value product of B is equal to $60, which is the same figure given above for rent calculated as a residual.

The Alternative Cost of Land. The Ricardian theory, however, has one feature not shared by modern productivity analysis. The only kind of rent considered in the Ricardian theory is agricultural rent; moreover, it is rent for the "raw produce" of agriculture as a whole, not rent for land devoted to particular products. Land used for tillage is thought to have no competing uses for grazing; labor and capital shift from one unit of land to another, but land itself never shifts between alternative uses. This explains the presence of the extensive margin in classical rent theory: land is supposed to be taken up freely when needed, not from some other rent-paying alternative, but from non-paying idleness. And, since land is completely specialized and fixed in supply, it follows that rent is price determined, not price determining: as Ricardo has it, "corn is not high because a rent is paid, but a rent is paid because corn is high." But Adam Smith pointed out in Book I, chapter 5, of the *Wealth of Nations* that when the market price of a commodity sinks below its natural price, "the interest of the landlords will immediately prompt them to withdraw a part of their land" into better-rental uses than this low-price commodity affords. Here rent is a cost to the individual producer that enters into the determination of price. In his formal chapter on rent, however, Smith lost sight of the plurality of uses of land and slipped imperceptibly into considering rent for land as a whole. His followers emphasized the latter half of Smith's reasoning and without further explanation deduced bold practical maxims from the assumption that the opportunity cost of land is zero.

This explains Ricardo's careful definition of rent as a payment for "the use of the original and indestructible powers of the soil." This excludes from contractual rent payment any interest on the capital invested by the landlord in the form of buildings, drains, hedges, and the like, as well as the gains resulting from the removal of timber or the extraction of minerals. What is left is pure rent to "land" considered as virgin territory and untapped mineral wealth; it is an inexhaustible and nonreproducible agent, unalterably fixed in supply, completely specialized in the production of one crop, and homogeneous in quality except for differences in fertility and location. Rent, therefore, arises for two reasons. If land is homogeneous, the limitation of supply would still create scarcity rents. Rent would still be the difference between the product of all capital-and-labor and the product of the final dose at the intensive margin. When land differs in quality, the scarcity of acres of a particular quality gives rise to differential rents. Ricardo thought that extensive no-rent land did exist in contemporary Europe, but clearly it would make no difference to the theory if this were not true. Rent would no longer constitute a pure differential, but scarcity rents would still exist.

From the notion that "rent does not enter into price," that rent is not a payment for the using-up of resources, the classical economists drew the practical corollary that it would make no difference if landlords were thrown to the wolves. The expropriation of rents by the state would not affect production, provided, of course, it were only pure economic rents that were being confiscated. Similarly, if rents were remitted from landlords to tenants, the price of agricultural products and the average rate of profit in agriculture would be exactly the same because the transfer of income would not affect the marginal cost of producing corn. But, of course, the remission of rents would probably alter the spending pattern of landlords and tenants and hence the demand for agricultural product. Since the location of the margin of cultivation is itself a function of the level of demand for corn, the marginal cost of producing corn would alter. In principle, Ricardo closed this gap in the theory by assuming demand to be perfectly inelastic—

"the desire of food is limited in every man by the narrow capacity of the human stomach"—so that whatever determines the size of population determines the volume of demand for "raw produce." But, in practice, the problem of explaining the location of the margin was simply ignored.

Land as a Factor of Production. The core of the Ricardian doctrine of rent is still with us, though in an attenuated form. John Stuart Mill was the first to admit that the rent that land could earn in one use forms a cost that must be paid when it is used in some other employment. Jevons seized upon this statement to show that land does have a supply price like any other agent and that all agents, when completely specialized, earn a differential rent. The cost of any agent cannot be less than what the agent can earn in the most remunerative alternative use. In recent times this has been called the "transfer price" of an agent. The earnings of any agent in excess of its transfer price constitute rent; from the viewpoint of the firm hiring the agent, rents are part of costs of production; but from the point of view of the industry or of society as a whole, they are price determined and may be taxed away without affecting the supply of the agent. If the supply of an agent is fixed, and if its services are specific to one use, transfer earnings are zero and the whole of its reward is rent, both from the individual and from the social point of view. But no agent is ever completely nonreproducible or incapable of being adapted to other uses; it all depends on the time period relevant to the case. In the short run, for example, fixed capital earns quasi-rents, not interest, for the supply of machines is nonaugmentable and nonadaptable. But, in the long run, new machines can be built and old machines put to new purposes, so quasi-rents are always in the process of being eroded.

In practice, the distinction between transfer earnings and rents will leave considerable room for doubt, which is to say that it is difficult accurately to estimate the price elasticity of supply of a factor of production. The perfect analogy to the Ricardian case is that of an industry made up of firms with a cost ladder determined by the unequal managerial talent available to each firm. The price of the industry's product is determined by the no-rent marginal firm; low cost producers earn an economic rent attributable to superior management. As long as managers may be bid away by other firms, their earnings will entirely absorb these rentals. From a social point of view, it would make no difference if they were taxed away. But this might well affect the supply of talent in the future, so in the long run these implicit rentals must be viewed as entering into the supply price of management. The state would have to experiment with various tax rates to discover the degree of elasticity of supply of managerial talent.

The classical authors treated land as a "free gift of Nature," a special factor of production distinct from man-made means of production and reproducible human labor. But in reality natural resources do not differ from the general run of capital goods in requiring initial development and subsequent maintenance charges. If by "land" we mean resources given by nature and available for use without cost, a very large part of the territorial resources of a society are not "land" at all: fields that have been drained, cleared, and manured are as much the product of past labor as are machines. If "land" is a factor of production, it must be said to consist of the heritage of equipment and improvements of the past given to the present generation as free goods. In this sense "land" is not a commodity at all and has nothing to do with agricultural production. Marshall argued, however, that territory does have some claim to be considered as a special factor of production. For one thing, it has the characteristic of certain long-lived goods— such as railway embankment, bridges, and some buildings—of being maintainable by relatively small expenditures on running repairs. In addition, it is expensive and sometimes even impossible in a settled country to augment the supply of land by draining swamps or irrigating deserts. Consequently, the supply of land is typically much less elastic than the supply of capital goods. In this sense, Marshall thought that the classical analysis of rent, particularly with reference to the circumstances of a country like Great Britain, was not in essence misleading. Some British economists share Marshall's sympathy with the Ricardian approach to rent, but, for the most part, modern economics has abandoned the notion that there is any need for a special theory of ground rent. In long-run stationary equilibrium the total product is resolvable into wages and interest and the theory of differential rent is interesting only because it marks the appearance of the marginal principle in economic theory.

NOTES FOR FURTHER READING

1. *The Theory of Population.* The reader should peruse the last published statement of Malthus' theory, an article of some fifty pages written for the 1830 edition of the *Encyclopaedia Britannica,* conveniently reprinted in *Introduction to Malthus,* ed. D. V. Glass (1953). The first edition of Malthus' *Essay* (1798) is now available in paperback. The second edition, quadrupled in length and significantly revised, appeared in 1803. The main text was never substantially

altered until the sixth and last edition in 1826, but the appendixes to the third and fifth editions of 1806 and 1817 contain important defenses against contemporary criticism. This edition, without the appendixes, is reprinted in Everyman's Library. The first two chapters, embracing less than 3 per cent of the total work, state the whole of the theory; the bulk of the book is devoted to rather tedious descriptive accounts of population in various societies that illustrate the thesis laid down in the first two chapters. There is some typical Smithian economic theory in the chapters on the Poor Laws, the Corn Laws, and the proper mixture of industry and agriculture in an economic system: Book III, chaps. 6–12; the first few chapters of Book IV, and particularly the last few pages of the book, throw light on Malthus' vision of the good society. The reader should consult the highly revealing correspondence between Senior and Malthus, reprinted in G. F. McCleary's *The Malthusian Theory of Population* (1953).

Cannan's incisive critique of Malthus has stood the test of time wonderfully well: *Theories of Production and Distribution,* chap. 5, and *Review of Economic Theory* (1929), chap. 4. Schumpeter's *History,* pp. 250–58, 578–84, covers the same ground, and from nearly the same viewpoint. G. J. Stigler, "The Ricardian Theory of Value and Distribution," *JPE,* 1952, reprinted in *EET,* adds emphasis to Cannan. The logical structure of Malthus' theory is brilliantly exposed in K. Davis, "Malthus and the Theory of Population," *The Language of Social Research,* ed. P. F. Lazarsfeld (1955). In an article that suffers from its excessive length, J. J. Spengler attempts to reconcile Malthus' *Essay* with Malthus' *Principles of Political Economy:* "Malthus' Total Population Theory: A Restatement and Reappraisal," *CJEPS,* 1945, reprinted in *EET.* The standard biography, J. Bonar, *Malthus and His Work* (1924), is spoiled by what Macaulay aptly called *Boswelliana:* the disease of biographers who get too close to their subject. G. F. McCleary, *The Malthusian Theory of Population* (1953), offers a spirited defense of the theory; the hostile reader should test his critical faculties on this book. J. Stassart, *Malthus et la population* (1957), provides an excellent guide to "what Malthus really said."

For a fascinating review of the great nineteenth-century debate in England on the Malthusian theory see K. Smith, *The Malthusian Controversy* (1951). D. E. Eversley, *Social Theories of Fertility and the Malthusian Debate* (1959), supplements Smith's account by emphasizing the development of the standard-of-living theory. M. Blaug, *Ricardian Economics* (1958), chap. 6, sketches the virtual abandonment of the Malthusian theory by Ricardo's early followers. The controversy over the nature of the population explosion of the 1790's is reviewed by H. J. Habakkuk, "The Economic History of Modern Britain," *JEH,* December, 1958. *Marx and Engels on Malthus,* ed. R. L. Meek (1953), is rich in invective but surprisingly thin in substance; the shrill Stalinist introduction by the editor is a good example of how the subject is nowadays discussed in Communist countries.

P. H. Douglas, *The Theory of Wages* (1934), chap. 13, surveys the work done on the long-run supply curve of labor since Malthus. For an excellent historical and critical account of the optimum population theory see M. Gottlieb, "The Theory of Optimum Population for a Closed Economy," *JPE,* 1945, reprinted in *Population Theory and Policy,* ed. J. J. Spengler and O. D. Duncan (1956). The use of Malthusian-type models in modern economics is demonstrated by A. T. Peacock, "The Theory of Population and Modern Economic Analysis," *PS*, 1952, reprinted in the Spengler-Duncan volume; see also E. E. Hagen, "Population and Economic Growth," *AER*, June, 1959. For a theory of declining fertility in terms of "utility" and "cost," see H. Leibenstein, *Economic Backwardness and Economic Growth* (1957), chap. 10.

2. *Diminishing Returns and Rent.* Most of the great economists in the latter half of the nineteenth century commented extensively on the Ricardian theory of rent; among these, Marshall and Wicksteed are the most illuminating. There is an outstanding discussion of the mixed static-dynamic character of Ricardo's rent theory in H. Sidgwick, *Principles of Political Economy* (1883), Book II, chap. 7. The crucial distinction between the alternative cost of land to an individual producer and the social cost of land to the whole community is brought out by D. H. Buchanan in a review of the rent theories of Smith, Ricardo, Mill, Jevons, and Marshall: "The Historical Approach to Rent and Price Theory," *Ec.*, 1929, reprinted in *Readings in the Theory of Income Distribution,* ed. W. Fellner and B. F. Haley (1946). An excellent treatment of Ricardian rent theory from the standpoint of modern economics will be found in A. W. Stonier and D. C. Hague, *A Textbook of Economic Theory* (1953), chap. 13; see also Schumpeter, *History*, pp. 671–79. For an ingenious resolution of the famous Carey-Mill dispute with reference to the order in which different types of land will be cultivated under the assumptions of Ricardian rent theory see the note by R. Turvey, "A Finnish Contribution to Rent Theory," *EJ*, June, 1955. For a critical discussion of Fabian economics, steeped as it was in Ricardian rent theory as adapted by Henry George, see G. J. Stigler, "B. Shaw, S. Webb, and the Theory of Fabian Socialism," *PAPS*, June 15, 1959.

Chapter 4

RICARDO'S SYSTEM

THE BARE outline of Ricardo's system can be grasped by supposing that the whole economy consists of a giant farm engaged in producing wheat by applying homogeneous doses of "capital-and-labor" to a fixed supply of land subject to diminishing returns. We have already seen how Ricardo avoids the necessity of handling three variables at one and the same time by reducing capital and labor to one variable input. The argument contains one further simplifying assumption: the demand for wheat is perfectly inelastic, being a simple function of the size of the population. The moment we posit a certain population, the output of wheat is determined. At this point we apply the marginal productivity theory to show that the variable input will obtain its marginal product and the fixed factor will earn a "surplus," determined by the gap between the average and the marginal product of the variable input for both extensive and intensive cultivation (Fig. 7). Rent is equal to the total product (OD) minus the marginal product of capital-and-labor (AM) multiplied by the number of doses applied (OM). Since the total product is given either by the area under the marginal product curve or by the rectangle under the average product curve, rent can be read off the diagram as the indicated shaded area or as the rent box so labeled. The magnitude of rent is determined solely by the gap between the average and the marginal product, by the strength of the forces making for diminishing returns. The curves are drawn as straight lines in the diagram for the sake of convenience only, although, as we shall see, Ricardo's arithmetical examples do assume straight-line productivity functions.

The Theory of Wheat Profits. So much for straightforward marginal productivity theory. Now for the strictly classical part of the argument: since capital and labor are combined in fixed proportions, the marginal productivity theory cannot determine the division of the product-less-rent between capital and labor. The subsistence theory of wages is now introduced to determine the wage rate by the constant supply price of labor in terms of wheat (OW). The supply curve of labor (WK) is infinitely elastic at the subsistence wage rate. Total profits are a residual equal to the total product-less-rent minus the wage bill (OK); per unit of capital-and-labor, profits are equal to the marginal product of the composite dose minus the wage rate. This composite dose is, strictly speaking, a dose of capital, consisting of fixed capital and circulating capital, with the proportions between the two kept constant. In physical terms, the rate of growth of tools and implements is always equal to the rate of growth of the labor force, and the proportions in

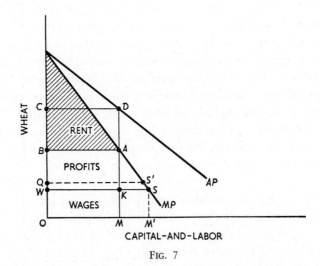

Fig. 7

which they are combined, together with the postulated subsistence wage rate, determines the amount of circulating capital required. So long as the turnover period of capital is one year—think of the harvest of agriculture—capital consists solely of annual advances to labor. In other words, capital is equal to the wage bill or wages fund (OK), the aggregate demand for labor in terms of wheat. This is the third "trick" in the argument: fixed capital is made to disappear by the proviso that implements wear out in one year. The *rate* of profit is given by the ratio of total profits to capital invested, and, since capital here consists solely of working capital, it follows that the ratio of total profits to the wages bill determines the wheat rate of profit per cent on capital employed. Thus, the rate of profit

$$r = \frac{\text{Profits}}{\text{Wages}} = \left(\frac{AM - KM}{KM}\right) 100\,\% = \left(\frac{AM}{KM} - 1\right) 100\,\%.$$

KM, the subsistence wage rate, is taken to be a constant, and hence the wheat rate of profit varies directly with the marginal product of capital-and-labor.

As long as the rate of profit is positive, capitalists are induced to accumulate. In the course of capital accumulation, the labor force will grow proportionately, *OM* will move to the right, the marginal product of capital-and-labor will fall and so will the wheat rate of profits until at last the stationary state (*S*) is reached. We may qualify the argument by supposing that there is a minimum rate of profit (say, *QW*) below which capitalists will not be willing to incur the risk of investment: the simplest assumption consonant with Ricardo's *obiter dicta* is that this minimum-of-existence reward for capital is a constant. This does

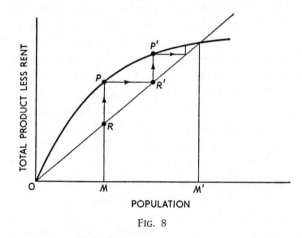

FIG. 8

not affect the argument in the slightest. Furthermore, technical progress must be admitted to shift the productivity functions upward, which serves to stave off the stationary state. This is partially offset by the fact that the long-run supply curve of labor is drifting upward through time as workers become accustomed to a higher standard of living. The subsistence rate of wages is, after all, that rate at which population growth would cease (*OM′*), but this does not happen until the economy has attained the stationary state. The accumulation of capital is continually raising the "market price" of labor above its "natural price"; this induces population growth, whereupon the market wage is bid down again to the natural wage. The process comes to a halt only when wages have eaten up the whole of the product-less-rent.

To illustrate what will happen, we plot the curve of total product-less-rent as a function of population (Fig. 8). The constant real wage is shown by a straight line through the origin. When population = *OM,* the wage bill $= RM$ (equal to our previous rectangle OK), and total profits $= PR$ (equal to our previous rectangle WA). The wage rate is equal to the wage bill divided by the number of workers $RM/OM =$ a constant. The existence of positive profits induces investment, and market wages rise above RM; by itself, this would choke off investment, but the growth of population forces market wages back to the natural wage; profits are now $= P'R'$, which gives rise to further investment, and so on until the stationary state is reached. If capital accumulation is taking place all the time, the market wage may never have time to fall back to the natural wage; the demand for labor is continually outrunning the supply. The result of this is that workers come to expect a higher minimum of existence, defined as that rate at which they have no incentive to "produce" more labor. The wage line in our last diagram would rotate counterclockwise, and the stationary state would be that much nearer. All this is ignored for the purpose of the argument: the subsistence wage rate is simply a datum, given by "habit and custom." Capital accumulation is what propels the system toward the stable equilibrium of the stationary state; population growth is merely a by-product of this adjustment. In the Ricardian system, therefore, economic growth is viewed as if all demographic adjustments to a long-run equilibrium had already taken place, while the process of capital accumulation has not yet been completed.

To return to our central conclusion: the farmer's rate of profit varies directly with the strength of diminishing returns. But what if the economy consists of two sectors, a wage-good industry, like agriculture, producing "corn" and a manufacturing industry producing "cloth." This does not affect the point, argued Ricardo in his 1815 pamphlet: "The profits of the farmer regulate the profits of all other trades." The money rate of profit earned on capital must in equilibrium be equal between the two industries. In agriculture, however, corn is both the input and the only output. It is capital as well as product; hence, the money rate of profit in agriculture cannot diverge from the corn rate of profit; any change in the price of corn affects inputs and outputs in the same degree. Manufacturing uses corn only as an input, as capital, and therefore equality in the rate of profit throughout the economy implies a definite relationship between the price of cloth and the price of corn. If the corn rate of profit declines, the price of cloth in terms of corn must fall. To reiterate: all prices are measured in terms of corn, and the "money" rate of profit in industry is governed by the corn rate in agriculture, which in turn depends entirely on corn.

By this ingenious argument Ricardo established the central tenet of his system without entering at all into the question of valuation. But the argument, as it stood, was vulnerable in the extreme. It assumed not only that wages are fixed in terms of wheat but that they are entirely spent on wheat. All agricultural products are wage goods, and all manufactured products are luxuries never consumed by workers. When this is not true, a change in the terms of trade between "corn" and "cloth" alters real wages and makes it impossible to deduce the average rate of profit merely from the wheat rate of profit in agriculture. Clearly, the problem had to be worked out on less heroic assumptions, and in so doing the problem of value had to come to the fore. But even in the *Principles* Ricardo clung to a model that rigidly distinguished between wage goods and nonwage goods, with the result that the rate of profit in the economy as a whole is still exclusively determined by the cost of production of wage goods. This is a feature of all theoretical models that distinguish between wage goods and luxuries, simply because wage goods enter into the production of all goods, while luxuries do not.

The Labor Theory of Value. Adam Smith confined the application of a labor theory of relative price to a conjectural "rude and original state of society." Ricardo went a step further and argued that a one-factor theory of value is capable of explaining price determination in the real world. But Ricardo's doubts have more significance in the history of the labor theory of value than do his positive assertions. He was the first to show just why a labor-cost theory cannot really determine the relative prices of reproducible commodities under perfect competition. If he adhered to the labor theory at all, he did so only as a rough approximation and because it served as a convenient device for expounding his model. His central purpose was not to explain relative prices but "to determine the laws which regulate the distribution of the produce of industry." Nevertheless, let us consider for a moment why any one-factor hypothesis fails to account for the relative prices we observe about us.

With one factor of production, the price of a product is equal to the average input requirement of the factor per unit of output multiplied by its money rate of reward. Let there be two goods X_1 and X_2. Let each require a_1 and a_2 of labor inputs per unit of output, rewarded at the rate w_1 and w_2. Then the cost of production equations for long-run prices are

$$p_1 = w_1 a_1 \qquad p_2 = w_2 a_2 .$$

Since $w_1 = w_2$ under perfect competition, relative prices are entirely determined by relative labor-input requirements, independent of demand

$$(p_1/p_2) = (a_1/a_2) .$$

Since labor costs usually bulk large in total costs, a pure labor-cost theory of value will still more or less accurately predict all *significant* changes in relative prices even when two or three factors are employed. As Samuelson put it: "the operational significance of a one-factor hypothesis lies in the powerful predictive value that it gives to technology alone."

But the presence of capital does imply that a simple labor theory can never *exactly* predict changes in relative price. Consider capital in the Ricardian sense as consisting solely of working capital. Production is time-consuming and workers need finished consumer goods today; they cannot wait to be paid out of the finished product of today's labor when it is actually sold. So the employer "advances" finished goods to the worker, the sum of which constitutes the so-called "wages fund" or circulating capital. The capitalist must earn interest on the money value of the goods-in-process that he has "advanced" to workers. The money flow of the final product, made up of finished consumer goods and investment goods, exceeds the sum of wages paid out by the interest returns of the capitalists. That interest exists is due simply to the lapse of time that always occurs between the application of inputs and the appearance of output. Who receives it is a matter of who can afford to do the requisite "waiting." In the language of Böhm-Bawerk, workers are forced to pay a premium on present goods because they cannot wait for the completion of the productive process; the present value of future output discounted at the ruling rate of interest equals the present value of wages; but current wages are paid for the sake of future output, and the future value of output normally exceeds its present value precisely because the rate of interest is positive. Whether "waiting" is a factor of production that requires a minimum rate of reward to be forthcoming at all is a question that we can leave open for the moment—this problem, to which Marx devoted his entire theoretical effort, never troubled Ricardo in the slightest. All we need for the purpose of the present argument is that a positive market rate of interest, or, to use classical language, a positive rate of profit, exists.[1]

[1] The classical theory of business profits refers to what we would now call the "pure" rate of interest, the rate on riskless perpetual bonds, which, in equilibrium and at a constant price level, equals the marginal productivity of capital. This does not mean that the classical economists failed to distinguish between the rate of return on real capital and the market rate of interest. But in equilibrium the two rates are equal, and therefore in their theory of value and distribution they ignored the distinction. Nowadays we draw a distinction between the capitalist earning interest and the entrepreneur earning profit. This distinction goes back to Adam Smith, who spoke of "the monied interests" of inactive investors in contrast to businessmen who actively employ their own or borrowed capital. But, for the most part, the classical writers had in mind the owner-manager of a firm, earning both implicit interest and profit. In the modern sense of the term, profits as

With a positive rate of interest, the price of a commodity is influenced not merely by the amount of labor required to produce it but also by the length of time for which it is embodied in production. The price of a product in the long run is equal to its wage cost plus a profit margin on the capital advanced. If one worker produces one bushel of wheat in *one* year, and two workers a yard of cloth in *one* year, the relative price of the two goods is equal to the ratio of the amounts of labor required to produce each of them: cloth will be twice as expensive as wheat. At any given rate of profit, the amount of profits earned on cloth are always just twice the amount earned on wheat, and no change in the rate of profit will alter this result. But if one worker can produce a bushel of wheat in *one* year, while it requires two workers *two* years to produce a yard of cloth, the profits earned on the wages of the first year will themselves have to earn profits for the second year; instead of cloth now being four times as expensive as wheat (two workers for two years as against one worker for one year), its relative price in terms of wheat will in fact be greater than four. And a change in the rate of profit will now affect relative prices even though the relative quantities of labor required to produce the two goods remain the same. To put it more tersely, if X_1 and X_2 are produced in unequal periods of time t_1 and t_2 with $t_1 > t_2$, then if r is the rate of profit per period, the cost-of-production equations for long-run prices are

$$p_1 = wa_1(1+r)^{t_1} \qquad p_2 = wa_2(1+r)^{t_2},$$

with $(p_1/p_2) = (a_1/a_2)(1+r)^{t_1-t_2}$.

It follows that we can no longer predict relative prices from the labor coefficients alone unless $t_1 = t_2$.

Capital Costs and Labor Value. The whole of the first chapter in Ricardo's *Principles* is devoted to the point we have just been making. Instead of speaking of unequal production periods, Ricardo prefers to group the objections to the pure labor-cost theory under the heading of "The different proportions of fixed and circulating capital," "The unequal durability of fixed capital," "the time which must elapse before it (the product) can be brought to market," and "The rapidity which it (the capital) is returned to the employer"; but all these objections, as he himself explained, "come under one of time." And it makes no

---

such consist partly of monopoly returns due to imperfect competition, partly of "rents" to factors in inelastic supply, and partly of rewards to uncertainty-bearing. In the classical period theorems about profits do not touch upon any of these three considerations, being in fact theorems about interest rather than profit. If we nevertheless continue to talk about the classical theory of profit, it is only because of customary usage; it would be much better if we spoke of the classical theory of interest.

difference whether we speak of different periods of production of commodities or of its reciprocal, the different turnover rates of capital. The
latter way of speaking has the advantage of translating Ricardo's insight into the common parlance of business. Commodities produced at
equal unit cost sell at equal prices when profits on turnover are also
equal. The rate of profit on turnover tends to equality in a competitive
system for the same unit period, not for different periods. If a capital
sum yields $10 every year, it must yield more than $20 every two years,
otherwise it will not be invested in the two-year period. Equality in the
annual rate of profit will in fact insure that the longer process is no
more profitable than the shorter process.

Actually, the problem is a little more complicated than Ricardo
made out. By confining capital to working capital, the problem is indeed reduced to one of "time." But fixed capital cannot be distinguished
from working capital merely on grounds of its greater durability, as
Ricardo thought. Labor working with fixed capital in the shape of a
machine produces as a by-product a slightly older machine, which gets
embodied in subsequent production. The used machine has a price determined by its initial cost, by the wage and interest rates that ruled
during its period of operation, and by the method that was employed to
charge depreciation. This creates difficulties of a kind that are even now
not completely resolved. The history of capital theory after Ricardo,
through Böhm-Bawerk and up to Wicksell, was confined for that reason to the examination of working capital, not fixed capital. Still, for
our purposes, the use of fixed capital does not alter the point being
made. Goods are produced at different ratios of fixed capital to labor,
and capital sunk in durable machines must have earned the going rate
of profit each year over the whole length of life of the machines. The
more machines per worker, the greater the weight of nonlabor income
in the cost price, the lower the ratio of wage costs to sales price. Hence,
goods produced with equal amounts of direct labor, but with unequal
amounts of machinery of unequal durability, cannot sell at the same
price. It is useless to reply that machines are only embodied labor, for
the whole point is that the present value of a machine exceeds the value
of all the wages expended on its production in the past by the amount
of annual interest charges or profit markups. It is not necessary to argue
that capital goods cannot be reduced solely to labor, that yesterday's
labor, which produced today's capital goods, was itself working with
capital goods and land existing yesterday, and so on back to the Garden
of Eden. Even if it were true that the first machine was produced by
labor alone eons ago, the fact remains that from that point onward the

labor theory of value consistently neglects at least one element deter-mining current prices. Notice that this kind of difficulty has nothing to do with the neglect of demand; it is a difficulty that remains even when the supply curve of every product in the economy is perfectly horizontal.

No labor theory of value is analytically satisfactory that does not address itself to this fatal objection. Peculiarly enough, after having discovered the exception to the rule, Ricardo shrugged his shoulders at it, saying in effect that the magnitude of the deviations that it caused was of a minor order of significance next to changes in the quantities of labor required to produce goods. This statement will not do if we are trying to explain how relative prices are determined at any moment of time. But if, like Ricardo, this question does not interest us, then it is true that a knowledge of the respective labor coefficients alone can ex-plain a good deal of price variation, particularly if r is small. Under certain circumstances, the labor theory of value may serve as a useful first approximation to the problem of price determination. But never more than a first approximation.

The Ricardian Theory of Value. The way Ricardo approached the problem of value theory is characteristic of his preoccupation with distribution. He assumed at the outset that the value of money is con-stant and hence that distribution is a matter of dividing a real national product among landlords, capitalists, and laborers. Rent, being an intra-marginal surplus, does not enter into the determination of prices. The value of a commodity, therefore, is determined by the variable inputs applied on no-rent land, and distribution is in the first instance a prob-lem in dividing a product-less-rent between capital and labor. The fact that capital-labor ratios differ among industries means that any change in money wage rates or in the rate of profit necessarily alters the struc-ture of prices and therefore the valuation of the product-less-rent. A change in the level of prices owing to a change in money wages has already been ruled out by the assumption of the constant purchasing power of money: a truly general rise of wages in all industries, includ-ing the gold-mining industry, cannot raise prices. It is impossible to raise both the gold price of commodities and the commodity price of gold. A rise of wages excluding the gold industry lowers the value of money, which is excluded by definition. Even if gold is not domestically mined, the argument holds good if the country is on the gold standard and paper notes are fully convertible in gold; all we need to do in such a case is apply Hume's price specie-flow mechanism. This leaves only the effect on the price structure to worry about.

As Sraffa has said: "The effects on value of different proportions or durabilities of capital can be looked upon from two distinct aspects. First, that of occasioning a *difference* in the relative values of two commodities which are produced by equal quantities of labor. Second, that of the effect which a rise of wages has in producing a *change* in their relative value." We have been emphasizing the first, but it was the second that really interested Ricardo. He was struck by the fact that, measured in money of constant purchasing power, a rise in wages would raise the price of labor-intensive goods relative to the price of capital-intensive goods or, to put it differently, lower the relative price of capital-intensive goods. Since average prices are being held constant, a commodity produced with an average ratio of capital to labor will not alter in price as a consequence of an increase in wage rates. Measured in terms of such a commodity, a labor-intensive good like wheat rises, while a capital-intensive good like cloth falls in price. We need a name for this effect, for it will come up frequently in our story. Fortunately, it already has a name. It is the so-called "Ricardo Effect." The Ricardo Effect, as Hayek has called it, states that a rise in real wages will lengthen the average period of production in an economy. When the price level is constant, a rise in real wages must entail a rise in money wages. A rise in money wages raises the price of labor-intensive goods relative to capital-intensive goods; its impact effect is to raise costs of production in "wheat" more than in "cloth" and hence to stimulate the output of "cloth." The composition of output, therefore, swings in favor of "cloth," a capital-intensive good. If we agree with Ricardo, and with Hayek, that an increase of capital means an increase of time for which labor is locked up in the productive process, the result is to lengthen the average period of production in the economy.

The Invariable Measure of Value. A commodity produced with a period of production that is a mean for the economy as a whole will, Ricardo now realized, provide an "invariable measure of value": a unit of account invariant to changes in factor rewards. If the total product-less-rent is measured in terms of this yardstick, its value will not alter with every change in its distribution between capital and labor. For a given quantity of capital and labor, that total product will always have the same value. Ricardo decided arbitrarily that "gold" is the commodity that most closely approaches the requirement of an invariable measuring rod, and in places he ventured to suggest that a year was probably the "average period of production" in the economy. But the principle remains the same whatever commodity is said to be representative of the general degree of "roundaboutness" in the economy.

So far, so good. Instead of deflating national income with a weighted index of prices, we deflate it with the hypothetical price of "gold." This solution to the index-number problem seems, however, to have got mixed up in Ricardo's mind with the problem of locating the source of variations in the ratios of exchange between two goods. Normally, a change in the money price of wheat will tell us nothing about conditions of production in agriculture. Under a gold standard, the money price of wheat may rise because wheat is more costly to produce, but equally well because of technical improvements in gold mining. Or it may be that a rise in the demand for labor is pushing up money wage rates and wheat happens to be a more labor-intensive good than gold. But Ricardo wanted to be able to speak unambiguously about a rise in the price of wheat caused by rising input requirements in agriculture. To do so, he took a further step and stipulated that the invariable yardstick must be conceived as being produced at all times by a constant quantity of capital and labor.

By itself this is still not enough. A change in the rate of wages or the rate of profit will still alter the price of wheat, measured in terms of the invariable standard, if the capital intensity of wheat production departs from the social average. Suppose that the relative price of wheat increases owing to the pressure of diminishing returns. Money wages must now rise to keep real wages constant, and in consequence the price of wheat in terms of the invariable standard alters once again for reasons having nothing to do this time with the inputs embodied in the production of wheat. If workers consume manufactured products, which have fallen in price measured in terms of the yardstick, the problem gets even more complicated. It is clear that the invariable standard does not really help to solve this problem even though it succeeds in valuing the national product irrespective of its distribution among the participating factors of production.

It is apparent that Ricardo realized this, and he got round it by collapsing the two problems into one. The invariable yardstick is not only produced with an "average period of production" and a fixed amount of capital and labor, but this average period is taken to be equal to the annual production cycle of agriculture. Thus, when wheat sells at $1 in terms of the measure of value, this means that the production of a bushel of wheat requires the same quantity of capital and labor as the production of gold designated as $1. The price of wheat is not affected by the wage rate and is determined soley by two labor coefficients, its own and the fixed coefficient of the "ideal money." After a long journey we have come right back to the original wheat model.

The whole of the famous chapter on value in the *Principles,* as well as the last paper Ricardo wrote, is concerned with justifying this procedure. It is a muddle because Ricardo is trying to resolve two different problems at one and the same time: on the one hand, to find an appropriate unit of social accounting to add up the real net national product and, on the other hand, to attach an absolute number to every economic good expressing its "difficulty or facility of production." Underlying both problems is the fatal objection to the labor theory of value: the value of a single good or of the total national product is influenced by the division of outlays between capital and labor. Ricardo cut this Gordian knot by ignoring capital, which can be done just as successfully by comparing goods produced by the same average ratio of capital to labor as by neglecting capital outright. We blow up the average and arrive at the total produced with the same proportion of capital to labor. Only a change in the amounts of labor or capital can now alter the value of the total product. Since capital turns over once a year, it consists solely of the wage bill. It follows that the value of every good and the value of the total product is solely determined by labor requirements. Marx read Ricardo carefully and used precisely the same sleight-of-hand to substantiate the labor theory of value.

Indeed, if Ricardo had not encountered so much criticism, he might have retained the definition of the invariable standard advanced in the first edition of the *Principles,* to wit, a commodity that would require at any time the same amount of labor unassisted by capital. Wheat was then said to be likewise produced by labor alone, and thereafter the whole argument ran on exactly as in the third edition. What Ricardo wanted to do in the chapter on value was to show that the labor theory, despite its flaws, provides a convenient short cut for expounding the "real" nature of distribution in a growing economy. The chapter is tortuous to read because it still shows marks of the process of thinking through an assumption without facing up to the fact that assumptions have meaning only in terms of their implications.

The Fundamental Theorem of Distribution. We saw earlier that if all capital consists of wheat advanced as wages, the rate of profit varies directly with the marginal product of capital-and-labor when the real wage rate is given

$$r = \left(\frac{AM}{KM} - 1\right) 100\% \, .$$

But AM/KM is the ratio of the total product-less-rent to total wages, whose reciprocal is labor's share of the final product minus rent. The rate of profit then varies inversely to wages if by "wages" we mean the relative share of labor in the final product (less rent) of a one-year investment. This is Ricardo's "fundamental theorem." When we introduce money into the system, this theorem must be assumed to apply to the money rate of profit and the rate of money wages. It is not merely a matter of relative shares as is sometimes alleged. Ricardo would hardly have gone to the length of emphasizing such a truism over and over again. Moreover, it is a truism only if we ignore the rental share: obviously, the share of capital in the total product-less-rent varies inversely with the share of labor. It is *not* a truism with respect to the total national product, however, since the rental share has yet to be determined. Be that as it may, let us now set forth the fundamental theorem that the rate of profit varies inversely to money wages for an economy whose output consists of more than wheat.

If the price of wheat is determined at the margins of cultivation,[2] rent must be spent on some good other than wheat. Let us introduce "gold," consumed by landlords, which we use at the same time as a *numéraire* in which to express all prices. There are two production functions in the economy:

$$\text{Wheat:} \quad X_1 = f(N_1) ,$$
$$\text{Gold:} \quad X_2 = f(N_2) ,$$

with $N_1 + N_2 = N$ being the number of doses of capital-and-labor required to produce wheat and gold. We assume $t_1 = t_2$—the crucial step in Ricardo's use of an invariable yardstick—and hence

$$(p_1/p_2) = (a_1/a_2) .$$

But a_2, the capital-and-labor required to produce one unit of gold, is assumed constant by definition. So the relative price of wheat is entirely determined by a_1, the capital-and-labor required to produce one unit of wheat on no-rent land.

To standardize our notation:

(1) The production function of wheat: $X_1 = f(N_1)$, subject to $f'(N) > 0$ and $f''(N) < 0$.
(2) The production function of gold: $X_2 = N_2/a_2$.
(3) The total number of workers: $N = N_1 + N_2$.

[2] The Ricardian method of "getting rid of rent" in determining relative prices is not really legitimate, since the location of the margin is itself a function of demand and hence of wage and profit rates; the lower the rate of profit, for example, the more profitable it is to cultivate land hitherto regarded as uncultivatable. But substitution in consumption is ruled out in the Ricardian model, for, as we recall, the output of wheat, and hence the classification of land in order of its fertility, is determined by the size of population and by the technical conditions of production in agriculture. We can get rid of rent because land is fixed in supply *and* because final demand for the product of land is fixed.

(4) The real wages bill: $W = wN$, with w = the constant real wage rate in terms of wheat.

(5) The physical stock of capital: $K = W$.

(6) The real annual rental: $R = X_1 - N_1f'(N_1) = f(N_1) - N_1f'(N_1)$.

(7) Real annual profits in agriculture: $P_1 = X_1 - R - wN_1$.

(8) The price of corn: $p_1 = a_1 = N_1/X_1 - R$.

After substituting from (6), equation (8) may also be written

(8a) $p_1 = 1/f'(N_1)$.

(9) The price of gold: $p_2 = a_2$.

(10) Money profits in the gold industry in which no rent is earned: $p_2P_2 = p_2X_2 - p_1wN_2$.

(11) Money profits in the whole economy: $P = (p_1X_1 - p_1R) + p_2X_2 - p_1W$.

The expression in parentheses is the value of the wheat product-less-rent. Substituting equation (8), it turns out that this is equal to N_1. From (9) and (2) the value of the total gold product $p_2X_2 = N_2$. This apparently peculiar conclusion is the result of our choice of a monetary unit, namely, the amount of labor required to produce a unit of gold. Naturally, since $p_1/p_2 = a_1/a_2$, $p_1(X_1 - R)/p_2X_2 = N_1/N_2$. Finally, the total wage bill $p_1W = p_1K = (N_1 + N_2)wp_1$. Hence, total money profits can also be written:

(11a) $P = (N_1 + N_2)(1 - wp_1)$.

(12) total money rent: $p_1R = p_2X_2 = N_2$.

(13) the money wage rate: $w = p_1w = w/f'(N_1) = wa_1$.

(14) the rate of profit: $r = P/p_1K$
$$= (N_1 + N_2)(1 - wp_1)/wp_1(N_1 + N_2)$$
$$= 1 - wp_1/wp_1 = (1/wp_1) - 1 = (f'(N_1)/w) - 1.$$

The conclusion we reach is identical to the simple corn model considered earlier: the rate of profit varies directly with the marginal product of N_1, given the real wage rate, and—we can now add—inversely to the price of wheat as well as to the money wage rate. We can express the corn model now in similar terms. The long-run cost of production equation for the price of wheat in such a system is

$$p_1 = a_1w(1 + r)^t \qquad (t = 1).$$

The money wage rate: $w = wp_1$. And so the price of corn is

$$p_1 = a_1(wp_1)(1 + r)$$

and

$$r = \frac{1}{a_1w} - 1.$$

The rate of profit, therefore, varies inversely with a_1, and a_1 is not the reciprocal of the average product of capital-and-labor but of its marginal product, since we are looking at the margin of cultivation after deducting rent. The conclusion for the one-good case is the same as for the two-goods case: the rate of profit is completely independent of the conditions of production outside the wage-good industry.

The Effect of Capital Accumulation. The system is now subject to three possible dynamic adjustments: the population adjustment when the market wage differs from the natural wage; the capital accumulation adjustment when r exceeds the minimum rate necessary to induce investment; and technical progress, which shifts the production function X_1. The first is put aside by Ricardo for purposes of establishing "strong conclusions"; the third is dealt with parenthetically, but the core of the argument abstracts from technical change; it is the second mechanism alone that produces the Ricardian conclusions for a growing economy. His effort is confined to describing what happens to product and factor prices and to factor shares in the process of capital accumulation. His results are simply expressed by taking the derivative of all the crucial variables with respect to capital and inspecting the sign of the derivatives. Recalling that $K = W = \bar{w}N$ or $N = K/\bar{w}$, we have from equations (4) and (5) the following trends over time:

(15) $dN/dK = 1/w > o$, employment increases.

From (5) we have

(16) $dW/dK = 1 > o$, the wage bill increases.

From (6) we have

(17) $dR/dK = -N_1 f''(N_1) \dfrac{dN_1}{dK} > o$, total rents rise.

This follows from the fact that the production function is at diminishing returns, i.e., $f''(N_1) < o$, so that $-N_1 f''(N_1) > o$ and $dN_1/dK > o$.

From (8a) we have

(18) $dp_1/dK_1 = \{-f''(N_1)/[f'(N_1)]^2\}dN_1/dK > o$, the price of corn rises.

From (13) we have

(19) $dw/dK = w(dp_1/dK) > o$, the money wage rate increases.

From (14) we have

(20) $dp/dK = f''(N_1)/w \cdot dN_1/dK < o$, the rate of profit falls.

Noticing that the value of total output is $(p_1 X_1 - p_1 R) + p_2 X_2 = p_1 X_1 = N$, we could go on to define the share of wages, profits, and rent in total income = total output, taking the derivative with res-spect to capital and inspecting the sign of the derivative to see what will happen to relative shares. But the expressions we would get would be extremely messy to interpret. It is simpler, and will serve the same purpose, to revert to a one-commodity corn model, keeping the same notation but dropping the subscripts. Ricardo, we know, argued not only that the profit rate would fall in a growing economy but also that the relative share of profits in total income would fall and that both labor's and land's share of income would rise. The proof of these propositions takes three chapters in the *Principles* but turns out to be dependent upon the particular production function of wheat that Ricardo selected for his arithmetical examples.

The Trend of Relative Shares. Taking the general case, we have a given production function for corn $X = f(N)$, subject to $f'(N) > o$ and $f''(N) < o$. What happens to relative shares as N, the number of doses of capital-and-labor, increases? We begin with labor's relative share. It is clear without any mathematics that the share of wages in total income must rise as income increases: at a given real wage rate, the wage bill grows proportionately to the number of labor inputs; output or income, however, grows less than proportionately owing to the postulate of diminishing returns. Spelling it out,

(21) labor's relative share: $W/X = wN/f(N)$.

$$(22) \quad \frac{d}{dN}\left(\frac{W}{X}\right) = \frac{w}{[f(N)]^2} [f(N) - Nf'(N)] > o .$$

The bracketed expression $[f(N) - Nf'(N)] = R$ and therefore, so long as land commands a rental, the whole expression is positive: the share of wages in total income rises with every increase in N.

Now for the rental share.

$$(23) \quad \frac{R}{X} = \frac{f(N) - Nf'(N)}{f(N)} = 1 - \frac{Nf'(N)}{f(N)} .$$

Rather than taking the derivative with respect to N, let us convert this expression. Dividing both numerator and denominator by N, we get

$$\frac{R}{X} = 1 - \frac{f'(N)}{f(N)/N} .$$

But $f'(N)$ is the marginal product and $f(N)/N$ the average product of the variable input N.

Thus,
$$\frac{R}{X} = 1 - \frac{M}{A} .$$

The ratio M/A is conventionally defined as the elasticity of the production function: the relative change in the total product associated with the relative change in the variable input. Using the standard notation for elasticity,

$$\epsilon = \frac{N}{X}\frac{dX}{dN} = \frac{N}{f(N)} f'(N) = \frac{M}{A}.$$

We note now that $N(M/A) = X - R/X$. So the share of the total product which capital and labor together receive is exactly equal to the ratio M/A. It follows, of course, that $R/X = 1 - \epsilon$ will rise only if the absolute value of ϵ falls in the course of capital accumulation. It is hard to visualize ϵ, so we shall translate it into the elasticity of the average product curve. For any pair of marginal and average curves, there is a formula, owing to Mrs. Robinson, which says that $M/A = 1 - 1/\eta = \epsilon$, where η is the absolute value of the elasticity of A at that point; accordingly, η varies directly with ϵ.[3] The translation reads: the rental share will rise along a given invariable production function if the absolute value of the elasticity of the average product curve falls. In general, η does not necessarily fall along a production function showing diminishing returns to the variable input. Diminishing returns is a necessary but not a sufficient condition for an increase in the rental share. It is possible that the added increment of output on no-rent land increases total output by a proportion greater than the percentage increment in rental payment on intramarginal land. Rents rise as a share of output only if returns diminish at a constant or increasing rate: it depends not on the sign of the slope of the M curve but on the rate of change of the slope; the production function has to be subject to the condition $f'(N) > 0$, $f''(N) < 0$, and $f'''(N) \leq 0$; the average product curve must be linear or concave to the origin.[4]

To illustrate, consider the three production functions shown in Figure 9, all obeying diminishing returns to the variable input. Pro-

---

[3] To avoid confusion, notice that if we spell out η we get

$$\eta = \frac{N}{X/N}\frac{d(X/N)}{dN} = \frac{N^2}{X}\frac{d}{dN}\frac{(X)}{(N)} = \frac{N^2}{X}\frac{1}{N^2}\left(N\frac{dX}{dX} - X\right)$$
$$= \frac{N}{X}\frac{dX}{dN} - 1 = \epsilon - 1, \text{ not } 1 - \frac{1}{\epsilon}.$$

This is because we have taken the ordinate value X/N as the dependent variable and the abscissa value N as the independent variable, whereas ever since Marshall, formulas for the price-elasticity of demand (the average revenue curve) treat price along the ordinate as the independent variable and quantity demanded along the abscissa as the dependent variable—instead of $(q/p)(dp/dq)$, the price-elasticity of demand is defined as $(p/q)(dq/dp)$. If we treat out η in the same way, we arrive at the result $\eta = 1 - 1/\epsilon$.

[4] The reader is warned, however, that convexity of the A curve does not by itself *insure* a falling rental share. For instance, a convex M curve which was a rectangular hyperbola would leave the total reward of the variable input constant, i.e., $Nf'(N) = $ a constant at every point. In that case, every increase of N increases the total product but leaves the absolute income of the composite dose unchanged; obviously, the rental share would increase.

ductivity curves I and II obey the stricter condition $f'''(N) \leqq o$, but productivity curve III does not, yet all obey $f''(N) < o$. The total product curve I, being a parabola, has no inflection point; total product curves II and III have indicated inflection points, an inflection point being a point where the corresponding marginal curve is at a maximum or minimum depending on whether $f'''(N) < o$ or $> o$. It is easy to see why R/X is inversely related to η and ϵ. In cases I and II the relative gap between A and M widens, i.e., $\epsilon = (M/A)$ falls. But in case III the relative gap diminishes, and ϵ and η rise along the production function. The arithmetical examples upon which Ricardo based his arguments implicitly assume linear productivity functions (case I), so no wonder he concluded that the rental share will increase: as we move down a straight-line A curve, its elasticity (η) falls.

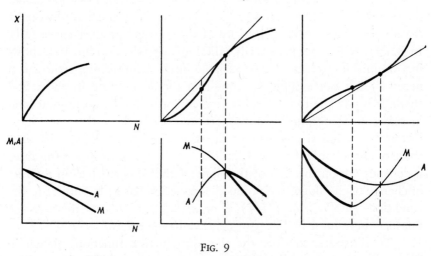

Fig. 9

Unless we are going to commit ourselves to a particular quadratic production function, we must conclude that the rental share is indeterminate. If the rental share is indeterminate, so is the share of wages plus profits in total income. We know that labor's share will rise, but the share of residual profits may go either way.[5] Thus, contrary to what

---

[5] We could prove this formula by proceeding as before. Recall that in Equation (23) $(R/X) = 1 - Nf'(N)/f(N)$, hence,

$$(24) \qquad \frac{d}{dN}\left(\frac{R}{X}\right) = \frac{1}{[f(N)]^2}\{-f(N)[Nf''(N) + f'(N)] - N[f'(N)]^2\}$$

$$= \frac{1}{f(N)} Nf''(N) - f'(N)\left[\frac{Nf'(N)}{f(N)} - 1\right].$$

Substituting $-1/\eta$ for the bracket expression, we have

$$\frac{d}{dN}\left(\frac{R}{X}\right) = -\frac{1}{f(N)}\left[Nf''(N) - f'(N)\left(-\frac{1}{\eta}\right)\right].$$

To evaluate the sign: $f'(N) > o$ and $\eta > 1$ by definition; hence, $-f'(N)(-1/\eta) > o$. Now

Ricardo thought he had demonstrated, the postulate of diminishing returns is insufficient to derive his general theorems about the pattern of income shares in a growing economy. Commentators ever since Ricardo's time have tried to simplify the fundamental theorem that "profits vary inversely with wages" by saying it refers to relative shares, not wages per man and profits per cent on capital invested. But, surprisingly enough, the theorem does hold on his own assumptions for money wages and the rate of profit, but it does not hold for the relative shares of labor and capital.

Technical Change. A growing economy is likely to experience technological progress, which will shift the M and A curves upward. What will happen to factor rewards and relative shares in that case? On this question the Ricardian system is vacuous. There are some general remarks in *Principles* on the effect of improved methods in manufacturing upon real wages and in the chapter on rent there is a formal discussion of the effect of improvements in agriculture upon rents. Let us look briefly at Ricardo's theory of agricultural improvements for what it is worth. His argument is that the short-run effect of such improvements is to lower rents and therefore that landlords will have no incentive to introduce them. He divides the changes in techniques into two types: (1) land-saving innovations that increase the output from given land, by "more skilfull rotation of crops, or the better choice of manure"; (2) innovations that reduce the doses of capital-and-labor required to produce a given output on a given amount of land, such as "improvements in agricultural implements, . . . economies in the use of horses employed in husbandry, and better knowledge of the veterinary arts." The first of the two types, he concludes, lowers rents per acre as well as the rental share, while the second lowers money rents but not necessarily corn rents.

$f''(N) < o$; therefore, $Nf''(N) < o$. The whole of the expression in the brackets may be positive or negative and so the sign of $(d/dN)(R/X)$ is indeterminate.

Now for the profit share.

(25) Total profits:

$$P = N[f'(N) - w]$$

(26) The profit share:

$$\frac{P}{X} = \frac{N[f'(N) - w]}{f(N)}$$

(27)

$$\frac{d}{dN}\left(\frac{P}{X}\right) = \frac{f(N)[Nf''(N) + f'(N) - w] - N[f'(N)]^2 - wNf'(N)}{[f(N)]^2}$$

$$= \frac{1}{f(N)}\left\{Nf''(N) - [f'(N) - w]\left[\frac{Nf'(N)}{f(N)} - 1\right]\right\}$$

$$= \frac{1}{f(N)}\left\{Nf''(N) - [f'(N) - w]\left[-\frac{1}{\eta}\right]\right\}.$$

It is hardly surprising that this expression is identical to the previous equation for the rental share, except for w, which is a constant. Since the rate of profit $r = [f'(N) - w] > o$, $(1/\eta)r > o$, but $Nf''(N) < o$, and hence $(d/dN)(P/X)$ may, like $(d/dN)(R/X)$, go either way.

Let us consider first a land-saving innovation. Obviously, its immediate effect is to lower rents per acre, but is it necessarily true that total rents and the rental share will fall? Ricardo assumes that the productivity of each grade of soil is raised equiproportionately. Raising the productivity of each grade of soil by an equal percentage amount necessarily means that the innovation raises output per unit of cost less on the margins of cultivation than on the intramargins. Referring back to our numerical example in chapter 3, a 10 per cent increase in output of land E constitutes a smaller absolute cost-reducing improvement than a 10 per cent increase in output on land A. To illustrate the argument graphically, we need to draw the productivity functions of land, holding capital-and-labor constant (Fig. 10). The new curves must stand higher above the old at the left than at the right. The demand for wheat

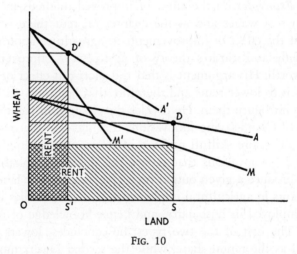

FIG. 10

is perfectly inelastic, so the total product remains unchanged $(OD = OD')$. As long as the curves are straight lines, it is indeed true that total rents as well as the rental share will fall. But the conclusion is dependent, in the first place, upon the fact that the marginal and average product of land are linear functions—convex productivity functions would produce precisely the opposite effect—and, in the second place, upon the fact that the improvement raises output per unit of land by a constant percentage amount. If, instead, Ricardo had assumed that output is raised by equal absolute amounts per unit of land —an iso-elastic upward shift in the productivity curves—the result would have been to increase rents. The reader can prove these propositions for himself by using the rule that the elasticity of the average product curve of a factor varies in the same direction as the relative share of a factor; and as we move back on a straight line from right to left we can translate every statement about relative shares into a statement about the absolute share.

Ricardo's analysis of innovations to save capital-and-labor is no more conclusive. Here he begins by assuming that innovations raise the productivity of capital-and-labor by equal absolute amounts—in which case rents fall—and then passes on to an example in which productivity is raised by equal percentage amounts—in which case rents rise. Even in the latter case, it is only corn rents that rise, not money rents, for the innovation causes the price of corn to fall. Ricardo does not consider what will happen to the now displaced capital and labor. Presumably, wage and profit rates will fall again, inducing the cultivation of new land, and hence rents will rise whatever the immediate effect of the innovation.

In general, the striking feature of Ricardo's analysis of improvements is his emphasis upon the short run, while elsewhere he concentrates upon long-run effects. He admitted that the fall in rents is really temporary: the fall in the price of corn stimulates population by raising real wages, and so rents per acre will eventually rise again. This curious reversal of method may have something to do with Ricardo's ideological bias against landlords. But we must not forget that, in spite of the numerous references to the accumulation of capital and the growth of population, Ricardo's model is not actually concerned with economic growth in the long run. The purpose of the model is to demonstrate the inexpediency of the Corn Laws. Restrictions on the importation of cheap wheat *tend* to reduce the rate of profit by forcing the rapid extension of cultivation to successively less fertile areas of land at home. The summary treatment given to technical change may be due to the fact that Ricardo really had his eye on the effects that a Corn Law imposes in a comparatively short period of time. Certainly he shows very little interest in the structural changes of an economy over long periods, a subject to which Adam Smith had given some of his best analysis. Even Ricardo's so-called pessimism is entirely contingent upon the maintenance of the Corn Laws. There is no indication whatever that he regarded the stationary state as imminent. After all, in the *Principles* the fundamental theorem of distribution is coupled with the Law of Comparative Cost to show that welfare is increased by free trade and that repeal of the Corn Laws would permit a country like Britain to reap the benefit of her comparative advantage in manufacturing.

We have reviewed the analytical skeleton of Ricardo's system.

The qualifications that he made, the frequent recognition of the restrictive assumptions of his model, are best examined in a reader's guide to the *Principles,* to which we now turn.

READER'S GUIDE TO PRINCIPLES OF POLITICAL ECONOMY

Value. The first chapter of the book consists of seven sections, the first of which states without compromise that relative prices are determined by the relative amounts of labor required to produce commodities independent of the rate of reward to labor. Adam Smith's water-diamond paradox is quoted, and Ricardo immediately alters the implicit meaning of Smith's "use value," defining it as "utility," the capacity of a product to "contribute to our gratification." The theory of exchange value is restricted to reproducible goods under conditions of perfect competition. Nonreproducible goods are called "scarce," meaning goods fixed in supply. In chapter 17 such goods are described as selling at a "monopoly price" entirely determined by demand. The rest of section 1 is devoted to attacking the doctrine that outlays on wages determine relative prices, a doctrine that Ricardo attributes to Adam Smith. The problem of value, Ricardo notes, is this: "two commodities vary in relative value, and we wish to know in which the variation has really taken place." Smith's measuring rod, the purchasing power of a commodity over labor, will not illuminate this problem. Smith identified a labor-embodied with a labor-commanded theory, observes Ricardo. This criticism makes sense only if we assume that Smith was trying to *explain* relative prices with a labor-commanded theory. Actually, Ricardo's quarrel with Smith is that the amount of labor that a product can command in exchange constitutes a poor *measure* of value.

	Wages in Corn	Corn Price per Bushel	Money Wages	Expend. on Corn	Expend. on Other Things
I.....	1 bu.	80*s.*	80*s.*	40*s.*	40*s.*
II.....	1¼ bu.	40*s.*	50*s.*	20*s.*	30*s.*

Ricardo now constructs a numerical example (see accompanying table) to show that Smith's yardstick cannot distinguish between "a rise in the value of labor" and "a fall in the value of things . . . on which wages are expended." Suppose that labor is paid in corn and consumes a half-bushel of corn per week, trading the rest for "other things." Corn now falls in price for any reason whatever, and labor receives more corn but not enough to maintain a constant market basket of the same goods. (Despite changes in relative prices, the composition of the market basket remains unchanged; Ricardo always ignores the possibility of commodity substitution.) In this case, Ricardo alleges, Smith would have to say that labor had risen in value because "his standard is corn," whereas he should have said that the value of labor had fallen because labor's real wages have decreased; labor has less purchasing power over all goods. Obviously, this criticism is unfair because it ignores the fact that Smith's standard is designed for long-run comparisons, and a huge long run at that. Naturally, if the price elasticity of demand for corn is zero and the cross-elasticity of demand for all goods is also zero, a fall in money wages leaves the laborer worse off. But what of the subsequent repercussions of the fall in money wages? Population growth would slacken, Smith might have argued, the demand for corn would fall off, corn prices would rise, followed by money wages, and, ultimately, real wages must rise back to previous levels. What irritated Ricardo was Smith's assumption that the wages of labor can be measured in corn because the price of corn stays constant through time. It would have been a simple matter, however, to have shown that Smith's belief in the stability of corn prices "from century to century" is irrelevant to the effects of such policy measures as the Corn Law of 1815. Instead, Ricardo chose to attack Smith on Ricardian grounds, completely ignoring the underlying rationale of Smith's measure, the idea that the disutility of labor is invariant at all times and all places.

Relative Wages. It is becoming clear that Ricardo is not in fact concerned with explaining why relative prices are what they are. Throughout this chapter he is really discussing the choice of a proper standard of value for the purpose of explaining shifts in the structure of prices through time. When he states that "the inquiry to which I wish to draw the reader's attention relates to the effect of the variations in the relative value of commodities, and not in their absolute value," he means *temporal* variations in relative value. This impression is confirmed by section 2, which dismisses the problem of wage differentials between labor of different skills with the argument that the occupational structure does not vary significantly over periods of moderate lengths: the scale of wages continues "nearly the same from one generation to another; or at least the variation is very inconsiderable from year to year, and, therefore, can have little effect, for short periods, on the relative value of commodities." This consideration has relevance only within the context of intertemporal comparisons of value—notice, however, Ricardo's careless and undecided attitude about the exact time span to which his argument applies.

Ricardo's chapter on value, therefore, is not subject to the common charge that a labor theory of value involves circular reasoning. The alleged circular argument is this: relative values are explained on the basis of the labor hours embodied in goods, and then the higher price of goods produced by skilled labor is explained by the higher wage rates of skilled over unskilled labor. But why is the value of skilled labor greater than the value of unskilled labor? Because the product it produces is more valuable. Smith, Ricardo, and Marx have been ridiculed for relying on "the higgling and bargaining of the market" to establish a quantitative relation of equivalence between skilled and unskilled labor. But criticism of the labor theory of value on this score is at best superficial. Differences in the productivity of different types of labor are due either to differences in natural ability or to superior training. Unless the subject under investigation is relative wages, it is perfectly legitimate to assume all labor to be homogeneous, ignoring specialized talents and treating skilled labor as a common multiple of unskilled labor. When relative wages come to the forefront, we may resort to Adam Smith's demonstration that perfect competition yields a wage scale in which an hour of labor, no matter how priced, expresses the same unit of disutility of labor at any time. This does imply that the common unit of labor time, which is said to determine value, is itself a subjective phenomenon, a consideration that Marx consistenly ignored. But Smith's theory of relative wages does at any rate resolve the problem of circularity.

The Invariable Measure of Value. The third section of chapter 1 reduces the value of capital goods to labor expended in the past. By "embodied labor," then, is meant both the direct and the indirect labor applied via the use of machines. We are told that only a commodity produced with a constant quantity of direct and indirect labor furnishes an invariable standard for locating the source of a change in the ratios of exchange between any two commodities. In sections 4 and 5 we meet with the difficulties created by the different proportions in which fixed and circulating capital are combined in different industries, compounded by the difficulty that the two kinds of capital might differ in their durability. The distinction between fixed and working capital is said to be a matter solely of degrees of durability; this reduces the whole problem to the different time periods for which working capital is locked up in the productive process.

Since production cycles differ widely in the length of time required for their completion, relative prices are never strictly determined by relative labor time. This fundamental finding is brought out with the aid of four numerical examples—three in section 4 and a fourth in section 5. In each example a comparison is drawn between the value of "corn" produced by labor alone for one year and the value of "cloth" requiring exactly the same amount of labor in year 1 to build a machine, or an inventory of semifinished goods, by means of which cloth is produced in year 2. In the first case the value of cloth at the end of year 2 is greater than twice the value of a year's corn crop because the profit on cloth production at the end of year 1 is reinvested in year 2; the capital of the clothier earns interest for two years. The second example is identical to the first except that labor is now expressed in money terms and a rate of profit is stipulated. The machine considered so far does not depreciate at all. In the third example an inventory of goods rather than a machine is produced, but in the fourth example the rate of annual depreciation is supposed to be 100 per cent, so the machine is fully used up in year 2. The conclusions drawn from the third and fourth examples are, of course, the same as that drawn from the first.

Thus, goods embodying equal quantities of direct and indirect labor will differ in exchange value when the time required for their production differs, and a uniform change in money wages will alter their exchange ratios even though there has been no change in the labor expended upon them. A rise in money wages will raise the value of goods made with short-lived capital or with little machinery relative to goods made with long-lived capital or much machinery: this is the only way that the rate of profit can be kept at equality between all trades, irrespective of differences in cost outlays. The Ricardo Effect, however, is dismissed as slight in magnitude: even if money wages rose enough to cause the rate of profit to fall by 6 or 7 per cent—"for profits could not, probably, under any circumstances, admit of a greater general and permanent depression than to that amount"—relative prices would not vary more than 6 or 7 per cent, a conclusion based on the second of the four examples. This has led one commentator to speak of Ricardo's "93% labor theory of value." Ricardo is satisfied that the labor-cost theory provides a good first approximation to secular shifts in relative prices.

Early in section 5 Ricardo indicates his method of treating depreciation. It is supposed that a quantity of labor is employed to maintain capital intact; depreciation costs are thus shared as direct wage costs by each manufacturer in proportion to the durability of his equipment. This explains why Ricardo rarely mentions depreciation as a separate business expense. The rest of section 5 examines a case in which a rise in money wages raises the price of most goods relative to that of machines, because of the fact that the "machine" is not produced entirely by direct labor. "Machines," he concludes, "would not rise in (relative) price, in consequence of a rise of wages." The result is, of course, to induce the substitution of machines for labor. In section 6 we are at last provided with an invariable measure of value. Ricardo postulates that "gold" is produced with an average ratio of labor to capital of average durability. All values are to be expressed in terms of this invariant yardstick. It follows now that any change in wages can affect prices only in terms of "gold." Since gold is produced with a capital structure that is an average for the economy as a whole, its value never varies when wages rise or fall, being strictly determined by the labor required to produce it. This makes it "a perfect measure of value for all things produced under the same conditions precisely as itself, but for no other." The operative assumption for Ricardo's system, which is nowhere stated in so many words in the *Principles,* is that wheat is to be produced under the same circumstances as the invariable yardstick. Thereby, the relative price of wheat in terms of "gold" is made a function solely of the man-hours embodied in its production.

Section 7 briefly relaxes the general assumption throughout the book of a constant value of money. The last pages of the chapter explain with marvelous confusion what is meant by "a rise or fall in wages, profits and rent." A fall in wages means a fall in the labor inputs required to produce wage goods. Upon Ricardo's assumptions, this is tantamount to a fall in labor's share but not a fall in money wages. In his example, however, money wages do fall, and in general the money wage rate in Ricardo's model does vary directly with the labor inputs required to produce wheat. In the third edition of the *Principles,* Ricardo altered this section to make the product that is being divided refer to the product of a single farm rather than the national output. Apparently, Ricardo had realized that all his conclusions depended upon wheat's being produced with the same production period as the invariable yardstick.

Demand and Supply. To round off the subject of value, the reader should turn now to chapter 4, on natural and market price, which is intended to justify concentration upon long-period prices, and then to chapter 30 on demand and supply. Ricardo had no patience for mere demand-and-supply explanations of price, for, with the exception of wheat, all goods are supposed to be produced under conditions of constant costs. Unfortunately, this chapter fosters the impression that cost of production is something separate and apart from demand and supply, although in his *Notes on Malthus* Ricardo does say that "market price will depend on supply and demand—the supply will be finally determined by the natural price—that is to say by the cost of production." Throughout chapter 30 Ricardo speaks of demand and supply, not as schedules, but as quantities actually bought and sold. To prove that price cannot be explained merely by demand and supply, he postulates the case in which a perfectly inelastic demand curve intersects a perfectly elastic supply curve (Fig. 11); the supply curve shifts down, the price falls, but the quantity bought and sold remains the same. "Here, then, we have a case where the supply and demand has scarcely varied . . . and yet the price of bread will have fallen 50 per cent."

Social Accounting. From chapter 30 we turn back to chapter 20 on "value and riches," which employs man-hours per unit of output as a standard to evaluate net national product. By "riches" Ricardo means the magnitude of physical output; more riches mean more real income. Value, however, varies inversely to the labor time required per unit of product. For Ricardo "value" is an inverse index of the average productivity of labor and therefore of economic welfare; welfare is a matter of minimizing human effort per unit of output. For Adam Smith "value" is also an inverse index of economic welfare: as output per man rises, the amount of labor commanded by the total product falls—to put it less paradoxically, labor's purchasing power over real income rises—and welfare is a matter of maximizing labor's purchasing power over real income. At face value, Ricardo's standard should give the same answer as Smith's standard, but Smith's standard, it is true, becomes ambiguous when real wages are themselves rising or falling. On the other hand, Smith's standard digs deeper than does Ricardo's. Why should a reduction in efforts per unit of product constitute an improvement in welfare unless labor is painful and equally painful through time?

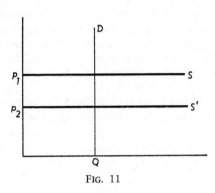

FIG. 11

This chapter contains Ricardo's only reference to the doctrine of productive labor, though it is obvious elsewhere that he accepts it uncritically. In the last paragraph of the chapter, having criticized Say's identification of value, riches, and utility, Ricardo implicitly denies the principle of diminishing marginal utility.

Did Ricardo Hold a Labor Theory?

Before proceeding to other topics, we should pause for a moment to ask ourselves just what kind of value theory Ricardo advances. Certainly, he does not adhere to what Stigler has called an *analytical* labor theory of value, the theory that labor is the sole determinant of relative prices. A consistent analytical labor theory must face the problem of explaining the nature of nonlabor income, a subject to which Ricardo gives no attention. Indeed, Ricardo must be credited with the decisive argument against a pure labor-cost theory: the so-called Ricardo Effect. He did advance an *empirical* labor theory, emphasizing the quantitative importance of labor inputs and in particular their strategic role in bringing about changes in relative prices over time. This involves nothing more than the belief that the approximate ratios in which goods exchanged are quantitatively influenced more by relative labor costs than by, say, relative interest charges. This type of theory is perfectly compatible with a Marshallian short-run theory, in which the existence of scarce factors in fixed supply will cause relative prices to vary with the rate of output of goods and hence with the pattern of demand. The difference is simply one of emphasis.

The great advantage of a one-factor theory is its tractability for purposes of popular exposition. But why a *labor* theory? The most obvious reason is that labor costs do dominate total costs in almost all industries. Land was of course regarded in Ricardo's day as a free "gift of Nature," while capital, as distinct from individual capital goods, cannot be measured in terms of homogeneous physical units. Individual capital goods, on the other hand, are too heterogeneous to be reducible to a common physical unit. This left physical man-hours as a rough-and-ready yardstick for explaining changes in relative prices.

Adam Smith, we have seen, could not swallow even an empirical labor theory, but, like Ricardo, he was in search of an appropriate unit of social accounting and found it in the number of wage units that the product can command in exchange. The common element in the labor theories of Smith and Ricardo was that both proposed what has been called a "labor theory of absolute value": "the notion that an absolute number may be attached to any economic good, independently of any other economic good." This is welfare economics, not value theory. Whether we should use money wages, man-hours, or relative prices as the weights to add up to real net national product is a question not of empirical fact or logical deduction but of normative judgment. Normative judgments are open to discussion but not to scientific proof or disproof. In the course of a particular normative judgment, however, writers are likely to claim analytical virtue for their position. When Ricardo, in the last months of his life, sat down to write a paper on "Absolute and Exchange Value," he used language as emotive as anything written by Marx: labor is the best measure of value, labor is the "cause" and "substance" of value, labor is the original purchase price of everything, and the like. For the first time Ricardo referred to "what I mean by the word value" and explained that it meant not labor and waiting but labor alone. But, unconnected with the problem of explaining relative prices, such assertions should not be taken seriously. When Keynes came to justify his choice of a wage unit to measure output in the *General Theory,* he spoke with sympathy of the classical doctrine that the expenditure of human labor constitutes a unique social cost in terms of which all other productive contributions can be expressed. He categorically denied that capital is "productive." But obviously Keynes did not hold an *analytical* labor theory of relative price. No more did Ricardo.

Rent. Chapters 2 and 3 distinguish rent from profit on capital as a return to an indestructible nonaugmentable factor of production. At the end of chapter 28, however, Ricardo observes that returns to capital sunk in the exploration and preparation of land for cultivation partake of the nature of rent, in that the yield of such capital is not an incentive reward. Enough has been said about Ricardo's rent theory to make unnecessary a préçis of his argument. The upshot of the chapter, of course, is that rent can be eliminated as an element in the pricing of goods.

For a moment in chapter 2 Ricardo generalizes the concept of marginal cost to all industry, but later, in chapter 17, he asserts definitely that manufacturing operates under constant returns to scale, marginal cost therefore being equal to average cost. Rent is said to be due to the niggardliness of nature—the scarcity of land—and not, as the physiocrats have it, the bounty of nature (its physical productivity). If land were not physically productive, capable of producing a surplus over the maintenance needs of the cultivators, no rent would arise. But unless land is also scarce in relation to demand, physical productivity will not result in value productivity. In a footnote Adam Smith's preference for agriculture as the most productive sector in the economy is soundly condemned. The fact that a like amount of labor and capital yields wages, profits, *and* rent in agriculture but only wages and profits in manufacturing is no evidence that land is more productive. On the margins of cultivation the value of wheat is in fact exhausted by the returns to labor and capital.

Agricultural Improvements. The effect of improvements in agriculture is discussed in chapter 2. We have seen that improvements need not reduce total rents, even in the short run. In the course of examining the second type of improvement, a capital-and-laborsaving innovation, Ricardo commits an interesting mistake, so easy to overlook that even Marshall missed it in his comments. Ricardo assumes that four portions of capital (and labor) are employed, 50, 60, 70, 80, each of which produces the same output. Any improvement that permits the same output, but with 45, 55, 65, 75 units of capital, will not affect corn rents but will lower money rents, Ricardo asserts. We might think that this is one of those improvements that raises productivity by equal absolute amounts; the productivity curves shift upward iso-elastically and corn rents fall. But Ricardo says corn rents are not affected. The trouble is that he has lowered costs per unit of output, not raised output per unit of cost, by equal absolute amounts. This makes all the difference. Rent in Ricardian theory is determined by output per unit of cost and to lower costs per unit of output by equal absolute amounts, leaving cost differentials unaffected, is tantamount to raising output per unit of cost more on the intramarginal applications of capital than on the marginal application. This will *raise* corn rents and leave money rents constant rather than lower them as Ricardo predicted. As a matter of fact, Ricardo himself gives the right answer to his problem in chapter 9, "Taxes on Raw Produce." To show that corn rents will rise in Ricardo's example, we translate from cost per unit of output to its reciprocal, output per unit of cost. At the margin, rents are zero, so 80 units of capital must receive 80 quarters of wheat. If x is the constant amount of wheat produced by the successively larger portions of capital applied to different plots of land, corn rents summed over the four plots in the two cases are:

(1) $$\tfrac{30}{80}x + \tfrac{20}{80}x + \tfrac{10}{80}x + 0 = \tfrac{3}{4}x .$$
(2) $$\tfrac{30}{75}x + \tfrac{20}{75}x + \tfrac{10}{75}x + 0 = \tfrac{4}{5}x .$$

Corn rents rise because $\tfrac{4}{5} > \tfrac{3}{4}$. It is assumed that the initial price of corn is £ 4 per quarter. Since corn is produced with $\tfrac{5}{80}$ less capital, the price of corn falls $\tfrac{1}{16}$, from £ 4 to £ 3.75. Total money rents, therefore, remain the same:

(3) $$\tfrac{3}{4} \cdot £4 = £3$$
(4) $$\tfrac{4}{5} \cdot £3.75 = £3 .$$

To complete the topic of rent, we go to chapter 24, in which the theory of differential rent is employed to point up contradictions in the *Wealth of Nations*. Noteworthy is Ricardo's insistence upon the fact that no-rent land does exist in England. In one place Ricardo considers the repercussions of an autonomous shift to a potato diet on the part of the working class; the analysis reveals the full sweep of Ricardo's macroeconomic generalizations—these pages bear rereading after chapters 5 and 6. A rising price of corn is shown to involve a fatal conflict of interests. Last there is chapter 32, which attacks Malthus' belief that rent is a genuine addition to wealth, not merely a transfer of purchasing power from wheat-consumers to landlords. Actually, Ricardo is attacking the political rather than the theoretical implications of Malthus' rent theory. In the middle of the chapter a passage considers the possibility of permanently raising the standard of living of workers; Ricardo's conclusion is somewhat ambiguous here—as in chapter 5, on wages, where the same topic is discussed at greater length. The distinction between gross and net revenue, taken up in chapter 26, is briefly touched upon. The last passage in chapter 32 denies that utility is measurable.

Wages. Chapter 5, on wages, and chapter 6, on profits, together contain the heart of Ricardo's system. At the outset of chapter 5 Ricardo defines "natural wages" as that wage which will keep population stationary in contrast to short-run "market wages." While money wages rise through time because of the rising price of wheat, the wages-population mechanism will keep real wages constant. But the subsistence minimum is held to be a matter of "habit and custom," which takes the sting out of the alleged constancy of real wages. Since manufactured goods tend to fall in price, Ricardo observes, a rising price of wheat need not prevent a gradual rise in real wages. Some comments in the middle of the chapter about young countries like Ireland and Poland with an abundance of fertile land show that Ricardo regarded overpopulation in underdeveloped countries as the result, not the cause, of backwardness and poverty. Reducing population in such cases, he points out, would merely cause wages to rise and the supply of effort to fall.

There follows a discussion of the relation between the rate of capital accumulation and the trend of market wages. Laborers spend half their income on wheat. When the price of wheat rises, money wages rise only half as fast: the composition of labor's market basket is never affected by changes in the price of wheat relative to other things. This means that wages in terms of wheat

—money wages divided by the respective price of wheat—fall. This leads Ricardo to draw a contrast between workers whose money wages rise but whose wheat wages fall and landlords for whom both money and wheat rents rise. The closing portion of the chapter, dealing with the Poor Laws, was written by James Mill. In the manner of Malthus, it holds out for total abolition of public relief.

We may wonder why Ricardo is so careful in this fifth chapter and again in chapter 22 to avoid assuming that money wages rise proportionately with the price of wheat. It is not merely because he realized that workers in fact consume other things than wheat. The assumption that money wages rise at the same rate as wheat prices, that workers, as it were, are being paid a constant amount of wheat, produces the paradox that the worker's welfare improves with a higher cost of living. Malthus actually advanced this paradox in his 1815 pamphlet on rent but withdrew it later on Ricardo's prompting. Suppose workers do consume cloth as well as bread but that money wages rise proportionately with the price of bread. Then every increase in the price of bread relative to cloth raises the worker's money income in the same proportion as the bread part of his diet and hence increases his real income or command over both bread and cloth. Presumably, he will substitute cheap cloth for dear bread, but, even if his demand for bread is perfectly inelastic, the relative price of cloth has fallen, and hence his real income is improved. Contrariwise, a fall in the price of bread would actually be harmful to workers.[6] To avoid such anomalies, Ricardo makes money

[6] This is easy to prove by means of indifference curves allowing for substitution in consumption. If *AB* is the relative price of bread in terms of cloth, a rise in the relative price of bread shifts the price line to *CB*. The condition that money wages rise proportionately to the price of bread means that bread wages are constant and fixed at *OA*. The price line *AE* parallel to *CB* is tangent to a higher indifference curve than *1*. Thus, the paradox that welfare improves with a rise in the price of bread. Surprisingly enough, however, *if* intercommodity substitution were permitted, Ricardo's solution would not resolve the paradox. His solution is to let money wages rise with the price of bread so as to enable a worker always to buy the same amount of bread as well as cloth. A rise in the price of bread, the price of cloth being constant, is shown by *FG* passing through *Q* because real income always consists of a fixed amount of bread and cloth. But *FG* is tangent to *2*, a higher indifference curve than *1*. This is the old paradox again. A fall in the relative price of bread

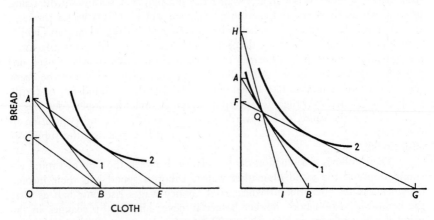

FIG. 12

wages rise less than proportionately to the price of wheat. This did not stop him, however, from talking about "deterioration" in living standards when wages constant in terms of the whole basket of goods have fallen measured in terms of wheat alone.

Profits. Chapter 6, on profits, is undoubtedly the most difficult chapter in the whole book. It expounds the fundamental theorem that "profits depend on high or low wages" with the aid of a single example whose implications are not as obvious as Ricardo makes out. Before discussing the example, let us reiterate the logic of the fundamental theorem. The problem is to show that, despite the fact that capital and labor grow at the same rate, the rate of profit on capital tends to fall solely because wage goods are more costly to produce. With the extension of cultivation, given amounts of newly employed capital-and-labor produce only diminishing increments of output. The price of wheat must now increase so that the amount of value produced by equal successive inputs of capital-and-labor remain the same; that is, the price of wheat rises to the extent of the diminution in the marginal physical product of capital-and-labor in order to keep profits in agriculture at a level with those in industry. Owing to the fact that wheat is measured in terms of the invariable standard, the product of a given quantity of capital and labor always has the same value regardless of its productivity. Therefore, the larger the value of labor, the smaller the value of capital, and the rise in the price of wheat has raised the value of labor by raising money wages. Thus, wages as a proportion of the product of marginal investment have risen, and with it the rate of profit has fallen in all sectors. This is not equivalent to a fall in capital's relative share because Ricardo has no determinate theory of the share going to rent.

RICARDO'S NUMERICAL EXAMPLE

1	2	3	4	5	6	7	8	9	10	11	12
						Wheat Wages		Wheat Profits		Wheat Rents	
Inputs (10 Workers per Dose)	MP in x Units of Wheat	Price of Wheat ($£.s.d.$)	Wheat Wages $= 3x$ ($£.s.d.$)	Cloth Wages of Constant Value ($£.s.d.$)	Money Wage Rate $(4) + (5)$ ($£.s.d.$)	$10 \cdot \frac{(6)}{(3)}$	Wage Share $W/180$	$(7)-(2)$	Profit Share $P/180$	First Difference of (2)	Rental Share $R/180$
1......	180	4.0.0	12.0.0	12.0.0	24.0.0	60	0.333	120	0.666	—	—
2......	170	4.4.8	12.14.0	12.0.0	24.14.0	58.3	0.323	111.7	0.622	10	0.055
3......	160	4.10.0	13.10.0	12.0.0	25.10.0	56.6	0.314	103.4	0.586	20	0.111
4......	150	4.16.0	14.8.6	12.0.0	26.8.0	55	0.301	95	0.529	30	0.170
5......	140	5.2.10	15.8.6	12.0.0	27.8.6	53.3	0.298	86.7	0.492	40	0.220

In Ricardo's numerical example (shown in the accompanying tabulation), Columns 1–7 incorporate Ricardo's own example in the previous chapter, on wages, and the last footnote to chapter 2, on rent. Columns 9 and 11 appear in the chapter on profits. Columns 8, 10, and 12 have been added and are not given by Ricardo. A word on column 3, which alone is not self-explanatory: The ini-

would shift the price-line to *HI*, passing through *Q*, which is also tangent to a higher indifference curve. We now have a double paradox: money wages rising just enough to compensate for an increased cost of bread and no more implies that a worker is better off when the price of bread rises *and* when it falls.

tial price of wheat is £4 per quarter. When 2 doses of variable inputs are applied, the price of wheat must rise $^{18}\!/_{17}$ because the quantity of capital-and-labor per quarter has risen in this proportion: $\dfrac{18}{17} \cdot £4 = £4.4.8$. Thus, column 3 is obtained by multiplying the ratio of the initial marginal product to the subsequent marginal products by the initial price of wheat.

We notice that, expressed in terms of wheat, the share of wages and the share of profits fall and the share of rents rises. Ricardo now expresses his results in terms of money and calculates the money rate of profit per cent on an assumed amount of capital fixed at £3,000 (see table). The rate of profit falls even as

1	13	14	15	16
Inputs	Money Rents (11)(3) (£.s.d.)	Money Profits (9)(3) (£.s.d.)	Money Wages 10(6) (£.s.d.)	Rate of Profit on $K = £3,000$ (Per Cent)
1..........	—	480.0.0	240.0.0	16
2..........	42.7.6	473.0.0	247.0.0	15.7
3..........	90.0.0	465.0.0	255.0.0	15.5
4..........	144.0.0	456.0.0	264.0.0	15.2
5..........	205.13.4	445.15.0	274.5.0	14.8

money wages per man rise. This assumes that the amount of capital invested remains the same. But, as Ricardo observes, rising wheat prices will call for an increase in the amount of capital, which further depresses the rate of profit. Notice that columns 14 and 15 summed across the rows always add up to £720, and so forth. The product-less-rent is measured in terms of the invariable standard, which has the property of keeping the total value of the product constant or, as Ricardo says, "the real value" of the product constant.

This demonstration of the fundamental theorem, however, has a fatal flaw, as Cannan pointed out long ago. The share of the factors is computed, not as a percentage of what the total product would be as more inputs are applied, but as a percentage of $180x$, the marginal product of the first dose, which is equal to the total product when one dose is applied. The value of the total product-less-rent (£720) is always the same as the value of the product of the first dose, and the rate of profit falls only because the value increments of the subsequent doses are not added to total money profits. Ricardo purports to explain the pattern of factor rewards and income distribution in an economy whose total income is growing and proves his case by explaining the distribution of the product at a fixed margin when inputs increase.

Column 8, showing a falling share of wages, is subject to another criticism. We know that, if real wages are constant, the share of wages in total income ought to rise, for the total product is rising less than proportionately to the doses of labor applied. But real wages are constant in terms of a market basket of wheat plus cloth, while in columns 7 and 8 we are looking at real wages in terms of wheat alone. Real wages, even when expressed in wheat alone, rise as a share of output when output is defined as the actually growing product of successive inputs, not as the output of the first dose of capital-and-labor.

N	X	W at $w = 6x$	W/X
1.........	180	60	0.333
2.........	350	120	0.343
3.........	510	180	0.353
4.........	660	240	0.364
5.........	800	300	0.374

Nevertheless, Ricardo is right in spite of himself. For his table of total products (see table) assumes that

$$f'(N) = 190 - 10N , \qquad (o < N < 19)$$

therefore,

$$X = \int (190 - 10N)dN = 190N - 5N^2$$

with $f''(N) = -10 < o$ and $f'''(N) = o$. This is a parabolic production function with linear average and marginal product curves. The average product: $(X/N) = 190 - 5N$. By the definition adopted above, the elasticity of this curve is

$$|\eta| = \frac{X/N}{N} \frac{dN}{d(X/N)} = \frac{190 - 5 N}{5 N} .$$

Within the relevant range of the independent variable, $|\eta| > 1$ and $d(\eta)/dN < o$, which is to say that the rental share rises as N increases. Since the wage share also rises, the share of profits does fall with every increase in N. The amount of capital grows at the same rate as labor, and the average product of capital declines at the same rate as that of labor. If P/X falls and X/K falls, $r = (P/X) (X/K)$ also falls. Q.E.D.

Foreign Trade. Chapter 7, on foreign trade, attempts to prove two propositions: (1) the "value" of the national product is the same for a closed economy as for an open one: foreign trade as such will not affect wage rates or the rate of profit; (2) foreign trade does increase a country's "riches," and real income will always be higher with free trade than without. The first proposition is directed against Smith's view that a high rate of profit in foreign trade pulls up profits in home industries. Smith ignores the shift in demand to foreign goods, argues Ricardo. Ricardo now distinguishes between three kinds of goods, analyzing each in turn: (1) home-produced goods for home consumption, such as cloth, shoes, corn, and hats; (2) home-produced goods for export; and (3) imported luxuries, such as wine—the demand for wine is assumed to be elastic. The gist of the argument is that the rate of profit will not be raised unless imports consist of wage goods, a simple deduction from the fundamental theorem. But at one point Ricardo does admit that the importation of cheaper luxury goods enables capitalists as consumers to save more; this stimulates capital accumulation, and in this way foreign trade, even when it does not involve the import of wheat, would seem capable of affecting the rate of profit.

This brings us to the Law of Comparative Cost, which demonstrates the general advantages of what Torrens called the "territorial division of labor." Ricardo was virtually the first economist to advocate a separate theory of international as against intranational trade. The basis of this separate theory is the relative immobility of capital between nations. The labor theory of value cannot pertain to goods traded across national boundaries because the rate of profit does not tend to equality between countries. But, in that case, what determines the movement of goods between countries, and on what basis will the barter terms of trade be decided? The answer to both questions, of course, is comparative cost advantages.

There are three kinds of differences in cost ratios for pairs of goods between countries: equal differences, absolute differences, and comparative differences. Supposing that both cloth and wine are produced in two countries, England and Portugal, by labor alone, the distinction is set out in the accompanying table.

Labor hours required to produce a unit of

	EQUAL DIFFERENCES			ABSOLUTE DIFFERENCES			COMPARATIVE DIFFERENCES		
	Cloth	Wine	Relative Prices p_w/p_c	Cloth	Wine	p_w/p_c	Cloth	Wine	p_w/p_c
England............	100	88	0.88	100	60	0.6	100	120	1.2
Portugal..........	90	80	0.88	90	80	0.88	90	80	0.88

Even Adam Smith knew that no foreign trade could arise when the cost ratios for two goods between two countries were equal. He thought that trade took place only when both countries had an absolute cost advantage in one good: in our example, England has an absolute advantage in wine, and Portugal in cloth. In the eighteenth century a few authors began to advance the rule that each country would find it profitable to import those goods which could be obtained in exchange for exports at less cost than their home production would entail. But almost no one, not even Adam Smith, realized that this meant that under free trade all goods are not necessarily produced in countries where their real costs of production are lowest: it might pay a country to import a product even though it could be produced at less cost at home than abroad. The doctrine of comparative cost is simply a rigorous statement of the informal eighteenth-century rule.

In Ricardo's example Portugal has a comparative advantage in wine, since the cost-difference here is relatively greater than in the case of cloth: $^{80}/_{120} < {}^{90}/_{100}$. What has to be compared is not costs but ratios of costs, and it does not matter whether we compare cost ratios of producing the same good in different countries or of producing different goods within the same country. An obscure pamphlet published in 1818 gave a simple algebraic statement of the necessary conditions. Let W and C denote the number of labor hours required to produce one unit of wine and cloth, the subscripts p and e identifying the respective countries. Then:

(1)   Equal cost-differences: $W_p/W_e = C_p/C_e$.
(2)   Absolute cost-differences: $W_p/W_e < 1 < C_p/C_e$.
(3)   Comparative cost-differences: $W_p/W_e < C_p/C_e < 1$.

To return to Ricardo's example: it is clearly to Portugal's advantage to send wine to England, where a unit of it commands 1.2 units of cloth, as long as 1 unit of wine can be traded with England for more than 0.88 units of cloth; it is to England's advantage to specialize in cloth if less than 1.2 units of cloth must be given for 1 unit of wine. Hence, the comparative-cost doctrine states the upper and lower limits within which exchange can take place between countries to their mutual benefit. If 1 unit of British cloth were exchanged for $^9/_8$ units of Portuguese wine, all gains from trade would go to England. If, instead, the ratio were $1:{}^5/_6$ all gains would go to Portugal. Ricardo assumes a $1:1$ ratio. England produces cloth with 100 man-hours and receives 1 unit of wine, which would have cost her 120 man-hours, and Portugal obtains cloth for 80 man-hours, which would have cost her 90 man-hours. Clearly, the comparative-cost case is much subtler than the absolute-cost case. In the latter it is self-evident that an international division of labor leads to an increase in total output. The "gains of trade" in Ricardo show up as an over-all saving in cost per unit of product; before trade, it took 390 labor days for England and Portugal each to produce one unit of cloth and wine; after trade, these four units require only 360 labor days. The point of Ricardo's analysis is to show that the conditions that make international trade possible are quite different from the conditions under which domestic trade will rise. If England and Portugal were two regions in the same country, all capital and labor would migrate to Portugal and both goods would be produced there. Within a nation, trade between two places requires an absolute difference in costs, but a comparative difference is a sufficient condition for the existence of international trade.

Ricardo's doctrine is incomplete: it shows how nations may gain by trade but it fails to tell us how the gain from trade is divided among the trading countries. The actual barter terms of trade, as John Stuart Mill was soon to show, depend not only on the cost conditions but also on the patterns of demand. Since Ricardo's theory requires that all goods are produced at constant costs—there is only one factor of pro-

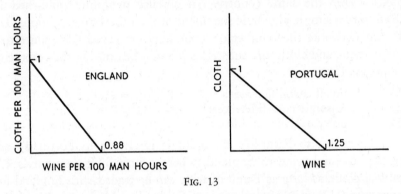

FIG. 13

duction—one may wonder why demand has anything to do with international prices, when, under the same conditions, domestic prices are entirely determined by supply. The reason lies in the fact that goods are produced at constant costs *within* countries but not *between* countries.

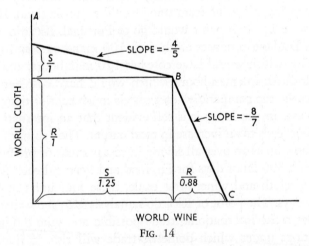

FIG. 14

This is easy to show if we render Ricardo's argument in strictly modern terms (Fig. 13). Portugal can convert 1 unit of cloth into 1.25 units of wine. England can covert 1 unit of cloth into 0.88 units of wine. The barter terms of trade will lie somewhere between 1 wine: 1.25 cloth and 1 wine: 0.88 cloth. We can now construct the production-transformation curve for the world (Fig. 14). The broken line *ABC* is

R = total man-hours available for cloth and wine in England.
S = total man-hours available for cloth and wine in Portugal.

the world's transformation curve, giving the maximum possible world output of wine for each given level of cloth, and conversely. The point at which both countries would specialize completely in one good is point B. The pattern of world demand for wine and cloth will be shown by an indifference curve that must be tangent either to the line segment AB, the point B, or the line segment BC. The resulting barter-price line will permit both countries to produce at B when each maximizes her comparative advantage by complete specialization. The exact slope of the barter-price line, however, can vary between $-1\frac{1}{7}$ and $-\frac{4}{5}$, depending upon the location of the particular tangency point. Despite the fact that constant costs pertain within each country, the world production-possibility frontier between cloth and wine is concave and the cost of converting one good into another for the world as a whole is increasing, although not continuously. International prices are governed by supply *and* demand even in the long run, despite the fact that relative prices within countries are assumed to be determined by labor alone.

It is clear that the doctrine of comparative cost would hold even if the production-possibility frontier were smoothly concave to the origin in which case specialization would rarely be carried to the limit. A smooth concave curve with the marginal cost of converting one good into another rising continuously in either direction implies that goods are produced at increasing cost within countries. In other words, abandoning the labor theory of value, and with it the assumption of constant costs, would in no way affect the validity of Ricardo's doctrine. The Law of Comparative Cost can be expressed succinctly as stating that each country will produce those goods whose alternative costs are relatively lowest, alternative costs being the number of units of one good that must be forgone to produce a unit of another good. This way of putting it covers every possible cost situation.

The Natural Distribution of Specie. Ricardo did much more than state the Law of Comparative Cost. He also saw its implications for international wage and price levels, although it was Nassau Senior who ten years later developed Ricardo's hints into a fully fashioned theory of relations between price levels in different countries. Ricardo realized that, if Portugal had an absolute advantage in both wine and cloth but a greater relative advantage in wine, foreign trade with England is only possible if money wage rates in Portugal are higher than in England. If the hourly wage rate in terms of gold is the same,

Portugal will not import cloth, since every Portuguese consumer can then get cloth more cheaply from domestic suppliers. England would have to ship gold to Portugal to pay for wine imports until hourly gold wages in Portugal rose enough to make it profitable for Portuguese consumers to import English cloth. In general, then, the low-cost country has the higher hourly gold wage and, hence, a higher money price for similar goods. Hume's "natural distribution of specie" therefore not only works to balance each country's exports and imports but results in such relative price levels between countries as to induce each country to produce those goods in which it has a comparative advantage. In Senior's memorable phrase, relative price levels between countries are determined by differences in "the cost of obtaining gold": the greater the efficiency of labor in the export industries of a country possessing no gold mines and the less the expense of conveying gold, the lower the cost of obtaining precious metals, the higher the level of average wages and prices relative to countries exporting bullion. This argument has an important practical implication: a high level of wages in a country is the result of higher efficiency and by no means prevents that country from competing with foreign producers. To put the same thing a little differently: an over-all disadvantage in productivity in a particular country relative to the rest of the world need not prevent her from participating in international trade; there is always a rate of exchange that would permit her to export those goods in which she had the least comparative disadvantage, while importing those in which she had the greatest disadvantage.

To drive the point home, consider the following example, as Ricardo himself might have given it. Suppose that 1 man-hour in both countries can produce the following amounts of cloth and wine:

In England, 16 cloth and 8 wine.
In Portugal, 20 cloth and 15 wine.

Comparative cost ratios are as follows:

Cloth, Portugal to England as $10:8$.
Wine, Portugal to England as $10:5\frac{1}{3}$.

From the cost differences it follows immediately that average hourly money wages in England must be between $53\frac{1}{3}$ and 80 per cent of money wages in Portugal.

Let us suppose that the wage rate in Portugal is $5.00 per man-hour. We know that the price ratio between cloth and wine in Portugal is $4:3$. Then, in Portugal, if

the money price per unit of cloth is, say, $3.00,
the money price per unit of wine is $4.00.

If England's wages were equal to wages in Portugal, then in England, at the existing exchange rate,

the money price per unit of cloth is $3.75;
the money price per unit of wine is $7.50.

These prices are fixed by the given domestic cost ratios of cloth and wine in England ($2:1$) and by the given cost ratios for the two goods between the two countries (for cloth $5:4$ and for wine $10:5\frac{1}{3}$). But at these prices it would pay England to import both goods from Portugal. Her balance of payments would become unfavorable, and gold would flow out of the country, thus deflating British wages. If wages fell 20 per cent to $4.00 per man-hour, then in England

the money price per unit of cloth is $3.00,
the money price per unit of wine is $6.00,

and now it would be possible for her to reap the benefits of her comparative advantage in cloth. Likewise, if England paid still lower wages, $2.66 per man-hour of $53\frac{1}{3}$ per cent of hourly wages in Portugal, then in England

the price per unit of cloth is $2.00,
the price per unit of wine is $4.00,

and both countries would still find it to their advantage to specialize in one product.

It may be noted that when England's wage level reaches its upper limit, the barter terms of trade are exclusively in her favor (4 cloth:3 wine). When it reaches its lower limit, the barter terms are exclusively in Portugal's favor (2 cloth:1 wine). It seems, therefore, that the relative efficiency of labor in the two countries influences the relations of wage and price levels between them in two ways: (1) the country with the more generally efficient labor will have a higher wage and price level than the other country; (2) the difference so established takes place within definite limits determined by comparative cost ratios. This is the gist of the classical theory of international prices.

The Purchasing Power Parity Theory. To conclude our discussion of chapter 7, it is noteworthy that Ricardo denies what has since been called the "purchasing power parity theory" of exchange rates. It was standard classical doctrine that "the value of money is everywhere the same": with free trade and a metallic standard, the rate of exchange between two currencies depends solely on their relative purchasing power over identical exportable goods. But, of course, the prices of nonexportable goods differ between countries. Hence, the doctrine that an equilibrium rate of exchange is to be found at the quotient between the price levels of different countries—the so-called "purchasing power parity theory"—ignores everything that creates discrepancies in the average prices of all goods between two countries. The last few pages of chapter 7 relate to the difficulty of proving the depreciation of an inconvertible currency such as England experienced between 1797 and 1819. This topic is best considered later, when we look at Ricardo's monetary theory. Chapter 25 on colonial trade should be read after chapter 7; it is largely devoted to showing that any tax or bounty upon exports or imports alters the international distribution of specie and therefore comparative cost ratios expressed in money terms between countries.

Say's Law. The Ricardian theory of profits is contrasted with Adam Smith's theory in chapter 21, on the effects of accumulation upon profits and interest. Smith's theory of declining profits, Ricardo correctly observes, assumes a definite limit to the number of investment opportunities available at any time. But, in the absence of rising costs in the wage-goods industry, full-capacity use of any amount of capital is possible: there are no inherent barriers to production on the side of demand. This leads to a statement of Say's Law of Markets and a denial that hoarding—an excess demand for money to hold—can be a permanent problem in a growing economy. In a footnote on Say, Ricardo even denies the need for price-interest adjustments to assure full investment of savings, but this is an overzealous comment because the mechanism of interest variations, acting upon the demand for loanable funds, is explained later in the same chapter. "Gluts," by which Ricardo seems to mean "secular stagnation," are impossible because demand is insatiable: although the demand for corn is inelastic, the demand for most consumer goods is highly elastic and will expand with every increase in the productivity of labor. Ricardo admits that a sudden upward shift in the propensity to save might produce a temporary "general glut": but, as capital would then be growing faster than population, market wages would rise above natural wages and purchasing power would increase once again. With Ricardo, therefore, the economy is conceived as descending smoothly into the stationary state without any hitch from a failure of effective demand.

It is evident from the context in which Say's Law first arises in the *Principles* that Ricardo believed that Smith and Malthus had already been refuted by the fundamental theorem on distribution presented in the preceding chapters without any mention of the Law of Markets. Say's Law now appears, not as a basic premise in the Ricardian system, but merely to confirm the theory that "the increased difficulty of obtaining food" is the only permanently operative cause of a fall in the rate of profit.

In the latter part of chapter 21 Ricardo points out that the ruling rate of profit cannot in practice be estimated from the market rate of interest as Adam Smith believed, not only because of the intrinsic difficulty of calculating the trend value of the rate of interest, but also because of the disturbing effect of the Usury Laws. In a classic passage Ricardo presents the germ of Wicksell's theory of the divergence between the natural and the market rate of interest, an argument that Ricardo repeats in chapter 28, "On Currency and Banks." In a trade depression, when prices fall, the market rate of interest will rise temporarily owing to involuntary accumulation of inventories. Likewise, an increase in the quantity of money will temporarily depress interest rates, but, as soon as the new money has acted on prices, the interest rate will rise back to its "natural rate," the rate of profit on capital. This is the classical doctrine of the "real" nature of the interest rate about which we will have more to say in the next chapter; its central idea is that monetary forces act upon the rate of interest only when the money market is in disequilibrium.

Pessimism? Turning back to chapter 19, on sudden changes in the channels of trade, we meet with Ricardo's views on Britain's long-term growth prospects. Writing in the difficult years of postwar conversion, Ricardo is anxious to discourage the belief that the current "revulsion of trade" marks the onset of secular stagnation. If the Corn Laws are repealed, Britain's prospects for growth are actually very favorable. He does not insist upon immediate total repeal, as did Cobden and Bright twenty years later. Since the poor rates fall heaviest on land, as argued in chapter 18, landlords are entitled to some relief for special tax burdens. Hence, Ricardo calls for gradual reductions in import duties on grain over a ten-year period coupled with a small bounty on exportation in years of bumper crops. Gradual repeal would have the additional advantage of cushioning the blow of disinvestment in agriculture. Nevertheless, rents would fall and landlords would sustain losses in consequence of repeal. But the loss to landlords would be more than offset by the welfare gains from free trade to other classes; this argument reminds one immediately of the Hicks-Kaldor "compensation principle" in modern welfare economics.

Monetary Theory. Chapter 27, "On Currency and Banks," seems to stand apart from the rest of the book and, unfortunately, gives an entirely inadequate impression of Ricardo's theory of money. Ricardo is a "metallist" and naturally expounds a labor theory of the value of the monetary metal. This is by no means contradictory to the quantity theory of money. Given unhampered coinage and melting-down, the quantity of money in the long run is governed by its cost of production. If the value of money in circulation exceeds its cost of production, mining is stimulated and more metal is presented for coinage, and, when the reverse holds true, mining contracts, and money is melted down for nonmonetary use. In this way the value of money is controlled by its cost of prodution. Owing to the large stock of gold and silver in existence, however, the rate of current output of gold and silver mines actually has a negligible effect upon the value of money. In that sense, the metallist theory of the value of money has very little significance for monetary problems. For all practical purposes, the quantity of money in a country is given at any time and is likely to alter only because her external account becomes unbalanced or possibly because of a change in velocity. Hence, the peculiar importance attached to the quantity theory, which is essentially a theory of the demand for money. In the years 1797–1819 Britain was off the gold standard and on an inconvertible paper standard. Under those conditions, the cost of manufacturing paper currency being too small to exercise any effective control over its quantity, the value of the currency is entirely a matter of its quantity as determined by banking policy. Thus, the classical theory of

value of money in the short run is the quantity theory, for both specie
and paper, with the cost-of-production theory reserved for the long run
and for specie money only.

The Bullionist Controversy. It is very difficult to follow Ricardo's attack on the Bank of England in this chapter without some
knowledge of the issues that animated the so-called "Bullionist Controversy" during the Napoleonic wars. A brief statement of the debate
must suffice for present purposes. In 1797, war with France had
brought a suspension of specie payments: the Bank of England was authorized to refuse payments for its notes in gold. Inconvertibility of
notes coincided with a state of war involving heavy remittances by the
United Kingdom to its allies and large-scale borrowing by the government. In addition, an unusual series of bad harvests led to abnormal imports of wheat, with consequent disturbing effects on the balance of
payments. Prices rose gradually, and gold commanded a premium in
the market over the quoted mint price.

Under a convertible paper currency, a premium on gold or a discount on paper cannot rise. Under a gold standard, the exchange rate
with any other country cannot fall below the gold export point—below the mint parity by more than the cost of shipping gold.[7] If an over-

[7] Under a gold standard, the exchange rate between two currencies is determined by
the ratio of the gold prices of the two currencies plus or minus the cost of handling and
shipping gold. When a country promises to sell gold freely in unlimited amounts at a fixed
price, the supply of currencies of other gold standard countries becomes perfectly elastic at
the gold export or upper gold points. In our illustration, the supply of dollars on foreign
exchange markets becomes perfectly elastic at $2 = £1. At $4 = £1, the demand for dollars also becomes perfectly elastic because the Bank of England stands ready to buy any
amount of gold offered at the gold-dollar parity. Within the narrow range between the gold
points the exchange rate is flexible. An export surplus *raises* exchange rates in favor of
England—*lowers* the price of dollars per pound sterling—thus stimulating imports. Simi-

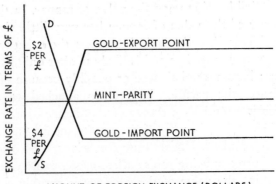

AMOUNT OF FOREIGN EXCHANGE (DOLLARS)

FIG. 14A

issue of notes depresses the value of paper below bullion, causing the exchange rate to fall below the gold export point, it would be more profitable to ship gold than to buy foreign bills to pay for imports. Notes would then be presented to banks for payment in gold, and the banks would be obliged to protect their reserves by contracting the volume of note issue. This would tend to raise the value of money, putting an end to the outflow of gold and restoring the exchanges to par. Convertibility of a paper currency therefore provides an automatic check to overissue or paper inflation. When a paper currency is made inconvertible, the paper price of gold is still governed by the exchange rates with countries on a metallic standard, but there is no longer any automatic check to fall, in the exchanges below the metallic parity, to a permanent premium of bullion over paper. This does not mean, however, that a "premium on bullion" is just shorthand for domestic inflation under inconvertibility. The title of one of Ricardo's famous tracts, *The High Price of Bullion: A Proof of the Depreciation of Bank Notes,* is quite misleading. Even without inflation, heavy foreign lending and grain imports can produce an unfavorable balance of payments, a fall in the foreign exchange value of the pound below the current gold export point, and a rise in the market price of gold beyond its mint price. The central issue in the debate was just this: Is the premium on gold over paper evidence of inflation, and if so is it due to reckless monetary policy on the part of the Bank of England?

Ricardo led the bullionists with the argument that the Bank had overissued and that this was the cause of inflation or, to use the language of the day, the cause of "the depreciation of bank notes." In the absence of any confidence in the then little-used tool of an index number of prices, the first problem was to prove that British prices had risen relative to other trading countries. Ricardo's test was the premium actually quoted on bullion. The cause of the inflation was the excess issue of notes by the Bank of England; the country banks were exonerated because they had to maintain a fixed percentage of reserves against their own notes in the form of Bank of England notes, while the Bank itself was not subject to any limitation. The Directors of the Bank and the anti-bullionists argued that it was impossible to overissue paper money even when it was inconvertible as long as new notes were issued only on discount of sound short-term commercial paper. This is the real-bills doctrine famous in the history of banking, of which more later; it had little relevance here because the Bank got its notes into cir-

---

larly, an import surplus leads automatically to *falling* exchange rates for England—*raises* the price of dollars in terms of pounds.

culation not only by commercial discounting but also by purchase of public bonds. The anti-bullionists argued, in the main, that the terms of trade had moved against England not because of monetary inflation but owing to the state of the balance of payments. But, if home prices were not rising, Ricardo retorted, an adverse balance of payments with the exchanges turning against England would stimulate exports and cause the foreign remittances to be transferred in goods. Therefore, the fall in the exchanges and the premium on bullion had nothing to do with heavy foreign lending.

This touches on a difference in approach to the corrective mechanism of disturbances in the balance of payments, which we will consider subsequently. In a sense, both sides avoided the real issues. The premium of gold over paper was caused in part, and perhaps in large part, not by an excess currency or by an unfavorable balance of payments but by a speculative flight to hoarded bullion and hoarded foreign currency. Added to this, the velocity of circulation must have risen with the rising price level. It is obvious, however, that, at bottom, government expenditures were behind the inflation and that the Bank of England avoided acknowledging its responsibility as a central bank, clinging to the notion that it was no more than *primus inter pares* passively serving "the needs of trade." Ricardo's plan to nationalize the Bank, therefore, was a recognition on his part of the necessity for clearly defined monetary policy by a central monetary authority.

The Machinery Question. In chapter 31, "On Machinery," added in the third edition of the *Principles,* Ricardo broke new ground and shocked his contemporaries by maintaining that new machinery might be injurious to workers. The basic argument is that if the introduction of machinery involves the diversion of labor previously required to produce wage goods, if instead of new machines being financed out of retained earnings they are financed by drawing down the wages fund, then output may fall for a time and produce unemployment. Ricardo's proof is by way of a single example, that of a farmer who diverts half his annual labor force, hitherto employed to make finished goods, to the construction of a machine (see accompanying table).

Year	Gross Product (£)	Net Product (£)	Wages Fund (£)	Value of Machine (£)
1...............	15,000	2,000	13,000	0
2...............	15,000	2,000	5,500	7,500
3...............	7,500	2,000	?	?

It is immediately conceded that the fall in price consequent upon the introduction of the machine would expand output so that some workers would be reabsorbed. Whether wage cuts would stimulate the re-employment of displaced labor, Ricardo does not say. In fact, his analysis is so severely short run that he does not trouble to spell out any of the adjustments to a new state of equilibrium. The argument is peculiar because it supposes a contraction of output and claims at best that the demand for labor is lessened for "a considerable interval." In the closing pages of the chapter Ricardo scuttles his own argument by pointing out that when machinery is financed out of previous earnings it involves none of these dire effects and indeed only rapid technical advance insures continuous economic growth. A warning against state intervention to discourage technical progress brings the chapter to a close.

The significance of this chapter is that it relaxes the two-factor assumption maintained elsewhere in the book and analyzes, not the effect of innovations, but the substitution of capital for labor along given production functions. He seems to have realized by this time that the rise in money wages and the fall in the rate of profit implied in his model leads to a constantly rising ratio of machinery to labor. This contradicts his usual assumption that capital and labor grows at equal rates and creates new complications. No wonder this chapter seems glued on to the rest of the book as an afterthought.

Toward the end of the chapter Ricardo introduces the notion that laborers have an interest in the pattern of luxury spending by the rich because spending on "menial servants" increases the demand for labor more than an equivalent amount of spending on luxury goods, assuming that luxury goods are not produced entirely by labor. This is a proposition that, transmuted by John Stuart Mill, became the maxim, "demand for commodities is not demand for labor."

Taxation. The tax chapters in Ricardo's book contain much additional insight into his system. They represent a rigorous working-out of his theory of factor shares, with a notable emphasis upon the short run. First, there is chapter 26, "On gross and net revenue," which defines taxable capacity as depending exclusively upon net revenue. Ricardo takes the concept of subsistence wages seriously and deducts from gross revenue all output necessary to maintain human as well as physical capital intact, leaving the sum of profits and rents as net revenue. But a footnote early in the chapter mentions a difficulty in this concept of the net returns to economic activity: market wages often exceed the minimum necessary to maintain labor. Chapter 8, "On Taxes," lays down the tautological rule that all taxes hamper capital accumulation unless met by "an increased production, or by a diminished unproductive consumption." It is not conceded that taxes ever stimulate effort. Chapter 9 deals with specific taxes on the raw produce of agriculture. Two numerical examples are used to show that a specific tax will raise the price of grain by the amount of the tax: the money expenditures of consumers rise, but total money rents are unaffected. An unchanged aggregate money rent means a fall in corn rents, however, since the tax falls heavier on the superior acres where the total corn produced is larger. Since the supply curve of labor is perfectly elastic, real wages net of tax remain the same, and if landlords do not themselves consume grain the whole burden of the tax falls on profits. Ricardo goes on to consider possible causes for a rise in the price of wage goods. In the course of the analysis he commits himself to the notion of a predetermined wages fund and admits that the supply of labor is actually relatively inelastic: labor is singularly slow to respond to a change in its price. At the close of the chapter Ricardo points out that taxes distort the structure of prices, hence the ratios of comparative costs, which in turn alter the level of prices by altering the international distribution of specie.

Chapter 10 develops the theory that a tax on rent cannot be shifted simply because it is a tax on a product in fixed supply, and it is only by varying the supply that the incidence of a tax is made to fall on the buyer. A tax on rent would tax all contractual rent and, since not all contractual rent is "pure economic rent," some part of the tax would fall on profits.

Chapters 11 and 12, on tithes and land taxes, raise no new issues. Chapters 13 and 14 provide an interesting discussion of the movement in the price of a taxed commodity toward its equilibrium level: the adjustment takes longer, the more durable the commodity in question, the more inelastic its supply, and the more elastic its demand.

The next chapter, "Taxes on Profits," contains an important discussion of the effect of a uniform profits tax upon the supply prices of products. Although the tax will be shifted forward, it will have an unequal effect on the selling prices of different products because of differences in the composition and turn-over rates of capital. Owing to the differential effect of taxes, an increase in the quantity of money will affect the structure as well as the level of prices; the level of prices, however, will ultimately return to its pretax level because of the specie-flow mechanism. Chapter 29 covers much the same points as chapter 15 but from a different viewpoint.

The thesis of chapter 9, that real wages cannot be taxed, is revised in chapter 16, "Taxes on Wages." Tax revenues spent by the government raise the demand for labor and hence money wages. Money wages rise by less than the tax, and therefore real wages fall. This rather odd argument rests on the idea that the private demand for labor is unaffected by government spending: the wage bill net of tax remains unchanged. If the wage bill net of tax is to remain unchanged, money wages must rise. As Musgrave points out, the only way insertion of the circuit of taxes and public expenditures could raise the total spending on labor is that it somehow increases the velocity of circulation; Ricardo's argument is an early and peculiar version of the balanced-budget multiplier. The views of Adam Smith and several other writers on the question of taxes on wages and on wage goods are then examined. Ricardo employs the standard eighteenth-century view that the demand for "necessaries" displays little elasticity as against the demand for "luxuries."

Chapter 17 is perhaps the most interesting of the tax chapters; it contains the famous defense of taxation in contrast to borrowing as a method of financing a war. The classical case against public debts is developed at length: a public debt invites flight of capital, and deficit financing cuts into private thrift; the burden of the debt is not so much the annual interest charges as the squandering of resources that the debt represents.

The Lasting Influence of Ricardo. As a rigorous theorist, Ricardo is obviously Adam Smith's superior. On the other hand, the *Wealth of Nations* contains more in the way of substantive generalizations on the workings of economic systems than does Ricardo's *Principles,* more, perhaps, than any other treatise in the nineteenth century, with the exception of Marshall's book. If *the* problem of economics is the allocation of limited means among unlimited competing ends, then Adam Smith contributed more to economics than did Ricardo—the only place where Ricardo addressed himself specifically to the allocation problem is in the chapter on foreign trade, but here, at any rate, he saw further and deeper than did Adam Smith. If *the* problem of economics is growth and development, as is sometimes said, there is again more in Smith than in Ricardo. But if economics is essentially an engine of analysis, a method of thinking rather than a body of substantive results, Ricardo literally invented the technique. His gift for heroic abstraction produced one of the most impressive models, judged by its scope and practical import, in the entire history of economic theory. Not everyone will consider this praiseworthy. Even Schumpeter calls Ricardo's habit of applying severely simplified abstractions to the solution of practical problems "the Ricardian Vice." And to the Historical School and the American Institutionalists, Ricardo has always stood for everything detestable in orthodox economics.

Until 1870 Ricardo thoroughly dominated British economic thought, and even those who turned against him on particular questions —Bailey, Scrope, Read, Jones, Longfield, Senior, Whately—succumbed to the leading Ricardian doctrine that the productivity of labor in agriculture governs the general rate of return on capital as well as secular changes in the distributive shares. As long as the Corn Laws remained on the statute books, the issue of free trade gave practical significance to the Ricardian system. And, when repeal came in 1846, Mill's *Principles,* published two years later, brought new authority to Ricardo's ideas suitably amended. After 1870, however, most economists turned their backs on what they understood to be the Ricardian theory of value and distribution and agreed with Jevons that Ricardo had "shunted the car" along the wrong track. Marx's warm praise for Ricardo did not enhance Ricardo's reputation with academic economists, though Ricardo could hardly have been more innocent than he was of paternity to the Marxian offspring. Marshall, Wicksell, and Cassel, however, retained a profound respect for Ricardo, and Marshall went so far as to argue that the foundation of Ricardo's theory of "cost of production in relation to value" remained intact. Still, the problem of macroeconomic class distribution, which struck Ricardo as "the principal problem in Political Economy," disappeared in neoclassical economics; marginal productivity theory approached the problem of distribution from a very different angle. In recent years, concern over effective demand has caused many economists to agree with Keynes that "the complete domination of Ricardo's approach for a period of 100 years has been a disaster to the progress of economics." What has really survived is the Law of Comparative Cost and the method of comparative static analysis that Ricardo invented, that and the unqualified horror of numerical proofs.

NOTES FOR FURTHER READING

Ricardo's *Principles of Political Economy and Taxation* is available cheaply in Everyman's Library, but the version edited by Sraffa is well worth the extra cost: *The Works of David Ricardo*, ed. P. Sraffa and M. Dobb, Vol. I (1951). Ricardo's "Essay on the Influence of a Low Price of Corn on the Profits of Stock," *Works*, Vol. IV, provides a useful brief introduction to the *Principles*. Nothing that Ricardo wrote is without interest, and a perusal of his "Notes on Malthus," *Works*, Vol. II, the Parliamentary speeches, *Works*, Vol. V, and the fascinating letters, *Works*, Vols. VI–X, will convey the flavor of Ricardian economics in a way that all the commentaries in the world cannot do.

There is no standard biography of Ricardo. The first part of J. H. Hollander, *David Ricardo: A Centenary Estimate* (1910), supplies an excellent biographical sketch; this should be supplemented by Sraffa's *Biographical Miscellany*, *Works*, Vol. X. The second half of Hollander's book may be recommended as the best nontechnical account of Ricardo's general views and opinions.

The failure to distinguish between a positive theory of relative price and a normative theory of social accounting has been the source of infinite confusion in commentaries upon Ricardo's theory of value. Like Smith, Ricardo did not hold an "analytical" labor theory of value, as G. J. Stigler shows: "Ricardo and the 93% Labor Theory of Value," *AER*, June, 1958; also D. F. Gordon, "What Was the Labor Theory of Value?" *AER*, May, 1959. Ricardo's value theory is really concerned with intertemporal variations in the normal prices of broad groups of commodities. This was pointed out for the first time by J. M. Cassels, "A Re-interpretation of Ricardo on Value," *QJE*, 1935, reprinted in *EET*. See also Sraffa's Introduction to Ricardo's *Principles*, *Works*, Vol. I, Secs. IV–V. There is hardly an economist of note in the nineteenth century who did not criticize Ricardo's writings on the problem of value; the reader should at least look at Marshall's "Notes on Ricardo's Theory of Value," *Principles of Economics*, Appendix I. G. Myrdal, *The Political Element in the Development of Economic Theory* (1953), chap. 3, argues that the classical labor theory of value and the notion of an invariable measure of value stem from natural-law doctrine. W. C. Mitchell, "The Postulates and Preconceptions of Ricardian Economics," *The Backward Art of Spending Money* (1937), has something to contribute to this question.

In a brilliant article V. Edelberg defends Ricardo's dictum that profits vary inversely with wages: "The Ricardian Theory of Profits," *Ec.*, February, 1933; this article is, unfortunately, couched in the language of the Austrian theory of capital and may mean little to the reader unacquainted with Böhm-Bawerk. Tucker gives a lucid exposition of Ricardo's theory of profits in *Progress and Profits in British Economic Thought*, chap. 6. For a general treatment of Ricardo's system see Cannan's *Production and Distribution Theories*, chaps. 7

and 8, particularly pp. 193–202, 220–28, 253–62, and 268–78. Deservedly famous as Cannan's discussion is, it is only fair to say that he is likely at times to lose sight of the logic of theories in the effort to run down every last contradiction in the writings of the classical economists. See also Schumpeter's unsympathetic and occasionally misleading comments in his *History*, pp. 471–75, 590–96, 636–37, 671–76, and 680–85.

In recent years a number of writers have tried their hand at mathematical formulations of Ricardo's system. L. L. Pasinetti and H. Brems focus on the determinacy and stability of Ricardo's model: "A Mathematical Formulation of the Ricardian System," *REStud*, XXVII, 1960, 2; "An Attempt at a Rigorous Restatement of Ricardo's Long-Run Equilibrium," *CJEPS*, February, 1960. H. Barkai deals with the Ricardian theory of relative shares: "Ricardo on Factor Prices and Income Distribution in a Growing Economy," *Ec.*, August, 1959. P. A. Samuelson presents a Ricardo-like linear programming model to show that one cannot "get rid of rent" by going to the margins of cultivation once commodity substitution is allowed for. Each of these articles throws light in its own way on Ricardo's arguments and my exposition has borrowed something from all of them. With the exception of the appendixes to the articles by Pasinetti and Samuelson, none of the four authors employs mathematics beyond calculus.

O. St. Clair, *A Key to Ricardo* (1957), is an excellent guide to "what Ricardo actually said": it is virtually a collation of Ricardo's opinions on every economic topic. Some useful pieces on special topics are: R. A. MacDonald, "Ricardo's Criticisms of Adam Smith," *QJE*, August, 1912; R. O. Roberts, "Ricardo's Theory of Public Debts," *Ec.*, August, 1942; A. Marshall, "Ricardo's Doctrine As to Taxes and Improvements in Agriculture," *Principles of Economics*, Appendix L, as amended by H. G. Johnson, "An Error in Ricardo's Exposition of His Theory of Rent," *QJE*, November, 1948; and W. D. Grampp, "Malthus on Money Wages and Welfare," *AER*, December, 1956. The definitive treatment of the classical theory of international trade is by Viner, *Studies in the Theory of International Trade;* chap. 8, secs. 1 and 2, and chap. 9, sec. 1, deal specifically with Ricardo. Wu, *An Outline of International Price Theories,* chaps. 3 and 4, supplements Viner's analysis. See R. Dorfman, P. A. Samuelson, and R. M. Solow, *Linear Programming and Economic Analysis* (1958), chaps. 2 and 3, for an illuminating presentation of the classical theory of international trade in terms of linear programming concepts. The tax chapters in Ricardo's *Principles* are carefully analyzed and evaluated by C. S. Shoup, *Ricardo on Taxation* (1960), but even the general reader will learn much from watching Ricardo at work, as it were, on specific problems. The same ground is covered with extraordinary succinctness by R. A. Musgrave, *The Theory of Public Finance* (1959), pp. 385–92.

A great deal has been written on the background of the Bank Restriction Period. For a convenient brief account see E. V. Morgan, *The Theory and Practice of Central Banking, 1797–1913* (1943), chap. 2. The most authoritative account of the bullionist controversy is by Viner, *Studies,* chap. 3. See also R. S. Sayers, "Ricardo's Views on Monetary Questions," *QJE,* 1953, reprinted in *Papers on English Monetary History,* ed. T. S. Ashton and R. S. Sayers (1953). T. W. Hutchison, "Some Questions about Ricardo," *Ec.,* November, 1952, raises provocative doubts about the value of Ricardo's influence.

Chapter 5 : SAY'S LAW AND CLASSICAL MONETARY THEORY

1. THE LAW OF MARKETS

IN AN economy with a developed division of labor the means normally available to anyone for acquiring goods and services is the power to produce equivalent goods and services. Production increases not only the supply of goods but, by virtue of the requisite cost payments to the factors of production, also creates the demand to purchase these goods. "Products are paid for by products" in domestic as much as in foreign trade; this is the gist of Say's Law of Markets.

This notion has at least one important consequence. It is one thing to speak of one industry producing "too little" or "too much" in terms of its independently given demand and supply curves: the demand curve for an industry is derived from the incomes generated by all other industries and is given independently of its own supply. But we cannot speak in the same sense of an entire economy producing too little or too much because aggregate demand and aggregate supply are not independent of each other. The component demands for the output of any one industry must increase in real terms when the supplies of all industries increase, since these are precisely what generate demand for an industry's product. Say's Law, therefore, warns us not to apply to aggregates propositions derived from partial analysis. While it is possible for a particular good to be produced in excess relative to all other goods, it is impossible for all goods to be produced in relative excess.

We seem to be talking about words: one must not *say* "general overproduction" for that is a logical impossibility. But, of course, it is only a logical impossibility in a barter economy. Overproduction must be relative to something, and, by talking of all goods in an economy without money, we have excluded anything relative to which goods can be produced in excess. An oversupply of one particular product means an underdemand for it in terms of all other products, for the supply of other products given in exchange for it represents the de-

130

mand for this product; the excess supply of one good means an excess demand for some other; hence, in a barter economy there can be no such thing as an excess of supply over demand for all goods. But in a monetary economy a general excess supply of *commodities* is a logical possibility, for it simply implies that there is an excess demand for money. If Say's Law is meant to be applicable to the real world, therefore, it states the impossibility of an excess demand for money. "Impossibility" in this case cannot mean logical impossibility. It must mean that the demand for money cannot be permanently in excess because this is a situation of disequilibrium. Before deciding just what Say did mean, we have to nail down the notion of equilibrium in the money market. Having done this, the role of Say's Law in classical theory becomes much simpler to explain.

Say's Identity. Assume that there are n goods in a closed economy. If we select any one of the n goods to be a *numéraire* by setting its price identically equal to unity and expressing all other prices in terms of it, there will be $n - 1$ exchange ratios or relative prices to be determined. For example, imagine that x_1 is wheat, x_2 apples, and x_3 nuts, and that 2 apples exchange for 1 bushel of wheat ($p_2/p_1 = 0.5$) and 1 nut for 2 bushels of wheat ($p_3/p_1 = 2$). So 4 apples will exchange for 1 nut ($p_3/p_2 = 4$). The complete set of exchange ratios for our 3-commodity system is given directly by 2 exchange ratios and the identity of the *numéraire,* which in this case is wheat. The numéraire may be set equal to unity or to any other specified number, say, a specified number of dollars. The fact remains that this kind of money serves only as an abstract unit of account; it does not exist in a physical sense, and trade is really barter. No one holds this money and no one desires to hold it. This kind of accounting money is quite different from circulating money, which people do want to hold in an actual monetary economy because it serves as a store of value as well as a unit of account.

In an economy in which only accounting money is used—the medium of exchange being an arbitrary commodity like any other—the total value of all goods demanded is always identically equal to the total value of all goods supplied. Summing over all the n goods (commodities plus money) demanded and supplied, this identity can be written as

$$\sum_{i=1}^{n} p_i D_i \equiv \sum_{i=1}^{n} p_i S_i .$$

This identity is called Walras's Law and in our context simply states the *logical* impossibility of oversupply of all goods in a barter economy. However, as soon as we have one good acting not only as a medium of exchange but also as a store of value, the amount demanded of the $n - 1$ commodities will be equal to the total value of the $n - 1$ commodities supplied only if the demand for money is equal to the supply of money. We substitute an equality sign for the identity sign and write

$$\sum_{i=1}^{n-1} p_i D_i = \sum_{i=1}^{n-1} p_i S_i ,$$

if and only if $D_n = S_n$. This follows from the fact that the total demand for money is equal to the value of all the commodities offered in exchange for money.

$$D_n = p_1 S_1 + p_2 S_2 + \cdots + p_{n-1} S_{n-1} = \sum_{i=1}^{n-1} p_i S_i .$$

And the total supply of money is equal to the value of all the commodities demanded with money.

$$S_n = p_1 D_1 + p_2 D_2 + \cdots + p_{n-1} D_{n-1} = \sum_{i=1}^{n-1} p_i D_i .$$

During a specified time period, therefore, any difference between the demand and the supply of commodities must reveal itself as a positive or negative excess demand for money—either $D_n > S_n$ or $D_n < S_n$. An excess supply of all commodities *means* an excess demand for money. If X_{n-1} stands for excess demand for commodities, and X_n for an excess demand for money, then

$$\sum_{i=1}^{n-1} p_i D_i - \sum_{i=1}^{n-1} p_i S_i \equiv \sum_{i=1}^{n-1} X_i \equiv -X_{n-1} \equiv X_n .$$

What meaning has the phrase "excess demand for money"? It means that people want to add to their stock of cash balances in the current period, and this they can do only by demanding fewer goods than are being supplied. We now see that to assert the *logical* impossibility of general overproduction in a monetary economy is tantamount to asserting $X \equiv o$: people hold the amount of money in existence in the form of cash balances and never want to alter these balances by financing a purchase out of them or by using the proceeds from a sale to add to them. Following current practice, we will call this strong proposition *Say's Identity*.

Say's Identity states that the money market is always in equilibrium because, regardless of prices, people supply commodities only to use the money received to demand other commodities "immediately," no matter how short the time period under consideration. It may not be apparent at first glance how strong an assumption this is. It implies that a change in level of prices in no way disturbs the relations between commodity markets and the money market; the marginal rate of substitution of commodities for money is by definition equal to zero. This, in turn, implies that commodity markets themselves are undisturbed: a change in the price level never leads to intercommodity substitution.

Say's Identity can be translated into the so-called "homogeneity postulate": the excess demand functions for commodities depend only on relative prices not on the absolute price level, or, as the saying goes, the demand functions are "homogeneous of degree zero in money prices." Homogeneous functions have the property that if each of the variables in the function is multiplied by a constant, the total function is increased by some power of that constant. The degree of a homogeneous function denotes the value of the power by which the constant is raised. For example, for a homogeneous function $f(x,y)$ and a constant $= 2$,

$$0°: f(2x,2y) = f(x,y) \,,$$
$$1°: f(2x,2y) = 2f(x,y) \,,$$
$$2°: f(2x,2y) = 2^2 f(x,y) = 4f(x,y) \,,$$

or, in general, $\lambda^m f(\lambda x, \lambda y)$ where λ is any arbitrary positive constant. We have already encountered first-degree homogeneous production functions, defined as obeying constant costs or constant returns to scale: double the inputs x and y, and the output is just doubled. Here, however, $f(x,y)$ is a demand function of a commodity whose price is x, the prices of all other goods being represented by y. If this demand function is homogeneous of degree zero, the doubling of prices leaves the amount demanded unchanged. The demand function is independent of absolute prices and depends only on relative prices. This is easy to show. Given a homogeneous zero-degree demand function for x, $D_x = f(\lambda x, \lambda y, \ldots \lambda z)$. Putting $\lambda = (1/x)$, we have $D_x = f(1, y/x, \ldots z/x)$. The function of z independent variables has been replaced by an equivalent function in which the independent variables are ratios, of which there are $z - 1$. These ratios are relative prices, and the demand function varies only with the $z - 1$ relative prices, not with the z absolute prices. Notice that we are right back to accounting money with the price of x as the numéraire. Obviously, if there is only accounting money in the system, the demand functions are homogeneous of degree zero in absolute money prices, and vice versa.

In a world in which Say's Identity holds, money really is a "veil," which can be lifted without affecting the analysis of relative prices.

But, surely, this is true only because we have created a money economy and then imposed upon it a condition that equates it in operation to a barter economy? In a barter economy people would never change their money balances, because there are none. To introduce money but to abstract from its store-of-value function does not get us any further. Why, then, all the rigmarole about Say's Identity? The classical economists frequently asserted the impossibility of general overproduction in a monetary economy. Say's Identity spells out the meaning of such assertions. But before we ask whether Say, Ricardo, and John Stuart Mill actually held Say's Identity, we need to consider the role of monetary theory in a system for which $X_n \equiv 0$.

Dichotomization of the Pricing Process. To say that the market for a product is always in equilibrium, that excess demand for it is identically equal to zero, is to imply that the price of the product is indeterminate. Whatever the forces that determine that price, they are nonmarket forces. Say's Identity, therefore, which asserts that the money market is always in equilibrium, leaves the value of money indeterminate. Mathematically, this indeterminacy is the result of not having enough equations to solve for the given unknowns. With n goods, we have n known demand and supply functions. Actually, only $n - 1$ of these functions are independent. Given $n - 1$ of these functions, the nth function is completely determined: any set of prices that satisfies the $n - 1$ functions necessarily satisfies the nth. By Walras's Law we can always eliminate an equation. So we have $n - 1$ unknown goods prices, or $n - 2$ unknown money prices of commodities plus an unknown price of money, and $n - 2$ known excess demand functions for commodities plus a known excess demand function for money. But the latter is not a genuine equation, for by Say's Identity $X_n \equiv 0$. And so we have only $n - 2$ equations to determine $n - 1$ unknowns; the system is indeterminate.

This is the basis of the Lange-Patinkin charge that the classical and the neoclassical economists "dichotomized the pricing process": they determined relative prices in commodity markets and absolute prices in the money market, which necessarily assumes that the money stock in the hands of the public remains invariant regardless of prices. But if people do have a demand for nominal money holdings because receipts and payments cannot be perfectly synchronized—the transactions motive for holding cash—or because of uncertainty about the future—the precautionary and speculative motives—it is a demand that will vary with every change in the price level; it is a demand for *real* balances. The "missing equation" we spoke of above is the Cambridge equation:

$$D_n = k \sum_{i=1}^{n-1} p_i S_i = M \, ,$$

where k is the proportion of the total supply of goods measured in money that people will want to hold as cash balances. If prices rise, individuals seek to add to their cash balances to compensate for the reduction in their real value. This means that they increase the quantity of the commodities or services they supply and reduce the quantities they demand. The demand functions alter because of the increase in absolute prices and "the homogeneity postulate" ceases to hold.

Say's Identity and the Quantity Theory. We now take the last step in the long story of spelling out the implications of Say's Identity. The pure Lockean version of the quantity theory of money—the value of money is determined by the quantity of money in circulation and by nothing else—implies Say's Identity, and vice versa. Indeed, the quantity theory was the chief element making for a dichotomization of the pricing process. The merit of the quantity theory had been to demonstrate that money as such does not constitute wealth; its weakness, however, in focusing exclusive attention on the medium-of-exchange function of money, led to a neglect of the interdependence between commodity and money markets deriving from the function of money as a store of value. With Locke, the constancy of the ratio M/P, denoting the strictly proportional variation in money and prices is a truism because his money is akin to accounting money. People demand a given amount of *real* balances for transactions purposes; this demand varies with the level of real income, and its elasticity with respect to the price level is always equal to unity. Thus, the demand curve for money is a rectangular hyperbola, a constant-outlay curve, as Marshall would say. But as soon as we add the demand for money to hold as a store of value, the demand curve for *all* money will not be a rectangular hyperbola.

In Figure 15 the left-hand diagram shows Locke's truistic quantity theory, where M and P always vary proportionately. In the right-hand diagram we add $M_2 + M_3 =$ the demand for inactive money balances or "hoards" for precautionary and speculative motives as a function of the level of income and the rate of interest. $M_1 =$ the transactions demand for active money balances, a rectangular hyperbola. Summing the three demand curves horizontally we get M, which is no longer a rectangular hyperbola. In fact, it shows the ratio M/P falling, every increase in M raises prices more than proportionately. This is just what we would expect: the "larger" the stock of money in circulation, the 'larger' the rise in prices required to get people to hold more cash. Incidentally, it is still true that the value of money varies proportionately to its quantity, *if everything else remains the same.* Through every point of M there is a rectangular hyperbola given by the condition $(M/P) \equiv (T/V)$. But the point we have been making is that a change in M in a real-world monetary economy necessarily affects V.

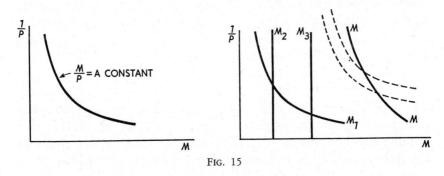

FIG. 15

We have good reasons to be suspicious of any theory that asserts that the price level is determined by M alone. Since the value of money is a relationship between money and goods, one of them cannot be described as *the* determinant of the relationship. All factors influencing MV/T determine the price level. Irving Fisher, a hundred years later, tried to show empirically that V is an institutional datum and that T is determined by real or nonmonetary forces. Formally, the Cambridge equation $M = kPT$ is identical to the Fisherian Equation $M = PT/V$; one can say that people, on the average, want to hold a certain proportion $k = \frac{1}{12}$ of their total transactions T, or one can say that M turns over 12 times a year, $V = 12$. The former expresses the rest theory and the latter the motion theory of velocity. The Cambridge approach, however, has the advantage of suggesting by its very formulation that $(1/k) \equiv V$ is not institutionally given. However, the real difficulty in both versions of the quantity theory is the idea that T is determined solely by real forces: total output and relative prices are determined in the commodity markets, and then the quantity theory is introduced to determine absolute prices in the money market as if the two markets were entirely independent of each other.

Say's Equality. We have now amassed all the pieces with which to categorize classical monetary theory. Is it true that the classical economists held Say's Identity? We have seen that statements denying that there are any reasons for holding money, that money is only a medium of exchange, that money is a veil because relative prices are exclusively determined by real forces, that supply automatically creates its own demand irrespective of what happens to the quantity of money or the price level, that absolute prices always vary in proportion to the quantity of money—are all expressions of Say's Identity. Many classical economists did in fact say such things: we would have no difficulty in culling numerous assertions of this kind from the writings of Ricardo, McCulloch, Senior, Torrens, James Mill, and John Stuart Mill. But before we leap to the conclusion that they were guilty of dichotomizing the pricing process we must distinguish between blanket assertions about the unimportance of money as such, when an author is not aware of the logical implications of such a statement, and explicit analyses of the problem of a general glut in a monetary economy.

We know that every one of the classical economists was aware of the occurrence of business depressions. Ricardo wrote a special chapter on the setbacks to trade in the postwar period and contemplated the possibility that technical change might give rise to unemployment. His followers lived through the slumps of 1825, 1836, and 1847, and each one of them recognized that a free market economy is subject to periodic fluctuations in business activity. Whatever Say's Law meant to them, it was not that gluts cannot possibly occur in the real world. Moreover, they were all acquainted with the Cantillon Effect, which denies "the homogeneity postulate" by asserting that a change in the price level produced by means of a cash injection varies with the nature of the injection and that a change in absolute prices is very often associated with alterations in relative prices. Unless they were merely talking nonsense, they could not have meant that aggregate demand is always equal to the total income of the economy, regardless of variations in prices, that no departures from full employment equilibrium can possibly take place. Rather, they were driving at the idea that a perfectly competitive economy always *tends* to full or maximum employment.

Depressions cannot be permanent because supply creates its own demand on a micro- and a macroeconomic level through automatic price and interest variations. This proposition has been called *Say's Equality* and asserts that an excess supply of goods, or an excess demand for money, tends to be self-correcting. If demand proves insufficient to sell all goods at cost-covering prices, including the going rate of profit, prices must fall. The purchasing power of nominal cash holdings will rise, and everyone will find himself holding excess real balances; there is an excess demand for money. In the effort to reduce the level of individual cash holdings, the demand for commodities increases until the excess supply in commodity markets is eliminated. A zero excess demand for money is an equilibrium condition because prices will continue to fall and the rate of interest will continue to rise as long as there is an excess demand for cash. The same argument holds in reverse for a rise in prices owing to a positive excess demand for commodities. "Supply creates its own demand," therefore, not despite the behavior of prices but because of them. On this argument, absolute prices are determined by the same set of forces as determine relative prices: for every set of relative prices there is a corresponding unique absolute price level at which the money market will be in equilibrium. This is true for a closed economy as much as for an open economy, except that for an open economy the price level has the additional task of bringing exports and imports into balance. Thus, it is clear that Say's Equality does not dichotomize the pricing process.

Say's Equality in Classical Writings. The classical economists never spelled out Say's Equality. But their writings are replete with references to a vaguely stated process of adjustment by which deviations from full employment tend to be self-correcting. We have already witnessed Ricardo defending Say's Law as valid irrespective of price-interest variations in the very same chapter in which he explains how variations in the rate of interest govern the demand for investment funds. Surprisingly enough, Jean Baptiste Say criticized Ricardo for stating Say's Identity and emphasized the function of the interest mechanism in equilibrating saving and investment. Elsewhere he himself was satisfied with the almost Keynesian assertion that production cannot be increased without generating new income with which additional output can be bought. James Mill and McCulloch discussed the question at various places in their writings, sometimes expressing Say's Identity, sometimes Say's Equality. But the one classical author who gave a really lucid presentation of the problem was John Stuart Mill. In the second essay in his *Unsettled Questions of Political Economy,* published in 1844 but written as early as 1830, he showed, first of all, complete awareness that Say's Identity holds only for accounting money in a barter-type economy:

> In order to render the argument for the impossibility of an excess of all commodities applicable to the case in which a circulating medium is employed, money must itself be considered as a commodity. It must undoubtedly be admitted that there cannot be an excess of all other commodities and an excess of money at the same time.

The "utility of money," however, consists in the possibility of being able to sell without having to buy and

> . . . it may very well occur, that there may be, at some given time, a very general inclination to sell with as little delay as possible, accompanied with a general inclination to defer all purchases as long as possible [an excess demand for money]. This is always actually the case in those periods which are described as periods of general excess. And no one, after sufficient explanation, will contest the possibility of general excess, in this sense of the word.

There follows a detailed explanation of why "under-supply of money' must be temporary, and, while the argument is somewhat loose, the distinction between Say's Identity and Say's Equality could hardly be drawn in clearer terms. Mill does not state the real-balance effect in so many words: a fall in absolute prices decreases the public's demand for cash, not because of its effect in raising the real value of cash balances, but because of the expectation that the fall in prices cannot continue. Still, an automatic equilibrating mechanism is contemplated. The discussion in Mill's *Principles* on this point is identical in content to the *Essays*. It is true that very early in the book he argues that "money, as money, satisfies no want." This occurs in a section deprecating the mercantilist identification of wealth with money, and Mill immediately proceeds to say that money derives its "utility" from the fact that it permits a seller to buy "at the times which suit him best." The first three sections of the chapter "Of Excess Supply" restate Say's Identity. It is here that Mill says that "all sellers are inevitably, and by the meaning of the word, buyers," a statement that Keynes quoted to show that Mill's exposition of Say's Law in no way differed from Ricardo's. But in the fourth section of the chapter Mill speaks once again of the "under-supply of money" during a commercial crisis, and elsewhere in the book he provides a vivid description, but not a theory, of the onset of a slump and the restoration of equilibrium.

Keynes and Say's Law. When a classical economist asserted the impossibility of "gluts" he had in mind not periodic crises but secular stagnation. Could the capitalist system absorb the constant increases in productive capacity without breakdown from limits inherent in the system? Say's Equality supplied an affirmative answer to this question: with flexible prices the system does tend to full-capacity equilibrium. The classical economists never established this proposition with any rigor, but they appealed to what are at any rate valid comparative static arguments.

It was Keynes's contention that a perfectly competitive "mature" economy does not in fact tend automatically toward full employment.

Inflexibility of wages and prices, low interest elasticity of investment demand, rigidities in monetary institutions, the "liquidity trap"—any of these might suffice to prevent attainment of full-employment equilibrium. In addition, even if Say's Equality were a valid comparative static argument, it had never been shown that full-employment equilibrium is dynamically attainable, that the process of moving toward equilibrium *through time* did not displace the equilibrium point itself. But, instead of granting the theoretical validity of Say's Equality as far as it goes—and it goes far enough to refute dire predictions of permanent overproduction—and then pointing to the qualifications that deprive it of practical significance, Keynes chooses instead to attack Say's Identity, which he ascribes to every economist before him.[1] As a result of Keynes's criticism, Say's Law has been given an importance out of all proportion to its actual role in classical and neoclassical theory.

It must have struck many readers of the *General Theory* as odd that a proposition supposedly so basic to Marshallian reasoning as Say's Law is covered in Marshall's *Principles* in one paragraph. The Keynesian explanation is that Say's Law was so implicit an assumption that Marshall never really thought it out. But a much more convincing explanation is that the possibility or impossibility of permanent overproduction was a dead issue by 1890. Instead of asserting that "if people do not spend their money in one way they will spend it in another," which is one of Keynes's versions of Say's Identity, Marshall declared that "though men have the power to purchase they may not choose to use it," and left it at that. The failure to pursue the argument may have been misleading, but certainly there is no suggestion here that $X_n = o$.

The Direct Mechanism. We must now look a little more closely at the classical conception of Say's Equality. Just what is the mechanism that brings markets once disturbed back to equilibrium? We have already seen that Say's Identity would preclude the need for any monetary theory. Contrariwise, belief in Say's Equality implies concern with the operation of money markets. It is in the realm of classical monetary theory that we must look for the reasoning behind Say's Equality.

---

[1] This explains Keynes's term "classical economics" as meaning the broad stream of orthodox economics from Smith to Pigou that fell victim to Say's Law. We have been using "classical economics" in the traditional sense to mean all the followers of Adam Smith through J. S. Mill and Cairnes. The term "classical economics" was first used by Marx in a peculiar sense to mean the school of political economy, from Petty to Ricardo in England and from Boisguilbert to Sismondi in France, that "investigated the real relations of production in bourgeois society."

Classical monetary theory consists essentially of two strands of thought, both of which relate the quantity of money to the price level: the "direct mechanism" expounded by Cantillon and Hume and the "indirect mechanism" first stated by Thornton and then reiterated by Ricardo. It was a commonplace of classical analysis that an increase in the quantity of money affects prices directly through its prior effect on demand: the increase in money receipts generates an increase in the outflow of expenditures because people are satisfied with their existing holdings of cash balances. The eighteenth-century doctrine that the quantity of money is determined by the "needs of trade" was based on the recognition that a stable demand for working balances preserves a certain proportion of the quantity of money to the value of trade: "Every man must have at least so much money, or so much timely recruits, as may in hand, or in a short distance of time, satisfy his creditor who supplies him with the necessaries of life, or of his trade," wrote John Locke in 1691. As we have seen, both Hume and Cantillon paid attention to the manner in which a cash injection is disbursed and to the various lags involved in the process. They showed, in effect, that an increase of money raises prices equiproportionately only if the extra cash is neutrally distributed, if everyone's initial money holdings are increased equiproportionately, so that, we should add, creditors and debtors cancel out. As Hume put it, imagine everyone's money holdings doubled overnight; prices would begin rising and in this special case would rise until prices had exactly doubled.

This special case has a particular significance in the history of monetary theory, and we must establish it with some care. We showed earlier that the demand curve for *all* money to hold is not a rectangular hyperbola: it does not show money and prices varying proportionately. It shows the change in the demand for money as prices change when the level of nominal balances is given. An increase of prices at a given amount of money in the hands of the public will, however, reduce desired real-balance holdings. The demand curve for money, therefore, has a steeper slope than a rectangular hyperbola—curve M in Figure 15. Through every point of this curve there passes a rectangular hyperbola that is the locus of demand-supply equilibria, showing the effect, *ceteris paribus,* of a neutral increase in the quantity of money upon absolute prices. We start from an equilibrium relationship between money and prices, introduce a change in one of the independent variables—in this case the quantity of money—and show that the system returns to equilibrium with prices rising proportionately to the increase in money. This is typical comparative static reasoning.

For a proportionate increase in the money holdings of every individual, prices must rise in the same proportion. This was never proved rigorously by the classical economists, but it was asserted again and again. The best way of motivating the proof is to ask why an increase in money, once it has ceased, should cause prices to remain at a permanently higher level? The answer must be that people apparently want to hold a certain proportion of their total transactions in the form of *real* balances as a reserve against the embarrassment of default. Let us follow Patinkin in a proof based on a simple Keynesian model (see Fig. 16). If the aggregate demand curve E cuts the $45°$ line at full em-

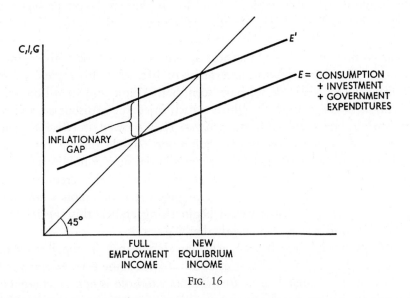

FIG. 16

ployment, a once-and-for-all increase in government expenditures financed by printing money will shift the aggregate effective demand curve E upward, creating an inflationary gap. Even when the government reverts to a balanced budget, the inflationary gap persists because individuals feel that their money holdings are too large for their needs: E has shifted upward not just because government expenditures have increased but also because the total real value of cash balances in the economy has stimulated consumption and investment. Now prices begin to rise, thereby reducing the real value of cash balances and causing E to shift down again. If the new money was distributed neutrally, prices must double, no more, no less. For, if prices less than double, the real value of the doubled cash balances will be greater than the real value of the original balances and E will be such as to leave an inflationary gap. And if prices more than double, the same consideration will show that a deflationary gap will result. Both these outcomes are disequilibrium situations. Hence, in equilibrium prices just double.

The Indirect Mechanism. Now for the indirect mechanism connecting money and prices. It has been said that the quantity theory of money assigns no explicit role to the rate of interest and that no monetary theory is worth very much if it neglects to introduce the interest rate. Now it is true that the Equation of Exchange does not refer to the interest rate, but then the quantity *theory* of money is a different thing from the identity $MV \equiv PT$. At any rate, the classical theory of the indirect mechanism connecting M to P refers specifically to the loan rate of interest. The indirect mechanism was first stated by Henry Thornton in his *Nature of the Paper Credit of Great Britain* (1802), the greatest single work on monetary theory produced in the classical period, and was then taken over verbatim by Ricardo and Mill. The argument is that monetary equilibrium in an economy with nonmonetary assets exists only when the money rate in the loan market equals the rate of return on capital in commodity markets. A cash injection must come into the loan market via the banking system; the increased supply of loanable funds causes the market rate of interest to fall below the yield of capital; the volume of borrowing rises as the price of investment goods increases, and the demand for loans is stimulated. Eventually, the increased demand for loans will catch up with the supply of loans. However, as long as the bank rate remains below the rate of profit on capital, the demand for loans is insatiable. Soon the demand for loans overtakes the supply and the bank rate will begin to rise again. If the real rate of return on capital has remained invariant, equilibrium is restored only when the bank rate has returned to its previous level. Prices are higher, but the rate of interest is as before. Ergo, in equilibrium, the rate of interest is independent of the quantity of money in circulation.

This theory of the two rates—the natural and the market rate of interest—was independently rediscovered a century later by Wicksell, who was surprised to find that it was an old idea. Ricardo had used it to show that the note issue of the Bank of England may expand beyond all assignable limits if the bank rate can be kept low enough; convertibility of the note issue would deprive the Bank of power to regulate the discount rate, at least below the 5 per cent limit of the Usury Laws; inconvertibility, however, in effect gave the Bank the capacity to maintain inflation by artificially depressing the discount rate. Quite apart from that, Thornton's argument emphasizes the connection between money and commodity markets and hence shows that classical theory, fairly interpreted, does not dichotomize the pricing process.

Saving, Investment, and Hoarding. In the standard interpretation, the rate of interest in classical economics is determined in the loan market, or what Keynes calls the "bond market." The money rate of interest depends on the demand and supply of loanable funds, identified, respectively, with investment and saving. It was rarely pointed out that investment may be financed out of hoards or out of inflationary bank credit. Ricardo, for one, strenuously denied that "credit can create capital." The notion that inflationary credit expansion cannot foster growth we will examine in a moment: it is nothing less than the controversial "forced saving" doctrine. The idea that investment is never financed out of hoards is much easier to deal with. By "hoarding" we mean withdrawing money income from current expenditure without diverting it to nonconsumption purposes; in other words, the building-up of cash balances. In the classical period, the term was always used in a pejorative sense: only a "miser" wants to increase his monetary holdings above the minimum required for transactions purposes. Taken strictly, the typical classical comment to the effect that hoarding is "abnormal" would imply that people never add their savings to cash balances and never finance investment out of cash balances. The excess demand for money is identically equal to zero, and we are back to Say's Identity and indeterminate prices.

In a money economy, therefore, savings and investment cannot always and necessarily be equal to the supply and demand for loans. But in equilibrium this will be true because equilibrium is given by the condition that people are satisfied with their cash holdings. It is evident, then, that classical economics does not maintain that planned saving is always and necessarily equal to planned investment. This kind of statement is simply a Keynesian translation of the language of loanable funds. To assert the impossibility of a discrepancy between intended saving and investment is to assert that the aggregate demand curve lies along the 45° line: the economy is always in equilibrium—in which case, of course, the level of income and employment is indeterminate. Since the classical economists held Say's Equality rather than Say's Identity, they must have allowed for the possibility that intended saving may not be realized. The "indirect mechanism" has the virtue of focusing attention on the demand side of the loan market as a function of the rate of interest. For every supply of real saving and flow of bank credit there is a price level that will maintain the rate of interest at a given rate of return on capital, thus insuring equilibrium in the loan market. Clearly, if intended saving exceeds intended investment, the rate of interest will fall and the price level will rise, working to restore equilibrium. The only difference between this kind of argument and the Keynesian is that saving, in Keynes, is a function of income, whereas in classical analysis saving is a complicated function of the interest rate and the level of prices via the state of investment opportunities. Income variations produce equilibrium in Keynes; price and interest variations produce equilibrium in classical theory. All this is disguised by the fact that the classical economists almost never use the word "investment" and speak of "saving" to denote not the process but rather the result of saving, the actual resources saved: with them "saving" already implies the issuance into additional capital equipment. This suggests that saving is actually identified with investment, but this cannot be what they had in mind. It is perfectly true, however, that the failure to spell out equilibrium adjustments often led classical writers to assume the comparative static result at the outset and to argue about relations between variables as if they were always in equilibrium.

Although most classical writers did not explicitly distinguish between saving and lending, on the one hand, and investment and borrowing, on the other, they did not argue that saving and investment alone determine the rate of interest. The loanable-funds theory, with its implication that the rate of interest is influenced by the state of the money market, is contained in Thornton and even in Ricardo and is ably expounded in Book III, chapter 23, of J. S. Mill's *Principles*. When John Stuart Mill defined saving as income "not consumed by the person who saves it" and hoarding as income "not consumed at all," we can conclude only that "intended saving" in the modern sense is equivalent to classical saving plus hoarding, for the excess of intended saving over intended investment in modern analysis produces the same economic effects as an increase of hoarding in classical economics.

The Real Interest Rate. The market rate of interest in classical theory is not determined by the quantity of money in circulation: they held a real theory of interest. The interest rate is ultimately determined by the same real forces that govern the rate of profit upon capital, for in equilibrium the two rates are equal. This result is really a corollary of the previous argument that a neutral doubling of M will double P. If $2 M = 2 P$ then people will supply and demand exactly double the value of loanable funds upon which the rate of interest depends. It is the initial excess supply of loans that depresses the rate of interest. When the price level has finally doubled, the *real* quantity of money in

the economy is the same, and so the demand and supply of loans intersect at the same interest rate. With costs twice as high, any given investment requires twice as many money loans. The rate of return on investment is not affected, for with the doubling of cost goes a doubling
of anticipated money returns. When the additional cash has been absorbed into circulation by the price increase, people increase their demand for loans to the same extent that the banks originally increased
their supply, and the equilibrium rate is ultimately unchanged.

This is the pure logic of the real theory of interest held by the
classical school. The individual demand curve for money with respect
to the interest rate is negatively sloped, but the market-equilibrium
curve is always horizontal (see Fig. 17). An individual will demand

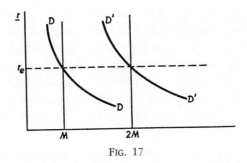

FIG. 17

more money when the rate of interest falls, everything else, including
absolute prices, remaining constant. But if he holds money for the rational reason of enabling him to conduct a certain *real* value of transactions, he will want to hold exactly twice as much money at a given
rate of interest when prices have doubled. Aggregate this result for all
individuals and we reach the classical conclusion.

The Exceptions. In Keynesian theory doubling the money stock
does not double the price level and does affect the rate of interest. This
is because Keynes's demand function for money, in particular his speculative demand, contains a "money illusion," a tendency to react to
changes in money balances even when they are not associated with
changes in real balances. Whenever there is money illusion in either
the money, loans, or commodity markets, the classical theorems do not
hold.

Likewise, if the monetary increase is not distributed equiproportionately to the initial money holdings, the argument loses all sem-
blance of precision. Suppose the extra cash flows into the hands of capitalists with a relatively low propensity to consume. The rise in prices

will then alter the composition of total output in favor of investment and cause the rate of interest to decline permanently. This, of course, is the Cantillon Effect. The classical economists were, therefore, perfectly aware that certain kinds of cash injection can "create capital" and thus permanently lower the rate of interest. All such exceptions come under the heading of "forced saving," a possibility generally admitted, though with various degrees of emphasis, by all the classical writers.

Forced Saving. Among the many theoretical contributions of the Bullionist Controversy was the doctrine of forced saving. The central idea is very simple: suppose there is an excess supply of loans in a fully employed economy resulting from a cash injection or the drawing-down of idle balances, so that investment is no longer limited by voluntary decisions of income recipients to save; the market rate of interest falls, and the demand for investment funds rises. But, if the capital stock is already utilized at capacity, where do the real resources required by additional investment come from? If they do not come from voluntary saving, they must be the result of involuntary saving. And this is exactly what does happen. The extra capital formation is "forced" from fixed-income recipients through a rise in prices.

Thornton called it saving arising from "defalcation of revenue." Bentham called it "forced frugality." Malthus dubbed it "fictitious capital." Mill labeled it "forced accumulation." Since Mill, it has been called "enforced saving" by Wicksell, "automatic stinting" or "imposed lacking" by D. H. Robertson, and "real levies" or "doctoring of contracts" by Pigou. All these writers agree about the meaning of the doctrine, at least in its monetary aspects.

The only major writer who was reluctant to accept the thesis was Ricardo. After attacking the Bank for issuing notes in excess, he was not likely to be sympathetic to the notion that inflation can increase investment in real terms. Still, he admitted that an increase in paper-money circulation may redistribute income to entrepreneurs from wages lagging behind prices; this is not quite the same thing as "forced saving" because the increase in saving here is perfectly voluntary. Ricardo relegated forced saving proper to the short run, arguing that the squeeze on consumption causes consumer goods prices to rise, thus limiting the degree to which the excess supply of funds actually materializes in additional real investment. Moreover, as money incomes rise in the process of inflation, increased consumption demand will eventually transfer resources back again to the consumer goods sector.

Whether Ricardo was justified in his skepticism it would be difficult to say. It is apparent that the forced-saving doctrine is the more convincing, the more elastic the supply of goods, the more elastic the supply of productive services, the more gradual the cash injection, and the greater the number of fixed-income recipients. Generally, inflation promotes growth in real output by absorbing hitherto idle resources into employment. The forced-saving doctrine, restricted as it is to the case of full employment, is probably of very little significance. The fact remains, however, that all the classical economists, including Ricardo, granted the possibility of an effect, however small, upon the long-run rate of interest and hence upon the rate of return to real capital from monetary expansion alone. There was disagreement over the significance of the Cantillon Effect, Ricardo and James Mill minimizing its importance. But there was no dogmatic denial of the partial validity of a monetary theory of interest properly stated.

Conclusion. In retrospect it is all too obvious that the confusion about classical monetary theory is solely due to the superficial resemblance between the valid comparative statics assertion that in equilibrium relative prices are unaffected by the quantity of money, when money is injected into the system in an appropriately neutral manner, and statements denying the generally beneficial effects of an influx of money. Even an unqualified statement that the quantity of money does not affect relative prices did not necessarily mean that the author subscribed to Say's Identity. Both Ricardo and Mill made such assertions in places where they were concerned with equilibrium relative prices; elsewhere, sometimes a few pages later, they are found discussing the time path between two equilibria in which relative prices, including the interest rate, *are* disturbed by an injection of cash. It is true that they were not aware, with the exception of Mill, of the entire logical structure of the problem and frequently expressed themselves in a misleading manner. But, whenever the problem of Say's Equality arose explicitly, it was analyzed in a manner that is at least formally valid, though incomplete.

The Mercantilists held a monetary theory of interest. The classical school held a real theory. Who was right? It is easy to see now that this is really a false issue because it already implies dichotomization of markets. Nevertheless, if the interest rate in question is an equilibrium interest rate, then there can be no doubt that it is determined in the "real" sector, not in the monetary sector. Furthermore, the classical theory of interest is more general because it encompasses all the elements of a monetary theory, while a monetary theory, particularly under a metallic standard, leaves the quantity of money itself undetermined and disconnected from commodity markets. It is for good reason that we spoke earlier of the theoretical advance brought about by "real" analysis.

2. MALTHUS' ATTACK ON SAY'S LAW

It has been said that just as free traders give the best arguments for protection, defenders of Say's Law give the best arguments for the possibility of a general glut. Malthus himself never produced a logical refutation of the Law, probably because he did not really understand the theory at the back of it. If he had merely wanted to argue that gluts are possible and very likely to occur, he had any number of arguments to appeal to. He could have argued that investors are very sensitive to future profit expectations and that loss of confidence resulting from a bad harvest or an external gold drain was enough to cause them to retain income in the form of idle balances; no doubt falling prices would eventually restore equilibrium, but the process of deflation itself might sap confidence, and in this way the process of adjustment could be a long and painful one. Or he could have argued that a sticky bank rate causes the stock of money to lag behind the growing volume of output; this leads to a falling price level—after all, prices did fall steadily in the British economy after 1821—and since wages are rigid downward or have a floor at the subsistence level, this leads to losses throughout the economy. But Malthus had no truck with any of these explanations for the simple reason that he wanted to demonstrate, not the possibility of temporary overproduction, but the possibility of permanent overproduction of all commodities. Without exogenous spending by "unproductive consumers" the process of capital accumulation leads inherently to secular stagnation; this is Malthus' case.

Malthus' Case. Malthus made things difficult for himself by rejecting all purely monetary explanations of gluts. Nor did he resort to inflexibility of wages and prices to justify his argument. Worst of all, he assumed, as did all his contemporaries, that saving means "the conversion of revenue into capital"; saving is a synonym for accumulation. "No political economist of the present day," he remarked, "can by saving mean mere hoarding." An excess supply of loanable funds created by bank credit is presumably absorbed by a fall in the market rate of interest and a rise in the price level; at any rate, Malthus did not dispute the Thornton-Ricardo argument of the "indirect mechanism." There is no hint whatever in his writings of the decisive Keynesian break with orthodox analysis, making saving a function of income rather than the rate of interest, so that oversaving is eliminated by a fall in the level of income. Malthus consistently adhered to the Smithian saving-is-spending theorem. Within such a model it would have been difficult to deduce even temporary lack of effective demand caused by oversaving. As it was, Malthus' aim was more ambitious. At the root of his thinking is a typical underconsumptionist fallacy, and his writings at best represent an important chapter in the long history of this "underworld" doctrine. To show what is meant, let us digress for a moment to consider the standard argument of the underconsumptionist.

The Doctrine of Underconsumption. The underconsumptionist position is that aggregate demand in the private sector of a closed economy is *always* insufficient, or forever threatening to become insufficient, to buy all goods at cost-covering prices. This position has crude and sophisticated versions. The crudest version simply ignores the fact that aggregate demand equals consumption plus investment. It appeals to the fact that most consumers are workers who can never buy back the products they produce because the value of output necessarily exceeds the value of wages paid out. Hence a certain volume of spending on luxury articles and labor services out of profits and rents is necessary to insure continued reproduction. Malthus actually used this argument in a few places but did not rest his case on it. It is easy to show, of course, that the consumption of capitalists and landlords and the investment of capitalists is precisely what causes consumer goods to be so priced that workers alone can never buy them back. Nevertheless, this does not prevent the total value of output from being exactly equal to total income. The accompanying tabulation gives a simple example for a two-sector economy. The sales value of con-

	Consumer Goods	Capital Goods	Total
Wages..................	40	10	50
Profits and rents........	40	10	50
Value of output.........	80	20	100

sumer goods = the consumption expenditures of workers (50) plus the consumption expenditures of capitalists and landlords (30). Since nonlabor income is 50, saving = investment is 20. Consumption (80) + investment (20) = total output = total income. This conclusion holds equally well for a stationary economy, in which investment is merely replacement demand for capital goods used up, as for a growing economy in which net investment is positive. It holds, among other reasons, because landlords do spend all their receipts; but, if they did not, output and income would merely be proportionately lower. Malthus was no doubt influenced by the argument of Cantillon that the spending of rental receipts depends upon the disposition of landlords because rent, unlike wages and profit, is not a necessary expense of production. But as long as landlord spending habits are stable, the failure to spend all rentals causes no deadlock. By itself, instability of spending patterns can explain cyclical fluctuations but not secular stagnation, and it is the latter that concerns us here.

The more sophisticated versions of the underconsumptionist thesis agree that total income is equal to total cost payments in an economy for any given period. And as long as investment in every period fills the gap between income and consumption, any given income level can be maintained indefinitely. However, investment not only creates income but also adds to capacity in subsequent periods. If next year's consumption and investment are identical to this year's, excess capacity must appear. The existence of excess capacity discourages investment because it makes it possible for producers to meet existing demand with smaller outlays of capital. As soon as investment falls, incomes fall, and the slump is on. Now it is true that the fall in income cures the difficulty in time by absorbing capacity. As soon as the economy swings up again, however, the problem reappears. It is clear that what is needed to absorb constantly increasing capacity is constantly increasing incomes. It is not enough for consumption and investment to repeat themselves period after period; they must increase exponentially. Now comes the clinching argument that produces underconsumptionist conclusions. Surely, it is absurd to expect either consumption or investment to rise by a constant percentage amount year after year? For notice that every act of saving tends to cut down the demand for consumer goods, and, when these savings are invested, the supply of goods is simultaneously augmented. Paradoxically, it is just when saving and investment are interdependent that the problem seems most intractable. Now we are at the heart of Malthus' position: an underconsumption theory of the oversaving type.

The paradox that saving as such creates trouble is easy to resolve. For one thing it proves too much: it suggests that purchasing power is *always* insufficient to absorb available output and hence would shift the problem to explaining why there are booms at all. Initially, the gap caused by saving is filled by equivalent investment; in the next period the supply of consumers goods rises, but costs usually fall precisely because of the previous investment; this frees purchasing power and permits the absorption of additional output. Still, costs may not fall sufficiently, and hence investment must rise to generate additional purchasing power. We are back at the incredible notion of investment's rising by increasing absolute amounts year after year.

The Malthusian oversaving argument is only one version of the underconsumptionist theory. The socialist version holds that stagnation sets in because the share of wages in total income tends to fall as income increases. The Hansen-Keynes version holds that stagnation is the result of a declining rate of return on investment. But the core of all these versions is the idea that consumption and investment cannot be expected to grow indefinitely like a geometric progression.

Exponential Growth. The impossibility of exponential growth is so intuitively appealing that most people are surprised that consumption, saving, investment, and income have grown at an exponential rate over long periods of time. The saving-income or consumption-income ratio has remained practically constant in the British and American economies since 1870—there is no reliable data, unfortunately, for the earlier period. Since real income has been growing at about 2 per cent per annum, investment and consumption must also have grown at 2 per cent per annum. Along the trend line, investment and consumption have increased in absolute amounts year after year.

This proves that it can happen, but it does not prove that it has to happen. However, we are not trying to prove the impossibility of secular stagnation but rather to disprove its inevitable occurrence. Investment is indeed capacity-adding, but this does not necessarily spell breakdown at some future point. There is always some rate of investment sufficiently high to create demand for the additional output of a previous period's investment. This can be shown by the now familiar Harrodian growth equation. Equilibrium requires that planned saving equals planned investment. Dividing by Y = income, we have

$$\frac{S}{Y} = \frac{I}{Y} = \frac{\Delta K}{Y}.$$

Let ΔY stand for the increment of income in a period. Then

$$\frac{S}{Y} = \frac{\Delta K}{Y} \frac{\Delta Y}{\Delta Y},$$

$$\frac{S}{Y} = \frac{\Delta Y}{Y} \frac{\Delta K}{\Delta Y},$$

or, $G = (s/k)$, where G = the rate of growth of income, s = the saving-income ratio, and k = the incremental capital-output ratio. Assume that intentions to save are always realized but that investment intentions may be frustrated. Realized saving must equal realized investment, by definition. The reciprocal of k tells us what increment of output is produced by an increment of capital. Now, if planned saving or investment in any one year $= I$, capacity in the next year will rise by I/k, and the growth of income must equal the increase of capacity. So, if there is sufficient demand to maintain full capacity use of the capital stock in any one year, it can be maintained by increasing the rate of investment by I/kY or s/k per cent the next year. The argument so far implies that all investment is induced by the growth of output; as soon as income increases, the "accelerator" k shows how investment must increase to accommodate the larger output. But there is also "autonomous" investment resulting from changes in productive techniques or in the range of available products. Writing d for autonomous investment, we have

$$G_w = \frac{s - d}{k} \, .$$

G_w is the warranted rate of growth of income required to absorb into production the annual increments in productive capacity provided by each year's net investment; it is the only income-growth rate at which intended investment is realizable. Harrod now introduces G_n, the natural rate of growth, being the maximum permissible rate of growth that the economy can achieve with its available resources. Secular stagnation corresponds to the case $G_w > G_n$: the full-capacity rate of growth cannot be maintained because it lies above the full employment ceiling. The actual growth rate therefore falls short of G_w; there is insufficient acceleration-induced planned investment or inadequate autonomous investment to absorb planned saving, and the result is a chronic tendency to unemployment and excess capacity.[2]

[2] The argument can be illustrated graphically by a slight elaboration of the ordinary short-run income-determination diagram found in elementary textbooks (Fig. 18). Assuming that the average and marginal propensity to save are equal, we draw the saving function through the origin. The investment functions are drawn in the usual manner and the intersection of the two functions determines the equilibrium level of income. Now we measure the capital stock along the vertical axis and superimpose a third function P, whose slope is $\Delta K / \Delta Y = k$. With respect to the saving function, Y is the independent variable; with respect to the P function, it is the dependent variable.

Assume that OY_1 is an initial full-capacity income in year 1. As a result of investment, the capital stock at the end of year 1 has increased by amount $S_1Y_1 = \Delta K$. Thus, productive capacity has increased by an amount $S_1P_1 = Y_1Y_2 = \Delta Y$. The capital coefficient is given by the ratio $S_1Y_1/Y_1Y_2 = k$. Full-capacity income has now increased from OY_1 in year 1 to OY_2 in year 2. Unless equilibrium income grows to OY_2, excess capacity will develop. With a given saving function, income will grow only if investment rises from I' to I''. This insures new full-capacity income OY_2 at end of year 2, by which time the economy's capital stock has risen by amount S_2Y_2. Drawing a new function P'', parallel to P' for convenience, we find productive capacity has increased by amount $S_2P_2 = Y_2Y_3$, the new full capacity income being OY_3. It is evident that $Y_3 - Y_2 > Y_2 - Y_1$, that is, full capacity is

The Harrodian analysis provides a convenient framework for discussing the issue of secular stagnation. As such it proves nothing one way or the other. It may be that the propensity to save as well as the acceleration coefficient k are subject to automatic correcting forces whenever $G_w > G_n$. Or perhaps autonomous investment tends to adjust to variations in k. The character of innovations also provides room for adjustment: laborsaving innovations would reduce G_w and thus lessen the tendency to stagnation. We cannot enter into these issues here, for they are still very controversial. The upshot of this long digression into modern economics is to show that there is an argument for secular stagnation and that even our recent experience with inflation is too brief to permit generalizations about the normal state of a "mature" economy. As for a century of steady expansion, it is always possible to plead special noneconomic factors. It is true that no one has ever proved the necessity of stagnation, but that does not preclude discussion of its possibility.

---

growing by increasing absolute amounts, which requires that the investment schedule is also rising by increasing absolute amounts. Both investment and income are growing at an increasing absolute rate or a constant geometric rate.

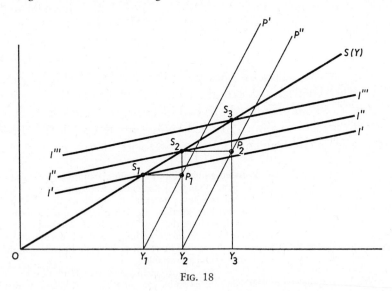

FIG. 18

This argument assumes that saving is a given constant percentage of income and that investment depends in a simple unique way upon the rate at which income increases, that is, the capital coefficient or the so-called accelerator coefficient—the ratio between investment and the increment of income which induces it—is a constant. But the method can easily be generalized to allow for saving and investment functions that are not linear and that contain autonomous components, as well as for curvilinear P functions with k declining as investment increases in value. This may mean that investment and income will not have to grow by greater and greater absolute amounts to preserve equilibrium. But we are not trying to prove the *necessity* of exponential growth but only its *possibility*.

If the reader recalls the earlier distinction between Keynesian and Marxian unemployment, he will realize that stagnation in Malthus' day was a rather different matter from Keynesian stagnation. For our times, the growth ceiling G_n is defined by the labor supply. But in the classical period the supply of labor was for all practical purposes unlimited, and in theory it was certainly regarded as infinitely elastic. But natural resource scarcities also enter into G_n. The Malthusian situation may be likened to the case in which $G_w > G_n$ because the absence of free trade holds down G_n. With free trade there is every reason to believe that planned investment would have tended to run ahead of planned saving, that is $G_w < G_n$. The situation accorded much more with secular exhilaration than with secular stagnation. It was a particularly inappropriate time in history to decry oversaving and to advocate a lower rate of capital accumulation. Thus, whatever we may conclude about the real dangers of stagnation in the twentieth century, it hardly induces a more sympathetic attitude to Malthus' theory. When secular rates of saving are deficient relative to the secular capital requirements of a growing population, saving is indeed a virtue.

What Malthus Actually Said. Book I of Malthus' *Principles,* devoted to value and distribution theory, makes much more difficult reading than Book II, which deals specifically with the question of general overproduction. Ostensibly, it is a typical Ricardian treatment, with an emphasis on the perfect measure of value, the theory of differential rent and the relation between profits and wages sharing a total product less rent. At various points, however, Malthus takes issue with Ricardo so as to bring out the pivotal role of effective demand. He distinguishes between Ricardo's "extent of demand" as the quantity actually bought on the market at a given price and the "intensity of demand" as "the will and power to make a greater sacrifice in order to obtain the object wanted." The purpose of this distinction is to clarify the meaning of glut, denoting an excess of supply relative to the intensity of demand, which causes price to fall below cost. The implied distinction between a shift and a movement along a demand curve, however, is not pushed further. Malthus shows no interest in demand theory as such and made no substantive use of his terminological clarification. He likewise rejected Ricardo's measure of value and went back to Smith's standard, the number of wage units that a product can command. His defense of this standard of value is extremely confusing, and his preference for it seems based on little else than that it permitted him to define a general glut as a case in which the number of wage units currently commanded by present output falls short of the quantity of the direct and indirect labor embodied in its production. Throughout

Book I Malthus seems to be trying to break away from the Ricardian postulates, while in fact remaining thoroughly imprisoned in them.

Very early in the *Principles,* and again in the concluding chapter of the work, we meet one of Malthus' favorite subsidiary arguments, to the effect that spending on productive labor (*read:* investment) necessarily creates a deficiency of effective demand. Since workers receive less than the value of the product they produce, "no power of consumption on the part of the laboring classes can ever alone furnish an encouragement to the employment of capital." Nor can the gap be filled by the demand of capitalists for "they have, by the supposition, agreed to be parsimonious, and by depriving themselves of their usual conveniences and luxuries to save from their revenue and add to their luxuries." It followed that there would be a general glut of commodities unless purchasing power were sustained by additional "unproductive consumption" on the part of some group other than capitalists and workers. This is the "saving defeats itself" fallacy mentioned earlier.

But the argument that Malthus seems to have in mind most of the time is the case of an increase of saving and investment, with profits at a minimum and the supply of labor given in the short run. We will recall that the Ricardian theory of the falling rate of profit is based on capital and labor, growing at the same rate, encountering increasing costs of producing wage goods. At one point in his book, Ricardo speculated briefly on the effects of a sudden increase in capital accumulation with population lagging behind; this, he admitted, would produce a fall in the rate of profit unconnected with a rising cost of producing wheat, and in the short run this situation would correspond to "an universal glut." This is in itself curious language, for profits fall only because wages rise. However, we are concerned not with Ricardo's argument but rather with what Malthus made of it. In Ricardo's argument, the glut is temporary because the increase in wages elicits population growth, which raises short-run profits once again. Malthus, however, stresses the inelastic supply of labor in the short run: "an increase of laborers cannot be brought into the market, in consequence of a particular demand, till after a lapse of sixteen or eighteen years." The argument is then immediately generalized: "a country is always liable to an increase in the quantity of the funds for the maintenance of labor faster than the increase of population." Whenever this happens, increased wage rates put the capitalists in a price-cost squeeze, and investment falls off. Increased wages do not add to effective demand because workers prefer leisure to increased consumption. In this way, Malthus thought he had shown that "an inordinate passion for accumulation must inevitably lead to a supply of commodities beyond what the structure and habits of such a society will permit to be profitably consumed."

We have seen that if the propensity to save in an economy is such that the realization of saving and investment intentions requires a rate of growth of income in excess of the growth rate of labor, the actual rate of growth of income will produce excess capacity and unemployment. Malthus seems to be pleading a short-run version of this kind of secular oversaving. It is a curious argument indeed for the author of the *Essay on the Principle of Population,* but, quite apart from that, it made little sense in an economy in which as much as 6–10 per cent of the population was on public relief. The one factor that was not in scarce supply at the time was labor.

The central idea to which Malthus returns again and again is that "saving, pushed to excess, would destroy the motive to production." Even if he meant that planned saving, as distinct from planned investment, when pushed to excess would destroy "the motive to production," his argument would be suspect under the circumstances then prevailing. But "the principle of saving" for Malthus always means "saving from the stock which might have been destined for immediate consumption, and adding it to that which is to yield a profit; or in other words, . . . the conversion of revenue into capital." And so his conclusion is that too high a propensity to save and invest causes trouble by encroaching upon consumption. This fallacious argument is summed up in a nutshell in the last pages of his book, where he decries the tendency "to recommend saving" while "under-stocked employments" are "glutting the markets of Europe." "As soon as the capitalists can begin to save from steady and improving profits, instead of from diminished expenditure . . . we may then begin safely and effectively to recover our lost capital by the usual process of saving a portion of our increased revenue to add to it."

Malthus' policy recommendations are designed to slow down the rate of capital accumulation and to encourage "unproductive consumption" on the part of landlords. His earlier defense of the Corn Laws, therefore, fitted in very nicely with the reasoning of his general treatise. He suggested public work schemes to alleviate unemployment, but on grounds that bear no resemblance to Keynes's proposals. In private correspondence Ricardo and Malthus had discussed the advisability of putting idle labor to work on public projects like road building. Ricardo, of course, did not think that public works would remedy the postwar depression. If capital were being used to capacity, spending on public works would simply raise the demand for consumer goods; inflation would then transfer resources from the private to the public sector without affecting the total volume of employment. Though this sounds like the discredited "Treasury View" of the 1930's, it had some merit in the circumstances of the day. Malthus, at any rate, agreed with Ricardo, adding that public projects created no additional spending. In his *Principles,* Malthus swung over to public work spending as a temporary measure of relief for unemployment. The proposal had two objections, he noted. It might prevent labor from "gradually accommodating itself to a reduced demand." This he thought could be corrected by giving low wages. Second, it would require an increase of taxation to finance the project, and this could well have the effect of reducing private investment. This objection, however, is precisely the virtue of public works for Malthus: "The objection to employing a large sum in this way, raised by taxes, would not be its tendency to diminish the capital employed by productive labor; because this, to a certain extent, is exactly what is wanted."

Ricardo and Malthus. The debate between Ricardo and Malthus on the possibility of general gluts would never have caused the confusion it did if both participants had made up their minds as to what Say's Law really implied. Ricardo did not regard the postwar depression as a harbinger of secular stagnation, as Malthus most certainly did. "You often appear to me to contend," wrote Ricardo to Malthus, "not only that production can go on so far without an adequate motive, but that it has actually done so lately, and that we are now suffering the consequences of it in stagnation." As a result, Ricardo was driven to insist on Say's Law as fully operative at every moment in time; this in itself suggests that he thought of Say's Law, not as denying the possibility of depression, but as affirming the long-run tendency of the economy to full-employment equilibrium. But instead of spelling out the process that would lead to automatic absorption of a constantly expanding output, Ricardo took refuge in the dogmatic assertion of Say's Identity. Malthus failed to challenge Say's Law effectively and provided no incentive to put the case correctly. Moreover, rarely mentioned, but always immediately below the surface of discussion, was the question of political bias. In Malthus, so far from the interests of landlords being always opposed to the rest of the community, economic prosperity is made to depend upon a prosperous landlord class. There is no doubt that Ricardo's advocacy of a rigid version of Say's Law, quite as much as his doctrine of the effect of improvements in agriculture, was motivated by a strong bias against landowners. The Law of

Comparative Cost demonstrated the advantages of repeal of the Corn Laws; observation of the political scene strongly suggested that repeal was impossible without weakening the influence of the landowning interests. In that sense, Malthus' opinions were politically dangerous and had to be opposed.

Such considerations, while they serve to explain the vehemence with which the problem of Say's Law was discussed, should not influence our judgment of the analytical issues. Malthus saw a problem, the problem of stagnation resulting from inadequate demand. He did not conceive the problem accurately and in analyzing it committed one analytical blunder after another. Ricardo's defense of Say's Law was dogmatic and hardly impeccable, but it was logical, given his premises and assumptions. Robert Torrens, a contemporary economist, summed it up when he said: "As presented by Mr. Ricardo, Political Economy possesses a regularity and simplicity beyond what exists in nature; as exhibited by Mr. Malthus, it is a chaos of original and unconnected elements." It is fortunate for the history of economics that good logic triumphed over bad. A victory for Malthus would have made economics the happy hunting-ground of every quack with panaceas designed to shore up the allegedly defective market economy. One can only marvel at Keynes's astounding assertion that "if only Malthus, instead of Ricardo, had been the parent stem from which 19th-century economics proceeded, what a much wiser and richer place the world would be today." No doubt, economic theory would have benefited from a continuing discussion over the meaning of Say's Law; the flaws in Malthus' argument, its unpalatable political overtones, and the anxiety to give "scientific" status to the case for a free market economy, unfortunately made such a constructive debate impossible. It took many years to realize that, as Hansen put it in his *Business Cycles* (1927): "The Say-Ricardo school, while fundamentally sound, left the problem [of business cycles] unsolved. As has so frequently been true of economic generalizations, it tackled the problem in terms of long-run tendencies, which in effect meant that it refused to recognize the problem at all. On the other hand, the Lauderdale-Malthus-Sismondi solution is logically untenable to anyone who will take the pains to think the problem through to the end."

NOTES FOR FURTHER READING

1. *The Law of Markets.* Apart from the relevant chapters in Ricardo's and in Mill's *Principles,* the outstanding primary sources on the Law of Markets are Say's *Letter to Malthus* (1820; reprinted 1936) and the essay by J. S. Mill,

"Of the Influence of Production on Consumption," *Essays on Some Unsettled Questions of Political Economy* (1844; reprinted 1948). There is also the famous exchange of letters between Malthus and Ricardo, which has to be read to be believed.

Schumpeter wrote what is probably the most brilliant single commentary on the role of Say's Law in classical economics: *History,* pp. 615–25. G. S. Becker and W. J. Baumol, "The Classical Monetary Theory: The Outcome of the Discussion," *Ec.,* 1952, reprinted with revisions in *EET,* is an important article in which the distinction between Say's Identity and Say's Equality was first broached. The Becker-Baumol article constitutes a prolegomena to D. Patinkin, *Money, Interest, and Prices* (1956), a book that ranks with Hicks's *Value and Capital* as a significant contribution to modern microeconomics; with reference to our theme, see pp. 44–45, 119–21, 181–84, and note L. Patinkin objects to Say's Equality as a misleading term because no classical economist showed exactly how the positive real-balance effect of a declining price level brings about recovery from a slump. This is perfectly true, but the same purist insistence on rigor would lead one to deny that there is such a thing as a classical theory of long-run prices, for no classical economist really demonstrated the existence, determinacy, and stability of equilibrium in a *single* commodity market. The classical writers did contemplate equilibrating adjustments in expenditure levels in response to variations of absolute prices and of the rate of interest. Their reasoning is loose and incomplete, but it is never inconsistent with Say's Equality as we would now state it.

J. S. Mill's position is analyzed in some detail by B. A. Belassa, "Mill and the Law of Markets," *QJE,* May, 1959; this article uses the terms "commodity-money" and "credit money" for what we have called "accounting money" and "circulating money." L. C. Hunter in a "Comment," *QJE,* February, 1960, delves deeper into the classical theory of saving and investment. In an article on "Mill and Cairnes on the Rate of Interest," *OEP,* February, 1959, the same author examines a set of unpublished notes that Cairnes sent to Mill as the latter was preparing the sixth edition of *Principles.* Cairnes held out for more emphasis on short-run monetary influences on the rate of interest, and Mill met him part way. Hunter is surprised that Cairnes's *Leading Principles* (1874) in no way reverts to this topic. But, in fact, the difference between Cairnes and Mill on this question is a minor one. Hunter exaggerates the inflexibility of classical real-interest theory. D. H. MacGregor, *Economic Thought and Policy* (1949), pp. 111–26, shows that many of Say's statements of the Law of Markets came close to expressing the Keynesian income = output concept.

A. W. Marget, *The Theory of Prices* (1942), Vol. II, chap. 1, subjects Keynes's allegation that all economists before him divorced value and monetary theory to an exhaustive examination. One of the "lessons of doctrinal history," Marget concludes, is that monetary theory in fact never lagged far behind developments in general value theory. There is additional material in Volume II that pertains to this theme (see, in particular, pp. 606–20 on Keynes's Law) but it must be read in its entirety. Whatever the ultimate verdict on Marget's attempt to resuscitate the quantity theory of money, no student should miss this supreme example of polemical scholarship, so amply documented that the footnotes virtually swallow the text. For an excellent account of Thornton's work and classical monetary theory in general see Schumpeter, *History,* pp. 276–99, 314–34 and 688–738; see also F. A. Hayek's introduction to the 1939 reprint of Thornton's *Paper Credit* (1802), pp. 36–58. M. W. Holtrop, "Theories of the Velocity of Circulation of Money in Earlier Economic Literature," *EH,* January, 1929, touches on a topic closely related to the theme of Say's Law. On the history of the forced-saving doctrine see F. A. Hayek, "The Development of the Doctrine of Forced Saving," *QJE,* November, 1932, and *Profits, Interest and Investment* (1939), chap. 7; and Viner, *Studies in the Theory of International Trade,* chap. 4, sec. 3. F. Machlup, "Forced or Induced Savings: An Exploration into Its Synonyms and Homonyms," *REStat,* February, 1943, relates the older versions to the more recent statements of the thesis.

2. *Malthus' Attack on Say's Law.* Keynes's famous eulogy on Malthus is to be found in his *Essays in Biography* (1933). Hutchison, following in Keynes's footsteps, traces a line of eighteenth-century underconsumptionists who were driven underground by Smith's theory of saving culminating in Say's Law: *A Review of Economic Doctrines, 1870–1929* (1953), pp. 346–56. Hutchison cites Mill as exposing the "trivial verbal character" and "extremely unrealistic assumptions" of the Law of Markets. Everyone must make up his own mind whether the denial of the possibility of secular stagnation from purely automatic market forces can ever be a "trivial" issue. See also Hutchison, "Bentham as an Economist," *EJ,* 1956, reprinted in *EET.* Bentham did most of his work in economics in the last two decades of the eighteenth century and carried on the kind of macroeconomic monetary analysis that Cantillon and his contemporaries had developed.

For the historical and intellectual context in which the controversy on gluts was fought out after Ricardo's death see Blaug, *Ricardian Economics,* chap. 5. G. J. Stigler, "Sraffa's Ricardo," *AER,* September, 1953, offers some cogent comments on the inconclusive debate between Ricardo and Malthus. Malthus' arguments are examined afresh and with great clarity by R. G. Link, *Theories of Economic Fluctuations* (1959), chap. 2. See also Schumpeter, *History,* pp. 480–83. Several commentators claim to have found many of the "building blocks" of the *General Theory* in Malthus. R. W. Corry, however, demonstrates succinctly that Malthus cannot be regarded as a precursor of Keynes: "Malthus and Keynes—A Reconsideration," *EJ,* December, 1953; see also Blaug, *Ricardian Economics,* Appendix B. Nor was Malthus a strong advocate of government spending; his views on this question were perfectly in keeping with majority opinion in his day: R. W. Corry, "The Theory of Economic Effects of Government Expenditure in English Classical Political Economy," *Ec.,* May, 1958.

Malthus' use of a particular standard of value to establish the possibility of general gluts is explained by Myint, *Theories of Welfare Economics,* chap. 3. Malthus' contributions to demand theory are analyzed in two valuable articles by V. E. Smith, "The Classicists's Use of 'Demand,'" *JPE,* June, 1951, and "Malthus's Theory of Demand and Its Influence on Value Theory," *SJPE,* October, 1956. The first of these two pieces is particularly useful for a review of all the leading classical writers on demand.

For a discussion of Harrodian dynamics with references to the recent literature see D. Hamberg, *Economic Growth and Instability* (1956), chap. 3, and H. Pilvin, "A Geometric Analysis of Recent Growth Models," *AER,* September, 1952.

The real anti-saver of the age was not Malthus but the Earl of Lauderdale, whose oft-mentioned but little read *Inquiry* was published in 1804. Fetter gives an excellent critique of Lauderdale's attack on Smith's doctrine of thrift: "Lauderdale's Oversaving Theory," *AER,* June, 1945. For a lighter article considering the causes of Lauderdale's neglect see A. V. Cole, "Lord Lauderdale and his 'Inquiry,'" *SJPE.* June, 1956. Finally, there is R. L. Meek, "Thomas Joplin and the Theory of Interest," *REStud,* XVII, 1950–51, 3, No. 47. Joplin was a contemporary writer on currency questions who, unlike Malthus, did treat saving as a function of income. The opening section of Meek's article, however, contains some doubtful comments on Ricardo's theory of saving.

Chapter 6

JOHN STUART MILL

ALL THROUGH the second half of the nineteenth century Mill's *Principles of Political Economy* was the undisputed bible of economists. In the 1890's Marshall's treatise began to dislodge Mill in the English-speaking countries, but as late as 1900 Mill's work was still the basic textbook in elementary courses in both British and American universities. The extraordinary durability of the book was due in large part to its blending of classical and anticlassical elements. It represented the final synthesis of Ricardian doctrine with many of the qualifications and refinements introduced by Ricardo's critics, hinting just enough at the "real cost" of capital and the role of demand in determining prices to reconcile Ricardian notions with the subjective theory of value. Its comprehensive treatment of almost all branches of the subject gave it a unique place in economic literature. And its loftiness of tone and elegance of style further enhanced its authority.

It is an easy book to read. Indeed, it is too readable. The argument flows along so smoothly that the reader is lulled into agreement. The whole book exudes immense confidence, and even when Mill is uncertain about a particular question—as we now know he was from his private correspondence with Cairnes—he does not permit the text to be affected by theoretical doubt. Disparate ideas drawn from divergent lines of approach are allowed to co-exist without any attempt at unification. Mill studiously avoids any claim to analytical originality, although such claims would have been justified. The aim was simply, as he says in the Preface, to write an up-to-date *Wealth of Nations* "adapted to the more extended knowledge and improved idea of the present age." The subtitle of the book reveals his intention to treat abstract principles in relation to "their applications to social philosophy," and, while he does not slight theoretical problems, the tone of the book subtly suggests the unimportance of rigorous analysis for its own sake.

But for all its theoretical eclecticism, or perhaps just because of it,

Mill's *Principles* affords the best opportunity for a review of classical theory as a whole. Bailey's *Critical Dissertation on the Nature of Value* (1825), Longfield's *Lectures on Political Economy* (1834), and Senior's *Outline of the Science of Political Economy* (1836) are more exciting to read. They cover only part of the ground, however, and do not adequately convey the flavor of classical economics applied to practical problems, without which the postponement of "the marginal revolution" to the 1870's becomes difficult to understand. For better or for worse, it was primarily in Mill's formulation that the ideas of the writers in the first half of the nineteenth century reached the founders of the "new economics" in the second half.

READER'S GUIDE

Laws of Production and Distribution. The "Preliminary Remarks" that open the book launch straightway into a condemnation of mercantilism, concluding in a passage emphasizing the "realness" of economic relationships: "money, as money, satisfies no want." In his anxiety to discredit monetary panaceas, Mill forgets the store-of-value function of money, although, as we shall see, he is perfectly aware of it elsewhere in the book. Wealth (*read:* income) is defined as the sum of all goods bought and sold in the market; the question as to whether services are to be included is postponed to Book I, chapter 3. There follows a brief sketch of economic development since ancient times, issuing in the famous distinction between the laws of production, given by technical conditions, and the laws of distribution, governed by "human institutions" and "the laws and customs of society." By this distinction Mill means not that the pricing of productive factors—functional distribution—is independent of the technical conditions of production, but that the personal distribution of income among "the three main classes of society" is influenced by the distribution of property, itself the product of historical change. Nothing can be done about the laws of production, for they partake of "the character of physical truths." But the laws of distribution are subject to human decision and are capable of being altered even under a regime of private property. This distinction became one of the chief props of Mill's thinking, reconciling the ideas of Ricardo and Malthus with his own comprehensive reform proposals.

Strictly interpreted, the distinction between the two kind of laws is untenable, for it implies independence of the forces determining the size of "the cake" from those governing its "slices." But, taken loosely, it says nothing more than that propositions about productive efficiency hold true in a way that propositions about distributive equity do not. Everything depends on how such a distinction is actually applied in a particular case. Mill's division of subject matter into "production" and "distribution," treated, respectively, in Books I and II, is open to question even when the distinction between the two kinds of laws is accepted. By treating the problem of value in Book III *after* discussing production and distribution, he more or less suggests that distribution has nothing to do with valuation, being a product of historical accident.

The Doctrine of Productive Labor. The first chapter of Book I considers the relationship between land and labor as the two "original" factors of production. Chapter 2 deals with labor alone and section 2 gives an excellent statement of the classical notion of a wages fund: the time-consuming discontinuous character of the productive process requires "food produced in advance." From this it follows that profit = interest must be a reward for the sacrifice of "abstinence" on the part of those who can afford to wait for the final product. No passage in the entire book shows more clearly that the wages fund doctrine, based as it is on the idea that capital is nothing but a series of "advances," logically implies a waiting theory of interest.

Chapter 2, sections 7–8, and the whole of chapter 3 are devoted to a defense of Smith's concept of productive labor. At the outset Mill dismisses the controversy over what constitutes productive labor as semantic and taxonomic, involving no question of substance. Productive labor is productive of "wealth," and "it is essential to the idea of wealth to be susceptible of accumulation." Wealth, he notes, consists, in essence, of tools, machines, and the skill of the labor force, the stock of what we would now call nonhuman plus human capital. Although it is "permanence" not "materiality" that is decisive, Mill feels that no great harm is done by following traditional usage and defining productive labor as productive of "material objects." He adds, however, that labor services expended in acquiring skills or in protecting property are to be considered as productive. Mill leaves no doubt about the purpose of the distinction. It is to show that the rate of capital accumulation is a function of the proportion of the labor force employed "productively." Profits earned by employing unproductive labor are merely transfers of income; unproductive labor does not generate net value added.

The distinction between the two kinds of labor is applied to consumption in section 5 of chapter 3. The only productive consumers are productive laborers, but not all consumption by productive laborers is productive consumption: "that alone is productive consumption, which goes to maintain and increase the productive powers of the community." This idea goes back to the physiocrats; it is the notion that a certain quantity of the consumer goods produced in an economy, namely wage goods, enters as necessary inputs into the production of manpower itself in the household sector. Productive consumption is simply an input necessary to maintain human capital intact. If wages are at subsistence, the whole of the wages bill is required for productive consumption. Mill concedes, however, that workers do consume some "luxuries," and in that sense a portion of wages is consumed unproductively. The fact remains that consistent classical income accounting implies deducting all productive consumption from the gross national product to arrive at the true net national product = profits plus rent; this net product is entirely created by productive labor and is spent entirely on investment goods and *true* consumption goods, that is, nonwage goods. The logic of this is impeccable, although the statistical difficulty of segregating wages into its productive and unproductive components might be insurmountable. The point is, however, that only a society bent on maximizing capital accumulation would want to adopt this kind of accounting. And Mill is not at all sure, as Smith was, that it is really desirable to try to increase the rate of growth. The closing passage of chapter 3 conveys his characteristic emphasis on distribution.

Theory of Capital. The next three chapters contain Mill's theory of capital, "a stock, previously accumulated, of the products of former labor." Chapter 4, section 1, develops Ricardo's proposition that the demand for labor is greater, the greater the capitalist's reinvestment of earnings and the smaller his expenditure on goods for personal consumption. Section 2 notes that wages generally exceed the physiological minimum and continues to drive home the idea that wages are "paid out of capital," that capital consists essentially of advances to workers. This chapter is a preliminary to the celebrated fifth chapter, which contains the four "fundamental propositions respecting capital."

The first of these propositions is that "industry is limited by capital," which seems to mean that employment cannot be augmented except by capital formation. In the course of expounding this proposition Mill assumes that capital is fully employed, but he goes on immediately to discuss the possibility of excess capacity (sec. 2). When there is excess capacity, governments can "create" capital, an idea that Ricardo had strenuously denied. Capital formation as such never produces unemployment (sec. 3). Here we have the first of a series of barbs at "authors of the highest name" who have held out the prospect of investment running into the barrier of limited demand, arguing that therefore "the unproductive expenditure of the rich is necessary to the employment of the poor."

The second fundamental proposition states that "capital is the result of saving," which links up with the third proposition that "capital, although the result of saving, is nevertheless consumed." This is of course Adam Smith's saving-is-spending theorem, which underlies Say's Law of Markets. Taken strictly, it implies Say's Identity. But Say's Identity denies the possibility of excess capacity, which has already been admitted under the first proposition. It should be evident now that, however much the saving-is-spending theorem encouraged thinkers to ignore "hoarding," its essential meaning was that saving and investment created effective demand just as surely as did consumption expenditures.

In sections 6 and 7 Mill notes that "the great part" of the income of the current year is currently produced: the average durability of capital goods is only about ten years. This accounts for the fact that countries recover so quickly after destructive wars; skills, technical knowledge, and the more durable buildings usually remain unimpaired and make possible a rapid recovery.

Mill turns now to the surprising growth of wealth during the Napoleonic Wars, surprising because classical theory suggests that wartime spending by the state on armaments reduces capital investment in the private sector. The war, Mill declares, gave rise to "unfounded theories . . . tending to exalt unproductive expenditure, at the expense of productive"—another jibe at Malthus. In his youth Mill had joined Ricardo in denying the stimulating effects of war expenditures. Now, however, he was prepared to admit the income-generating effects of public spending. Suppose, for the sake of argument, he begins, we assume that capital is fully employed during a war. Then, why prosperity? Because government loans for war purposes reduce wages and the workers in this way really pay for the war. The only reason given for this peculiar conclusion is that "the loan cannot have been taken from that portion of the capital of the country which consists of tools, machinery and buildings," a dogmatic assertion that contradicts the fact, stated a few pages earlier, that the maintenance of capital involves annual charges on production. Mill then goes on to show that in rich countries government loans do not in fact siphon off funds that would have been invested in the private sector but, rather, absorb excess capital that would have flowed abroad or have been spent on luxury goods. In a footnote, he grants that war can divert labor as well as capital from productive employment and hence that wages need not fall in wartime. This possibility is dismissed in the case of England, which had a comparatively small standing army: government revenues during the Napoleonic Wars were derived from taxes on circulating capital, at the expense of the civilian labor force.

The most controversial proposition in the chapter on capital is the fourth: "demand for commodities is not demand for labour" (sec. 9). Sir Leslie Stephen described it as a "doctrine so rarely understood, that its complete apprehension, is, perhaps, the best test of an economist." But Cannan called it "the biggest blunder made in economic theory in modern times," and Jevons, Sidgwick, and Nicholson all commented adversely on it. Even Marshall, always partial to Mill, agreed that it "expresses his meaning badly." What Mill was driving at was the idea that the total volume of employment is a direct function of the rate of capital accumulation and that consumers' demand, while it determines the allocation of labor between different industries, influences total employment only at one remove. Since the decision as to whether the proceeds of sales will be used to reconstitute the wages fund rests with the capitalist, demand for commodities is not *necessarily* demand for labor. Having made the decision to save a certain portion of his income, the only way in which an individual can *directly* influence the demand for labor is by substituting labor services for commodities in his own consumption. This is Ricardo's old argument, laid down in the chapter on machinery, that the interest of labor is best served by the most labor-intensive kind of spending on personal consumption.

All this is unobjectionable when properly interpreted, but the dozen pages explaining this proposition in Mill's book are among the most tortuous in the whole literature of economics. Among other things, it is never made clear whether it is supposed to hold regardless of the existence of unemployed resources. Mill seems to be assuming full employment by affirming that an increased demand for labor in one industry must draw labor out of another. In that case it seems to follow tautologically that an increased demand for consumer goods cannot increase the demand for labor. But Mill's object is to show that the demand for labor will in fact fall off under full employment when resources are shifted into the manufacture of additional consumer goods: an increase in consumption means a decrease of investment, and investment under the wages fund doctrine can only mean "advancing" more wage goods to labor in subsequent periods.

Given the rigid discontinuity of production implied in the wages fund doctrine, it is perfectly true that an increase in aggregate consumption demand under full employment impairs the wages fund and so leads to a decline in the amount of employment demanded at any given wage rate.[1] But on the same grounds, the Ricardian redistribution of "unproductive consumption" from commodities of personal consumption to the purchase of direct labor services cannot add to employment but will in effect raise wages, which in turn redounds unfavorably upon the production of wage goods. But Ricardo, of course, applied the argument to a situation in which some labor is unemployed, from which it follows that demand for commodities *is* demand for labor. Mill's proposition would have seemed less paradoxical if he had carefully distinguished between the cases of full employment and underemployment.

The Wages Fund Doctrine. Before proceeding further we must consider the wages fund doctrine in a little more detail. This doctrine has been so frequently ridiculed that it is difficult nowadays to appreciate its partial validity and in particular to realize that it marks the beginning of all sound thinking on the nature of capital. Usually we think of capital as a sum of money, the total value of assets of a business firm. But if we lift the "veil" of money, what are the characteristics of the real capital stock that the sum of money represents? Production is time-consuming, but workers must be hired and equipment installed before there are final products ready for sale. The capital fund of a firm, therefore, is nothing but the power to purchase labor and the products

---

[1] Mill's argument implies a difference equation. If W = the total output of wheat available as a wages fund, N = the total amount of labor employed (ignoring fixed capital), a = the labor-input coefficient, and w = the real wage rate, then this year's employment depends upon last year's harvest and upon the real wage rate.

$$(1) \qquad N_t = W_{t-1} w .$$

This year's harvest = the wages fund is determined by the labor-input coefficients and the total amount of labor available.

$$(2) \qquad W_t = N_t \cdot a .$$

Substituting, we have

$$(3) \qquad W_t = W_{t-1} \left(\frac{a}{w}\right) .$$

The reduced form of this difference equation is

$$(4) \qquad W_t = W_o \left(\frac{a}{w}\right)^t .$$

But in fact a certain proportion u of W is spent on luxury goods and labor services. Eq. (1) should be rewritten as

$$(5) \qquad N_t = \frac{W_{t-1}}{w} - W_{t-1}\left(\frac{u}{w}\right) = W_{t-1}\left(\frac{1-u}{w}\right) .$$

The amount of labor producing wage goods equals the total amount of labor supported out of W minus the amount of unproductive labor. Substituting (5) into (2) and writing it in reduced form we have

$$(6) \qquad W_t = W_o \frac{a(1-u)^t}{w} .$$

With sample values of $w = 2$, $a = 4$, $u = \frac{1}{3}$, we have $[a(1-u)^t]/w = (1.33)^t$: W and N grow at a compound rate of 33 per cent per year and any increase in u lowers the rate of growth.

of other firms over the period during which the firm has no output to sell. Since labor itself spends its wages on finished goods, the firm's capital in real terms consists simply of other firms' products. If we add together the capital of all the firms in the economy, we arrive at society's real capital stock as the sum of all intermediate products on the way to consumption.

The real meaning of capital emerges even more clearly if we think of the whole economy as a giant firm. This giant firm, like any other firm, must pay workers for their services as they are rendered before the services have ripened into consumers' goods. To tide itself over this period, the firm must be in possession of a stock of finished consumer goods as well as semifinished goods capable of being added to inventories as they are depleted. All these goods, whether finished or unfinished, represent produced "means of production" in the sense that they are all in the process of being converted into final output. In other words, the real capital fund of a society can be defined as the sum total of all produced goods-in-process in the hands of producers, wholesalers, and retailers; in practice, this amounts to an inventory of consumer goods and raw materials as well as plant and equipment.

What the classical economists did was to seize on a part of the total stock of produced inputs, namely, wage goods consumed by workers, identifying the part with the whole. On the notion that a worker's staple article of consumption is wheat, they treated agriculture as the wage-goods industry. The fact that wheat becomes available in the form of annual harvests, which must be willy-nilly stored as a "fund" for future consumption if its actual use is to be more or less continuous throughout the year, made it possible to define capital simply as "advances" to workers to support them from seedtime to harvest. In practice, the employer does not "advance" anything; he merely buys labor services. But in real terms, he does exchange past output for current labor before current labor has produced anything: wages are paid out of "capital" and capital is nothing but "inchoate wealth" entering into the production of current goods and services. Marx objected to the wages fund doctrine on the grounds that capitalists do not really "advance" wages to workers; on the contrary, since wages are usually paid after they are earned—at the end of the week—workers are invariably creditors of their employers. But the question is whether workers get paid before the output that they have produced has been sold. In some cases, only a few days are required to produce an article, in which case the employer benefits from the convention of paying workers every seven days. But, on the average, the period of fabrication greatly exceeds a week even in manufacturing, and the employer does, in fact, advance wages to the workers.

The idea that capital is to be understood in terms of a time interval between production and consumption is implicit in the wages fund doctrine, and it is from this idea that all later work on capital stems. But the proposition that this time interval can be identified with the annual period of production in agriculture invested the whole analysis with artificiality. At best, the theory emphasizes the complementarity of capital and labor, insisting that in the absence of an increase in the rate of capital accumulation aggregate wages can not be permanently raised. The wage rate, it implies, is not subject to an arbitrary bargaining decision but depends upon the growth of previous investment. But, at worst, it suggests that the whole of the wages fund is necessarily exhausted in any period and that the fund is rigidly predetermined by technical conditions; it indicates the impossibility of increasing payrolls by curtailing the "unproductive consumption" of capitalists and seems to depict the aggregate demand for labor as perfectly inelastic at any moment in time.

In point of fact, however, the wages fund doctrine was rarely employed by the leading economists to deprecate trade-union action to raise wages. The more common practice was to exploit the doctrine to emphasize the necessity for family limitation. The wages fund as "demand" for labor was set against the existing "supply"; the wage rate was said to be determined by dividing the number of workers into the total sum of money available for wage payments; it followed that to raise wages it was necessary either to raise the dividend or to lessen the divisor, to produce more or to procreate less. Although the theory was frequently presented as an ordinary case of the working of the law of demand and supply, no notion of a schedule of demand and supply prices was presented and no attempt was made to define a true equilibrium wage rate. Nor was it made clear how the wages fund theory was related to the subsistence theory of wages. It is tempting to say that the wages fund doctrine accounts for the demand side, while the subsistence theory is concerned with the supply side. But, since the latter holds in the long run, while the former pertains to the short run, this raises as many questions as it settles. It is true to say, however, that the wages fund doctrine contains whatever theory of the demand for labor was developed by the classical economists.

A good example of how a wages fund theorist might combine classical doctrine with sympathy for trade unions is Mill's own treatment of the Combination Laws in one of the last chapters of the *Principles* (Book V, chap. 10, sec. 5). "It is a great error," he remarks, "to condemn *per se* and absolutely, either trade unions or the collective action of strikes." In the absence of unions, the monopsony power of the employer—shades of Adam Smith's "tacit and universal combination not to raise wages"—frequently results in wages below the competitive level. Unions, therefore, are to be welcomed as a countervailing force: "far from a hindrance to a free market for labor, [they] are the necessary instrumentality of that free market." When Mill retracted the wages fund doctrine in *Fortnightly Review* (1869), he interpreted it as denying that unions could raise wages, or at least "limited their operations in that respect to the somewhat earlier attainment of a rise which the competition of the market would have produced without them." But his discussion in the *Principles* belies this interpretation. And, lest it be thought that Mill is unique, it is worth mentioning that the so-called founder of the wages fund doctrine, John Ramsay McCulloch, advanced the same argument about monopsony in the labor market in his influential *Essay on Wages* (1826).

Advance Economics and Synchronization Economics. What, if anything, remains of the wages fund doctrine? In a developed economy, goods that can be produced only at comparatively long intervals do not form a very large part of society's consumable output; most goods can be produced fairly continuously throughout the year. It would be unrealistic to think that "roundabout production" depends on the prior existence of a stock of such goods. But the fact remains that such accumulated stocks of consumer goods are constituents of capital and that the amount payable in wages during any slice of time is limited by the quantity of wage goods that can be produced during its course with the aid of equipment inherited from the past. In a stationary state this consideration would have no significance. Although production is time consuming, a stationary economy functions *as if* output in every period is consumed in the same period: the stock of consumer goods available at the beginning of each year is used up through the year, but it is always exactly replaced at the end. In the stationary state the flow of consumption and the flow of productive services are perfectly synchronized. In this kind of economy it is strictly true that wages are paid out of current product. But in a growing economy wages are in part paid out of past product and the stock of goods-in-the-pipelines has real significance for the functioning of the system. This assertion is sometimes denied, and it is useful to categorize the denial as involving "synchronization economics." The opposite view, which insists on the importance of the time structure of production, we will call "advance economics." The coinage is Schumpeter's, and it will serve us in good stead when we come to consider the controversy that raged over the Austrian theory of capital at the end of the century. Suffice it to say that the Austrian theory rests upon "advance economics" and in this way links up with the wages fund doctrine. To throw out the wages fund theory *in toto* is to cut oneself off from the key to the meaning of real capital that it furnished. It was a bad theory of wages, but it had the ingredients of a good theory of capital.

The Machinery Question. Chapter 6, section 1, distinguishes between fixed and circulating capital in the traditional manner, with special emphasis, however, upon fixed capital sunk in land. Section 2 takes up Ricardo's doctrine about the adverse effect upon employment of increasing the ratio of fixed to working capital. The argument is dismissed as being inapplicable to cases other than the conversion of arable land into pasture. But the thesis that the introduction of machinery leads automatically to the reabsorption of displaced labor through price reductions stimulating demand is also rejected; lowered prices do not by themselves foster additional investment because "demand for commodities is not demand for labor." The increased demand consequent upon lower prices must be set against the loss in purchasing power of displaced workers. Still, in the end, Mill does grant the gist of the theory of "automatic compensation" and denies that the substitution of machinery for labor injures the working class even in the short run (sec. 3). Moreover, he concludes that "there is probably no country whose fixed capital increases in a ratio more proportional to its circulating." And, while Ricardo had frowned on state interference with the rate of technical advance, Mill does not hesitate to recommend measures to moderate its rapidity.

Notice that the closing page of this chapter makes the ratio of fixed to circulating capital a technical matter, not a function of relative factor prices. This implies that the portion of the accumulated capital stock actually used as a counterpart of wage payments is not a function of the wage rate and hence that there is no such thing as a demand curve for labor. The rate of growth of total capital is a function of the rate of profit; it is only by affecting the rate of profit that changes in wage rates influence the demand for labor. Apparently, once the capital stock is given, purely technical conditions determine the proportion devoted to "supporting" labor.

There is a certain confusion in Mill's presentation of the machinery question because, like Ricardo, he seems at one point to be analyzing the substitution of capital for labor at a given state of technical knowledge, and then suddenly to address himself to genuine innovations, cost-reducing improvements in techniques. The theory of "automatic compensation," framed for the first time by McCulloch in the 1820's, is certainly intended to apply to labor-saving innovations. This theory, incidentally, is more than the naïve argument that all technically displaced labor will necessarily be absorbed in the making of the machines themselves. The argument rests on the idea that innovations must under perfect competition result in price reductions and the expansion of output. If demand is at all elastic, total receipts rise and the employer will increase his expenditures either on consumption or on investment. If demand is unresponsive to lower prices, purchasing power in the hands of consumers is freed for spending on other goods. Directly or indirectly, laborsaving machinery entails the increase of output and the consequent reabsorption of displaced labor. The adjustment is a slow one and may leave pockets of unemployment for some periods of time. For this reason, most classical economists, including McCulloch, recommended government assistance to the victims of technological unemployment. No one went as far as Mill did, however, in suggesting direct interference with private decisions to introduce new machinery.

The Rate of Growth of the Factors of Production. Chapter 7, section 1, contains the offhand remark that "by far the largest portion" of total capital consists of working capital, although in the previous chapter Mill remarks upon "the enormous fixed capital now embarked in the cotton manufacture." This chapter is devoted to a consideration of the forces determining the general productivity of resources in different countries. It is full of good sense, though the subject does not lend itself to rigorous treatment. What is emphasized throughout is the crucial element of people's attitudes to pecuniary goals. In section 4, Mill implicitly classifies innovations into laborsaving, landsaving, and capitalsaving, although the terminology used is different. Chapter 8, on the division of labor, adds little to Adam Smith's treatment and may be passed over without loss. The next chapter contains one of the first discussions in economic literature on the forces making for increasing returns of scale. It is heavily indebted to a remarkable book, *Economy of Machinery and Manufactures* (1833), by Charles Babbage, which is quoted without stint. Mill predicts an increase in the scale of business firms in the course of economic progress, a prediction that is often attributed to Marx. The advantages of scale, Mill suggests, must be set off against the dangers of oligopoly and spontaneous agreement to restrict entry and keep up prices: "where competitors are so few, they always end up by agreeing not to compete. They may run a race of cheapness to ruin a new candidate, but as soon as he has established his footing they come to terms with him." (sec. 3). Natural monopolies should be nationalized, Mill concludes. The last section (sec. 4) of chapter 9 lays the groundwork for the case in favor of *petite culture,* which Mill develops at greater length in Book II.

Chapter 10 takes up the Malthusian theory of population, laid down as an axiomatic truth (secs. 2–3). Mill denies that the desire to "keep up with the Joneses" is an effective force for family limitation among the working class in England—this assertion is retracted in Book IV, chapter 7, sec. 3. The elasticity of supply of labor in response to a rise in wages is said to be very high. Nevertheless, the rate of population growth has been slackening since the census of 1821 and "subsistence and employment in England have never increased more rapidly than in the last forty years [1862]" (sec. 3).

Chapter 11 is taken up with the theory of saving: "abstinence from present consumption for the sake of future goods." The rate of saving is made a function of the rate of interest (sec. 2), but the parameters of the functions are discussed in detail under the heading of "the effective desire of accumulation" (sec. 3). This chapter, together with the earlier chapter 7 and section 1 of chapter 13, contains the essence of the classical contribution to the theory of economic development.

In chapter 12 we meet at last with the law of diminishing returns to labor in the cultivation of given land, stated in terms of a "given state of agricultural skill and knowledge"—an improvement in presentation due to Senior—and verified by the extension of cultivation to inferior soil. Mill leaves no doubt that he is a disciple of Ricardo when he declares this general law of agricultural industry to be "the most important proposition in political economy." Section 3 takes up the cudgels against Carey for holding that land in a young country is actually taken up in inverse order of its fertility. Mill goes on to reiterate Ricardo's analysis of improvements in agriculture but goes much deeper in tracing the forces offsetting diminishing returns. Indeed, his list of offsetting factors is so impressive as to throw doubt on the existence of historically diminishing returns in agriculture. Chapter 13 reviews the previous three chapters and concludes that economic progress must be conceived as a race between technical change and diminishing returns in agriculture. In section 2 Mill concedes that, since the 1820's, technical change in England has outstripped the forces making for rising wheat prices; capital has increased faster than population, and the standard of living has risen.

Socialism. We come now to Book II, dealing with the laws of distribution. The first chapter, "Of Property," defies a précis. It is deservedly the most famous chapter in the book and marks the first appearance of the subject of socialism in a major treatise on economics. In many ways it is less dated than other parts of Mill's book. No doubt the ideas of Saint-Simon and Fourier, which Mill discusses, bear little resemblance to the more familiar doctrines of Marx. And Mill's critique of contemporary objections to socialism have little relevance today. Likewise, the dismissal of the problem of central planning strikes the modern reader as superficial. But now that most economists are agreed that economic theory as such can say little of general validity about the respective merits of capitalism and socialism, the final passage of section 3 has all the more bearing on the great debate. Mill's treatment of socialist theory is extremely sympathetic, but he really differs from socialists on the fundamental question: the social ills experienced under capitalism are not traced by Mill to the private ownership of property but rather to rampant individualism and inadequate safeguards against the abuse of property rights. Notice, too, the distinction that Mill draws between communism—a society in which income is equalized regardless of productivity—and socialism, which retains the incentives of differential pecuniary rewards. This distinction is identical to the one Marx drew between "each according to his ability" under socialism and "each according to his need" under communism.

Custom and the Laws of Distribution. Chapter 2 continues the theme and argues that labor does not have a "right to the whole product" because the supply price of abstinence is in fact positive (sec. 1). Section 3 opens Mill's attack on the institution of inheritance with a plea for progressive death duties to reduce inequalities in the distribution of income. The supply price of land is zero, and hence property rights in land are sanctioned only by expediency; but, in fact, landlords are poor improvers (secs. 5–6). Chapter 3 notes briefly that few land-tenure systems in the world, other than the English and the Scottish, duplicate the tripartite class structure of society as a whole in agriculture alone. This is precisely why the Ricardian system proved difficult to export and never won general acceptance on the Continent. Chapter 4, on competition and custom, is a characteristic Millian warning against the hasty application of competitive models to the real world. Mill's distinction between custom and competition as stages in world history was very probably the source of inspiration for Maine's well-known contrast between "status" and "contract." Chapter 5 deals with slavery but says very little about the economics of a slave state. Chapters 6 and 7 take up the issue of peasant proprietorship, a cause that Mill made his own. The topic has no contemporary interest and may be skipped. The same holds true of the next three chapters, which discuss other systems of land tenure.

The Distributive Shares. Chapters 11–16 deal with the theory of class income distribution. In chapter 11 Mill defines that "elliptical" expression, the wages fund, as that part of working capital used to pay wages plus all expenditures on unproductive labor (sec. 1). The wages bill, being a flow, is equal to the wages fund multiplied by its turnover rate. Mill concedes that the entire wages fund need not be used up in any period but does not deduce the practical implications of this admission (sec. 2). He proceeds to deny what German writers have called the *Paralleltheorie*—that money wages always vary in the same direction as the price of food. But wages do follow the price of food "after an interval of almost a generation." Ricardo, Mill observes, assumed that wages are at long-run equilibrium, an assumption which "contains sufficient truth to render it permissible for the purposes of abstract science." Surprisingly enough, Mill minimizes the benefits of repeal of the Corn Laws on the living standards of the working class: unless workers restrict their numbers, real wages will rise only as long as it takes to "people down to their old scale of living." Sections 3–6 come back to the Malthusian theory of population. In the last pages of the chapter Mill reduces the whole debate over the theory to the question whether a slackening in the growth of population would or would not raise wages. He thinks it obvious that it would and rests his argument on that. He assumes as a matter of course that England is overpopulated but fails to distinguish between the advantages of *being* a smaller population and the advantages of *reducing the rate of growth* of population.

Chapters 12–13 spell out the practical implications of the Malthusian theory. In Mill's hands the Malthusian theory becomes a relentless argument in favor of family limitation, and every conceivable policy measure is judged in the light of its effects upon the birth rate. "Little improvement in morality can be expected until the producing [of] large families is regarded with the same feeling as drunkenness or any other physical excess." Mill never wrote better and with more fervor than in these chapters. He joins the hope of voluntary family limitation with the demand for female emancipation, and in chapter 13, section 1, comes close to hinting at the necessity for birth control.

Chapter 14 is a series of glosses on Book I, chapter 10, of the *Wealth of Nations*. But a new idea is now added to Smith's theory of the structure of wages, the concept of noncompeting groups. Mill seems to have arrived at this distinction by considering Smith's jewelers, in whom "great trust" is placed. Generalizing from this case, he concludes that there is a "hereditary distinction of caste" between different grades of labor, "a class of considerations which Adam Smith, and other political economists, have taken into far too little account" (sec. 2).

Chapter 15 rounds off the subject of distribution by analyzing profits as the "remuneration of abstinence," measured by "the current rate of interest on the best security," and expressing "the comparative value placed in the given society upon the present and the future" (sec. 1)—a good illustration of our earlier contention that the classical theory of profit is really a theory of interest. Section 5 states that "the cause of profit is, that labor produces more than is required for its support." This is no Marxian exploitation theory, different from the abstinence theory. The fact that labor is *physically* productive does not, in the absence of other considerations, prove that it is productive of *value*. The whole of capital is now said to consist of working capital; fixed capital itself is broken down to wages advanced in the past (sec. 6). In this sense, the rate of profit is made dependent after Ricardo on the ratio of profits to wages. Mill suggests amending Ricardo's dictum that profits depend on wages to read: profits depend upon the cost of labor. The cost of labor to the employer—by which Mill seems to mean wage costs per unit of output—is in turn explained as being a function of money wages and the average productivity of labor. This reformulation of Ricardo's fundamental theorem is grossly misleading: the rate of profit depends upon wage costs per unit of output only when the average productivity of capital is constant. Chapter 16 provides an excellent review of Ricardian rent theory, with a rebuttal of some of the more popular contemporary objections to it.

The Abstinence Theory of Interest. While we are in no position as yet to do justice to different theories of interest, it would be a pity to pass by the abstinence theory without further comment. The abstinence theory is not a complete theory of interest. It is merely a theory of the supply of savings and does not explicitly relate thriftiness to the demand for investment based upon productivity. Mill took the idea from Nassau Senior but improved its formulation. Senior talked of saving as if it were carried out under conditions of constant subjective cost; he completely ignored individual differences in the relative sacrifice involved in saving. This opened the theory to ridicule on the grounds that abstaining from the present enjoyment of income is hardly a pain cost to the average saver in the upper income brackets. The very phrase "reward for abstinence" suggested a glib justification for rentier income. But the supply schedule of savings is positively sloped, not perfectly horizontal, and the rate of interest is governed by the *marginal* supply price of abstinence. In a rich economy, this marginal sacrifice may well be very small and will certainly exceed the rate necessary to induce saving on the part of most individuals. The bulk of rentier income, as Mill makes clear, will consist of intramarginal surpluses, pure Ricardian "rents," which accrue to the saver through no effort of his own. And, of course, there is nothing in the theory that justifies the private ownership of property as such. If abstinence is required for capital accumulation, society as a whole can bear the burden just as well.

Abstinence has two possible meanings. It may refer to a sacrifice incurred in *creating* capital: by saving we add to the value of property, which we can do only by abstaining from consuming the current income of property. This is the meaning that Senior gave to "abstinence." But the present owner of property may have inherited his wealth, thus enjoying income from someone else's abstinence. Hence, Senior had to argue that return on inherited property is of the nature of rent, not interest. In Senior's version, abstinence would disappear in the stationary economy where net saving is zero by definition. Not until Mill do we get the Casselian notion of abstinence: a reward for forbearing to *consume* one's capital. Property confers on the owner the right of consuming his property; if he fails to do so, he is abstaining from exercising that power. But why should it be necessary to reward an owner for not consuming his wealth? Because everyone prefers consumption now to consumption later, partly on the rational ground that he may be dead before the later date comes and partly from a weak-minded failure to value future consumption at its true worth. The reasons for "time preference" are not very clearly indicated either by Senior or by Mill, but the essential idea is there. People will not refrain from using purchasing power they command unless they are assured of more consumption in the future for every amount given up in the present. They will insist on earning interest, and we can say that the rate of interest measures, as Mill put it, "the comparative value placed, in the given society, upon the present and the future."

It is sometimes said that the only reason the rate of interest is normally positive in a capitalist society is that the rate of profit is expected to be positive. When the productive advantage of utilizing capital is positive, present purchasing power is necessarily more valuable than an equal future amount because it permits its owner to invest in production and to earn a net surplus of receipts over costs. Hence, in a growing economy it is hardly surprising that people have positive time preference; the fact that the rate of interest is positive does not prove that people would consume their capital in the absence of a reward for holding it intact. But this argument is misleading, for it amounts to saying that the rate of interest is determined solely by productivity considerations, by the demand side in the loan market. The rate of interest is determined by both productivity and thrift. The role of abstinence is to act as a brake on the investment process; if saving involved no sacrifice whatever, its supply could presumably be augmented indefinitely. Hence, the mere fact that investment yielded a net return should produce a flow of savings large enough to permit investment to depress the net yield of capital to zero.

Moreover, interest created by pure time preference could exist in Adam Smith's "rude" society, where there is no property in capital and hence no profit. Suppose that some of the hunters want to consume more than their catch of deers, while others are willing to postpone consumption of their present catch. Then the latter could lend to the former out of today's catch against a promise of larger repayment in the future. If the "improvident" hunters exceeded the "provident," the rate of interest would be positive: a deer today would be more expensive than a deer tomorrow, and hence the prices of deers would no longer be determined by the quantity of labor required to produce them.

The abstinence theory of interest, like any theory of interest, attempts to explain the scarcity of capital. Why does the possession of capital yield an income? To say that capital is scarce is to imply that saving does involve some kind of social cost. The social cost of adding to the stock of capital is that of diverting current consumption to investment.

It is always possible indefinitely to increase future output by investing more and consuming less in the present. But the results of present investment become available only after a lapse of time: "waiting" is involved in every act of investment. It is because the supply of "waiting" is limited that capital is scarce.

"Waiting," no doubt, is merely a neutral synonym for "abstinence" when abstinence is given its Seniorian meaning of "the conduct of a person who abstains from the unproductive use of what he can command." But the waiting theory avoids the weaknesses of the abstinence theory *sensu stricto*. The abstinence theory assumes that saving is a function of the interest rate and stands or falls upon that ground. But it has always been recognized that the bulk of saving in a capitalist economy is business saving out of previously earned profits that may be little influenced by the rate of interest. Even Senior conceded that "capitals are generally formed from small beginnings by acts of accumulation, which become in time habitual. The capitalist soon regards the increase of his capital as the great business of his life; and considers the greater part of his profit more a means to an end than as a subject of enjoyment." Moreover, personal saving in the upper income brackets is largely involuntary, the result of income exceeding customary levels of expenditure. The effect of social taboos on the squandering of capital and the halo that surrounds the practice of saving is such as to leave little scope for interest-induced saving. Mill observed that "the savings by which an addition is made to the national capital usually emanate from the desire of persons to improve what is termed their conditions of life, or to make a provision for children or others." Still, this argument can be pressed too far. Saving is no doubt a function of the level of income and of its distribution, but it is also dependent upon the rate of interest. The advantage of speaking of waiting rather than abstinence is that we do not commit ourselves in advance on the nature of the supply curve of savings and, in addition, lay appropriate stress on the fundamental element of time, which alone creates the social sacrifice of adding to the stock of capital.

The abstinence theory of interest is more than a piece of crude apologetics. In essence, it is simply a logical deduction of the view of capital contained in the classical wages fund doctrine. If capital consists principally of "advances" to workers, the rate of interest is the reward of those who can afford to lend present goods in return for future goods.

The Theory of Value. Owing to the peculiar construction of Mill's book, factor pricing has already been discussed before anything has yet been said about the principles determining relative prices. Book III, chapter 1, at last plunges into the subject of value, beginning with a clarification of the meaning of such terms as "use value," "exchange value," "general exchange value," "price," and the like. Mill suggests that it is convenient to consider the absolute value of a commodity in relation to its purchasing power over all other goods whose relative prices do not vary. In other words, the price of wheat is compared to the fixed price of a composite commodity bundle. This will permit one to speak of a cost-reducing improvement in agriculture lowering the value of wheat, without having to specify all its attendant effects on other commodities (sec. 2). This is nothing but Marshall's method of partial equilibrium analysis. Mill goes on to point out that value is essentially a relative concept: "there cannot be a general rise of values" (sec. 4). He confines his discussion to goods produced under conditions of competition (sec. 5).

Chapter 2 introduces the concept of demand and supply. Manufacturing is carried on at constant cost, agriculture at increasing cost (sec. 2). Demand is defined as "effectual demand," not in Adam Smith's sense of the demand, which realizes the "natural price" of a commodity, but in the ordinary sense of desire backed up by purchasing power. Supply being the quantity offered for sale, and demand being the desire to purchase on the part of those who have the power, how can there be a ratio between a quantity and a desire, "two things not of the same denomination"? (sec. 3). Without drawing a demand curve, Mill is clearly cognizant of the fact that demand determines price because it is a schedule of quantities, itself a function of price. And, indeed, he shows quite clearly that an equilibrium price is one that equates demand and supply; it is not a ratio between demand and supply that determines prices: "the proper mathematical analogy is that of an *equation*" (sec. 4).

For the purpose of explaining relative prices he classifies goods into three groups: (1) perfectly inelastic supply or "absolutely limited in supply"; (2) perfectly elastic supply or "susceptible of indefinite multiplication without increase of cost"; and (3) relatively elastic supply or "susceptible of indefinite multiplication but not without increase of cost" (Chap. 2, secs. 3, 5, and chap. 3). (See Fig. 19.). The value of goods of the first class, he notes, is determined solely by demand and supply; that of the second class, by "another law," namely cost of production; and the third class by cost of production "in the most unfavorable existing circumstances." He has in mind the distinction between demand-determined prices (case 1) and supply-determined prices (case 2) but fails to point out that the law of demand and supply is perfectly

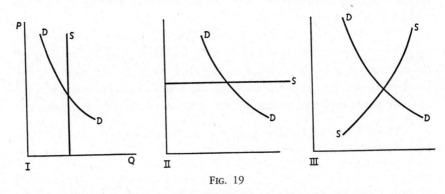

FIG. 19

general and embraces both cases. Moreover, he leaves no doubt that zero elasticity of supply is a phenomenon of the short run—all reproducible goods may be augmented in quantity, given sufficient time—while constant costs occur only in the long period. But Mill perpetuates Ricardo's misleading distinction between long-run prices determined by costs and short-run prices determined by demand and supply. This seems to be a mistake in terminology, however, not in substance. Although Mill spoke awkwardly of the law of demand and supply as a "law of value anterior to cost of production," in chapter 9 of Book III he observed that "cost of production would have no effect on value if it could have none on supply."

Toward the end of chapter 3, section 1, Mill mistakenly defines the long-run price as average trend value of a series of short-run market prices. The distinction between the short and the long run is not in principle a distinction between a brief and a long period of time. And the least-square trend of a time series of prices does not represent the price in stationary long-run equilibrium.

Chapter 4 lays down the doctrine that value depends principally, and almost solely, on the quantity of labor required to produce goods (sec. 1). With equal ratios of capital to labor in all industries, relative prices are not affected by changes in wage rates (sec. 2). The prices of commodities produced by labor of different skills are affected by differences in relative wages, but, in considering "the causes of *variations* in value, quantity of labor is the thing of chief importance" (sec. 3). But wine and cloth produced by equal amounts of homogeneous labor will not sell at equal prices because wine is "called upon to yield profit during a longer period of time than the other," and "all commodities made by machinery are assimilated, at least approximately, to the wine in the preceding example" (sec. 5). The whole of section 5 is, in fact, an excellent review of Ricardo's first chapter on value—it takes Mill three pages to say what Ricardo said in thirty.

Chapter 4, section 6, and chapter 5 generalize the concept of rent to all goods and factors in inelastic supply. In such cases, prices are always determined by marginal costs, and "the price paid for a differential advantage in producing a commodity cannot enter into the general cost of production of the commodity." On the other hand, rent *is* an expense of production that affects price when the factor in question is subject to alternative uses. Chapter 6 summarizes the previous five chapters and calls for no special comments.

To round off the topic, the reader should turn now to chapters 15 and 16. Chapter 15 is a brief but interesting review of the old problem of the Ricardian quest for the philosopher's stone: an invariant unit of measurement by which to reduce the various productive services to a homogeneous amount of "productive power." "The desideratum sought by political economists," Mill remarks, "is not a measure of the value of things at the same time and place, but a measure of the value of the same thing at different times and places." This "desideratum" is impossible to attain, Mill contends. It is significant that he did not even contemplate the idea that the difficulty could be solved by a price index. He was perfectly well acquainted with the concept of index numbers but, like most of his contemporaries, did not believe it feasible to construct a price index of all goods. A "general measure of exchange value" being out of the question, Mill goes on to say, "writers have formed a notion, under the name of a measure of value which could be more properly termed a measure of cost of production," that is, "some means of ascertaining the value of a commodity by merely comparing it with the measure, without referring it specially to any other given commodity." This is an excellent statement of the meaning of Ricardo's "invariable measure of value." Mill does not explain, however, how such a "measure of cost of production" can be constructed.

Chapter 16, "Some Peculiar Cases of Value," marks the first appearance in economic literature of the problem of joint costs (sec. 1). Mill considers the case in which two goods are produced in fixed proportions, and he shows that the price of each product must be such as to clear its market, subject to the condition that the sum of the two prices equals their joint cost. The case of joint costs presents a new qualification to the labor theory of value. Even in a one-factor economy the relative prices of joint products—say, venison and deer skins—are determined by demand as well as by supply.

The Quantity Theory of Money. Chapter 7 is a standard nineteenth-century textbook treatment of the advantages of the precious metals as a medium of exchange. The closing page of this chapter states the "neutrality" of money in the most uncompromising fashion, but in chapter 8, section 2, we are told that people normally hold cash balances as "a reserve for future contingencies." An increase in the supply of money raises the level of prices proportionately *if* there are "no alterations of the proportions in the demand for different commodities." This is a perfect statement of what we earlier called a "neutral" distribution of extra cash in proportion to individual holdings. As did Cantillon, Mill realized that the process of increasing the quantity of money may alter relative prices. Barring that possibility and provided that the only means of payment are coins and redeemable paper, the value of money varies inversely with the quantity in circulation. Velocity is discussed in section 3, and the distinction between the motion theory and the rest theory of velocity is drawn. The Equation of Exchange $MV = PT$ is clearly expressed in words. Bank credit, which Mill excludes from M, complicates matters, and he is not willing simply to add bank credit to currency in circulation on the grounds that bank reserves consisting of legal tender money bear a constant ratio to deposits (sec. 4). He points out that a mere increase in M does not raise prices if the money is hoarded and that an increase of M that keeps pace with a rising T does not affect prices.

The Quantity Theory is said to be a straightforward application of the law of demand and supply, but in the next chapter the long-run value of gold and silver is made dependent upon cost of production. We have already noted that the quantity theory is not incompatible with "metallism," that is, the labor theory of value applied to the monetary metal. If gold rises above its "natural" price, the level of prices falls and gold producers can purchase all inputs for less gold; the output of gold then rises until gold is once again at its natural value. But, as Mill himself observes, gold being extremely durable and the gold stock large relative to the annual output of gold mines, such an adjustment takes place only slowly. Hence, the cost of production of gold has little influence on prices, which are largely governed by the quantity of money actually in circulation. But in long-run equilibrium a country will tend to circulate an amount of money consistent with a value of money corresponding to its cost of production (sec. 3).

Chapter 10, on bimetallism, contains nothing of importance. In the eagerness to refute the popular fallacy that capital can be created simply by turning the money crank, Mill denies that credit can do more than divert capital from one field to another—the full-capacity assumption he had earlier discarded in Book I (chap. 11, sec. 1). In his 1844 *Essays* Mill had accepted the forced-saving doctrine. In the first edition of the *Principles* he made no mention of it. But in the sixth edition, published in 1865, he added a footnote admitting that inflation can "create capital," even if the capital stock is already utilized at capacity, by drawing resources from the luxury-goods sector to the sector producing capital goods.

The rest of chapter 11 describes the nature of contemporary credit instruments, with copious quotations from Thornton. Chapter 12 shows that bank credit would act on prices just as would an increase in the supply of metals if the supply of credit were tied to the gold supply. Under a convertible paper standard, prices cannot rise for long without inducing a compensatory outflow of gold. But, when paper is inconvertible, an elastic currency may promote a speculative boom such as took place in 1824 leading to collapse in the following year: "this is the ideal extreme case of what is called a commercial crisis" (sec. 2). The crisis of 1847, however, was the result of a sharp rise in interest rates owing to a heavy draft on the money market produced by the railway boom and the unprecedented importation of corn. From section 4 on, chapter 12 contains little of interest, except for section 8, which denies the doctrine of the Currency School that a control of bank notes would in effect control checkbook credit.

Inflation. Chapter 13 deals at length with inconvertible paper currencies. A convertible currency cannot be issued to excess because the advantage of turning coins and notes into bullion keeps it in check (sec. 1). An inconvertible currency can be issued to excess, the test being whether the market price of bullion has risen above the mint price fixed prior to suspension of specie payments (sec. 2). This is merely a reproduction of Ricardo's argument, and a very uncritical reproduction at that. Sections 3 and 4 attack inflationary paper-money schemes on comparative static grounds. The Hume-Cantillon argument that the process of increasing M may stimulate T is paraphrased but dogmatically rejected on the grounds that the gains of some are matched by the losses of others: "there is no way in which a general and permanent rise of prices . . . can benefit anybody, except at the expense of somebody else" (sec. 5). Without making any reference to the existence or nonexistence of idle resources, Mill suddenly introduces a new proinflationary argument never contemplated by eighteenth-century economists. A rise in prices lowers the real value of debt and hence favors debtors against creditors; now "the productive class . . . generally owe large debts to the unproductive . . . especially if the national debt be included." We recognize this as an argument that has since become the stock-in-trade of the doctrine of beneficial inflation. But Mill has no sooner presented it than he dismisses it on grounds of equity. The denial of the doctrine that "money stimulates trade" is therefore allowed to stand side by side with the footnote admission of forced saving and the debtor-creditor argument without any effort at reconciliation. This is all the more remarkable since the fourth edition of the *Principles* came out in 1857, by which time "The Currency Extension Act of Nature"—the gold discoveries of 1848 in California and Australia—had added about 30 per cent to the gold coinage of the United Kingdom. These eight years were extremely prosperous, and the boom was widely attributed to the beneficial effects of the gold inflow.

The Loanable Funds Theory. We pass on to chapter 23, which deals with the determination of the rate of interest. Gross profits on capital, Mill observes, consist of wages of management, a risk premium, and interest (sec. 1). He distinguishes in so many words between the capitalist earning interest for abstinence and "the employer"—we would say "entrepreneur"—earning a compensation for risk. The rate of interest is determined by the demand and supply of loanable funds. The demand for loans consists of investment demand plus government demand plus landlord demand for unproductive consumption; the supply of funds is made up of savings plus bank notes plus bank deposits (sec. 2). The rate of interest is subject to alteration owing to changes in the demand and supply of funds, independent of the rate of profit (secs. 3–4). This section should dispel the notion that the classical economists never distinguished between the market rate of interest and the yield of capital. The quantity of money as such has no influence on the rate of interest, but a change in the quantity of money necessarily alters the interest rate (sec. 4). Inflation "while in process" *raises* the interest rate when the inflation is due to government expenditure financed by issuing inconvertible paper, but additional bank credit or an inflow of gold tends to *lower* the rate of interest. In equilibrium, the market rate of interest must equal the rate of return on capital; the rate of interest is therefore ultimately determined by real forces.

Say's Law. We turn back to chapter 14, which refutes the thesis that oversaving is possible. The doctrine of Malthus, Chalmers, and Sismondi, Mill confesses, "involves so much inconsistency in its very conception, that I feel considerable difficulty in giving any statement of it." The essence of the argument, he goes on to show, is that all producers may fail to sell at cost-covering prices owing to the failure of purchasing power to absorb the extra capacity created by rapid capital accumulation. Note the statement in section 4, which observes that during a commercial crisis "there is really an excess of all commodities above the money-demand: in other words, there is an undersupply of money." Mill expresses the fear that the theory of oversaving may give comfort to restrictionist policies: Chalmers, says Mill, "inculcates on capitalists the practice of moral restraint in the pursuit of gain; while Sismondi deprecates machinery."

The Currency-Banking Controversy. Chapters 22 and 24 should be read consecutively, dealing as they do with the question of how to assure stability under a mixed paper currency. For an appreciation of Mill's position, it is necessary to sketch the background of the great controversy that divided his generation on the issue of currency regulation. Ricardo had laid down *the* currency principle: a mixed paper currency should be made to vary in the same way as a purely metallic currency so that it responds automatically to any inflow or outflow of gold. In his day, the fact that the note issue was inconvertible made some kind of regulation of the currency mandatory. With the resumption of specie payments in 1821, the question arose whether convertibility as such provided an automatic mechanism to stabilize the currency. Ricardo's writings suggested that this was not so, and the so-called Currency School, led by Overstone, Normans, and Torrens, took its stand on a regulated note issue that would tie the currency to the movement of the foreign exchanges. The Bank leaned toward the views of the Currency School and under the guidance of one of its great Governors, Horsley Palmer, followed the rule of maintaining a constant ratio of security holdings—loans, investments, and discounted paper—to total liabilities. This rule seemed to make regulation an automatic matter, for it tended to maintain a constant internal circulation unless acted upon by external gold movements. The Charter Act of 1844 achieved the same effect by centralizing the note issue in the hands of the Bank and by limiting the power to issue against securities up to a fixed amount, above which notes could be issued only in exchange for gold and silver. Moreover, the Act formally separated the

Issue Department from the Banking Department and left the function of discounting entirely unregulated on the strength of the notion that changes in deposits would follow changes in the note issue.

In contrast to the Currency School, the Banking School, numbering Tooke and Fullarton among its most prominent advocates, denied that it was possible to overissue a convertible paper currency inasmuch as "the needs of trade" automatically controlled the volume of notes issued. There was no need for statutory control of the currency as long as convertibility was maintained. In addition, it was argued that the use of bank deposits, bills of exchange, and other forms of credit as substitutes for Bank notes would defeat the Currency School's efforts to control the money supply through the control of Bank notes only.

It is clear that at bottom neither school recognized the necessity for discretionary management of the currency. The Currency School wanted to regulate the note issue in order to leave central banking free, while the Banking School balked at the idea of any monetary management whatever. Neither side recognized the essential functions of a central bank, a fact which gives the entire controversy a somewhat dated appearance. But underlying the debate were important differences of opinion about the definition of money that persist to this day. The Currency School has been characterized as asserting that only gold and redeemable notes are money and that their total circulation should be made to reflect the changes in gold supply. But, in effect, their argument was more subtle. Just as Thornton and the Bullion Report had argued earlier that the issues of country banks were substantially governed by Bank of England notes so the protagonists of the currency principle argued that the superstructure of credit could not for long get out of line with the supply of gold and Bank notes; the latter were the basic monetary instruments because they were always demanded for final payments in a crisis. Moreover, they held that the low velocity of circulation of bank deposits and bills of exchange rendered these credit instruments a quantitatively unimportant part of the money supply. On the other hand, the Banking School's stress on the variety of sources of credit, and their insistence that it was necessary to control near-money as well as money proper, is relevant once again in view of the current debate over the role of financial intermediaries in monetary policy.

The Real-Bills Doctrine. The Banking School based its contention that a mixed currency will expand and contract with the needs of business on the fact that a bank's assets will normally consist of "real bills." If banks restrict their loans to self-liquidating commercial paper, that is, to discounting short-term notes based on goods-in-process, the means of payment in an economy will necessarily expand in pace with the volume of goods produced. This doctrine is stated quite plainly in the *Wealth of Nations* and was attacked by Thornton, Ricardo, and the Bullion Committee as being the standard view of the Directors of the Bank of England. The Banking School held the real-bills doctrine in the form a Law of Reflux: if banks should ignore the policy of real bills only and lend on long terms or for speculative purposes, the rise in prices would cause the "excess issue" to flow back to the banks through repayment of loans or conversion into specie. The Law of Reflux thus assures the impossibility of inflation produced by overexpansion of bank credit. Some exponents of the real-bills doctrine conceded that loans to the government by the central bank might be inflationary. Barring the last contingency, however, it followed that a rise in prices is not typically preceded but, on the contrary, is followed by an increase in the circulating media. It is easy to see why the Banking School and, in particular, Thomas Tooke is associated with the contraquantity theory of money.

In opposition to the Law of Reflux stands the Thornton-Ricardo doctrine of the market rate of interest as the connecting link between money and prices: at any bank rate below the long-term equilibrium rate, the demand for loans and discounts is insatiable. Confining loans or discounts to bona fide commercial paper does not furnish a check to overissue, even when the currency is convertible. Most of the good arguments against the real-bills doctrine are already found in Thornton's *Nature of the Paper Credit* (1802). First of all, the same product may be sold a number of times, each sale giving rise to a new real bill. In this way the money supply may expand far beyond the needs of business, even though each loan is made on short-term commercial paper. Second, bankers may have difficulty in distinguishing real from speculative bills, and anyway tend to regard customers' loans as the least liquid of their assets. Most important of all, the current volume of bills is a function not merely of the volume of transactions but also of the length of time for which the bill must run, that is, the velocity of circulation. Since commercial bills are near-money, a bill may be spent several times during its life, and each time it is spent it acts on prices. Inasmuch as velocity tends to rise in a boom, banking in terms of real bills will not prevent the ratio of bills to currency from rising at the very time when the money supply ought to be contracted. The expansion of loans increases money incomes, raises demand, and so justifies additional borrowing. Neither in the quantity of money nor in the volume of credit can stability be achieved by restriction of discounts to real bills. The real-bills doctrine entirely ignores the rate at which bills, real or not, are discounted. An expansion of loans can always be induced by a reduction in the bank rate or by a failure to raise the bank rate when profits are rising. But despite Thornton's impressive rebuttal of the Law of Reflux, the real-bills doctrine lived on into the twentieth century to be written into the Federal Reserve Act of 1913.

Mill's Position on Monetary Management. Mill starts out by endorsing the real-bills doctrine: the Law of Reflux is "far nearer to being the expression of the whole truth than any form whatever of the currency theory" (chap. 24, sec. 2). In chapter 13, and again in chapter 22, Mill had pointed out that the overissue of a convertible currency leads either to the outflow of gold via a deficit in the balance of payments or to the melting-down of coin for conversion to industrial use, made profitable by the rising price of industrial gold against a fixed money value of gold coin. This contention is qualified in chapter 24, section 2, by the distinction between the two states of markets: "the quiescent" and "the speculative"—this is as near as Mill ever came to a statement of turning points in the business cycle. In a quiescent state the Law of Reflux would provide an automatic check to overissue. But in the speculative state, when everyone expects prices to rise, bank credit may indeed rise without limit even if the banks obey the rule of real-bills-only. He takes note of the Tooke-Fullarton objection that speculative purchases are typically financed by checks and that the note issue begins to expand only *after* prices have risen. When speculation has spread from dealers to producers, however, Mill declares, the volume of Bank notes begins to rise, and it is only then that the inflationary upsurge takes hold. In this way, Mill appears to effect a compromise between the views of the Banking School—valid for quiescent states—and the Currency School—valid for speculative states. His own leanings are clearly toward the Banking School however—with Adam Smith and against Thornton and Ricardo—as is made clear in his negative evaluation of the Charter Act of 1844 (chap. 24, secs. 3–6). The comments on the speculative state, nevertheless, grant the gist of the Currency School's criticism of the real-bills doctrine.

Theory of International Values. Chapter 17 provides a good review of the Law of Comparative Advantage. In chapter 18 it is shown that the barter terms of trade depend not only on cost conditions but also on "reciprocal demand." The "equation of international demand" stipulates equality in the value of exports and imports, and the terms of trade are therefore determined by "the amount and extensibility of demand," or what we would now call the level and elasticity of demand in each country (sec. 2). The greater and more elastic the foreign demand, the more favorable the terms of trade to the home country. In section 3 Mill introduces the cost of carriage and notes that every increase of transport costs means a lessening of the gains from foreign trade. Moreover, once transport costs are present, the ratios of exchange between the two products is no longer the same in both countries. Finally, transport costs give rise to goods of domestic trade that are never exported or imported. The argument is generalized to more than two commodities and two countries in section 4.

In section 5 it is argued that a cost-reducing improvement in the linen industry of "Germany" may turn the barter terms of trade in favor of "England" by more than the fall in linen's relative price. In the last paragraph of section 5, where this argument is considered, Mill comes closer to expressing the concept of price elasticity than does any other economist before him. He divides all exports into three classes: (1) those in which "the demand is increased in greater ratio than the fall of price"—elast. > 1; (2) those in which total receipts remain constant, when the price falls because the quantity demanded increases in "the same proportion with the cheapness"—elast. $= 1$; and (3) those in which receipts fall because the quantity demand increases in a smaller "ratio" than the fall in price—elast. < 1. Edgeworth dismissed sections 6–9 of this chapter as "laborious and confusing"; it was added in later editions in response to the criticism that multiple equilibria are possible when either country has an inelastic demand for the other country's product.

Later neoclassical writers added little to Mill's pure theory of international values except to allow for varying costs in either country. The only real point of substance concerned the relative size of the two countries and the relative importance of the two traded commodities, an addition made in the 1920's. A small country producing an item important in international trade may be able to specialize exclusively in its production and so turn the terms of trade in its favor: the demand for its exports will be inelastic relative to its demand for imports. If one country is large relative to another, it can force exchange at the limit of the range of comparative costs; though both countries produce under constant costs, they specialize completely. The formal presentation of Mill's argument, however, was considerably improved. In the late 1870's Marshall devised an elegant geometrical illustration of the action of reciprocal demand. He measured all exports goods in terms of a common unit—the "representative bale"—and constructed each country's offer curve for the other country's exports.

Offer curves are peculiar demand curves because they express demand not in terms of the price per unit of the other good, but in terms of the total supply of the other good; they are analogous to a total, instead of an average, revenue curve. The British offer curve (Fig. 20) shows that in exchange for OM amount of linen England is

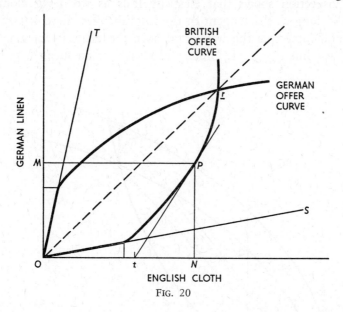

Fig. 20

willing to offer ON amount of cloth, in other words, that in exchange for ON cloth England demands OM linen. The price lines OS and OT represent the terms on which England could obtain linen and Germany could obtain cloth in the absence of trade, denoting the comparative-cost ratios of linen to cloth for the two countries, respectively. They are straight lines because of the assumption of constant costs. The offer curves follow the price line in the absence of trade and then move away from the price line, showing each country's willingness to offer less exports for every increment in imports. The price lines are the limit beyond which the offer curve cannot go, for no country will offer less exports for imports than it can produce in import-competing goods at home. The actual equilibrium position of trade is at r, where the two offer curves intersect, the slope of Or representing the equilibrium terms of trade.

Mill's argument can now be demonstrated graphically (Fig. 21). Notice first that the elasticity of each offer curve falls as we move along it. The price of, say, M linen in terms of N cloth is represented by tan angle $POM = (MP/OM) = (ON/PN)$. The elasticity of the offer curve at that point is, by the Robinson formula, equal to $A/(A - M)$, where A and M stand for average and marginal revenue.

$$\frac{A}{A - M} = \frac{ON/PN}{(ON/PN) - (tN/PN)} = \frac{ON}{ON - tN} = \frac{ON}{Ot}.$$

Casual inspection shows that elasticity falls as we move along the curves. So long as the tangent to the English offer curve is positively sloped and intercepts the horizontal axis, the elasticity of England's demand for linen is > 1. Unitary elasticity would mean a perfectly

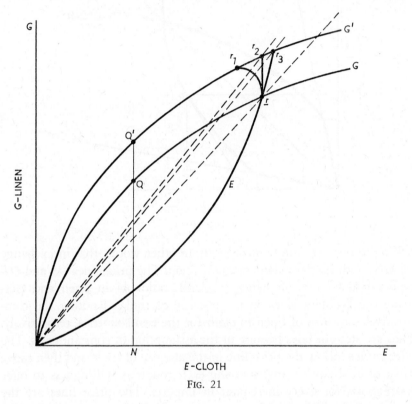

Fig. 21

vertical offer curve and inelastic demand implies a backward-bending offer curve. A technical improvement in Germany's linen-export in-dustry would alter the conditions of supply as shown by the displaced curve OG': whereas Germany was willing initially to offer NQ linen for ON cloth, she is now prepared to offer as much as NQ'. The effect of the cost reduction on the rate of exchange clearly depends on the shape of the curve OE. If it is a straight vertical line beyond Or, the case of unitary elasticity where the English demand for linen increases in "the same proportion with the cheapness," the terms of trade do not turn in England's favor as much as when her demand for linen is inelastic (Or_1). If her demand is highly elastic, we have the case in which the terms of trade move in her favor by less than the initial fall in linen's relative price.

Later, in Book V, chapter 4, section 6, Mill takes up the question of the effect of a tax on exports and imports. The same diagram will do duty for that problem. If OG' represents the intial untaxed offer curve, then OG is the displaced offer curve net of tax when Germany taxes English imports and/or Germany's exports. According to the position of the original intersection, we have the three cases Mill distinguishes in his discussion.

It is also evident from Marshall's diagram that when England's or Germany's offer curve bends backward because of inelasticity of demand, multiple equilibria are possible and the terms of trade become indeterminate, as Mill realized (chap. 18, sec. 6).

International Wage and Price Levels. In chapter 19 and chapter 25, section 2, Mill elaborates upon the Seniorian doctrine of the relative value of money in open economies: the price level will be highest in the country where export industries are most efficient. But Mill goes further than Senior in demonstrating that a country's relative "cost of obtaining gold" varies also with the cost of transportation: if the cost of carrying linen to England is increased, the price of linen in Germany, and hence the general price level in Germany, will fall relative to England via the operation of the specie-flow mechanism. Moreover, those countries where exportable goods are most in demand and which have the least home demand for foreign goods will have relatively higher price levels.

Senior's doctrine with respect to relative wage levels between countries also needs amendment in the light of reciprocal demands. First, when demand and supply conditions promote favorable barter terms of trade for a country, the level of wages in that country will be high relative to other trading nations. Second, the greater the relative importance in trade of cloth relative to linen, the higher the wage level in Britain relative to the wage level in Germany. And, last, the less elastic the demand of England for German linen, or the more elastic Germany's demand for English cloth, the higher the English wage level relative to Germany. Recalling the numerical example employed in our previous exposition of Senior's doctrine, we found that the average wage in England could vary between 80 and 53⅓ per cent of that in Portugal. We have now shown that it is likely to be closer to 80 than to 53⅓ per cent when Portugal has a greater absolute demand for English cloth than England has for Port wine and when England has few alternative sources of supply for Port, while Portugal can turn elsewhere for cloth at slightly less advantageous terms.

Senior had shown that wages in the different countries must be proportional to the value productivity of labor in the export industries of the respective countries. But what determines the character and number of the export industries? Surely, the level of wages and the resulting wage costs per unit of output in various industries will determine the number of industries that can profitably export their products. To the solution of this apparently vicious circle, Mill gives no assistance. It was Longfield who posed the problem correctly: if we imagine a range of products for a given country varying with their comparative advantage in real costs against some other country, exports will be in the upper and imports in the lower range of the hierarchy. Comparative money wage rates in the two countries will provide the line of division between export and import commodities. The final solution of this problem, taking into account not only scales of comparative advantage and wage structure but also reciprocal demands for the products of the respective countries, was not given until much later by Edgeworth.

Hume's Law. Chapter 20 is taken up with the elementary principles of foreign exchange adjustments under a gold standard, emphasizing the role of prices in bringing about equilibrium in the balance of payments. Chapter 21 discusses the international distribution of specie. Mill's version of Hume's Law is much broader than that of any previous author. He shows that an inflow of gold lowers interest rates even as it raises prices (see also chap. 24, sec. 4). As the interest rate falls, short-term capital will flow abroad, thus promoting an adjustment of the exchange. Mill was one of the first authors to emphasize the fact that the central bank can protect its reserves during an external drain by raising the bank rate, thus assisting a rise in the market rate of interest, which is already taking place as a result of the gold outflow. The rise in interest rates attracts capital from abroad; the demand for British bills of exchange rises, and as the price of bills increases it becomes profitable to ship bullion instead; and so the exchanges turn in favor of England. This mechanism, linking the bank rate to international movements of specie, was stated systematically by Goschen in the 1860's. The essence of it, however, is in Mill and to some extent even in Thornton.

Section 2 of chapter 21 takes up the effect of technical improvements in an export industry upon the gains of trade shared by each country: the whole of the gain of a reduction in the cost of making English cloth goes to Germany if German demand for English cloth is of unitary elasticity. If the German demand is inelastic, the price to German buyers will be greater than to English buyers. The gains to England exceed the gains to Germany only if the German demand is relatively elastic. If "gain" is measured by the fall in the price of cloth relative to a given amount of linen, this result is obvious and can be read off the Marshall offer curves.

Transfer Payments. Section 4 takes up the question of unilateral transfers. It is significant that Mill does not select the export of capital as an example of a transfer payment—possibly because of the fundamental classical assumption of the immobility of capital between countries. Instead, he cites government remittances abroad and interest payments to foreign creditors as examples of capital transfers. Mill treats the whole question very briefly and solely in terms of price adjustments, although later in the book he gives a clear statement of the role of income changes as a corrective force to a disturbance in the balance of payment (Book III, chap. 24, sec. 4). Under a gold standard the attempt to transfer capital to another country leads, in the first place, to a rise in the price of bills drawn on the borrowing country. There follows a flow of gold from lender to borrower—the rate of exchange being at the lending country's gold export point—then a rise in prices in the borrowing country relative to the lending country, with the lender acquiring a favorable balance and the borrower an unfavorable balance of trade, which tends to become equal to the rate of borrowing, at which point the exchanges return to parity and relative prices stabilize at new levels. Here price changes and gold flows bring about adjustments on the assumption that the conditions of international demand in the trading countries remain unaffected by the capital transfer—*the* classical theory of transfer payments. This theory is to be contrasted with the modern theory of transfers, which emphasizes shifts in demand and income changes.

In the classical theory the change in imports and exports is accompanied by movements in their prices along given demand curves. The transfer of capital therefore leads to a shift in the barter terms of trade in favor of the receiving country. According to the "modern" theory, this shift in the barter terms of trade is not a necessary consequence of the transfer. When a payment is made to foreigners unaccompanied by an equivalent receipt, the aggregate expenditure of the home country exceeds its income. The tendency to contract outlays at home, while foreigners are spending more, causes the demand for imports in both paying and receiving countries to shift and, necessarily, to shift in the direction of restoring equilibrium in the balance of payments. This shift in the demand curves may be sufficient to permit the transfer to be made in the form of goods without any change in prices.

We have seen that Mill was aware of the role of income changes in adjusting the balance of payments but that he slighted its importance. This seems to be the typical procedure of most classical economists. Henry Thornton, in whose hands the transfer problem was first subjected to careful analysis, subscribed to both the classical and the "modern" theory but regarded the latter as being of negligible importance in the long run. Thornton took a failure of the harvest requiring heavy imports of wheat as an example of a transfer payment. This turns the exchanges against England and, under a convertible standard, leads either to the export of gold or to a contraction of the note issue; in either way the shift in the relative prices of the trading nations restores the balance. Under an inconvertible paper standard, an unprecedented importation of corn results in an excess supply of bills drawn on London in foreign markets. These bills can be exchanged for Bank of England notes only when presented for payment in London. Foreigners are willing to pay a premium for gold; therefore, Bank notes sell at a discount in terms of gold as well as in terms of foreign currency, that is, there is a "premium on bullion" and the exchanges have become unfavorable. This reduces the price of English goods to foreigners, which tends to restore equilibrium just as gold flows do under a convertible standard.

Ricardo took Thornton to task for suggesting that a transfer would cause a shift in the terms of trade against the paying country. If the exchanges were unfavorable to England, this was not due to a failure of the harvest or to government subsidies to allies—disturbances from the commodity side—but solely to overissue of the currency—disturbances from the money side. Oddly enough, Ricardo's argument could be justified by assuming that he has in mind the "modern" theory of transfer payments and assumes it to be operative immediately. In other words, if a failure of harvest would immediately and automatically bring about a proportionate change in the reciprocal demands of countries for each other's products, no alteration whatever would take place in the exchanges. On this ground, some authors have credited Ricardo with extraordinary prescience. But it is more plausible to assume that Ricardo met Thornton's argument by looking at the long run. A crop failure is only a temporary condition, he said, which tends to raise prices by lowering the level of real income in the economy. In terms of the previous price level, gold is now in excess, and the balance of trade will become unfavorable. The root of the trouble is that the note issue is excessive relative to current needs, and in this sense the disturbance is really a monetary rather than a commodity disturbance. The whole argument is somewhat forced, and Ricardo would hardly have adopted it had he not been so anxious to attribute the entire "premium on bullion" to an excessive issue of Bank notes. To improve his presentation by crediting him with the "modern" theory of transfers seems to miss the point. Apart from Ricardo, however, most classical writers did make some allowance for income adjustments, but, like Mill, did so only occasionally in connection with special problems.

The Vent-for-Surplus Doctrine. In chapter 17, sections 4 and 5, Mill dismisses Smith's "vent-for-surplus" argument in favor of foreign trade as "a surviving relic of the Mercantile theory." Comparative cost analysis regards the territorial division of labor as a matter of moving along a static production-transformation curve constructed on the basis of the given resources and the given techniques of the trading country; specialization is conceived as a fully reversible process of reallocating resources. In the vent-for-surplus theory of international trade, emphasis is put upon the indirect gains of foreign trade conceived as a dynamic force widening the extent of the market and generating new wants. It is a consideration, as Mill says, "principally applicable to an early stage of industrial advancement"; the opening up of a backward country to foreign trade "sometimes works a sort of industrial revolution." These remarks touch upon the whole question of secular changes in comparative advantage, to which none of the classical economists gave very much attention. It is curious that classical theory, generally oriented as it was to problems of long-run development, should have developed an almost wholly static theory of international trade. But here, as elsewhere, it must be recognized that much of what appears to be development economics in this period is nothing but a special form of comparative static analysis in which the passage of time is irrelevant to the outcome of the adjustment process.

The Basis of a Theory of International Trade. Before passing on to other questions, we must raise the issue whether there is in fact any basis for a separate theory of international trade. The classical economists advocated a special theory of international, as distinct from intranational, trade because of the relative immobility of resources between nations. This meets with the objection that the difference is one of degree, not of kind: there is much immobility within an economy—recall Smith's remark that "men are of all luggage the most difficult to transport"—and capital and labor do at times move across national boundaries. Either, it is said, we assume for theoretical purposes perfect mobility in domestic as well as in foreign trade, or, if we must be realistic, we should assume imperfect mobility in all cases. Cairnes, following Mill's own suggestion, argued that labor within a country is in fact immobile between noncompeting occupations. Exchange between such groups is therefore exactly like exchange between countries, that is, wages and profits are not equalized by the movement of labor and capital. Hence, it is not true that domestic trade takes place on the basis of cost of production, while international trade is governed by reciprocal demand; between noncompeting groups of domestic industries, value is also regulated by reciprocal demand. Cairnes thus took the first step toward a general theory of value in which domestic trade and international trade are merely special cases depending upon the prevailing degree of factor mobility.

It would probably avoid misunderstanding if we followed Bastable and spoke of a classical theory of "interregional" trade rather than of "international" trade. The classical economists never claimed that their definition of "nation" coincided with the political boundaries of countries. Mill advisedly used the term "distant places" and pointed out that trade with the colonies is really internal trade, not subject to the law of international values (chap. 25, sec. 5). At all events, we can agree that nations are conspicuous examples of noncompeting groups, and the case for a separate theory of international trade rests on that claim. There is nothing to prevent one from applying the doctrine to regions within a country when the relevant conditions hold. Even the classical economists applied the specie-flow mechanism to trade between London and the provinces, arguing that the country banks could not overissue without losing gold to London.

Statics and Dynamics. The last chapter of Book III lays down the Ricardian view of economic development as a race between "population and agricultural skill," repeating the gist of Book I, chapter 13. Ostensibly, its purpose is to show that the "laws of distribution" are not affected by the presence of money in the economy, being the result of "real" forces. The whole of Book IV is devoted to analyzing the nature of these forces determining the secular changes in factor prices and in distributive shares. In chapter 1 Mill announces the distinction between "statics" and "dynamics," which he had borrowed from Comte. So far, he declares, we have examined "the economical laws of a stationary and unchanging society," a rather surprising assertion in view of the discussion of the Malthusian theory of population, the laws of historical returns, and socialism in Book I. Now, he goes on to say, we add the "dynamics of political economy to the Statics." It is hardly necessary to say that the terms "statics" and "dynamics" have undergone considerable changes of meaning since Mill's day. "Dynamics" now denotes analysis that takes explicit account of leads and lags in economic relationships—witness current models employing difference equations—as against "statics," in which all the variables refer to the same point of time. Quesnay's Tableau Économique, though it employs the concept of the stationary state as an expository device, is primitive "dynamics" in the modern sense of the word because of the assumption of a one-year income-spending lag. The wages fund doctrine represents another example of elementary economic dynamics. For Mill, however, "dynamics" means analysis of historical change, whereas "statics" seems to denote what we now call comparative static analysis: the comparision of an initial equilibrium situation disturbed by an exogeneous event with the subsequent equilibrium situation after the disturbance has worked itself out. But Mill is by no means consistent in this; we have already seen examples of his "dynamics," and numerous examples of static reasoning occur in Books IV and V.

The Falling Rate of Profit. Chapter 2 of Book IV treats the Smithian problem of secular changes in the structure of prices from the Ricardian viewpoint. As in Book I, chapter 13, Mill concedes that a strong "impulse" toward agricultural improvements has shown itself since 1830 or thereabouts, such that the tendency to diminishing returns has been more than offset. He suggests that a time series of agricultural prices, adjusted for seasonal variation and changes in the value of money, will reveal which of the two opposing forces, diminishing returns or technical changes, has in fact predominated (sec. 3). This is a new note in the literature. The Ricardian system predicted rising wheat prices in the absence of free trade, and no one before Mill had proposed submitting this proposition to an empirical test.

The rest of chapter 2 (secs. 4 and 5) defends commodity speculation as a method of ironing out fluctuations in prices. Chapter 3 looks at the possible changes in the distributive shares under four conditions: (1) when population increases faster than capital (sec. 1); (2) when capital increases faster than population (sec. 2); (3) the Ricardian case, when capital and population increase proportionately (sec. 3); and (4) when capital and population are constant but technical change is reducing the inputs required to produce output (sec. 4). Section 4 contains an analysis of the effects of laborsaving innovations in agriculture upon land rentals. It adds nothing to Ricardo's presentation except an emphasis upon the short-run nature of the argument.

Chapter 4 provides an original treatment of "the tendency of profits to a minimum." Mill notes that there is a minimum supply price of capital, namely "a rate which the average person will deem an equivalent for abstinence." This rate tends to fall with economic progress because "mankind becomes more willing to sacrifice present indulgence for future objects": the larger the annual output, the less anxious people are to supplement current consumption by drawing on accumulated savings. In addition, the growth of capital depresses its productivity. As Mill points out, riskless consols stand at 3 per cent in England. The present rate of capital accumulation must, *in the absence of technical change,* reduce this "in a small number of years" to 1 per cent, which he takes to be the minimum supply price of capital. The rate of profit is, therefore, habitually witin "a hand's breadth of the minimum," and the country is forever on the verge of stationariness (sec. 4). The counteracting forces to this tendency are examined in section 5. They consist of (1) capital losses during a crisis (sec. 5); (2) technical improvements, particularly in the production of wage goods (sec. 6); (3) the extension of foreign trade insofar as it lowers the real cost of obtaining wage goods (sec. 7); and (4) the export of capital (sec. 8). Capital exports offset the declining rate of profit not because they provide a "vent-for-surplus" but because they are typically sent to the colonies to produce primary goods for export to the home country, the ultimate effect of which is to lower the real cost of obtaining wage goods. In section 5, Mill links the periodicity of crises to the very tendency of the rate of profit to fall, with the waste of capital in the slump preparing the way for a recovery of profit expectations. In the following chapter (chap. 5), Mill concludes that the tendency of the rate of profit to fall weakens the case against government spending in such countries, a point which he had already made in Book I, chapter 4, section 8. All through Books IV and V there is a continuous repetition of materials discussed at an earlier stage. This is partly the result of Mill's haste in composition (the whole of the *Principles* was said to have been written in eighteen months) but probably more the result of his double distinction between Production versus Distribution and Statics versus Dynamics, which imposed a peculiar structure on the order of presentation.

The Stationary State. Chapter 6, on the stationary state, is strongly colored by Mill's social views. He divorces himself at the outset from "political economists of the old school," citing McCulloch, Smith, and Malthus, which identifies all that is "economically desirable" with "the progressive state" and regards the approach of stationary conditions as the coming of the day of judgment. "I am not charmed," Mill remarks, "with the ideal of life held out by those who think that the normal state of human beings is that of struggling to get on." American readers will note the comments on America in the first edition, which Mill later struck out (sec. 2). The whole of this chapter is nothing so much as a prolegomenon to Galbraith's *Affluent Society.* Witness the Galbraithian assertion that "it is only in the backward countries of the world that increased production is still an important object: in those most advanced, what is economically needed is better distribution."

Chapter 7, on the "Probable Futurity of the Labouring Class," starts out by rejecting Carlyle's theory of the élite, the rich guiding the poor in paternal obligation: "the poor have come out of leading-strings, and cannot any longer be governed or treated like children" (sec. 1). Mill's favorite schemes are discussed in sections 4–6: peasant proprietorship, profit-sharing, and consumer co-operatives. His detailed illustrations of profit-sharing schemes and early co-operative ventures make tedious reading. The last section (sec. 7) criticizes

socialists for declaiming against competition; this, it may be assumed. is tantamount to accusing them of ignorance of economics.

Taxation. Book V, on the scope of government launches, after some preliminary remarks in chapter 1, into the question of taxation. Chapter 2, on
Smith's canons of taxation, defends the ability-to-pay theory on the grounds that
sacrifices ought to be equalized. It is not made clear whether the sacrifices in
question are total, average, or marginal sacrifices. Mill rejects the benefit theory
of taxation grounded upon the *quid pro quo* principle (sec. 2). Equality of
sacrifices, Mill notes, means a progressive tax on incomes above subsistence
because of the law of diminishing marginal utility of income; the law is clearly
suggested in section 3. He condemns progressive taxation on incentive grounds,
however, although he favors progressive death duties because they represent a
tax on "unearned income." If it were possible to separate consumption from
investment spending, an expenditure tax would be preferable to an income tax
(sec. 4). In section 5 we come at last to the famous proposal to tax the "unearned increment" of rental values, which is worth a few remarks by itself.

Taxing the Unearned Increment.

Ricardian theory suggested
that ground rent, being a return to a nonreproducible natural agent,
was eminently suitable for taxation. James Mill was the first to draw
the obvious corollary that all future increments in rent from some current base year ought to be taxed away on grounds of equity. Ricardo
himself was not happy with the proposal, but it remained an academic
question in his lifetime. With the publication of J. S. Mill's book, however, and the subsequent formation of the Land Tenure Reform Association under Mill's aegis, the idea caught on with the public. Mill
proposes to exempt present rents and to tax "the future increment of
unearned rent" by taxing increments in the value of land as judged by
the trend in the price of land sales. Henry George in the 1870's went
a little further and proposed confiscating present rents in the manner
of the physiocrats, a measure that he claimed would abolish poverty
and economic crises, the latter being simply the result of speculation
in land values. This would be a "single tax" because its proceeds would
be sufficient to defray the entire expenses of the state.

The Marshallian objection to the "single tax" is obvious: all
agents may earn rents in the short run, and even Ricardian rents are
incentive payments in the long run. Mill might have replied that no
quasi-rent has either the persistence or the generality of ground rent,
and Marshall would probably have agreed with that. At any rate, England did adopt Mill's scheme in the Budget of 1909 for urban lands not
used for building purposes, and in the Town and Country Planning Act
of 1947 it applied the principle of taxing rental increments to all land.

The idea that Ricardo had planted proved to be as irresistible to
the early exponents of marginal utility as to Ricardo's immediate fol-

lowers. Walras and Wicksteed were both advocates of land nationoliza-tion, albeit with full compensation. Walras's scheme was to pay the proprietors with bonds, using future rents to pay interest and to redeem the loan. But if future rents are properly discounted, the present value of the land will just equal the price paid: rental receipts will be entirely swallowed up by meeting annual interest payments, and the state will never be able to redeem the bonds. Walras solved this problem by believing with Ricardo that rents tend to rise in a growing economy: he proposed to pay the proprietors a price on the basis of 99 years' pur-chase—the equivalent of perpetuity as far as the individual is con-cerned—and thereafter all rents would accrue to the state.

The Incidence of Taxes. Chapter 3, concerned with direct taxes on in-come, continues in the vein of chapter 2. Chapter 4, on excises taxes, is full of interesting asides. In section 2 Mill asserts that a specific or ad valorem tax will raise the price of a good by at least the amount of the tax and usually by more. In the short run it is impossible that this be true: even if demand is perfectly inelastic, the tax can raise price only by the amount of the tax. But, it soon be-comes clear that demand is not taken to be typically inelastic. Mill has in mind long-run downward-sloping supply curves, on the assumption that the industry in question is operating under increasing returns to scale. In that case a tax that shifts the supply curve to the left will indeed raise the price of the product by more than the amount of the tax. Section 3 treats of a tax on wheat and shows that any tax that does not affect intramarginal differentials will leave corn rents the same. A tithe would lower corn rents because it would fall more heavily on intramarginal land. A specific tax per unit of wheat produced lowers corn rents, but not money rents, because corn prices rise to the extent that output is reduced. All this is straightforward Ricardian tax analysis.

Section 4 of chapter 4 discusses the effect of commuting tithes to money payments, a subject of interest to Mill's generation because of the Commutation of Tithes Act of 1834. Section 5 contains yet another deprecatory remark on the benefits of repealing the Corn Laws—recall Book I, chapter 11, section 4. Mill denies that the Corn Laws have kept up rents and wheat prices, but he con-cedes that they have retarded growth. Section 6, on export and import taxes, were discussed above in connection with the theory of international trade.

Chapter 5, on taxes on contracts, is uninteresting. The next chapter is an early contribution to the much-vexed question, which has flared up again in the "new" welfare economics, of the advantages of direct versus indirect taxes. Mill's comments hardly come to grips with the issues, but he does discount the so-called "optional" argument in favor of indirect taxes, on which both Smith and Ricardo had relied.

The Public Debt. Chapter 7 represents Mill's final summing-up of the case against government spending considered in the light of capital abundance in wealthy countries: the subject had been touched upon in Book I, chapter 4, section 8, and again in Book IV, chapter 5. The test of whether government spending is hampering private capital formation is the rate of interest—notice again Mill's inclination to subject theoretical arguments to an operational test.

If the government is actually siphoning off funds from the private sector, the rate of interest will rise (sec. 1). Ricardo's recommendation of a capital levy to redeem the public debt is discussed inconclusively (sec. 2). Budgetary surpluses should be applied to redeeming taxes, not the public debt, because all taxes are objectionable in principle (sec. 3).

The Scope of Government. Chapters 8 and 9 consider the efficiency with which the British government has executed its indisputably legitimate functions; ineffectively, is the verdict. Chapter 8, section 3, on the need for law reform, is in the best manner of Bentham. Chapter 9, section 1, reiterates the proposal to revise the inheritance laws, sketched earlier in Book II, chapter 2. His friend Alexander Bain recalled that Mill anticipated a "tremendous outcry" over his legislative recommendations on inherited wealth: "He frequently spoke of his proposals as to Inheritance and Bequest, which, if carried out, would pull down all large fortunes in two generations. To his surprise, however, this part of the book made no sensation." Sections 2 and 3 of chapter 9 attack primogeniture and entails; section 6 gives reluctant approval to the Limited Liabilities Act of 1855, which Mill had opposed before its introduction.

With chapter 10 we pass over to the disputable sphere of government action. Section 1 dismisses protectionism but allows the infant-industry argument, a concession that Mill came to regret, as it was seized upon in America and Australia to justify protective tariffs. Section 2 deals with the Usury Laws, section 4 with the Patent Laws, and section 5 with the Combination Laws, which we have already discussed. The last chapter in the book provides an excellent exercise in political theory: sections 1–6 review virtually every cogent argument ever advanced against the extension of government intervention in economic affairs. In Book V, chapter 1, section 2, Mill had rejected any rule that limited the interference of government save "the simple and vague one" of expediency. Now he concludes that *"laissez faire, in short, should be the general practice; every departure from it, unless required by some greater good, is a certain evil."* And, to show what he means, he proceeds to recommend free education provided by the state, a case in which "the consumer is an incompetent judge of the commodity," and to approve the regulation of the hours of work on the ground that public action is sometimes "necessary to give effects to the wishes of the persons interested."

Concluding Remarks. Is the economics of Mill's *Principles* Ricardian economics? Mill himself thought that he was only qualifying Ricardo. But his qualifications at times affect essentials of theory, and in the sphere of policy he carried Ricordo's system to lengths undreamed of by Ricardo. Schumpeter argues that, despite Mill's reverence for Ricardo, he cannot be considered a disciple. Nevertheless, the fact remains that on all important questions, such as the determination of factor prices and their variations in the course of economic progress, Mill adhered to Ricardo's postulates. Everything is traced back to the cost of producing wage goods, the crucial element in determining the rate of profit; under the portmanteau of "corn," wage goods are identified as the product of agriculture; and the law of diminishing returns to scale as well as to technical progress is regarded as uniquely applicable to agricultural production. This is the framework of Ricardo's system, and, once present, no admissions of the "real cost" of capital or of the role of demand—so important to later generations preoccupied with the determination of relative prices under static conditions—can prevent the emergence of typically Ricardian conclusions. Nassau Senior, one of Ricardo's leading critics, was surely right when he remarked in a review of Mill's book that "Mr. Mill's exposition of the theory of Profit and of Rent . . . does not differ materially from that of Ricardo."

Mill's *Principles* is more than an *œuvre d'assemblage,* a mere restatement of what has gone before. Even on a purely theoretical level it is full of genuine novelties. The Equation of International Demand is an obvious example, but in addition there is the concept of noncompeting groups; the correct statement of the law of supply and demand with what amounts to a definition of price elasticity of demand in terms of total-revenue effect of a change in price, the treatment of economies of scale, the analysis of the problem of joint products, and, finally, the concept of opportunity costs. Moreover, Mill's theory of interest is nearly forty years ahead of his time. Even when he draws specific ideas from his predecessor, he almost always improves upon their presentation: this shows up in his statement of the abstinence theory of profit and the generalization of the rent concept, borrowed from Bailey and Senior, and again in his emphasis upon the role of "custom," particularly with respect to land tenure, derived from Richard Jones. The quality of theoretical eclecticism, which so irritates the modern reader, worked, in the final analysis, to Mill's advantage. For a period of two generations he taught England its economics, and the multiplicity of analytical ideas, often running in opposite directions, opened the way to subsequent refinement and development.

The essential Mill, however, is to be found in his proposals for economic reform and in the pervasive moral tone, at once sentimental and austere, with the flourishes of abstract theory kept in check by a desire to preach improvement. It is exactly the same flavor that imbues Marshall's *Principles.* And, just as Marshall, with his genius for pure theory and his competence in mathematics, spoke disparagingly of abstract analysis and mathematical economics, so Mill, with all his flair for theoretical work, told a friend: "I regard the purely abstract investigation of political economy . . . as of very minor importance compared to the great practical questions which the progress of democracy and the spread of socialist opinion are pressing on."

NOTES FOR FURTHER READING

The most useful edition of Mill's *Principles* is the *ad variorum* edition by W. J. Ashley, with an introduction describing Mill's intellectual development and appendixes containing excerpts from his other writings on the wages fund doctrine and on socialism. Unfortunately, this edition is very scarce. But the sixth *People's Edition* (1865) or the seventh edition (1871), the last to be revised by Mill, are easy to come by in secondhand book shops. There is little point in reading any edition earlier than the third (1852), for there are significant alterations in the second and third editions.

Of all the classical economists, none had so varied and rich a career as John Stuart Mill. We are fortunate in having a fascinating recent biography of him: *The Life of John Stuart Mill,* by M. St. J. Packe (1954). Packe's treatment of Mill's philosophical, political, and economic ideas, however, leaves something to be desired. For a general account of Mill's intellectual position see L. Stephen, *The English Utilitarians* (1900), vol. III, chaps. 3 and 4. Mill's relation to Bentham is explored in a brilliant article by J. Viner, "Bentam and J. S. Mill: the Utilitarian Background," *AER,* 1949, reprinted in *The Long View and the Short.* The same terrain is covered from a wider angle by P. Streeten, "Keynes and the Classical Tradition," *Post-Keynesian Economics,* ed. K. Kurihara (1954). Both authors take pains to correct Halévy's misleading dichotomy of Bentham's juristic theory, in which the state is assigned the function of harmonizing private and public interests, from Bentham's economic theory in which laissez faire is advocated on the basis of spontaneous harmony of interests. (See E. Halévy, *The Growth of Philosophical Radicalism,* 1901; reprinted, 1949). But in fact there is no evidence of any belief in natural harmony in Bentham's writings. This is only one of the many differences between Bentham and Mill. Mill did believe in "natural harmony," if this phrase be interpreted to mean that a decentralized competitive economy does harmonize private and public gains over a large area of economic life. Laissez faire *is* the general rule, Mill declared, although the exceptions to it are numerous.

Anyone who still believes that the classical conception of the scope of government was wholly negative and based on *Harmonielehre* must read L. Robbins, *The Theory of Economic Policy in English Classical Political Economy* (1952), particularly the concluding lecture "The Classical Theory in General Perspective." S. G. Checkland reviews Robbins' book and raises some further questions: "The Prescriptions of the Classical Economics," *Ec.,* February, 1953. The dogmatic espousal of laissez faire was found not in the treatises of economists but in the journals and popular magazines: see S. Gordon, "The London *Economist* and the High Tide of Laissez-Faire," *JPE,* December, 1955. D. H. MacGregor, *Economic Thought and Policy,* chap. 3, gives an interesting history of the maxim of laissez faire supplemented by general comments on the attitude of nineteenth-century British economists toward state intervention. Blaug, *Ricardian Economics,* chap. 10, discusses the position of the leading Ricardian economists on prominent issues of public policy, such as the Poor Laws, the Corn Laws, and the Factory Acts. An excellent recent book by R. D. C. Black, *The Classical Economists and the Irish Problem* (1960) examines classical policy proposals for a unique backward area, illuminating both the strengths and peculiar weakness of Ricardian economics.

As to Mill's specific economic opinions, see Taussig's classic study of the wages fund doctrine, which covers everyone from Adam Smith through John Stuart Mill to Amasa Walker: *Wages and Capital* (1896), in particular pp. 181–82, 214–15, 235–36, 263–65, and 319–25. Taussig shows that, contrary to popular belief, the wages fund doctrine was employed primarily to analyze problems of population control rather than to discourage trade-union action to raise wages. See also Schumpeter, *History,* pp. 662–71. There is a vast body of commentary on what Edgeworth called the *locus vexatissimus* of economics, Mill's fourth proposition on capital. But see Marshall, *Principles,* Appen. J; F. A. Hayek, *The Pure Theory of Capital* (1941), Appen. III; A. C. Pigou, "Mill and the Wages Fund," *EJ,* June, 1945; H. G. Johnson, "Demand for Commodities is *Not* Demand for Labour," *EJ,* December, 1949. G. O'Brien, "J. S. Mill and J. E. Cairnes," *Ec.,* November, 1943, presents extracts from a correspondence between the two men covering a variety of economic topics, in particular the wages fund doctrine and the theory of value. In a provocative article on "Originality in Scientific Progress," *Ec.,* November, 1955, G. J. Stigler shows that in terms of identifiable theories Mill must rank as one of the most original writers in the history of economics. Schumpeter's comments on Mill are scattered throughout Part III, chaps. 6 and 7, of his *History:* see pp. 527–34, 541–50, 603–5 and 640–45. But the reader should really *study* the whole of chapter 6, running well over a hundred pages, which contains the bulk of Schumpeter's discussion of classical economics.

Mill's work on the theory of international trade is critically reviewed by F. Y. Edgeworth, "The Pure Theory of International Values," *EJ,* 1894, reprinted in *Papers Relating to Political Economy* (1925), II, pp. 20–25. The basic commentary on the classical theory of international trade as summed up by Mill is Viner, *Studies in the Theory of International Trade,* chap. 6. See also Schumpeter, *History,* pp. 605–15; Wu, *An Outline of International Price Theories,* chap. 3, secs. 3 and 6 and chap. 7, sec. 1; C. Iversen, *International Capital Movements* (1935), chaps. 4–6; two articles by W. E. Mason, "The Stereotypes of Classical Transfer Theory," *JPE,* December, 1956; "Ricardo's Transfer-Mechanism Theory," *QJE,* February, 1957; and H. Grubel, "Ricardo and Thornton on the Transfer Mechanism," *QJE,* May, 1960. Wu and Grubel credit Ricardo with the modern income theory of transfer payments, but Mason argues convincingly that Ricardo's long-run bilateral-trade reasoning really abstracted from the transfer problem, which is essentially a short-run question.

On the much-discussed controversy between the Currency School and the Banking School see, first of all, Viner, *Studies,* chap. 5, and the lucid and comprehensive discussion by M. R. Daugherty, "The Currency-Banking Controversy," *SEJ,* October, 1942, and January, 1943. There is a highly compressed and rather cutting treatment by E. V. Morgan, *The Theory and Practice of Central Banking 1797–1913* (1943), chaps. 5 and 6. V. C. Smith, *The Rationale of Central Banking* (1936), chaps. 6 and 9, and E. Wood, *English Theories of Central Banking Control 1819–1858* (1939), chaps. 3, 4, 11, and 14, adds valuable detail. Among the leading exponents of the Banking School was Thomas Tooke, whose *History of Prices* left a profound impression on all writing in this period. In a brilliant *Introduction to Tooke's History* (1928) T. E. Gregory reviews monetary controversy in the whole period from the Suspension of Cash Payments in 1797 to the passage of the Bank Charter Act in 1844, analyzing Tooke's position on all the leading topics under debate. On the early history of the real-bills doctrine see two articles by J. K. Horsefield, "The Duties of a Banker," *Ec.,* 1941 and 1944, reprinted in *Papers in English Monetary History,* ed. T. S. Ashton and R. S. Sayers. The first of these articles discusses Adam Smith's theory of banking and the second focuses on Thornton. There is also the ponderous but painstaking study of the evolution of the real-bills doctrine through the nineteenth century: L. W. Mints, *A History of Banking Theory* (1945), particularly chaps. 4, 6, and 7.

Mill's tergiversations over socialism are discussed by L. Robbins, *The Theory of Economic Policy,* Lecture 5. A. L. Harris, *Economics and Social Reform* (1958), chap. 2, reviews Mill's views on social reform.

The classical theory of public finance, emphasizing the views of Mill, is surveyed in Myrdal, *Political Elements in the Development of Economic Thought,* chap. 7. J. Burkhead, "The Balanced Budget," *QJE,* 1954, reprinted in *Readings in Fiscal Policy* (1955), ed. A. Smithies and J. K. Butters, traces the prevailing opinions on the budget from Adam Smith to the present day.

The name of Nassau William Senior has come up frequently in the course of the text. There is a comprehensive study of Senior's many incisive but fragmented contributions to classical theory: M. Bowley, *Nassau Senior and Classical Economics* (1937). The book suffers, however, from a tendency to modernize Senior's presentation and to exaggerate his emancipation from Ricardian assumptions. Senior had a checkered career as a civil servant. S. L. Levy's biography, despite its absurd title, makes absorbing reading: *Nassau Senior: The Prophet of Modern Capitalism* (1949). G. J. Stigler, "The Classical Economists: An Alternative View," *Lectures on Economic Problems* (1949), analyzes the famous Handloom Weaver's Report, written under Senior's direction, and shows that it displays analytical insights not found in the formal treatises of the period.

Senior was only one of the many able economists writing in this period. L. Robbins has recently published a full-length study of Robert Torrens: *Robert Torrens and the Evolution of Classical Economics* (1958). Chaps. 4 and 5 and pp. 251–54, dealing with Torrens' banking theory, presents the Currency-Banking controversy with great clarity. Torrens is best remembered for the terms-of-trade argument in favor of protective tariffs: his argument is taken apart and put back together in chapter 7.

On the successive occupants of the Chair of Political Economy at Dublin, who from the 1830's onward developed the subjective value theory, see R. D. Black, "Trinity College, Dublin, and the Theory of Value, 1832–63," *Ec.,* August, 1945. The failure of the subjective theory of value to catch on and the tendency of all Ricardo's critics to compromise, and to compromise fatally, with Ricardian economics is considered in Blaug, *Ricardian Economics,* chap. 8.

J. N. Keynes, *The Scope and Method of Political Economy* (1904), particularly chaps. 1 and 7, discusses classical views on methodology, a subject on which nothing has been said in this chapter. Bowley, *Nassau Senior,* chap. 1, and Schumpeter, *History,* pp. 534–41, are also instructive on this question. On factual work in the period, for this is the era in which fact-finding caught on, see Schumpeter, *History,* pp. 519–26. For the bearing of empirical findings on the development of Ricardian doctrine see Blaug, *Ricardian Economics,* chap. 9, secs. 5 and 6.

In view of the current interest in problems of growth and development, some readers may want to look at E. McKinley, "The Problem of 'Under-development' in the English Classical School," *QJE,* May, 1955. This article presents a compendium of classical ideas on development. For the construction of a classical model of the growth process, see A. Lowe, "The Classical Theory of Economic Growth," *SR,* Summer, 1954. Comparative cost theory is contrasted with Smith's dynamic approach to international trade in H. Myint, "The 'Classical Theory' of International Trade and the Underdeveloped Countries," *EJ,* June, 1958.

In a long article, F. H. Knight ranges over the whole of classical economic theory in the manner of Cannan: "The Ricardian Theory of Production and Distribution," *CJEP,* 1935, reprinted in *On the History and Method of Economics* (1956). This is not an essay for the tyro, for it presumes thorough acquaintance with modern economics, but it is a brilliant review of the subject from the standpoint of absolutism.

Chapter 7 MARXIAN ECONOMICS

THE TWENTIETH century has witnessed a strong revolt against great philosophical systems, such as Marxism, which purport to explain the nature of reality in all its aspects. We live in an age of specialization, no less in technology than in social science. But this is precisely why we should study Marx. His attempt to embrace historical, sociological, and economic elements in one theoretical framework provides a useful antidote. Whatever one may think of the ultimate validity of Marxism, it is a dull mind that fails to be inspired by Marx's heroic attempt to project a systematic general account of "the economic laws of motion of modern society."

Terminology. Since most of Marxian economics thrives in a cloud of terminological confusion, the first step is to agree on a set of definitions. We will use capital letters for stocks, lower-case letters for flows, and primed letters for ratios per unit of time. Marx's "constant capital" c is defined as the sum of depreciation charges on fixed capital and inputs of raw materials. Adding the wages of production workers v, Marx's "variable capital," we get the flow of outlays k. Dividing the components of k by the appropriate annual rates of turnover t_c and t_v, or multiplying by the appropriate durabilities in years d_c and d_v, we get the stock of capital invested K. $K = C + V$, where C stands for the value of the stock of durable equipment and inventories of raw materials and V stands for the working capital required to meet weekly payrolls. Following Marx, surplus value is defined on a flow basis as the excess of gross receipts over variable and fixed costs. For the economy as a whole this amounts to the excess of net national product over the wages bill. The gross national product $= c + v + s$, but the net national product $= v + s$. The "rate of surplus-value" $s' = s/v$. The rate of profit p', as Marx defined it, is s/k; on a stock basis it is s/K.

Apart from s' and p', another fundamental ratio in the Marxian system is the "organic composition of capital," q. Marx never explicitly defines this concept, sometimes writing $c/c + v$ and in one case $v/c + v$. What he has in mind, however, is clearly the ratio of machine costs to labor costs C/v. When multiplied by the wage rate v/L —the total wage bill divided by the number of workers—and ignoring V as negligibly small, this becomes the familiar concept of the amount of capital per man:

$$K/v \cdot v/L = K/L = Q \, .$$

At all times Marx shuffles freely between stocks and flows without warning the reader. His expression for p' is actually the share of profits in the turnover of capital; it is only equal to the rate of profit on capital invested on the assumption that the whole of the capital stock turns over once a year. Thus,

$$p' = \frac{s}{c/t_c + v/t_v} = \frac{s}{c + v}$$

when $t_c = t_v = 1$. Marx discusses the different turnover rates of c and v at great length in Volume II of *Capital*—writing n for our t_c—but elsewhere he loses sight of the distinction between stocks and flows. For the time being we shall follow Marx's procedure in Volume I and set $t_c = t_v = 1$: society's capital stock, therefore, is entirely consumed and reconstituted each year.

Value and Surplus Value. The first volume of *Capital* is so framed as to bring out the essential nature of profit as a surplus value produced by labor. It is assumed at the beginning that the capital-labor ratio is identical in every industry. Hence, the ratio of interest to wage charges is the same for every product, and commodity prices differ only because some employ more direct plus indirect labor—more labor and more capital—than others. In short, all products exchange in proportion to the labor embodied in their production. Now, if all prices correspond to labor values, how is it that a surplus value results when employers buy labor inputs to produce final output? The answer is not that employers pay workers just enough to live on and no more. This ignores the fact that it is the force of competition that compels employers to pay the economic value of services received. Whatever the source of surplus value, it must come about because, not in spite of, competition.

The answer that Marx gives runs in terms of the historical dispossession of a large group in society that is impelled to live by the sale of personal services as a result of the concentration of property in the hands of a few. Labor power becomes a commodity, traded on the market like any other at a normal price governed by the labor time necessary to produce it, that is, by the labor time necessary to produce the wage goods which go to maintain labor. The commodity labor power is bought and sold at its full value, but the value of the products of labor exceeds its own value. As Marx would say, the "exchange-value of labor-power" is bought and paid for, but what is actually acquired is "the use-value of labor." In Marxian imagery, only a part of the worker's working day is spent in replacing the equivalent of his own value, namely, the subsistence goods that go to maintain him; during the remainder of the day, the worker works for the capitalist. Surplus value is nothing but "unpaid labor."

Marx concludes, as does Ricardo, that profits or total surplus value depend on the cost of wage goods. Surplus value can be increased by lengthening the working day: "absolute surplus-value"; or by an increase in the productivity of labor, which lessens the time required to produce wage goods—"relative surplus-value." The "rate of exploitation" or "rate of surplus-value" is solely a function of the direct labor employed; constant capital in the form of machinery and raw materials only transmits its own value to the product; it does not create additional value. It is true that machinery enhances the productivity of labor and that insofar as depreciation charges and raw material costs enter into the total value of the final product, they *add* to the value produced by labor. But the value that machines and raw materials add to labor is no more than the value at which they were purchased. This is why the value of the total net national product consists entirely of wages plus a mark-up proportional to labor time: $v + s'(v)$. In the language of social accounting, raw materials as well as the current services of machines constitute intermediate products that are netted out of gross income. Interest on fixed capital, however, is present in the Marxian schema, but it is subsumed under surplus value on the premise—which is yet to be proved—that it is really a function of the employment of direct labor.

The Great Contradiction. So far, we have faithfully followed Marx's own exposition. It is evident that, as matters stand, the argument is unsatisfactory. In a system in which relative prices correspond to relative labor values, the net product of equal quantities of labor is sold for equal quantities of money; given uniform money wage rates between industries, the rate of surplus value is everywhere the same. But the organic composition of capital is not the same in different industries. If profits per man s' are everywhere the same, while capital per man q varies from industry to industry, the rate of profit per unit of capital p' will vary inversely with capital per man. This implies that the higher the degree of mechanization, the lower the rate of profit, which flies in the face of the fact that capitalists are motivated to substitute capital for labor by the prospect of earning higher profits. In other words, if s/v is uniform between industries, but c/v is not, $s/c + v$ will also differ between industries. But competition between capitalists does in fact establish a uniform rate of profit on capital regardless of its composition. We are now caught in a contradiction: with a uniform p' and with different q's, we cannot logically have a uniform s'. Recall that $p' = s/(c + v) = s'/(q + 1)$: if one ratio is equal between industries, the other two ratios must be equal between industries. Since q in fact differs between industries, so must s'. This implies, however, that the net product of equal quantities of labor cannot sell for equal quantities of money: relative prices cannot correspond to relative labor values.

On Marx's own grounds, the labor theory of value is only formally correct if we assume that there are no differences in the ratio of capital to labor between industries. Anyone who has read Ricardo will hardly be surprised by this conclusion.

In view of the fact that widely different capital-labor ratios are observed in the real world, it would seem that we must abandon the labor theory of value as a theory of relative prices: the pressures that equalize the rate of profit necessarily produce different rates of surplus value between industries. This is just what we would expect: profits per man employed are surely a function of output per man that is greater where capital per man is greater. But if labor values do not correspond to prices, owing to variations in s' between different products, the theory of surplus value will also have to be abandoned. The amount of surplus value that a worker produces is apparently influenced by the amount of capital with which he is furnished: surplus value is not simply "expropriated labor." But Marx, of course, does not give up the assumption that profits depend upon human labor employed and upon nothing else: s' *must* be equal in all industries irrespective of the observed variations in the ratio of capital to labor and despite the fact that profits per unit of total capital tend to equality. The solution to the problem is given in the third volume of *Capital,* in which Marx transforms "values" into "prices." The so-called Transformation Problem is worth careful consideration, not only for its own sake but because it marks the first and only attempt in the history of economic thought to carry the labor theory of value to its logical conclusion.

The Transformation Problem. Marx's solution to the "great contradiction" is best approached by looking at his own numerical example (see accompanying table). The economy consists of five indus-

Capitals	Used up *c*	Cost Price	*s* at $s' = 1$	Value	Profit at $p' = .22$	"Price of Prod."	Price > Value
I. $80C + 20V$	50	70	20	90	22	92	+ 2
II. $70C + 30V$	51	81	30	111	22	103	− 8
III. $60C + 40V$	51	91	40	131	22	113	−18
IV. $85C + 15V$	40	55	15	70	22	77	+ 7
V. $95C + 5V$	10	15	5	20	22	37	+17
Σ $390C + 110V$ 202		312	110	422	110	422	0

tries, and none of the products of the five industries enters into the production of any other. The capital invested in every industry is the same and is equal to 100 units. The turnover rate of variable capital is everywhere equal to unity, but the turnover rates of constant capital differ considerably from industry to industry. Adding the value of the fixed capital actually consumed to the wages paid out, we arrive at the "cost price" of a commodity. With $s' = 100$ per cent, the labor value of each commodity is equal to the cost price plus a uniform mark-up proportional to outlays on wages. So far the argument is that of Volume I. At this point we take account of the fact that capitalists actually sell products at "prices of production": to the "cost price" they add a uniform mark-up proportional to the total capital invested, regardless of the degree of mechanization in the industry. Thus, "prices of production" are equal to $c + v + p' (C + V)$.

We find that in no case does "value" correspond to "price of production." But, lo and behold, the sum total of deviations of prices from values is equal to zero. Moreover, the deviations are uniquely related to the organic composition of capital in each industry. The average composition of capital in the whole economy $q_0 = 390/110 = 3.5$. When the composition of capital in an industry exceeds this average, as with q_1, q_4, and q_5, the product sells at a price in excess of its value; contrariwise, when the composition of capital is below the social average, price is less than value. Apparently, if we had an industry whose composition equaled the social average, prices would actually correspond to values. Let us bring this out by constructing a simple three-sector model upon Marx's assumptions, setting both t_c and t_v equal to unity for convenience (see accompanying table).

Capitals	Cost Price	s at $s' = 1$	Value	Profit at $p' = 33.3$	"Price of Prod."	Price > Value	q
I. $250C + 75V$ 325		75	400	108.3	433.3	+33.3	3.3
II. $100C + 50V$.........150		50	200	50	200	0	2.0
III. $50C + 75V$..........125		75	200	41.6	166.6	−33.3	0.7
$\Sigma\ 400C + 200V$........600		200	800	200	800	0	

How is it that in Department II the price of the product is exactly equal to its labor value? Obviously, because $q_2 = q_0$, which means that the share of labor in the cost price of Department II is identical to the share of labor in the cost price of output as a whole, namely one third. The trick in Marx's argument is very simple: first, we derive the total amount of surplus value from the amount of variable capital employed; next, we calculate the average rate of profit on total capital invested by dividing the total surplus value by the amount of capital in the economy; and then we add profits at the going rate to the cost price. Obviously, the deviations of price so determined from value must cancel out in the aggregate, because we have defined total profits to be equal to total surplus value. Different industries share in a pool of surplus value, not in proportion to their variable capital, but in proportion to their quotient of the total capital invested in the economy. Nevertheless, by setting $\Sigma s = \Sigma\sigma$, where $\sigma = $ total profits, we insure that the industry whose $q = q_0$ will sell its product at a price equal to its value simply because it earns profits exactly equal to its surplus value. The total surplus is derived by applying a given s' to v; total profits are derived by applying the given s' to $v/c + v$. An industry in which $q = q_0$ is a scalar model of the whole economy and naturally shares the attributes of the aggregate economy. But how do we know that profits in the aggregate are determined by applying a coefficient s' to variable capital alone? We do not know. This precisely what is to be proved. Instead of proving it, Marx assumes it at the outset.

Let us restate the logic of the argument. Price will be higher or lower than value depending on whether $q > q_0$ or $q < q_0$; when $q = q_0$, price = value. Since value $= c + v + s$ and $\Sigma s = \Sigma\sigma$, it follows that with a given s' any industry for which $q < q_0$ would earn a higher rate of profit. As it can earn only the average rate, the profits it does obtain are less than the surplus value generated in the industry; this is what causes the price of its product to be less than its value. Conversely, industries with a high degree of mechanization sell at prices in excess of value by appropriating surplus value from

other industries. Interindustry equality in the rate of profit causes surplus value to be redistributed from labor-intensive industries to capital-
intensive industries. The industry with an average degree of mechanization is unaffected by this process. And so Marx concludes that "the sum
of prices equals the sum of values." Since it is nonsense to speak of a
sum of relative prices, it would be better to say "average prices equal
average values."

Solutions of the Transformation Problem. Quite apart from
the actual meaning of Marx's argument, it remains to be shown that the
problem admits of a uniquely determined solution when both output
and input values are transformed into prices. In Marx's solution the
equal rate of profit is calculated in relation to the *value* of invested
capital, and then outputs are expressed in terms of prices instead of in
values. But, obviously, the price calculation ought to transform inputs
as well as outputs. Marx himself did not give the general solution, but
it is easy to show that it is in fact possible to transform *all* values into
prices (see accompanying tabulations). Reading across the rows, we

Values	Prices
I. $c_1 + v_1 + s_1 = a_1$	I. $c_1 p_1 + v_1 p_2 + \sigma_1 = a_1 p_1$
II. $c_2 + v_2 + s_2 = a_2$	II. $c_2 p_1 + v_2 p_2 + \sigma_2 = a_2 p_2$
III. $c_3 + v_3 + s_3 = a_3$	III. $c_3 p_1 + v_3 p_2 + \sigma_3 = a_3 p_3$
$\Sigma\ a_1 + a_2 + a_3 = \Sigma a$	$\Sigma\ c\ p_1 + v\ p_2 + \sigma p_3 = \Sigma ap$

have each industry's cost input according to its origin, including the
surplus accruing to it; reading down the columns, we have the allocation of each department's output according to its destination. Under
stationary conditions, Marx's "simple reproduction," in which all surplus value is spent by capitalists on luxury goods, the sum of each row
would equal the sum of the corresponding column. But under conditions of "expanded reproduction," this will not be true. Department I
produces capital goods used for further processing, Department II produces wage goods consumed by workers, and Department III produces
luxury goods consumed by capitalists. Now $\sigma_i = p'\ (c_i p_1 + v_i p_2)$,
and the principle of equal profitability says that $p' = \sigma_1 / c_1 p_1 + v_1 p_2 =
\sigma_2 / c_2 p_1 + v_2 p_2$. Since $a_1 p_1 = (1 + p')\ (c_1 p_1 + v_1 p_2)$ and $a_2 p_2 =
(1 + p')\ (c_2 p_1 + v_2 p_2)$, whereas luxury goods do not function as
cost inputs, we can write

$$(1) \qquad 1 + p' = \frac{a_1 p_1}{c_1 p_1 + v_1 p_2} = \frac{a_2 p_2}{c_2 p_1 + v_2 p_2}$$
$$= (a_1 c_2) p_1^2 + (a_1 v_2 - a_2 c_1) p_1 p_2 - (a_2 v_1) p_2^2 \ .$$

Dividing through by p_2^2, we have the familiar quadratic equation of general form $ax^2 + bx + c$, whose solution is $x = (-b \pm \sqrt{b^2 - 4ac})/2a$. Therefore,

$$(2) \qquad x = \frac{p_1}{p_2} = \frac{a_2 c_1 - a_1 v_2 + \sqrt{(a_2 c_1 - a_1 v_2)^2 + 4 a_1 a_2 v_1 c_2}}{2 a_1 c_2}.$$

With x determined, the average rate of profit is therefore given by

$$(3) \qquad p' = \frac{a_1 x}{c_1 x + v_1} - 1.$$

If (3) is substituted into the original set of price equations, the system will uniquely determine the three prices except for a proportionality factor; that is, we obtain unique solutions for relative prices in terms of any one commodity. This is as far as the principle of equal profitability will take us by itself.

The three-industry model is unnecessarily restrictive: it assumes that the ultimate use of any product is predetermined by its department of origin. But it has been shown that the transformation of values into prices based upon equal profitability can be carried out even for an n-fold subdivision of the economy with all possible uses for each product. As long as we stay with relative prices, there is no problem. To determine absolute prices, however, we need an invariant characteristic of the value system, and in principle the selection of such a characteristic is entirely arbitrary. Marx himself suggests two definite aggregate characteristics of the value system that are said to remain invariant to the transformation into prices: (a) "total value equals total price," which is tantamount to selecting the weighted average of all prices as the *numéraire* = 1; and (b) the total surplus in value terms is equal to total profit in price terms. Interestingly enough, it turns out that both conditions cannot hold simultaneously. This can be demonstrated by a single numerical example.

Let us begin with the first postulate. The condition is that $\Sigma a = \Sigma ap$ or

$$(4) \qquad a_1 p_1 + a_2 p_2 + a_3 p_3 = a_1 + a_2 + a_3.$$

Eliminate p_2 by $p_2 = p_1/x$ and p_3 by setting p' in Department III equal to the average rate. Thus,

$$\frac{a_3 p_3}{c_3 p_1 + v_3 p_2} = \frac{a_1 x}{c_1 x + v_1} = p' + 1.$$

Hence

$$(5) \qquad p_3 = \frac{a_1 (c_3 x + v_3)}{a_3 (c_1 x + v_1)} p_2.$$

Rewriting (4), we have

$$(6) \qquad a_1p_1 + a_2p_1/x + \frac{a_1(c_3x + v_3)p_2}{(c_1x + v_1)} = \Sigma a .$$

It is an easy matter to solve for p_1 and then in turn for p_2 and p_3. With a given value system we can substitute the results.

Take a typical Marxian three-sector model in which $s' = 100$ per cent and $q_2 = q_0$.

$$
\begin{array}{rl}
\text{I.} & 3c_1 + 4v_1 + 4s_1 = 11a_1 \\
\text{II.} & 18c_2 + 15v_2 + 15s_2 = 48a_2 \\
\text{III.} & 9c_3 + 6v_3 + 6s_3 = 21a_3 \\
\hline
\Sigma & 30c + 25v + 25s = 80a
\end{array}
$$

Applying these values to equation (2), we obtain $x = 0.94$, which, after substitution in (6), yields $p_1 = 0.94$, $p_2 = 1$, and $p_3 = 1.04$. The results of the entire calculation are as follows:

$$
\begin{array}{rl}
\text{I.} & 2.82c_1p_1 + 4v_1p_2 + 3.52\sigma_1 = 10.34a_1p_1 \\
\text{II.} & 16.92c_2p_1 + 15v_2p_2 + 16.08\sigma_2 = 48.00a_2p_2 \\
\text{III.} & 8.46c_3p_1 + 6v_3p_2 + 7.38\sigma_3 = 21.84a_3p_3 \\
\hline
\Sigma & 28.20cp_1 + 25vp_2 + 26.98\sigma = 80.18\Sigma ap
\end{array}
$$

We see that although the solution naturally leaves the sum of prices equal to the sum of values, total profit diverges from total surplus value.

Likewise, if we start out by postulating the invariance of total profits by the condition $\Sigma s = \Sigma \sigma$, we arrive at the following results:

$$
\begin{array}{rl}
\text{I.} & 2.59c_1p_1 + 3.71v_1p_2 + 3.20\sigma_1 = 9.50a_1p_1 \\
\text{II.} & 15.55c_2p_1 + 13.91v_2p_2 + 15.05\sigma_2 = 44.52a_2p_2 \\
\text{III.} & 7.77c_3p_1 + 5.56v_3p_2 + 6.78\sigma_3 = 20.12a_3p_3 \\
\hline
\Sigma & 25.91cp_1 + 23.18vp_2 + 25.03\sigma = 74.14\Sigma ap
\end{array}
$$

A fixed aggregate of surplus value is reallocated in the form of profit at the average rate among the various capitals concerned, but the sum of prices diverges from the sum of values. We conclude that Marx is mistaken: when both input and output values are appropriately transformed into prices, we may retain either the aggregate version of the theory of surplus value ($\Sigma s = \Sigma p$) or the aggregate version of the labor theory of prices ($\Sigma a = ap$), but we cannot have both.

Since Marx's day other invariance postulates have been proposed. The first author to treat the transformation problem after Marx was Bortkiewicz, writing in the first decade of this century. Bortkiewicz claimed invariance for the unit value of luxury goods, the products of

Department III in the traditional three-sector breakdown of the economy: $p_3 = 1$. Taking a leaf out of Ricardo's book, he identified luxury goods with gold and thus insured that money prices were expressed in terms of the labor value of gold. On applying Bortkiewicz's solutions to a given value system, it is seen that total profits come out equal to total surplus value but that total prices normally diverge from total values. This is a consequence of the fact that $q_3 < q_0$. If Bortkiewicz had followed Ricardo the whole way, he would have made wage goods the "invariable measure of value" by setting $p_2 = 1$ and assuming $q_2 = q_0$. And, indeed, this is the only case in which the sum of prices does come out equal to the sum of values.

In recent years some Marxists have advocated postulating the equality of total value with total price in terms of wage goods, without necessarily assuming that $q_2 = q_0$. That is, the ratio of the man-hours required to produce all goods to the man-hours required to produce wage goods is said to be equal to the ratio of the money value of the total product to the money value of wages. Hence,

$$\frac{\Sigma a}{\Sigma v} = \frac{\Sigma ap}{p_2 \Sigma v} = \frac{\Sigma ap}{\Sigma vp} \,.$$

In the same way, and still more in keeping with the spirit of Marxism, we could postulate the invariance of the output-surplus ratio:

$$\frac{\Sigma a}{\Sigma s} = \frac{\Sigma ap}{p_3 \Sigma s} = \frac{\Sigma ap}{\Sigma sp} \,.$$

Both these postulates, however, ask us to hold price *ratios* constant and tell us nothing about *absolute* prices. They merely impose an additional constraint on the relative prices, which are already determined by the principle of equal profitability. Hence, by themselves they do not solve the transformation problem.

It is interesting to ask, however, under what conditions the output-wages and output-surplus ratios hold necessarily. The requisite condition for strict invariance of the output-wages ratio is simply that Department II reflects all the relevant characteristics of the economy as a whole, that is, $q_2 = q_0$ and $s_2/v_2 = \Sigma s/\Sigma v = s'$. When this is true we can write

$$c_2 p_1 + v_2 p_2 + \sigma_2 = (\Sigma c)p_1 + (\Sigma v)p_2 + (\Sigma \sigma) = (\Sigma a)p_2 = \Sigma ap \,.$$

Therefore,

$$\frac{\Sigma ap}{\Sigma v} = \frac{\Sigma ap_2}{\Sigma v} = \frac{\Sigma ap}{\Sigma vp} = \frac{\Sigma a}{\Sigma v} \,.$$

The ratio of output to wages is unaffected by transformation of values into prices when the value structure of the wage-goods industry conforms to the national average and the rate of surplus per man is equal in all industries. The additional assumption $p_2 = 1$, to determine absolute prices, will then necessarily imply invariance of the aggregate output value $\Sigma a = \Sigma ap$.

In exactly the same way, we can make the luxury industry representative of the economy as a whole by the postulate $q_3 = q_0$. And if all surplus value is wholly absorbed by capitalists' consumption, we necessarily have invariance of the output-surplus ratio.

$$\frac{\Sigma ap}{\Sigma s} = \frac{(\Sigma a)p_3}{\Sigma s} = \frac{\Sigma ap}{\Sigma sp} = \frac{\Sigma a}{\Sigma s} \,.$$

Setting $p_3 = 1$, we get the best of all possible results: "total value equals total price," total surplus value equals total profit, and all money prices are expressed in terms of the labor value of gold.

All this is strongly reminiscent of something we have already encountered. The Marxian quest for the appropriate transformation of values into prices is nothing else than the Ricardian hunt for a perfect "invariable measure of value." The whole problem is derived from Ricardo, a fact that emerges more clearly in Bortkiewicz's solution than in Marx's own. The divergence of prices from values does not appear as such in Ricardo: only the case of alteration of prices by various wages and profits when values remain the same. It was Ricardo who in effect was the first to ask: Will propositions about the rate of profit laid down in a world in which commodities sell at labor values hold as well as the real world in which commodities sell at "normal prices"? We can now see that, when Ricardo measured all values in terms of gold and assumed that gold was produced with an average ratio of capital to labor, he was in fact assuming $q_3 = q_0$ and $p_3 = 1$. At times he made things even simpler for himself by simultaneously assuming that $q_2 = q_0$ and $p_2 = 1$. The logic of Ricardo's procedure, its formal validity, as well as its incredibly restrictive character, emerge very clearly in the light of the Marxist transformation problem. That is why we have taken so much care to spell it out.

Historical Transformation. By now the reader has surely grown weary of juggling to and fro with averages and ratios. It is time to ask what all this is supposed to prove. It was Marx's intention to show that the average rate of profit, calculated as it is on total capital invested, hides the true nature of profit, namely, its sole dependence on capital expended to purchase direct labor services. In the first volume of *Capi-*

tal we get an analysis of *s'* stripped of all disguises: surplus value accrues to each capitalist in accordance with his outlays on labor. But,
since capital-labor ratios differ between industries, while *p'* tends to be
uniform, it cannot be true that profits in each industry depend solely
on wage capital. So let us translate into the price calculus of capitalists
and show that, despite all appearance to the contrary, the average rate
of profit depends on an average rate of surplus value as a function of
the size of the labor force. It is quite clear that Marx thought he had
actually demonstrated that total profits equal total surplus value. Were
this not so, he argued, the average rate of profit would be indeterminate: producers add a mark-up to the cost price of a commodity, but
how is this mark-up itself determined? "The sum of the profits of all
spheres of production must be equal to the sum of surplus-values"; to
deny this is to leave "political economy . . . without a rational basis."

And yet nowhere does Marx give any reason for believing that
the rate of surplus value is in fact uniform between industries. What we
actually observe is that profit per worker varies with capital per worker
in each industry. The "strong" assumption that each worker generates
a constant surplus no matter where he is employed requires proof to be
credible. And the proof is never forthcoming. The whole of *Capital* is
in fact a long-drawn-out *petitio principii*. The rate of surplus value is
not observable in the market; no one acts in response to changes in that
rate; workers are interested in maximizing wages, and capitalists are
motivated by the rate of profit. Marx merely *attributes* all income to
labor and so presumes the existence of a purely fictitious ratio s/v. If,
instead, he had operated with a capital theory of value, attributing the
whole of the surplus solely to machinery and implements, and defined
the rate of surplus value as s/c, he could have carried on transforming
values into prices in exactly the same way as he did. It is not always
appreciated that, under the assumptions of Volume I of *Capital*, not
only is s/v equal between all industries, but so is s/c. With a capital
theory of value we can say that all capitalists share in a pool of surplus
value, a pool created solely by the nonhuman factors of production; in
the process of equating profit margins per unit of capital invested in
both labor and machines, capitalists necessarily cause prices to fall below value in capital-intensive industries and to rise above value in
labor-intensive industries. But this argument would no more prove that
surplus value is created only by machines than Marx's own argument
proves that surplus value is created only by labor.

The only place in which Marx approaches something like a substantive argument is in his contention that "value" exists not only theo-

retically, but also historically, prior to "prices of production." Prices were at one time in accordance with the labor theory of value; just as ontogeny repeats phylogeny in biology, the capitalist system grew in the same way as Volume III succeeded Volume I. Under "simple commodity production," in which each worker owns his own tools, everyone earns the same income for equal working time. Here unequal capital-labor ratios do not come in to plague us because there is no tendency toward equal profitability and the movement of workers between occupations merely establishes an equal rate of surplus value. Marx supposes that this condition actually prevailed in ancient and medieval economies. Engels went so far as to say that "the law of value has prevailed during a period of from 5 to 7000 years." Soviet writers have pointed out that this accounts for the fact that the process of industrialization in capitalist countries always begins with the development of light industry. At early stages of capitalist development, when the transformation into prices has not yet been affected and the rate of profit is still unequal between industries, capital will naturally be attracted to labor-intensive consumer-goods industries, where the rate of profit is higher than in capital-intensive industries producing machinery.

This extraordinary argument is not without significance for an understanding of Marx's preconceptions. Taken at its face value, it is untenable: all societies that have even approximated the conditions of "simple commodity production" have been custom ridden. Competition was never allowed to equate skilled labor to so many units of unskilled labor, and hence the ratios at which products exchanged could not have corresponded to the quantities of "socially necessary simple" labor required to produce them. Moreover, what has happened to what Marx called "primitive accumulation"? Instead of capitalism arising out of colonial plunder, piracy, the slave trade, debasement of the currency, and enclosures, we suddenly have an orderly historical process of the transformation of values into prices. The interesting implication of the argument, however, is that it admits that the labor theory of value can be operative even when the sociological spectrum of capitalism is missing. All that is really necessary is the presence of competition. "Simple commodity production" is nothing else than Adam Smith's "early and rude state of society," in which commodities exchange at ratios proportional to embodied labor because there is no capital. Adam Smith conjectured the existence of such a society only to illustrate the action of competition under simplified assumptions. But Marx, in a thoroughly un-Marxist fashion, actually supposes that a precapitalist economy functions in the same way that a Smithian society of beaver and deer hunters does.

What Price Value? It should now be obvious that the labor theory of value is not a theory of value at all in the now accepted use of the term. It does not claim that the price of a commodity is equal to the labor embodied in its production or that competition enforces such a distribution of productive resources between various industries that relative prices in the long run tend to be proportional to labor inputs. Long-run prices in Marx are determined in the same way as in orthodox theory, that is, by long-run costs of production, including profit at the ruling rate. But an adequate theory of value must explain how market forces produce such an equilibrium "normal price." This involves an explanation of how the values of the factors of production are determined and how the level of prices, including factor prices, results from the supply of factors and the pattern of demand for finished goods. On all these counts, we get no assistance from *Capital*. What Marx means by the value of a commodity is its price in terms of labor time if the share of wages in total costs for this commodity is equal to that of output as a whole. Moreover, the commodity in question must be reproducible at constant cost and sold within a perfectly competitive closed economy. It is clear, therefore, that for any detailed pricing problem of the microscopic kind, the Marxist theory of value will prove worse than useless.

It has been argued that it was not Marx's intention to supply a detailed theory of relative prices. The Marxian system is fundamentally concerned with macroeconomic relationships and, in particular, with the distribution of income between property owners and wage earners. Some Marxists have expressed their discomfort at this face-saving argument. A theory of class-income distribution that is economic and not ethical in content must have *some* reference to actual prices. The whole point of Volume I of *Capital* is to show how the existence of surplus value is consistent with a state of affairs in which commodities exchange according to the quantity of labor embodied in them. The theory of surplus value is essentially a statement about the relationship of the value of labor power to the value of the final product; surely, this is a statement about relative prices.

Nevertheless, it would seem that Marx's constant harking back to the basic division between "paid" and "unpaid" labor refers to the aggregate output of the entire economy: in any developed economy workers do not spend part of their time producing their own consumption goods. What Marx seems to be saying, therefore, is something like this: If a given net national product requires 100 man-hours to produce, and if 60 per cent of output goes to wages, then the value of the surplus is 40 man-hours; in a particular capital-intensive industry in which wages absorb only half of net output, the extra 10 man-hours of profit are to be attributed to the fact that the price of the product exceeds its value. Put this way, it is seen that total profits in the system are limited by the amount of unpaid labor that can be squeezed from the working class. Marx's "value," therefore, is not a ratio at which products exchange but purely an abstraction that is posited, not observed, by crediting each worker with an average rate s'. When the total surplus formed from this average is broken up and redistributed among industries, it is possible to *say* that prices diverge from value and that profits are, in the last analysis, simply unpaid labor.

It has also been held, but not by Marxists, that the theory of surplus value is merely an expression of the particular ethical or political viewpoint that property income *ought* to accrue to workers rather than to capitalists, landlords, and rentiers. The labor theory of value, according to this interpretation, is a theory of natural rights rather than a theory of prices. But however much every sentence of *Capital* radiates moral zeal, Marx did not write three volumes to furnish a *positive* demonstration of a *normative* proposition. The labor theory of value may be associated with definite moral sentiments, but it does not rest upon them. At bottom, its appeal is to science, not to ethics. A wholly different question is whether labor values should play a normative pricing role in a socialist economy: instead of charging profit against each product in proportion to cost, it is possible to calculate profit margins in proportion to outlays on direct labor. The dominant point of view among Soviet economists is that actual prices should deviate from labor values only in a planned, orderly fashion, which implies the use of the labor theory of value as a pricing norm. It is evident, however, that this has nothing to do with the validity of the labor theory of value in a capitalist economy.

The Marxist Case for the Labor Theory.   We have seen that the labor theory of value can in some fashion explain all observed price phenomena in a capitalist economy. The skeptic would say that any schema can be made to work at the cost of theoretical complexity: given enough epicycles, the Ptolemaic hypothesis can be upheld. But Marxists retort that economics is replete with theories that require substantial qualification before they can be applied to real-world situations: it is all a matter of the degree of appropriate abstraction, about which no rules can be laid down. But economy of logic does have its virtue:

the fewer the epicycles the better. Should we not apply Occam's Razor to the troublesome assumption that only labor adds value to the product, the value of raw materials and machinery being merely passed on? By dropping this notion we excise the arbitrary assumption that the ratio of value added by labor to wages tends to equality between industries and so dispense with the formalistic transformation problem. After all, a good many economists have used the labor theory of value as a rough approximation of the secular trend in "real costs" of production, without all the rigmarole of transforming value into price. Even Keynes expressed "sympathy" with the labor theory of value in the *General Theory* on the grounds that in the short run relative prices are determined by prime or variable costs and that, over the economy as a whole, prime costs are all wage costs. This is not strictly true, for demand plays a role in determining price in the short run, but it will suffice for general purposes. It is clear, however, that Marxists mean more than this by the labor theory of value. Why do they cling to it?

When pressed, Marxist writers concede the limited importance of the labor theory as a theory of relative prices. But they insist that this theory throws into sharp relief, in a way no other does, the fundamental division of income between wage earners and property owners. The point is that the labor theory, and the labor theory alone, leads to the theory of surplus value, and it is the latter that appeals. A review of recent writings by Anglo-American Marxists yields a series of defensive arguments: only the labor theory of value is based on the fact that labor is a unique social cost, it alone starts from the firm bedrock of *objective* costs, it alone emphasizes that production and exchange involve social relations between men and not just technical relations between things, and so on. In part, this seems to be a reaction against the colorless neutrality of modern economics, with its rigid divorce of price theory from welfare economics. But, on a deeper level, what Marxists are saying is that unless we begin with a labor theory of value we cannot argue that capitalists get a part of the total product without working. But what evidence do we have that profit is an "unearned income"? This question, which seems to be at the bottom of the debate between Marxists and non-Marxists, is almost never raised explicitly in the literature.

Profit as Unearned Income. The first point to note is that the concept of surplus value in Marx is not formally derived from the labor theory of value at all. For labor power to sell at its value, there must be an equilibrating mechanism in the labor market that causes the "market price" to conform to the "natural price" of labor services.

The classical economists found such a mechanism in the theory of population, but Marx rejected the Malthusian theory and denied that labor is produced in accordance with rational cost calculations. What he puts into its place is "the reserve army" of the unemployed, which has no necessary tendency to preserve wages at the "value" of labor power, however effective it may be in holding wages down. In short, without being aware of it, Marx denies the applicability of the labor theory of value to wages because the equilibrating mechanism that is the foundation of this theory does not work in the labor market. This is all to the good, for it permits us to discuss the theory of surplus value on its own merits without any connection with the vexed questions of value theory.

Marx's problem is to show how surplus value, a costless gain to the capitalist, is preserved in an economy in which prices are determined by impersonal forces and the relation between employer and worker is based on contract rather than status. Under perfect competition one might think that capitalists—whose individual contributions to total output are too small to influence price—would expand output in the effort to reap more surplus value, until wages are bid up so as to reduce the surplus to zero. Having discarded the Malthusian wages-population mechanism, Marx cannot argue that population pressures will maintain wage rates at the subsistence level. Instead, he postulates the existence of "the industrial reserve army," a chronic excess supply of labor. Excess supply of labor implies that the equilibrium wage rate lies below the ruling rate. If factor substitution is possible, the artificially high wage rate results in the adoption of capital-intensive methods. As the demand for labor falls off, wages decline and continue to decline until the labor market is cleared. But this may not happen in an underdeveloped economy in which the equilibrium wage rate that would clear the market is well below the subsistence wage rate. The wage rate will then be kept artificially high by all kinds of social conventions favoring a "fair wage." The result is hidden as well as open unemployment resulting from inappropriate factor endowments combined with limited possibilities of factor substitution. This is what we have earlier described as Marxian unemployment: full-capacity use of the capital stock is nevertheless insufficient to absorb the available labor supply.

But surely this kind of structural unemployment must eventually disappear? Marx argues, however, that an excess supply of labor is required to prevent wages from eating into profits. Thus, capital accumulation in an advanced economy must involve a sufficient flow of laborsaving innovations to produce chronic unemployment. Booms deplete the reserve army, and slumps replenish it, but secular growth at full employment is a contradiction in terms.

For the moment let us accept this theory of the dynamic process that keeps capitalism going. In what sense can we now say that surplus value or profit is an unearned income? In describing surplus value as "expropriated labor time," Marx apparently means to imply that surplus value does not remunerate a productive effort; it is not a payment that is technically necessary to enable production to go on; it is merely the result of the fact that means of production are privately owned under capitalism. Does this contradict the teachings of "bourgeois" economics? Let us take the most apologetic of all interest theories, the abstinence theory of interest as held by Nassau Senior. The capitalist has practiced abstinence from present consumption and may therefore demand interest or profit as a "just reward" for his pains. He may demand all he will, but why does competition allow him to earn interest? Obviously, because workers do not possess the wherewithal to wait until the goods they are currently producing are ready for sale; it is only because capitalists can advance wages that they receive interest as their personal income. Does this theory "justify" the payment of interest? In one sense, yes: positive net investment cannot take place unless some people are willing to postpone present consumption; since no one is apparently willing to do so without a reward, elimination of interest would mean cessation of investment. But this in no way justifies *private* ownership of means of production. If postponement of the present enjoyment of income is really a sacrifice, the abstinence theory of interest will justify a positive interest rate on money loans just as well under socialism as under capitalism. In general, all theories of interest, whether a marginal productivity theory or a time-preference theory or what have you, must explain the receipt of surplus value by capitalists, landlords, and rentiers in terms of the fundamental institutional fact that workers do not own the means of production.

The issue is not how to justify interest or profit but how to justify private property of productive equipment. Acceptance of one or another bourgeois theory of interest implies nothing about the institutional structure of a society. To rationalize private ownership of the means of production, we need an additional argument designed to show that private decision making is more efficient than central planning. Contrariwise, arguments in favor of socialism require demonstration that public ownership and central direction are more efficient or better in some well-defined way than is decentralized decision making.

It is curious that Marx, the prophet of socialism, gave the whole dispute about the respective merits of capitalism and socialism a wrong slant by confusing the social and the economic implications of a theory of interest. The debate about capitalism versus socialism revolves around the question of how certain functions can be most efficiently performed, functions bound up with the ownership of property. Instead, Marx is caught up in the purely metaphysical problem of whether capital is barren or productive, whether interest or profit is a payment for services rendered or merely income stolen from workers. Marx admits that, though all value is produced by labor, labor's capacity to create value is enhanced by working with capital equipment. But to say that the output of labor is greater with than without capital is to say that capital is productive. This proves nothing about the merits of capitalism. One may believe that capital is productive, and even that capitalists are productive—another proposition altogether—and yet believe that the price we pay for free enterprise in the form of recurrent slumps and gross inequalities in the distribution of income is too great to warrant its perpetuation. In other words, it is not necessary to be a Marxist to believe in socialism, nor does approval of capitalism imply denial of the facts from which Marx drew the unwarranted conclusion that profit is legalized plunder of workers.[1]

Marx and Böhm-Bawerk. The distinction between interest as a distributive share and interest as a necessary cost payment is well brought out by contrasting Marx's theory of interest with Böhm-Bawerk's. The "dean of bourgeois economists" regarded labor and land as the only primary factors of production and treated capital as produced

---

[1] The same facts can be made to look quite different when seen through different lenses. Here is Keynes describing the flourishing capitalism of the nineteenth century in his *Economic Consequences of the Peace:*

"Europe was so organized socially and economically as to secure the maximum accumulation of capital. While there was some continuous improvement in the daily conditions of the life of the mass of the population, Society was so framed as to throw a great part of the increased income into the control of the class least likely to consume it. The new rich of the nineteenth century were not brought up to large expenditures, and preferred the power which investment gave them to the pleasures of immediate consumption. In fact, it was precisely the *inequality* of the distribution of wealth which made possible those vast accumulations of fixed wealth and of capital improvements which distinguished that age from all others. Herein lay, in fact, the main justification of the Capitalist System. If the rich had spent their new wealth on their own enjoyment, the world would long ago have found such a régime intolerable. But like bees they saved and accumulated, not less to the advantage of the whole community because they themselves had narrower ends in prospect.

"The immense accumulations of fixed capital which, to the great benefit of mankind, were built up during the half-century before the war, could never have come about in a Society where wealth was divided equally. The railways of the world, which that age built as a monument to posterity, were, not less than the Pyramids of Egypt, the work of 'labour' which was not free to consume in immediate enjoyment the full equivalent of its efforts."

means of production that merely transmit value to the product; he denied that abstinence is an independent entity in production or that interest owed its existence to any personal activity of capitalists. Surplus value is produced by labor and land alone, but it accrues only after the passage of time. Workers do receive the entire *present* value of their future output, properly discounted at the going rate of interest; the *future* value of that output, however, will necessarily exceed its present value. The central task of the theory of interest is to show why there is such a difference in the value of labor's product over time. But, whatever the reason, this discounting of the future value of goods is possible only because workers' lack of reserves forces them to pay a premium on present goods. Insofar as interest is a distributive share, therefore, Marx's and Böhm-Bawerk's explanations do not differ significantly.

But interest is also a price that governs the distribution of the income stream of a community over time. It acts to allocate resources between current and future consumption. And it is one of Böhm-Bawerk's contentions that interest is a general economic category, not peculiar to capitalism but obtaining whenever present and future goods are exchanged. By way of contrast, Marx completely neglects the problem of resource allocation over time under socialism. It is not merely that Marx is reluctant, as he puts it, to write "recipes for the cook-shops of the future," but rather that Marxian economics falls down just where it is most needed, namely, to provide an economic rationale for a socialist economy.

Surplus Value and Economic Surplus. Marx's "proof" of the exploitative character of surplus value runs in terms of the reiterated assertion that workers produce more than the cost of their own maintenance and replacement. But all that this proves is that capitalism produces a surplus product over and above the biosocial minimum standard of life of the population. Again and again Marx thinks he is showing us that the surplus is attributable to labor alone, when all he is demonstrating is that the productive process generates a surplus. On Marx's definition, "exploitation" can cease only when the whole current net output of labor accrues to labor as current consumption: "exploitation" means positive net investment.

If there is any economic sense in giving the name of "surplus value" to the incomes of capitalists and landlords, it must be because such payments, unlike the wages of workers, are not necessary to call forth the sources of capital and land. A "surplus" in economic theory can only mean an excess of the receipts of an agent over its supply price. The classic example of such a surplus is Ricardo's rental payments to landlords in possession of superior land. The question of what constitutes a Ricardian rent depends entirely upon the point of view we take. As long as an agent has alternative uses, its earnings are necessary from the viewpoint of the firm—the narrowest point of view. But if an agent is committed to the industry, or if the "net disadvantages" of transferring to other industries are prohibitively high, payments to the agent may be higher than is necessary to keep the services of the agent in the industry: since competition between firms in the industry will assure equalization in the price of every unit of the productive service, marginal and intramarginal units alike, the agent may well earn a surplus from the viewpoint of the industry. As we take a wider and wider view, from the firm to the industry to the economy as a whole, the alternatives available to a productive agent become more restricted in scope, and the payment necessary to keep a unit of the productive service within the economic area considered becomes smaller. For the economy as a whole and in the short run, there are no alternative opportunities and the whole of an agent's reward is a surplus: payments for services yielded by property in the short run are economically unnecessary because the property is already in existence and "bygones are forever bygones." In the short run, as Marshall would say, all interest is in the nature of a quasi-rent. The same is true of the bulk of wages in the short run except that labor needs some daily maintenance payments.

But if we now give our attention to the long run, we "narrow" our point of view by considering the possibility of new alternative earnings for the factors of production. Payments for the use of property do now appear to be economically necessary, even from the point of view of society as a whole. Payments to the owner of a requisite productive service to compensate him for the loss of an alternative use constitute the supply price of the service. The sacrifice of a future use for a present one is just as real and necessary a social cost as the payments that go to workers to enable them to rear a new generation of workers. Surpluses may and do exist, but they may exist just as much in a society that has abolished private property in the means of production.

With this lesson in Marshallian economics in mind, we can now restate the Marxist theory of profit as a "surplus" income. The only condition under which the supply price of capital is always zero, no matter how narrow or wide our point of view, is when neither saving nor investment is in any way connected with the interest rate or the profit rate—let us agree to speak of these as synonyms from now on. If a fall in the rate of profit depresses saving or investment, then the supply price of capital is in fact positive, meaning by supply price simply the payment that induces capital to be supplied.

The reader may be tempted to think that this proves our point: profit is not merely surplus income. But, as a matter of fact, Marx seems to have foreseen the Marshallian objection, for he argues that all saving is carried out by capitalists for the purpose of reinvestment and that capitalists automatically reinvest all profits regardless of prospective returns. There is no problem of inducement to invest in Marx, and, if the theory of surplus value is really taken seriously, there cannot logically be any problem of investment incentives. Unfortunately, this view destroys Marx's theory of business cycles and indeed his whole conception of the "breakdown" of capitalism.

We have reached an intriguing result, which we will pursue further: either the theory of surplus value is untenable or Marx's prediction of the increasing instability of a capitalist economy must be abandoned.

The Laws of Motion of Capitalism. It is clear that Marx's attack on capitalism has actually nothing to do with the essence of property income as "unpaid labor." Labor does not receive the whole product under capitalism, but it would not receive the whole product under socialism: even a socialist society will have to allot part of the product to investment and collective consumption. Capitalism has to be abolished, argues Marx, not because of any inherent injustice in the prevailing class distribution of income, not because workers' consumption might conceivably be raised by the 10 or 20 per cent of the national income now consumed by capitalists, but because the system results in wars, in colonial exploitation, and, above all, in a waste of human resources through unemployment. In the same way, he sees socialism as bringing full employment, increased control of workers over their working conditions, emancipation of the individual, release of new cultural energies, and international peace. This means that we can examine Marx's analysis of the "laws of motion of capitalism" without regard for the emotive arguments about the nature of surplus value. In fact, Marx's analysis of the structural development of capitalism at no point hinges on acceptance or rejection of the labor theory of value.

But here we encounter a difficulty not experienced before. For, no matter which of Marx's predictions we examine—absolute or relative impoverishment, increasing severity of business cycles, absolute growth of unemployment, gradual elimination of small and medium-sized enterprises, falling rate of profit—we find no complete analysis of the phenomenon in question. In some cases all we have to go by is a series of vague and even contradictory statements. If we leave Marx, we find a mass of literature by his disciples, who offer a bewildering variety of interpretations of the basic historical drives of capitalism. In the end, we must conclude that some of the predictions have been refuted by the course of events, while others remain suggestive and debatable, but none of them can be regarded as having been theoretically established. Nevertheless, this part of Marx's writings is in many ways the most fecund, abounding as it does in provocative hypotheses.

The Law of the Falling Rate of Profit. We will recall that the rate of profit p' varies inversely with "the organic composition of capital" and directly with the rate of surplus value s'.

$$p' = \frac{s}{c + v} = \frac{s'}{q + 1} .$$

At this point we drop the assumption that the whole of the capital stock is consumed each year and explicitly introduce variations in the turnover rate or durability of capital.

$$p' = \frac{s}{K} = \frac{s}{c/t_c + v/t_v} = \left(\frac{s}{c + v}\right)t = \left(\frac{s'}{q + 1}\right)t = \frac{s'}{Q} ;$$

t_c and t_v are the respective turnover rates of constant and variable capital; t is a weighted average of these two turnover rates; $Q = (q + 1)d$ where d is a weighted average of the durabilities of c and v. This formulation has the advantage of emphasizing what every businessman knows: any increase in the turnover rate of capital, or, what is the same thing, any reduction in its durability, increases the rate of profit.[2]

The expression $p' = s'/Q$ is equivalent to the more familiar expression that makes the rate of profit a function of the amount of surplus per man—a flow per unit of stock—and the ratio of capital to

[2] An example may clarify the problem. Let $K = 500$, consisting of $C = 400$, $V = 100$. C consists of fixed assets plus a stock of raw materials and V consists of a sum of money or a stock of wage goods to make wage payments until the product is sold. Suppose it takes six months to manufacture the finished product. The stock of raw materials and wage goods turn over twice a year: $t_r = t_v = 2$. Suppose, in addition, that fixed assets have an average durability of 10 years: $t_f = \frac{1}{10}$. If the total value of fixed assets is 300, outlays on depreciation per cycle of production lasting 6 months will equal 15. Outlays on raw materials and wages over the same period will both equal 100. Therefore, $c = 115$ and $v = 100$. Assume that s' for one turnover of c is 100 per cent. Then the value of the finished product $= c + v + s = 315$. For one turnover of c we have $s/c + v = 100/215 = 46.5\%$. The annual rate $s/c + v$ will be twice this, or 93 per cent. Since s per annum $= 200$, the rate of profit, however, is $p' = s/K = 200/500 = 40$ per cent. This may also be expressed in terms of the average turnover rate t calculated as the weighted average of t_f, t_r, and t_v. We have $t = 300 \ t_f + 100 \ t_r + 100 \ t_v/500 = 0.86$. Then p' is given by $s/c + v$ for one turnover of c multiplied by t, i.e., $(46.5)(0.86) = 40$ per cent as before.

labor—a ratio of two stock. We simply start with Marx's expression and divide through by wages per man:

$$p' = \frac{s/v \cdot v/L}{K/v \cdot v/L} = \frac{s/L}{K/L}.$$

As far as Marx was concerned, the very expression $p' = s'/Q$ establishes the law that the rate of return on capital must fall with the increased mechanization of industry. Having concluded that the wage rate rises little, if at all, in the course of capital accumulation, while technical change constantly raises the stock of equipment per worker, he thought it obvious that Q, the organic composition of capital, must show a steady upward trend. It is true that this will not lower p' if the rate at which s' is rising exceeds that of Q. And, since mechanization raises the productivity of labor, it can hardly fail to raise s'. Marx realized that there was some functional connection between Q and s', but, after satisfying himself that s' could rise only within "certain impassable limits," he assumed it to be constant. He did recognize the influence of *autonomous* increases in s' which he handled under the label of "absolute and relative surplus value," but these too he dismissed, with more justification, as having definite physical limits.

The constancy of s' was only a simplifying assumption, but, as has been frequently pointed out, it was a particularly clumsy simplification for the Marxian system. Since wages and profits exhaust total income, a constant s' implies constant relative shares. This means that real wages rise as fast as the average productivity of labor. Writing o for net output and o/L for the average productivity of labor, we have

$$s' = \frac{s}{v} = \frac{s/o}{v/L \cdot L/o}.$$

Not only did Marx state in so many words that labor's share would decline, but it is implied by the notion that "the reserve army" keeps wages down to something like subsistence. However interpreted, this presumably means that wages do not rise as fast as the average productivity of labor. And as long as this is true, every increase in output per man raises s'. A fortiori, if real wages are constant, s' will rise sharply as K/L increases. Thus, the tendency for p' to fall is indeterminate: it all depends on the nature of the explicit function $s' = f(Q)$.

Marx's attempt to demonstrate the existence of an upper bound to this function is hopelessly muddled, reflecting the difficulty of measuring prices with a yardstick that is itself changing through time. As time goes by, the average productivity of labor rises and the "value" of products measured in embodied labor falls. This rise in productivity, however, is the result of a rising organic composition of capital. With a constant rate of profit, a rising Q entails falling prices but not falling as fast as labor values—just as the price for a particular commodity exceeds its value when it is produced with a Q in excess of the national average. It is quite clear, therefore, why Marx operates with a constant s' in his numerical examples: it insures prices moving proportionately to values. Nevertheless, in principle he was bound to agree that a rising s' was an integral part of the general process of rising productivity engendered by the steady increase of Q. The only question is: are there any limits to the rising rate of surplus value?

Most of us would be prepared to say that profits per man cannot rise without limits. Workers will certainly enforce a rise in money wages as productivity increases through trade-union action. This is an argument Marx does not use because the assumption of perfect competition eliminates the possibility of trade unions. But even in a perfectly competitive economy, real wages must rise as more complex machinery requires more highly trained workers to operate it, while increased intensity of labor requires more or better food and clothing to maintain workers' energies. More complex machinery, however, also works to raise the gap between output and wages upon which s' depends. The fact that the increased productivity of labor also reduces the money value of output is irrelevant, because at the same time it is also cheapening the goods bought by workers. We end up with the proposition that s' will rise if productivity increases faster in the wage-goods industries than in other sectors; it will fall if productivity increases are confined to the making of machines and luxury goods.

Marx, we see, should have claimed that the value of wage goods lags behind the fall in the value of the total product. But on logical and on empirical grounds, this would be a weak argument. The best argument he comes up with is this: the 24-hour limit to the working day makes it impossible to raise s' beyond a definite amount; at the same time, the rise in Q involves a reduction in the amount of employment associated with each unit of capital, so a rise in s' may not raise the total surplus associated with that capital. These two arguments are apparently additive: there will eventually come a point at which no conceivable rise in s' can possibly prevent the total quantity of surplus produced by a given capital from falling below its original level; at that point p' will fall. What Marx is forgetting here is that "value" is constant only when the productivity of labor is constant. At any moment in time $s + v$ is a given amount for a given amount of labor;

hence, the 24-hour limit to the working day prevents s' from rising to infinity (assuming $v > o$). But with a rising productivity of labor there is nothing to stop s' from increasing indefinitely. With constant real wages, both the "value" of s and the "value" of v are falling but, by definition of rising output per man, s/v is always increasing. It may be true that c/v is also rising, but an infinitely high s' is always capable of offsetting the increase in q. Marx's law of the falling rate of profit, therefore, even when accepted on its own grounds, is caught up in a bewildering mesh of opposing forces whose outcome is not deducible from elements supplied by the theory.

It is possible, however, to make out a case for Marx's law on orthodox grounds. First, we must rigidly distinguish between movements along production functions at given states of technical knowledge and shifts in the production functions themselves in the form of technical change. In Marx these two are considered together, implying that capital is not normally increased without altering "the state of the arts" and, likewise, that innovations always require some investment. Assuming that we can in principle distinguish capital investment at a constant state of technique, we define an aggregate production function obeying constant returns to scale—constant costs or constant returns to scale is the natural assumption for a labor theory of value. By the properties of this function, output rises for every increase in capital per man along the given function but less than proportionate to the increase in capital. As the capital-output ratio rises, the increase in capital will entail a fall in p' even though $s' = f(Q)$.[3] Innovations may offset this tendency but not all innovations will do so necessarily. If technical change does not work to reduce capital per unit of output, p' will nevertheless fall. This is because the capital-absorbing effects of the innovational process govern the degree to which wages rise as capital increases. If wages rise as fast as output per man, relative shares are unaffected and the rising capital-output ratio alone leads directly to a fall in p'. In the Marxian system, labor's share is alleged to fall through time; therefore, a rising capital-output ratio here does not necessarily imply a falling p'. But this is only to say that the Marxian law of the falling rate of profit is predicated upon a very rapidly rising capital-output ratio, which implies in turn that technical change is heavily slanted toward laborsaving improvements. For the claim that capital

[3] This can be shown by drawing the total product function with respect to capital. For equal increases in both capital and labor, the total product increases proportionately: that is what we mean by constant returns to scale. An increase in capital per man, however, will increase the total product at a decreasing rate, as shown in Figure 22. As a result, the capital-output ratio will rise. This is shown by the increase in $\cot \theta = (K/L)/o/L = K/o$

per man rises faster than profits per man, or in Marxian terms that Q rises faster than s', is tantamount to claiming that the capital-output ratio rises faster than the property share of output:

$$p' = \frac{s'}{Q} = \frac{s/L}{K/L}.$$

Dividing through L/o, we get

$$p' = \frac{s/o}{K/o}.$$

The fact that the aggregate capital-output ratio has remained practically unchanged in advanced economies over the last seventy-five years is fatal to the Marxist schema. Together with the observed long-run stability in relative shares, it leads directly to the conclusion that profits per man have risen as fast as capital per man and hence that p' has not declined.

A Glance at the Data. Is it in fact true that p' has not fallen in the history of capitalism? This is not the place for a thorough discussion of the evidence, but let us glance briefly at a recent effort by an American Marxist to submit the falling rate of profit to a statistical test. Using census data for American manufacturing over the period

---

as we move along the function. At the same time, the rate of profit or the marginal productivity of capital RS/oT—shown by the slope of the tangent to the production function—falls, and the wage rate w—shown by the intercept of the tangent with the ordinate—rises.

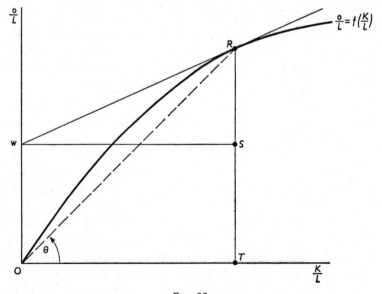

FIG. 22

1849–1939, the author starts out by accepting Marx's categories on a flow basis. The results are very disquieting: although q showed a fairly strong tendency to rise until the turn of the century, the trend value through 1919–39 was constant. Since s' rose persistently, the trend in s/k was decidedly upward over the whole of the ninety-year period.

When the ratios are converted to a stock basis, however, the data breaks clearly into two historical phases. Until 1919 capitalism in manufacture behaved very nearly as Marx had predicted: Q rose significantly and s' did not increase sufficiently to prevent p' from falling. Then something went wrong. The organic composition of capital stabilized in the 1920's at levels reached in 1919 and fluctuated countercyclically in the 1930's; it fell all through World War II and had risen little by 1950. If the decade of the 1930's is excluded, there is in fact some indication of a secular decline in Q. In addition, neither s' nor p' showed any definite trend over the years 1919–50.

These findings are complemented by evidence with respect to the capital-output ratio in American manufacturing: estimated in 1929 prices, the ratio rose through 1880–1919 and has fallen continuously since that time. The decline since 1919 is all the more remarkable if it is true, as Marxists allege, that "mature" capitalism reveals a chronic tendency toward underutilization of capacity. Since capital is measured as capital in existence, whether utilized or not, a fall in the utilization of capacity should, everything else being the same, increase the capital-output ratio.

Capitalsaving Innovations. The reasons Marxists themselves give for the decline in Q since 1919 is the increasing importance of capitalsaving innovations. There is a certain tendency to regard these innovations as novel manifestations of a complex technology that Marx could not possibly have foreseen: laborsaving improvements are *induced* by rising wages' eating into profit margins, but capitalsaving improvements just happen, for technical reasons, to occur only in late-stage capitalism.

Such was not Marx's own attitude, however. In Volume III of *Capital* he gives great prominence to "cheapening the elements of constant capital" as one of the "counteracting causes" to the falling rate of profit. And, to show what he means, he devotes two chapters to the tendency of certain inventions to shorten the time of production, thus raising profits by reducing the stock of goods that must be carried for a given output. "Cheapening the elements of constant capital," that is, raising t_c, evidently refers to innovations that release fixed capital. Apart from better-quality machines, any improvement that widens the scope of auxiliary instruments, reduces the need for floor space, or lengthens the physical life of a plant belongs to this class of innovations. Under the same heading, Marx also discusses innovations that save working capital by lowering freight charges, reducing delivery time, and effecting fuel savings through recovery and use of waste products. Marx is not only aware of the importance of capital saving changes but regards them as the product of automatic market forces. "Capitalist production," he writes, "enforces economies in the employment of constant capital" which tend "to check the fall in the rate of profit." But the decline in the value of "the elements of constant capital" is not a "counteracting cause" at all: it is a necessary element of the rising productivity of labor in all sectors, and particularly in the capital goods sector. The steady tendency of the capital-labor ratio to rise through time not only automatically increases s/v but also automatically reduces c/v, all variables being measured in terms of labor. There is nothing in Marx that would stop us from assuming that technical progress is neutral on balance, the productivity of labor rising just as fast in the capital goods industries as in the consumer goods industries. And this would mean that economic progress constantly raises productivity, and hence s', but leaves the "value" of Q unchanged.

The Reproduction Schema. The law of the falling rate of profit is fundamental to Marx's analysis of the cyclical character of economic growth under capitalism. But, before we turn to his theory of business cycles, we must pause a moment with the famous reproduction schema of Volume II. These have a particular historical interest not only because they have never ceased to fascinate Marx's followers but because they represent the first example of an analysis associated with the names of Harrod and Domar in our own times. The problem is to state the macroeconomic conditions for smooth growth of the system, so as to raise the question whether hitchless expansion is possible.

Marx begins by dividing the economy into two sectors producing capital and consumer goods, respectively. He then distinguishes between simple and expanded reproduction. Simple reproduction denotes a condition of stationariness in which net investment is zero. What conditions are required to keep a stationary economy stationary? The answer is seen by noting that the whole output of Department I must be devoted to capital replacement in both departments: $c_1 + v_1 + s_1 = c_1 + c_2$. Simultaneously, the whole output of Department I must match the wages bill plus property income: $c_2 + v_2 + s_2 = (v_1 + v_2) + (s_1 + s_2) =$ net national product. Both these equations upon cancellation reduce to the condition: $v_1 + s_1 = c_2$, that is, the net output of

Department I must be matched by the replacement demand of Department II; or, the only part of the gross value of capital goods not retained by Department I must be exchanged for that part of the gross value of the consumer goods industries not used to buy the goods which it itself produces. If $v_1 + s_1 > c_2$, it signifies that outlays on replacement of fixed capital exceed depreciation allowances, that is, net investment is positive. On the other hand, the failure to use depreciation accruals for replacement of worn-out capital must cause output to shrink. This demonstration brings out basic macroeconomic relationships: it shows, for example, that while total outlays must equal total income for the economy as a whole, income may exceed outlays in some industries without causing any difficulty; or, similarly, the fact that workers cannot buy back the total product does not by itself cause disequilibrium.

Unfortunately, Marx does not explicitly state the conditions for expanded reproduction to occur smoothly. Moreover, he examines growth only at a constant rate, the case in which growth does not involve a change in Q. With respect to an increasing rate of growth, he merely suggests that if saving increases without concurrent investment, this need not spell deadlock if new money is being introduced into the system or if capital is being exported. Formally, however, the equations for expanded reproduction at a constant rate are similar to those for simple reproduction. Breaking up surplus value into its constituent parts, we have s_v spent on hiring labor, s_k spent on consumer goods, and s_e spent on capital goods. Hence, the output of Department I must be equal to the total demand for capital goods:

$$c_1 + v_1 + s_{k_1} + s_{c_1} + s_{v_1} = (c_1 + s_{c_1}) + (c_2 + s_{c_2}) .$$

Also, the output of Department II must be equal to the total demand for consumer goods:

$$c_2 + v_2 + s_{k_2} + s_{c_2} + s_{v_2} = (v_1 + s_{k_1} + s_{v_1}) + (v_2 + s_{k_2} + s_{v_2}) ;$$

canceling out, both equations yield

$$v_1 + s_{k_2} + s_{v_1} = c_2 + s_{c_2} .$$

The demand for consumer goods emanating from Department I must equal the demand for capital goods on the part of Department II; the net output of Department I must equal gross investment in Department II. We can go a step further and define

$$h = v_2/v_1, \quad x_1 = s_{c_1}/s_1, \quad \text{and} \quad x_2 = s_{c_2}/s_2 .$$

Dividing the equation for smooth expanded reproduction by v_1 and rewriting, we have

$$1 + s' - s'x_1 = hq_2 + s'hx_2$$

or

$$h = \frac{1 + s' - s'x_1}{s'x_2 + q_2}.$$

At a uniform rate of wages, h defines the proportion in which the total labor force is divided between the two sectors. The equation, therefore, makes balanced growth depend upon a definite distribution of labor between the two sectors as a function of the ratio of profits to wages (s'), the propensity to save and invest (x_1, x_2) and the capital intensity of production in the consumer goods industries (q_2).

This construction can be made to yield a few insights, but on the whole it is based on assumption so restrictive as to deprive the argument of much illumination. The economy is closed, all products sell at long-run "normal prices"; the rates of turnover of capital are identical in the two departments; the workers' average and marginal propensity to save is unity; savings in each department are always fully invested in the same department; there is no technical change; real wages are constant; real surplus per man is constant; and so on. Moreover, a two-sector model is a treacherous instrument for analyzing a real economy in motion. Many industries do not fall neatly into either category, producing both capital and consumer goods—think of coal, transport, and chemicals. Moreover, the division within such industries between the two categories varies through time as a result of changes in the pattern of demand. This works havoc in our simple conditions for expanded reproduction. Nevertheless, they play a role in the Marxian system by suggesting the great improbability of smooth expansion. Most of what Marx has to say about business cycles arises out of consideration of the causes of disequilibrium under conditions of expanded reproduction.

Business Cycles. Marx does not have a special theory of business cycles and in fact specifically disavows any attempt to provide such a theory. His view seems to be that crises are merely expressions of the "fundamental contradiction of capitalism," namely, that production is carried on for profit, not for use, and that the very drive for increased profits destroys investment opportunities. Marx's theory of the business cycle is coextensive with his general analysis of capital accumulation.

His picture of the cyclical process, however, runs something like this: In a boom the demand for labor resulting from accumulation will run ahead of the available supply; the reserve army is depleted, and the relative scarcity of labor causes wages to rise; hence, profits fall and accumulation slows down. A reduction in the rate of capital accumulation leads to a fall in aggregate demand and hence to a downturn. In the slump, capital values are written off and the reserve army is recruited, driving wages down. This restores the profitability of production and sets the stage for a resumption of accumulation: the slump is both a retribution and a catharsis.

This cyclical reserve-army theory is joined to the secular tendency of the rate of profit to fall combined with the possibility of disproportionate rates of growth of capital goods and consumer goods industries. "The last cause of all crisis," Marx remarks, is the maldistribution of income under capitalism owing to the failure of real wages to rise as fast as output per man. This does not mean that Marx held an underconsumption theory either in the sense that saving and investment cause overproduction unless some new source of consumption demand appears, or in the sense that a deficiency of consumption demand is always the initiating cause of a slump. The first version, held by Malthus, is refuted by the reproduction schema, which shows that expanded reproduction at a constant rate is theoretically possible. The second version is refuted by Marx's penetrating observation that wages are never higher than right before the crash. Raising wages will not of itself perpetuate the boom because it merely creates a situation in which capitalists are dissatisfied with existing wage-price relations. What Marx seems to have in mind is that capitalism tends continually to expand production without any reference to the effective demand that alone can give it meaning. The expansion of production does not automatically generate a proportionate increase in effective demand because the excessive rate of capital formation lowers the rate of profit even while the innovations embodied in the increments of capital hold down wage rates by being largely laborsaving.

The Investment Function. The first thing to notice by way of criticism of Marx's conception of the business cycle is that it assumes too glibly that money wages vary inversely with the rate of profit in the short run. In the boom a rise in money wages caused by falling unemployment raises money costs of production. Before we conclude, however, that this implies a reduction in profit margins, we must take account of the effect of higher money wages upon effective demand. The rise in demand for consumers' goods is bound to raise prices in the short run, particularly because Marx supposes that the marginal propensity to consume of workers is always equal to unity. In the short run, all variable costs of production over the economy as a whole consist of wage costs. Hence, on the average, we would expect that rising money wages would raise prices as much as average costs, leaving profits per unit of output as well as real wages unaffected. Likewise, in the slump, cutting wages will not raise profit margins if workers habitually spend all their income. Realistically, the workers' marginal propensity to consume is less than unity, but, on the other hand, wage costs are only a fraction of total costs in the long run; given time to adjust the size of the plant, it is not at all clear that cutting wages in the slump works to restore profits.

Be that as it may, the profit margin is not the same thing as the rate of profit on capital. Suppose an increase of money wages in the boom does reduce gross and net profit margins; as long as capitalists are the only savers and invest without fail, there is no reason why the increase in money wages should affect the rate of profit. Likewise, the fall in money wages in the slump may act to increase profit margins, but if effective demand falls off in proportion to the reduction in payrolls, investment will not be encouraged.

Capitalists, Keynes has taught us, can pull themselves up by their own bootstraps via the multiplier. The crucial question is the inducement to invest. This brings us at last to the deepest problem in the Marxian system. Precisely what does govern the willingness to invest? We have seen that Marx pictures capitalists as reducing investment at the peak of the boom in response to falling rates of return to capital. Apparently, then, capitalists do not always invest the whole of nonlabor income; if they did, crises could never take place. Yet elsewhere Marx views capitalists as caught up in a dynamic race that forces them to accumulate on pain of elimination. And, as we know, the theory of surplus values implies as much: investment is not a function of a rate of reward to capital. How do we resolve this contradiction?

What Marx is saying is that the pursuit of wealth in a capitalist society is regarded as an end in and of itself. Capitalists save and invest for reasons of prestige and social status, a way of "keeping up with the Rockefellers." Hence, changes in the rate of profit will have little effect on investment, except insofar as low profit rates, by reducing the income of the wealthy, leave them with less to save. Investment demand will continue high, and the capital stock will be used to capacity as long as investment yields any positive return, however small. This is not incompatible with periodic shrinking of investment due to the shock effect of a fall in the rate of profit. In other words, whereas we usually think of factor demand and supply curves as being *more* elastic in the long run than in the short run, Marx suggests that the demand for investment and the supply of business saving is actually *less* elastic in the long run. As Keynes once observe: "It is not necessary . . . that the game should be played for such high stakes as at present. Much lower stakes will serve the purpose equally well, as soon as the players are accustomed to them."

The Marxist view of the mainsprings of capital accumulation makes excellent sociological sense. The typical businessman in the heyday of nineteenth-century capitalism was not interested in pecuniary profit for what it would buy in the way of personal consumption. The motive that produced economic development under capitalism was "conspicuous accumulation" for its own sake, not maximum profits to increase personal spending power. In this sense, and taking the widest view, it is indeed true that the supply price of capital was effectively zero. But this does not mean that the "real cost" of saving was zero, that society effortlessly converted present income into future income at will. It is simply that the institutions and social climate of nineteenth-century capitalism in effect shifted this burden onto wage earners by producing sharp inequalities in the distribution of income. The removal of these sharp inequalities by means of redistributive taxation and social welfare legislation has not reduced the rate of interest to zero. Nor would socialism tomorrow do so. Nothing can reduce the rate of interest to zero except capital saturation: a state of affairs in which real incomes are so high that postponement of present consumption is painless. To test the theory of surplus value, we must ask: is the failure to pay workers the whole national product in the form of wages and collective consumption *merely* a matter of institutional considerations? The institutions of capitalism actually disguise the nature of interest as an index of the cost of "waiting," and it would seem that a satisfactory theory of the rate of interest must begin by abstracting from the specific sociological characteristics of capitalism.

The Myth of a Laborsaving Bias. Accepting Marx's picture of the investment process, however, implies abandonment of his dire predictions about the imminent breakdown of capitalism, predictions based upon a belief in the predominantly laborsaving slant of technical change, which grinds down rates of reward to both capital and labor. In orthodox theory it is possible to conceive of an aggregate production function with diminishing returns to scale so sharp that an increase in capital per man lowers both profit and wage rates. Technical progress can offset this tendency, but if it saves both factors in the same proportion and is only forthcoming at very low levels, it may not upset the perverse result of unfavorable trends in both profit and wage rates.

In Marx there can be no question of insufficient offsets to diminishing returns to scale or diminishing returns to the faster-growing factor, for technical change is indissolubly connected with increases in capital per man. It is plausible that capital accumulation lowers the rate of profit, but in that case it should at least raise wages. On the contrary, "the passion for accumulation" expresses itself in innovations that are heavily slanted in the laborsaving direction; the wage rate *must* be kept down to keep profits up, but the scramble for more profits defeats its own purpose.

This "paradox of accumulation" colors the whole of Marx's analysis of the laws of motion of capitalism. It is indeed the contradiction to end all contradictions. The easy retort is to say that it has not happened. But let us give the argument a run for its money. Under perfect competition, capital accumulation cannot for long lower both profit and wage rates.[4] First of all, the fall in the rate of profit depresses saving, not because it affects the willingness to save, but because it affects the

[4] Given that technical change is irreversible, it is *theoretically* possible for both wage and interest rates to fall simultaneously through time with the increase in capital per man. This can be shown by using the same diagram as in the last footnote F_2 shows the output-increasing result of an innovation: the wage rate has fallen, as shown by the lower tangent *intercept* on the ordinate; the profit rate has also fallen, as shown by the reduced *slope* of the tangent; the capital-output ratio is higher for K_2/L than for K_1/L. But what if capitalists

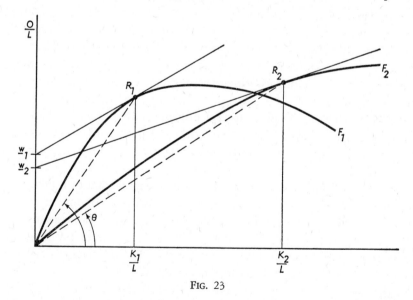

FIG. 23

now try to revert to the old technology to reap the higher profit rate associated with it? This would create excess capacity $K_2 - K_1$ and would therefore depress the rate of profit further; this is why it is never feasible to return to old technology when new technology has been capacity-adding. Marx's case *is* possible, but it does leave p' falling relative to w and hence promotes the economizing of the relatively dearer labor.

ability to do so. Recall that all savings come out of profits in the Marxian system. As business saving falls, so does investment, and the system settles down to a slower rate of growth, which brings the rate of profit back to previous levels. Second, if capital is being incessantly invested in laborsaving improvements, the capital-output ratio must be rising. This means a higher share of depreciation and interest charges in total costs, with consequent pressures to effect economies in the use of capital: innovations become less and less laborsaving, and wages start rising. Similarly, "the passion for accumulation" entails a chronic excess demand for capital; consequent difficulties in obtaining finance, expressing itself in an upward-sloping supply curve of funds available to the firm, should make capitalists alert to every possibility to save capital. Finally, laborsaving technical change implies that the rise in man-hour productivity is concentrated in the finishing stages of production. All cost-reducing changes in the capital goods industries release capital for the economy as a whole: they lower machine prices and bring about substitution of capital for labor. Therefore, if technical change in the economy as a whole is slanted in the laborsaving direction, it must be concentrated in the consumer goods industries. Hence, prices of consumer goods fall faster than machine prices, and this induces substitution of cheap labor for dear capital all round. The rate at which labor is being displaced in the economy falls off, the reserve army stops growing, and wages rise. It is possible that the scope for factor substitution is so limited that the mechanism just outlined would not work. But in a developed multi-industry economy it is difficult to believe that factor endowments could long continue to be grossly inappropriate to available technology.

The idea that the innovational process as a whole is the outcome of responses to market pressures should have been congenial to Marx, who may be said to have discovered it. We may sum up by noting that if technical progress is plentiful and yet produces a fall in the rate of return to capital, it suggests that the factorsaving slant of innovations is out of line with relative factor scarcities. In an economy in which capital is the scarcer factor, a persistent bias toward laborsaving improvements must erode the profits that each individual producer expects to reap from an improvement; this is the Marxian case. When labor is the scarcer factor, as in advanced Western economies, a bias toward capitalsaving improvements likewise works to reduce the yield of capital. The reason that technical change has not exhibited either bias to any marked degree is that the long-term pattern of innovations is the outcome of successive adjustments to differential rates of growth in the factor supplies as reflected in relative prices. Producers in a perfectly competitive market face infinitely elastic factor-supply curves, that is, factor prices are given to them. It would seem, therefore, that the perfectly competitive market provides no signal to induce the "appropriate" factorsaving innovation. But the factor-supply curves do shift through time, and there is nothing in the static theory of the competitive firm that leads us to deny that firms will learn to adapt themselves to a persistent trend in the shifting of factor-supply curves. Producers simply become conditioned by experience to avoid disappointment by choosing improvements that save the relatively scarcer factor.

It is not necessary to assume that factor prices have a *conscious* redirecting effect on firms. The argument rests essentially on competitive survival, regardless of the nature of individual motivation and foresight. Firms adopting, say, laborsaving devices in the light of falling wage rates and rising interest charges will not prove viable. The successful innovator will be saving capital and absorbing labor, and the economist looking on will find the system as a whole adapting technical change to relative factor scarcities.

Impoverishment of the Working Class. Having banished the bogey of falling profit and wage rates, we can make short shrift of most of Marx's secular predictions, such as the increasing amplitude of business cycles, the growing volume of chronic unemployment, the decline in domestic investment outlets, and the law of the absolute and relative "immiserization of the proletariat."

The last, however, is worth special consideration. Marx never denies that real wages may rise under capitalism. He strongly implies that labor's relative share would fall but in fact never uses the phrase "relative impoverishment." The notion that he propounds a theory of the growing poverty of the working class is just folklore Marxism. The doctrine of absolute impoverishment is actually an argument about quality, not quantity. Marx spoke, not of material poverty, but of "pauperization," of the growing "misery" and "mental degradation" of the working class: "in proportion as capital accumulates, the lot of the laborer, be his payment high or low, must grow worse." Presumably, Marx is referring to the fact that mechanization destroys the demand for skills, reduces the worker to a mechanical cipher, and tends to deteriorate the conditions of work. Nevertheless, the failure of wages to rise with the productivity of labor is an element in the doctrine of absolute impoverishment. The fact that labor's relative share under capitalism has remained remarkably constant for a half-century or more, and in the case of Britain and the United States has actually increased, would surely have surprised Marx.

Marx's followers have advanced a number of explanations of the tendency for living standards to rise under capitalism, two of which we will examine in some detail. First, there is the popular contention that Marx's mistake was political, not economic. This starts from the constancy of relative shares and then asks how this can be squared with the conscious action that has been taken over the last century to redistribute income in favor of labor: factory legislation, minimum wage acts, the growth of social services, the progressive income tax, the rise of inheritance taxation, the voluntary redistribution of great fortunes through public foundations, and, last, the growth of trade unions. And all that this has done is to leave relative shares constant and to slightly equalize the distribution of personal income. Does this not show that Marx's analysis of the basic tendencies of capitalism was sound? To be sure, he underestimated the economic consequences of trade unions and the rising labor vote. But, if we switched off the heavy counter pressures of state action and labor organizations, who would doubt that the basic tendency of wages to hover about subsistence levels would reassert itself?

Apart from the fact that this argument explains the facts only by the miracle of two equally opposing forces, there is something about this way of looking at things that is essentially alien to the spirit of Marxism. It implies that the division of the product between capital and labor is fundamentally a matter of the political wage bargain, that competitive pressures in the labor market exert no influence on wage rates, and that the "rate of exploitation" is not subject to any general rule. If this is so, a theory purporting to describe capitalism's laws of motion should provide an analysis of the bargaining process that on this view is as fundamental to the system as the economic tendency toward subsistence wages. It is Marx, more than any other writer, who claims to have shown that trade unions can never do more than ameliorate the fundamental contradictions of capitalism. In the context of Marxism it is not legitimate to drag in trade unions as a *deus ex machina* to rescue Marx's falsified predictions. One could understand a bourgeois economist drawing a rigid line of division between economic and political forces; but if Marxism is all it claims to be, a science of society, we cannot accept the idea that wages are determined by inexorable economic forces, which unions then "offset" or "counteract." Unions are not fortuitous institutions but are generated by forces inherent in capitalism: a mature capitalist economy without unions is almost as difficult to imagine as capitalism with a negative rate of interest. In general, Marxists in the wake of Marx himself have carried the game of shifting levels of discourse in the middle of an argument to a fine science: one moment something is an "absolute law," the next it is a "counteracting cause"; it is an "inherent economic tendency" for one purpose and a political accident for another. The Marxist theory of trade unions and government intervention under capitalism remains to be written.

The second and equally popular argument suggests that the high standard of living of workers in advanced countries is somehow due to the exploitation of the colonial masses. This notion is almost impossible to get hold of because its meaning is not at all clear. Lenin talked vaguely of the "aristocracy of labor" in the home country, sharing in the superprofits of imperialism, but the extra yield of foreign over domestic investment has not been such as reasonably to account for a tripling of real wages over the last century. Moreover, taken at face value, it would mean that the rise in living standards in the advanced countries has been matched by a deterioration of standards in the colonies. One German Marxist did argue that the law of absolute impoverishment holds strictly, not for individual countries, but for the whole labor force employed within a given capitalist society both at home and abroad. He carried out a series of statistical studies designed to verify the thesis but, after a number of inconclusive volumes, abandoned the project.

Nevertheless, the general argument cannot be so easily dismissed. It might be reinterpreted to mean that unemployment in the major capitalist countries would have been much worse in the absence of imperialism. After all, Great Britain in the years 1870–1914 did invest abroad something like half her domestic savings, whose interests and dividends amounted to one tenth of her national income. Surely, the transfer of so much saving must have reduced potential domestic deflationary pressures and stabilized national income? But it is a mistake to assume that savings that went overseas would have existed at all in the absence of capital exports: foreign investment, by stimulating exports, generates income and hence saving just as much as does domestic investment. Without foreign investment, British income would no doubt have grown less rapidly, but so would domestic savings. Moreover, most overseas investment in the heyday of Edwardian imperialism did not offset domestic saving in any sense whatever; the bulk of it was due to the reinvestment of undistributed profits on previous investment. Be that as it may, the idea that the British worker was better off at the expense of the Indian peasant or African miner carries little conviction.

The Role of Institutional Assumptions. We conclude our discussion by raising a difficult question provoked by the study of Marxian economics. What is the appropriate level of abstraction for an economic theory? Debates between Marxist and Orthodox economists invariably break down over the nature of the questions that economics ought to answer. When both schools of thought turn to the same questions, they do not really differ in results. As a theory of relative prices, for example, the labor theory of value is nothing but a static theory of general equilibrium, applicable to any closed exchange economy regardless of the character of property ownership, as long as the input coefficients of production are given by technical considerations and perfect competition prevails. The labor theory of value is a special case of the more general Walrasian theory. Marxists themselves do not argue that orthodox price theory is wrong, but merely that its results are not very interesting. Similarly, when a Marxist and a bourgeois economist turn to the question of long-run economic development under capitalism, their disagreements are not traceable to matters of fact and logic but to specific sociological assumptions that each regards as appropriate to a meaningful analysis of the problem.

Let us take a typical example: the theory of profit. The orthodox economist starts with certain data, such as the preference scales of households, production functions, factor endowments, including forms and distributions of property, all of which he regards as outside the scope of economic theory. On the basis of the data he develops a theory of factor prices in which a hiring agent, the entrepreneur, purchases the services of hired agents, workers, and capital owners. In a stationary economy, this gives rise to equilibrium wage and interest rates. In a growing economy, it may leave a residual as profit to the entrepreneur. Imperfect competition in product markets or monopsony in the labor market may enhance this residual and distort factor prices. Changes in the data themselves must now be introduced to analyze the effects of advertising, technical change, saving propensities, and population growth. Finally, to explain the wages, interest, and profit that are actually received by flesh-and-blood workers and capitalists, we must take into account inheritance laws, the tax structure, monetary institutions, and so forth. The process, therefore, of moving from functional to personal income distribution takes the form of progressively relaxing more and more of the data given at the outset of the analysis.

Marxists, on the other hand, introduce the distinction between the haves and the have-nots at the outset of the argument, operating on the ground floor with personal income aggregated into class types. It is illegitimate, they argue, to regard the distribution of property as a datum, for it is not given independently of the determination of wages and interest. It is only by specifying the property relations that distinguish a capitalist economy from an ordinary exchange economy, and making this the cornerstone of the analysis, that we can explain the historical performance of the capitalist system, the utter dependence of profits upon continuous technical progress, the relentless pressure to increase capital equipment per worker, the evident tendency toward concentration of production, the economic function of unemployment, and the general role of business cycles in governing the form which long-run development takes. But for this hardheaded realism Marxian economics pays a price. Lange made this point very strikingly:

> . . . Let us imagine two persons: one who has learned his economics only from the Austrian School, Pareto and Marshall, without ever having seen or even heard a sentence of Marx or his disciples; the other one who, on the contrary, knows his economics exclusively from Marx and the Marxists and does not even suspect that there may have been economists outside the Marxist School. Which of the two will be able to account better for the fundamental tendencies of the evolution of Capitalism? To put the question is to answer it.

> But this superiority of Marxian economics is only a partial one. There are some problems before which Marxian economics is quite powerless, while "bourgeois" economics solves them easily. What can Marxian economics say about monopoly prices? What has it to say on the fundamental problems of monetary and credit theory? What apparatus has it to offer for analysing the incidence of a tax, or the effect of a certain technical innovation on wages? And (irony of Fate!) what can Marxian economics contribute to the problem of the optimum distribution of productive resources in a socialist economy?

> Clearly the relative merits of Marxian economics and of modern "bourgeois" economic theory belong to different "ranges." Marxian economics can work the economic evolution of capitalist society into a consistent theory from which its necessity is deduced, while "bourgeois" economists get no further than mere historical description. On the other hand, "bourgeois" economics is able to grasp the phenomena of the every-day life of a capitalist economy in a manner that is far superior to anything the Marxists can produce. Further, the anticipations which can be deduced from the two types of economic theory refer to a different range of time. If people want to anticipate the development of capitalism over a long period a knowledge of Marx is a much more effective starting point than a knowledge of Wieser, Boehm-Bawerk, Pareto or even Marshall (though the last-named is in this respect much superior).

> But Marxian economics would be a poor basis for running a central bank or anticipating the effects of a change in the rate of discount.

The formal principles of the theory of economic equilibrium are the same for any exchange economy, and the economic problem in a capitalist system has characteristics shared by a socialist economy. In refusing to abstract at any point from the institutional framework in which the economic process is embedded in a capitalist society, Marxists have cut themselves off from the task of clarifying the pure logic of economic relationships. Their strength has lain in providing a systematic account of the evolutionary process of capitalism. In recent years their monopoly has been challenged. Orthodox economics has come to devote more attention to explaining the hitherto successful performance of the capitalist system so as to discover what light past trends may shed on future prospects. For the first time in a century of debate between Marxian economics and orthodox economics, the nature of the central issue is not in dispute. For the first time there is the real possibility that the cold war between the two schools of thought may be settled once and for all.

READER'S GUIDE TO *CAPITAL*

To read *Capital* is a major undertaking. It is a badly arranged work, excessively repetitious, and replete with special terminology. Every page bears testimony to the author's obsession with analytical riddles and Hegelian "contradictions." When the reader is not driven to despair by the lengths to which a chain of arguments is pursued, he is irritated by the author's condescending tone toward his adversaries or put off by the moral fervor that surrounds even the most abstract propositions. Nevertheless, *Capital* should hold no terrors for anyone who has managed to get through Ricardo's *Principles*. The method of reasoning—the abstract deductive method—is the same, and the whole analysis is steeped in Ricardian assumptions. Moreover, Marx's style, at least in the first volume that he completed and finished for the press, is a great deal more animated than is Ricardo's. There is the difficulty of Marx's Hegelian jargon; but too much has been made of that. One soon grows used to it, and it is no more than an outer dressing: Marx himself speaks of "coquetting" with "the modes of expression" peculiar to Hegel. Furthermore, the flow of argument is relieved, as it never is in Ricardo, by the incursion of historical material. The reader might indeed follow Marx's own advice to a friend and begin, not with the difficult first chapter of Volume I, but with the historical chapters 10, 13–15, and 25–33.

Value. Chapter 1 begins with the distinction between use value and exchange value and immediately lays down the unqualified proposition that goods exchange at ratios that are reciprocals of the ratios of labor required to produce them. Marx approaches the question in an Aristotelian fashion by asking: What have commodities in common by virtue of which they can be equated one to another as exchange values? This common element must be capable of being quantified and, at the same time, it cannot itself have exchange value, for then it would explain nothing; it must be, as Marx says, something "contained in . . . yet distinguishable from" the exchange value of commodities and representing "a greater or less quantity." A modern reader might be tempted to say that the "common property" is in fact the equal ratios of marginal utility of goods offered to goods demanded for both parties. But this approach entails the notion of utility measured in incremental amounts as well as the concept of diminishing marginal utility as a function of the amount of goods offered and demanded. For Marx, "the exchange of commodities is evidently an act characterized by a total abstraction from use-value," and in his sense of the term, namely, total utility, it undoubtedly is. Like Ricardo, he assumes as a matter of course that a product's "worth" to an individual bears no relationship to the price that the individual is willing to pay and that, whatever the relationship, "worth" cannot be quantified.

Socially Necessary Labor. Nowhere in the first chapter does Marx state the conditions under which competitive rates of exchange correspond to the labor embodied in commodities: equal capital-labor ratios in all industries and constant costs of production. The absence of any qualification in the initial statement of the labor theory of value is precisely what puzzles the reader. But, in fact, the assumption of constant costs is already tucked inside the concept of "socially necessary labor," which Marx introduces immediately after his "proof" of the labor theory of value. Value is determined by the man-hours required to produce commodities. The intensity of effort, however, is not constant per unit of time, either for one individual or between individuals. Shall we choose the labor effort of the best man or the worst man, the first or the last hour in the day, as our common unit of labor time? Marx selects the "labor-time socially necessary," that is, "with the average degree of skill and intensity prevalent at the time." He takes it for granted, however, that each employer attempts to use labor at its maximum intensity in the long run. In marginal terms, this amounts to taking the least intensive man-hour applied as the common unit. The only condition under which the least intensity of labor applied is equal to the average intensity is that of constant costs: each plant is operated at optimum capacity where average and marginal costs are equal and the average costs of all plants within an industry are identical. It follows that the long-run supply curve of the industry is horizontal and that demand, and hence utility, has no influence on price.

Apart from the intensity of effort, there is the quite different problem of labor of different skills. In section 2 of chapter 1, Marx decides to treat unskilled common labor as the fundamental value-creating unit, regarding skilled labor as a simple multiple of unskilled labor. Later, in chapter 7, he defends this procedure by the argument that the "production" of skilled labor involves the expenditure of labor time in the form of training; skilled labor is more valuable than unskilled labor because these "commodities" also exchange for one another according to the man-hours required to produce them. This ignores the fact that training takes time and the outlay on training must earn interest for the training period. The difference between the wages of skilled and unskilled workers is a function of the man-hours required to produce the two types of labor *and* of the time for which they are produced. Furthermore, there are reasons for differences in wages other than differences in the cost of training. In the whole of *Capital* there is only one reference to Smith's equalization of "net advantages" in the labor market. In Volume III, chapter 8, Marx points out that "the surplus labor of the goldsmith produces correspondingly more surplus-value than that of the day-laborer." The study of such "frictions," Marx goes on to say, "may be dispensed with as being accidental and unessential in a general analysis of capitalist production." It is easy to see why Marx ignored Smith's argument, for it implies that the choice of *workers* among occupations has something to do with the determination of the average wage rate. Moreover, it would mean that the standard unit of labor was a unit of disutility, not an objective "expenditure of human brains, nerves, and muscles."

However, the assumptions of homogeneous labor and a given wage structure—for this is all that Marx's argument amounts to—are perfectly legitimate as first approximations in the explanation of relative prices. The proper criticism of Marx is not that he made these assumptions, but that he never relaxed them anywhere to ask how relative wages themselves are determined. Marx simply posits a situation in which the conditions of equilibrium have been reached, without explaining how they are reached, how the amount of labor "socially necessary" is determined.

Commodity Fetishism. The reader will miss little by skipping the pedantic third section of chapter 1, on which the hands of Hegel lie all too heavily. Section 4, on "the fetishism of commodities," however, is crucial to an understanding of the Marxist attitude to "bourgeois" economics. Commodity "fetishism" refers to the tendency to reify commodities, to treat what are in fact social relations between men as relations between things. In a footnote Marx attacks "vulgar economy," as distinguished from "classical Political Economy." Instead of penetrating below the surface to "real" or "ultimate" determinants, as did Adam Smith and Ricardo, the vulgar economist operates with the superficial concepts of demand and supply, with the subjective attitudes of economic agents toward money costs. In the minds of individuals, the mental relations between goods acquire the quality of independent forces that dominate market reactions. Yet actually they are nothing but the products of the independent actions of all individuals in a market that holds sway despite the deliberate intent of each economic agent.

If this is what Marx meant by his doctrine of "fetishism," it would seem to indict modern economics even more than the theories of such "vulgar economists" as Malthus, Senior, and Mill. And yet the indictment seems to rest upon a misunderstanding of the procedure of price theory. Marx's concept of commodity fetishism sounds very much like the current distinction between price-determined behavior as seen by individuals and behavior-determined price as it appears in the market. Modern price theory begins with entrepreneurs and households facing given prices and adjusting the quantity supplied and demanded in accordance with their own "maximand." The summation of the resulting individual supply and demand schedules constitutes the market schedules that determine prices. Individuals do in fact act in terms of their own mental beliefs and fetishes, but prices are determined by the objective outcome of individual actions. If the agents in the process were aware of the consequences of their actions, economics would be a branch of psychoanalysis. The whole point of the theory of perfect competition is to analyze the wholly objective outcome of purely subjective actions and reactions. There is nothing "superficial" about lifting the veil of objective determination to penetrate to the "ultimate" subjective motivations and beliefs from which the whole process stems. In comparison with orthodox economics, it is Marxian economics that seems prone to the sin of "vulgarity." Marx's retort, no doubt, would be that class relationships do not appear in orthodox economics and that these constitute the "real" elements of an economic situation. But this is a different charge. The reader should now turn to the Preface to the second German edition of Volume I, in which Marx explains why "scientific" bourgeois economics came to an end in 1830: "Political Economy can remain a science only so long as the class-struggle is latent or manifests itself only in isolated and sporadic phenomena." In point of fact, however, the decade of the 1830's is the high point of classical economics in terms of vigor of debate and appearance of new ideas: among the outstanding works of this decade are Lloyd's *Lecture on the Notion of Value* (1833) and Longfield's *Lectures* (1834)—neither of which is cited by Marx—as well as Scrope's *Principles* (1833), Jones's *Essay on the Distribution of Wealth* (1831), and Senior's *Outline* (1836).

Theory of Money. Chapter 2 and 3 contain Marx's theory of money, a subject that he dealt with at greater length in *Critique of Political Economy* (1859). There is nothing in these chapters not found in Ricardo or Mill. The Equation of Exchange is very clearly stated in verbal terms, but the quantity *theory* of money is rejected on the grounds that V and T are variables (chap. 3, sec. 2b). The store-of-value function of money is discussed under the heading of "hoarding" (chap. 3, sec. 3a). Say's Identity is repudiated (chap. 3, sec. 2a), and Marx gives a vivid description of the liquidity panic that marks the onset of a depression (chap. 3, sec. 3b). A footnote in chapter 3, section 2c, contains one of Marx's many derogatory comments on J. S. Mill.

Surplus Value. Part II, chapters 4 and 5, set the stage for the solution of the riddle of surplus value. The exchange of goods begins with a sale and ends with a purchase $(C - M - C)$ but the process of production begins with a purchase and ends with a sale $(M - C - M)$. How is it that a surplus value is produced in the act of turning money capital into commodities and back into money again? It cannot be because goods are bought below their value and sold above their value, for in that case the sum of all individual gains would be zero. Surplus value has to be explained in terms of "an exchange of equivalents," everything being bought and sold at its value. Having posed the problem, Marx proceeds to the answer in chapters 6 and 7—there is real art of presentation in these chapters. Labor itself cannot be bought and sold in a nonslave economy. What is in fact bought are the services of labor, or labor power, "a commodity, whose use-value possesses the peculiar property of being a source of value." The value of labor power, "as in the case of every other commodity," is determined by the labor required to produce it, that is, the labor required to produce means of subsistence. Since labor is *physically* productive, it follows, Marx suggests, that the value of labor's output will exceed the value of labor services, hence, the existence of surplus value is compatible with "the exchange of equivalents."

Marx was very proud of the distinction between labor and labor power, which he thought cleared up Smith's confusion between embodied labor and commanded labor. But the contrast between the two kinds of labor is purely terminological: labor, as distinct from labor power, is a Marxian abstraction. Moreover, if workers really sell their labor power, and not their labor, the favorite phrase "unpaid labor" is subtly misleading, assuming as fact something that is supposed to be proved. Marx notes that "a historical and moral element" enters into the determination of the value of labor power, something that is not true of other commodities (chap. 6). But he fails to point out that competition provides no mechanism to reduce the "market price" of labor power to its "natural price." The labor theory of value as such does not guarantee that labor power will sell at its value.

Chapter 8 defines constant and variable capital; chapter 9 defines the rate of surplus value. Notice the footnote at the close of chapter 9, section 1, as well as the last footnote to chapter 5, both of which point out that prices are assumed equal to values: "we shall, however, see, in Book III, that even in the case of average prices the assumption cannot be made in this very simple manner." This, apart from any other evidence, shows clearly that Marx was aware from the outset of the so-called "great contradiction."

Chapter 9, section 3, contains Marx's famous attack on Senior's last-hour theory, a superb example of Marx's polemical powers. But for Marx's criticism, Senior's pamphlet would long ago have passed into oblivion. It met with the unanimous condemnation of all Senior's fellow economists: they objected to the unrealistic numerical example upon which his conclusions were grounded. Ironically enough, Senior's calculations do not in fact show that all net profits are produced in the "last hour": on his own assumptions, he merely showed that a shortening of the work day by one hour, given constant output per man-hour, will reduce the rate of profit from 10 to 8 per cent. Marx discusses Senior's figures but fails to make this point.

The Factory Acts. The long tenth chapter, entirely historical in character, contains Marx's indictment of contemporary factory conditions and tells the story of the long struggle to regulate hours and to eliminate the employment of children. The purpose of this chapter is to suggest that capitalists resist the passage of Factory Acts because they strive to maximize the rate and amount of surplus value. It is only in chapter 11 that Marx admits that this cannot in fact be true. If employers really maximized $s' = s/v$, it would be hard to explain why they ever substitute capital for labor. The fact is that they want to maximize $p' = s/v + c$ and that lengthening the working day does not necessarily raise p'. Although it always pays, *ceteris paribus,* to work machines as intensively as possible, extra hours do involve extra overhead costs and usually lead to a reduction in output per man-hour. The resistance of capitalists to hours legislation is not due to a "were-wolf's hunger for surplus-labor." It is the result of the divergence between private and social costs and the failure of atomistic competition to put a price on the social cost of overutilizing labor. As Marx himself points out: *"Après moi le déluge!* is the watchword of every capitalist. . . . Hence Capital is reckless of the health or length of life of the laborer, unless under compulsion from society"; and again, "the English Factory Acts . . . curb the passion of capital for a limitless draining of labor-power by forcibly limiting the working-day by state regulations, made by a state that is ruled by capitalists and landlords. Apart from the working-class movement that daily grew more threatening, the limiting of factory labor was dictated by the same necessity which spread guano over the English fields." This is a striking observation, for it is not always realized that there is nothing in the Marxist theory of the state—the state is simply the executive committee of the ruling class—that precludes social legislation in the public interest.

In the case of Factory Acts, it is clear that no individual employer can benefit from a reduction in hours unless it is enforced upon everyone. Even if he realizes that output per man-hour in his own plant might rise if hours were cut, the immediate effect would always be to decrease total output and hence to increase costs per unit; in the short run, profits would fall. But if the reduction in hours is general, his competitive situation would not be affected and, even at constant wages, the stimulus given to labor efficiency might maintain or possibly raise the rate of profit. The length of the working day, therefore, is merely one of the many examples of the failure of competition to produce optimum results owing to a divergence between the private and the social cost of production.

Marx's Use of Historical Material. Although Marx was much more aware of methodological issues than, say, Ricardo, he made no serious effort in his writings to verify his conclusions or to check his predictions against the available body of data. This may seem a strange statement in view of the wealth of empirical material in *Capital*. But the statistical and historical data is used, not to test the conclusions of theory, but to build up a graphic picture of capitalist society. Marx is never ashamed to admit that the data is selective; it is meant to illustrate a thesis, not to establish it. By virtue of its nature, however, it has a powerful effect upon the reader. The suggestion is that the conditions depicted are a necessary product of capitalism, generated by the peculiar nature of that system, and that similar conditions will be found wherever such a system is in force. But the chapter on "The Working Day," considered above, suggests the necessity to ask in every case what conclusions can be legitimately drawn from the material presented.

Division of Labor and Machinery. Chapter 12 distinguishes between "absolute surplus value" obtained by lengthening the working day and "relative surplus value" produced by an increase in the productivity of labor, which cheapens wage goods. There follows what is in effect a digression from the main theme: chapters 13 and 14 deal with the advantages of the division of labor. Marx's treatment is much more erudite than Smith's but, on the whole, adds detail rather than new insights. Chapter 13 provides a striking illustration of Marx's tendency to hypostasize the rate of surplus value. "The directing motive, the end and aim of capitalist production," he remarks, "is to extract the greatest possible amount of surplus-value." But in fact the motive of the capitalist, on Marx's own showing, is to maximize, not the sum of profits or the total amount of surplus value, nor even the rate of surplus value, but the rate of profit on total capital invested. Chapter 13 also contains one of Marx's rare remarks on the nature of entrepreneurship.

Chapter 15, the longest in the book, is again largely historical in character, treating of the effects of machinery on working conditions, on the composition of the labor force, and on the total volume of employment. Section 6, on the theory of "compensation," is of theoretical interest. Marx alleges that Mill, McCulloch, Senior, and Torrens held the view that all technically displaced labor must necessarily be reabsorbed in the making of laborsaving machines. This is a travesty of the classical theory of technological unemployment. Nowhere does Marx mention the effect of lower prices upon the demand for goods, a consideration that is an essential element in the classical theory. The last footnote in chapter 15 deals with Mill's statement of the law of diminishing returns and affords a representative example of Marx's style of criticism. In chapter 24, however, Marx concedes that Mill should not be classed with "the herd of vulgar economic apologists."

Surplus Value and Labor Productivity. Part V is devoted to the effect of changes in absolute and relative surplus value. The opening pages of chapter 16 define "productive labor" as labor that produces surplus value; this question is dealt with at greater length in Volume II of *Capital* and in *Theories of Surplus Value*. The last few pages of the chapter ridicule Mill's theory of profit; while Mill's language is hardly felicitous, his views are not as absurd as Marx makes out. Chapter 17 considers the combined effect of a change in hours and in the productivity of labor. Notice the proposition that "a working-day of given length always creates the same amount of value, no matter how the productiveness of labor, and, with it, the mass of the product, and the price of each single commodity produced, may vary." Value per unit of output falls as productivity rises, but the total value of output remains unchanged. This assumes that the ratio of capital to labor is equal in all industries—the unstated general assumption of volume I—so that a given rise in the productivity of labor entails an equal rise in the productivity of capital.

Chapter 19 plays hard and fast with the distinction between labor and labor power. "Labor is the substance, and the immanent measure of value, but *has itself no value*," meaning that the worker as such has no value, it is only his services that are valuable. Ricardo expressed the same thing by saying that the price of labor depends on the quantity of labor required to produce wage goods. This chapter also contains one of Marx's characteristic assertions about the law of demand and supply: "If demand and supply balance, . . . then demand and supply cease to explain anything. The price of labor, at the moment when demand and supply are in equilibrium, is its natural price, determined independently of the relation of demand and supply" (see also Volume III, chap. 10). This marks a retrogression from Ricardo, who at least adhered to the implicit notion of market schedules; given Mill's exposition in his *Principles,* Marx's misunderstanding is really unpardonable. It is difficult to say, however, how much it led him astray. He operates throughout with the case of constant costs, and completely ignores short-run pricing, but seems totally unaware of the restricted scope of his theory. Chapter 20 is uninteresting, but chapter 21, on "Piece-Wages," is worthy of mention. Chapter 22 provides a superficial and very much watered-down version of Senior's doctrine of international wage levels.

The Accumulation of Capital. After the rather slack Parts V and VI of the book, the argument moves into high gear in Part VII. Chapter 23 takes up the stationary state, "simple reproduction" Marx calls it. Notice that surplus value is said to be positive even under stationary conditions. Chapter 24 is full of interesting material, criticizing in turn the saving-is-spending theorem (sec. 2), the abstinence theory of interest (sec. 3), and the wages fund doctrine (sec. 5). Marx's criticism of the abstinence theory falls below all acceptable standards: the notion of time preference, without which the theory is meaningless, is not even mentioned. Saving for the purpose of productive investment, Marx explains, is virtually automatic under capitalism, the result of the competitive race to take advantage of the latest improvements in technique: "Accumulate, accumulate! That is Moses and the prophets!" Oddly enough, he does admit what he calls "a Faustian conflict between the passion for accumulation, and the desire for enjoyment," that is, the concept of abstinence in disguise.

The only point that Marx makes against the wages fund doctrine, which he attributes for no apparent reason to Bentham, is that the wages fund is not fixed or predetermined at the beginning of a production period. The classical doctrine that "what is saved is spent" or "consumed by productive laborers" is denied on the grounds that savings are invested in constant as well as variable capital.

Chapter 25 introduces the concept of the organic composition of labor, distinguishing between the ratio of capital to labor in physical terms and in value terms. This chapter lays down Marx's conception of the determination of real wages (sec. 1). He takes pains to point out that both money wages and real wages can rise, and rise indefinitely as long as it does not "threaten the system itself." Marx's hesitation about the nature of the investment function comes out clearly when he supposes at one point that a rise in wages results in a slackening of accumulation "because the stimulus to gain is blunted." This implies that investment is a function of the going rate of profit, but immediately thereafter he goes on to advance the more typical view that there is no problem about the inducement to invest: "The rate of accumulation is the independent, not the dependent variable; the rate of wages, the dependent, not the independent, variable." This is followed once again by the notion that wages rise in the boom, choking off investment, whereupon wages fall again: "the rise of wages is therefore confined within limits that not only leave intact the foundations of the capitalist system, but also secure its reproduction on a progressive scale." A curious footnote in this section remarks on the monopoly of the theory of population by "Reverends of Protestant Theology."

Absolute and Relative Impoverishment. Section 2 discusses the increasing organic composition of capital as a fundamental law of capitalist development. Accompanying this process is the "concentration and centralization" of capital, the growth in size of firms, and the reduction in the number of firms in an industry—Volume III, chapter 27, has some additional comments on the "formation of stock companies." Section 3 is devoted to the concept of the "industrial reserve army" of the unemployed. Marx cites Malthus on the slow adjustment of population to changes in wages and on this ground rejects the classical wages-population mechanism. In several places Marx suggests that the absolute amount of unemployment grows in the course of capital accumulation. The greater the industrial reserve army, the greater is "official pauperism": "This is the absolute general law of capitalist accumulation." Marx adds cautiously: "Like all other laws it is modified in its working by many circumstances, the analysis of which does not concern us here." He proceeds, two paragraphs later, to enumerate the action of the law in bringing about "misery, agony of toil, slavery, ignorance, brutality, mental degradation." It is evident that the so-called doctrine of "absolute impoverishment"—a phrase that Marx does not use—does not mean, or even necessarily entail, a fall in real wages. Marx did believe, however, that labor's share would fall—he remarks casually in chapter 24, section 4, that "real wages . . . never rise proportionally to the productive power of labor." Section 5 is designed to supply illustrative material of "the absolute general law," but, shocking as are the conditions Marx reveals, the working of the law is not really clarified by the selective evidence he presents (see also Vol. II, chaps. 4 and 5).

It is worth remarking that in some ways Marx's notion of "absolute impoverishment" is not very different from Adam Smith's description of the disadvantages of the division of labor that deprives "the laboring poor" of "intellectual, social, and martial virtues."

Primitive Accumulation. Instead of capitalism's growing naturally out of feudalism by the gradual emergence of a "spirit of rational calculation," it comes into the world "dripping from head to foot, from every pore, with blood and dirt." By means of the slave trade, piracy, and colonial plunder, wealth is concentrated in the hands of the few, while forcible enclosures of arable land create a propertyless proletariat. The whole of Part VIII of Volume I (see also Vol. III, chaps. 20, 36, and 47), is given over to a description of this historical process of "primitive accumulation" in the fourteenth and fifteenth centuries: "the capitalistic era dates from the 16th century." It is doubtful whether Marx's account of the slave trade and colonial booty bears the weight he puts upon it. Moreover, his treatment of the role of enclosures indiscriminately identifies enclosures of arable land with the enclosures of wasteland— by the eighteenth century most enclosures served to *raise* the total acreage under cultivation. Chapter 32 contains the most frequently quoted passage in *Capital* on the eventual "expropriation of the expropriators."

The Costs of Distribution. One of the problems left over for solution from Volume I is the question whether the distribution, as distinct from the production, of commodities creates surplus value. This problem is discussed in Volume II, Part I, and again in Volume III, chapters 16–19. The reader should pass over Volume II, chapters 1–5, which are immensely tedious and add little to an understanding of Marx's system; it is chapter 6 in Volume II and the four chapters in Volume III that are relevent for our purpose.

On the face of it, the "circulation" as well as the production of commodities enhances their value, since there is a visible difference between "the purchase price" paid by the merchant and the realized "sales price" to consumers. Nevertheless, Marx contends, the labor expended in distributing commodities does not add value to the product; clerks, typists, bookkeepers, and salesmen are "unproductive" workers. Commercial capital merely appropriates part of the surplus value produced in the industrial sphere: the merchant buys commodities below their labor value and sells them at their value; the difference constitutes his gross profit margin. It makes no difference whether distribution is actually handled by independent middlemen; an office staff and a sales force attached to the factory are just as "unproductive" as the workers employed by wholesalers and retailers. The transportation, shipping, warehousing, and packing of goods are parts of the productive process and, hence, do create value; but true selling costs in the Marxian sense, that is, office and clerical overheads, promotional expenses, and the financing of goods in transit, are all "dead expenses" (Vol. II, chap. 6, secs. 2 and 3).

Like Smith, Marx disavows any connection between "productive" labor and "useful" labor. There is no questioning the usefulness of the unproductive function of merchandizing in a highly specialized economy, where buyers and sellers must be brought together. And any reduction in the "time of circulation" raises the average rate of profit in the economy (Vol. III, chap. 16). Marx clearly adopts the "value-version" of Smith's doctrine of productive labor, but the concept plays a role in *Capital* different from that in the *Wealth of Nations*. The proposition that the rate of capital accumulation is a function of the ratio of productive to unproductive labor, which is in the foreground in Smith's treatment, hardly appears in *Capital*. In Marx the problem is a purely formal one: is the "value" of a commodity proportional to all the labor expended on its production and distribution, in which case the denominator in the expression s' refers to the total wage bill in the economy, or is it merely a function of the labor expended in manufacturing and transportation so that a portion of the total capital of a society "must be set aside for secondary operations, which are no part of the process of creating value" (Vol. III, chap. 17)? Marx's distinction between productive and unproductive labor, therefore, stands or falls with the labor theory of value, and has no interest apart from it. Hence, we need not trouble ourselves with Marx's occasional inconsistencies when he speaks of wage workers in service industries as productive workers merely because they are hired to create marketable services (Vol. I, chap. 16; Vol. III, chap. 17). If this line of thought were pursued, only the government sector would prove to be unproductive. The import of Marx's doctrine of productive labor for his system is that the rate of profit is not equal to s/K, but rather $\bar{s}/K$, where $\bar{s}$ stands for nonlabor income minus administrative overhead, sales and advertising expenses, rents and indirect business taxes. Likewise, $s' \neq s/v$, but $s' = \bar{s}/\bar{v}$ where $\bar{v}$ excludes what we may roughly call salaried personnel. The national income of the economy is now $= \bar{v} + \bar{s}$, the wage bill of productive workers plus the surplus value generated by them.

The Turnover of Capital. In chapter 8 Marx defends his distinction between constant and variable capital against the orthodox distinction between fixed and circulating capital, the former transferring only part of its value to the product during each turnover, while the latter has to be renewed after each turnover. The only difference between the two distinctions lies in the treatment of raw materials. Chapter 8, section 2, provides an excellent "bourgeois" account of the subject of depreciation of capital, separating user's cost and depreciation proper. To this is added the problem of obsolescence (chap. 9). Marx explains in chapter 9 how to calculate the average period of turnover of all capital when its various components turn over at different rates. Adam Smith's and Ricardo's theory of capital are criticized in chapters 10 and 11. Chapter 12 considers differences in the turnover rate or durability of capital invested in different industries, irrespective of the organic composition of capital in these industries. What Marx calls "the working period" is what Böhm-Bawerk later called "the period of fabrication" of goods. Marx goes on in the next chapter to treat "the time of production" with reference to such goods as wine and timber, which require aging or finishing after their manufacture; chapter 14 introduces the further consideration of "the time of selling," the time interval between the completion of the product and the receipt of sales proceeds. These three chapters (12–14) are remarkable for their clarity and adroit use of historical examples.

The *fact* of the time-consuming character of the productive process has never been better described, not even by Böhm-Bawerk. But what is striking about the treatment is Marx's failure to relate the fact of differences in the durability of capital in different industries in any way to the problem of price determination, getting sidetracked instead by the spurious problem of the periodic "release" of money capital—Engels' refreshing postscript to chapter 15, section 4, is warning enough to pass over Marx's calculations in the preceding sections. Chapter 16 shows Marx's awareness of the necessity to re-define all the ratios in Volume I to take account of differences in the turnover rate of capital: "the annual rate of surplus-value coincides only in one single case with the current rate of surplus-value . . . in the case that the advanced capital is turned over only once a year" (sec. 1). Chapter 16, sections 2 and 3, contain nothing of interest. Chapter 17 turns to the questions raised at length in Part III of the book: the realization of surplus value under conditions of simple and of expanded reproduction.

The Reproduction Schema. After some initial procrastination in chapters 18 and 19, Marx gets down to the task in chapter 20. No part of *Capital* is as difficult to follow as this chapter. The essence of the matter is stated in sections 2 and 3, but the remaining sections are full of interesting hints. Unfortunately, chapter 21, on expanded reproduction, is even less finished than chapter 20, on simple reproduction. Marx's refutation of the vulgar under-consumptionist theory of crises occurs in chapter 20, section 4, but an earlier footnote in chapter 16, section 3, nevertheless gives credence to some version of underconsumption.

The Transformation Problem. If surplus value is proportional to varia-ble capital employed, why is it that the more mechanized processes earn the same rate of profit on total capital invested as do the less mechanized processes? Profits per cent of capital tend toward equality regardless of the technique in which the capital is invested. This implies that surplus value is not a function of v alone, in which case commodities apparently do not exchange according to the total labor embodied in them. This is the so-called "Great Contradiction," whose resolution Marx had promised for Volume III. His occasional remarks in Volume I show that he had worked out the solution before 1867. We have Engels' word that the draft of Volume III was in fact completed in 1865, two years before Volume I was published; in addition, we have a letter from Marx to Engels written in 1862, outlining the solution. In the Preface to Volume II (1885) Engels dared Marx's critics to show how "an equal average rate of profit can and must come about, not only without a violation of the law of value, but by means of it." In the decade that intervened between the publication of Volumes II and III, the prize essay competition drew several contributions from leading German economists vying with one another to solve the puzzle posed by Marx. According to Engels, who reviewed some of the essays in the Preface to Volume III, no one succeeded in carrying off the prize. But Engels' protests notwithstanding, it is evident that Schmidt and Fireman each gave a possible solution and that Lexis solved the problem in the same way as Marx did. This is hardly surprising: anyone who knew his Ricardo should have had no trouble in resolving the Marxian dilemma.

Midway through the Preface, Engels refers parenthetically to "Jevons' and Menger's theory of use-value and marginal profits" on which G. B. Shaw was erecting "the Fabian church of the future." The *Fabian Essays,* in which Sidney Webb and G. B. Shaw fused George's theory of rent and the Jevons-Wicksteed theory of value into a new brand of English socialist theory, had appeared in 1888. This remark of Engels is the only notice that either Marx or Engels ever took of the new departure in economic thought, despite the fact that Marx died nine years after Jevons' *Political Economy* (1874). By the time Engels edited Volume II of *Capital,* Böhm-Bawerk's attack on Marx in *Capital and Interest* (1884) was already attracting attention on the Continent. Volume III of *Capital* was published in 1894, six years after Böhm-Bawerk's *Positive Theory of Capital* (1889) and Wieser's *Natural Value* (1889), with their frequent attacks on the labor theory of value, and five years after Marshall's *Principles* (1890). But Engels had long before lost interest in economic theory and made no mention of the new currents of thought.

Chapters 1–3 of Volume III make the transition from the labor theory of the value to the theory of "prices of production"; the unqualified term "price of production" always refers to the "purchase price" at which the merchant buys the good. Chapters 4–6 digress from this theme and should be read in conjunction with Part III, which discusses the law of the declining rate of profit. Chapters 8–12 show how values can be transformed into prices without violating the labor theory of value applied to output as a whole. Throughout the early chapters of the third volume, Marx displays a lively sense of the paradoxical character of his theory of surplus value. "It is immaterial for the capitalist," he notes in chapter 2, "whether he is supposed to advance constant capital in order to make a profit out of his variable capital, or whether he advances variable capital in order to make a profit out of the constant capital. . . . Although it is only the variable portion of capital which creates surplus-value, it does so only on condition that the other portions, the material requirements of production, are likewise advanced." And again, in the last pages of chapter 9, he declares that "in its disguise of profit, the surplus-value had actually concealed its origin, lost its character, and become unrecognizable"; "the capitalist had a practical interest only in the rate of profit"; "by the transformation of value into prices of production, the basis of the determination of value is itself removed from direct observation"; and so on. Marx is proud of the paradox. The bourgeois economist is a "vulgar" economist because he refuses "to penetrate through the outward disguise into the internal essence and the inner form of the capitalist process of production," meaning he refuses to see that equality of the rate of profit on total capital invested is really predicated upon a uniform rate of surplus on variable capital. The total surplus is determined by the size of the labor force, and this surplus is then shared out among each capitalist in proportion to his share of the total capital stock of the community, "a process which takes place behind his back, which he does not see, nor understand, and which indeed does not interest him at all."

Marx steadily ignores the fact that he has not yet given any reason to believe that the rate of surplus value is in fact uniform between industries. There is a paragraph in chapter 10 in which he admits that a uniform rate of surplus value "has been assumed by us," presupposing "a competition among the laborers and an equilibration by means of their continual emigration from one sphere of production to another." He proceeds to make "the essential point . . . visible" by examining production in a noncapitalist society in which "the laborers themselves are in possession of their respective means of production." This is the only place in the 2,000 pages of *Capital* where Marx recognizes that the concept of a determinate rate of surplus per man requires defense. But the idea that the mobility of labor between industries establishes such a rate is a fallacy of the first order: mobility of labor produces a uniform rate of reward for labor but no more equalizes the rate of surplus per man than it equalizes total output per man between industries.

In the short chapter 7 Marx comments briefly on differences in managerial ability within an industry, suggesting that the going rate of profit is earned by the marginal firm, while firms with superior management earn what we now call "rents of management." The technical, as distinct from the organic, composition of capital, Marx declares, is governed by strictly technical conditions (chap. 8 and opening sentence of chap. 9). Marx's assumption, therefore, is that of fixed coefficients of production. But, elsewhere, he speaks of laborsaving technical change induced by a rise of wages (Vol. III, chap. 14, sec. 4). Thus, the ratios of capital to labor observed in different industries are, as a matter of fact, functions of relative factor prices.

The transformation of labor values into normal prices in chapter 9 is carried out only in terms of output. Marx was aware of the necessity of transforming input as well as output values but apparently found the task beyond him: "it is necessary . . . to bear in mind that there is always the possibility of an error, if we assume that the cost price of commodities of any particular sphere is equal to the value of the means of production consumed by it. Our present analysis does not necessitate a closer examination of this point." The transformation is carried out on the *assumption* that "the sum of the profits of all spheres of production must be equal to the sum of surplus-values, and the sum of the prices of production of the total social product equal to the sum of its values" (chap. 10). Without this assumption, Marx contends, "political economy would be without a rational basis." We would be back with Adam Smith, for whom prices are determined by "adding a more or less arbitrary amount of profit to the actual value of commodities" (chap. 13).

In chapter 10 Marx suggests that "it is quite appropriate . . . to regard the value of commodities not only theoretically, but also historically, as existing prior to prices of production." In societies in which "the laborer owns his means of production"—"and this is the condition of the landowning farmer and of the craftsman in the old world as well as the new"—prices are indeed governed solely by the "law of value." In a developed capitalist economy this is true only for "capitals of average composition" (chap. 9).

The last half of chapter 10 is concerned with deviations of the actual price from long-run normal levels. "Price of production" is what "Adam Smith calls *natural price,* Ricardo *price of production,* or *cost of production,* and the Physiocrats *prix necessaire,* because it is in the long run a prerequisite of supply." Nevertheless, Marx heaps ridicule on Malthus' suggestion that "the great principle of demand and supply is called into action to determine what A. Smith calls natural price as well as market price" because "if demand and supply balance, then they cease to have any effect."

Chapters 11 and 12 criticize Ricardo's dictum that "profits vary inversely as wages" but in point of fact come to exactly the same conclusion as Ricardo: a rise in money wages leaves the price of goods produced with average technique unaffected while changing other prices inversely to the degree of mechanization.

The Law of the Falling Rate of Profit. The whole of Part III, chapters 13–15, as well as chapters 4–6 of Part I, are concerned with the "mystery" of the falling rate of profit "whose solution has been the goal of the entire political economy since Adam Smith." Chapter 14 on the "Counteracting Causes" is particularly interesting. Marx lists five offsetting forces to the falling profit rate and in four of the five cases emphasizes that "the same causes which produce a falling tendency in the rate of profit, also call forth counter-effects." This is a very peculiar use of the term "tendency to fall." We would be inclined to say that there is a tendency for the rate of profit to be constant when some forces act to reduce the rate while other forces act automatically to raise it, unless of course we have reasons to believe that one set of forces tends to predominate over the other. In one respect, Marx thought he had created a presumption that the rate of profit would fall, the case in which the rising organic composition of capital increases the rate of surplus value by raising the productivity of labor but not proportionately to the rise in q. First, Marx does admit, in chapter 14, that s' tends to rise with q. In chapter 15, section 2, he gives the argument that s' will not rise as rapidly as q, an argument that he had already stated in Volume I, chapter 11: "to the extent that the development of the productive power reduces the paid portion of the employed labor, it raises the surplus-value by raising its rate; but to the extent that it reduces the total mass of labor employed by a certain capital, it reduces the factor of numbers with which the rate of surplus-value is multiplied in order to calculate its mass. Two laborers, each working 12 hours daily, cannot produce the same mass of surplus-value as 24 laborers each working only 2 hours, even if they could live on air. . . . In this respect, then, the compensation of the reduction in the number of laborers by means of intensification of exploitation has certain impassable limits." In the first case total surplus value = 48 man-hours; in the second case it is at best = 24 man-hours. Hence, an increase in q cannot be compensated beyond a certain point by an increase in s'.

This argument is not only farfetched but is in fact fallacious. First, the total size of the labor force does increase in the course of development despite the rise in q; as Marx points out toward the end of the chapter, "it is but a requirement of the capitalist mode of production that the number of wage workers should increase absolutely." Moreover, at constant real wages, s' rises at the same rate as the productivity of labor in the wage-goods industries. If the average product of labor can in principle rise to infinity, so can s'. A rising rate of s' applied to a rising quantity of v, owing to the growth of the labor force at constant real wages, is perfectly capable of offsetting an ever rising q.

It is worth noting that Marx never links the process of a rising q specifically to the rise in s' and certainly does not emphasize the functional relationship between them. In Volume I, chapter 12, Marx noted that relative surplus value is "directly proportional" to the productivity of labor. But this point is not mentioned in Volume I, chapter 25, which introduces the organic composition of capital. In Volume III, chapter 3, Marx remarks that "we shall see that alterations affecting the factors c, v, and s imply also changes in the productivity of labor," but although this chapter considers almost every possible combination of changes in the fundamental ratios p', s', and q, the promise is never fulfilled. Again, in Volume III, chapter 14, the tendency of s' to rise is not related functionally in any way to the increase in q. This leaves only the passage in chapter 15, which we have just considered. It is difficult to escape the conviction that Marx was deliberately misleading the reader in order to cover up a loose end in the argument.

Capitalsaving Innovations. The third counteracting cause, "cheapening of the elements of the constant capital," is nothing else but capitalsaving innovations. We turn back to chapters 4 and 5, which deal at length with "economies in the employment of constant capital," marking the first explicit discussion of capitalsaving innovations in the literature of economics. Chapter 4, contributed by Engels, refers both to the release of working capital by improved means of communication and transportation, which have "in the last fifty years doubled or trebled . . . the productive capacity" of the capital engaged in world commerce, and to economies of fixed capital in "the recently discovered methods of making iron and steel, such as the processes of Bessemer, Siemens, Gilchrist-Thomas, etc." At the close of the chapter Engels illustrates the importance of turnover rates of capital on the rate of profit by data drawn from an actual cotton-spinning firm. With a profit rate of 33.3 per cent, the annual rate of $s' = 1307$ per cent, due to the fact that payrolls turn over 8½ times in one year. Notice too the negligible portion of the stock of working capital required (2½ per cent of total capital). Chapter 5 begins by noting that double work shifts save capital. It quotes a Report of the Factory Inspectors that neatly distinguishes fixed and variable costs of operation—could Marshall have learned his theory of the firm by reading Blue Books? Marx also comments upon the tendency to increasing returns of scale: expenses of fuel, power, light, and buildings do not rise proportionately with output. Capitalsaving innovations take the form of (1) "progressive improvements of machinery" (see in particular chap. 3, on steam engines); (2) the use of waste products previously discarded (sec. 4); and (3) the reduction in annual repair and maintenance charges owing to the greater durability of machines. Marx even makes the point that all cost-reducing improvements in the machinery industries release capital in all industries using machinery. This leads him to say, although he obviously did not realize what he was conceding, that the capital-output ratio tends to decline through time: "While the circulating part of constant capital, such as raw material, etc., continually increases in mass to the extent that the productivity of labor grows, it is not so with the fixed capital, such as buildings, machinery, apparatus for lighting, heating, etc. Although a machine becomes absolutely dearer with the growth of its bodily mass, it becomes relatively cheaper. If five laborers produce ten times as many commodities as formerly, this does not increase the outlay for fixed capital tenfold; although the value of this part of constant capital increases with the development of the productive forces, it does not increase by any means in the same proportion with them." (chap. 15). Marx also makes the interesting observation in the last paragraph of the chapter that "the first leaders in a new enterprise are generally bankrupted" owing to the bottlenecks in a new invention that need time to be ironed out.

Foreign Trade. One of the counteracting causes is foreign trade, insofar as it cheapens wage goods and raw materials. Capitals invested in foreign trade may yield a higher rate of profit because "an advanced country is able to sell its goods above their value even when it sells them cheaper than the competing countries." It is not clear what this means, inasmuch as the labor theory of value is not applicable to trade between countries. Moreover, capital invested in colonies may yield a higher rate of profit "for the simple reason that the rate of profit is higher there on account of the backward development, and for the added reason, that slaves, coolies, etc., permit a better exploitation of labor." This is the foundation of Lenin's theory of imperialism, but, as it stands, it is singularly unconvincing. As Marx had shown elsewhere, it is not low real wages but low wage costs per unit of output that govern profits; backward countries have low wages, but, owing to the low productivity of labor, costs of production may well be prohibitively high. And there is no "simple reason" why the rate of profit should be higher in backward than in advanced countries; in general, the absence of social overhead capital in backward countries makes most investment unprofitable.

Business Cycles. Chapter 15, section 3, contains the bulk of Marx's comments on business cycles in *Capital* (see also Vol. I, chap. 25, and Vol. III, chap. 30), a subject which he discussed more fully in *Theories of Surplus Value.* Here we get further hints of "the narrow basis on which the conditions of consumption rest," which is made "the cause of crises" in the ultimate paragraph of chapter 15. And again, in chapter 30: "the last cause of all real crises always remains the poverty and restricted consumption of the masses as compared with the tendency of capitalist production to develop the productive forces in such a way, that only the absolute power of consumption of the entire society would be their limit." The productivity of crises is linked with the falling rate of profit à la Mill. Marx points out in several places that innovators reap surplus profits until the innovation is adopted by others. Capitalists innovate "for the sake of self-preservation and on penalty of failure." There are some typical Malthusian remarks in this chapter as well as in chapter 13: "the time of prosperity would have promoted marriages among the laborers and reduced the decimation of the offspring." At the beginning of the chapter Marx remarks that "the rate of accumulation falls with the rate of profit," but at the end he declares: "in spite of the falling rate of profit the inducements and facilities to accumulate are augmented." His hazy conception of the inducement to investment is never more strikingly revealed than here.

There is a useful review of the history of booms and slumps in the cotton industry through 1845–60 (chap. 6, sec. 3); see also Engels' description of the crash of 1847 (chap. 25).

Say's Law of Markets is briefly discussed in chapter 15, and Marx attacks Ricardo's followers for admitting "periodic overabundance of capital," while denying "general overproduction of commodities." But there is no contradiction between the recognition of recurring crises and the assertion of Say's Equality, namely, the possibility of full employment equilibrium at all levels of output and the unlimited development of an inherently adaptive economy. Marx supposes that a "general glut" refers to business depressions, instead of to secular stagnation. Despite Mill's treatment of the question, Marx interprets the Law of Markets as an identity, and hence his criticism of Say's Law, both in *Capital* and in *Theories of Surplus Value,* never gets beyond an attack on the fallacy of abstracting from money.

Money and Interest. Part V of Volume III is extremely uneven, consisting for the most part of disconnected observations on monetary disturbances and the rate of interest, and a running logic-chopping commentary on parliamentary testimony about currency management. The only chapters worth reading with any attention in this section are chapters 21–23 and 25; chapter 30 has already been referred to as containing some of Marx's important observations on the business cycle.

For Marx, the rate of interest is essentially a monetary phenomenon; although interest is a derived income from profit—the average rate of profit in Marx always means profit inclusive of interest—it is only tenuously connected with the rate of return on capital. Marx holds that "the rate of interest in capitalist countries is overwhelmingly determined by conditions (loans granted by usurers to owners of large estates who draw ground rent) which have nothing to do with profit" (chap. 13). The demand for loanable funds is dominated by consumption loans, and since most profits are automatically plowed back into the industry in which they are earned, even the supply of loans is little influenced by business savings. Hence, the loan market is affected by business activity only in the last stages of the boom and at the onset of a slump, when the rising preference for liquidity leaves the loan market glutted with idle funds. Moreover, "there is no such thing as a natural rate of interest," that is, the interest rate is a short-run phenomenon and there is no tendency toward long-run equilibrium. Marx's remarks on the determination of the rate of interest are made incidentally in chapter 22, for he disavows any interest in what he describes as "minor fluctuations of the money-market." The rate of interest, however, does exhibit a secular tendency to decline, not only because of the tendency of the rate of profit to fall, but also because of the development of credit institutions and the efficient concentration of "the money savings of all classes of society" into the hands of the bankers.

Chapters 25–35 touch in one way or another upon all the issues dividing the Currency from the Banking School. Marx's sympathies lie with the Banking School. As early as 1859 he had taken his stand against the quantity theory of money, probably because he believed it to be at variance with the labor theory of value applied to money. Like Tooke, Marx argued that the quantity of money in circulation was governed by the flow of money expenditures; although he does not commit himself explicitly, Marx gives credence to the Law of Reflux based on the real-bills doctrine: "the quantity of circulating notes is regulated by the requirements of commerce, and every superfluous note wanders back immediately to the issuing party" (chap. 33).

In the absence of details, there is nothing to choose between a quantity theory and a contraquantity theory of money. Under a convertible paper standard *and a passive monetary policy,* the quantity of money in circulation is indeed the result, not the cause, of the level of prices; "real" forces, acting through the volume of trade and the demand for money-to-hold, generate a flow of money demands that determines absolute prices; the elasticity of the money supply is no doubt an element in the price-setting process, but it is a purely passive element. This kind of formulation has its advantages over a simple quantity theory because it is more likely to avoid "dichotomization" of the pricing process. But when the quantity of monetary metals is increasing sharply owing to the discovery of new gold mines, the quantity theory comes into its own. Furthermore, as soon as the monetary authorities practice an active monetary policy, the contraquantity theory is bound to lead to misunderstanding. At the time Marx was writing, the Bank of England was in fact practicing monetary management. The practice of using the Bank's discount rate as an instrument of credit regulation may be said to start from the Bank Charter Act of 1833, which repealed the Usury Laws. After 1844 the Bank also practiced something like "open market policy" by the device of "borrowing on Consols." The theory of monetary management by means of the bank rate had been advanced a half-century earlier by Thornton. It is noteworthy that Marx nowhere refers to the Thornton analysis of the two rates, which decisively refutes the theory of the Banking School (see in particular chap. 24, in which Marx summarizes Ricardo's theory of money). The Thornton-Ricardo argument would have supplied a definition of the long-run equilibrium rate of interest, whose existence Marx denied. In long-run equilibrium, the rate of interest is equal to the yield on real capital; at any lower rate the demand for lonable funds for investment purposes is insatiable, and at any higher rate the supply of loanable funds increases indefinitely. If the money market is dominated by investment loans, the money rate of interest will tend to be governed by the rate of return on real capital, despite the autonomous influence of monetary policy. We must conclude, therefore, that Marx's theory of money, even on its own reading, fares badly next to the best work of his predecessors.

Theory of Rent. Marx's theory of rent, developed in loving detail through chapters 37–43 is simplicity itself. First, there is differential rent, owing, as in Ricardo, to differences in the fertility and location of different grades of land. If the price of production of an individual capitalist is lower than the average price of production of the product—Marx uses the example of a power-driven mill enjoying the advantage of a waterfall—he will earn a surplus over and above the average rate, assuming that demand is high enough to allow him to participate in the market. Competition for the use of the waterfall will permit its owner to charge a rent, thus equalizing the rate of profit earned by capitalists. The rate of profit is now given by $p' = (s - r)/(c + v)$, and the "rate of rent" by $r' = r/(c + v)$. Thus, $p' = (s'/[q + 1]) - r'$. Differences in s' owing to differences in site value or fertility of land will be compensated by differences in r', so as to leave p' uniform between industries. Second, there may be absolute rent, something not found in Ricardo, owing to the fact that agriculture operates with an organic composition of capital below the social average. As a result, the "value" of agricultural products is in excess of its "price of production." Normally, the flow of capital would reduce the rate of profit in agriculture to the average rate, but, owing to the existence of landed property, the landowner is able to charge the tenant an extra rental equal to the abnormal surplus earned in agriculture. Marx is careful to avoid commitment to the view that the organic composition of capital in agriculture is in fact below the average: this is "a question which can be decided only by statistics" (chap. 45). If this is not so, absolute rent disappears and all rent is differential rent.

Marx's theory of absolute rent has no validity except in terms of his theory of surplus value and the resulting necessity of transforming value into prices. We will therefore pass it by without comment. Marx's discussion of differential rent is more detailed than is Ricardo's but adds nothing new— Marx gives a convenient summary of the argument in the closing pages of chapter 43. Two special points are worthy of mention. In chapter 39 Marx denies that the demand for wheat is perfectly inelastic, as Ricardo had assumed. The Ricardian view, Marx asserts, is due to observing the impact-effect of drought or bumper crops, in which "the sudden and short cheapness does not get time to exert its full effect upon the extension of consumption." Moreover, the amount of wheat used to produce whisky or beer varies with the price of wheat, and a falling price of wheat brings about the substitution of wheaten bread for bread made out of rye and oats. One hardly expects such comments from Marx. Equally surprising are the remarks made in chapter 45 on the opportunity cost of using land for pasture instead of for tillage, drawn from the *Wealth of Nations*.

The Trinitarian Formula. Part VII contains discursive notes on the classical concept of the productive triad, land, labor, and capital. Chapter 48 clarifies Marx's attack on vulgar political economy. The other three chapters merely repeat earlier material.

NOTES FOR FURTHER READING

There is nothing to choose between any of the English editions of *Capital:* each follows the same translation. There is a modern edition of Volume I, however, edited by D. Torr, which is distinctly superior to the Engels edition. There is no point in reading just Volume I of *Capital*. Volumes II and III are not addenda; they are vital to the story. Rather than reading only the first volume, it would be better to read Borchardt's adroitly arranged selections from the three volumes in the Modern Library edition of *Capital and Other Writings*, ed. M. Eastman. A revealing supplement to *Capital* is Marx's *Theories of Surplus-Value*, planned as a fourth volume to *Capital*. After Engels' death the manuscript passed into Kautsky's hands and he published it in three volumes (1905–11). An English translation of selections from this work appeared in 1951. There are innumerable biographical studies of Marx; the standard biography is by F. Mehring (1948). The chapters on Marx's economic ideas in the Mehring biography were written by Rosa Luxemburg and are marked by certain inaccuracies of exposition and an overemphasis upon the "reproduction schema."

P. M. Sweezy, *The Theory of Capitalist Development* (1942), and J. Robinson, *An Essay on Marxian Economics* (1942), provide the most satisfactory accounts of Marxian economics. Sweezy's invaluable book has shortcomings, which its author has since acknowledged: it improves Marx by Keynesian embellishments and contains an untenable "proof" of underconsumption (see N. Georgescu-Roegen, "Mathematical Proofs of the Breakdown of Capitalism," *Ecom.*, April, 1960, and the references cited there). Chapter 7 of Sweezy's book reintroduced the Transformation Problem in the Marxist literature; since then the subject has been worked on by others, and to that extent Sweezy's treatment is now outdated. In addition, the book is not a complete study of Marxian economic theory: it neglects Marx's theory of rent, of interest, and of productive labor, and says little on Marx's conception of the investment function. The core of the book is Parts I and II; Part III, on business cycles, is much less satisfactory. Part III, chapter 11, however, is about the only account in English of the important "breakdown controversy" among German Marxists. (See also the introduction by J. Robinson to the English edition of R. Luxemburg, *The Accumulation of Capital* [1951], reprinted in *Collected Economic Papers* [1960], Vol. II).

Mrs. Robinson's essay, written in a mood of bitter dissatisfaction with modern economics, is lucid and penetrating. The chapter on "Real and Money Wages," however, suffers from a failure to appreciate the Ricardian basis of Marx's argument about wages and prices. Nevertheless, if the reader has only a limited interest in Marx, this is the one book to read. It closes with the comment that "if there is any hope of progress in economics at all, it must be in using academic methods to solve the problems posed by Marx." Mrs. Robinson has gone on to solve Marx's problems in her *Accumulation of Capital* (1956). The reader who wants to gain a quick impression of her results should consult M. Bronfenbrenner, "Academic Methods for Marxian Problems," *JPE*, December, 1957.

J. A. Schumpeter has written a keen appreciation of Marxian economics in *Capitalism, Socialism, and Democracy* (1942), chap. 3, reprinted in *Ten Great Economists* (1951). Marx is also discussed in various places in Schumpeter's *History*, in particular pp. 383–92, 438–42, 596–98, 647–52, 661–62, 681–87, 747–50, 877–80, and 1131–32. An excellent exposition of Marx's ideas, and a virtual précis of the difficult opening chapters of Volume I of *Capital*, will be found in E. Roll, *History of Economic Thought* (3d ed., 1956). In the first edition, Roll took an orthodox Marxist position. Since then he has had second thoughts but has wisely left the chapter unaltered, adding a candid new "appraisal" to the third edition. Rogin, *The Meaning and Validity of Economic Theory,* chap. 9, ranges far and wide through Marxian economics and, despite its turgid style, is particularly useful on Marx's theory of business cycles and on the Marxian conception of the role of the state in capitalist development.

The classic critique of Marx is by Böhm-Bawerk, *Karl Marx and the Close of His System* (1898). P. M. Sweezy has republished Böhm-Bawerk's tract together with the equally famous reply by R. Hilferding (1949). Böhn-Bawerk criticizes Marxian economics considered as a theory of relative prices and makes heavy weather of the "great contradiction" between Volumes I and III of *Capital.* In some ways the chapter on Marx in Böhm-Bawerk's *Capital and Interest* (1932), Book IV, chap. 3, is more to the point. P. H. Wicksteed, "The Marxian Theory of Value" (1884), reprinted in *The Common Sense of Political Economy* (1933), Vol. II, confronts the labor theory of value as an explanation of relative prices with the marginal utility theory. The Lausanne version of Böhm-Bawerk's critique is by V. Pareto, *Les Systèmes Socialistes* (1926); on the whole, it is surprisingly ineffectual. For a review of these and other criticisms from a Marxist standpoint see Meek, *Studies in the Labour Theory of Value,* chap. 6, and W. J. Blake, *An American Looks at Karl Marx,* also published under the title *Elements of Marxian Economic Theory and Its Criticism* (1939). Blake's study contains an excellent annotated bibliography of the Continental literature covering all phases of Marxist thought.

The debate between Marxist and orthodox economics flared up again in the 1930's, led by O. Lange's brilliant essay, "Marxian Economics and Modern Economic Theory," *REStud,* June, 1935. Lange argued that the superiority of Marxian economics in analyzing capitalist evolution is due not to the technically invalid labor theory of value but to the exact specification of the institutional features of capitalism. M. Dobb drives this point home in a forceful Marxist attack on modern economics: *Political Economy and Capitalism* (1937), chap. 5; see also Dobb, "On Some Tendencies in Modern Economic Theory," *Economic Theory and Socialism* (1955). No student should fail to read this chapter and to ask himself whether he is prepared to meet the charges. For an instructive exchange of opinions occasioned by Dobb's book see A. P. Lerner, "From Vulgar Political Economy to Vulgar Marxism," *JPE,* August, 1939, and "A Reply" by Dobb, August, 1940.

On recent discussions in Marxist circles concerning the Transformation Problem see R. L. Meek, "Some Notes on the Transformation Problem," *EJ,* 1956, reprinted in *EET,* and the literature cited there. J. Robinson supplies a skeptical note on the significance of the problem: "The Labour Theory of Value," *EJ,* 1950, reprinted in *Collected Economic Papers* (1951), Vol. I. Marx's abuse of the concept of averages and ratios in his value theory is emphasized by H. W. B. Joseph, *The Labour Theory of Value of Karl Marx* (1923), chap. 3. The three-sector solution of the transformation problem given in this text is due to J. Winternitz, "Values and Prices: A Solution of the So-Called Transformation Problem," *EJ,* June, 1948. The general n-industry solution is given by F. Seton, "The Transformation Problem," *REStud,* June, 1957, an article which may be said to be the last word on the problem.

Both Sweezy and Robinson agreed in 1942 that Marx's "law" of the declining rate of profit was no law at all. R. Rosdolsky, "Zur neuern Kritik des

Marxschen Gesetzes der fallenden Profitrate," *KYK,* IX, 2, 1956, joins issue with Sweezy and Robinson, skating on some very thin ice in the process. H. D. Dickinson, "The Falling Rate of Profit in Marxian Economics," *REStud,* February, 1957, comes to Marx's defense with the aid of a mathematical reconstruction, but insofar as he abstracts from technical change he merely succeeds in proving the orthodox argument. The falling rate of profit is submitted to a statistical test with negative results by J. M. Gillmann, *The Falling Rate of Profit* (1956).

An old article that still bears careful rereading is L. v. Bortkiewicz, "Value and Price in the Marxian System" (1907), reprinted in *IEP,* No. 2, 1952. The first part of the article deals with the Transformation Problem; the second with the theory of the declining rate of profit. It also contains a scathing review of Marx's tendentious criticism of Ricardo. Ricardo was perhaps the only bourgeois economist whom Marx admired, and yet Marx's comments on Ricardo are not only petty but grossly unfair. Marx regarded himself as Ricardo's intellectual heir and all too many commentators have taken him at his word: see G. S. L. Tucker, "Ricardo and Marx," *Ec,* August, 1961. Marx's treatment of J. S. Mill is even worse and disguises his debt to Mill's *Principles* on several counts: see B. Balassa, "Karl Marx and John Stuart Mill," *WA,* Bd. 83, 2, 1959. Most of Marx's commentary on his predecessors is spoiled by his supposition that everyone was in search of, or was covering up, the puzzle of surplus value.

Marx's view of the process of capital accumulation is analyzed by J. Steindl, *Maturity and Stagnation in American Capitalism* (1952), chap. 14. W. J. Fellner, "Marxian Hypotheses and Observable Trends under Capitalism: A 'Modernised' Interpretation," *EJ,* March, 1957, shows under what conditions it is possible to have both the rate of profit and the rate of real wages falling through time. This theoretical possibility is denied by P. A. Samuelson, "Wages and Interest: Marxian Economic Models," *AER,* December, 1957; "Comment" by F. M. Gottheil and "Reply" by Samuelson, September, 1960. Samuelson's article is primarily an exercise in thinking through a Marx-like model, but it abounds in incisive comments upon Marx's system.

On the Marxian theory of the business cycle see, in addition to Sweezy and Robinson, Dobb, *Political Economy and Capitalism,* chap. 4, which disposes of the allegation that Marx held a simple underconsumptionist theory; H. Smith, "Marx and the Trade Cycle," *REStud,* June, 1937; J. D. Wilson, "Marx and the Trade Cycle," *REStud,* February, 1938; and "A Reply" by Smith, October, 1938. Wilson stresses the fallacy of looking for a monocausal explanation of business cycles in the writings of Marx.

On the relationship between Marx and Keynes see E. F. Ward, "Marx and Keynes," *ER,* April, 1939; S. Alexander, "Mr. Keynes and Mr. Marx," *RESTUD,* February, 1940; L. R. Klein, "Theories of Effective Demand and Employment," *JPE,* 1947, reprinted in *REA,* Vol. II; S. Tsuru, "Keynes versus Marx: the Methodology of Aggregates," *Post-Keynesian Economics* (1954); J. Robinson, "Marx and Keynes," *Economica Critica,* 1948, reprinted in *Collected Economic Papers,* Vol. I, and the delightful "Open Letter from a Keynesian to a Marxist" in *On Re-reading Marx* (1953). Most authors are impressed by the similarities between the two thinkers: two-way disaggregation on the product side of the social accounts; a monetary theory of the rate of interest; the rejection of Say's Law; emphasis on the declining marginal efficiency of capital; and a chronic tendency toward oversaving in a mature economy. But the differences are more profound than the similarities, as Robinson and Tsuru point out. Klein's essay is particularly valuable for its attempt to recast the Marxian system into an econometric model with specific behavioral assumptions.

Much has been written on the validity of Marx's predictions, most of which are worthless because they fail to consider the exact nature of the prognosis. Consider, for example, the prediction of the disappearance of the "middle classes." It turns out that Marx had in mind the "old" middle class of independent shopkeepers, merchants, and farmers, and commented at length on the rise of a "new" white-collar class of executives, salesmen, and office workers. On this question see A. L. Harris, "Pure Capitalism and the Disappearance of the Middle Class," *JPE*, June, 1939. J. Kuczynski's interpretation of Marx's doctrine of absolute impoverishment is to be found in his introduction to *Labour Conditions in Great Britain* (2d ed., 1946). But see T. Sowell, "Marx's 'Increasing Misery' Doctrine," *AER*, March, 1960. H. Gottlieb argues that the whole of Marx's system should be understood as a sociological bargaining theory of wages, and in that sense his predictions do not have the force of economic laws: "Marx's Mehrwert Concept and the Theory of Pure Capitalism," *REStud*, XVIII, 3, No. 47, 1950–51, and "A Reply" by R. L. Meek, XIX, No. 2, 1951–52.

Unfortunately, there is no single critical account of Marx's contributions to economic history, particularly his discussion of "primitive accumulation" in Volume I of *Capital*. It is probably fair to say that the emphasis he gave to certain kinds of historical phenomena in the fifteenth, sixteenth, and seventeenth centuries is highly misleading. The reader may want to compare Marx's treatment with a modern Marxist account: M. Dobb, *Studies in the Development of Capitalism* (1946), chap. 5. The Marx-Hobson-Lenin theory of imperialism is critically analyzed by M. Blaug, "Economic Imperialism Revisited," *Yale Review*, Spring, 1961.

Chapter 8

JEVONS AND THE
MARGINAL REVOLUTION

1. THE MARGINAL REVOLUTION

THE YEAR 1871 saw the publication of Menger's *Grundsätze* and Jevons' *Theory,* followed three years later by Walras's *Éléments.* The striking similarity in approach of these three books, coupled with the fact that each writer developed his ideas in total ignorance of the others' works, strongly suggests the existence of an underlying historical trend that made for common results. It is not at all clear, however, that there is such a historical trend. Menger, Jevons, and Walras each made subjective satisfactions the starting point of the explanation of relative prices. The leading novelty in their works was the replacement of the labor theory by the marginal utility theory of value. The discovery of the concept of marginal utility, however, goes back to the writings of Senior, Lloyd, and Longfield in the 1830's, although only Lloyd made any substantive use of the notion. It was independently rediscovered by Dupuit in 1844, by Gossen in 1854, and by Jennings in 1855, and in this case all three writers employed it to throw light on consumer behavior. And while Jevons, Menger, and Walras published their works almost simultaneously in the 1870's, Jevons had publicly announced his discoveries as early as 1862. If there is any unique historical cause for the rise of marginal utility economics, it is to be found somewhere around the middle of the century rather than in the 1870's.

To speak of a marginal *revolution* is in itself somewhat misleading. Marginal utility theory spread very slowly and did not effectively replace classical economics until the last decade of the century. Indeed, in France and Germany it never won wholehearted acceptance. For almost fifteen years after 1871 no one recognized the similarity of the books written by the three "revolutionaries." Jevons died in 1882 without knowing that Menger had published a work on utility theory in 1871 strikingly similar to his own. Walras, in 1886, seems to have been the first to link the names of the "triumvirate" together, but for some time the Austrian accounts of the history of marginal utility theory did not recognize Walras's own claim as a pioneer. Most of the general histories of economic thought published between the years 1870 and 1890 did not even mention marginal utility, and no complete account of the theory appeared in any history of economic thought until after the turn of the century. Here was a revolution that was not generally admitted to have taken place until more than a generation after its occurrence.

As with all revolutionary movements, marginal utility economics altered in character as it conquered the field. In retrospect, it is evident that, as one commentator put it recently, "what was important in marginal utility was the adjective rather than the noun." In Menger, Jevons, and Walras, marginal utility is the unifying principle of all economic reasoning. By the 1890's it had been reduced to the status of providing a somewhat questionable rationale for the slope of demand curves. The significance of marginal utility theory was that it provided the archetype of the problem of allocating with maximum effect. It was not long before the same approach was extended from the household to the firm, from the theory of consumption to the theory of production. The theory of utility supplied most of the excitement of discovery in the seventies and eighties, but it was the introduction of marginal analysis as such that marked the true dividing line between classical theory and modern economics.

The New Departure. Let us recall the main lines of classical economics. Whether we look at Smith, Ricardo, or John Stuart Mill, the economic problem is seen in essence as a contrast between nonaugmentable land and augmentable labor, with capital subsumed under the latter as stored-up wealth. The function of economic analysis is to reveal the effects of changes in the quantity and quality of the labor force upon the rate of growth of aggregate output. Since the rate of growth of output was held to be a function of the rate of profit on capital, secular trends in factor prices and in distributive shares naturally came to the fore as key elements in the economic process. The accent was on capital accumulation and economic growth in the context of a private enterprise economy. In classical economics, free competition was thought to be desirable because it tended to expand the area of the market by bringing about an improved division of labor: economic welfare was treated, in physical terms, as roughly proportional to the volume of output.

After 1870, however, economists typically posited some given supply of productive factors, determined independently by elements outside the purview of analysis. The essence of the economic problem was to search for the conditions under which given productive services were allocated with optimal results among competing uses, optimal in the sense of maximizing consumers' satisfactions. This ruled out consideration of the effects of increases in the quantity and quality of resources and the dynamic expansion of wants, effects that the classical economists had regarded as the *sine qua non* of rising economic welfare. For the first time, economics truly became the science that studies the relationship between *given* ends and *given* scarce means that have alternative uses. The classical theory of economic development was replaced by the concept of general equilibrium within an essentially static framework.

All this is nicely exhibited in the attitude of the "new economics" to the Malthusian theory of population. With the advent of marginal analysis, the Malthusian theory disappeared from economics. But not because economists ceased to believe in it. Most of the great figures of this period—Jevons, Marshall, Wicksteed, Walras, Wicksell, Clark—regarded the Malthusian theory as valid in the main. But the growth of population was treated as an exogenous variable in the new economics. As Jevons said, the "problem of economics" was: "Given, a certain population, with various needs and powers of production, in possession of certain lands and other sources of material: required, the mode of employing their labor which will maximize the utility of the produce."

The emphasis on allocation with maximum effect is much stronger in the Lausanne and Austrian schools than in the English School dominated by Marshall. Marshall learned his economics from Mill and retained a link with classical thought via the "real cost" theory of value. Moreover, he never entirely abandoned the deep-rooted classical belief that economic welfare depends as much on capital accumulation and population growth as on efficiency in resource allocation. He shied away from the heroic abstractions of general equilibrium, stationary conditions, and perfect competition in favor of partial analysis of particular sectors with special emphasis on the long-run adjustments of industries expanding under loosely competitive conditions. But even Marshall devoted more attention to the action of competition in tightening up the allocation of resources within a given market environment than to the expansion of the market area itself. His long-run theorizing is essentially static, as he himself would have been the first to admit.

The Use of Mathematics. The dominant role of the concept of substitution at the margin in the new economics accounts for the sudden appearance of explicitly mathematical reasoning. Again, it is not utility theory but marginalism that gives mathematics its prominent role in economics after 1870. It is no accident that the Austrians, who were always insistent on the primary role of utility, were wholly innocent of any mathematics. Neither Menger nor Wieser nor Böhm-Bawerk ever employed a genuine algebraic equation in any of their writings. More than that: they were opposed on methodological grounds to mathematics as a tool of economic analysis. In a letter to Walras in 1884, Menger insisted that mathematics was of no use in helping the economist to get at the qualitative "essence" of phenomena like value, rent, and profit. This attitude remained characteristic of the Austrian writers, who went so far as to eschew all emphasis on the mutual determination of dependent economic variables.

With this exception, however, all the great economic theorists of this period had at least an intermediate training in mathematics. Jevons, Marshall, Wicksteed, Wicksell, and Cassel are examples among the so-called literary economists, although among these only Marshall and Wicksell can be said to have been technically competent mathematicians. Economists like Cournot, Walras, Edgeworth, and Pareto were, of course, avowedly mathematical economists. It is a striking fact that among the great economists of the latter half of the nineteenth century only J. B. Clark and Böhm-Bawerk managed to make fundamental contributions to economic theory without use or knowledge of mathematics.

The Maximization Principle. The kind of mathematics that economists employed in this period was confined to calculus. Economic functions were invariably assumed to be differentiable continuous functions. The underlying principle of maximization, however, is equally applicable to discontinuous functions. The general principle is that of ordering a series of attainable positions in terms of the respective associated values of a relevant maximand, the optimum position being one that assigns the greatest possible value to the maximand. Whether the maximand is utility, or profits, or physical product, the analysis remains formally identical. Marginal analysis proper applies only when the maximand function is continuous at the maximand. But discontinuities present only a formal, not a substantive, difficulty in the analysis.

To become somewhat more explicit, the principle at issue is that of equalizing marginal values: in dividing a fixed quantity of anything among a number of competing uses, "efficient" allocation implies that each unit of the dividend is apportioned in such a way that the gain of transferring it to one use will just equal the loss involved in withdrawing it from another. Whether we refer to allocating a fixed income among a number of consumer goods, or a fixed amount of outlays among a number of productive factors, or a given amount of time between work and leisure, the principle always remains the same. Moreover, in each case the allocation problem has a maximum solution if and only if the process of transferring a unit of the dividend to a single use among all the possible uses is subject to diminishing results. In the theory of the household an optimum situation obtains when the consumer has distributed his given income in such a way that the marginal utility of each dollar of purchase is equal; the law of diminishing marginal utility insures that such an optimum exists. In the theory of the firm an optimum result is obtained when the marginal physical product of each dollar's worth of factor purchases is equalized; the law of diminishing marginal productivity plays the same role here as diminishing marginal utility in the theory of demand. Both examples are merely particular applications of the equimarginal principle. The whole of neoclassical economics is nothing more than the spelling-out of this principle in ever wider contexts joined with the demonstration that, under definite conditions, perfect competition does in fact produce equimarginal allocation of expenditures and resources.

It is easy to see that the equimarginal principle refers only to definite quantities of money, resources, or time to be distributed, and has only as much significance as the initial assumption of a fixed dividend. In our own time, we have become acquainted with a kind of economics that does not rest on maximization analysis. In modern macroeconomics we simply posit an aggregate outcome of individual choices in accordance with a definite global rule: Keynes's consumption function, for example, is not built up from individual maximizing behavior. In classical economics, analysis does ultimately hark back to the maximizing actions of individuals, but instead of investigating resource allocation at a moment of time, it emphasizes the time paths of successive equilibria. For better or for worse, however, economic theory in the period 1870–1914 consisted almost wholly of static microeconomics based squarely on the equimarginal rule.

Value and Distribution. Classical economics derived the prices of products from the so-called "natural" rates of reward of the three factors of production. These were in turn explained by special theories: land rentals were determined as a differential surplus over the marginal cost of cultivation, wages of labor were governed by the long-run cost of subsistence, and the rate of profit on capital was treated as a residual element. Only in the case of labor was the problem of distribution solved by a straightforward application of value theory. The value of land and of capital had to be explained by principles quite different from those used to account for the relative prices of products.

In the "new economics," distribution theory was treated as nothing more than an aspect of general value theory. Factors are rewarded because they are scarce relative to consumers' wants for the products that they can produce. The process of production and distribution has significance only insofar as it modifies the possibility of consumers' choice. The demand for factors is a derived demand; given the supply of factors and their technical rates of transformation, the prices of productive services and the prices of consumer goods alike are determined by consumers' wants. Hence, there is no room for a special analysis of the value of each factor of production. That the classical authors provided a special theory of distribution is precisely the criticism leveled against them by the writers of the present period.

The classical economists frequently wrote as if distribution preceded the valuation of products in a causative sense. The early marginalists, and particularly the members of the Austrian School, on the other hand, seemed to argue that the causal order should be reversed, the income of productive factors being the resultant of prices in the product market. In point of fact, of course, both product and factor prices are mutually and simultaneously determined. The real claim of the new economics was that it broke down the departmentalized approach of Ricardian economics. Ricardo, Mill, and Marx treated all commodities as produced under conditions of constant costs and fixed technical coefficients. Ricardo admitted the variability of factor proportions in the chapter on "Machinery," but this concession was never incorporated into the main stream of classical theory. Even so, generality was sacrificed in the case of agricultural goods where marginal costs of production diverged from average costs. Classical economics, therefore, was forced to operate with two theories of value: the price of industrial goods depended solely upon conditions of supply, but the price of agricultural goods varied with the scale of output and hence the pattern of demand. This implied a fatal indeterminacy in classical distribution theory. Since wage goods consist largely of the products of agriculture, real wages depend on the position of the "margin of cultivation" and hence on the length to which investment is carried in agriculture. This is true even if real wages are taken to be constant in the long run.

Thus, long-run wages in the classical system depend on the rate at which capital accumulation proceeds, which in turn depends on the state of demand. But it is at this point that classical theory breaks down. Ricardo and Marx were inclined to treat the supply of capital as being governed by a minimum-of-existence rate of profit on lines analogous to the wages-population mechanism. Above this minimum rate, the supply of capital is stimulated by a rise and checked by a fall in the rate of profit, via its effects on the power to invest. Mill suggests instead that the supply of capital is a function of the rate of profit through the incentive effect, but this leaves the notion of a long-run supply price of capital hanging in the air. Ultimately, classical economics provided no determinate analysis of the conditions governing the supply of capital and never gave the state of demand a position co-ordinate with the conditions of supply. In this sense, the Ricardian theory of distribution not only lacked generality but stopped short of fulfilling its own promise.

Neoclassical theory achieved greater generality and economy of argument by explaining both factor and product prices on the basis of a single principle. The new theory encompassed both reproducible and nonreproducible goods, both constant and varying costs. Ricardo's differential rent theory was generalized to all nontransferable resources, while the postulate that value is determined by production under "the least favorable circumstances" was made the basis for the determination of all prices. Greater generality, however, is rarely an unambiguous achievement. Unless a new theory encompasses all the variables of the old, the order of generality will vary with the question under analysis. Neoclassical economics was in some ways more restrictive than was classical theory: for example, it took the supply of labor as given. Moreover, its boast of greater economy of theoretical means was largely whittled away in subsequent decades. Böhm-Bawerk's contribution to the theory of interest can be boiled down to the proposition that the capital market presents unique problems because of the omnipresence of the time-discount factor. The "peculiarities of labor" are noted and discussed by Marshall. In each case, special elements, missing in most product markets, are adduced to account for the characteristics of capital and labor markets. When the supply of resources is given at the outset of the analysis, these difficulties largely disappear. But, as soon as we leave the realm of short-run analysis and take up classical questions about capital accumulation and population growth, the claim that distribution theory is nothing more than a particular aspect of value theory seems to have only formal significance. An unkind critic might say that neoclassical economics indeed achieved greater generality, but only by asking easier questions.

The Genesis of Marginal Utility Theory. Having delineated the leading features of the new economics, we are now in a position to speculate briefly on the origins of the marginal revolution. The explanations that have been advanced fall roughly into four classes: (1) an autonomous intellectual development within the discipline of economics, (2) the product of philosophical currents, (3) the product of definite institutional changes in the economy, and (4) a counterblast to socialism, particularly in its Marxist variety.

Let us examine these in turn. The first is the most plausible single explanation and is indeed the most widely held of the four given above. It points to the bankruptcy and disintegration of classical economics in the fifties and sixties, to the virtual abandonment of the labor theory of value in Mill's *Principles,* and, in particular, to Mill's recantation of the wages fund doctrine in the late sixties. In the process of attacking the wages fund doctrine, Thornton and Longe drew attention to the possibility of perverse demand and supply functions in the labor market; inspired by this controversy Fleeming Jenkin drew demand and supply curves in a paper published in 1870—Cournot had done so as early as 1838, but he was almost unknown in England. Jevons had been working on his book since 1860 and had already published a "Notice of a General Mathematical Theory of Political Economy," which outlined the marginal utility theory of value. The fifties had seen a revival of interest in the writings of Bentham: following in Bentham's footsteps, Richard Jennings stated the principle of diminishing marginal utility in 1855 in the form of a "law of the variation of sensations," and McLeod foreshadowed Jevons' concept of discommodity and disutility in his discussion of zero and negative value (1858). These were the writers from which, as Jevons said, "my system was, more or less consciously, developed."

So far as England is concerned, then, we can detect something like a pure filiation of ideas under the impulse of a growing sense of dissatisfaction with older views. The fact that Jevons' book was poorly received lends support to this interpretation. Marginal utility doctrine made its way slowly against persistent opposition; the new and the old continued to exist side by side. Marshall's *Economics of Industry* (1879) shows the influence of the "revolution," and Edgeworth's *Mathematical Psychics* (1881) is a speculative excursion into the higher realms of the new theory. But Cairnes's *Leading Principles* (1874) and Sidgwick's *Principles* (1883) were entirely cast in the old mold. The dominant view among English economists in the seventies and eighties was that of the Historical School. English historicism was an indigenous growth, whose roots go back to Carlyle's and Ruskin's protests against the narrow scope of classical political economy. It represented a reaction not only to classical economics but to all abstract economic theory of any variety. This English *Methodenstreit* was put to rest by J. N. Keynes's *Scope and Method of Political Economy* (1890) and by Marshall's conciliatory attitude in the *Principles* (1890), by which time the new movement had successfully vanquished all vestiges of classical economics.

The difficulty with the "absolutist" explanation is that of applying it to the Continent. Neither Menger nor Walras was stimulated, as was Jevons, by writers who hinted at the idea of *marginal* utility; nor were they reacting to a well-entrenched school of ideas such as dominated the British universities in the fifties and sixties. Walras was building on the ideas of his father, Auguste Walras, in the light of the inspiration he received from studying Cournot and possibly Dupuit. Menger credited a long list of eighteenth- and nineteenth-century writers with the utility theory of value, but none of the authors he mentioned had connected the idea of diminishing marginal utility with the problem of price determination. Gossen's remarkable book, published in 1854, which clearly formulated the law of diminishing marginal utility and applied it to individual acts of consumption, escaped his attention. Nevertheless, despite the diversity of background and tradition, Menger and Walras hit upon the idea of marginal utility almost at the same time. It is difficult to believe that this was entirely due to adventitious intellectual forces.

This leads one to look for some general movement in philosophy or in social science that might have promoted an emphasis on introspection as an instrument for forming hypotheses about economic behavior. Some authors have been struck by the renaissance of Kantian philosophy somewhere around the middle of the century, beginning in Germany and spreading out over the Continent. "Back to introspection and sense-impression" was the watchword of this philosophical trend. There is no evidence, however, that Menger himself was motivated by any such philosophical leanings, and in the case of Walras there is no indication whatever of any interest in contemporary philosophical debates. Once again, it is the British scene that alone lends support to the argument: hedonism enjoyed considerable vogue in England in the 1850's and must be put down as one of the germinal influences on Jevons' thinking.

A different argument along the same lines accounts for the delayed acceptance of utility theory in England on the grounds that the subjective value theory is the product of a Catholic culture, whereas the labor theory of value naturally emanates from a Calvinist outlook on the world. Calvinism places work and labor at the center of theology, while Catholic philosophy is supposed to exalt modern pleasure-seeking instead of work and money-making. Since Catholicism dominated the Continent, we have here an explanation of the prevalence of utility theory in French and Italian economics and the long delay in its acceptance in Great Britain. It is not obvious, however, how this helps to explain the rise of *marginal* utility theory on the Continent and in England. Moreover, many of the nineteenth-century forerunners of the new theory of value do not fit the pattern: Lloyd, Longfield, and Senior were Protestants, and Gossen was notoriously anti-Catholic.

This leaves the possibility of accounting for the rise of marginal utility theory by changes in the economic environment. A bold attempt along these lines was made by the most provocative of all Bolshevik thinkers, Nikolai Bukharin. In a book entitled *Economic Theory of the Leisure Class* (1927), Bukharin explained the marginal revolution in "relativist" terms on the basis of two very questionable assumptions: (1) "the psychology of the consumer is characteristic of the *rentier*," and (2) marginal utility theory is "the ideology of the bourgeoisie who has already been eliminated from the process of production." Any amateur historian can see the flaw in this argument. Nevertheless, it has a certain force: the consumer and not the capitalist is the dominant figure in neoclassical economics; the employer of labor is no longer identified with the investor of capital; the manager, the entrepreneur, and the rentier have become separate individuals, and personal saving, not business saving, is regarded as the typical source of investment funds. All this involves a conception of economic institutions different from that found in the writings of Smith and Ricardo. Economic growth is now taken for granted, and problems of secular stagnation or technological unemployment disappear in economic literature. It is not farfetched to see a connection between changes in the economic structure of society around the middle of the century and the theoretical innovations of the subjective value trio. The trouble here is of making the connection concretely in terms of personal intellectual awareness of institutional changes—something that no student has so far attempted—and at the same time of taking account of differences in the economic structure of Austria, France, and England.

It has been argued that there was in fact only one institutional problem that colored the work of all the three pioneers of marginal analysis. This was the problem of the pricing policies of public utilities where large fixed costs gave prominence to divergences between average and marginal costs. Railway economics was indeed a subject of great interest at this time in England as well as in France and Germany. Other less obvious changes in the historical environment, however, may have been more significant in producing new ways of thinking. In the absence of a definitive treatment of the question, mere speculation will carry us no further.

Finally, there is the argument that marginal utility theory was nothing but the bourgeois answer to Marxism. Here, at any rate, it is possible to be quite definite. The first volume of *Capital* appeared in 1867; it was not translated into English until 1887. Jevons' "Notice" was written in 1862 and published in 1863; it shows him in full possession of the theory of marginal utility and even of the marginal productivity theory of capital. Marshall began his work in 1867, and the outline of his system is already discernible in his review of Jevons' book in 1872. All the evidence suggests that neither Jevons, nor Marshall, nor Menger, nor Walras had ever heard of Marx in their formative years. Later in the 1880's, when Marxism spread through the European labor movement, Böhm-Bawerk, Wicksteed, Pareto, and Wieser employed the new theory to attack Marxian economics. But there is nothing unusual about the attempt to fortify a line of thought by turning it against contemporary rivals. Böhm-Bawerk may be said to have set out more or less deliberately in his work on interest theory to provide an alternative solution to the Marxist concept of exploitation. But this concerns the development of marginal economics, not its genesis. The first generation of economists in the new tradition had no knowledge of socialist thought, much less of Marxism.

Marginal utility theory was ideologically neutral in that it emerged without any direct reference to practical questions and was compatible with any position on social and political issues. But Marxists do not claim that the subjective value trio was actuated by a sinister desire to come to the defense of capitalism, but rather that marginal utility theory naturally supports a faith in things as they are, being readily employable to defend the status quo. Actually, classical economics was a far better instrument for defending private property. It would be difficult to think of an argument more agreeable to business interests than the classical wages fund doctrine. The nomenclature of utility and disutility, on the other hand, leads one immediately to ask whether a free enterprise system represents such a use of resources in satisfying wants as to insure society the greatest surplus of utility over disutility. It is true that both Jevons and Walras thought they had demonstrated that perfect competition does maximize satisfactions over all the members of society. But this piece of apologetics was roundly condemned by the second generation of economists in the utility tradition. Indeed, one of the uncomfortable aspects of utility theory seemed to be the implication that only egalitarianism maximizes satisfactions. Most writers after 1870 were extremely critical of existing inequalities in income distribution and did not hesitate to use utility theory to fortify their critical outlook.

In general, we find great differences in the political attitudes of economists within the main stream of neoclassical economics. The Marshallian tradition culminated in Pigou's *Wealth and Welfare* (1912), which is virtually a blueprint for the welfare state. The Fabians adopted the utility theory in *Fabian Essays* (1889) to display the systematic inequities of the market mechanism. The reformist element was equally strong in the Lausanne School: Walras was a land reformer and Pareto grew increasingly sympathetic to the idea of a corporate state. It was the Austrian School that was markedly conservative and given over to attacks on socialism and the espousal of laissez faire. The aversion to radical politics was a characteristic note of economists trained in Vienna seminars, just as interventionism and a bored attitude to Marxism was characteristic of the Cambridge economist. If the argument is that politics entered into the development of modern economics, one can only concur. But the idea that modern economics has no other *raison d'être* than to provide an apologetic for capitalism is too farfetched to be entertained.

2. JEVONS

As Whitehead once remarked: "Everything of importance has been said before by somebody who did not discover it." This aphorism aptly describes Jevons' indebtedness to a host of forerunners. Oddly enough, however, Jevons never drew a demand curve and did not develop a theory of the firm—this despite the fact that Jenkin's paper on trade unions, published in 1870, made use of the graphic device of demand and supply curves. Moreover, Jevons declared that he owed the idea of investigating economics mathematically to Lardner's *Railway Economy* (1850). This book contained the first exposition in England of what approximates to the modern theory of the firm. Lardner drew total cost and total revenue functions and showed that profits are maximized at a level of output at which tangents to the two functions are parallel, that is, the output level at which marginal cost and marginal revenue are equal. Jevons apparently failed to see the significance of this argument, for he never referred to it.

It is not merely that Jevons overlooked some of Lardner's ideas but that he showed no awareness of the need for a theory of the firm. Cost was a bygone by the time an article came on the market, and its relationship to revenue seemed insignificant. Jevons concentrated instead on the willingness of the holder to sell out of a given stock; costs are indeed irrelevant when sales are made out of a given stock, the typical case Jevons had in mind. Hence, it never occurred to him to build up a supply curve out of cost curves. Jevons was not alone in this. Menger also failed to apply marginalism to production and, like Jevons, did not draw demand and supply curves despite the fact that the fourth edition of Rau's *Grundsätze* (1844) and Mangoldt's *Grundrisse* (1863) both used demand and supply curves to demonstrate the formation of price.

The Theory of Exchange. Jevons approaches value theory by way of two individuals engaging in exchange. Exchange cannot take place unless the relative marginal significance of the commodity received exceeds that of the commodity given up in exchange for each party in the exchange. This marginal significance is not a constant magnitude but changes with different persons and with different circumstances. What the classical writers called value in use or total utility is an abstraction. All we know is the relative significance of an increment of one commodity to a decrement of another. In modern parlance, we can obtain the *total* utility of a commodity for an individual only by integrating the differential coefficient, the *marginal* utility of the stock of the commodity.

At this point Jevons formulated the Law of Diminishing Marginal Utility. He appealed to a physiological law, citing Jennings as his authority, that the strength of the response to a stimulus diminishes with each repetition of that stimulus within some specified time period. With the publication of Fechner's *Elemente der Psychophysik* (1860), this kind of statement came to be known as the Weber-Fechner Law. Jevons was the only economist in this period to base the law of diminishing marginal utility on a physiological principle. Edgeworth, Pareto, and Wicksell noticed the Weber-Fechner Law but made no real use of it. The typical practice was to establish the law on purely intuitive grounds.

With the aid of the law of diminishing marginal utility Jevons proceeded to the "equation of exchange." The ratios of increments of commodities consumed must, in equilibrium, be equal to the ratios of the intensities of last wants satisfied, or, as Jevons put it, to the final degrees of utility. And the ratios at which the two goods exchange must be inversely proportional to the final degrees of utility. By introducing a *numéraire,* whose price is unity, this equilibrium equation turns into the familiar modern textbook condition of the proportionality of marginal utilities to relative prices.

As Jevons expressed it: let *a* and *b* represent the quantities of the two goods held initially by the two parties, let *x* and *y* be the actual quantities exchanged and ϕ and ψ the final degrees of utility to the respective parties. Then

$$\frac{\phi_1(a-x)}{\psi_1(y)} = \frac{y}{x} = \frac{\phi_2(x)}{\psi_2(b-y)}.$$

For the first individual, for example, the marginal utility of $(a-x)$ goods left over after exchange—or the marginal utility of x goods given up—to the marginal utility of y goods acquired in exchange is inversely proportional to the ratios at which the goods have been exchanged. The higher the importance ascribed to a good, the less of that good anyone is willing to offer in exchange for something else; marginal utility is inversely related to the quantity of goods possessed and therefore to the goods given up in exchange. To convert Jevons' expression to the modern consumer's allocation formula, we look at the first party and observe that an equilibrium allocation of expenditures implies that

$$\frac{MU_x}{MU_y} = \frac{y}{x} = \frac{p_x}{p_y} \quad \text{or} \quad \frac{MU_x}{p_x} = \frac{MU_y}{p_y} = \frac{y}{x}$$

when the two prices are expressed in terms of a *numéraire.*[1]

---

[1] A terminological note: Jevons' final degree of utility was written du/dx; it is the same thing as Menger's "lowest importance of satisfactions" or Walras's *rareté,* "the intensity of the last want satisfied by any given quantity consumed of a commodity." It indicates the rate of increase of total utility per unit of the commodity acquired. The Austrians later spoke of *Grenznutzen,* the modern equivalent of marginal utility. But marginal utility is not the derivative of utility with respect to quantity but the differential increment of utility. As Marshall points out in the first mathematical note to his *Principles,* marginal utility is not du/dx, but $(du/dx)\delta x$ where $u = f(x)$ is the total utility function of commodity x; it can be represented by a "thick straight line," of which the breadth measures the unit affording marginal satisfaction. Jevons' final degree of utility is our marginal utility divided by the size of the marginal increment. Present-day textbooks still sometimes speak of marginal utility as the utility of the marginal unit. This is likely to be misunderstood: the marginal utility of the last unit is the utility of every unit, because any unit can be last; thus we can obtain total utility by multiplying marginal utility by the number of

Isolated and Competitive Exchange. Jevons had seized upon the case of isolated exchange in the belief that it permitted a simple demonstration of the pure logic of price determination, which might then be carried over to the more complicated case of competitive exchange. But, in point of fact, isolated exchange has properties not found in competitive exchange. Exactly ten years after the publication of Jevons' book, Edgeworth showed that isolated exchange, or what he called "bilateral monopoly," does not yield a unique and determinate equilibrium price. His demonstration of the indeterminacy of bilateral monopoly in *Mathematical Psychics,* apart from its intrinsic interest, has an important place in our story, for it marks the introduction of in-

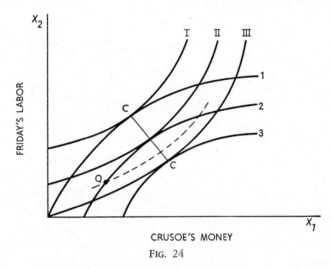

CRUSOE'S MONEY

FIG. 24

difference curves into economics. Edgeworth defined an indifference curve as denoting a combination of two goods, x_1 and x_2, such that they yield equal utility. Instead of the now conventional box diagram introduced by Fisher, in which the different quantities of both goods that each individual holds appear on all axes, Edgeworth lets the abscissa represent the money offered by Crusoe for Friday's labor—the quantity of x_1 obtained by the individual—and the ordinate the labor offered by Friday—the quantity of x_2 given up (see Fig. 24). Since the individual

units consumed. This creates what has come to be known as "Wieser's Paradox": it implies that total utility may fall as more units of a good are consumed, despite the fact that marginal utility is still positive. Marginal utility is the utility of the last unit minus the change in utility of the preceding unit, and so on for every unit, when the last unit is added. Thus, marginal utility $= (du/dx)\,\delta x$ and total utility $=$

$$\int_o^x \frac{du}{dx}\,\delta x\,.$$

will insist upon additional x_1 to offset the loss of any amount of x_2, the slope of the indifference curves will be positive. Since $dx_1 MU_1$ will be the gain of utility from an increment dx_1 and $dx_2 MU_2$ will be the loss of utility from a decrement dx_2, the slope of the indifference curves with respect to x_1 axis will be

$$\frac{dx_2}{dx_1} = \frac{MU_1}{MU_2},$$

as given by the condition that $dx_1 MU_1 = dx_2 MU_2$ for movements along an indifference curve. Although Edgeworth drew only one curve for each trader, a family of indifference curves fills the plane.

The "curves of indifference" 1, 2, 3 are those of Friday possessing x_2 but no x_1; curves I, II, III are those of Crusoe possessing x_1 but no x_2. Edgeworth assumed without proof that these curves are concave, respectively, to the x_1 and x_2 axes. The loci of tangency points of the two sets of indifference curves form what Edgeworth called "the contract curve" *CC*. The final contract between the two traders must take place on *CC* because any other point is such that one party may improve his situation without harming the other by moving back to the contract curve. Thus from point *Q,* Crusoe can move to a higher indifference curve II while Friday remains on the same indifference curve 2. Any point on the *CC* curve is a possible equilibrium, and the precise position depends on bargaining and strategy. This problem of indeterminacy does not arise under competitive exchange because all traders then face the same given prices for all goods.

Having analyzed two-party, two-commodity barter trade, Jevons tried to generalize the equation of exchange by introducing the concept of "trading bodies," letting ϕ and ψ stand for the collective marginal utilities of buyers and sellers. This is, of course, completely unsatisfactory, as Edgeworth soon pointed out. First of all, we are not told how the utility functions are aggregated. Second, the marginal utility of a product for a trading body is the average of the individual marginal utilities of its members; exchange cannot be considered a simple function of the size of the initial supply of goods as with isolated exchange. The average marginal utility depends also on the distribution of this supply before and after the exchange. Be that as it may, from the rule that both parties maximize satisfaction in isolated exchange when each person "procures such quantities of commodities that the final degree of utility of any pair of commodities are inversely as the ratios of exchange of the commodities," Jevons quickly concluded that "so far as is consistent with the inequality of wealth in every community, all commodities are distributed by exchange so as to produce the maximum of benefit." The operative clause here is "so far as is consistent with the inequality of wealth in every community." But even if we take the distribution of income as given, it is not possible to assume from an analysis of isolated exchange that competitive exchange maximizes satisfactions all round. Jevons forgot that in equilibrium it is not the marginal utility of each good by itself that must be the same for both parties to the exchange but the ratio of the marginal utilities of the two goods. The former condition would include the latter, but the latter does not include the former. Since utility is measurable only in terms of comparisons of two or more goods, and since Jevons denied the possibility of making interpersonal comparisons of utility, the conclusion that "a perfect freedom of exchange must be to the advantage of all" has no clearly assignable meaning.

The Catena. Jevons' "equation of exchange" assumes a given initial stock of commodities in the possession of the parties engaged in trade. Only then are unspecified utility functions adequate by themselves to determine ratios of exchange or relative prices. When output is known, we might paraphrase, marginal utility determines value. What determines output? Jevons' answer is given in the well-known catena:

> Cost of production determines supply;
> Supply determines final degree of utility;
> Final degree of utility determines value.

This chain of causation is not only naïve but conflicts with the claim that value is determined by utility. The first two steps are merely suggestions, since Jevons supplied no theory of production. His only explanation of the connection between costs of production and utility is that the marginal utility of the product obtained in equilibrium must equal the marginal disutility of producing it. This hardly depicts equilibrium for the entrepreneur because it depicts "feelings" as one of the co-ordinates. Even the last step in the argument is not quite right. Those engaged in exchange compare final degrees of utility of both goods traded, and from these comparisons every individual arrives at a set of demand prices. It is these scales of demand that determine prices. But Jevons expressed utility schedules in pecuniary terms without explicitly introducing demand curves and reasoned directly from the equivalence of marginal utilities to the equivalence of price offers. When money is one of the two goods being traded, it is possible to construct a demand curve for the commodity in question by assuming that the marginal utility of money remains constant. Jevons realized that this assumption is legitimate only when additional expenditures on the commodity do not "appreciably affect the possessions of the purchaser." But he made no effort to show how market demand curves are built up on the basis of individual demand curves constructed on such *ceteris paribus* assumptions.

   Disutility of Labor.   Jevons' theory of labor supply is his most important contribution to the main stream of neoclassical economics. If human effort has a positive value on account of its pecuniary reward and a negative value on account of the pain accompanying it, he argued, labor will be supplied as long as the individual contemplates a preponderance of satisfaction over dissatisfaction. On the assumption that the disutility of labor first decreases and then increases with the duration of effort, while the marginal utility of the product falls monotonically, Jevons illustrated the argument graphically (see Fig. 25). The upper curve expresses the decreasing final utility of the

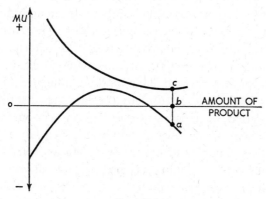

FIG. 25

product on the supposition that the product increment is due solely to additional labor. The lower curve shows the disutility of labor per units of product. When $ab = bc$, the utility of the product equals the disutility of labor; hence, ob units of labor will be supplied in equilibrium.

   Jevons' statement of the theory requires that units of painful effort remain of the same efficiency throughout the working day. Moreover, it assumes a nonexisting symmetry between the factors governing the demand for labor and the supply of labor. The argument could be restated, however, to overcome these objections. The more serious criticism is that Jevons' theory does not seem to be in accord with typical methods of hiring labor in a modern economy. The idea that workers can balance efforts against rewards is realistic enough for piecework, where the worker faces given rates of pay and adjusts his supply of effort so as to maximize income and minimize subjective sacrifice. But, under modern factory conditions, labor services are generally sold in lump amounts; the laborer may have to work far in excess of the point at which the marginal utility of income equals the marginal disutility of effort. The indivisibility of labor may be lessened by absenteeism and lateness, but this may not be enough to equate irksomeness to the rate of reward. Furthermore, the disutility of work is a function not only of duration and intensity but also of environment and the quality of work to be done. Almost all of these are in some degree beyond the control of workers. Jevons' notion of workers freely determining the hours they will work simply does not fit the facts of the labor market.

Despite these objections, Marshall and Edgeworth accepted Jevons' analysis of the short-run supply curve of labor. They insisted that the possibility of varying the intensity of work, the existence of piece-rate wages, the flexibility of overtime hours, and the possibility of choosing different occupations are important enough to endow the Jevonian conception with general applicability. The Austrian writers, insisting that the utility of the product is the sole determinant of value, refused to admit that the individual workman can effectively vary the daily amounts of his physical labor and so influence product prices. Böhm-Bawerk went so far as to deny the fact that disutility can influence the allocation of labor services between various uses, arguing that skilled labor is better rewarded than unskilled labor although it is no more irksome. But this comes down to the assertion that competition fails to equalize the money incomes of alternative occupations; it should have been clear from the *Wealth of Nations* that even if the disutility of labor does not directly affect the quantity of effort supplied, its influence on the choice of occupations does affect wage rates and therefore relative prices. The upshot of this debate was that the English School at least attempted to discuss the supply curve of labor, whereas the Austrians closed the door on the subject.

Negatively or Positively Sloped Labor Supply Curves. All through this period economists could not make up their minds whether the short-run supply curve of labor is positively or negatively inclined. In *Risk, Uncertainty, and Profit* (1921), Frank Knight contended that it is always negatively inclined. At the margin of indifference, he said, the rational worker will equate the marginal disutility of labor and the marginal utility of income. If wages are raised, the marginal utility of income will be reduced. Thus, the added disutility of the last unit of labor time will now exceed the added utility of the last unit of money wage. Hence, the worker will want to shorten his working day when wages rise.

Knight's argument is that a rise in wage rates lowers the worker's schedule of the marginal utility of money, which is therefore cut by the curve of marginal disutility at a point indicating fewer hours. The negative supply curve of labor is then deduced by correlating hours and wage rates. In a now classic article, Lionel Robbins showed that the labor supply curve may be backward bending, positively sloped over a range, then becoming negatively sloped. It all depends on the elasticity of the supply of effort, or, as he put it, the elasticity of demand for income in terms of effort. Probably, for the mass of workers, this elasticity is greater than unity, meaning that a unit of extra effort will be ex-

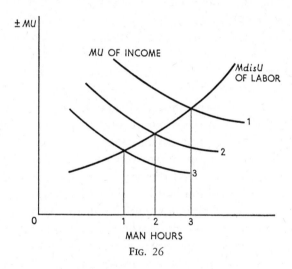

FIG. 26

pended only if income rises thereby more than proportionately. In that case, the supply curve of labor will be positively sloped. If the elasticity coefficient is less than unity, however, the supply curve will be negatively sloped.

Since the advent of the indifference-curve technique, the matter can be put even more simply: it all depends on the relative weight of the substitution effects versus the income effect of a rise in wage rates. If labor is specific to an occupation and perfectly immobile, the supply curve of labor may be negatively sloped. Having no alternatives, the worker is likely to relax his efforts when returns to labor increase. There being no substitution effect, the income effect is supreme—Knight's case. But whenever it is possible to switch employment or freely to substitute work and leisure, the supply curve *may* be positively sloped. Needless to say, all this concerns the supply curve of individual workers. Even if all the individual supply curves are negatively inclined, the aggregate short-run supply of labor may vary positively with the wage rate owing to variations in the school-leaving age and in the female-participation rate in the labor force.

Capital Theory. Little need be said about Jevons' other contributions. His essay on "A Serious Fall in the Value of Gold" would have given him a place in the history of economic thought even if he had written nothing else: it probed deeply into the problems of index numbers and for the first time constructed a weighted price index for a period as long as a half-century. Among his other pioneering inductive studies was that of the connection between cycles in sunspots and business activity. The idea that there are rhythms of temperature caused by solar activity that affect crop yields and, in this fashion, economic activity in general, is by no means implausible. But Jevons' statistical case was singularly unconvincing, and he failed to show theoretically how this or any other exogenous disturbance is capable of generating endogenous fluctuations.

Finally, there is Jevons' theory of capital, which contains all the ingredients of Böhm-Bawerk's theory except the stress on time preference. Jevons treated the productivity of capital as a function of time alone; investment is a quantity of two dimensions, the amount of investment and the period for which the amount is invested. Jevons in effect laid down the proposition that is at the core of the Austrian theory of capital: an increase of capital is tantamount to a lengthening of the period of investment. As Jevons showed, the rate of interest depends on the ratio of the product increment to the increment of capital. Let $F(t)$ be the production function, giving the product of a given amount of labor as a monotonically increasing function of t. For $t + \Delta t$, the total product $= F(t + \Delta t)$, and the marginal product $= F(t + \Delta t) - F(t)$. When we extend the time of production by Δt, Jevons argued, we allow the product $F(t)$ which we could have received at end of time t to remain invested for the extra period Δt. Hence, the increase of capital in this case $= \Delta t \cdot F(t)$. Dividing the increment output by the amount of additional investment, we have

$$\frac{F(t + \Delta t) - F(t)}{\Delta t} \cdot \frac{1}{F(t)}.$$

In the continuous case, the limit of this ratio gives the instantaneous rate of interest

$$r = \frac{dF(t)}{dt} \cdot \frac{1}{F(t)} = \frac{F'(t)}{F(t)} \, .$$

This is clearly a marginal productivity theory of capital, though of an oversimplified kind. Jevons never applied this kind of argument to wages and rents. He seems to have been aware of the general application of marginal productivity analysis to all the factors of production, but he never worked it out. There is reason to think, however, that if he had not died prematurely in 1882 at the age of 46 he would have joined Wicksteed and Marshall in England, John Bates Clark in America, Wicksell in Sweden, and Walras in Lausanne, in formulating the general marginal productivity theory of distribution.

3. OTHER FORERUNNERS

Marshall's early works are all of a later date than the treatises of the subjective value trio, but we have Marshall's own authority for the assertion that his theory of value and distribution was "practically completed in the years 1867 to 1870." It was not to Jevons, but to Cournot and von Thünen, that Marshall was indebted for his leading ideas. "Under the guidance of Cournot, and in a less degree of von Thünen, I was led to attach great importance to the fact that . . . the demand for a thing is a continuous function, of which the 'marginal' increment is, in stable equilibrium, balanced against the corresponding increment of its cost."

Cournot on Profit Maximization. Cournot, in a book that for sheer originality and boldness of conception has no equal in the history of economic theory, was the first writer to define and to draw a demand function. He took no interest in utility theory but assumed as a matter of course that the demand curve was negatively inclined. He treated monopoly as the pure case and defined a demand function, $D = F(p)$, a total revenue function, $R = pF(p)$, and a marginal revenue function, $M = F(p) + pF'(p)$, objectively given to the monopolist. The given revenue functions are then confronted with total and marginal cost functions, and it is shown that instantaneous gains will be maximized if the monopolist produces an output at which marginal cost equals marginal revenue. To prove the existence and uniqueness of this maximum, Cournot employed the familiar tests of calculus: the first derivative of the total profit function must vanish, and the second derivative must be negative. All this in 1838!

In Book V, chapter 13, of his *Principles,* Marshall adopted Cournot's analysis of profit maximization but expressed the equilibrium conditions in terms of the monopolist's total costs and revenue rather than in terms of the marginal conditions. And so the concept of marginal revenue had to be rediscovered in the 1920's, when the case of imperfect competition drew theorists' attention to the possibility of a downward-sloping demand curve confronting the individual firm.

Duopoly Theory. Cournot not only founded the theory of pure monopoly but also the theory of duopoly. His theory of duopoly is based on the competitive assumption that buyers name prices and that sellers merely adjust their output to given prices. Each duopolist estimates the demand function for the product and then sets the quantity sold, on the assumption that his rival's output remains fixed. Although each

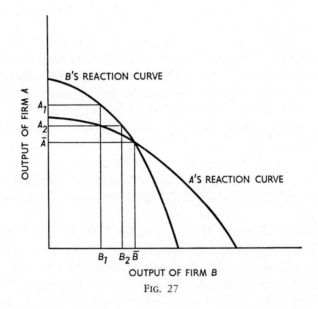

FIG. 27

duopolist adjusts his output simultaneously to the output of the other, each assuming at every point that the rival's output is constant, a determinate solution nevertheless emerges. Cournot demonstrated this result graphically by means of reaction curves (Fig. 27). Each reaction curve shows the optimum output of one duopolist as a function of the output of its rival. Assume that firm A is producing A_1; then firm B will produce B_1, whereupon A will produce A_2, and B will produce B_2, and so forth. Outputs tend toward the equilibrium values $\bar{A}$ and $\bar{B}$.

In the 1880's the French mathematician Bertrand criticized Cournot's solution and suggested instead that sellers set prices and that each seller determines his price on the assumption that his rival's price, rather than his output, remains constant. Edgeworth, in the "Theory of Monopoly" (1897), carried the argument one step further and introduced uncertainty of mutual reactions, concluding that this rendered the solution indeterminate. In the 1920's, the reaction patterns were made to include sales, costs, quality of product, and service competition. Cournot's symmetry assumption about the intentions and policies of the two firms, grounded on the arbitrary notion that firms never test each other's reactions, was discarded once and for all. As soon as it is admitted that the two parties will indeed try to test each other's reactions, we have a whole catalogue of cases, depending upon what we assume about their behavior. They may go to the Cournot point, the case of nonco-operative equilibrium in which each party maximizes subject to some notion about the other party's reactions; they may go to the "minimax point" and maximize subject to the assumption that the rival will adopt the most damaging policy; or they may go to the Fellner point of co-operative equilibrium and maximize joint profits. Each of these assumptions entails different price-quantity outcomes, and on a priori grounds there is no reason for believing that one outcome is more likely than another.

Von Thünen's Marginal Productivity Theory. Remarkable as is Cournot's work, no one has more claim to be considered the founder of marginal analysis than von Thünen. Throughout his writings he relentlessly applied the principle that all forms of expenditure should be carried to the point at which the product of the last unit equals its cost: the total product is maximized only when resources are allocated equimarginally. A simplified version of his doctrine of the "natural wage" illustrates his procedure and affords us at the same time an example, the first of its kind, of the use of differential calculus to solve a maximization problem.

Consider an isolated state where all land is of equal fertility. At its outer edge land rent is zero, so the entire product of estates located in this outer ring of cultivation is divided between workers and owners of capital. Workers cultivating existing estates are free to leave their present employments to take up new land; the wages of such workers are in excess of their subsistence needs; and wages are the only expense of production. Since any worker possessing sufficient capital is free to move from the hired-worker status to the capital-producing status, wages on the old estates must be equal to what the worker and his capital can earn by cultivating new land. Let p represent the annual product that one family working for one year can obtain when assisted by capital; w, the annual wages bill; total profits, $y = p - w$; and the rate of profit or interest, $z = (p - w)/w$. All variables are measured in terms of wheat. The necessary wage at the boundary of the isolated state is then $w + zw = p$. Workers spend a per year, investing the rest, $y = w - a$, at the current rate of profit. Thünen assumes that it is to the interest of the capital-producing workers who invest their surplus earnings and the hired workers who loan out their surplus earning that the value of w be such as to maximize, not their total annual incomes, as might be expected, but the revenue zy that each can earn by investing one year's surplus.

Investing $y = w - a$, workers will earn $(p - w/w)(w - a)$ $=: p - w - (ap/w) + a$. Treating p and a as constants, we maximize this expression with respect to w by setting the first derivative equal to zero.

$$d\frac{\left(p - w - \dfrac{ap}{w} + a\right)}{dw} = -1 + \frac{ap}{w^2} = 0 \; ;$$

$$1 = \frac{ap}{w^2} \quad \text{or} \quad w = \sqrt{ap} \; .$$

Similarly, if $z = (p - w)/w = p - (a + y)/(a + y)$, then the worker's yearly surplus $y = (p/[1 + z]) - a$, and the revenue that the worker receives by investing his year's surplus $yz = (pz/[1 + z]) - az$. To find the rate of profit at which this revenue reaches a maximum, Thünen sets the first derivative of the expression for yz equal to zero, and solves for z.

$$\frac{d(yz)}{dz} = \frac{(1 + z)p - pz}{(1 + z)^2} - a = 0 \; ;$$

$$\frac{p}{(1 + z)^2} = a \; ;$$

$$1 + z = \sqrt{p/a} \; ;$$

$$z = \frac{\sqrt{ap} - a}{a} \; .$$

Substituting this value for z into the equation for wages $w = (a + y) = p/(1 + z) = ap/\sqrt{ap} = \sqrt{ap}$, which agrees with the maximizing value for wages obtained above.

The wage that would maximize the worker's income from investment is $\sqrt{ap}$, the geometric mean between the subsistence needs and the average annual product of a working family. This "natural wage" is established not by the market but by the voluntary self-determination of workers who are trying to maximize the surplus y available for capital accumulation.

This argument cannot be taken seriously. It is a model of *a*capitalistic production, which treats subsistence spending as if it were subject to precise measurement. Since a has no definite meaning, neither has $\sqrt{ap}$. Moreover, the marginal productivity of labor, which von Thünen defined elsewhere correctly as the ratio between an infinitesimal increase of product and an infinitesimal increment of labor giving rise to it, does not even enter in to his basic equation of the "natural wage." Furthermore, there is no reason to believe that capital-producing workers would want to maximize the algebraic expression zy, the revenue obtained by investing the surplus of one year's wages, rather than to maximize the total income from labor and the capital they already possess. Nevertheless, von Thünen's rudimentary development of the concept of marginal productivity, applied to wages as well as to the revenue of capital; his use of differential calculus and marginal reasoning to provide equilibrium solutions of economic variables; and his general statement of the principle of variable proportions, make him the first truly modern economist.

Dupuit and Gossen. Two other pioneers of marginal utility theory deserve mention here. In 1844 Dupuit, a well-known French engineer, stumbled upon the distinction between total and marginal utility in an effort to find a measure of the social benefit of such colleclective goods as roads, canals, and bridges. He realized that the benefit was greater than that shown by the price actually paid for the service inasmuch as most people would be willing to pay more for the service than they actually did pay. Tacitly identifying utility and demand curves, he constructed a marginal utility curve for a collective good by supposing that the state charges the maximum toll for each additional unit of the service, lowering the toll by small steps as it offers additional units. In this way total receipts from the service are equal to the whole area under the demand curve; in utility terms, the total benefit from the existence of the facility is measured by the area under the marginal utility curve. The "relative utility," or what we now call consumers' surplus, is equal to the excess of total utility over the marginal utility multiplied by the number of units of the service. It is measured by the roughly triangular area under the demand curve in excess of the price times quantity rectangle.

Dupuit's own diagram, with the axes transposed, is shown in Figure 28. NP is the marginal utility or demand curve for the services of a bridge. Op is the price, $OrnP$ is the total utility obtained from the bridge, and pnP is the consumers' surplus. A reduction in the toll by pp' results in a net gain of consumers' surplus of qnn': the total gain to consumers of $p'pnn'$ minus the loss in receipts of $p'pnq$.

Without drawing a supply curve, Dupuit went on to consider the producers' surplus from selling the services of a bridge at a uniform price per unit. If the supply curve represents the marginal cost curve of the industry, the producers' surplus is equal to the excess of the money received in the industry over the aggregate marginal costs. The total benefit of the bridge to the community is the sum of consumers' and producers' surplus represented by the large curvilinear triangle

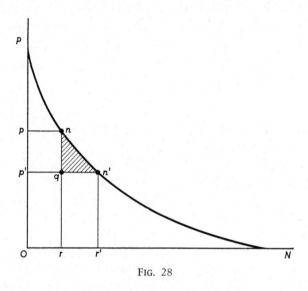

FIG. 28

sPn (Fig. 29). With the aid of some such implicit construction, Dupuit proceeded to develop some elementary theorems about the net social loss of a tax or a rise in tolls on public services.

When we compare Dupuit's original paper with Marshall's refinement of the same concept, we are struck by the inadequacy of Dupuit's discussion. Dupuit never realized that the argument hinges on the measurability of utility. A consumer's surplus from one particular service may be dependent on surpluses arising from other services and commodities consumed. Moreover, the surpluses of different persons may not be addible: the placing of the apostrophe in consumers' surplus tacitly assumes interpersonal comparisons of utility. There are further problems connected with the measurement of producers' surpluses. Nevertheless, Dupuit's paper, primitive as it is, should have aroused interest in the possibilities of a utility approach to value. In point of fact, it went neglected until the 1870's, when both Jevons and Walras paid tribute to its pioneering qualities.

Little need be said of Gossen, whose work attracted no attention whatever at the time of its publication. His neglect is only too easy to explain: the method of exposition was such that few readers even now could follow the argument. The whole of the book was taken up with the theory of consumption, supplemented by a theory of the marginal disutility of labor very similar to that presented by Jevons. Gossen's statement of the principle of diminishing marginal utility is concerned solely with individual acts of consuming specific goods. From the principle of diminishing utility he proceeded to examine the equilibrium conditions of exchange, concluding that each individual will continue trading "until the values of the last units of the two commodities in his

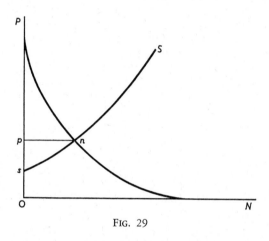

Fig. 29

possession have become equal." Generalizing the argument, he arrived at the succinct formulation of the theory of rational consumer choice, a formulation that has ever since been known as Gossen's second law: "A person maximizes his utility when he distributes his available money among the various goods so that he obtains the same amount of satisfaction from the last unit of money spent upon each commodity."

NOTES FOR FURTHER READING

1. *The Marginal Revolution.* Extraordinarily little has been written on the causes of "the marginal revolution." What little has been done is almost solely concerned with the English scene. The most useful general survey of the state of British economics in the critical years 1850–75 is Hutchison, *Review of Economic Doctrine,* chap. 1. Hutchison denies any institutional basis for the rise of marginal economics, other than the pricing problems of public utilities: "Insularity and Cosmopolitanism in Economic Ideas, 1870–1914," *AER,* May, 1955. The rise of the English Historical School is traced by A. W. Coates, "The Historicist Reaction in English Political Economy, 1870–1890," *Ec,* May, 1954.

S. G. Checkland attributes the intellectual stagnation of the 1860's to the hegemony of Mill and the academic authority of Fawcett and Cairnes: "Economic Opinion in England as Jevons Found It," *MS*, May, 1951. E. Kauder, however, argues that the delayed acceptance of utility theory in England was due to its predominantly Protestant culture: "The Retarded Acceptance of Marginal Utility Theory," *QJE*, November, 1953; "Comment" by J. P. Henderson, August, 1955. On Menger and the background of German economics before 1870 see Hutchison, *Review of Economic Doctrines,* chaps. 8 and 9; F. A. Hayek, "Carl Menger," *Ec*, 1934, reprinted in *DET;* and E. Schneider, "Hans v. Mangoldt on Price Theory," *Ecom*, April, 1960. G. J. Stigler's treatment of Menger in *Production and Distribution Theories* (1948), chap. 6, seems excessively generous and one may question his unfavorable comparison of Jevons to Menger. By way of contrast, see F. H. Knight's introduction to the English translation of Menger's *Principles* (1950). The ideas of the subjective-value trio, their sources and inspirations, the reviews that their books received, the slow spread and subsequent refinement of marginal utility theory, are all analyzed in great detail by R. S. Howey, *The Rise of the Marginal Utility School 1870–1889* (1960). G. J. Stigler, "The Influence of Events and Policies on Economic Theory," *AER*, May, 1960, analyzes such problems as the origin of "the marginal revolution" in broad terms.

2. *Jevons.* First, there is J. M. Keynes's sparkling essay in *Essays in Biography* (1951), chap. 4, reprinted in *DET*. L. Robbins discusses "The Place of Jevons in the History of Economic Thought," *MS*, 1936, Vol. VIII, No. 1, emphasizing Jevons' contributions to capital theory. B. H. Higgins stresses Jevons' views on utility theory: "Jevons—A Centenary Estimate," *MS*, 1935, Vol. VI, No. 2. Stigler, *Production and Distribution Theories*, chap. 2, is particularly useful on Jevons' theory of labor.

Marshall's review of Jevons' *Theory* (1872), reprinted in *Memorials of Alfred Marshall*, ed. A. C. Pigou (1925), makes an interesting contrast with the later treatment in the *Principles,* Appen. I. See also P. H. Wicksteed, "On Certain Passages in Jevons' *Theory of Political Economy*," *QJE*, 1889, reprinted in *Commonsense of Political Economy*, Vol. II. Jevons' "Brief Account of a General Mathematical Theory of Political Economy" (1862) is reprinted as an appendix to the fifth edition of his *Theory of Political Economy* (1957). On the Knight-Robbins controversy over the supply curve of labor see Douglas, *Theory of Wages,* chap. 12.

3. *Other Forerunners.* R. M. Robertson discusses Jevons' English forerunners in a brilliant essay: "Jevons and his Precursors," *Ecom*, July, 1951. F. Y. Edgeworth's articles in *PDPE* on Dupuit, Cournot, and Gossen are well worth perusal. On Gossen see also W. Stark, *The Ideal Foundations of Economic Thought* (1943), chap. 3. On the history of mathematical economics before Cournot, an esoteric subject at best, see R. M. Robertson, "Mathematical Economics before Cournot," *JPE*, December, 1949; C. D. Calsoyas, "The Mathematical Theory of Monopoly in 1839: Charles Ellet, Jr.," *JPE*, April, 1950; and the recent monograph by R. D. Theocharis, *Early Developments in Mathematical Economics* (1961). I. Fisher supplies a preçis of Cournot's book in *QJE*, 1898, reprinted in *DET*. Much has been written on Cournot's duopoly theory. For a review of the Cournot-Bertrand-Edgeworth debate see A. J. Nichol,

"A Re-appraisal of Cournot's Theory of Duopoly Price," *JPE*, 1934, reprinted in *EET*, and "Edgeworth's Theory of Duopoly Price," *EJ*, March, 1935; see also Schumpeter, *History*, pp. 954–63, 976–85. A. H. Leigh gives an excellent connected account of von Thünen's theoretical contributions: "Von Thünen's Theory of Distribution and the Advent of Marginal Analysis," *JPE*, 1946, reprinted in *EET;* see also Schumpeter, *History*, pp. 465–68. R. W. Houghton, "A Note on the Early History of Consumer's Surplus," *Ec.*, February, 1958, discusses Dupuit, Jenkin, and the development of Dupuit's work by Auspitz and Lieben in the 1880's. Dupuit's remarkable essay is reprinted in *IEP*, No. 2 (1952). Jenkin's paper, published in 1871, is reprinted in *Readings in the Economics of Taxation,* ed. R. A. Musgrave and C. S. Shoup (1959).

Chapter 9

MARSHALLIAN ECONOMICS: UTILITY AND DEMAND

1. UTILITY THEORY

THE FOUNDERS of marginal utility theory accepted the existence of a unit of measure of utility as a self-evident fact. Menger and Walras never seriously raised the question of measurability. Jevons expressly denied that utility was measurable but, in fact, suggested a way of measuring utility via the approximate constancy of the marginal utility of money, a procedure that Marshall later adopted and refined. Jevons likewise denied the possibility of making interpersonal comparisons of utility, pointing out that price theory did not require such comparisons, but then went on to make statements about welfare that involved both cardinal measurement and interpersonal comparisons. Menger and Walras, on the other hand, saw no difficulty in comparing the utility of different individuals. All the three founders of utility theory worked with a so-called additive utility function, treating the utility of a commodity as a function only of the quantity of that commodity. They paid very little attention to the precise shape of the utility function and assumed a law of diminishing marginal utility as a matter of common experience. Walras drew linear marginal utility functions in his book. Menger's tabular representations implied linear functions. Most of Jevons' curves were drawn convex from below. None of them admitted any exception to the fundamental law of diminishing marginal utility, and Jevons went out of his way to deny that there were any exceptions.

Furthermore, Walras alone succeeded in linking utility to demand, although even he did not rigorously derive the implications of diminishing marginal utility with respect to demand curves. He began his analysis with given demand curves and obtained his equilibrium market conditions before he ever said a word about utility. Jevons, on the other hand, bridged utility and demand by the illegitimate concept of Trading Bodies, and Menger simply postulated certain demand prices that were somehow representative of marginal utilities. None of these technical issues in utility theory was cleared up until the 1890's, and some were not elucidated until well past the turn of the century. Marshall's statement of utility theory is superior to either Jevons' or Walras's, but succeeding editions of the *Principles* were marked by increasing caution and reticence as the work of Edgeworth, Fisher, and Pareto began to undermine the earlier notions of measurability, additivity, and comparability. Before examining Marshall's resolution of some of the technical difficulties in utility theory, we must review the theoretical issues that plagued analytical progress in this area.

The Measurability of Utility. Suppose a consumer chooses A, B, C, and D according to his preferences. Given consistent ranking of the four, we can construct the consumer's utility index by attaching arbitrary numbers of ascending order to the various outcomes. An indefinite number of such indices will rank the four outcomes in the same way. If order alone is the same among all these possible indices, we have ordinal utility, a function "unique up to a monotonic transforma-

Ordinal Utility Monotonic Transformations				Cardinal Utility Linear Transformations			
	I	II	III		I	II	III
A............	16	5	...	A............	16	33	...
B............	8	4	...	B............	8	17	...
C............	4	3	...	C............	4	9	...
D............	2	2	...	D............	2	5	...

tion." Suppose we construct a new series indicating the same order of preference among A, B, C, and D. But now we ask something more restrictive of these indices: they must all be the same but for an additive and multiplicative constant. That is, if x is one index, and y another, y satisfies the equation $y = ax + b$, where a and b are constants. The only difference, then, between two indices related in this way is the point of origin and the arbitrary units of the scale. Such indices are for obvious reasons called "unique up to a linear transformation."

These two types of utility scales differ strikingly in one respect. Scales that are monotone transformations of each other vary together in the same direction: this is the only property that they have in common. But scales that are linear transformations of each other assert something much stronger: when the interval differences of one scale increase or decrease successively, the interval differences of the others also increase or decrease successively to the same extent. When we have picked one of the million arbitrary utility functions that will satisfy $A > B >$

$C > D$ up to a linear transformation, we can compare *differences* between the successive intervals so as to conclude, say, that $U_A > U_B$ more than $U_B > U_C$. In our example, we can say that $U_A > U_B$ twice as much as $U_B > U_C$, a statement that is meaningless when applied to utility functions unique up to a monotone transformation.

Measurability up to a linear transformation involves knowledge not only of the signs of the first differences of the utility scales but also of the signs of the second differences; the first differences tell us about the *direction* of preference, the second differences tell us about the *intensity* of preference. If we can do no more than rank utilities ordinally, marginal utility has meaning only in being positive or negative but diminishing or increasing marginal utility has no meaning. But, if utility is cardinally measurable, the first and second derivatives of the utility function do have meaning; the value of the first derivative is an index of marginal utility, and the law of diminishing marginal utility is defined by the negative sign of the second derivative. Utility measured in this way is analogous to heat registered by a centigrade or a Fahrenheit thermometer. Since a Fahrenheit scale is related to a centigrade scale by the linear equation $\frac{9}{5}° \, C + 32° = F°$, it is possible to make statements about variations in the intensity of heat regardless of the type of thermometer employed.

Operational Measurement of Utility. The operational construction of an ordinal utility scale would seem to be a simple matter: we simply let the individual choose between goods and write down a series of numbers expressing the ranking of utilities along the scale according to magnitude. But, in order to construct a cardinal utility scale, we have to ask the individual to perform a *Gedankenexperimente,* projecting himself in two different situations. Having chosen A over B, we must give him B again and ask him to choose between B and C, comparing the intensity of preference in the two situations. This is a purely subjective procedure, but, as long as the utility of one good is entirely independent of all other goods, it is in fact possible in principle to construct a cardinal utility scale.

This was first demonstrated by Fisher in his essay, "A Statistical Method of Measuring 'Marginal Utility' and Testing the Justice of a Progressive Income Tax" (1927). Fisher's method ran as follows: endow an individual with an arbitrary quantity of any commodity, say, 100 loaves of bread. Let the marginal utility of the 100 loaves be equal to one "util," the units of the utility scale. Starting with no milk, find the minimum amount of milk the individual will accept in exchange for the hundredth loaf of bread worth 1 util. Given the possession of the first increment of milk, repeat the experiment for a second increment, and so forth. We thus obtain a schedule giving the amounts of milk necessary to obtain equal increments of utility. By inverting the series and interpolating, we find the amount of utility obtained from equal increments of milk (see Tables 1 and 2).

TABLE 1			TABLE 2		
Increments of Milk (Cu. In.)	Utility of Increments of Milk	Total Utility of Milk	Quantity of Milk (Cu. In.)	TU of Milk	MU of Milk (Per 3 Cu. In.)
3	1	1	3	1.0000*	....
4	1	2	6	1.7667	.7667
5	1	3	9	2.4333	.6667
6	1	4	12	3.000*	.5667
7	1	5	15	3.4667	.4667

* From Table 1.

Granting the ability of the individual to choose consistently between specified amounts of two goods, this utility function is determined up to a linear transformation. But, if the marginal utility of milk depends not only on the quantity of milk but also on the quantities of other foodstuffs consumed, Fisher showed, we will get an entirely new utility function whenever we change the commodity in terms of which the utility of milk is measured. If we drop the notion of one-variable additive utility function, $U_A = f(A)$, $U_B = f(B)$, *ad infinitum*, and adopt a generalized utility function, $U_A = f(A, B, C, \ldots)$, $U_B = f(B, A, C, \ldots)$, we can no longer measure utility cardinally by the method of pairwise choices.

The generalized utility function was reached independently by Fisher. Edgeworth had already introduced it in *Mathematical Psychics*. But, although most economists conceded the interdependence and, hence, the nonadditivity of utility functions, the additive utility function was only slowly and very reluctantly abandoned. The hypothesis of universal "independence" has, as we shall see, the implication that no particular good is an "inferior" good—the kind of good of which less is bought as income increases. This implication is contradicted by evidence showing that many goods, if narrowly enough defined, are "inferior" for some ranges of income. The hypothesis of universal "independence" therefore, must be rejected. A generalized utility function, however, makes it impossible to devise a *simple* operational procedure for measuring cardinal utility. Even if the measurability of utility is taken for granted, it makes it impossible rigorously to deduce upward-sloping income curves and downward-sloping demand curves from the law of diminishing marginal utility; a richer but a much more complicated theory of demand is the result. It is not difficult to understand, therefore, why most writers in this period, and particularly the nonmathematical writers, preferred to work with one-variable utility functions.

Although we can devise a measurement unique up to a linear transformation if the utility functions are additive, it does not follow that we can integrate the marginal utility curves and so obtain the corresponding total utilities. Sums obtained by adding interval differences based on two indices identical up to a linear transformation do not yield equal totals, owing to the fact that both the zero point of the scale and the unit of measurement are arbitrary. We can say that temperature rose twice as much from Sunday to Monday as from Monday to Tuesday, and this statement holds true whether we use a Fahrenheit or a centigrade thermometer. But we cannot say that temperature was twice as high on Monday as on Sunday, for this statement depends on which thermometer we use: for example, $20°$ C $= 68°$ F, but $40°$ C $=$ $104°$ F. Sums of measurement of temperature make no sense because the results differ according to the scale chosen. With reference to utility, measurability up to a linear transformation gives us the sign of marginal utility as well as its rate of change but does not allow us to find the total utility of a group of objects or bundle of goods by an additive process.

To obtain the absolute value of the individual's total utility from a bundle of goods, we would have to be able to calculate ratios, not merely between the interval differences among the numbers assigned to the utility scale, but between the numbers themselves. This implies measurement "unique up to a proportionate transformation": the indices differ only by a multiplicative constant. If utility were measurable in this sense, it would belong to the field of weights and lengths, in which the zero point of measurement is well defined, instead of to the field of temperature measurement. To put the same point somewhat differently, in *ordinal* utility theory we know only the successive contour lines on the map of an individual's utility mountain without being able to judge whether the mountain in question is Mount Everest or a molehill. In *cardinal* utility theory we can at least compare the distances between the contour lines to get a picture of the shape and slope of the mountain. We still do not know, however, how high it is because the unit and the origin of measurement are entirely arbitrary. Under certain restricted conditions, however, Marshall argued, we can determine the absolute height of the mountain. By assuming constancy in the marginal utility of money, Marshallian welfare economics did achieve the strongest possible measurement of utility, namely, measurement unique up to a multiplicative constant.

The Bernoulli Hypothesis. Up to this point we have been concerned with utility theory as a rationalization of commodity-demand curves, a means of predicting how consumers choose among a number of "sure prospects." But how do we explain consumers' behavior in the presence of uncertainty? People buy insurance, thus choosing certainty over uncertainty, but they also engage in gambling, choosing uncertainty over certainty. Is it possible to rationalize this kind of behavior by assuming that people act so as to maximize their expected income?

All attempts to define a utility function by observing the reaction of individuals to probability situations go back to Bernoulli's memoir on the St. Petersburg Paradox (1738). The nature of the paradox is this: a coin is tossed until heads appears; if heads appears on the first toss, A pays B \$1; if heads appears for the first time on the second toss, A pays B \$2, and so on, always paying $\$2^{n-1}$ for each toss if heads appears. What fee should B be willing to pay for the privilege of playing the game if it is to be a "fair game"? A "fair game" is one in which the player pays no more than the total mathematical expectation of success, the actuarial value of the gamble, at each stage of the game. The expected gain or loss of income from a "fair bet," therefore, always equals zero. The mathematical expectation of success on the first toss is $p \cdot \$1 = (\frac{1}{2}) \cdot \$1 = \$0.50$; on the second toss $(1 - p)\,(p) \cdot \$2 = (\frac{1}{2})(\frac{1}{2}) \cdot \$2 = \$0.50$; on the nth toss $(\frac{1}{2})^n \cdot \$2^{n-1} = \$2^{n-1}/2^n = \$0.50$. Since the total expectation E is the sum of the expectations at each state, $E = \$0.50 + \$0.50 + \ldots$. The sum of this infinite series is infinite and so B must pay A an infinite sum of money for the privilege of playing this "fair game." Since people are clearly not willing to pay any stake no matter how large, the assumption that people act as if they were maximizing expected income produces a contradiction.

Bernoulli's solution was to argue that people are guided, not by the "mathematical expectation," but by the "moral expectation" of success, the probabilities being weighted by the utility of income. Moreover, the marginal utility of income declines with every increment of income. Given diminishing marginal utility of money income, people will insist on a larger gain to compensate them for the risk of a given loss: no one will pay as much as \$1 for the 50–50 chance of winning \$2. He illustrated the argument graphically (see Fig. 30). The individual's wealth at the outset is *AB,* and the chance of winning *BP* is 50 per cent. The total utility of a gain and the total disutility of the fee paid for the privilege of playing the game are measured along the ordinate. If *sBS* were a straight line, an individual would pay a fee *pB* equal to the expected gain *BP*. Since the utility-of-income curve is concave from above, *pB* is the largest amount that should be paid for a 50 per cent chance of winning *BP*, being the point where the utility of gain *PO* is equal to the disutility of the fee *po*. Bernoulli then went on to assume that the curve is a logarithmic one. If *rH* is the utility of an infinitely small gain *PD* to an individual who possesses *AP*, Bernoulli conjectured that *rH* is directly proportional to *PD* and inversely proportional to *AP*. That is, letting *F* be the amount of an individual's "for-

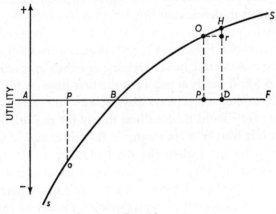

FIG. 30

tune" and *dF* the increment to his fortune, then

$$dU = K \frac{dF}{F} \quad \text{or} \quad \frac{dU}{dF} = \frac{K}{F}.$$

Assuming with Bernoulli that *c* is the amount of "fortune" necessary for existence, the total utility derived from income *F* may be represented by the definite integral

$$\int_c^F K \frac{dF}{F} = K(\log F - \log c) = K \log \frac{F}{c}.$$

The "Bernoulli hypothesis" states that dU/dF, the marginal utility of income, declines at the same percentage rate at which income increases; the schedule of the marginal utility of income thus takes the form of a rectangular hyperbola. Here, incidentally, we have the first use of calculus in anything resembling an economic problem.

Gambling and Insurance. In the 1860's Bernoulli's hypothesis received some corroboration from the newly emerging field of psychophysics. The so-called Weber-Fechner Law held that a just noticeable difference in sensation is inversely proportional to the stimulus received; sensation is a logarithmic function of the stimulus. Fechner's experiments seem to confirm Bernoulli's hypothesis if stimulus is identified with increments of income and sensation with utility. Neither Jevons nor Menger nor Walras, however, paid any attention to the Weber-Fechner Law. But Jevons was acquainted with Bernoulli's hypothesis and accepted its implication that "gaming is, in the long run, a sure way to lose utility." Marshall followed him in this and agreed that utility maximization must be rejected as an explanation of choices involving uncertainty. If the utility of a given sum gained is always less than the utility of the same sum lost, the rational individual will take out "fair" or slightly "unfair" insurance but will never gamble at "fair" odds: he will be willing to pay more than $1 as a premium to protect himself against the 1 per cent probability of a loss of $100, but he will not be willing to pay $1 for the 1 per cent chance of winning $100. The widespread phenomenon of buying lottery tickets at less than fair odds must be explained by the "love of gambling." In other words, people do not seem to behave as if they were maximizing the expected utility of income.

The Marshallian ban on the utility analysis of choice under uncertainty lasted until recent times, when Neumann and Morgenstern showed that this is precisely the case in which it is possible to devise an operational procedure for measuring utility up to a linear transformation. This is of little help in the theory of consumption in which individuals typically choose among sure alternatives. But it does imply that we may some day be able to measure the income-utility curve in cardinal terms. Empirical work along the lines of Neumann and Morgenstern has not yet yielded any conclusive evidence, and so investigators have turned back to the problem of rationalizing the seemingly contradictory behavior of individuals who hedge against large losses and at the same time gamble at "fair" odds. One such hypothesis, the Friedman-Savage hypothesis, is that the total income-utility curve is concave from above in the lower and upper ranges, but convex from above in the middle ranges. Let us return to the Bernoulli hypothesis that it is concave throughout its entire range. An individual is at Y_2 (Fig. 31) and acts to maximize the expected utility of income. A "fair bet" is given by the condition $pY_3 + (1 - p)Y_1 = Y_2$. The individual compares the utility Y_2 with the weighted average utility from the gamble, the weights being probabilities. He will accept "fair bets" if $pU(Y_3) + (1 - p)U(Y_1) > U(Y_2)$, that is, if a line connecting $U(Y_1)$ and

$U(Y_3)$ passes above $U(Y_2)$. With Bernoulli's hypothesis, therefore, he will always decline "fair bets." He will accept insurance, however. If his present income is Y_3 and the insurance premium is equal to Y_2Y_3, he will accept the certainty of Y_2 over the chance of falling to Y_1. If

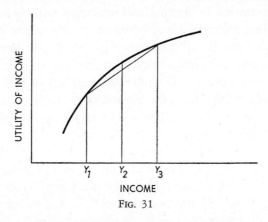

INCOME

FIG. 31

the curve were convex—increasing marginal utility of income—the individual would gamble but would refuse to take out "fair" insurance. That is, he would pay $Y'_1Y'_2$ for a lottery ticket in the hope of winning $Y'_1Y'_3$. By supposing that the entire curve is first concave, then convex,

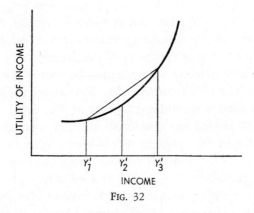

INCOME

FIG. 32

and finally concave, the Friedman-Savage hypothesis (Fig. 33, *left*) explains both the buying of insurance and the buying of lottery tickets; the "poor" are to the left of *A*, the "rich" are to the right of *B*, and the "middle classes" are in between.

Both the Bernoulli hypothesis and the Friedman-Savage hypothesis imply that utility is dependent on levels of income rather than on changes in income. Once the curve is constructed, individuals choose among alternative situations by moving along the curve. The utility of income, however, may be related to changes in the level of income, in which case a much simpler rationalization of individuals, both insuring and gambling, suggests itself. The Markowitz hypothesis (Fig. 33, *right*) explains this phenomenon without the uncomfortable implication of the Friedman-Savage hypothesis that the "poor" will not accept "fair bets." Instead of two inflection points, Markowitz assumes that there are three, with present income at the middle inflection point. Small increments in income yield increasing marginal utility, but large

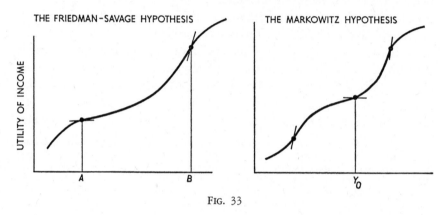

FIG. 33

gains in income yield diminishing marginal utility; this accounts for people's reluctance to accept large "fair bets." On the other hand, small decrements in income result in increasing marginal disutility, while large losses in income result in diminishing marginal disutility; hence, the eagerness to hedge against small losses.

The point of this recent development is to indicate that diminishing marginal utility of money income is a very different thing from diminishing marginal utility for a specific commodity. Even if all the things money income can buy are subject to a law of diminishing marginal utility, it does not follow that money income itself is. It is possible to rationalize people's behavior by a particular income-utility curve and it may even be possible some day to measure the utility of income cardinally. When an individual is willing to pay a fee of $10 for the 50–50 chance of winning $20, we can conclude that the marginal utility of money is constant to him in the relevant income range. If he insists on better-than-fair odds, we can conclude that he weighs the loss of $10 more than the gain of $10, that the marginal utility of money to him declines within the relevant range.[1] But the theory of demand does not require cardinal measurement of utility, and no one has yet found an operational procedure that would permit us to measure people's choices among sure alternatives in a way that would be "unique up to a linear transformation." In Marshallian theory this problem is neatly circumvented by confining the analysis to goods that absorb a small portion of the consumer's total expenditure. For such goods, the marginal utility of money income may be considered approximately constant, clearing the way for a simple transition from utility to demand.

The Bernoulli Hypothesis and Progressive Taxation. Before passing on to the theory of demand, let us briefly consider one of the popular uses of Bernoulli's hypothesis in this period, namely, to justify progressive income taxation. It may seem, at first glance, that the notion of declining marginal utility of income always justifies tax progression. But this is not so. Assuming that all individuals have equal capacities of want satisfactions for equal incomes, so that the same income-utility schedules may be applied to all taxpayers, and, assuming we want to distribute the tax bill so as to inflict "equal sacrifice" on everyone,

[1] This is the essence of the Neumann-Morgenstern procedure for measuring utility. Suppose an individual finds $U_A > U_B > U_C$. Form a lottery ticket of A and C and offer him a choice between the certainty of B and either A with probability p or C with probability $(1 - p)$. Find that p which would make $pU_A + (1 - p) \ U_C = U_B$. If $p = 1$, the individual would choose the lottery ticket. For example, the individual is given a one-fifth chance of winning nothing and a four-fifths chance of winning $10. The "mathe-

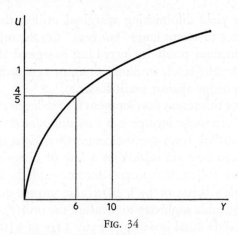

FIG. 34

matical expectation" of the lottery ticket is $(1/5 \cdot \$0) + (4/5 \cdot \$10) = \$8$; the "moral expectation," however, is $(1/5 \cdot 0) + (4/5 \cdot 1) = 4/5$, where U, the utility of winning $10, is arbitrarily set equal to unity. Suppose we find the individual is indifferent between $6 and the lottery ticket—apparently, when $B = \$6$, $U_B = 4/5$ of U_A. By varying the probabilities in the gamble and setting the average utility of the outcomes equal to different B's we can elicit the entire utility curve with zero and unity arbitrarily defined.

measured in terms of income surrendered, we arrive at different conclusions depending on whether we select equal absolute, equal proportional, or equal marginal sacrifice. Under equal *absolute* sacrifice, the tax bill is so distributed as to extract the same absolute amount of total income utility from each individual. Under equal *proportional* sacrifice, we try to extract the same proportion of total income utility from each individual; hence, the "rich" pay more and the "poor" pay less under this scheme than under the former. Under equal *marginal* sacrifice we minimize aggregate sacrifice by inflicting the same loss of marginal utility on all individuals. On a priori grounds it is not clear which concept of equal sacrifice should be applied; Sidgwick and Marshall favored the first; Cohen-Stuart, an important Dutch writer on public finance, preferred the second; and Edgeworth and Pigou held out for the third. Whichever concept is chosen, the actual rate structure required to implement it still depends on the precise shape of the income-utility curve.

If all that is known is that the marginal utility of income declines at some undetermined rate over its entire range, progression is only clearly justified by the concept of equal *marginal* sacrifice. Whatever the negative shape of the curve, this theory would proceed by leveling the highest income down to the next highest, and so on, until the necessary revenue had been raised. To get progression from the equal absolute and equal proportional standards requires that the marginal utility-of-income curve be steeper than a Bernoulli curve, that is, a rectangular hyperbola. The Bernoulli hypothesis implies that a given percentage increase of income results in the same increase in total utility, whatever the level of income. It follows that in this case the principle of equal *absolute* sacrifice calls for a proportionate tax: an individual with twice as much income as another should pay twice the number of dollars in tax. Even with equal *proportional* sacrifice, declining marginal utility of income as such does not necessarily lead to progression, as Cohen-Stuart and Edgeworth have shown.

Moreover, although the marginal utility of income may decline at a given income level, every increase in income might cause the schedule to shift upward owing to a rise in aspiration levels. If the long-run schedule is constant, none of the three concepts will justify a progressive tax, and the case of equal absolute sacrifice will now require a regressive tax. Further complications result if the individual utility schedules are interdependent so that the satisfactions derived from income depend not only on total income but also on one's place in the income-distribution scale. And, last, differences in tastes and hence differences in the income-utility schedules preclude *any* deduction about rate structure from any concept of equal sacrifice without interpersonal comparisons of utility. As soon as we admit that people differ in their capacities for want satisfaction, we are driven to the conclusion that an optimal income distribution would award larger incomes to the efficient utility engines.

It has been argued that, in the absence of specific knowledge, we should assume that "all men are equal." But this is the fallacy of equiprobabilities. In the face of ignorance it is no more plausible to assume that the income-utility curves are the same than that they are different, for each has a 50 per cent chance of happening. On a priori grounds we cannot deny Edgeworth's famous observation in *Mathematical Psychics:* "If we suppose that capacity for pleasure is an attribute of skill and talent . . . we may see a reason deeper than Economics may afford for the larger pay, though often more agreeable work, of the aristocracy of skill and talent. The aristocracy of sex is similarly grounded upon the supposed superior capacity of the man for happiness. . . . Altogether . . . there appears a nice conciliance between the deductions from the utilitarian principle and the disabilities and privileges which hedge round modern womanhood."

Perhaps the only way to rescue the assumption that men are alike in their capacity for enjoying income is to adopt the one-vote principle upon which our political institutions are based. Taxation is a matter of political consensus, and here we may legitimately take refuge in truths that are said to be self-evident. This disposes of the problem of interpersonal comparisons but still leaves us with the problem of which concept of equal sacrifice to apply.

Derivation of Demand Curves. Marshall was virtually the first author after Walras clearly and explicitly to derive demand curves from utility functions. In Mathematical Appendix II of the *Principles,* Marshall gives the equilibrium condition for the consumption of commodity x as $MU_x = p_x \cdot MU_m$. Taken across all goods this gives the familiar equimarginal rule:

$$\frac{MU_x}{p_x} = \frac{MU_y}{p_y} = \frac{MU_n}{p_n} = \lambda,$$

λ being what Marshall calls the marginal utility of money. The "marginal utility of money" is a confusing phrase because what Marshall had in mind was not the marginal utility of an individual's money stock but the marginal utility of his money income flow. In equilibrium an individual will want to hold a stock of money that gives him ready command over a certain desired proportion k of his real income.

$$\frac{M}{P} = k\frac{Y}{P},$$

where P is a general price index. Formally, therefore, we should write a separate fraction in the consumer-allocation formula, representing the marginal utility of a dollar held in idle money balances at given market prices. If the individual saves, we have another equation giving the present marginal utility of the future yield of earning assets over their current prices. For convenience, however, we may assume that all expenditure is on current consumption goods. A rise in money income flows initially into an individual's money-stock holding, lowers the marginal utility of these holdings, and then raises expenditures until the marginal utility of money *held* is once again equal to the marginal utility of money *spent*. In other words, in disequilibrium, the marginal utility of money holdings regulates expenditures and the marginal utility of money spent gives the equilibrium level to which the marginal utility of money holdings tends to move. To avoid future confusion, we will label λ the marginal utility of money expenditures in general MU_e. It is not necessary to divide this marginal utility by a general price index because the price of money in terms of dollars is unity. MU_e is thus the common value of the ratios of the marginal utilities of commodities to their prices, the uniform utility of a dollar on the margin of expenditure in all directions.

We can now restate the equimarginal rule for consumer equilibrium in three ways: the consumer maximizes satisfactions when (1) he equalizes weighted marginal utilities over all goods, that is, the marginal utility of each good weighted by its price; (2) he equalizes the ratio of marginal utilities with the ratio of the corresponding prices for every pair of goods consumed; and (3) he equalizes the marginal utility of a dollar's worth of each commodity purchased at given market prices, that is, he equalizes the marginal utility of dollars spent in all markets.

Suppose the consumer has achieved equilibrium and p_x falls: immediately, the equality $MU_x = p_x \cdot MU_e$ becomes an inequality. To restore equilibrium, more of x must be bought to reduce MU_x. There is no doubt that the consumer will buy more of x when the price falls because at lower p_x he obtains a larger marginal utility per dollar from x than from any other commodity. The law of diminishing marginal utility guarantees that MU_x falls as more x is bought to restore equilibrium. The substitution effect of the fall in price, therefore, yields a negatively inclined demand curve on the assumption that the consumer always acts so as to maximize his satisfactions within the restraints of his given income and given prices. This argument assumes, however, that the individual is deprived of the increase in real income owing to the fall in p_x, so that MU_e remained constant through the adjustment process. Once the individual has again equalized the marginal utility of expenditures in all directions, we restore the nominal increment of real income: this lowers the marginal utility of money holdings and thereby leads to an increase in the purchase of every commodity, including x. The income effect in this case is positive, and we obtain a negatively inclined demand curve as well as a positively sloped income curve for x.

The typical Marshallian method of deriving demand curves from the underlying utility curves is based on the notion of additive utility functions: the utility function of each commodity purchased by the individual is independent of every other. An additive utility function does not permit consideration of substitution and complementarity between commodities. But Marshall realized that some commodities are rivals in consumption while others are complementary: x and y are substitutes when MU_x decreases as the quantity of y increases; they are complements when MU_x increases as the quantity of y increases. Recognition of such interrelations among commodities leads straightway to a generalized utility function, the utility of x being a function of $x, y, z,$ . . . n. With a generalized utility function, however, diminishing marginal utility no longer has the necessary corollary that all demand curves have negative and all income curves have positive slopes. When we restore the increment in real income resulting from a reduction in p_x, we cannot be sure that *all* commodities will be consumed in larger quantities. Suppose an increase in y purchased not only reduced MU_y but also MU_x because x and y are substitutes. Then when a portion of the increment of real income is spent on y, MU_x may fall so much that the amount of x must be reduced below its original quantity to fulfil the conditions for maximum satisfaction. The income effect is negative and the demand curve for x *may* prove to be positively sloped; x is an "inferior good."

The Constancy of the Marginal Utility of Money. One way of resolving this problem is to eliminate the income effect by assumption. This is exactly what Marshall did when he argued that the marginal utility of money—our MU_e—is approximately constant in most cases. Of course, absolute constancy in MU_e would be a very rare case, as can be easily demonstrated. A price change that would leave MU_e unaffected could result only from a marginal utility function with an elasticity equal to unity in the relevant range. If a 1 per cent drop in p_x increases the quantity demanded of x by 1 per cent, total expenditures on x are unaffected by the fall in price; hence, real income is the same at the old price as at the new. If the elasticity of the utility function over the relevant range is less than unity, a fall in p_x reduces total expenditures on x, everything else being the same; the increase in real income lowers the marginal utility of money holdings and results in larger purchases of every commodity—all demand curves shift to the right. As a result, in the new equilibrium MU_e is other than it was before. Contrariwise, if the elasticity of the marginal utility curve is greater than unity, a fall in p_x, given MU_e, raises total expenditure. The marginal utility of money balances will now rise, thus shifting all demand curves to the left and altering the final equilibrium value of MU_e. The strict assumption of a constant MU_e, therefore, entails unitary price elasticity of the marginal utility and demand curves over the relevant range of price variations.

Unable to contend that MU_e is really constant, Marshall was satisfied to argue that MU_e is approximately constant for small changes in the price of "unimportant" commodities, commodities absorbing a negligible portion of an individual's total expenditures. For all practical purposes MU_e remains constant and may be employed as the unit of measurement of utility to the individual, representing the increase in total utility that results from adding one dollar to the consumer's total expenditure. Given the basic formula $p_x = (MU_x/MU_e)$, knowledge of MU_e, and knowledge of the individual's demand curve for commodity x, permit us to infer the underlying marginal utility function of x. In this way, without postulating that MU_e, or the marginal utility of money income, can in fact be measured cardinally, Marshall achieved something tantamount to cardinal measurement of the marginal utility functions of "unimportant" commodities.

The method is perfectly analogous to the way we usually derive the demand schedule for a factor. Marginal utility plays the same role in the theory of consumption as the marginal physical product of a factor in the theory of production. We convert marginal physical product into dollar terms by multiplying it by the marginal revenue of the product—under perfect competition, with firms facing given prices, marginal revenue is equal to average revenue is equal to the price of the product. The analogous concept in the theory of consumption is the reciprocal of MU_e: it might be called the marginal revenue of utility.

If MU_e is the increase in total utility resulting from the addition of one dollar to the consumer's total expenditure, then MR_u is the dollar value of adding one util to total utility. Suppose $MU = 20$ utils per dollar. Then, MR_u is 5 cents; adding a util to total utility is equivalent to adding 5 cents to total expenditures. $p_x = MU_x \cdot MR_u$ and $MU_x \cdot MR_u$ or MU_x/MU_e gives us the marginal rate of substitution between money and the commodity in question. MR_u is therefore related to MU as the marginal revenue product of a factor is related to its marginal physical product. The demand schedule for a factor is identical with its marginal revenue product schedule; in the same way, the demand schedule of the consumer *is* the marginal rate of substitution schedule. The analogy, however, is purely formal. The price of the product does

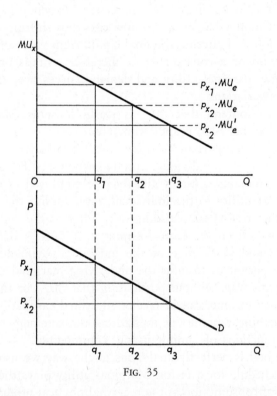

Fig. 35

indeed remain constant when the firm changes its purchases of factor inputs in response to a change in factor prices. But MR_u almost always alters somewhat when the price of a particular commodity changes— the only case in which this does not happen is when the marginal utility schedule, and hence the demand curve for a specific commodity, has unitary elasticity over the relevant range.

Restatement. Given a fall in price, the demand curve for x is derived from the marginal utility curve for x in two stages. In Figure 35 straight-line functions are drawn for geometrical convenience. In equilibrium, the consumer equates MU_x to $p_x \cdot MU_e$. When $p_x = p_{x_1}$, he buys q_1 amount of x. At a lower price p_{x_2} he moves down the marginal utility curve because of the substitution effect. If the elasticity of the MU_x curve is less than unity, the drop in price releases income for spending on other goods—that is, the rectangle $(p_{x_1} \cdot MU_e)O_{q_1} >$ the rectangle $(p_{x_2} \cdot MU_e)O_{q_2}$. More is bought of all goods, including x, and MU_e falls to MU'_e. In consequence of the substitution effect plus the income effect, the consumer buys q_3 of x at the lower price. In this way, we can derive the demand curve of every "superior" good.

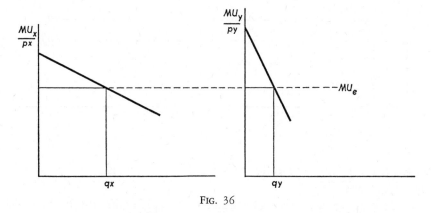

Fig. 36

Instead of confronting a given marginal utility function with various prices, we can adopt one of Jevons' diagrams and graph the moving ratio MU_x/p_x directly (Fig. 36). For two or more goods the equimarginal rule implies that q_x and q_y will be purchased. The rational consumer equates the weighted marginal utilities of all goods, making each equal to the common MU_e, so that his entire income is exhausted. A fall in p_x leads to an upward shift in the weighted marginal utility function of x. If we deprive the consumer of the nominal increase in real income owing to the fall in p_x, he buys more of x and less of y. Restoring the increment of real income, he will buy still more of x, as well as of y, if MU_e falls. (See Fig. 37.)

In principle, MU_e may either rise, fall, or remain the same. If the elasticity of demand in the range $p_{x_1} - p_{x_2}$ is equal to unity, the individual will spend as much on x at the new price as at the old; hence, MU_y/p_y, MU_n/p_n, and MU_e will not be affected; the income effect is zero, and the individual will end up buying q_{x_2} and q_{y_1}. If the demand is inelastic, the individual buys more of x at the lower price but still has income left for spending on other goods. In consequence, MU_e falls. Contrariwise, an elastic demand for x raises MU_e by pulling expenditure away from other goods. At given prices, MU_e is inversely related to the amount of real income. But every reduction in price raises the potential purchasing power of money income. The fact that an individual has more real income when he spends a marginal dollar lowers MU_e, but the fact that he can buy more goods for a marginal dollar

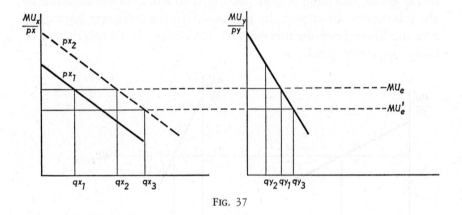

FIG. 37

when some prices have fallen raises MU_e. The balance of forces may go either way.

If x and y are either substitutes or complements, the problem is complicated by a new consideration. Each weighted marginal utility function is drawn up on the assumption of given tastes, a given money income, and a given set of prices of all goods, including the price of the good in question. (See Fig. 38.) If x and y are substitutes, MU_y and hence MU_y/p_y shift down as more x is acquired; if they are complements, MU_y and hence MU_y/p_y shift up as more x is acquired. Unless x and y are independent goods, therefore, every change in p_x involves a shift in *all* the weighted marginal utility functions. It is easy to see now how "Giffen's Paradox" might arise. The price of x falls, and more of x would be purchased owing to the substitution effect. The income effect of the price fall, however, leads to an increase in y purchased; x and y are strong rivals and the increase in the consumption of y sharply depresses MU_x. It is possible that the curve MU_x/p_{x_2} will fall so sharply that in equilibrium less of x is purchased than before. We conclude, therefore, that a positively inclined demand curve is the outcome of a significant income effect, which is negative owing to extreme rivalry between goods.

Inferior goods are goods whose income elasticity of demand is negative. If we hold MU_e constant by assuming with Marshall that the item in question is "unimportant," we eliminate the possibility of any income effect from a change in price and thus eliminate inferior goods by definition. Without adopting this approach *in sensu stricto,* we can generally say that we will rarely encounter inferior goods, provided we define commodities broadly enough. On the other hand, when goods are narrowly enough defined they are almost all inferior for some

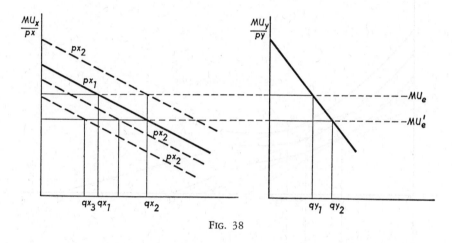

FIG. 38

ranges of income. Food as a whole is certainly not an inferior good: food is complementary to other broadly defined commodities, such as "clothing" and "housing," and the income effect of a change in the price of all foodstuffs is therefore bound to be positive. But margarine or any other cheap brand of a particular food may well be inferior because preferred substitutes are readily available.

The Indifference-Curve Approach. So far the exposition of the theory of consumer behavior has been Marshallian in spirit, implying cardinal measurement of utility. It is possible, however, to approach these problems from the viewpoint of ordinal utility theory by employing indifference curves. The technique of indifference curves was invented by Edgeworth and refined by Pareto and Fisher. But it had never become popular and subsequently fell into disuse. It was revived by A. Bowley in his *Mathematical Groundwork* (1924); Bowley did not, however, explore its implications for the measurability of utility. In 1934 Hicks and Allen showed that indifference curves can be employed to reconstruct the theory of consumer behavior on the basis of ordinal utility, only to discover that as early as 1913 and 1915 Johnson and Slutsky had independently demonstrated the same results.

The indifference-curve technique assumes that the individual can consistently rank his preferences and, moreover, that he can discern "indifference" between two given alternatives at a given time. What we actually observe is one point on the indifference curve, a point at which the slope of the price line between x and y equals the ratio of

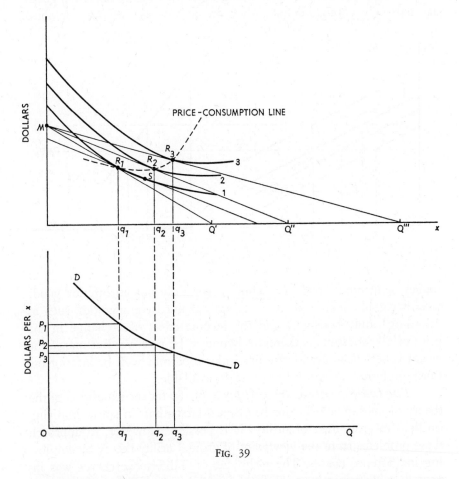

FIG. 39

the marginal utilities of x and y. But we *infer* that at other hypothetical ratios of exchange between x and y the individual could choose a combination of the two goods such that his level of total utility would be the same. An indifference curve, therefore, shows the various combinations of x and y yielding the same level of total satisfaction.

We can now derive the demand curve for x by placing money instead of another good on the y-axis. (See Fig. 39.) The individual finds himself initially at R_1, with a given income equal to OM, spending R_1q_1 on goods other than x. The price of $x = OM/OQ'$ is shown as p_1 in the price-quantity plane. If p_x falls, the budget line MQ' shifts to MQ'': with the same money income it is possible to buy a larger quantity of x. The individual once again equates the slope of the price line OM/OQ'' ($= p_x$) to the ratio of the marginal utility of x to the marginal utility of money: he moves to R_2 on the higher indifference curve 2. The income and substitution effect of the fall in p_x can now be broken up rather neatly. We deprive the individual of the gain in real in-

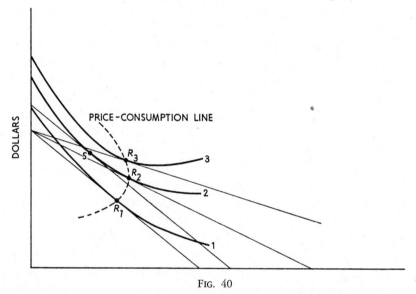

FIG. 40

come from the fall in p_x by shifting the budget line down, without changing its slope, until it is tangent to 1. Even if the individual were no better off from the fall in p_x, he would move to S and thus buy more of x. When we restore his income gain, he moves to R_2. Consequently, the fact that he buys more of x when the price falls is due to the combined impact of the substitution and the income effect. Graphic inspection (Fig. 40) will show that a positively sloped demand curve implies successively flatter indifference curves, so that the price-consumption line bends back on itself. This must mean that increments of money income are being spent on some substitute y, which makes the individual increasingly reluctant to acquire additional units of x at the same price.

The slope of an indifference curve expresses the marginal rate of substitution MRS of two goods. In our case $MRS = MU_x/MU_e$.

We have drawn the indifference curves as convex, showing a diminishing MRS as smaller and smaller amounts of money are offered for unit increments of x. It is sometimes asserted that convexity of an indifference curve is tantamount to assuming the law of diminishing marginal utility. This is a misunderstanding. If the consumer could compare the magnitude of the utility gained by moving from indifference curve 1 to curve 2 relative to the utility gained in moving from 2 to 3, then utility would be measurable in cardinal terms. Diminishing marginal utility would then be shown by successively closer indifference curves. But the indifference-curve approach assumes only that the individual can rank total utilities in order of magnitude: he knows that curve 2 is higher than curve 1 but he does not know how much higher. But what of the shape of a single indifference curve? For any bundle made up of two goods, more of at least one good raises the total utility of the bundle—on anybody's definition of utility—and moves the individual onto a higher indifference curve. But what happens if we move along an indifference curve by having more of one good but less of the other? Is it necessarily true that MRS diminishes?

The notion of "indifference" itself is not subject to direct measurement. Although choices between what we might call "unambiguously separate" bundles of goods—bundles that differ by having more of at least one of the goods—can be rationalized by an ordinal utility scale, no operational method for rationalizing the exact shape of an indifference curve has ever been devised. The indifference-curve technique requires us to compare *signs* of marginal utility: as we move along the curve toward the y-axis, MU_x is negative and MU_y is positive, but the relative value of the marginal utilities themselves are not defined. We know, that is to say, that indifference curves are negatively inclined, but their precise shape is not determined. The use of indifference curves by themselves implies nothing more than measurability of utility unique up to a monotone transformation. The individual states that he prefers $4x$ to $1y$ but not $2x$ to $1y$. We may infer that he would be indifferent between, say, $3x$ and $1y$. Furthermore, it follows that to be reduced to $2x$ he must be compensated by more than $1y$, but we do not presume that he can say how much more y would be equivalent to a unit reduction in x. To make that presumption is to suppose that the individual can compare increments and decrements of marginal utility and would thus imply cardinal measurement of utility.

Since indifference maps are not directly observable, convexity can be inferred only from observations of people's behavior. Concave indifference curves have the implication that the individual will succumb to monomania. If the budget line were given as shown in Figure 41, R would not be a stable equilibrium point, for the individual could get on a higher indifference curve by moving along his budget line. Maximizing utility, the individual would end up consuming only *x* and no *y;* if the budget line met the extremities of the same indifference curve, the

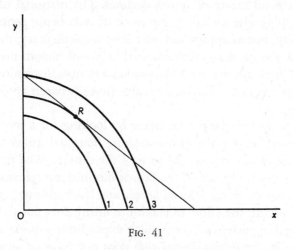

FIG. 41

individual could spend his income either entirely on *y* or entirely on *x*. Concavity seems to be equivalent to a distaste for variety and on a priori grounds this might occur. We must conclude that concave indifference maps cannot be ruled out. Nevertheless, distaste for variety cannot be considered modal behavior and so we *may* take convexity to be the general case.[2]

[2] We may assume that utility mountains have no dip in their surface. What we have is contour lines on which we cannot write absolute numbers. Only quadrant III is

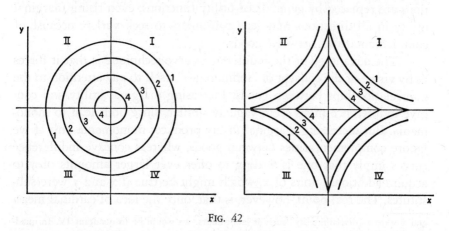

FIG. 42

relevant for the analysis of the usual case in which both *x* and *y* are what Jevons called "commodities": having more of at least one good increases total utility. If *y* were income

Granted that we may draw convex indifference maps, this does not mean that we are assuming diminishing marginal utility. To say that I will offer successively smaller amounts of nuts in exchange for additions to my stock of apples is not the same thing as saying that for me the marginal utility of apples declines. The marginal utility of apples, everything else including my stock of nuts being constant, might be increasing, but as apples and nuts are complementary, the more apples I have, the greater is the marginal utility of nuts to me and hence the less willing I am to offer equal amounts of nuts to acquire additional apples. In consequence, the indifference curves between apples and nuts will be convex.

This point may be driven home by looking for a moment at the kind of "proof" of the law of diminishing marginal utility that used to appear in textbooks around the turn of the century. The proof is modeled on the classical proof of the law of diminishing returns in agriculture and proceeds by *reductio ad absurdum*. If we assume that marginal utility is constant, the effort to maximize utility does not yield a unique and predictable pattern of consumer's expenditure among a variety of goods, that is, the equimarginal rule does not produce an equilibrium pattern of allocation. If we assume rising marginal utility, the consumer will buy the product with the highest or most rapidly rising marginal utility and thus succumb to monomania. Since people do, in fact, consume a large variety of goods, rising marginal utility must be rejected along with constant marginal utility. This proof shows at best that the marginal utility of some goods falls, not that it falls for every good. But what is worse is that the proof depends on the implicit assumption of independence among the utility functions. If the additive utility functions are replaced by generalized utility functions, even rising marginal utility in all directions may lead consumers to seek variety because of complementarities between goods.

The advantage of the indifference-curve technique is that it forces us by virtue of the concept of "indifference" itself to pay attention to the interrelationships between goods. Increasing marginal utility and concave indifference maps seem vaguely similar, since both lead to monomania. But increasing marginal utility produces monomania only if we ignore complementarities between goods, whereas concave indifference curves imply that one is willing to offer ever larger amounts of y to acquire additional units of x, which might be true if x and y were substitutes. The real point, however, is that, once the idea of cardinal meas-

---

and x were a "discommodity" such as labor-hours, we would be in quadrant IV. In quadrant I, both goods are "discommodities" or nuisances.

urement is dropped, the very notion of marginal utility as a uniquely determinable quantity loses all meaning. Diminishing marginal rate of substitution is *not* equivalent to diminishing marginal utility.

The Revealed Preference Approach. There is no doubt that we often prefer A to B much more strongly than we prefer B to C. Such introspective feelings, however, have no operational consequence. We would have chosen A over B and B over C even if he had preferred A to B much less than B to C. At the level of observation, the idea of preference intensity has no meaning. Furthermore, if we are going to dismiss introspective evidence, the notion of indifference is as objectionable as the concept of preference intensity. No *single* act of choice on the part of the consumer can prove his indifference between two situations. Unless we are going to give indifference a statistical meaning—the individual does not choose B over A more frequently than he chooses A over B in a large number of observations—we must dismiss the concept of indifference with the same behaviorist argument that we used against the notion of preference intensity. Samuelson has shown that it is possible to derive demand curves solely from an individual's "revealed preferences." The only assumption we must make is that of "transitivity": if the individual is found to have chosen A over B in a particular instance, then he cannot consistently choose B over A in any other instance. The assumption may be stated more simply: no two observations of choice behavior can provide conflicting evidence of an individual's preferences.

The "Fundamental Theorem of Consumption Theory," according to Samuelson, states that the demand for a commodity always changes in the same direction as that of a change in the income of the consumer; positively sloped income curves always imply negatively inclined demand curves. To demonstrate this theorem, let us suppose that the consumer devotes his entire income to the purchase of only two goods. The original price-income situation is represented in Figure 43 by AB, and the consumer is observed to have chosen the combination x and y represented by the point R. R is "revealed" to have been preferred to all other combinations of x and y within the area OAB available to him. Suppose that the price of x falls and that the new price-income line is AC. Let us now deprive the consumer of an amount of money income that would leave him with exactly enough to buy the same quantities of everything at the lower price of x. The new price-income line DE is parallel to the old line AC and passes through R. It is evident that the consumer cannot choose any point above R on DE for the simple reason that R was revealed to be preferred to any such point in the original price-income situation. To choose a point that was previously available but was revealed by his choice of R to have been worse than R is tantamount to inconsistent behavior. We rule out this possibility by assumption. Hence, the consumer must either choose R or a point in the newly available shaded area; he must choose to buy either the same amount of x or more. If we now grant him back the amount of money originally taken away from him, he will buy more of x if the income elasticity of demand for x is positive. We have, therefore, proved that the demand curve for x is negatively inclined if the income curve for x is positively inclined. On the same grounds, if the income

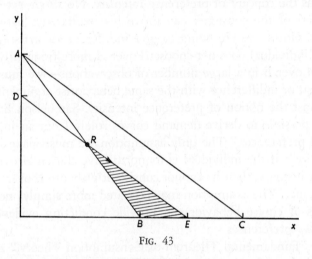

FIG. 43

effect is negative, the change in demand owing to a change in price is indeterminate. Since the substitution effect cannot be isolated from the income effect on the level of observation, the "revealed preference" approach cannot distinguish between the Giffen case of a negative income effect combined with a weak substitution effect and a negative income effect combined with a strong substitution effect.

Marshallian Demand Curves. It is possible, as we have seen, to rationalize the negative slope of the demand curve for "unimportant" goods by means of utility theory. But why not deduce the demand curve directly from recorded data? After all, the fact that quantity and price are generally inversely related had been known long before utility was thought to be measurable. Price-quantity data, however, refer to successive observations through time, whereas a demand curve refers to alternative intentions to purchase at one and the same time. To construct a Marshallian demand curve, we have to ask consumers how much they would purchase if prices were other than they are but other things were exactly the same. Obviously, their answers would constitute guesses. From casual observation we feel quite sure that most demand curves are negatively inclined. But this is hardly a satisfactory foundation for so important a concept. In the absence of elaborate econometric techniques, we have little alternative but to deduce the negative inclination of the demand curve from fundamental psychological postulates.

The effort to link utility to demand in the Marshallian manner via the "law of satiable wants" is beset by two difficulties. When we replace additive by generalized utility functions, the law of diminishing marginal utility does not furnish "one general Law of Demand." Moreover, a generalized utility function robs us of any operational procedure for the cardinal measurement of utility. With the elimination of cardinal measurement, the very notion of deriving *diminishing* increments of utility from additional units of a good loses all meaning and it is no longer possible to make statements about the welfare effects of a change in price.

No wonder then that Marshall tried to simplify his argument by the device of holding MU_e constant. Although he spoke of one general Law of Demand, he asserted that the whole aggregate demand curve for bread, and particularly the demand curve for bread among the poorer classes, is positively inclined, a proposition that has ever since been labeled "Giffen's Paradox." By abstracting from the income effect he eliminated all the practical consequences of intercommodity relationships and in this way rescued the additive utility function. If the utility functions for individual goods are additive, goods are necessarily independent of each other. And, if they are, utility can be cardinally measured along the lines proposed by Fisher.[3] It is true that we can "explain" consumer behavior just as well with ordinal as with cardinal measurement of utility. Consumers are expected only to equate ratios of marginal utility to ratios of prices, and the theory of price determination never requires either interpersonal comparisons of utility or intrapersonal comparisons of the utility differences between pair-wise choices. But Marshall was reluctant to abandon the use of the demand curve to measure the consumer's surplus from a change in price, and

---

[3] It must be kept in mind that we are concerned at this point with the derivation of *individual* demand curves from individual utility curves. A generalized utility function may also contain as one of its variables the effect of other people's utility functions. This poses a new additivity problem. Since each individual demand curve is drawn up on the assumption of given demand functions of other consumers in the same market, the market demand curve for the product can no longer be constructed by simply summing horizontally over the individual demand functions; this would be like explaining fashions by the summation of individual ideas about dress. Interdependence between the individual preference functions raises special problems in the interpretation of market-demand curves.

for that reason, despite all admissions to the contrary, he retained both the additive utility function and the concept of an approximately constant MU_e.

Marshall's uneasiness about the assumption of a constant MU_e may account for the failure to draw up an explicit list of the restrictions placed upon the demand curve for an individual commodity. The traditional description of the content of the pound of *ceteris paribus*, a description derived from Edgeworth and never repudiated by Marshall, includes such items as: (1) tastes, (2) money income, (3) the prices of closely related goods, (4) the prices of unrelated goods, and (5) expectations about future prices. The logical corollary of ignoring income effects is to hold real income, not money income, constant along the demand curve. In the foregoing list, however, (2), (3), and (4) together imply that real income varies with every change in the price of the product in question. Moreover, (3) and (4) violate the general assumption of the *Principles* that the purchasing power of money is to be kept constant; every change in the price of x unaccompanied by an opposite change in some other price alters the value of money.

There are two ways of resolving this dilemma. One is to argue that the real-income effect of a change in the price of an "unimportant" commodity, and the corresponding change in the purchasing power of money, is so small as to be negligible. The other, recently advocated by Friedman, is to replace (4) by the condition that the prices of all unrelated goods move inversely to the price of x so as to keep real income constant along the demand curve for x. The latter definition would indeed avoid most of the pitfalls in the usual Marshallian treatment. A Friedman-Marshall demand curve *must* slope negatively under the conditions implied in its very construction. Moreover, by freezing only the prices of obvious substitutes and complements, and by treating only the behavior of an average of all other prices, it claims to provide a more practical and useful concept of the demand curve. But, however impractical may be the usual injunction to keep each individual price constant, it is no less impractical to be told to keep *some* prices constant. Any specified set of price changes must be arbitrary, since the changes imposed are not necessarily those that would occur in the real world in association with changes in the price of x. The traditional approach is also arbitrary in specifying no change in any price, but at least it is not ambiguous. Moreover, it is not clear what starting price is to be considered for drawing up the Friedman-Marshall demand curve of a commodity; keeping the level of an individual's real income constant implies a different offsetting price variation for each different starting price.

In reality, the income effect is as inherent a part of the influences determining consumer behavior as is the substitution effect. It is true that a demand curve drawn up so as to allow for income effects may be either negatively or positively inclined; the usual Marshallian demand curve has no empirical implications that are capable of being contra- dicted. It is also true that Marshall himself occasionally entertained the idea of interpreting demand curves as constant real-income curves. Nevertheless, the traditional method of drawing demand curves has the advantage of focusing attention on the fact that price changes in the real world do invariably affect the real income of buyers in the market and so shift their demand curves in all other markets. Conceptually, the traditional demand curve is simpler to grasp and closer to the spirit of approximation that characterizes partial equilibrium analysis. Eco- nometrically, the overwhelming difficulties in the way of actually draw- ing up a demand curve constructed on the traditional interpretation are no greater than those involved in drawing it up on the Friedman inter- pretation.

The real world contains no objective entity corresponding to *the* demand curve. For some purposes it is conceivable that a constant real- income curve might prove more useful. For most purposes, however, the traditional interpretation provides a superior instrument for grasp- ing the inverse price-quantity relationship asserted by the Law of De- mand. The concept of a demand curve has, after all, only a limited practical applicability. A demand curve, like a supply curve, is an aid to straight thinking. It is nothing but a device for organizing the forces that influence price into one or another category. The Marshallian "cross" of demand and supply helps us understand why a free market tends to clear itself, why an equilibrium price once reached may be stable, and how prices act as signals transmitting relevant information to buyers and sellers. They permit us to indicate, without quantitative precision, what would happen to price and quantity if income or tech- nology underwent specified changes. They help us to grasp the conse- quences of taxes and subsidies, price floors and price ceilings. It is not too much to say that almost everything we know about the behavior of the economic system can be illuminated by way of reference to the fun- damental cross of demand and supply. Looked at in this way, there is nothing to choose between the two interpretations of the demand curve. The method of holding money income and all other individual prices constant yields a richer but also a more complicated theory of demand. That is all.

The Status of the Subjective Theory of Value. By making utility the "explanation" of consumer behavior, the sponsors of the subjective theory of value ran into a double-barreled opposition: it was argued that the underlying psychology of the theory is bad or at least questionable psychology and that, moreover, the psychological aspects of consumer behavior were irrelevant to the objective facts of the economic process, which runs its course irrespective of individual feelings. Much of this opposition was based on a confusion between the two meanings given to the word "utility." In the theory of consumer behavior, utility is a quantity that it is useful to regard an individual as maximizing in interpreting and predicting his behavior. A utility function is nothing more than a way of describing an individual's preferences between various real or hypothetical alternatives. Such a function no more "explains" an individual's choices than a production-transformation curve "explains" the state of technology. In welfare economics, however, utility is a quantity that an individual "should" maximize or that the social arrangement "should" help him to maximize. Here utility is indeed a quantitative concept, whereas, in the theory of consumer behavior resting on ordinal utility, utility is, strictly speaking, no quantity at all but simply a choice indicator.

As soon as this distinction is firmly grasped, most of the criticism that was at one time leveled against utility theory as a theory of consumer behavior falls to the ground. The most common objection found in the critical literature is the objection to the so-called hedonistic premise, the tendency to identify the desire that prompts an individual to purchase with the underlying "utility" or satisfaction that he derives from the purchase. Marginal utility theory, ignoring as it does the habitual and conventional forces that shape desires and wants, the critics argued, constitutes an inadequate explanation of consumer behavior. Now it is clear that price, if it measures any subjective quantity, measures desires; it is a measure of satisfactions only to the degree to which desire is an accurate reflection of satisfaction. The effect of ignorance on the part of buyers of the quality of the product, the effect of fraud or misrepresentation on the part of sellers, and possibly the effect of aggressive advertising as such is to increase the disparity between desire and satisfaction. These constitute important problems in welfare economics, not in the theory of demand. The law of diminishing marginal utility may be replaced by the law of diminishing marginal desire. The idea of diminishing marginal desire may be replaced by diminishing marginal rate of substitution; this would not alter by one jot the effort to deduce the Law of Demand from fundamental postulates about consumer behavior. The theory of price determination does not require the "hedonistic premise."

The defenders of the subjective theory of value were almost as confused on this point as the critics. After citing impulse, habits, self-denial, mistaken expectation, and other causes of disparity between desire and satisfaction, Marshall concluded that, in the absence of direct measurement of either desire or satisfaction, we must fall back on price and make it serve "with all its faults, *both* for desires which prompt activities, and for the satisfactions that result from them." This is a foot-note to the first page of a chapter devoted to the theory of demand! The tendency to draw facile welfare conclusions from utility theory, ignoring inequalities of the distribution of income, the inadequacy of price as a measure of welfare, the difficulties in making meaningful interpersonal comparisons—the chief offender being Marshall himself—was largely responsible for producing a skeptical attitude toward the achievements of marginal utility analysis.

When the misconceptions of the nature of utility theory are cleared away, what is left is a profound distaste for economic analysis that proceeds by drawing up demand and supply curves on the basis of *given* wants and *given* techniques. The theory of consumption, it has been argued, should throw light on the inherent tendency of wants to expand and change instead of being concerned with the mechanical process by which given wants are satisfied. With the growth of advertising and other forms of nonprice competition, business firms set out actively not only to create new wants but to foster "pecuniary canons of taste." Once consumers have developed the habit of judging quality by price, every change in price affects their tastes. There is no point in drawing up demand curves for homogeneous products on the basis of given tastes when every change in price alters the nature of the product in consumers' minds and so shifts the demand curves. The traditional theory of consumer behavior, based as it is on the belief that consumers' tastes are stable and independent of prices, must be abandoned in favor of a broad socioeconomic theory of consumption. With various degrees of vehemence, this kind of criticism has been voiced over and over again by almost every member of the American Institutionalist School and by Anglo-American Marxists.

In its extreme form, an emphasis upon the inherent instability of wants is destructive not only of the theory of demand but also of traditional welfare economics grounded upon the doctrine of "consumers' sovereignty." It is an objection that cannot be lightly dismissed. Insofar as demand theory is concerned, it is perfectly true that it cannot get along without the assumption of stable tastes. The fundamental principle of utility theory is that consumers act "as if" they were maximizing utility, and this principle can be translated into the "consistency postulate": if an individual prefers *A* to *B* in one situation, he will not be found to choose *B* in preference to *A* in another situation. It is clear that consistency means constant tastes and that inconsistency can be interpreted as a change in tastes. Indeed, the "consistency postulate" amounts to the proposition that a utility function exists, a question that has been discussed by mathematical economists since the days of Fisher and Pareto under the heading of "the problem of integrability." If it were really true that tastes were always in a process of flux, consumer behavior would be utterly unpredictable—at least in the absence of the broad theory of consumption that critics ask for—and none of the familiar propositions of the theory of demand would stand scientific scrutiny.

It is not clear how far the critics want to carry this argument. Even an Institutionalist may occasionally permit himself the luxury of drawing demand and supply curves to illustrate the workings of the market mechanism. If the pattern of wants is never stable in any market for at least a short period of time, it is difficult to see why businessmen spend so much money creating new wants; why generate new wants if their inherent instability makes it impossible to guarantee that they can be exploited for a definite period of time? Without denying that tastes are continuously being molded by the action of producers, it is still possible to investigate the pattern of consumers' demand on the provisional assumption of given wants. No doubt the formal theory of demand cannot be applied to the real world of imperfect competition without serious qualification. But that is hardly an argument for placing a ban on demand curves.

Acceptance of the concept of a demand function as a useful tool of analysis does not, of course, constitute an endorsement of traditional utility theory. We could follow Cournot's and Cassel's approach, employing demand functions directly without a utility substructure. The reason why most economists have rejected this approach is that it seems tantamount to throwing away information. Since demand curves cannot be simply observed, it is hoped that the specification of behavioral assumptions—and that is all utility theory is—will add information on the nature of demand functions. And yet the long and tortuous history of utility theory presents a disheartening picture. Few of the sponsors of utility theory bothered to test the implications of the theory, and, indeed, on the whole, utility theory was not a fruitful source of hypotheses about demand. The attitude was that utility theory was merely a matter of systematic common sense. The inadequacy of this criterion was demonstrated, as Stigler has said, by the slowness with which utility theory progressed: "The additive utility function was popularized in the 1870's; it was 1909 before the implication of positively sloped income curves was derived. The generalized utility function was proposed in 1881; it was 1915 before its implications were derived. The chief of these implications is that, if consumers do not buy less of a commodity when their incomes rise, they will surely buy less when the price of the commodity rises. This was the chief product—so far as hypotheses on economic behavior go—of the long labors of a very large number of able economists. These very able economists, and their predecessors, however, had known all along that demand curves have negative slopes, quite independently of their utility theorizing."

2. MARSHALLIAN WELFARE ECONOMICS

Consumer's Surplus. If it were possible to measure the marginal utility of money income by some such method as that suggested by Neumann and Morgenstern, it would be possible to trace the consumer's marginal-utility function for a particular good from his demand schedule by the equilibrium formula $MU_x = p_x \cdot MU_e$. But even without cardinal measurement of MU_e, we can say that the marginal utility of an "unimportant" commodity is equal to its price measured in terms of MU_e treated as a constant. For small variations in real income we can assume that the addition of one dollar to the consumer's total expenditure increases his total utility by a constant amount. Thus, the price that a consumer is willing to pay for a particular quantity of x directly expresses the marginal utility of x to him. Likewise, the *total* utility of acquiring a certain quantity of x, given the fact that x is "unimportant" in the budget of the consumer, may be derived by summing the marginal utilities associated with the successive increments of x from 0 to C (Fig. 44). With each thin parallelogram expressing the marginal utility of a finite increment of x, the total utility of the quantity $OC = OABC$. The consumer would be willing to pay the sum $OABC$, but he actually pays $OEBC$ for quantity OC. Hence, AEB equals the consumer's surplus from buying amount OC of x; this triangle measures the loss in the consumer's welfare if he were prevented from buying any quantity of x. The surplus is really a utility surplus, but it is expressible in pecuniary terms because of our invariable unit of measurement, namely, the marginal utility of expenditures in general.[4]

Marshall defines this kind of consumer's surplus as "the excess of the price which he would be willing to pay rather than go without the thing, over that which he actually does pay." We can think of it, in the manner of Dupuit, as the amount that can be extracted from the consumer by discriminatory pricing. If a monopolist could shade his price along the consumer's demand curve, his marginal revenue would be

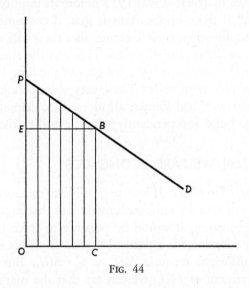

FIG. 44

equal to the price charged for the last unit sold, for he could always sell an extra unit at a lower price without lowering the price of every unit. The maximum possible gain from this kind of quantity discrimination is Dupuit's price surplus, being a money measure of the utility surplus to a consumer from being able to buy each unit of the commodity at the same price. Mathematically, the surplus is *estimated* as the sum of money represented by the definite integral, from zero to the given quantity, of the individual demand function minus the total outlay on the commodity in question.

[4] The marginal utility of money income is not the only invariable measure we might use. In his *Alphabet of Economic Science* (1889), Wicksteed suggested the use of "a given amount of work as the standard unit by which to estimate the magnitude of satisfaction. For example, one might express the utility of numbers of tons of coal by the lifting work one is willing to do to acquire another hundred weight." "In academical circles," Wicksteed remarked, "it is not unusual to take an hour of correcting exam papers as the standard measure of pleasure and pains." Despite this convincing piece of evidence, however, there is no reason to believe that it is possible to put Smithian welfare economics on a sound basis by defining an invariant unit of disutility of labor.

It is sometimes objected that demand curves are usually asymptotic to the price axis. If the individual's offer for the first unit is not finitely limited, so that the demand curve is open-topped, the integral under the curve is infinite. But this objection is easily overcome by measuring consumer's surplus from some selected value of $q_x > 0$. The more fatal objection to the estimate of the price surplus as the triangle under the demand curve is that it is difficult to believe that real income would remain constant along the whole of the demand curve even for "unimportant" commodities. If we start with a given income for the individual and let him buy successive units of x at the maximum price he will pay for each unit, we trace out a constant real-income curve, a Friedman-Marshall demand curve, or, as Hicks called it, a "marginal

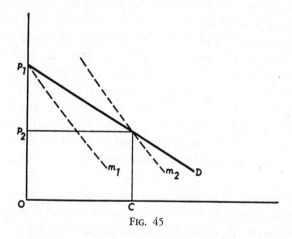

FIG. 45

valuation curve," which always lies below the Marshallian demand curve at lower prices and above it at higher prices. This is due to the fact that real income increases along a Marshallian demand curve as the price falls; at lower prices, the constant real income curve shifts, as it were, to the right; the loci of intersections of the shifting constant real-income curve with the successive horizontal price lines trace out a Marshallian demand curve. (See Fig. 45.) If the starting price is p_2, the marginal valuation curve is m_2; if the starting price is p_1, the maximum price the individual is willing to pay for the first unit of x, the marginal valuation curve is m_1. An unambiguous measure of consumer's surplus can be derived only from something like a marginal valuation curve that holds real income constant by showing all units purchased separately at their full marginal prices. For a given quantity of x purchased, the Marshallian demand curve overstates the amount of consumer's surplus.

It was partly in recognition of this objection that Marshall confined himself for all practical purposes to the measurement of the consumer's surplus from a given *change* in price. In all important applications of the concept of consumer's surplus, Marshall concerned himself solely with the range of normal price variations, defining the consumer's surplus from a change in price as the area between the demand curve and the price axis within the range of the price movement. We will follow Hicks in calling this "Marshall's measure." So long as we consider only small changes in the quantities consumed of an "unimportant" commodity, the marginal valuation curve practically coincides with the demand curve and the psychological gain or loss to the consumer of a small change in price may be read directly off the demand curve. This means that we cannot really employ the concept of consumer's surplus to measure the satisfaction afforded from being able to buy a given amount of x at a price below what one would be willing to pay rather than do without it altogether, at least not with usual Marshallian demand curves. It is true that the notion remains a useful one for demonstrating the fact that the price paid for an article is not a measure of the satisfaction it affords, but we cannot measure this surplus in any meaningful way. At best we can appraise the welfare effect of one price-quantity situation compared to another, provided the expenditure on the commodity in question is a small fraction of total expenditures.

Restatement. The difficulties in measuring consumer's surplus from a demand curve can be illustrated by means of indifference curves. Placing money on the vertical axis and the commodity x on the horizontal axis, Marshall's assumption of a constant marginal utility of money corresponds to indifference curves that are vertically parallel: at any given quantity of x the slope of the curves, expressing the marginal rate of substitution between money and x or MU_x/MU_e is the same no matter how large the quantity of money on the ordinate. *MRS* depends only on the quantity consumed and not on the amount of money spent on goods in general. The individual's money spending is so large that small changes in the volume of his spending do not affect his willingness to part with it; or else as MU_e falls with increases in the quantity of money, so does MU_x, even when its quantity is constant, because money and x are competitive goods. For either reason, as we proceed along any vertical line, *MRS* is constant because both MU_x and MU_e change in the same proportion. In consequence, at any given quantity of x, the *MRS* of every indifference curve is equal to p_x: the system of indifference curves reduces to a single *MRS* curve that is the same as the demand curve. (See Fig. 46.) Suppose the individual is at R, with given income M; at the price structure MQ he buys O_{q_1} of x, spending R_{q_1} on other goods and TR on x. The price of $x = TR/MT = OM/OQ$. Since the slopes of the indifference curves at S, R, and T are

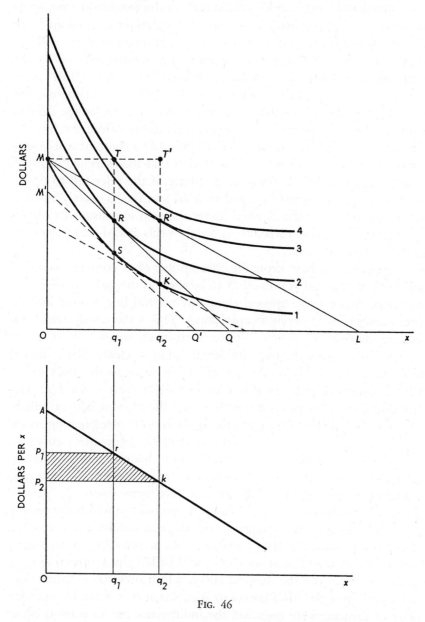

FIG. 46

the same, being equal to the slope of the price line MQ, the MRS of all the indifference curves at the quantity O_{q_1} are equal to p_1 in the price-quantity plane. At a lower price of x, given by the price line ML, the individual would move to R' and by analogous reasoning $OM/OL = p_2$. In this way the whole demand curve for x may be derived from the indifference map.

Marshall's price surplus corresponds to the maximum amount the consumer will offer when confronted with the choice of x on an all-or-nothing basis. If the consumer is at the initial situation R, he will at a maximum offer TS rather than go without x, for the offer of TS will leave him no worse off than being deprived of x. $RS = MM'$ measures the price surplus from being able to buy O_{q_1} of x at the uniform price p_1, and this is exactly equal to the area p_1Ar under the demand curve above the expenditure rectangle. This follows from the fact that the demand curve that we have derived is in fact a constant real-income curve, drawn up as it is on the assumption that the marginal utility of money income is strictly constant. Similarly, if the price fell to p_2, the new price surplus would be equal to $R'K$, and this is exactly equal to the area p_2Ak under the demand curve; the gain in consumer's surplus from the fall in price, therefore, is equal to the shaded area p_2p_1rk under the demand curve.

Suppose we now drop the assumption of a constant marginal utility of money and permit MRS to increase as the quantity of money increases. As we move upward along any vertical line, we cut indifference curves at successively steeper slopes. This is the case in which the income elasticity of demand for x is positive: parallel shifts in the budget line increase the quantity demanded of x. Hence, the system of indifference curves is no longer reducible to a single MRS curve. Each indifference curve now has its own MRS curve. (See Fig. 47.) For example, at the price-income line MQ the amount bought will be O_{q_1}. The dotted lines $m_{1,2,3}$, are the MRS curves corresponding to the indifference curves 1, 2, 3, for the amount O_{q_1} of x. MRS curve m_2 lies above m_1, m_3 lies above m_2, and so on, because the slope of the indifference curves at a given quantity of x rises with increasing amounts of money; the MRS curves have been drawn as parallel straight lines for convenience. Thus, p_2 is the price at which the amount O_{q_1} will be bought, being equal to the slope of indifference curve 2 at R. Similarly, p_1 on the MRS curve m_3 is the slope of indifference curve 3 at R' and is the price at which O_{q_2} will be bought. Connecting these points, we trace out the demand curve, which now has a flatter slope than any one of the MRS curves. It is apparent that if the income elasticity of demand were negative, the indifference curves converging to the left instead of to the right, the successive MRS curves would lie below one another and the demand curve would have a steeper slope than any one of the MRS curves.

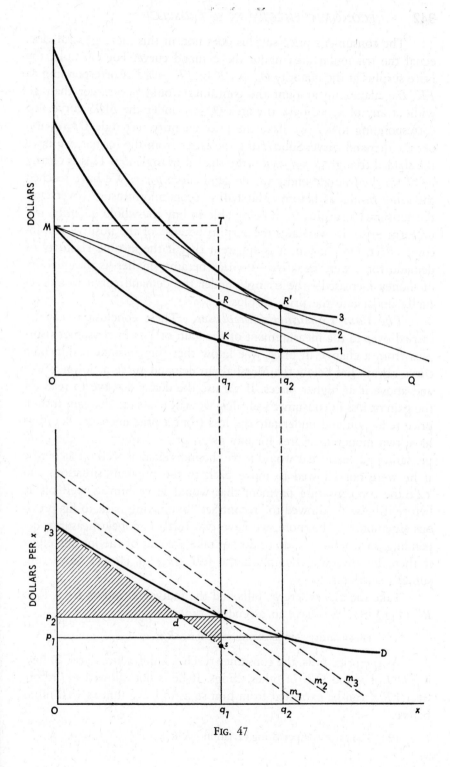

FIG. 47

The consumer's price surplus does not, in this more general case, equal the triangular area under the demand curve. For example, the price surplus at the quantity O_{q_1} is RK or $TK - RT$. Corresponding to TK, the maximum amount the consumer would pay rather than go without any of x, we have the area Op_3sq_1 under the MRS curve m_1; corresponding to RT we have the price-quantity rectangle Op_2rq_1 under the demand curve. Subtracting the latter from the former, we have the shaded triangle p_2p_3d *minus* the shaded triangle drs. This is clearly less than the triangle under the demand curve p_2p_3r. We have reached the same results as before: Marshall's "economic measure" overstates the consumer's surplus from being able to buy the whole quantity at a uniform price. It overstates the surplus because of the positive real-income effect. Once again, it is apparent that if the income elasticity of demand for x were negative—if MRS became smaller as the quantity of money increased—the triangle under the demand curve would actually understate the price surplus.

The Four Consumer's Surpluses. These conclusions can be carried over to the measurement of the gain or loss in consumer's surplus from a change in price. We know that the constant real-income curve always lies below the Marshallian demand curve at lower prices and above it at higher prices. If we use the demand curve to read off the gain or loss in consumer's surplus, we will overstate the gain from a price reduction and understate the loss from a price increase. We thus have two money measures for any given price change: (1) the compensating payment that would leave the individual as well off as before if he were not allowed to move back to the previous situation, and (2) the compensating payment that would leave him as well off as before if he were allowed to "recontract" by moving back to his previous situation. Furthermore, we have two further money measures, depending on whether we do or do not take account of the income effect if there be any. We thus reach the full array of Hicks's "four consumer's surpluses."

Take the case where p_x falls and the individual moves from R to R' (Fig. 48). We have in ascending order:

(1) The quantity-compensating variation—$R'r'$.

As the price falls, the consumer reaches indifference curve 2, buying OQ of x and QR' of other things. If he is not allowed to "recontract," $R'r'$ can be extracted from him so as to leave him as well off as before.

(2) The price-compensating variation—$R'R'_1$.

Actually, the consumer would be better off after losing $R'r'$ because a price line through r' would be tangent to a higher indifference curve than 1. A sum equal to $R'R_1'$ should be extracted from him to offset the initial gain in real income from the price fall. The distinction

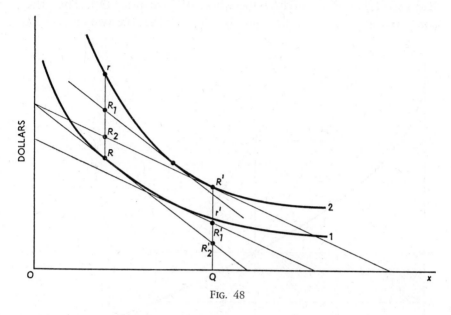

FIG. 48

between (1) and (2) would not occur if the indifference curves were vertically parallel.

(3) The price-equivalent variation—RR_1.

If the consumer were forced once again to pay the higher price but was allowed to move back to the price quantity point R, RR_1 is the gain in money income that would offset the loss of forgoing the reduction in p_x.

(4) The quantity-equivalent variation—Rr.

Again, (3) would put the individual on an indifference curve below 2. Rr is a measure of the full gain in real income from the fall in p_x. The distinction between (3) and (4), like that between (1) and (2), disappears if the indifference curves are vertically parallel.

Which of these four measures corresponds to "Marshall's measure": the area between the demand curve and the price axis within the range of the price movement? None of them precisely. (See Fig. 49.) If the *MRS* curve m_1 is drawn up for a constant real income the same as at price OB, the quantity-compensating variation is $ABCG$ minus GFL, the amount $OBCLq_2$ he would be willing to pay for q_2 to be as well off as before minus the amount $OAFq_2$, which he actually does pay. The individual would now be better off than if he had been compelled to purchase the extra quantity of q_1q_2 at price OB but worse off than if he had been allowed to purchase the whole of q_2 at price OA. The price-compensating variation, therefore, is $ABCG$. Thus, the two compensat-

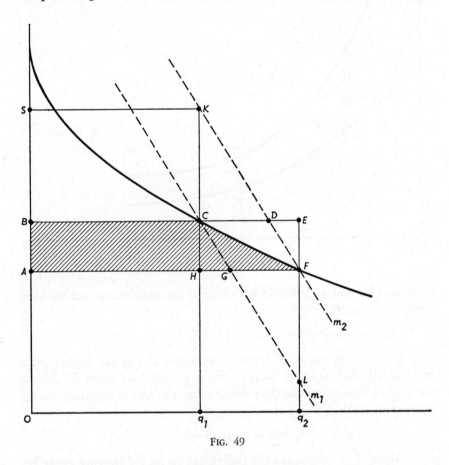

FIG. 49

ing payments fall short of "Marshall's measure." On the other hand, the two equivalent variations exceed "Marshall's measure." If m_2 is drawn up for a constant real income the same as at price OA, the price-equivalent variation evaluated at the lower quantity q_1 is $ABDF$ minus CKD. The individual loses $ABDF$ by being forced again to pay the higher price, but he gains CKD because he is also allowed to buy the smaller quantity associated with the higher price. The full quantity-equivalent variation, however, is $ABDF$ because CKD could be extracted from him without making him any worse off. Thus the two equivalent variations are greater than "Marshall's measure."

It should be noted that, for a rise in price, the gains and losses in terms of utility are the same as for an equivalent fall in price, but consumer's surplus measured in terms of money is not because the value of money in terms of goods is different in the two cases. In effect, for a rise in price, the compensating variations become equivalent variations and *vice versa*.

Tax-Bounty Analysis. Having exhausted our patience on the subtleties of *estimating* the consumer's surplus from a demand curve, we must now observe that if the fraction of expenditures devoted to the commodity in question is small, and if the demand curve over the range between the two prices is highly elastic, the four consumer's surpluses merge and become equal to Marshall's measure. Presuming this is so, we have not yet shown how we can add the individual consumer's surplus in a market to obtain a measure of the aggregate consumers' surplus from a change in price. In Marshall's practical use of the tool, the apostrophe always comes after the *s:* it is the collective gain of all the buyers in a market that interests him. He begins with the individual's surplus and then employs the argument that most markets are homogeneous with respect to the income class of the buyers to justify the idea that the individual is a modal representative of the group. In this way he achieves addibility without raising the question of how the aggregate surplus is distributed among the individual buyers. It is clear that Veblenesque effects—other people's utilities or incomes appearing in each individual's utility function—destroy the possibility of aggregating consumer's surpluses. Even with additive utility functions, the notion of consumers' surplus involves us in interpersonal comparisons.

Marshall's principal use of the concept in tax-bounty analysis affords a beautiful example of the careless way in which neoclassical economics arrived at welfare conclusions. Marshall begins by showing that a tax imposed on a commodity obeying the law of constant returns results in a loss of consumers' surplus greater than the amount of the tax receipts, and, conversely, a subsidy in this case exceeds the gain in consumers' surplus. We couple a demand curve with a horizontal long-run supply curve (Fig. 50) and impose a uniform tax LA per unit of the product purchased. The supply curve shifts up (supply decreases) by the amount of the tax, and the loss of consumers' surplus is expressed by the area $SsRA$ under the demand curve. Tax receipts are equal to $SsRK$. The difference is shown by the shaded triangle. Likewise, if a subsidy shifts the long-run supply curve down from ss' to SS (supply increases), the triangle *RAL* above the demand curve represents the excess of subsidies paid out over consumers' surplus gained.

In the case of an industry operating under diminishing returns to scale, the bounty gives the same results as above. To overcome the forces making for increasing costs, the subsidy must be proportionately larger; once again, the subsidy exceeds the gain in consumers' surplus from a fall in price. The effects of a tax, however, are now less certain. Tax receipts here are *BARK* and the loss in consumers' surplus is

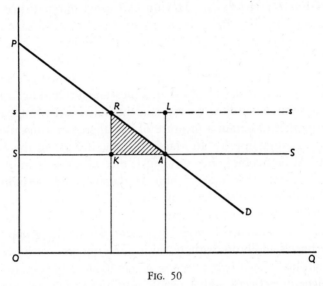

FIG. 50

CARD (Fig. 51). Since the rectangle *BCLK* exceeds the triangle *RDL,* tax receipts exceed the loss in consumers' surplus, the opposite result from what we obtained before. It is clear that this conclusion depends on the steepness of the long-run supply curves, on the strength of the forces making for diminishing returns.

With increasing returns, the long-run supply curve slopes downward. In this case loss in consumers' surplus must once again exceed tax receipts. Taxing a decreasing cost industry raises prices and thus raises the loss in consumers' surplus above tax receipts. The effect of a subsidy, however, depends entirely on the slope of the supply curve. (See Fig. 52.) The amount of the subsidy is *TREF* and the gain in consumers' surplus is *TRAC.* As shown, the shaded trapezoid is greater than the shaded triangle; therefore, the gain in consumers' surplus exceeds the subsidy payment. But if the supply curve were more elastic, we should approach the constant cost case: subsidy payments would exceed consumers' surplus.

The argument may be summed up by supposing that an increasing cost industry and a decreasing cost industry both face the same demand curve. (See Fig. 53.) Initially, the increasing cost industry produces Oq_2 and the decreasing cost industry produces Oq_1. A tax is placed on the first industry and the tax receipts are then used up to subsidize the

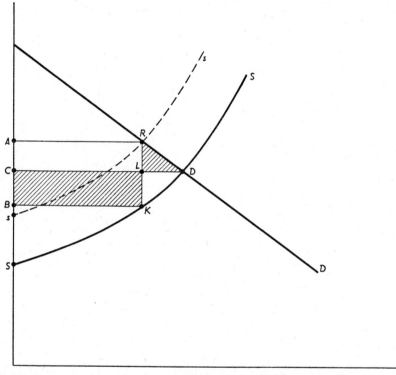

Fig. 51

second industry, that is, rectangle AG = rectangle CH. The *net* gain in consumers' surplus is shown by the shaded area $CBED$. The increasing cost industry now produces Oq_1 and the decreasing cost industry now produces Oq_3; the *net* gain in physical output is q_2q_3.

What may we conclude from all this? Apparently, it is possible for the state to increase consumers' welfare by taxing diminishing returns industries where the tax receipts *may* exceed the resulting loss in consumers' surplus, using the proceeds to subsidize increasing returns industries where the subsidy payment *may* be less than the resulting gain in consumers' surplus. The argument depends on the possibility of distinguishing diminishing from increasing returns industries, a formidable problem, as we shall come to see. Moreover, the forces making for diminishing or increasing returns must make themselves sharply felt in each group of industries. Marshall's proof is purely geometrical, but the underlying reasoning is perfectly simple. A tax on diminishing returns industries raises their supply prices and reduces the amount they supply; this makes it possible to produce the supply at lower cost, at a margin that represents a superior use of resources. The supply price rises, but by less than the tax, owing to the savings effected by pro-

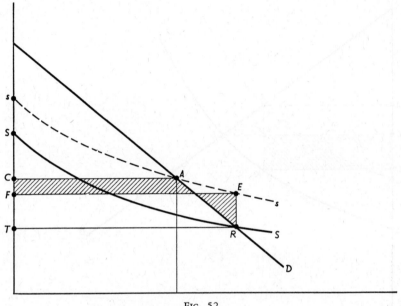

FIG. 52

ducing a superior marginal unit at lower cost. Tax proceeds are now used to subsidize increasing returns industries; their prices fall as the quantity supplied increases because the increased amount is supplied at lower costs per unit. Total satisfactions have increased all round because resources have been shifted from goods produced at rising supply prices to goods produced at falling supply prices.

Marshall expressed some caution about the practical applicability of this piece of reasoning. He warned of the administrative problems of collecting the tax and determining the level of the subsidy. It plays an important part, however, in his refutation of vulgar *Harmonielehre:* the doctrine that perfect competition necessarily maximizes the aggregate satisfactions of the community. This doctrine not only requires that income distribution be perfectly equal, he argued, but also assumes that all industries operate at constant cost. When the latter condition is not met, aggregate satisfactions can always be increased by pushing production in increasing returns industries at the expense of diminishing returns industries. In this sense, the tax-bounty analysis has at least negative significance in upsetting "the doctrine of maximum satisfactions."

The argument that we have outlined is drawn directly from Marshall's text. It is apparent, however, that it is incomplete because it fails

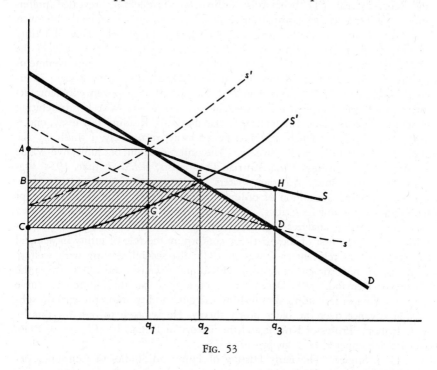

FIG. 53

to take into account the change in producers' as well as consumers' surplus resulting from a tax or subsidy. Marshall deals with the problem of producers' surplus in Appendix H to the *Principles,* but with considerable confusion. The confusion has to do with the dubious concept of a downward-sloping long-run supply curve. But before we can fruitfully examine this issue, we must digress to review Marshall's theory of short- and long-run price determination.

NOTES FOR FURTHER READING

1. *Utility and Demand.* The recent revival of cardinal utility in game theory has provoked a number of articles designed to clarify the meaning of utility measurement. The most useful of these is A. A. Alchian, "The Meaning of Utility Measurement," *AER,* March, 1953. The reader who wishes to pursue

the subject further is advised to look at S. A. Ozga, "Measurable Utility and Probability," *EJ*, September, 1956; D. Ellsberg, "Classic and Current Notions of Measurable Utility," *EJ*, September, 1954; and W. J. Baumol, "The Cardinal Utility Which is Ordinal," *EJ*, December, 1958—in that order. T. Majundar's controversial and lively monograph, *The Measurement of Utility* (1958), surveys the concepts of utility that have appeared in economic literature: in his own terminology, (1) introspective cardinalism—Jevons and Marshall; (2) introspective ordinalism—Hicks and Allen; (3) behaviorist cardinalism—Neumann and Morgenstern; (4) behaviorist ordinalism—Samuelson's revealed preference; (5) introspective cardinalism revived—Armstrong's marginal preference.

On the historical side there is G. J. Stigler, "The Development of Utility Theory," *JPE*, 1950, reprinted in *EET*, an important article that surveys the whole literature down to 1914 and concludes with some interesting comments on the characteristics of "successful" theories. D. N. Rosenstein-Rodan, "Marginal Utility" (1927), reprinted in *IEP*, No. 10, 1961 gives an excellent picture of European marginal utility doctrine around World War I, proliferating in subtle distinctions and metaphysical classifications. Reading this essay, one is made to realize how much has been swept away, fortunately, I think, by the Hicksian Revolution. A. R. Sweezy, "The Interpretation of Subjective Value Theory in the Writings of the Austrian Economists," *REStud*, June, 1934, suggests that the younger Austrian writers of the twenties were moving independently toward the notion of ordinal utility. J. Viner, "The Utility Concept in Value Theory and Its Critics," *JPE*, 1925, reprinted in *The Long View and the Short* (1958), analyzes the traditional criticisms that have been leveled at utility theory; the first of these articles, concerning the role of utility in demand theory, is still as relevant as it was in 1925; the second, dealing with welfare economics, is now somewhat dated. F. H. Knight, "Realism and Relevance in the Theory of Demand," *JPE*, December, 1944, argues that the indifference-curve approach does in fact imply diminishing marginal utility and represents no substantial advance over the older utility theory. He is taken to task for this by R. L. Bishop, "Professor Knight and the Theory of Demand," *JPE*, April, 1946. See also Schumpeter, *History*, pp. 1054–73.

G. J. Stigler, "The Early History of Empirical Studies of Consumer Behavior," *JPE*, April, 1954, reviews the early empirical work on income curves and demand curves; the latter did not begin in earnest until just before World War I. In "Notes on the History of the Giffen Paradox," *JPE*, April, 1947 ("Reply," by A. R. Prest, February, 1948), Stigler shows that Marshall read a positively sloped demand curve for bread into Giffen's "hint": Giffen's data on bread consumption do not positively establish the Paradox. M. Friedman, "The Marshallian Demand Curve," *JPE*, 1949, reprinted in *Essays in Positive Economics* (1953), argues that demand curves should be defined as constant real-income curves and that this interpretation comes closer to what Marshall really intended: the appendix to Friedman's essay contains a thorough exegesis of the relevant sections of the *Principles*. R. F. G. Alford, "Marshall's Demand Curve," *Ec.*, February, 1956, rejects Friedman's interpretation and restates the traditional position; as a piece of pedagogy, this article has much to recommend it. Along the same lines, see also W. Fellner, *Emergence and Content of Modern Economic Analysis* (1960), chaps. 14 and 15. L. B. Yeager, "*Methodenstreit* over

Demand Curves," *JPE,* February, 1960, raises the methodological issue inherent in the Friedman interpretation.

For a discussion of the history of the theory of progressive taxation in the utilty tradition see E. D. Fagan, "Theories of Progressive Taxation," *JPE,* 1948, reprinted in *Readings in the Economics of Taxation;* Musgrave, *Theory of Public Finance,* chap. 5. Fagan reviews the traditional arguments for and against the principle of diminishing marginal utility of income.

2. Marshallian Welfare Economics. R. L. Bishop, "Consumer's Surplus and Cardinal Utility," *QJE,* May, 1943, contains an excellent discussion of the difficulties in Marshall's concept, including some of the older objections thrown out by Nicholson and Cannan. Marshallian surplus analysis is examined by Myint, *Theories of Welfare Economics,* chap. 9; see also chap. 8, on the "Characteristics of Neo-Classical Welfare Economics." For a translation of the problem in terms of indifference curves see J. R. Hicks, "The Four Consumer's Surpluses," *REStud,* Winter, 1943, and K. E. Boulding, "The Concept of Economic Surplus," *AER,* 1945, reprinted in *Readings in the Theory of Income Distribution.* J. N. Morgan, "The Measurement of Gains and Losses," *QJE,* February, 1948, cites and reviews all the recent literature on consumer's surplus and suggests practical methods for measuring it. F. Machlup, "Professor Hicks' *Revision of Demand Theory,*" *AER,* March, 1957, discusses the treatment of the four consumer's surpluses and related matters in Hicks's new book. For a diagrammatic presentation of the four producer's surpluses on the same footing as the Hicksian treatment of consumer's surplus see E. J. Mishan, "Rent as a Measure of Welfare," *AER,* June, 1959. I. M. D. Little, *A Critique of Welfare Economics* (2d ed., 1957), chap. 10, throws doubt on the practical importance of surplus analysis in the "new welfare economics."

Chapter 10 · MARSHALLIAN ECONOMICS: COST AND SUPPLY

MARSHALL'S theory of price revolves around the distinction between (1) a market period, in which supplies are absolutely fixed in amount; (2) a short period, in which the quantities supplied can be augmented by increasing the variable elements of total costs; and (3) a long period, in which all costs, both variable and fixed, can be completely adjusted to meet any change in demand.

The time dimension that pervades Marshall's analysis has been aptly described as "operational time." Although the terminology employed conveys an air of clock time, the impression is deceiving. Periods are short or long, not according to the revolving hands of the clock, but according to the partial or the complete adaptations of producers and consumers to changing circumstances. The actual clock-time periods to which the curve construction applies are left undefined and must be separately specified for each particular industry.[1] To be sure, the short run normally does involve a shorter period of clock time than the long run, but this is not necessarily and always true. It is conceivable, for example, that the time needed to increase output from existing facilities exceeds the time required to install new equipment. We would then have a long run preceding a short run. Since time is conceived operationally, Marshallian analysis does not preclude such oddities.

The Short Run. Between the instantaneous market period and the long period lies the indefinite morass of the short run. This is a period too short to permit changes in capacity—the size of plant and amount of equipment of firms—but long enough to allow for changes in the degree of utilization of capacity. It is in the short run that the problem of time is most troublesome. In long-run equilibrium all ad-

---

[1] Modern economics abounds in definitions that conceive of time in operational terms: there is D. H. Robertson's "day," a period too short to dispose of earned income; there is Hicks's "week," a period during which variations in prices can be ignored; and so on. But the "stationary state" of classical economics is still the supreme example of a functional-time definition.

justments are complete and therefore independent of particular time periods. In the short run, however, the dynamic problems that characterize temporary adjustments are the heart of the matter. In the first place, we cannot just select any definite clock-time period and call it short run for the simple reason that expansion of capacity and changes in the degree of utilization of existing capacity are likely to proceed simultaneously. Second, adjustments that are made in the short run differ depending on whether the change in price is expected to be temporary or permanent; expectations of the future do affect the adjustment process, perhaps decisively so. Third, the responses of producers in a given time period are asymmetrical with respect to a rise and to a fall in price. Because of the durability of existing equipment, the short run may be much longer when the adjustment is a contraction than when it is an expansion, and this lack of symmetry is the sharper the longer lived is the equipment relative to its period of construction.

Provided these kinds of difficulties are kept in mind, we can now proceed to analyze the adjustment of industry toward short-period equilibrium. All costs can be classified into prime and supplementary costs, or, to use current American terminology, variable and fixed costs. In the short run, each firm is burdened with certain unalterable commitments in the form of existing facilities. Variations in the level of output will be accompanied by variations in certain prime costs, such as wages of production workers, expenses for raw materials, and users' cost of machinery. But, as long as plant and equipment themselves cannot be altered, some costs will remain fixed in amount regardless of the rate of output: the usual list of fixed costs contains such things as obsolescence charges on machinery, ground rent, property taxes, and possibly the salaries of supervisory personnel. Facing given prices, entrepreneurs maximize profits by producing that output at which total costs increase at the same rate as total receipts: in other words, they equate marginal cost to marginal revenue. Under perfect competition, price is not affected by the individual firm's decision to produce; hence, price or average revenue is always equal to marginal revenue. Profit-maximizing behavior under perfect competition may, therefore, be expressed succinctly as marginal cost pricing. Moreover, in the short-period situation marginal cost is in no way influenced by fixed costs. The rate at which total costs increase as a function of output is not affected by the addition of a lump sum to total costs at all levels of output. The economic sense of this is that the alternative costs of fixed investments in the short run are zero: bygones are forever bygones.

From data on total costs of production within a given plant we obtain the corresponding figures for average and marginal costs. The now familiar graphic illustration, not found in Marshall's *Principles,* shows the firm maximizing profits at $\bar{q}$. (See Fig. 54.) The total revenue curve is a straight line coming out of the origin because the slope of this

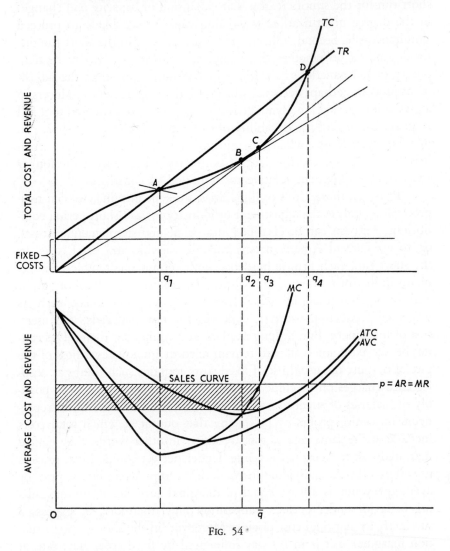

FIG. 54

line, which is price or average revenue, is constant at all levels of output. The total cost curve is given the usual plausible shape, based on the idea that the plant is designed to be operated under normal circumstances at something like 50–80 per cent of capacity. Drawing successive vectors from the origin to different points along the total cost curve, we obtain average total costs as the slope of the various vectors. Marginal cost is the slope of the total cost curve itself. A is an inflection point where marginal costs are at a minimum. Average total costs reach a minimum at B where $ATC = MC$. As long as an average value declines, the corresponding marginal value must be below the average; the average can be declining only because the marginal addition to the total is smaller than the average. Similarly, when an average value increases, the corresponding marginal value must lie above it. Hence, when the average has reached its minimum point, neither declining nor increasing, the marginal must equal the average value. The ATC curve must cut the AR curve at Q_1 and Q_4 because $TC = TR$ at these points. The average variable cost curve AVC is obtained by a parallel downward shift in the TC curve to eliminate the presence of fixed costs; it follows that the minimum point of the AVC curve is reached earlier than the minimum point of the ATC curve. Profit *per unit of output* is maximized at Q_2 where the gap between ATC and AR is at a maximum. At this point, however, the MR of additional output exceeds its MC. The firm maximizes *total* profits by producing $\bar{q}$, as shown by the shaded rectangle. Since the amount of capital invested is given in the short run, maximizing total profits is equivalent in this case to maximizing the rate of profit on capital.

The firm's supply curve is its marginal cost curve, at least insofar as marginal costs exceed average variable out-of-pocket costs: at various given prices the amount that the firm will produce can be read off the MC curve. Since this is true of one firm, it is true of all firms. The industry supply curve is simply the horizontal summation of individual firms' supply curves. Suppose there are three firms in the industry; arranging the firms in order of their average costs, we obtain an industry supply curve that is the cumulative array of the MC curves of the individual firms (Fig. 55). As long as the price is below p_2 but above p_1, only the first firm finds it profitable to operate. When the price is equal to p_2, firm 1 produces Oq_2 and firm 2 produces q_2q_3; together they produce Oq_3. As the price rises and reaches p_3, firm 3 enters the industry, producing q_4q_5. If the market demand curve for the industry is as shown, p_3 and q_5 will clear the market.

With the high-cost producer just covering out-of-pocket costs, the industry is in short-period equilibrium. The marginal firm is earning no profits whatever; indeed, it is not even recouping its fixed costs and at this rate will leave the industry in the long run. At p_3, the intramarginal firms are earning producers' surpluses. As we increase the number of firms to some large number, the supply curve smooths out and producers' surplus can be read off as a sum *in excess of* the roughly triangular area above the supply curve and below the horizontal line indicating the market price.

Quasi-Rents. It should be noticed, however, that on this interpretation producers' surplus in the short run includes not only what has since come to be called "economic rent"—total net revenue *CABD*—but also what Marshall called "quasi-rent"—the rectangle *ECDF*, being the difference between *AVC* and *ATC* multiplied by the quantity produced. The term "quasi-rents" is self-explanatory. Marshall reserves the

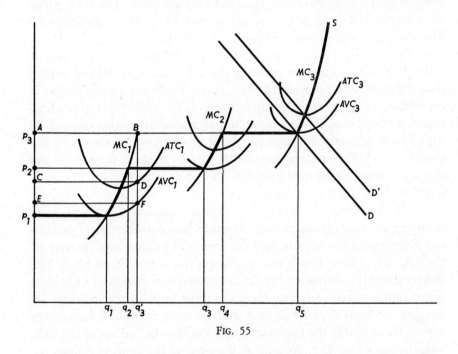

Fig. 55

term "rent" for the so-called "free gifts of nature." Like Ricardo, Marshall singles out land as a unique resource because it is virtually unresponsive to higher rates of reward. But income derived from man-made assets that are temporarily fixed in supply partakes of the nature of rent. The term "interest" is applicable to new prospective investment only. Sunk capital yields a value product net of maintenance and replacement, and this net value product on fixed investments we call "quasi-rents."

Like rents on superior grades of land, quasi-rents are price determined and not price determining. In other words, in the short run, the price paid for the services of capital goods is analogous to the price paid for the services of natural agents, because in each case the return is not necessary to call forth the corresponding service. The analogy to Ricardian rents is, however, somewhat misleading. Ricardian rents are only price-determined for the economy as a whole. If land has competing uses, as it usually has, Ricardian rents do enter into the costs of production of an individual farmer: the alternative costs of using a tract of land to an individual farmer are measured by the rental payments required to bid land away from competing uses. But Marshall's quasi-rents are price-determined both for society as a whole and for the individual entrepreneur; they are the result of the failure to achieve complete adjustment in any given slice of time and will disappear in the long run as all costs become variable.

It is clear that quasi-rents accrue to the individual entrepreneur. The same is not necessarily true of "economic rent." A firm may be a low-cost producer because of a favorable site that reduces its freight charges on raw materials or on shipping the product to market. In this case, part of the whole of its unimputed income or "profits" may go to the landlord as ground rent, even in the short run. In the long run it is, of course, bound to be swallowed up by rental payments as other firms compete for the favorable site. Possibly, the favorable cost position is due to superior management, in which case the recipient of "economic rent" is the manager. Whatever the reason, a period so short as to prevent the entrepreneur from adding to capacity may be long enough to overcome the resource immobilities that alone permit the entrepreneur to collect the intramarginal surplus. Be that as it may, in the long run the cost ladder must straighten out, and when all adjustments are completed each firm will produce along identical cost curves that include "rents."

The Long Run. So far we have traveled through familiar terrain because most of Marshall's short-period analysis has found its way into modern textbooks in a refined version. Marshall's long-period analysis, however, is not quite such smooth sailing because it has been largely discarded without anything else taking its place. Our first problem is to show how we obtain the long-run average cost curve of an individual firm, a subject that Marshall completely neglected to analyze. As was shown by Viner in the late 1920's, the long-run average cost curve of a firm is an envelope of all the short-run average cost curves.

Suppose the firm finds itself with plant 1, producing q_1 at p_1 (Fig. 56). The short-run curve MC_1 is upward sloping because, with a *given* plant, the employment of equal additional amounts of any variable factor results in diminishing increments of output. Since long-run marginal costs are below short-run marginal costs at the output level q_1, it will pay the firm to enlarge its plant or to build a new one capable of producing a larger output at lower per unit costs. Since *all* factors are now variable, the law of diminishing marginal productivity is not applicable to this case. What we have is a movement from one plant curve to another such that, when we increase all the factors by a given amount, output increases more than proportionately. As long as we are

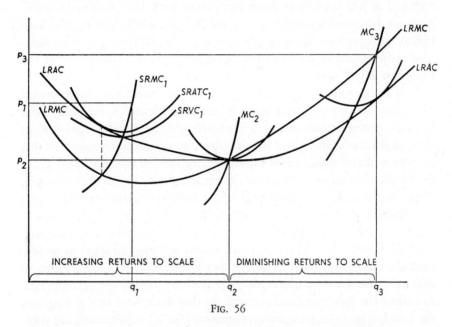

Fig. 56

moving along the downward-sloping portion of the *LRAC* curve, we are in the phase of increasing returns to scale. With a plant larger than plant 1, however, *SRMC* may still exceed *LRMC,* and so the firm is induced to build a still larger plant. This process will continue until the firm reaches plant 2. Beyond this point it incurs decreasing returns to scale. If the price rises sufficiently, it is willing to enter this phase because the *SRMC* of producing q_3 in plant 3 is still lower than it would be in plant 2, assuming that q_3 could be produced at all in plant 2. But as soon as the price falls again it is motivated to scrap plant 3 and to build a smaller plant that can produce a smaller quantity more efficiently. If the price is equal to p_2, the firm will settle down at plant 2, equating *SRMC* with *LRMC,* earning zero profits, and experiencing constant returns to scale.

The *LRMC* curve, it appears, is the firm's long-run supply curve. With respect to the long run, the firm tries to equate *LRMC* to price. If the price exceeds *LRMC,* the firm expands its scale of operations. When, with a given plant, short-run profit maximization causes the price to be less than *LRMC,* the firm contracts its scale and moves down to a smaller plant. Its long-run output response to a changing price can, therefore, be read off its *LRMC* curve. The *LRMC* curve begins to slope upward at some point, owing, presumably, to internal diseconomies associated with the entrepreneurial function that defines the firm.

It is to be noted that the minimum point of each short-run *ATC* curve always lies above the *LRATC* curve except at the output level at which the *LRATC* curve itself reaches a minimum. This is precisely what is meant by saying that the *LRATC* curve is an envelope curve: it is the locus of all the lowest possible average costs of producing any output when the entrepreneur is able to make all desired adjustments. If the *LRATC* curve went through the minimum point of each and every *SRATC* curve, it would have to lie above some portion of the *SRATC* curve. But this is economically absurd, for it would mean that cost per unit when capacity cannot be varied is less than when it can be varied. But, surely, it cannot be to a firm's advantage not to be able to vary all the elements in total costs?

When we draw upward-sloping long-run supply curves for an *industry,* we do not necessarily assume that the *firms* are operating under decreasing returns to scale. If a firm were operating along the rising portion of its *LRATC* curve, it would be earning positive profits. In the long run, returns owing to differential advantages are capitalized and imputed to costs. Hence, if one firm were earning positive profits, all firms would be earning positive profits, which is incompatible with long-run industry equilibrium under perfect competition. So long as entry into the industry is free, all firms must be operating at constant returns to scale equating price to *SRMC, SRATC, LRMC,* and *LRATC.* Provided all productive agents are available in infinitely elastic supply in the long run, the industry's *LRS* curve must be horizontal under perfect competition.

If some factor is limited in supply even in the long run, then the *LRS* curve of the industry may be upward sloping owing to the fact that the expansion of output raises the price of the scarce factor. We then have an increasing cost industry despite the fact that each firm operates under constant returns to scale at the minimum point of its envelope curve. There is one other possibility, however, that may produce a positively sloped *LRS* curve for the industry. Suppose that competition is "pure" but not "perfect" in Chamberlin's terminology, that is, the initial cost of operation to a new firm is such that profits in the industry must exceed a certain minimum amount to make it profitable for a new-comer to enter the industry. In that case, the firms in the industry will operate under diminishing returns to scale and the *LRS* curve of the industry, as the horizontal summation of the *LRMC* curves of the firms, will be positively inclined. The fact that an industry is an increasing cost industry therefore may, but need not, entail diminishing returns to scale on the firm level.

Whatever the reasons for increasing cost, an adjustment to an increase in demand may be conceived as taking place in two steps. First, all the firms produce more along their *SRMC* curves, and, second, new firms enter the industry and the existing firms build larger plants to accommodate the increase in demand. As the demand curve shifts, price rises from p_1 to p_2 and output increases from q_1 to q_2. (See Fig. 57.)

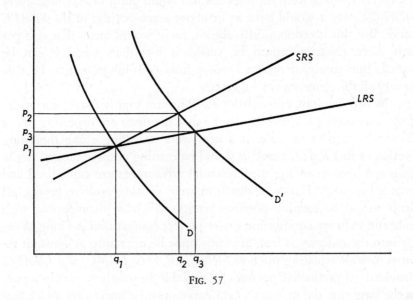

FIG. 57

Now the long-run adjustment shifts the short-run supply curve; output increases to q_3 and price falls to p_3. If competition is "perfect," the larger quantity requires a higher price because new firms have bid up the price of the scarce factor. If competition is "pure," the larger quantity requires a higher price because each firm is subject to diseconomies of scale. In either case, the increasing cost industry is in long-run equilibrium at p_3 and q_3 in the sense that no firms are induced to enter or leave the industry.

But suppose the industry is a decreasing cost industry. Can the long-run supply curve be downward as well as upward sloping, as Marshall believed? First, it is clear that the *short*-run supply curve for the industry cannot be downward sloping. Since the industry supply curve is the sum of the firms' supply curves, the industry supply curve cannot be negatively inclined unless at least some of the firms have negatively inclined supply curves. But this is impossible, since a necessary condition for internal equilibrium of the firm is that the firm's *MC* curve be rising at the point of equilibrium, that is, the *MC* curve must cut the *MR* curve from below. If net revenue π is equal to total cost minus total revenue, the condition for a maximum extremum value is that the first derivative of the net revenue function vanishes and that the second derivative is negative. That is, if $\pi = f(R - C)$, then the condition for maximizing profits is

$$f'(R - C) = 0 ;$$

$$f''(R - C) = \; < 0 .$$

But $(d/dx)(R - C) = 0$ if $(dR/dx) - (dC/dx) = 0$, if marginal revenue equals marginal cost. And $(d^2R/dx^2) - (d^2C/dx^2) < 0$,

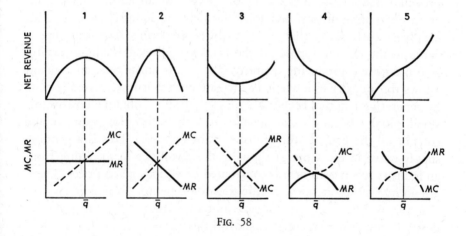

FIG. 58

if $(d^2R/dx^2) < (d^2C/dx^2)$, if marginal revenue increases less rapidly than marginal cost. Profits are maximized, then, only in diagrams 1 and 2, not in diagrams 3, 4, and 5 (Fig. 58).

Hence, the competitive industry's short-run supply curve must be positively inclined. But, as Cournot had shown, the same argument holds for the long-run supply curve. If the industry supply curve is declining in the long run, at least some of the firms must have negatively inclined *LRMC* curves. But this implies that the firms are not in equilibrium because declining *LRMC* means that $LRMC < LRAC$.

In trying to equate price with *LRMC,* the firms will expand their scale of operations. Indeed, they will go on expanding even if their *LRMC* curves turn up as long as $LRMC < LRAC$. In other words, as long as there are economies of scale, the *LRMC* curve is *not* a true supply curve in the sense of the schedule that traces out the quantities forthcoming from a firm when it is confronted with various prices. No firm can possibly be in long-run equilibrium unless $LRMC \geqslant LRAC$, unless it operates in the phase of constant or diminishing returns to scale. If this is true for each firm, it follows that it is also true for the industry supply curve in the long run. *Competitive equilibrium is incompatible with downward-sloping long-run supply curves.*

External Economies. The conclusion that decreasing cost industries cannot exist under perfect competition depends on the assumption that the supply curves of the individual firms are independent of one another. But, as Marshall first pointed out, competitive equilibrium may be compatible with falling supply curves if "external economies" make for interdependence between supply curves. External economies are present whenever an increase in the output of an entire industry increases the amount any individual firm in the industry is willing to supply at each price, that is, if it shifts the firm's short-run supply curve to the right. Suppose all the firms are all exactly alike, earning zero profits and producing quantity $Q = \Sigma q$. If an increase in demand allows the industry as a whole to increase output at lower average costs by generating external economies for each firm, we obtain a downward-sloping long-run supply curve made up of the falling long-run average costs of all the firms in the industry. (See Fig. 59.) This is a genuine supply curve in the sense of showing the quantities forthcoming from an industry when each firm is confronted by various given prices. There are no *internal* economies of scale that could permit an individual firm to cut its costs by enlarging its size. But when more firms enter the industry in response to rising demand, all the firms find that they are able to supply larger quantities at lower costs. In all cases in which the economies involved are *external,* output can vary only through variations in the number of firms.

When external economies prevail, we cannot obtain the industry supply curve by mere horizontal summation of the firms' supply curves. The curves now shift in the process of summation: the output of each and every firm depends on the output of the industry, and yet the industry's output is nothing more than the sum of the output of the firms. Theoretically, the problem requires the solution of a system of simultaneous equations; in practice, each firm assumes some value for total output, and the mutual adjustment of all the firms *may* then lead to convergence toward the true value.

Assuming, then, that external economies alone can account for downward-sloping industry supply curves, what are external economies and how frequently will they be encountered? This question has different answers depending on the scope of the inquiry. According to Marshall, external economies are dependent on (1) "the general development of the industry," and (2) the "general progress of the industrial environment." But, if we are dealing with competitive output from the standpoint of partial equilibrium analysis, we must ignore (2),

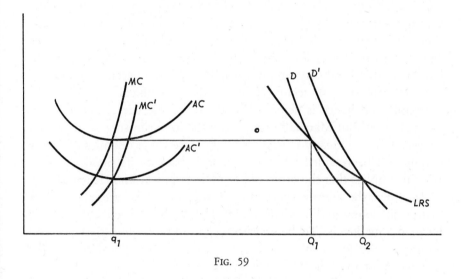

FIG. 59

which involves dynamic considerations that have no place in a static frame of reference. The economies appropriate to our analysis are reflected in the downward-shifting cost curves of individual firms as the industry's output expands. Lower costs may be due to the increased efficiency of each firm and/or lower factor prices. Lower factor prices imply external or internal economies in the supplying industry. If lower factor prices are due to internal economies in the supplying industry, that industry cannot be competitive. This condition is ruled out by the assumption that all industries operate under perfect competition, which we have seen is incompatible with internal economies of scale. Therefore, lower factor prices must be due to external economies in the supplying industry, which involves the same problem as the one we are trying to explain. Thus, what has to be explained is why each firm should become more efficient as the industry's output expands. The industry's output expands only if the output of at least one firm expands. So the question is: why do the costs of other firms fall when the output of a particular firm expands?

It is clear that the external economies we are after involve economies that are external to the firm but internal to the industry, involving a particular kind of interdependence between the member firms of an industry. Marshall's own examples are singularly unconvincing because they are not confined to single industries: he mentions economies arising from the localization of industry, from the development of auxiliary and subsidiary industries, from the increasing availability of skilled labor, and from the development of the means of transportation and communication. This list does not distinguish between ordinary reversible movements along a static curve and historical irreversible shifts in the curves themselves. Now, a long-run falling industry supply curve is reversible because it is drawn at a constant state of technical knowledge. Technical progress is irreversible and hence is depicted by a shift of the curve, not a movement along it. But Marshall argued that the long-run supply curve in a decreasing cost industry is irreversible because the economies of larger output will be retained when output falls back to its previous level. But this implies that the firms add to their technical knowledge as they move down the supply curve, for, if the economies were already a matter of common knowledge, they should have been exploited at lower output levels. To be consistent, we must assume that external economies are lost as the industry's output contracts, and this means that we must exclude all dynamic irreversible changes.

What Are External Economies? External economies or diseconomies exist whenever the production function of one firm contains noninput variables that express the effect of the activities of other firms. In effect, some firm is rendering a service to other firms without being able to appropriate to itself the value of these services, or else is inflicting a loss on other firms without having to pay a fee for its nuisance value. External economies or diseconomies therefore always involve some kind of nonmarket interdependence. Such technological economies," as they are called, are few and far between in a static context. Two examples of such economies satisfying the strict Marshallian condition of being fully reversible are (1) the labor-force case and (2) the trade-journal case. With the growth and localization of an industry in one particular area, all firms enjoy the benefit of an available supply of skilled labor and a well-informed and convenient labor market. The trade-journal case, on the other hand, exemplifies external economies arising from improved communication about market conditions and costs of production. When the industry reaches a certain size, it becomes feasible to publish information and to make it cheaply available to all. A third possible example, although it is not clear that this is always fully reversible, is that of the vertical disintegration that comes with a widened market. Since "the division of labor is limited by the extent of the market," the growth of industry brings into being a host of specialized auxiliary industries to service the need of the parent industry. Contrariwise, the classic example of a technological external *dis*economy, causing the long-run supply curve to be upward sloping, is the case in which the firms in an industry use a resource that is free but nevertheless scarce, such as a publicly owned road or a common geological oil field.

All such phenomena reflect hidden inputs or outputs the benefits or costs of which are not appropriable by the agents in the market. As long as we confine ourselves to particular industries and to cases in which the effect is reversible, we do have considerable difficulties in coming up with convincing examples. But if we include irreversible dynamic phenomena, we have no difficulty whatever in finding examples of technological external economies. The leading case is a change in technological knowledge itself; the full benefit of most changes in knowledge is not easily captured by the originator, even with strong patents and copyrights. Another favorite instance is that of labor-training: the social benefits of labor-training accrue over the lifetime service of the trainee, but the private benefit to the producer stops when the worker quits to go to work for a competitor. There is no doubt, therefore, of the importance of technological external economies, but one may well question their significance from the point of view of partial equilibrium analysis. It is possible to "save" the notion of a downward-sloping "forward-falling" industry supply curve by means of reversible external economies, but their exceptional occurrence explains why most modern economists are reluctant to endorse Marshall's belief in the existence of decreasing cost industries.

"Real" external economies must be kept distinct from "pecuniary external economies"—a vital point made by Viner. An industry that expands along a long-run falling unit cost curve can sell its products at lower and lower prices even though the prices of the services that it buys are rising as more services are purchased. This kind of effect may benefit other industries, but, unlike "real" external economies, these pecuniary external economies reflect an interdependence among producers that *is* transmitted through the price system. These kinds of economies are ubiquitous in any integrated economic system, but they present no problem for price theory because they will necessarily be fully exploited by the beneficiaries and therefore eliminated in the long run. In development economics, however, pecuniary external economies represent *the* problem.

Once again, we see that the kind of external economies admitted into the purview of analysis depends entirely upon the level of discourse we adopt. The common tendency in the interwar literature to regard external economies as economic curiosa reflected the limited scope and assumptions of partial equilibrium analysis. In recent years, however, the concept of external economies has emerged in a variety of disguises in discussions of the industrialization of backward areas. The meaning that the concept has now acquired in the "doctrine of balanced growth" is a very wide one, covering a number of quite distinct mechanisms by which investment in one field may give rise to nonappropriable benefits and hence new investment opportunities elsewhere.

Producers' Surplus. Having established what is meant by the notion of a falling supply curve for an industry, we can now return to the tax-bounty analysis. We recall that Marshall's text discusses only the gain or loss in *consumers'* surplus from a change in price. We must now take account of producers' surplus. Marshall defines a worker's surplus, a saver's surplus, and a producer's surplus, each being defined as the excess of actual earnings from a given quantity of work, saving, or output over the amount that the individual would accept rather than refuse to offer his services altogether. It is, in this sense, perfectly analogous to the consumer's price surplus. Having introduced producers' surplus in a footnote, Marshall does not take it up in detail until Appendix H, where it turns out to be something very different, namely, the "producers' surplus triangle." It has nothing now to do with the increasing marginal disutility of effort and is not the money measure of surplus satisfactions but, rather, the actual excess earnings obtained by the low-cost firms over the earnings of the marginal firm. It is a pure Ricardian differential rent.

Marshall defines this intramarginal surplus by means of a "particular expenses curve." This is not a supply curve but a cumulative array of the average costs of different firms. We know that at any point on the short-period supply curve of an industry, price is equal to the marginal cost of the individual producers as well as to the average cost of the marginal firm. The *PE* curve shows the firms' average costs for that price-output combination arranged in ascending order from left to right. Since for any other price each firm would produce a different output and incur a different average cost, it follows that there is a definable *PE* curve for each point on the supply curve. The end point of each *PE* curve shows the marginal = average cost of producing that output for the marginal firm. The industry supply curve is, thus, the locus of end points of the *PE* curves (Fig. 60).

The *PE* curves always lie below the short-period supply curve for the simple reason that each intramarginal firm's average cost curve lies below its marginal cost curve at the profit-maximizing output level. Since this is the short run, we might ask: What is the relevant

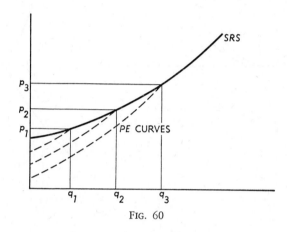

FIG. 60

average cost curve for measuring the producer's surplus—the average total cost curve or the average variable cost curve? The difference between *ATC* and *AVC* is average fixed cost on which, we recall, the entrepreneur may earn quasi-rents. Quasi-rents are scarcity rents, being the earnings of productive resources temporarily fixed in supply. What we are after, however, is a measure of differential rent. Therefore, the *PE* curve is a cumulative array of the average *total* costs of the firms in an industry. The roughly triangular area above the *PE* curve and below the horizontal price line shows the excess earnings of the better-placed firms over the earnings of the marginal firm.

Marshall applied the *PE* curve not only to short-run but also to long-run supply curves. Indeed, it was the latter application that really interested him. We know that the superior services to which the producers' surplus is due in the short run will tend to be capitalized in the long run and become permanently embodied in the supply curves. In the long run, therefore, all the firms will have identical cost curves inclusive of rent and the *PE* curve must coincide with the long-run industry supply curve.

Given perfect competition, there are two reasons why the long-run supply curve may be upward sloping and one reason why it may be downward sloping. Suppose some factor, say land, is nonreproducible or, at any rate, less than infinitely elastic in supply. As the industry expands, the average cost curves of each firm shift up owing to pecuniary external diseconomies in the form of rising scarcity rents. (See Fig. 61.) Assuming that there are *n* firms in the industry, we

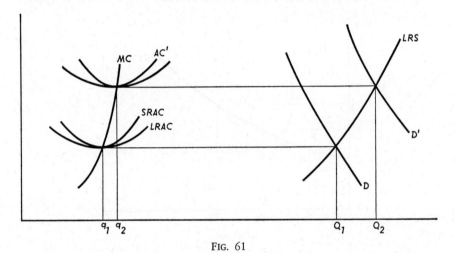

Fig. 61

show the short-run cost curve of one firm with its accompanying envelope curve and the resulting average cost curve of the industry as a whole blown up *n* times. The short-run supply curve of the firm does not change when scarcity rents rise because the total cost of producing all levels of output rises by a constant amount.

The same result, however, may be due not to pecuniary but to "real" external *dis*economies. As output of the industry expands, the supply curve of each firm shifts to the left, and hence the supply price of the industry as a whole rises. (See Fig. 62.) It is clear that in this case, as in all others involving "real" economies or diseconomies, the increase in output of the industry as a whole results in variations in the number of firms.

Finally, the presence of "real" external economies will cause the supply curve of each firm to shift to the right as the output of the industry increases and so yields a downward-sloping, forward-falling long-run supply curve (Fig. 63). This kind of supply curve is some-

what peculiar because it does not show the amount forthcoming from
the industry at various prices. A rise in demand will cause prices to
rise as each firm travels up its *SRS* curve. The *LRS* curve is an *ex post*

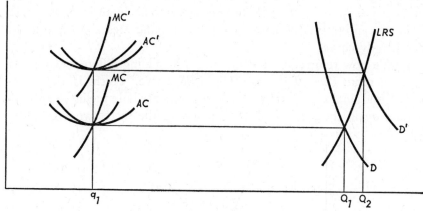

FIG. 62

curve, showing the average cost per unit after the industry has reaped
all the external economies appropriate to a particular output.

There is no need to go on to consider pecuniary external economies because these must be due to "real" economies somewhere in the

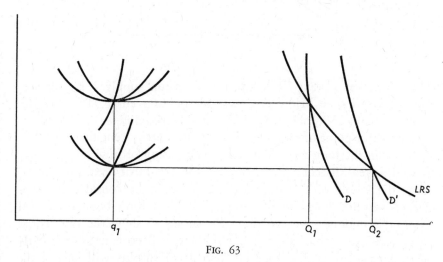

FIG. 63

system. Pecuniary diseconomies, however, need have no technological counterpart and therefore have to be treated separately.

Real external economies or diseconomies do not create "rent,"
and hence our discussion of producers' surplus in the long run is con-

fined to the case of pecuniary external diseconomies. The latter may be present, however, even when supply price is falling; a falling supply price simply means that the pecuniary diseconomies are outweighed by the real economies. As long as entry is free—competition is "perfect" and not just "pure"—the presence of scarcity rents in an increasing cost industry can be read off as the roughly triangular area above the long-run supply curve.

We now reintroduce the *PE* curves by adding differential rent to scarcity rent. (See Fig. 64.) The *LRS* curve, which is the average = marginal cost curve of the industry as a whole inclusive of rent, is once again the locus of the end points of the successive *PE* curves.

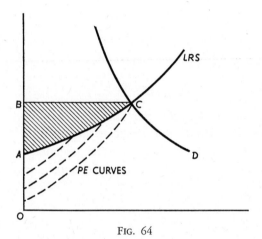

FIG. 64

The *PE* curves always lie below the short-run supply curve; hence, they necessarily lie below the more elastic *LRS* curve. The roughly triangular area *ABC* above the *LRS* curve is thus differential rent from the short-run point of view, but it contains scarcity rent that will persist even in the long run. If supply price is rising because of pecuniary as well as real diseconomies, however, the argument breaks down because the whole of the area *ABC* cannot now be considered a producers' surplus. Likewise, if supply price is falling because of real external economies, we can draw *PE* curves to show the differential rent accruing to the industry, but if these real economies are partly offset by pecuniary diseconomies, producers' surplus will exceed the triangle above the *PE* curve (Fig. 65).

Be that as it may, we can now complete the tax-bounty analysis by coupling producers' with consumers' surplus. Suppose we levy a per unit excise tax on an increasing cost industry. Ignoring differential rents and external effects for the moment, the loss in producers' surplus is given by *ADEB* (Fig. 66). This is derived in the following way: before the tax, producers' surplus was equal to *DEC;* after the tax it is

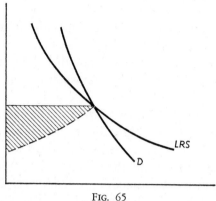

FIG. 65

equal to *abs = ABC. DEC* minus *ABC = ADEB.* We know that the loss in consumers' surplus, from the rise in price, ignoring real-income effects, is equal to *DabE.* Hence, the combined loss in producers' and consumers' surplus is *AabEB.* Tax receipts are equal to *AabB.* We

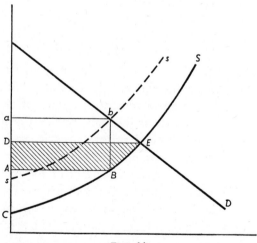

FIG. 66

reach the anti-Marshallian conclusion that the combined loss in consumers' and producers' surplus from a tax actually exceeds the amount of tax receipts. Even if all the revenue from the tax were returned as a lump sum to the buyers and sellers in the market, they would be worse off than before. If we use the tax receipts, instead, to subsidize a decreasing cost industry, we will certainly generate an increase in consumers' surplus and we *may* increase the producers' surplus in that industry. The net effect of the entire operation is thus highly uncertain.

All this does not even take into account the four consumers' surpluses! Suffice it to say that, as a piece of deductive reasoning, we have little reason for confidence in the theorem that the state can harmonize private production decisions with public welfare by taxing some industries and subsidizing others.

The Asymmetrical Welfare Effect. The skeptical reader may have wondered whether, all technicalities aside, it really made sense to add a money measure of consumers' satisfactions to an actual sum of producers' money. Surely, these two things are not on the same footing? And, indeed, there was something wrong here, which became apparent only when Pigou, in *Wealth and Welfare* (1912), translated Marshall's tax-bounty analysis into his own terminology of private and social costs. It is perfectly obvious from Pigou's comprehensive survey of the doctrine of consumers' and producers' surplus, published in the *Economic Journal* in 1910, that he was aware of the very ambiguous outcome of Marshall's line of argument. Possibly for that reason he discarded the doctrine in *Wealth and Welfare* and in its successor, *Economics of Welfare* (1919). The same essential conclusions, however, emerge in a new garb. In an increasing cost industry, argued Pigou, marginal social costs exceed marginal private costs. Marginal social cost may be defined as the sum of the marginal private cost of producing a commodity plus the nonrecoverable positive and negative effects associated with an increment of output of that commodity that accrue to or are borne by individuals outside the industry. Marginal social costs exceed marginal private costs in an increasing cost industry because the latter does not include the increase in costs to buyers as a result of the expansion of output of the industry in question. Production is carried too far in such industries on the supposition that economic welfare is maximized only when the marginal social cost of producing a commodity equals its marginal private cost. Marginal social cost is a measure of the alternative production forgone from the production of a particular commodity. Only when prices are everywhere reflective of social as well as private costs will a dollar expenditure by consumers purchase the same value worth of factor units irrespective of the commodity acquired. If an increasing cost industry is taxed, its marginal private cost will be raised to where it will equal marginal social cost. Likewise, a decreasing cost industry operates at an output level below the social optimum, since its marginal social cost of production falls short of its marginal private cost. Hence, its output must be expanded by a subsidy.

It took the better part of thirty years to unravel the thread of truth that runs through the Marshall-Pigou argument. The basic flaw, however, was pointed out as early as 1913 by Allyn Young: The causes of changes in long-run supply prices are not symmetrical in the two types of industries. In an increasing cost industry social costs exceed private costs because as the industry expands it raises its own costs as well as the cost of all other goods in which this factor is used. The effect is to transfer purchasing power from other industries to the industry in question. What is involved is a pecuniary external diseconomy: the expansion of the increasing cost industry does not represent a using-up of resources and hence does not result in a genuine social cost. But in the case of a decreasing cost industry, the expansion of output does involve a saving of resources because, Young might have added, such an industry expands only along a falling supply curve because of the presence of "real" external economies.

This argument is impeccable and requires only one addendum. If an industry expands at a rising supply price, it may be the result of pecuniary external diseconomies, but it may also be the result of "real" external diseconomies. In the latter case, forcing the industry to contract does represent a saving of resources. But, in general, it remains true that pecuniary external economies or diseconomies cannot create a divergence between private and social costs. Given the exceptional nature of genuine technological diseconomies and retaining the assumption of perfect competition, we may conclude that the proposal to contract increasing cost industries by taxes has no welfare significance. If we can find any decreasing cost industries, subsidizing their expansion will certainly raise economic welfare. But it is not possible to advocate subsidization on this score alone because we must necessarily reduce someone's welfare when we raise the required funds for the subsidy program.

To reiterate: the existence of producers' surplus in the sense of "rent" does not indicate a failure to achieve an optimum allocation of resources. On the contrary, competition will insure that the money costs to all producers in the industry will be equalized by imputing rent to scarce factors in inelastic supply. These Ricardian rents, or transfer costs, or producers' surplus, serve the social function of limiting the use of the scarce factor to the point at which its marginal value product is equal everywhere in the industry. In the case of land, for example, the exploitation of superior land is restricted by the landlord's rent to the point at which its marginal cost is equal to cost on the rentless inferior land. In consequence, equal additions of investment on superior or inferior land will make equal additions to output, and equal units of output will incur the same costs. The creation of differential as much as of scarcity rents, therefore, is one of the optimizing characteristics of a competitive market.

The Representative Firm. Marshall's "restless quest for realism," his refusal to be bound by static assumptions, is perfectly symbolized by his invention of the concept of the "representative firm." Despite the recourse to external economies to reconcile decreasing costs with competitive equilibrium, Marshall seems to have believed that business firms in most manufacturing industries are able to take advantage of internal economies of scale. He gave numerous examples of such internal economies and almost none of diseconomies that could not be overcome in time. The implication was that firms expand slowly but without any apparent limit. This creates a dilemma in stating the conditions of long-run equilibrium for an industry. The supply price of an industry in the long run is determined by the minimum average costs of the marginal firm, including "normal profits." "Normal profits," which Marshall defined as "the supply price of average business ability and energy," might be thought of as that level of profits that, if expected in the future, would lead to zero net investment. If firms enjoy internal economies, they must necessarily grow in size with the growth of the industry itself. Expansion by external economies will now favor the larger firms and so alter the size distribution of firms in the industry. The earning of "normal profits" now has no significance in limiting entry, since a still larger newcomer to the industry could always do better than the marginal firm. Marshall rescued himself from this difficulty, however, by a biological analogy. He claimed that firms go through cycles of energy and business initiative and are thus unable to take constant advantage of decreasing costs. Although he conceded later that the growth of joint stock companies mitigated the effect of the high mortality of unusual entrepreneurial ability, he never abandoned the conviction that the history of firms is characterized by a biological life-cycle.

Marshall's belief in the eventual senility of growing firms won very few adherents even in his own time. It is difficult to see what any assertion about the returns-to-age schedule of a firm—Marshall seems to be saying that the curve relating a firm's average costs to its age is U-shaped—has to do with static returns to scale. Once we accept Marshall's idea, however, we must reconstruct the usual formulation of long-period equilibrium and replace the idea of a marginal firm by a representative firm. The final equilibrium situation must now be defined as one in which a representative firm earns just normal profits and no more. The industry is in equilibrium and its output is constant through time, because the increase in output from firms that are growing and being "born" is matched by the loss in output from firms that are declining and "dying." The representative firm provides us with a miniature illustration of the supply curve of the industry; its unit costs represent the average unit costs of the firms in the industry, and its unit cost curve describes the reactions of supply, via the number and size of firms, in the process of long-period adjustment. Here, as elsewhere, it is not clear whether Marshall refers to a representative one-plant firm or a representative multiplant business unit. On the whole, however, it appears that the representative firm is a representative business organization, not a representative production unit. Marshall describes it as neither a newcomer nor a well-established firm, but one with an average access to internal and external economies. This has the danger of suggesting that it has a real existence. The representative firm, however, is an abstraction; it is neither an arithmetic average, nor a median, nor even a modal firm. It is representative not with respect to size but with respect to average costs. Marshall likens it to a typical tree of a virgin forest, for it always remains representative of the average life-cycle of the firms in industry, growing as does the industry itself.

The concept of a representative firm is one of Marshall's many concessions to brute facts. Much as he was preoccupied with supplying a purely formal body of analysis, he was, at the same time, attempting to account for the experience of his age. The growth in the size of firms, he thought, made it necessary to concede the existence of economies of scale. On the other hand, he was unwilling to accept the implication that this entailed the destruction of competition. Hence, the resort to biological analogies. It is obvious, however, that static theory has almost nothing of significance to say about the temporal process of growth in the size of firms: *being* large, yes, but not *growing* large. Marshall's device of the representative firm allowed him to state the conditions for equilibrium of total output of an industry without requiring at the same time that all the member-firms of the industry be in equilibrium. The trouble with the notion is that it is a purely *ex post* construction: it describes the features of an equilibrium situation but contains no analysis of the path toward equilibrium and fails in any way to demonstrate that the process will in fact converge to equilibrium. It yields a conception of long-run equilibrium that does not conform to stationary conditions but constitutes, in Guillebaud's words, a "sort of conceptual half-way house between the real dynamic world and the stationary hypothesis."

Monopolistic Competition. The concept of the representative firm retained its place in economic theory until an alternative reconciliation of increasing returns with competitive equilibrium suggested itself. Taking a hint from Marshall's suggestion of "the difficulties of marketing," the entire Marshallian theory of value was reconstructed by Sraffa, Harrod, Chamberlin, and Robinson on the basis of the individual firm as a monopolist of its own particular market. Marshall had toyed with this solution as a reinforcement for his other two explanations of increasing returns under competition but had apparently regarded it as a special case. The heated debate in the 1920's over "empty economic boxes" in Marshallian theory culminated in the triumphant generalization of Marshall's hint of the existence of product differentiation. The almost total rejection of long-period analysis that this entailed banished the concept of the representative firm and the associated problem of falling supply price from economic literature. Price theory ever since has been a theory of the firm in the short run, supplemented by an informal analysis of the entry conditions into loosely defined groups of enterprises. The gain in rigor from this piece of surgery has been immense, but the price in terms of a lopsided theory of competition has been equally great. In distribution theory or in welfare economics the argument is invariably carried through to the full long-period adjustment before being dropped, but in the theory of supply the long run is fuzzed over or entirely confined to the individual firm floating uneasily in a situation in which it can exclude rivals from duplicating its product but cannot prevent them from eroding its profit.

READER'S GUIDE TO THE *PRINCIPLES OF ECONOMICS*

The preface to the first edition pays tribute to the principle of continuity, exemplified in the motto *Natura non facit saltum,* as the unifying element in the treatment of the book. Running through the *Principles* is "one Fundamental Idea," namely, that of "the general theory of equilibrium of demand and supply." The final paragraph of the Preface contains one of Marshall's typical skeptical comments on mathematical economics: mathematics is at best a useful piece of scaffolding, which should be removed in the presentation of final arguments (see also Book III, chap. 1; Appen. D, sec. 1; Math. Appen. XIV).

The Preface to the eighth edition carries an apologetic note about the largely statical character of the analysis in *Principles*. Despite the frequent use of the device of *ceteris paribus,* the keynote of the book, Marshall insists, is dynamics rather than statics. Even so, statics and dynamics are not the whole of economics: "The Mecca of the economist lies in economic biology rather than in economic dynamics." The notion of a price-determining margin, Marshall observes, has received increasing stress in successive editions of the *Principles* and with it has come increasing emphasis on the fact that the relevant margin "varies with the conditions of the problem in hand, and in particular with the period of time to which reference is being made."

Introduction. It is characteristic of Marshall's approach to economics that the book begins with a statement of "the pains of poverty and the stagnating influences of excessive mechanical toil" whose elimination "gives to economic studies their chief and their highest interest" (chap. 1, sec. 2). The fundamental feature of modern industrial life, Marshall continues, is not competition but self-reliance, deliberate choice-making and rational forethought (sec. 4). Appendixes A and B complement the introductory chapter: the first gives a sketch of the growth of the free enterprise system, the second provides a capsule history of economic thought, notable for its conciliatory comments on the German Historical School.

Scope, Substance, and Method. Economics owes its progress to the fact that "money affords a fairly good measure of the moving force of a great part of the motives by which men's lives are fashioned." This thesis forms the burden of chapters 2–4. Marshall admits that the "desires" that prompt to action sometimes bear little relationship to the realized "satisfactions" from that action (sec. 1; see also Book III, chap. 3, n. 1). Price theory, however, can get along merely on the basis of "revealed desires." The divergence between desires and satisfactions raises no special problems until we get to welfare economics. But Marshall is reluctant to cede any ground whatever. After noting the real difficulties connected with intertemporal and interpersonal comparisons of utilities, he nevertheless concludes that "the money which people of equal incomes will give to obtain a benefit or avoid an injury is a good measure of the benefit or injury" (sec. 2). Similarly, after stating Bernoulli's hypothesis he avoids applying it directly to whole income classes, not because of the impossibility of aggregating individual utilities, but on the strength of the astonishing assertion that "by far the greater number of the events with which economics deals affect in about equal proportions all the different classes of society" (sec. 2).

Sections 3–7 defend the economist's concern with the sphere of rational action, that part of men's conduct that is dominated by deliberate choice. Appendixes C and D pursue the theme of the proper scope and method of economics. Chapter 3 defines the concept of an economic law. Chapter 4 touches on the relationship between pure economic theory and applied economics; section 3 contains an interesting list of the chief practical questions to which economists ought to address themselves. The four brief chapters which make up Book II deal with the definition of fundamental terms. Chapter 3, section 2, provides some very sensible comments on Smith's doctrine of productive labor. Chapter 4 and Appendix E introduce the reader to the much discussed question of the appropriate definition of capital.

Wants and Activities. Book III, chapter 1, introduces the theory of demand, a subject that "until recently . . . has been somewhat neglected." It is typical of Marshall's apologetic attitude to his English predecessors that he criticizes Ricardo and his followers merely for "laying disproportionate stress on the side of cost of production": they "were aware that the conditions of demand played as important a part as those of supply in determining value, yet they did not express their meaning with sufficient clearness" (see also Book III, chap. 3, sec. 6; Book V, chap. 5, sec. 5; Book VI, chap. 2, sec. 1; and Appen. I). Equally characteristic is the closing comment of the chapter to the effect that "the reaction against the comparative neglect of the study of wants by Ricardo and his followers shows signs of being carried to the opposite extreme."

Marshall's insistence on the importance of the supply side is central to his belief (developed in chap. 2 of Book III) that "activities"—questions involving the energy, efforts, and quality of human agents in the economic process—in some sense dominate and mold those very "wants," which are taken as data in static equilibrium analysis. Here and elsewhere in *Principles,* Marshall displays a reluctance to take wants as given. He inquires into the formation of consumers' preferences (chap. 2) before proceeding to develop the theory of value based on given tastes (chap. 3). Changes in the mode of production and their influence on human character, he seems to be saying in chapter 2, are more important determinants of economic welfare than the mechanical efficiency with which given resources are allocated to satisfy given wants. Despite his belief that a decentralized economy does within limits tend to produce optimum results, his faith in free enterprise is in fact grounded on the notion that certain superior qualities of human character—initiative, industry, frugality, and rationality—are invariably associated with such a system. He is firmly opposed to socialism, although sympathetic to some of the views of socialists, because he does not think that socialism will conduce to the development of that "firmness of character" that constitutes the springs of enterprise under a private property system. No doubt, this kind of thinking reflects what Schumpeter called "mid-Victorian morality, seasoned by Benthamism."

Marginal Utility. Chapter 3 opens with a statement of "the law of satiable wants or of diminishing utility" as a "familiar and fundamental tendency of human nature." Marshall gives no proof for the existence of such a law, but he does defend it against possible misinterpretations. Suppose it be argued that the marginal utility of the last necessary yard of wallpaper to cover a wall is greater than that of earlier yards; in that case, Marshall suggests, we must make the entire wall the unit of utility analysis. What of the case of the desire for music growing with the more music a man hears, or the virtue of cleanliness and the vice of drunkenness, which grow by what they feed upon? Here we must perforce conclude, according to Marshall, that the utility function has shifted. In the end we are left with a completely tautological definition of the law of diminishing marginal utility, referring to given tastes at an instantaneous moment of time, so stated as to include any and all eventualities.

Consumer's Demand. Having stated the law of diminishing marginal utility in section 1, Marshall proceeds immediately to deduce from it that demand schedules are negatively inclined (sec. 2). Employing an additive utility function and assuming that the marginal utility of money is "a fixed quantity," he shows that an individual's demand price for a commodity will fall with every addition to the amount of the commodity possessed or consumed. The underlying rationale of this procedure is given by the equation

$$\frac{MU_x}{p_x} = \frac{MU_y}{p_y} = MU_e ,$$

stated in Mathematical Appendix II. Marshall writes the marginal utility of money "or general purchasing power at a person's disposal at any time" as $d\mu/dm$, our MU_e. His du/dx and du'/dx' is our MU_x and MU_y. Defining p as "the price which he is just willing to pay for an amount x of the commodity which gives him a total pleasure μ," dp/dx is the price paid for an additional unit of x. And so we have in equilibrium

$$\frac{d\mu}{dm}\frac{dp}{dx} = \frac{du}{dx} ,$$

which is equivalent to our $MU_e \cdot p_x = MU_x$, and likewise for every other commodity. Jevons' equation for isolated exchange, namely that $(MU_x/p_x) = (MU_y/p_y)$, becomes

$$\frac{du/dx}{dp/dx} = \frac{du'/dx'}{dp'/dx'} .$$

A constant MU_e and a declining MU_x give a negatively declining demand curve; similarly, Marshall remarks, a constant MU_x and Bernoulli's hypothesis of a declining MU_e—$d^2\mu/dm^2 < 0$—give a positive income curve: "the marginal utility to him of an amount x of a commodity remaining unchanged, an increase in his means increases . . . the rate at which he is willing to pay for further supplies of it" (Math. Appen. II and chap. 3, sec. 3).

Marshall draws a demand curve in section 4. Cournot, following standard mathematical practice, had placed price, the independent variable, on the abscissa, and quantities demanded, the dependent variable, on the ordinate. Marshall established the now familiar arrangement showing price on the y-axis and quantity on the x-axis. His reason for violating common mathematical usage was to permit graphic derivation of market demand curves as the sum of individual demand curves (sec. 5); using the same co-ordinate system throughout, market demand curves could then be coupled with market supply curves, quantity now being the independent variable and price the dependent variable to be determined. Nevertheless, the Marshallian procedure is somewhat clumsy: in computing the price elasticity of demand of an individual demand curve, we have to accustom ourselves to inverting the first derivative of the demand function.

A demand curve for a commodity is drawn up on the basis of "other things remaining equal." Marshall never furnished an explicit list of the content of the pound of *ceteris paribus,* but he comes closer to doing this in section 6 than anywhere else in the book. A footnote touches upon the associated difficulty of defining a commodity.

Chapter 4 defines the concept of price elasticity algebraically as well as geometrically. Mathematical Appendix III introduces the notion of a constant-outlay curve, a demand curve whose elasticity is everywhere equal to unity. The demand for "necessaries" is shown to be typically inelastic, while the demand for "luxuries" is said to be highly elastic—an old idea in the history of economic thought (sec. 3). Elasticity of demand is governed by the ease of substitution in consumption (sec. 4); elasticity of demand for a commodity, therefore, has no meaning except in connction with a particular definition of the scope of the commodity in question (first footnote, sec. 3). The conceptual and statistical difficulties in measuring elasticity are discussed in sections 5–8.

The equimarginal principle with reference to consumption is stated in chapter 5, sections 1–2. It is then applied to the distribution of purchases through time. Given a subjective preference for present over future consumption, the marginal utility of a commodity will differ depending upon the date at which it is expected to be consumed (sec. 3). Although in principle intertemporal comparisons of utility, even for the same individual, have no scientific validity, it is possible to deduce the existence and shape of an individual's intertemporal utility curve from his willingness to pay interest for a money loan, assuming that his tastes and money income remain the same between two dates and ignoring the uncertainty that attaches to future events (sec. 4). The economy and care with which Marshall sets out the notion of time preference makes a striking contrast with Böhm-Bawerk's prolix and confusing exposition of the same idea (see also Book IV, chap. 7, sec. 8).

Consumer's Surplus. Consumer's surplus is defined in chapter 6, sec. 1, as the excess of what the consumer would pay for a commodity, rather than go without it, over what he does pay—in other words, the roughly triangular area under a demand curve above the price-quantity rectangle (see Math. Appen. VI). A similar utility surplus can be defined for the marginal utility curve that underlies the demand curve. Consumer's surplus becomes consumers' surplus in section 3, provided we "neglect for the moment the fact that the same sum of money represents different amounts of pleasure to different people." The first footnote in section 3 announces Marshall's intention "henceforward" to measure price per unit of the commodity demanded, in effect, to employ Jevons' "final utility" $(du/dx.)\,\delta x$ (see Math. Appen. I).

The chief difficulty in aggregating individual consumer's surpluses is the fact of different income-utility curves (sec. 3). Marshall brushes this objection aside on the grounds encountered earlier, that important economic events affect different income classes in about equal proportions. This paves the way for the application of consumer-surplus analysis in Book V, chapter 13, involving intergroup comparisons of utility. At this point Marshall encounters two further difficulties. First of all, the individual's utility function for a particular commodity varies with the amounts of other commodities consumed: consumer's surplus, therefore, can be estimated only on the static assumption that other commodities do not vary in price (sec. 3). Furthermore, it must be supposed that MU_e is constant along the demand curve (sec. 4), which is approximately true when the expenditure on the commodity in question involves only a small part of the total outlays of individuals (see Math. Appen. VI). For both these reasons, Marshall now abandons the previous concept of consumers' surplus and adopts instead a definition that limits the calculation of the surplus to "the neighborhood of the customary price" (sec. 4). Summing up, we conclude that consumer's surplus is approximately measurable when the commodity in question constitutes an insignificant item in the individual's budget and when the change in price is small. No particular reason has been given to lead one to believe that individual surpluses can be satisfactorily aggregated to form a consumers' surplus.

Having stated "one general law of demand" in Book III, chapter 3, Marshall now allows for the possibility of positively sloping demand curves, the so-called Giffen Paradox stated in section 4 of the present chapter. Giffen's Paradox, however, implies a generalized utility function, a conception that Marshall dimisses as "less adapted to express the every-day facts of economic life" than an additive utility function (see Math. Appen. XII). The closing section of this chapter once again postulates Bernoulli's hypothesis (see also Math. Appen. VIII). In a footnote Marshall draws attention to its implications with respect to gambling and insurance.

The Law of Diminishing Returns. Book IV, chapter 1, introduces the productive triad and the notion of the increasing marginal disutility of labor as one of the "fundamental principles of human nature," yielding a positively sloped supply curve of human efforts in the short run. "Land" is defined in chapter 2, section 1, as consisting of those resources given without cost or effort: "the fundamental attribute of land is its extension." This definition is, however, immediately fuzzed over, and by the end of the chapter we are back to agricultural land, for which the farmer pays a contractual rent to the landlord. This leads straightway to a statement of the law of diminishing returns à la Mill: not only is the law confined to the case in which capital and labor are jointly applied to land but, given a constant level of technical knowledge, it is proportionate rather than incremental returns that are said to be diminishing (chap. 3, sec. 1). An unambiguous incremental definition of the law is found later in the same chapter (secs. 3 and 8), but the proportional definition occurs again in Book V, chapter 2, section 1, and Book VI, chapter 10, section 8. Marshall's proof of the law is again perfectly classical in character: unless the law were in operation, cultivation would never have been extended to new land (sec. 1).

Marshall leaves no doubt that he regards the law of diminishing returns in this context as a historical law, for "whatever may be the future developments of the arts of agriculture, a continued increase in the application of labor to land must ultimately result in a diminution of the extra produce which can be obtained by a given extra amount of capital and labor" (sec. 2). The intramarginal surplus over and above the marginal cost of cultivation is only part of "the full rent of a farm in an old country" (sec. 2). The large variety of return schedules that are compatible with diminishing returns—if $x = f(N)$ is the production function, then $f'(N) < 0$ is compatible with $f''(N) \lessgtr 0$—are illustrated in section 3. Ricardo's assertions about the order of cultivation in a growing economy are defended against Carey's attack (sec. 5). Ricardo spoke carelessly "as though there were an absolute standard of fertility," ignoring the fact that "a mere increase in demand may invert the order in which two adjacent pieces of land rank as regards fertility" (sec. 3) and that "the order of fertility of different soils is liable to be changed by changes in the methods of cultivation and the relative values of different crops" (sec. 4). It is not to be doubted that there does exist something like a Malthusian pressure of population upon the means of subsistence; still, "Ricardo, and the economists of his time . . . did not allow enough for the increase of strength that comes from organization" (sec. 6; see also chap. 7, sec. 3).

So far, the whole of this third chapter in Book IV is entirely classical in tone, a somewhat improved version of J. S. Mill's treatment of the same subject. Near the end of the chapter, however, Marshall at last generalizes the law of diminishing returns to all the agents of production, making it applicable to manufacture as well as to agriculture (sec. 7). Nevertheless, "the fixedness of the whole stock of cultivable land in an old country" implies that "from the social point of view, land is not on exactly the same footing as those implements of production which a man can increase without limits" (sec. 8). In the final analysis, therefore, Marshall retains the classical notion that the "free gifts of Nature," which comprise land as a factor of production, are coterminous with the soil for which farmers pay rent.

The Growth of Population. As in Mill, the exposition of the law of historically diminishing returns leads on to a discussion of the dynamics of population growth (chap. 4). The Malthusian theory of population is set out with admirable succinctness, and its essential validity is boldly proclaimed: "there will probably be great improvements in the arts of agriculture; and, if so, the pressure of population on the means of subsistence may be held in check for about two hundred years, but not longer" (sec. 3). Sections 4–5 discuss the inverse relationship between fertility and the height of socioeconomic classes. Sections 6–7 provide a fairly pedestrian history of the growth of population in England since the Middle Ages. The whole of chapters 5 and 6 may be passed over, although the concluding sections at the end of both chapters give further evidence of Marshall's orthodox classical attitude to population problems.

The Growth of Capital. Chapter 7 pursues the subject of time preference and the supply of savings, broached early in Book III, chapter 5. Marshall notes that the classical economists regarded savings as made almost exclusively from business profits (sec. 7). But "in modern England rent and the earnings of professional men and hired workers are an important source of accumulation," particularly since "human faculties are as important a means of production as any other kind of capital." From the point of view of capital as it is conventionally defined, however, it would seem that Marshall, like most of the economists of his generation, exaggerated the significance of personal saving; his theory of saving completely neglects business saving, which probably accounted in his day for about half of all new funds.

"Human nature being what it is, we are justified in speaking of the interest on capital as the reward of the sacrifices involved in the waiting for the enjoyment of material resources" (sec. 8). The neutral term "waiting" is chosen in preference to "abstinence," though Marshall does not explain why Senior's term is likely to be misunderstood: it is not merely that the term "abstinence" seems to carry an honorific connotation but that it was difficult to break away from Senior's practice of speaking of average rather than marginal abstinence. The short-run supply curve of saving is said to be positively sloped (sec. 9). It may be backward bending, however, because of the Sargant Effect: individuals who are saving to provide a certain income for old age will find that they must save more if the rate of interest falls. Nevertheless, "while human nature remains as it is every fall in that rate is likely to cause many more people to save less than to save more than they otherwise would have done" (sec. 9). Moreover, the long-run supply curve of saving is also positively sloped, not so much because "a rise in the rate increases the *desire* to save" as because "it often increases the *power* to save, or rather it is often an indication of the increased efficiency of our productive resources."

The Division of Labor or Industrial Organization. Chapters 8–9 treat of a conventional subject in a conventional way. Chapter 8, however, contains some incisive comments on Social Darwinism, the working philosophy of businessmen everywhere at the turn of the century. At the close of chapter 9 economies of scale are divided into two classes: (1) external economies, dependent on the general development of the industry and (2) internal economies, "dependent on the resources of the individual houses of business engaged in it." Chapter 10 analyzes the localization of industry as a chief source of external economies (see in particular sec. 3). The growth of tertiary industries in England is discussed in section 4. Chapter 11 turns to internal economies as a source of the advantages of production on a large scale. Marshall's list of these economies indiscriminately mixes perfectly and imperfectly competitive conditions: (1) superior use of specialized machinery, (2) improved facilities for developing new machines and products, (3) discounts on bulk purchases, (4) greater opportunities for selecting managers and foremen with specialized skills, (5) favorable credit rating with bankers and, hence, ability to borrow on easier terms, and (6) ability to overcome marketing difficulties by spending on advertising (secs. 1–3 and 5).

This raises the question whether the growth of firms reaping the benefits of internal economies will destroy competition. Marshall's answer is that small firms do in fact survive because of the short-lived nature of dynamic entrepreneurship as well as the marketing difficulties that growing firms encounter (sec. 5).

The character of entrepreneurial ability and the context in which energetic innovators will come to the fore is further discussed in chapter 12. Marshall's explanation of the unique functions performed by the entrepreneur as distinct from the business manager is far from precise (secs. 2 and 5). Unusual business talents are rarely inherited; this accounts for the fact that firms in the hands of partners will rarely grow rapidly for more than a generation (sec. 6). But "since the joint-stock companies in the United Kingdom do a very great part of the business of all kinds that is done in the country," offering "very large opportunities to men with natural talents for business management, who have not inherited any material capital, or any business connection" (sec. 9), it is difficult to see how this chapter is supposed to live up to its promise of showing why large firms do not in fact drive their smaller rivals out of business. The famous "trees in the forest" paragraph in the following chapter (chap. 13, sec. 1) does little to clear up the difficulty. Despite "the great recent development of vast joint-stock companies, which often stagnate, but do not readily die. . . . Nature still presses on the private business by limiting the length of the life of its original founders, and by limiting even more narrowly that part of their lives in which their faculties retain full vigour." By some process of arithmetic addition, we are led to the conclusion that "in almost every trade there is a constant rise and fall of large businesses, some firms being in the ascending phase and others in the descending."

In the last paragraph of this chapter Marshall distinguishes between interest as "the supply price of capital," the net earnings of management as "the supply price of business ability and energy," and the gross earnings of management as the sum of the net earnings plus "the supply price of that organization by which the appropriate business ability and the requisite capital are brought together." Marshall's net earnings of management correspond to what other authors have called "wages of management." Marshall's gross earnings seems to correspond to the common definition of "profits" when it is calculated inclusive of wages of management.

So far we have met only one kind of external economy, that caused by the localization of industry. Chapter 11, sec. 4, briefly mentions another: the growth of trade knowledge as the result of more newspapers and technical publications. The summary in chapter 14, however, mentions a more comprehensive kind of external economy stemming from "the modern facilities for communication offered by steam transport, by the telegraph and by the printing-press" that accrues to an industry independently of its own growth. Section 2 defines the "representative firm" of an industry as "in a sense an average firm," whose expenses govern the supply price of the industry's product. This leads up to a statement of the Law of Increasing Return as a counterfoil to the Law of Diminishing Return. Marshall gives credence to the classical idea that agriculture is dominated by the latter, while manufacturing is largely subject to the former; in a footnote, however, he concedes that "the forces which make for Increasing Return are not of the same order as those that make for Diminishing Return." Section 3 virtually amounts to a statement of the optimum theory of population. "The accumulated wealth of civilized countries," Marshall concludes, "is at present growing faster than population."

Equilibrium of Demand and Supply. The bulk of Marshall's contributions to the theory of value and distribution are to be found in Book V. Chapter 1 gives a short account of the concept of a "market." Chapter 2 examines the simple case in which supply is perfectly inelastic and all sales are made out of fixed stocks. The proviso that the marginal utility of money must be supposed approximately constant is mentioned once again (sec. 3). The last paragraph of chapter 2 draws attention to an important "peculiarity" of the labor market. Low wages, stemming from initial monopsony in the labor market, may cause workers to attach a high marginal utility to money, which then perpetuates low wages by affecting workers' willingness to supply labor. Moreover, workers sell labor in a lump sum and are thus prevented from making marginal calculations of efforts and rewards. "These are two among many facts, in which we shall find, as we go on the explanation of much of that instinctive objection which the working classes have felt to the habit of some economists . . . of regarding the labor market as like every other market."

The efforts and sacrifices of labor and waiting together make up the "real cost of production" of a commodity (chap. 3, sec. 2). When the real-wage rate and the interest rate are constant, "the money measure of costs corresponds to the real cost" (chap. 3, sec. 7). The normal supply price of a commodity may be taken to be the "normal expenses of production (including *gross* earnings of management)" of the "representative firm"; it is a price that will preserve constancy in the aggregate output of an industry (sec. 5). Marshall defines equilibrium in terms, not of the equality of quantity demanded and supplied, but in terms of the equality of the demand and supply price (sec. 6). Market and normal prices are identified with Smith's market and natural price (sec. 6). There follows the famous "blade of a pair of scissors" paragraph, concluding with the assertion that "as a general rule, the shorter the period which we are considering, the greater must be the share of our attention which is given to influence of demand on value; and the longer the period, the more important will be the influence of cost of production on value."

Stability Conditions. The stability conditions in the market are touched on in a footnote to section 6 and again in Appendix H, section 2. Marshall insisted that his formulation of the problem was identical with that given by Walras. Walras, however, insisted that his approach did not yield the same results as Marshall's. And, in point of fact, Walras was right. The now standard Walrasian approach treats price as the independent and quantity as the dependent variable. It looks at the supply and demand curves as end points of horizontal lines corresponding to the quantity demanded or supplied at a given price. But Marshall views the schedules as end points of a set of vertical lines, each corresponding to the price at which a given quantity is produced or consumed; quantity is now the independent variable and price the dependent variable. Marshall talks about the supply price and demand price of a quantity; the individual is asked not how much he would demand at a given hypothetical price but what is the highest price he would be willing to pay for a certain amount of a commodity. Marshall's demand schedule should really be called a sales function, not a demand function, since it gives the price at which a certain quantity can be sold.[2]

The quantity-dependent Walrasian approach relies on movements of price to reach equilibrium while the price-dependent approach relies on movements of quantity. Of course, both price and quantity vary in disequilibrium, and for simple problems there is no difference between the two approaches. But the dynamic assumptions of the two systems are quite different, as can be easily shown.

Take the case of a normal demand curve and a forward-falling or backward-bending supply curve (see Fig. 68). In the Marshallian analysis a shift to the right of the demand curve, given the supply

[2] It is easy to misinterpret Marshall unless his special terminology is kept in mind. For instance, in *Money, Credit and Commerce* (1924), Appendix J, section 5, he poses the following paradox: if England's import-demand for German goods increases, England's terms of trade become less favorable the more elastic England's import-demand, everything

curve, always increases the quantity supplied if the supply curve is positively inclined. But if the supply curve is negatively inclined, this result occurs only if the algebraic slope of the supply curve is less than that of the demand curve. For Marshall, Ia is stable: the moment the demand curve shifts, the demand price exceeds the supply price for Q_1, causing the quantity supplied to rise, which steadily narrows the gap between demand and supply price, until a position of stable equilibrium is reached at Q_2. It is stable by the Marshallian criterion $\Delta EDP/\Delta Q > 0$: for larger quantities the excess demand price is negative, causing the quantity produced per unit of time to decrease, and vice versa for smaller quantities.

Ib is unstable on Marshallian grounds. As soon as demand shifts, the demand price > supply price, which increases the quantity produced per unit of time so that output moves away rather than toward the equilibrium value. Any position to the right of Q_1 increases

---

else being the same. One would think that the more elastic England's demand, the less, not the greater, the adverse change in the price of her imports. But Marshall succeeds in demon-

MARSHALL'S PRICE-DEPENDENT
APPROACH

WALRAS'S QUANTITY-DEPENDENT
APPROACH

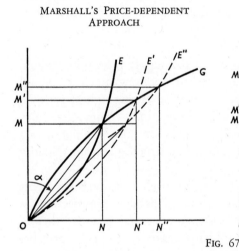

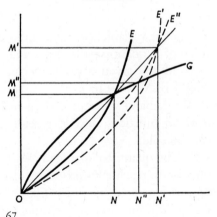

FIG. 67

$$\text{The terms of trade} = \frac{\text{England's exports}}{\text{England's imports}} = \frac{ON}{OM} = \tan \alpha .$$

strating that this is not so. E' shows the increase in England's import-demand at a given elasticity; E'' shows the increase at a greater elasticity. Hence, $ON'' > ON'$ and $OM'' > OM'$ and $ON'' - ON' > OM'' - OM'$, it follows that the terms of trade move against England by a greater amount for E'' than for E'. But a careful appraisal of the argument shows that Marshall obtains his paradoxical result by interpreting "an increase in England's import-demand" as an increase in the price (quantity of exports) that would be paid for a fixed amount of imports. If we interpret an increase in demand as an increase in imports taken at a given price, the conclusion is the exact opposite and the paradox disappears.

output, any position to the left decreases output: Q_1 is not a stable level of output.

Walras's stability condition is that excess demand equals zero at the equilibrium level and that $(\Delta ED/\Delta p) > 0$, such that a fall in

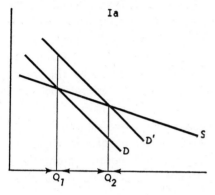
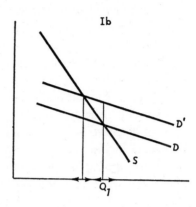

FIG. 68

price raises excess demand (Fig. 69). The dotted ED function illustrates this effect. When the demand curve shifts and the supply curve is positively sloped, $ED > 0$ makes the price rise to a new stable equilibrium. This is also true for negatively inclined supply curves but only if the algebraic slope of the supply curve is greater

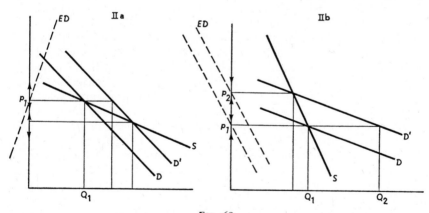

FIG. 69

than that of the demand curve. For Walras IIb is stable. As demand shifts, $ED > 0$, the price rises, reducing the supply and squeezing ED down to zero. The final price p_2 is stable because, at greater output, ED is positive: a positive rate of price change causes the supply to fall but by more than demand, thus eliminating excess demand. Similarly,

IIa is unstable. As demand shifts $ED > 0$, the price rises but the new equilibrium price is lower than the old equilibrium value; as the price moves away from the equilibrium value, supply falls faster than demand, increasing ED, which makes the price rise even faster.

Neither Marshall nor Walras realized why their approaches led to directly opposite results. Marshall never referred to the criterion of positive or negative excess demand. Walras, on the other hand, never understood the price-dependent approach. Who was right? Comparative statics shows that an equilibrium point is denoted by the intersection of a demand and supply curve. This tells us nothing about the way in which the system approaches a new equilibrium if the demand or supply curve shifts. This is true even when the supply curve is positively inclined, although we do not usually recognize it. Actually, of course, we do make certain implicit but nonrigorous assumptions about the dynamic properties of the market process even in static theory. But the Walrasian excess-demand assumption, which is usually implied in current textbook treatments, is no more plausible than the Marshallian excess-demand price assumption. The rigorous analysis of the stability conditions in terms of observable market behavior is the heart of economic dynamics, a branch of theory that hardly existed two decades ago.

Short Run and Long Run. Chapter 4 shows that all investment is carried to the point at which discounted future returns just equal accumulated cost outlays (sec. 2). The distribution of investment among alternative uses provides an illustration of the equimarginal principle (sec. 4). Prime and supplementary costs, or variable and fixed costs, are distinguished in section 5 of chapter 4. The complex problem of value must be broken down by means of the *ceteris paribus* method (chap. 5, sec. 2). The "famous fiction of the 'Stationary State'" has proved a convenient first step toward a solution of the problem of value. In a stationary state "the plain rule would be that cost of production governs value" because constant returns to scale would obtain (sec. 2). The assumption of a stationary state is "unconsciously implied in many popular renderings of Ricardo's theory of value, if not in his own versions of it" (footnote, sec. 8). The case of capital's growing at the same rate as labor, with land available in abundance and no technical change, exhibits all the distinctive features of a stationary state (sec. 3). Marshall then proceeds to define what he calls the statical method; it has since been called "partial equilibrium analysis" (sec. 3). The influence of the element of time on the relations between cost of production and value is illustrated with reference to the fishing industry.

In summarizing the nature of short-period adjustments, Marshall points out that producers often practice "restrictive strategy" when the going price fails to cover fixed costs. Instead of "spoiling the market" by supplying the amount called for by their marginal cost curves, they supply less so as to cause the price to rise. (See Fig. 70.) "In fact however they seldom pursue this policy constantly and without moderation." Reasons for employing the concept of a "representative firm" are reviewed in section 7. Section 8 classifies the problems of value by the periods to which they refer: market price, short-period normal price, long-period normal price, and secular movement of normal price. "The remainder of the volume is chiefly concerned with the third of the above classes: that is, with the normal relations of wages, profits, prices, etc., for rather long periods." The use of partial equilibrium analysis in problems relating to very long periods is "dangerous" (footnote, sec. 8). "In the opinion of the present writer the problem of normal value belongs to economic Dynamics" (footnote, sec. 2).

Joint and Composite Demand and Supply. When two or more productive factors are in joint demand, the demand schedule for any one factor can be derived from the demand curve of the final product by the vertical subtraction of the supply curves of the factors other than the one in question (chap. 6,

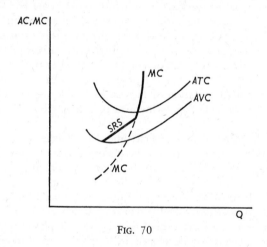

FIG. 70

sec. 1). The graphic illustration in the footnote assumes that the technical coefficients of production are fixed. The four laws of the elasticity of derived demand state that the elasticity of demand for a factor will be the lower: (1) the more indispensable the role of this factor in the production of the commodity, (2) the more inelastic the final demand for the product, (3) the smaller the share of this factor in total costs, and (4) the more inelastic the supply of co-operating factors (sec. 2, and Math. Note XV). The aggregate demand curve of a factor is the sum of its composite demands in various uses (sec. 3). The well-known difficulty, first discussed by J. S. Mill, of the impossibility of assigning separate supply prices to two or more joint products is mentioned in section 4. The last footnote in section 5 shows how to derive the composite supply curve of a factor and then goes on to comment on the instability of competitive equilibrium in cases in which some industries operate under increasing return. Foreshadowing the modern solution of the problem, Marshall notes that "product differentiation" may "keep many rivals in the field for a long time." Mathematical Appendix XXI shows that a general equilibrium of prices is theoretically determinate despite the existence of joint demand and supply.

Chapter 7 contains some general comments on the calculation of fixed costs for jointly produced goods. Section 2 considers once again the tendency toward oligopoly fostered by economies of scale. Section 3 broaches Knight's distinction between uncertainty and risk. If the individuals engaged in a certain industry are "gamblers"—for whom "the deterrent force of risks of loss in it is less than the attractive force of chances of great gain"—the presence of uncertainty may actually reduce average gains in the industry, as Adam Smith had once argued (sec. 4). Marshall ventures to say, however, that "in the large majority of cases the influence of risk is in the opposite direction," that is, most people are risk averters for whom "the total utility of increasing wealth increases less than in proportion to its amount."

Marginal Net Product. Chapter 8 opens with a statement of the concept of general equilibrium (sec. 1) and moves on to an exposition of the principle of substitution at the margin (sec. 2). The marginal product of a factor is defined as the marginal *net* product in an effort to overcome Hobson's objection that a single factor cannot be varied in amount without altering the amounts employed of all other factors; in mathematical terms, this reduces to the argument that a change in any one of the first partial derivatives of the production function involves significant changes in all the first-order differentials. Marshall points out correctly that the marginal product of any factor is defined on the basis of an optimum combination of factors, in which case the change in productivity of the nonvariable factors involves only negligible changes in higher-order differentials.

In section 4 Marshall for the first time distinguishes clearly between the static law of variable proportions and the historical law of diminishing returns. He takes the edge off the distinction, however, by confining his examples to agriculture. Marginal productivity theory is not a complete theory of distribution but rather a theory of the forces governing the demand for factors (sec. 5).

Rent and Quasi-Rent. The famous distinction between interest on new capital and quasi-rent on sunk capital, ground rent being merely "the leading species of a large genus," is developed in chapter 9. In a footnote, Marshall refers to Fetter's attack on "extension as the fundamental attribute of land, and the basis of rent." Marshall's reply is that the prominent role of ground rent in the development of rent theory is a historical accident: rent is a payment for *any* nonaugmentable resource. Scarcity rents are distinguished from differential rents in the concluding section of the chapter. Marshall warns, however, that "in a sense all rents are scarcity rents, and all rents are differential rents."

The final footnote of chapter 9 and the first few pages of chapter 10 are devoted to clearing up misconceptions with respect to the nature of quasi-rent: quasi-rents are once again defined as the total returns to temporarily specialized agents minus the cost of replacement and wear. Chapter 10, section 5, touches on the concept of opportunity or alternative costs, a phrase that Marshall never used. The footnote to this section, attacking Jevons' formulation of the rent problem, with its pointed comment that it is "inexpedient" to say that "rent does not enter into cost of production" but "it is worse than inexpedient" to say that it does, has been the subject of endless discussion. Marshall fails to point out that the problem can be looked at not only from the short-run and from the long-run point of view but also from the individual and the social point of view.

If "land in an old country is approximately (and in some senses absolutely) a *permanent and fixed stock,"* as Marshall claims (chap. 10, sec. 3), rent is price determined even in the long run. As long as land has alternative uses, however, rent is nevertheless price determining to the individual farmer.

Chapter 11 completes the discussion of rent with an analysis of urban site values. The footnote to section 1 states a simple theorem in location economics, one of "a great many fanciful, but not uninstructive, problems which readily suggest themselves."

Increasing Returns. Chapter 12 returns to a subject raised earlier in chapters 3 and 5 of Book V: the special difficulties connected with the idea of decreasing cost industries. Marshall notes that, on the face of it, "the elasticity of supply of a commodity which conforms to the law of Increasing Return . . . is theoretically infinite for long periods" (sec. 1). This implies that there are no limits to the growth in size of firms. But this is incompatible with the maintenance of competition in the industry. The resolution of this dilemma lies in some combination of: (1) "real" external economies, (2) the life-cycle of firms, and (3) "the difficulties of marketing." Section 2 of this chapter mentions all three theories in rapid succession. The first paragraph clearly implies the existence of "real" economies external to the firm but internal to the industry. In section 3 Marshall observes that "we expect the short-period supply price to increase with increasing output," but "we also expect a gradual increase in demand . . . to increase the economies both internal and external" at the disposal of most firms. The long-run supply curve will "exclude from view any economies that may result from substantive new inventions," but it will "include those that may be expected to arise naturally out of adaptations of existing ideas." In this sense the curve is not fully reversible. The second paragraph of section 2 sketches the reasons for "the rise and fall of individual firms." The third paragraph resorts to market imperfections to explain why firms cannot constantly take advantage of internal economies. A footnote provides the starting point for the theory of monopolistic competition: "when we are considering an individual producer, we must couple his supply curve—not with the general demand curve for his commodity in a wide market, but—with the particular demand curve of his own special market. And this particular demand curve will generally be very steep." The last footnote to this section seems to accuse Cournot of overlooking the incompatibility of internal economies to the firm and the maintenance of competition. But it was Cournot who first posed the problem explicitly.

The device of a representative firm is discussed once again in section 3. The chapter closes with the admission that the problem is one of "organic growth" not "statical equilibrium." "The Statical theory of equilibrium is only an introduction to economic studies, and it is barely even an introduction to the study of the progress and development of industries which show a tendency to increasing return." We pass on to Appendix H, where the problem is further discussed. In section 3 of this appendix, Marshall argues that *neither long-run demand nor long-run supply curves are really reversible* and that this is true whether the industry in question is a decreasing or an increasing cost industry. In a famous sentence he sums up the crucial difficulty in the concepts of short and long run, involving as they do operational time rather than clock time:

"We should have made a great advance if we could represent the normal demand price and supply price as functions both of the amount normally produced and of the time at which that amount became normal."

The Particular Expenses Curve. Section 4 introduces the concept of a particular expenses curve. Marshall's exposition of this tool is confusing in the extreme. He applies it to the short run only in the final paragraph of the appendix. His Figure 39 shows a demand curve and a *PE* curve for an industry in long-run equilibrium. The long-run supply curve for the industry is not drawn at all, but it is made quite clear that it would lie above the *PE* curve. "The difference between the particular expenses curve and a normal supply curve lies in this, that in the former we do, and in the latter we do not, take the general economies of production as fixed and uniform throughout"—that is, we must draw a different *PE* curve for each point on the supply curve. The reason Marshall makes use of a *PE* curve to show the producers' surplus or the "dif-

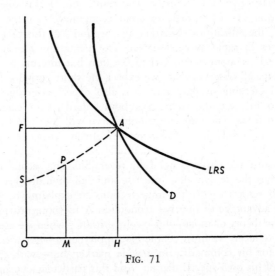

FIG. 71

ferential advantages" accruing to the industry in the long run is that he assumes that differences in average costs between the firms will persist in the long run. If he had drawn the supply curve of the industry, it would represent the unit costs of the representative firm. But this implies that "strong" or "mature" low-cost firms are earning a positive producer's surplus while "weak" or "senile" high-cost firms are earning negative producer's surplus. The firm that is representative of the industry should earn no producer's surplus whatever in the long run. Marshall concedes that "the producer of the *OH*th unit is supposed to have no differential advantage." In that case, the producer of the *OH*th unit is a marginal firm and the supply curve of the industry is the usual average = marginal cost curve of the industry as a whole. We can then interpret Marshall's Figure 39 in a straightforward fashion without assuming that the "producer's surplus" (notice the place of the apostrophe) accrues to the representative firm. It is not true, as Marshall argues in the opening paragraph of Appendix H, that the term "margin of production" has no significance for a decreasing cost industry. On the contrary, he himself suggests that we draw the *PE* curve so as to make the producer of the *OH*th unit the marginal producer. (See Fig. 71.) It would seem that if we are going to adhere to the notion of a representative firm we must permit the *PE* curve to cross the supply curve of the representative firm so as to make its producer's surplus equal to zero (Fig. 72).

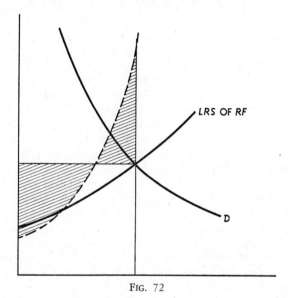

FIG. 72

Tax-Bounty Analysis. Marshall opens chapter 13 with a discussion of the various reasons that may cause demand and supply curves to shift (secs. 1 and 2). The effects of the shifts depend upon the elasticity of the curve that remains unchanged (sec. 3). In section 4 it is shown that a specific tax levied on increasing cost industries combined with a subsidy paid to decreasing cost industries increases aggregate consumers' surplus. The doctrine that "maximum satisfaction is *generally* to be attained by encouraging each individual to spend his own resources in that way which suits him best" is thus qualified even if we ignore inequalities of income distribution by assuming that "a shilling's worth of happiness is of equal importance to whomsoever it comes" (sec. 7). Marshall notes that the combined loss in producers' and consumers' surplus from a tax on an increasing cost industry actually exceeds the amount of the tax receipts (footnote to sec. 6), while a subsidy to a decreasing cost industry may not increase producers' surplus, though it must increase consumers' surplus (sec. 5). He argues that the latter difficulty could be overcome by a "compensating payment": "if a general agreement could be obtained among consumers, terms might be arranged which would make such action amply remunerative to the producers, at the same time that they left a large balance of advantage to the consumers" (sec. 5). The conclusions of this chapter, he warns in the closing paragraph, "do not by themselves afford a valid ground for government interference."

To avoid misunderstanding, the reader should turn now to Appendix K, where it is shown that consumers' surplus or producers' surplus cannot be added to workers' or savers' surpluses.

Theory of Monopoly. The net revenue of a monopolist producing at decreasing cost is maximized at the output level where the net revenue curve becomes tangent to a "constant outlay" curve (sec. 3). We may suppose that the monopolist has already exploited all the internal economies available to him and is producing in a plant of optimum size. The falling supply price is due to external economies, and hence the supply curve in Marshall's Figure 34 is the monopolist's long-run average cost curve. As Marshall remarks in Mathematical Appendix XXII, if $y = f_1(x)$ is the demand function and $y = f_2(x)$ is the supply function, the maximum net revenue is found by making $[xf_1(x) - xf_2(x)]$ a maximum. Since $xf_1(x)$ is total revenue and $xf_2(x)$ is total cost, this amounts to equating marginal revenue and marginal cost.

A lump-sum tax, such as a license duty on gross or on net revenue, will not alter the optimum output level (sec. 4 and Math. Appen. XXIII). But a tax proportional to output will induce the monopolist to raise his price and restrict output (sec. 4). Marshall is careful to discourage the idea that output is always less and price always higher under monopoly than under competition (sec. 5). One of the difficulties is that a monopolist may choose to suffer losses in the short run in order to maximize long-run profits (sec. 6).

Marshall adds the monopolist's net revenue to the consumers' surplus to form the "total benefit" accruing to producers and consumers together from the sale of the product. In a footnote he shows how to obtain a total benefit curve. It is hardly surprising that the decision, say, on the part of a nationalized industry, to maximize total benefit always results in a large output and lower price than the decision to maximize net revenue alone (sec. 7 and Math. Appen. XXIII).

These results, however, are used in section 8 to produce the interesting conclusion that it may be worthwhile to operate a government enterprise at a loss if the total benefit or at least the "compromise benefit"—consumers' surplus being discounted by the necessity to levy taxes to make up the deficiency—is positive. Marshall goes on to express the naïve hope that the future will produce statistical "demand schedules sufficiently trustworthy to show in diagrams that will appeal to the eye, the quantities of consumers' surplus that will result from different courses of public and private action," thus dispelling the suspicion that falls on all public projects that do not show a balance of pecuniary profit (sec. 9). The chapter closes with a brief note on the indeterminacy of duopoly and the pervasiveness of competitive forces even in industries that are technically "natural monopolies" (sec. 9).

Chapter 15 provides a serviceable summary of the whole of Book V but adds nothing new.

The Marginal Productivity Theory of Distribution. "The keynote" of Book VI, Marshall remarks, "is in the fact that free human beings are not brought up to their work on the same principles as a machine, a horse, or a slave. If they were there would be very little difference between the distribution and exchange side of value." The first chapter of Book VI abstracts from this difficulty as well as from all other aspects of factor supplies. After a brief history of wage theory (sec. 2) and a sketch of a simple Ricardian theory of distribution (secs. 3–6), we are given a succinct statement of marginal productivity theory as a theory of the demand for productive agents. The wage of a "marginal shepherd" is governed by his marginal product (sec. 7); this result is applied to the capital market in section 8 to show that the pure rate of interest is likewise regulated by the marginal productivity of capital. Marshall asserts that the marginal productivity theory "cannot be made into a theory of interest, any more than into a theory of wages, without reasoning into a circle." His objection is based, presumably, on the fact that the theory has nothing to say about the forces governing the supply of factors. But this is not how he expresses it at this point. On the contrary, he seems now to lend support to Hobson's criticism, which he had earlier rejected (see Book V, chap. 8, sec. 4): "The doctrine that the earnings of a worker tend to be equal to the net product of his work, has by itself no real meaning; since in order to estimate the net product, we have to take for granted all the expenses of production of the commodity on which he works, other than his own wages" (sec. 7). This statement is open to various interpretations, but it seems to deny the mutual and simultaneous determination of factor prices. The chapter closes with a brief comment on the calculation of national income (sec. 10).

The Supply of Productive Agents. Chapter 2 introduces "the reflex influence of remuneration on the supply of different agents of production." Marshall insists on the importance of Jevons' disutility of labor as governing the supply of productive effort in the short run: "There seems . . . to be no good foundation for the suggestion made by v. Böhm-Bawerk . . . that value must be determined generally by demand, without direct reference to cost, because the effective supply is a fixed quantity: for even if the number of hours of work in the year were rigidly fixed, which it is not, the intensity of work would remain elastic" (footnote, sec. 2). The short-run supply curve of labor is generally positively sloped, though it may be backward bending (sec. 2). The long-run supply curve of labor is also positively sloped (sec. 3). Every increase in earnings increases the supply of labor, yet the "iron law of wages" does not hold for "the modern western world." Wages have risen because wants have become adjusted to a higher level of "activities," meaning an increase in the energy and initiative of human agents and an increase in expenditures on rearing and training. Similarly, the supply of saving generally responds positively to the rate of interest, not because of a static principle of substitution, but because saving habits become increasingly rational as the future is more vividly regarded (sec. 4). Marshall's interest in "the high theme of economic progress" is never more evident than in this chapter. His final attitude to the marginal productivity theory of distribution is summed up in section 3: "Wages tend to equal the net product of labor; its marginal productivity rules the demand-price for it; and, on the other side, wages tend to retain a close though indirect and intricate relation with the cost of rearing, training and sustaining the energy of efficient labor."

The special character of land as a productive agent is stressed once again in section 5. Section 9 touches on the relations between wages and interest in an economy in which the capital stock is growing faster than the labor force: "the rate of interest will constantly fall, unless indeed invention opens new advantageous uses of roundabout methods of production." For all the crudities of the classical wages fund doctrine, "there is . . . a rather forced sense in which we may perhaps be justified in saying that the earnings of labor depend upon advances made to labor by capital." At any rate, "the modern doctrine of the relations between labor and capital is the outcome to which all the earlier doctrines on the subject were working their way; and differs only in its greater exactness, completeness and homogeneity, from that given by Mill in the third chapter of his fourth book; the only place in which he collects together all the various elements of the problem" (sec. 10).

The Peculiarities of Labor. Chapter 3 deals with the problem of relative wages and, apart from the clarifying distinction between time earnings, piecework earnings, and efficiency earnings, adds nothing to Adam Smith's famous discussion. Chapters 4 and 5, on the other hand, represent what is perhaps the most penetrating contribution to labor economics since the *Wealth of Nations*. In these chapters Marshall is concerned with those forces acting on the supply of labor that lead to cumulative disadvantages in labor's bargaining position. He distinguishes five "peculiarities." The first two have to do with the special role of nonpecuniary considerations in the supply of labor: (1) the absence of a "capital market for labor" (secs. 2–4), and (2) the inseparability of the worker from his services (sec. 5). The first of these had been discussed by J. S. Mill and Cairnes under the heading of noncompeting groups. Investment in human capital in the form of labor-training is not merely a function of the prospective earnings resulting from a given expenditure on education. Since "the worker . . . remains his own property: those who bear the expenses of rearing and educating him receive but very little of the price that is paid for his services in later years." Children of the working class generally receive inadequate education and labor-training and "this evil is cumulative" (sec. 2). Moreover, labor-training initiated by employers results in benefits which cannot be fully appropriated by the employer (sec. 4); labor-training constitutes an important example of irreversible "real" external economies. The second "peculiarity of labor" refers to the fact that the sale of labor always involves the "purchase" of working conditions. Sweated trades paying less than efficiency wages, therefore, may justify themselves in time by depressing the efficiency of labor.

The next two peculiarities are matters of degree, and their significance is debatable: (3) the perishability of labor and (4) the lack of a "reserve fund" (sec. 6). Marshall concludes, however, that "it is certain that manual laborers as a class are at a disadvantage in bargaining; and that the disadvantage wherever it exists is likely to be cumulative in its effect. . . . It lowers his wages; and as we have seen, this lowers his efficiency as a worker, and thereby lowers the normal value of his labor."

The fifth and most important of the peculiarities consists of the long period of time required to vary the supply of specialized labor: "Not much less than a generation elapses between the choice by parents of a skilled trade for one of their children, and his reaping the full results of their choice" (chap. 5, sec. 2). Furthermore, "the birth-rate in every grade of society is determined by many causes, among which deliberate calculations of the future hold but a secondary place" (sec. 3). But whatever the importance of this fifth peculiarity in limiting the action of competition in the labor market, it is difficult to see in what way it constitutes a cumulative force tending to increase labor's disadvantage in bargaining. Possibly this explains why Marshall held it over for separate discussion in chapter 5.

The Theory of Interest. The real rate of interest is governed on the supply side by "prospectiveness" or time preference and on the demand side by "productiveness" (chap. 6, sec. 1). Marshall minimizes Böhm-Bawerk's contributions to the theory of interest and in a footnote takes issue with the proposition that "every lengthening of a roundabout process is accompanied by a further increase in the technical result." On the contrary, Marshall argues, it is because the rate of interest is positive that technical processes are exploited in order of their roundaboutness. This point, however, was eventually conceded by Böhm-Bawerk himself and does not vitally affect his theory. A brief description of scholastic doctrine on interest (sec. 2) is followed by Marshall's only extended reference to Marx (sec. 3). Every attempt to establish the premise that interest is "unpaid labor," Marshall observes, "has necessarily assumed implicitly that the service performed by capital is a 'free' good, rendered without sacrifice, . . . and this is the very conclusion which the premise is wanted to prove." Gross and net interest are distinguished in sections 4 and 5. Fisher's distinction between the money and the real rate of interest is explained in section 7. A money rate of 5 per cent per annum corresponds to a real rate of 15.5 per cent when prices have fallen 10 per cent per annum, that is, the purchasing power of $105 at the beginning of the year is equivalent to that of $115.50 at the end of the year. Similarly, a money rate of 5 per cent corresponds to a negative real rate of 5.5 per cent when the annual rate at which prices are rising is 10 per cent.

The Theory of Profit. The next two chapters on business profits are extremely diffuse and difficult to summarize. A great many salient points are made, but the discussion lacks terminological clarity. Notice Marshall's doubt whether joint stock companies have "the enterprise, the energy, the unity of purpose and the quickness of action of a private business" (chap. 7, sec. 6); the importance of trusts and cartels, despite their recent growth, "is apt to be exaggerated" (chap. 8, sec. 10). The views of "some American writers" who regard profits as "remuneration of risk simply" are attacked on the ground that many risks can be insured against; Marshall comes close here to stating Knight's uncertainty theory of profits (chap. 8, sec. 2). Marshall attributes profits to a fourth factor of production, namely "organization," the institutional arrangements of modern business. In addition, he visualizes conjuncture or opportunity earnings, resulting from the fact that agents are more productive when combined in a going enterprise than when used separately (chap. 8, sec. 10). We will have occasion to examine the validity of these assertions in the next chapter. A footnote in chapter 8, section 3, concerning "fishmongers and green grocers in working-class quarters" deserves special mention. It contains a hint at the structure of Chamberlin's theory of monopolistic competition: despite geographical product differentiation and finite demand elasticities, profits are normal—the so-called tangency solution.

Theory of Rent. Chapters 10 and 11 may be passed over, concerned as they are with the familiar problem of different land tenure systems. Marshall observes that the distinctive features of English land tenure largely account for Ricardo's discovery of "the deepest and most important line of cleavage in economic theory": "the distinction between the quasi-rents which do not, and the profits which do, directly enter into the normal supply prices of produce for periods of moderate length" (chap. 9, sec. 5).

Chapter 11 provides an excellent summary of the whole of Book VI.

The Course of Economic Progress. The last two chapters of the book provide Marshall with the opportunity of looking both backward and forward, touching on the springs of secular growth and projecting the future. Chapter 12, sections 2–4, contains an interesting account of England's industrial development in the eighteenth and nineteenth centuries. "Probably more than three-fourths of the whole benefit she has derived from the progress of manufactures during the nineteenth century has been through its indirect influences in lowering the cost of transport of men and goods, of water and light, of electricity and news: for the dominant economic fact of our own age is the development not of the manufacturing, but of the transport industries" (sec. 4). Economic growth has brought an increase in the " 'telescopic' faculty" (chap. 12, sec. 8), a gradual narrowing of wage differentials (sec. 9), a discernible tendency toward income equalization, in England if not in America, and a decline in the "inconstancy of employment" (sec. 12).

Population prospects are reviewed once again in sections 1 and 2 of chapter 13. Some support is given to the shorter-hours movement (sec. 3). The lump-of-labor fallacy is attacked in section 4, followed by an agnostic discussion of the effects of trade unions (secs. 7–10). Mill's formulation of Say's Law is cited in section 10: "though men have the power to purchase," Marshall observes, "they may not choose to use it." The general characteristics of a boom and slump involving a multiplier process are then described. Section 11 states the case against socialism. But "this cautious attitude does not imply acquiescence in the present inequalities of wealth." Bernoulli's hypothesis suggests that every move toward income equalization raises economic welfare (sec. 13). The closing pages of the book contain some suggestions for extending the scope of government control over "medical and sanitary matters" and for increasing government aid to education.

The Greatness of Marshall's Contribution.

Judged by the exacting standards of present-day theory, Marshall's *Principles* is an unsatisfactory book. In the hope of being read by men of affairs, Marshall hid his diagrams and mathematics in footnotes and appendixes and covered up every knotty point in the analysis. Moreover, an ambivalent attitude on the part of the author toward his own subject matter pervades the entire book. Ostensibly, the *Principles* is a study of static microeconomic theory, but time after time the reader is told that the conclusions of static analysis are unreliable and that microeconomics fails to come to grips with the vital issues of economic policy. The "Mecca of the economist," says Marshall, lies not in comparative statics, nor even in dynamic analysis, but rather in "economic biology." By "economic biology," Marshall apparently means the study of the economic system as an organism evolving in historical time. This sounds very much like the methodological program of American Institutionalism. And yet Marshall's efforts throughout his life were devoted to teaching, expounding, and refining the very kind of theory that he deprecated repeatedly in his book.

More than one commentator has puzzled over Marshall's "schizoid" attitude toward partial equilibrium analysis. And yet there is nothing very mysterious in it: it is the typical attitude of the modern economist. The value of the neoclassical contribution to economics, in providing a rigorous explanation of the determination of prices in long-run stationary equilibrium, is rarely denied. But the limited scope of this kind of analysis and its ultimate remoteness from practical problems is now well understood, not least of all by those who continue to devote themselves to improving it. Marshall's greatness lies in possessing this type of perspective at a time when most of his contemporaries had almost completely lost sight of the age-old "inquiry into the causes of the wealth of nations."

This is not to deny, however, that Marshall's peculiar integration of static microeconomics with bits and pieces of the classical theory of economic development made it more difficult for subsequent writers to grasp the true significance of partial equilibrium analysis. On the positive side, the Marshallian distinction between the market period, the short period, and the long period provided a general framework in which all previous theories of value found a place. His repeated emphasis on the "two blades" of demand and supply brought home as nothing else had the action of both costs and preferences in determining relative prices. His analysis of the Laws of Return brought order and meaning to the theories of Smith, Ricardo, and Marx. But his reconciliation of decreasing cost and competitive equilibrium via the notions of external economies, monopolistic competition, and the representative firm, fruitful as were all but the last, raised false problems that took the best efforts of a generation of economists to solve. And his total neglect of monetary forces in a work on the principles of economics, however much he warned his readers of this failing, did much to persuade economists that monetary theory belonged to the periphery of the science.

Nevertheless, if a man's contribution is to be judged on the basis of his solution of old problems as well as the stimulus that he provides for subsequent students, Marshall's *Principles* must be considered one of the most durable and viable books in the history of economics: it is the only nineteenth-century treatise on economic theory that still sells in the hundreds every year.

NOTES FOR FURTHER READING

1. *The Theory of Supply.* R. Opie, "Marshall's Time Analysis," *EJ,* June, 1931, emphasizes Marshall's operational conception of time and discusses some of the difficulties created for his analysis by clock-time considerations. R. Frisch reconstructs Marshall's theory of short- and long-run supply price with the aid of current graphical techniques: "Alfred Marshall's Theory of Value," *QJE,* November, 1950. Frisch's rendering seems entirely faithful to Marshall's intention, but see some objections by D. H. Robertson, *Economic Commentaries* (1951), chap. 1. All the relevant articles in the Great Debate on increasing returns and falling supply price are included in *Readings in Price Theory,* ed. G. J. Stigler, K. E. Boulding (1953); see especially J. Viner, "Cost Curves and Supply Curves," and H. S. Ellis and W. Fellner, "External Economies and Diseconomies." The latter article should be read after perusal of chapter 10, on the "Four Cost Curves," in J. Robinson, *The Economics of Imperfect Competition* (1934). The Appendix to Mrs. Robinson's book provides an authoritative restatement of the issue of "Increasing and Diminishing Returns." Stigler, *Production and Distribution Theory,* chap. 4, covers a number of topics in Marshall's *Principles* but is particularly useful on Marshall's treatment of internal and external economies; see also chap. 5, pp. 112–25, for Edgeworth's pathbreaking clarification of the distinction between proportional and incremental returns as late as 1911! Stigler's article "The Division of Labor Is Limited by the Extent of the Market," *JPE,* June, 1951, analyzes the effects of vertical disintegration, the earliest recognized source of increasing returns in the broad sense. The recent flowering of external economies in writings on "balanced growth" and their relationship to strict Marshallian external economies is lucidly discussed by H. W. Arndt, "External Economies in Economic Growth," *ER,* November, 1955.

L. Robbins' critique of "The Representative Firm," *EJ,* September, 1928, succeeded in virtually eliminating the concept from the literature. In recent years, however, some Cambridge enthusiasts have attempted to revive the doctrine: see P. Newman, "The Erosion of Marshall's Theory of Value," *QJE,* November, 1960, and the literature cited there. "Nobody knows Marshall who knows only the *Principles,*" remarked Schumpeter. And, indeed, Marshall's *Industry and Trade* (1919) and *Money, Credit and Commerce* (1923) are indispensable to an understanding of his entire system. *Industry and Trade* is something of a prolegomena to Chamberlin's and Robinson's works, as H. H. Liebhafsky shows: "A Curious Case of Neglect: Marshall's *Industry and Trade,*" *CJEP,* August, 1955. But even the *Principles* shows awareness of product differentiation and market imperfections; see D. C. Hague "Alfred Marshall and the Competitive Firm," *EJ,* December, 1958, and S. Hollander, "The Representative Firm and Imperfect Competition," *CJEP,* August, 1961. The modern theory of "workable competition" is actually a natural outgrowth of the thinking fifty years ago of Marshall, Clark, and their contemporaries; see S. Peterson, "Antitrust and the Classic Model," *AER,* 1957, reprinted in *Readings in Industrial Organization,* ed. R. B. Heflebower and G. W. Stocking (1958).

2. *Miscellaneous Topics.* The long-awaited variorum edition of Marshall's *Principles,* prepared by C. W. Guillebaud, has finally appeared; see

especially the "Editorial Introduction," Vol. II (1961). F. W. Ogilvie's hyper-critical essay, "Marshall on Rent," provoked a sympathetic restatement by T. P. Hollond, *EJ*, March, September, 1930. C. W. Guillebaud, "Davenport on the Economics of Alfred Marshall," *EJ*, March, 1937, provides an excellent exposition of Marshall's concept of long-run equilibrium. Marshall's views on "the peculiarities of labor" are critically dissected by W. H. Hutt, *The Theory of Collective Bargaining* (1954). This book consists of two essays; the first discusses "Labor's Disadvantage" in bargaining, the second deals with "In-determinateness" resulting from bilateral monopoly in the labor market. The latter problem was the subject of a famous article by J. R. Hicks, "Edgeworth, Marshall and the Indeterminateness of Wages," *EJ*, June, 1930; "Reply," by M. H. Dobb, March, 1931. J. J. Spengler, "Marshall on the Population Question," *PS*, March, June, 1955, provides a good survey of the state of population theory between Mill and Marshall and furnishes a detailed précis of Marshall's views on demographic change. B. Glassburner, "Alfred Marshall on Economic History and Historical Development," *QJE*, November, 1955, and A. J. Johnson, "Marshall on Economic Growth," *SJPE*, February, 1956, discuss Marshall's work in economic history. J. N. Wolfe, "Marshall and the Trade Cycle," *OEP*, February, 1956, supplemented by A. H. Hansen, *Business Cycles and National Income*, pp. 270–76, contrasts Marshall's emphasis on price and credit fluctuations with Keynes's emphasis on variations in income.

3. *Marshall, the Man and His Book.* The classic biographical account is by J. M. Keynes, *Essays in Biography*. See also Hutchison, *Review of Economic Doctrines*, chap. 4. The pathbreaking study of Marshall's philosophical preconceptions and their influence on his economic views is by T. Parsons, "Wants and Activities in Marshall," *QJE*, 1931, reprinted in *The Structure of Social Action* (1937), chap. 4, and "Economics and Sociology in Relation to the Thought of His Time," *QJE*, February, 1932. The centenary of Marshall's birth produced a number of reassessments, the most important of which is G. F. Shove's long essay, "Marshall's *Principles* in the Development of Economic Theory," *EJ*, 1942, reprinted in *EET*. One of the aims of this essay is to dispel the popular notion that Marshallian economics represents a compromise be-tween Ricardian doctrines and those of the marginal utility school, instead of a generalization of Ricardo's theory of value and distribution as expounded by J. S. Mill; Marshall's *Principles*, argues Shove, is of the "true Ricardian stock, neither a cross-bred nor a sport." Shove defends Marshall's political attitudes as the attitudes of a liberal, in the Victorian sense of the word; see his "Mrs. Robinson on Marxian Economics," *EJ*, April, 1944. J. Viner, "Marshall's Economics, in Relation to the Man and to His Times," *AER*, 1941, reprinted in *DET*, is written with characteristic charm and wit, emphasizing the profound influence of J. S. Mill on Marshall's social views. Schumpeter writes of Marshall with a certain degree of revulsion: see "Alfred Marshall's *Principles*: A Semi-Centennial Appraisal," *AER*, 1941, reprinted in *Ten Great Economists* (1951), and *History*, pp. 833–40, 920–24, 932–38, 990–98, 1045–53, 1060–62, 1083–84—page 922 contains some typical misleading "Austrian" remarks on the causal influence of utility and page 995 n. upholds Schumpeter's lifelong view of the inadmissibility of static falling supply curves. D. H. Macgregor, "Marshall and His Book," *Ec*, November, 1942, and C. W. Guillebaud,

"Marshall's Principles of Economics in the Light of Contemporary Economic Thought," *Ec,* May, 1952, each contribute to the task of "explaining" Marshall to a generation bred on macroeconomics and the theory of the firm in the short run. A. C. Pigou, *Alfred Marshall and Current Thought* (1953) conjectures what Marshall might say, were he alive today, on such topics as mathematical economics, elasticity of demand, the rate of interest, measurability of utility, and socialism. L. E. Fouraker, "The Cambridge Didactic Style," *JPE,* February, 1958, holds that the difficulties in grasping Marshall's meaning are mainly a matter of style of presentation, but G. Pursell, "Unity in the Thought of Alfred Marshall," *QJE,* November, 1958, argues that Marshall's striving for a unified approach led him to minimize theoretical complications.

Chapter **MARGINAL PRODUCTIVITY**

11 **THEORY OF DISTRIBUTION**

1. THE DEMAND FOR FACTORS OF PRODUCTION

IN THE first edition of the *Principles,* Marshall used the term "consumer's rent" instead of consumer's surplus to emphasize the fact that the triangle under the demand curve is in some ways analogous to Ricardian rents earned by producers. Following on this thought, we might go so far as to say that the whole of the marginal utility theory of value is simply an application of Ricardian rent theory to consumption demand. It was not until the 1880's, however, that it suddenly dawned on economists that the Ricardian theory of differential rent is really a special case of a much more general theory. Ricardo had shown that the final dose of "labor-and-capital" on an intensively used rent-yielding piece of land adds nothing to rent but merely produces wages and interest, rent being due to the superior productivity of the intramarginal units. Wicksteed, Wicksell, and J. B. Clark, to cite only the most prominent names, now realized that when land had alternative uses there was nothing unique about a no-rent margin. It is equally possible to picture a no-interest margin where the total product is exhausted by wages and rent, or a no-wage margin where the entire price is resolvable into interest and rent.

But, whereas Ricardo had used the marginal principle to show that the fixed factor earns a residual surplus, determined by the gap between the average and marginal product of the variable factor, Wicksteed, Wicksell, and Clark emphasized the other side of the coin: any variable factor must obtain a reward equal to its marginal product. If we measure a factor along the abscissa, the quantities of the other factors being fixed, the demand price per unit of the factor is determined by its marginal productivity curve; given the supply of all the factors, the corresponding rectangle under the marginal productivity curve represents its share of the total product. If this is so, the

403

remaining rectangle under the average productivity curve must be sufficient to reward the fixed factors on the basis of their respective marginal productivities. Since this is true of one variable factor, it must be true of all, each considered in turn. Is this generally true? Will the total product be exhausted when each factor is rewarded its marginal product? The answer to the last question is affirmative, argued Wicksteed in the *Co-ordination of the Laws of Distribution* (1894), provided the production function is of a special kind, namely, linear and homogeneous. Whether production functions necessarily conform to this type or whether market forces can be expected to lead to product exhaustion were among the most keenly debated questions in eco-

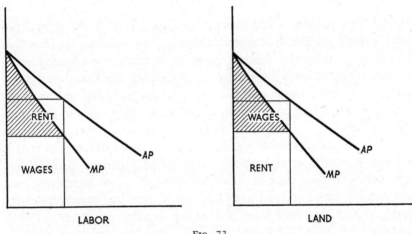

FIG. 73

nomics around the turn of the century. But before we examine this debate, it may be useful to review marginal productivity theory as such in the light of the standard objections that have been raised against it.

Marginal Productivity Theory. Marginal productivity theory states that each productive agent will be rewarded in equilibrium according to its marginal productivity as measured by the effect on the total product of the addition or withdrawal of a unit of that agent, the quantity of the other agents being held constant. With reference to labor, for example, the wage rate cannot exceed the marginal value product of labor: since any unit of labor may be the marginal unit, the rate of pay necessary to bring the marginal unit of labor into production marks the maximum the entrepreneur will pay to retain any other unit in employment. On the other hand, wages cannot in equilibrium be less than the marginal value product of labor: so long as additional labor adds more to revenue than to costs, it will pay to hire more labor; competition among employers, therefore, will bid up wages to the marginal value product of labor. *Ergo,* labor will be rewarded in accordance with its marginal productivity.

Marginal productivity theory may be described as a theory of distribution, provided we remember that it has nothing to say about the supply side in factor markets. Strictly speaking, it is only theory of the demand for a factor. This is why Marshall objected to statements implying that the marginal productivity of a factor "determines" its rate of reward. One might think that in the short run it would be legitimate to assume that the supply of a productive agent was given. Surely, the supply of labor is fixed in the short run, and hence wages are effectively governed by the demand price for labor. But if we define a unit of labor not as an individual worker but as an hour's work at the standard level of intensity, then the labor supply curve is by no means perfectly inelastic. If this is so, marginal productivity theory is unable alone to specify the rate of wages in the market. In the long run it is obvious, of course, that the rate of growth of the labor force is an independent element acting on wages. Indeed, in the extreme case of the subsistence theory of wages, the long-run supply curve of labor is infinitely elastic and labor's marginal product has no influence whatever upon the rate of wages.

The Normative Implications. J. B. Clark, the American founder of marginal productivity theory, regarded it as a normative principle of distributive justice, demonstrating that the returns to productive agents are not susceptible to change by human action. Although he developed the theory in the context of a stationary state with perfect competition, perfect foresight, and perfect mobility, fully realizing that these provide no more than the long-period equilibrium values toward which the actual values in the real dynamic world are continually tending, his formulation invited misunderstanding. It would be less misleading to say the very opposite: marginal productivity theory organizes the considerations relevant to a change in wages by human action. It tells us that wages may be raised by reducing the numbers available for hire, by raising the efficiency of workers, by increasing the quantity of capital they work with, and so forth, quite apart from the naked exercise of bargaining power.

Böhm-Bawerk once posed the following objection to the marginal productivity theory of wages: if the product of the marginal unit of labor governs the wage rate and labor works subject to diminishing returns, the intramarginal worker will receive less than the amount that he contributes to the total product; to the extent that labor fails to receive this intramarginal surplus, marginal productivity theory pictures the worker as subject to "exploitation." Clark replied to this objection in the *Distribution of Wealth* (1899) by pointing out that the theory assumes each factor to be homogeneous, all units of the factor being equally efficient; the marginal productivity of labor falls as more labor is added to a given amount of capital because capital per unit of labor is falling. In the same way, the greater marginal productivity of fewer workers is solely the result of the fact that they have more capital to work with; the greater productivity of fewer workers may just as well be attributed to the productivity of capital. Clark did not realize the full consequences of this reply, for it completely destroys the idea that a wage in accordance with the marginal productivity of labor is a "just wage." There is no such thing as a specific marginal product of a factor considered in isolation: the factors of production are basically complementary and the marginal product of one factor is a consequence of the marginal product of the other factors, and vice versa.

Payment in accordance with marginal productivity does have a normative function, however, but not in the Clarkian sense. A straightforward application of the equimarginal principle tells us that, but for nonpecuniary considerations, the whole of the labor force should be so distributed among alternative employments as to equalize the marginal value product of labor in all uses. In other words, the normative function of rewarding factors in accordance with marginal productivity is to achieve efficiency in resource allocation. To attack the theory by showing that it assumes perfect mobility of labor, perfect knowledge on the part of buyers and sellers, perfect competition, and full employment, assumptions that are not verified in real labor markets, is to miss the point. If there is immobility and ignorance of alternative wage rates, resulting in inequalities of wages for the same type of labor under identical working conditions in the same labor market, the total product is not being maximized; the total product is not maximized because labor is not being rewarded according to its marginal product. In each case, removal of a "friction" will improve the allocation of resources.

Exploitation. Pigou characterized a situation in which a factor receives less than the marginal increment it adds to the product as "exploitation." Pigovian exploitation is due to monopsony in the labor market, resulting in a divergence between average and marginal factor costs; that is, $MFC > AFC$. Instead of facing a given wage rate that it cannot affect by its own employment policy, the firm now finds that it bids up the wage rate as it expands its labor force. If perfect competition prevails in the product market, we have the situation depicted in the left-hand diagram of Figure 74. The firm multiplies labor's marginal physical product by the price per unit of final product to obtain the marginal value product of labor; it buys ON amount of labor, equating MVP to MFC. The difference between AFC and MFC represents the excess of labor's MVP to the firm over labor's average rate of reward. When there is both monopolistic competition and monopsony,

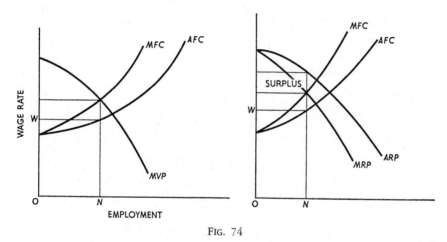

Fig. 74

we have the situation depicted in the right-hand diagram. Additional output can be sold only at lower prices; the firm faces a downward-sloping demand curve for its product, and the marginal revenue product curve —labor's marginal physical product multiplied by marginal revenue— lies below the average revenue product curve—the marginal physical product of labor multiplied by average revenue. The firm still determines the employment it will offer by equating MRP to MFC, but now it earns a surplus on the employment of each unit of labor, including the marginal unit.

The term "exploitation" to describe a situation in which labor receives less than its marginal value (or revenue) product conveys the unfortunate suggestion that labor's MVP or MRP constitutes its "just reward." But Pigou's point has nothing to do with equity. Pigovian exploitation differs from Marxian "exploitation" because, unlike the latter, it is due to imperfect competition in the labor market. It is designed to show that maximum efficiency in production is incompatible with a difference between labor's reward and the specific *MVP* of labor to the firm. It is the community and not the workers in question who are being exploited. Monopsony profits, like all other departures from perfect competition in factor markets, represent a failure to maximize welfare.

To avoid misunderstanding, we must remember that marginal productivity theory addresses itself only to static welfare considerations. The wage rate necessary to achieve optimum efficiency from the static point of view may fail to provide dynamic efficiency—say, an income adequate to educate children. But in the absence of knowledge of a specific divergence between static and dynamic efficiency, payment in accordance with marginal productivity must be assumed *prima facie* to contribute to the attainment of the optimum welfare conditions.

Is Continuous Substitution Possible? Almost at the outset, the marginal productivity theory met with the formal objection that inputs are not in fact fully variable. In the early versions of his general equilibrium model, Walras assumed that the input-output coefficients in each industry were rigidly fixed by technical considerations. This does not imply that wages are indeterminate because as long as the fixed input coefficients differ between industries it will still be true that only one wage rate can clear the market. Nevertheless, the assumption of technically fixed input coefficients is astonishingly restrictive: it not only eliminates the problem of optimum factor proportions but also the problem of choosing an optimum plant; no price or cost accounting is needed, and efficiency in production is achieved by the purely engineering conditions of avoiding outright waste. Walras eventually realized that the stringent condition of fixed coefficients was not required to demonstrate the existence of general equilibrium. But both he and Pareto continued to insist that conditions approximating to fixed input coefficients did occur. Although some coefficients of production are variable, others are fixed, and in the latter case marginal productivity fails to provide an explanation of how factor prices are determined.

The Theory of Imputation. The assumption of fixed coefficients also appears in Wieser's theory of imputation (1884), one of the earliest nonmathematical solutions to the problem of distributive shares. The germ of this theory is to be found in Menger's distinction between first-order goods (consumer goods) and high-order goods (intermediate goods) and the dependence of the want-satisfying power of the latter on the former. Although Wieser recognized the possibility of varying the proportions of the factors employed in the production of a good, he based his imputation theory on the postulate that the factors combine in fixed proportions in each industry, with the actual proportions varying between industries. Following Wieser, let us suppose that there are three factors, *x, y, z,* employed in the following proportions in three industries:

$$x + y = 100 \ ;$$
$$2x + 3z = 290 \ ;$$
$$4y + 5z = 590 \ .$$

The values on the right sides of the equations are the given prices of single units of the three final products; *x, y,* and *z* stand for the prices of the respective factor units. It is assumed that the value of the final product is equal to the value of the factors that enter into its production; that is, the final product is exhausted by the factor payments, which, as we will see, means that constant returns to scale prevail. Since we have three linearly independent equations in three unknowns, the system has a unique solution for *x, y,* and *z:* solving by the usual method, we obtain $x = 40$, $y = 60$, and $z = 70$. Since the input coefficients are fixed, the marginal product of a factor has no meaning. Nevertheless, the price of each factor and the allocation of factors between industries is perfectly determinate.

The assumption of perfect complementarity between the factors remained a favorite Austrian premise. Long after the "law of variable proportions" had become a standard feature of Marshallian and Walrasian economics, the Austrians retained the cumbrous doctrine of imputation. Even in the later editions of the *Positive Theory of Capital,* Böhm-Bawerk went no further than to admit partial factor substitutability. Some craven scruple of thinking too precisely about discontinuities and indivisibilities prevented him from accepting the "law of variable proportions" in its full generality. In its mature version, the Austrian theory of imputation might be characterized as a marginal productivity theory with a difference: the marginal value product of a factor is construed as the gain in consumers' satisfaction resulting from the addition of a *finite* unit of that factor; it is a factor's marginal physical product, inexactly defined, multiplied by the consumers' marginal utility from the extra product. Quite apart from the unnecessary concession to realism implied in making the increment of the factor a finite unit, the argument implies something like a social marginal utility and suggests that entrepreneurs impute consumers' satisfactions to the means of production. This clumsy formulation in terms of cause and effect can be avoided by recognition of the mutual and reciprocal determination of factor and product prices. The Austrian economists often implied that marginal utility is independent of factor prices, determining what product prices will be; but in fact the consumer's decision to purchase itself depends on the income that he has earned by selling productive services.

Linear Programming. The objection to the notion of complete variability in the factor proportions is nothing more than a questioning of the smoothness and continuity of production functions. Until recently the vested interest of economics in continuous differentiable functions has stood in the way of a fair appraisal of this objection. It

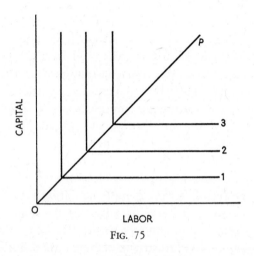

Fig. 75

is clear, however, that the general assumption of smooth continuous substitution renders marginal analysis inappropriate for most short-run situations in which a limited time horizon makes for rigidities in the productive process. In the last decade, however, a new type of analysis called linear programming has sprung up to deal practically with the case of discontinuous production functions. This approach consists essentially of applying Wieser's theory of imputation to a single firm. Without realizing it, Wieser had in fact stated a typical linear programming problem, defined as that of maximizing a linear relation, in his case the gross product of the economy, subject to a number of linear restraints.

The case of a firm faced with rigid technical coefficients of production is exemplified by a series of L-shaped isoquants whose vertices lie on a given vector *OP* (Fig. 75). An isoquant is analogous to an indifference curve except that a constant total product produced by various combinations of two productive agents replaces the constant total utility yielded by various combinations of two consumption goods. The distances between the isoquants along any ray from the origin show the returns to equiproportionate increases in *both* factors. If returns to scale are constant, every increase in labor and capital in the ratio t would raise output by the ratio $t;$ thus, the vertices of the L-shaped isoquants are equidistant from each other. Suppose now that the firm is faced not with one given technical alternative but with a number of alternatives, each characterized by fixed input coefficients. Every one of these "activities," so called, is characterized by a separate vector, and production can proceed by using two or more activities simultaneously and adding the results. For example, the final product can be produced by four different machines, each with a rigidly determined labor per machine ratio; the firm can choose between them or can elect to use them in combination. This idea of a set of additive activities is the basis of linear programming analysis. The firm is now faced with the same problem that Wieser posed for the total economy, that of maximizing its total product subject to a set of linear restraints.

An output of, say, 1 unit is obtained by the combination of inputs represented by A_1, B_1, C_1, D_1 (Fig. 76), an output of 2 units by A_2, B_2, C_2, D_2, and so on. By the property of constant returns to scale, A_1 and A_2 lie on a vector OA such that $A_1A_2 = A_2A_3$, etc., and similarly for the other activities. If the four activities are independent, such that they could be chosen alone, the corners always form a convex "cone." Any point within the cone is a possible combination of inputs. If C_2 lay above and to the right of B_2D_2, then a combination of the second and fourth activities would require fewer inputs per unit of output than the third activity, and hence the third activity would not be employed. The essence of linear programming analysis is that the firm is faced with given physical restraints in addition to given factor prices. Suppose labor is the limiting factor. At the indicated price line between labor and capital, activity A is optimal, and so is activity B or any combination of the two. But activity B is not feasible. With ON units of labor, the best the firm can do is to produce 2 units of output with activity A. Despite the positive price of capital, the marginal productivity of capital to the firm is zero.

It is easy to see that the case of complete variability of inputs, corresponding to a map of smooth isoquants, represents a generalization of activity analysis with the number of activities becoming infinitely large. Curiously enough, the development of economic theory reversed the logical order between the particular and the general case. It took more than half a century to show that marginal analysis can be applied to the concrete production problems of business firms only by recognizing that factor proportions are not in fact fully variable in the short run. Linear programming has already proved itself a power-ful tool of management science. More than that, however: by virtue of the ease with which it handles large numbers of variables, it has also shed new light on some traditional problems of economic analysis.

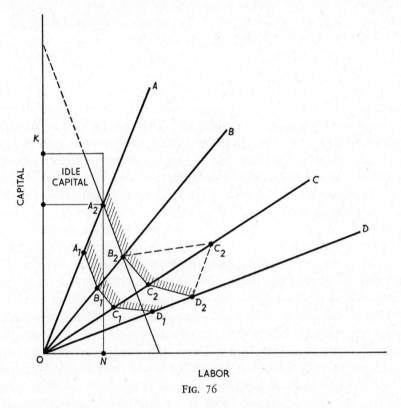

FIG. 76

The Hobson Objection. Marginal productivity theory assumes a constant amount of capital as the quantity of labor is varied. But if the *quantity* of labor is increased, the *quality* of capital will almost always undergo some change: more workers require more raw materials and more or different machines. If every change in the quantity of labor is accompanied by changes in the organization if not in the quantity of capital equipment—multiple-operator machines are not, after all, the same as single-operator machines—how can variations in output be attributed to labor alone? Is there a discernible and specific marginal product of labor?

This criticism was most vigorously stated by Hobson in *The Industrial System* (1909) and has since been echoed by many other gifted amateurs in economic theory. It is probably the oldest and most persistent objection advanced against marginal productivity theory. In a long unsatisfactory footnote in the *Principles*, Marshall replied to Hobson with a lesson in differential calculus. A factor's marginal product is not a finite amount of output; it is the rate of change of the total product with respect to the variable agent in question: the units are the infinitesimal ones of the calculus. If the production function is given by $Q = f(K, L)$, an increase in the quantity of labor will cause the marginal product of labor to fall, that is,

$$\frac{\partial Q}{\partial L} > 0 \quad \text{and} \quad \frac{\partial^2 Q}{\partial L^2} < 0,$$

and will usually increase the marginal productivity of the other factor, that is,

$$\frac{\partial^2 Q}{\partial L \partial K} > 0.$$

But the slight change in the productivity of the factor held constant when the variable agent is increased, as shown by the nonzero value of the cross-partial derivative, involves a higher order differential of "the second order of small" and hence may be neglected. This is particularly so since all marginal variations are assumed to take place around a previously established optimum combination of factors.

But despite this reply, Marshall in fact capitulated to Hobson by introducing the concept of the marginal *net* product of a factor. In his well-known example of the marginal shepherd he showed that the employer has a joint demand for labor and capital. Substitutability being limited in the short run, he recommended measuring the marginal product of joint additions of capital and labor and then subtracting the cost of one factor to determine the marginal net product of the other. This notion makes sense, however, only in the case of *strict* jointness—the case of fixed coefficients—and even then it is an illegitimate concept because we are assuming that we already know the cost of the co-operating factor to the industry as a whole. Since no separate productivity can be imputed when the two factors are combined in strictly fixed proportions, to talk of marginal product at all, net or gross, is misleading. Either factor substitution is possible, and a factor's marginal product can be defined, or factor substitution is ruled out, and the concept of a marginal product has no meaning.

The High-Wage Economy Theory. The chief critics of marginal productivity theory in its early days were the trade-union leaders and their spokesmen. Books like *Industrial Democracy* (1897) by the Webbs emphasized the influence of custom on wage determination and attacked the notion that unions cannot secure an increase in wages in excess of labor's marginal product in one industry except at the expense of workers in some other industry. The Webbs argued that an artificial wage rate, secured by union action, might justify itself by affecting the efficiency of the work force, stimulating entrepreneurs to rearrange their plant and equipment and so altering the equilibrium wage rate. This has ever since been known as the high-wage economy theory and to this day constitutes an important element in the creed of labor.

This is not the place to consider the argument in detail. Obviously, it proves too much. It is revealing, however, to strip this proposition down to its fundamentals. Marginal productivity theory is a wage theory on the industry level, the supply of labor to the industry being given; for the firm, it is an employment theory, the rate of wages being given. The high-wage economy theory alleges that an artificial increase in wages increases efficiency and leads to an expansion of output; the rise in demand for labor then justifies the rise in wages. Marginal productivity theory says that $w = f(M_L)$; the high-wage economy theory says that, on the contrary, $M_L = f(w)$. There are two possible situations in which both the first function and its inverse may hold. One is the case of a backward economy in which wages are at or above subsistence levels but in which an increase of wages raises labor's propensity to produce by overcoming dietary deficiencies; traditional marginal productivity theory cannot handle this case. The other possibility is that of an advanced economy in which the function is relevant to static analysis but its inverse pertains to dynamic changes; that is, $w = f(M_L)$ and $M_L = (\dot{w})$ where $\dot{w}$ indicates a time derivative. There is certainly nothing implausible about the latter case, but the marginal productivity theory of wages has had little to say about it. The Webbs had a point, as has always been conceded, but it was not clear even to them what it was. Recognition of the dynamic effects of wage changes, however, should suggest that the traditional marginal productivity theory, when properly understood, does not yield flat pronouncements on trade-union action.

The Present Status of Marginal Productivity Theory. When economics turned back in the 1890's to the classical problems of factor pricing, it took some time to realize that the new theory of distribution dealt with a much more restricted range of questions. The relative shares of land, labor, and capital, which had been at the heart of classical distribution theory, disappear as a problem in marginal productivity theory. The microeconomic focus of the new theory precluded conclusions about the tripartite division of revenues à la Adam Smith. With the demise of the wages fund theory, not only that theory but all the macroeconomic problems of distribution with which it was concerned were abandoned. It took a long time, however, before economists became fully aware of the limited content of marginal productivity theory. Right up to the 1920's it was not uncommon for economists to discuss such issues as the level of wages and of employment as a whole in terms of the operation of the entire economy conceived as a giant firm. But, obviously, the interdependence of aggregate demand and supply renders the theory inapplicable to such problems. Indeed, it is easy to show that marginal productivity analysis is necessarily based on the assumption of a given level of income in the economy as a whole.

The individual firm under perfect competition hires factors according to the equimarginal principle. An optimum combination of factors implies equalization of the weighted marginal physical products taken over all the factors, the weights being factor prices.

$$\frac{MP_L}{w} = \frac{MP_K}{r} = \cdots = \frac{1}{MC}.$$

The common ratio is the reciprocal of marginal cost, an analogue to the marginal revenue of utility in the theory of consumer behavior. We already know that the competitive firm maximizes profits by equating price to marginal cost. Profit maximization implies cost minimization, and the latter is a synonym for payment to factors in accordance with marginal productivity. If the firm obeys the equimarginal rule, it hires labor, for example, up to the point where $MC = w/MP_L$. If it maximizes profits, MC will equal p, the price of the final product. Hence $(MP_L/w) = 1/p$ and $(MP_L \cdot p) = w$: the wage rate will equal the marginal value product of labor.

The firm's demand curve for labor is given by the MP_L curve. Summing horizontally over all the firms in an industry, we obtain the industry's demand curve for labor. But we cannot obtain the market demand curve for labor simply by way of the horizontal summation of industry demand curves. That would imply that the product demand curves and hence the derived labor demand curves for each industry were independent of each other. But the product demand curve for each industry is drawn up on the basis of given incomes and given price configurations throughout the economy. Changes in the level of wages necessarily affect incomes and hence the pattern of consumer demand. But every change in the product demand curves alters the industry demand curves for labor. In short, we are caught in a web of interdependent relations.

The crucial hypothesis of traditional marginal productivity theory, therefore, is the assumption that consumer demand curves are invariant to the prices paid for the factors of production. Since the product demand curves are drawn up on the basis of fixed money incomes, at bottom, marginal productivity analysis proceeds by treating the level of income as a datum. This is the essence of Keynes's objection to wage cutting as a remedy for unemployment. On marginal productivity grounds, an excess supply of labor would seem to denote wage payments in excess of labor's marginal product somewhere in the economy. Cutting wage, therefore, appears to be the appropriate remedy. But wages are incomes as well as costs and a general decline in wages must lower the aggregate demand for final goods and services. There is no guarantee, therefore, that wage cutting will succeed in eliminating unemployment.

The failure of the marginal productivity theory to throw light on the determination of relative shares is not solely due to its microeconomic bias. Variations in factor prices, and hence in relative shares, are not only the result of movements along given production functions but also of shifts in the production functions themselves. Marginal productivity theory, however, has traditionally neglected the problem of technical change as falling outside the purview of economic analysis. Schumpeter, in his *Theory of Economic Development* (1912), tried to fill the gap, insisting on the importance of "innovations"—broadly defined as the introduction of new methods, new products, new sources of supply, and new forms of industrial organization—for the understanding of economic progress. But Schumpeter failed in any way to provide either a systematic theory or classification of innovations or an analysis of the manner in which innovating "entrepreneurs"—the source of all dynamic change in the Schumpeterian system—appear on the historical scene. And so economists continued by and large to abstract from technical progress.

Beginning with Hicks's *Theory of Wages* (1932), the problem of classifying innovations into mutually exclusive categories at last began to receive attention. Hicks confined himself to process innovations: improvements in techniques of production—the index-number problem has so far defied all efforts to analyze product innovations. He defined a laborsaving innovation as one that at a given capital-labor ratio raises the marginal product of capital relative to the marginal product of labor. Hence, laborsaving innovations raise capital's relative share of income. Similarly, capitalsaving innovations raise labor's relative share, while neutral innovations leave relative shares unaffected. Furthermore, he postulated that technical change leads to greater upward shifts in the marginal productivity curves of the relatively abundant and therefore cheaper factor. That is, a rise in the capital-labor ratio, tending to raise wage rates and depress interest rates, will *induce* offsetting laborsaving innovations. Here, he suggested, is the explanation of the comparatively small changes observed in the relative shares over the last one hundred years of capitalism and of the seemingly insignificant influence of trade-union action on wages.

The Hicksian argument meets with the objection that the tendency to substitute capital for labor when wage rates are rising constitutes factor substitution, not technical change. Technical change, after all, has always been defined as a cost-reducing improvement *not* caused by a change in factor prices. The Hicksian argument threatens to jettison the crucial distinction between substitution along given production functions and shifts in the functions themselves, without which marginal productivity analysis falls to the ground. Moreover, Hicks produces no reason why individual producers in a competitive economy should ignore dramatic capitalsaving innovations merely because interest rates are falling. The individual producer is interested in cutting costs and will appraise innovations in terms of their cost-cutting characteristics; even if wage rates are rising, dramatic capitalsaving innovations may raise profits much more than insignificant laborsaving innovations. If the engineers are coming up with startling capitalsaving improvements, technical change will be slanted in the capitalsaving direction, thus causing interest rates to fall and wage rates to rise even more.

But this line of reasoning is convincing only within the context of static theory, which assumes that producers never learn from experience. A persistent capitalsaving bias, with capital becoming cheaper all the time, must eventually disappoint producers' expectations of rising innovation profits. Thus, we may assume, firms will learn to adopt a pattern of innovations that will offset the influences of differential rates of growth in the factor supplies. And, in this sense, technical change is indeed a stabilizing influence on the relative shares.

The notion of an automatic inducement mechanism governing the factorsaving slant of technical change has been sketched before in the chapter on Marx. It is still a controversial issue. The trouble is that investment within given technical horizons and the advance of technical knowledge itself cannot be entirely separated because even routine investment always teaches new lessons. There is a growing conviction that the rigid divorce of factor substitution and technical change, sanctioned by a century of tradition, may be the crucial bottleneck that has held up analytical progress.

We have by now collected an extensive list of the shortcomings of marginal productivity theory: it is static, it is of little practical use in production problems, it neglects the supply side in factor markets, it cannot be applied to factor markets as a whole because of the interdependence of demand and supply, and it sheds no direct light on the problem of relative shares because it fails to analyze the nature of technical change. Nevertheless, contemporary distribution theory is a marginal productivity theory, properly qualified to make allowance for these objections. It is as secure from attack as any theory can be, for no alternative theory is in sight.

2. LINEAR HOMOGENEOUS PRODUCTION FUNCTIONS

In his brilliant *Essay on the Co-ordination of the Laws of Distribution,* Wicksteed tried, albeit unsuccessfully, to prove that the total product would be precisely exhausted when each factor was rewarded its marginal product. In a review of Wicksteed's book in the *Economic Journal,* A. W. Flux gave an elementary but elegant proof of Wicksteed's contention.

If $Q = f(x,y,z)$ then by assumption of constant returns to scale

(1)
$$\frac{dx}{x} = \frac{dy}{y} = \frac{dz}{z} = \frac{dQ}{Q} = \text{a constant } \lambda \, .$$

By the theorem of ratios, if

$$\lambda = \frac{a}{b} = \frac{c}{d} = \frac{e}{f} \quad \text{then} \quad \lambda = \frac{la + mc + ne}{lb + md + nf} \, .$$

Applying this theorem to (1) by multiplying each ratio by the first partial derivative of $Q,$ we have

(2)
$$\frac{dQ}{Q} = \frac{\frac{\partial Q}{\partial x} dx + \frac{\partial Q}{\partial y} dy + \frac{\partial Q}{\partial z} dz}{\frac{\partial Q}{\partial x} x + \frac{\partial Q}{\partial y} y + \frac{\partial Q}{\partial y} z} = \frac{dQ}{x \frac{\partial Q}{\partial x} + y \frac{\partial Q}{\partial y} + z \frac{\partial Q}{\partial z}} \, .$$

Hence, given (1) and (2),

(3)
$$x \frac{\partial Q}{\partial x} + y \frac{\partial Q}{\partial y} + z \frac{\partial Q}{\partial z} - Q \equiv 0$$

for all values of x, y, and z.

To illustrate: let Q be of the form $Ax^l y^m z^n$, where A is a constant and l, m, and n obey no law. In this case

$$\frac{\partial Q}{\partial x} = lAx^{l-1}y^m z^n$$

$$x \frac{\partial Q}{\partial x} = lAx^l y^m z^n = lQ .$$

Hence (3) takes the form

$$l(Ax^l y^m z^n) + m(Ax^l y^m z^n) + n(Ax^l y^m z^n) - (Ax^l y^m z^n)$$
$$= (l + m + n - 1)Ax^l y^m z^n .$$

This has to be zero for all values of x, y, and z, which is only possible if each of the numerical coefficients of the terms $(l + m + n - 1) = 0$. Hence, $l + m + n = 1$. Q must be a homogeneous function of the first degree. For example, one function satisfying this condition is $Q = Ax^{1/6} y^{1/3} z^{1/2}$.

Linear Homogeneous Production Functions. Flux was the first to relate the problem of product exhaustion explicitly to Euler's theorem on homogeneous functions. Euler's theorem states that a function is homogeneous in the tth degree if any real multiple $t > 0$ applied to each and every variable in the function increases the value of the total function by t^m, whatever m is. We have already encountered homogeneous demand functions of zero degree $(m = 0)$ in our discussion of Say's Law. Here we are concerned with production functions. It is obvious that the value of m determines the returns to scale that obtain for a particular production function. If we double all the inputs $(t = 2)$, will output double? If so, $m = 1$, and we have first-degree homogeneity, the linearity assumption. If output more than doubles $(m > 1)$, we have increasing returns to scale. If output less than doubles $(m < 1)$, we have diminishing returns to scale. It is also obvious that production functions will usually be homogeneous. Nonhomogeneous functions involve a constant term and a non-homogeneous production function would therefore imply some output even with zero inputs, which seems economically meaningless.

The proposition that factor payments in accordance with marginal productivity will exactly exhaust the total product when and only when the production function is linear and homogeneous can be easily proved. We prove first that the marginal product of each factor depends only on the *ratio* between the amounts of the factors employed. If $Q = f(x, y)$ is a linear homogeneous function, then

$$f(tx, ty) = t^m f(x, y) = tQ.$$

We choose $t = 1/x$, so that

$$f(1, y/x) = F\left(\frac{y}{x}\right) = tQ = \frac{Q}{x}.$$

From which we get

$$Q = xF\left(\frac{y}{x}\right).$$

The function $f(\quad)$ in two variables has been replaced by the function $F(\quad)$ in one variable.

Differentiating partially with respect to x, we find that neither x nor y appears alone in the expression for the marginal product of x

$$\frac{\partial Q}{\partial x} = F\left(\frac{y}{x}\right) + xF'\left(\frac{y}{x}\right)\frac{\partial}{\partial x}\left(\frac{y}{x}\right)$$

$$= F\left(\frac{y}{x}\right) + xF'\left(\frac{y}{x}\right)\left(-\frac{y}{x^2}\right)$$

$$= F\left(\frac{y}{x}\right) - \frac{y}{x}F'\left(\frac{y}{x}\right),$$

where

$$F'\left(\frac{y}{x}\right) = \frac{\partial F(y/x)}{\partial(y/x)}.$$

Thus, $\partial Q/\partial x$, the marginal product of x, is equal to the difference between two terms, both of which are a function of the ratio y/x. The distributive share of x is

$$x\frac{\partial Q}{\partial x} = xF\left(\frac{y}{x}\right) - yF'\left(\frac{y}{x}\right).$$

But we already know that $Q = xF(y/x)$. Hence,

$$x\frac{\partial Q}{\partial x} = Q - yF'\left(\frac{y}{x}\right).$$

On the other hand, for y we have

$$\frac{\partial Q}{\partial y} = 0 + xF'\left(\frac{y}{x}\right)\frac{\partial}{\partial y}\left(\frac{y}{x}\right)$$

$$= F'\left(\frac{y}{x}\right)$$

$$y\frac{\partial Q}{\partial y} = yF'\left(\frac{y}{x}\right).$$

And therefore the sum of the two distributive shares is exhausted by the total product.

$$x \frac{\partial Q}{\partial x} + y \frac{\partial Q}{\partial y} \equiv Q \cdot$$

In money terms we have to multiply through by the price of the product, but as long as competition is perfect this does not alter the result.[1]

$$pQ \equiv x \left(\frac{\partial Q}{\partial x} p \right) + y \left(\frac{\partial Q}{\partial y} p \right) \cdot$$

The Properties of Linear Homogeneous Production Functions. Before we examine the economic implications of a linear homogeneous production function, we would do well to spend a moment on its formal properties. The reader who does not care for mathematical reasoning may skip this section, but he is warned that in so doing he is bypassing the hard core of neoclassical economic theory. The first point to notice about first-degree homogeneous production functions is that the marginal product of the factors is invariant to the absolute amount of the factors employed: proportionate changes in the amounts of all the factors employed leave their marginal productivity unaffected. It follows from this that the composite marginal product of an extra dose of all the factors, leaving their proportions unchanged, equals the sum of the marginal products of the factors added separately. That is to say, when the production function obeys constant returns to scale, the factors are always complementary: increasing the amount of one factor in isolation lowers its own marginal product but necessarily raises the marginal product of the other factors.

To prove, note that if $Q = f(K, L)$, then $(\partial/\partial L)(Q) = (\partial Q/\partial L)$. From Euler's theorem

$$\frac{\partial}{\partial L} \left(L \frac{\partial Q}{\partial L} + K \frac{\partial Q}{\partial K} \right) = \frac{\partial Q}{\partial L} + L \frac{\partial^2 Q}{\partial L^2} + K \frac{\partial^2 Q}{\partial L \partial K} = \frac{\partial Q}{\partial L} \cdot$$

Hence,

$$\frac{\partial^2 Q}{\partial L^2} = - \frac{K}{L} \frac{\partial^2 Q}{\partial L \partial K} \cdot$$

---

[1] Under monopoly we have

$$pQ = x \left(p \frac{\partial Q}{\partial x} + Q \frac{\partial p}{\partial x} \right) + y \left(p \frac{\partial Q}{\partial y} + Q \frac{\partial p}{\partial y} \right).$$

In this case product exhaustion always implies higher than first-degree homogeneity. The explanation of this assertion will become apparent as we proceed.

Similarly,

$$\frac{\partial^2 Q}{\partial K^2} = -\frac{L}{K}\frac{\partial^2 Q}{\partial K \partial L}.$$

Now, $\partial^2 Q/\partial L^2$ and $\partial^2 Q/\partial K^2$, the second-order partial derivatives, are always less than zero because of the law of diminishing marginal productivity; because of the negative sign appearing in the right-hand expression, $\partial^2 Q/\partial L \partial K$ and $\partial^2 Q/\partial K \partial L$, the cross second-order partial derivatives, must be positive. This proves our contention because the cross second-order partial derivatives show the effect on the marginal product of the fixed factor when the amount of the variable factor is altered.

As soon as we have increasing or diminishing returns to scale, however, it is no longer necessarily true that all the cross-elasticities are positive. If $\partial^2 Q/\partial K \partial S$—where S is some third factor accounting for varying returns to scale—is large enough, $\partial^2 Q/\partial K \partial L$ may be negative: labor and capital are then rival factors because an increase in capital increases "rent" so much that the marginal product of labor falls.

The complementarity of labor and capital along any production function showing constant returns to scale implies that when the rate of interest r is falling, wages per man w must be rising, and vice versa. That is, from Euler's theorem

$$Q = wL + rK$$

Therefore, with $t = $ time,

$$\frac{dQ}{dt} = w\frac{dL}{dt} + L\frac{dw}{dt} + r\frac{dK}{dt} + K\frac{dr}{dt}$$

and

$$\frac{1}{Q}\frac{dQ}{dt} = \frac{1}{L}\frac{wL}{Q}\frac{dL}{dt} + \frac{1}{w}\frac{wL}{Q}\frac{dw}{dt} + \frac{1}{K}\frac{rK}{Q}\frac{dK}{dt} + \frac{1}{r}\frac{rK}{Q}\frac{dr}{dt}.$$

Defining

$$\alpha = \frac{L}{Q}\frac{\partial Q}{\partial L} = \frac{wL}{Q} \quad \text{and} \quad \beta = \frac{K}{Q}\frac{\partial Q}{\partial K} = \frac{rK}{Q}$$

as the elasticities of productivity with respect to labor and capital, respectively, and letting dots indicate time derivatives, we have

(1) $$\dot{Q} = \alpha\dot{L} + \alpha\dot{w} + \beta\dot{K} + \beta\dot{r}$$

Also from

$$dQ = \frac{\partial Q}{\partial L}dL + \frac{\partial Q}{\partial K}dK$$

we have

$$\dot{Q} = \frac{L}{Q}\frac{\partial Q}{\partial L}\dot{L} + \frac{K}{Q}\frac{\partial Q}{\partial K}\dot{K}$$

(2)
$$= \alpha\dot{L} + \beta\dot{K}$$

Subtracting (1) from (2) we get

$$\alpha\dot{w} + \beta\dot{r} = 0.$$

Hence, if capital is growing at a faster rate than the labor supply along a *given* production function, the rate of interest will be falling and wages per man will be rising, that is, if $\dot{r} < 0$ then $\dot{w} > 0$. This result does not hold when returns to scale are increasing or diminishing for the simple reason that capital and labor may then be rival factors.

From the above it appears that α and β, the elasticities of productivity, are independent both of the relative proportions of the factors employed and of total output. But $\alpha = (L/Q)(\partial Q/\partial L)$ and under perfect competition $w = (\partial Q/\partial L)$; hence, $\alpha = (Lw/Q) = (W/Q)$ = labor's share of total output. Likewise, β is equal to capital's relative share. Therefore, with linear homogeneous production functions the relative shares of the participating factors are constant and independent of the level of output. To illustrate this basic theorem, we select a class of linear homogeneous production functions of the form $Q = Ax^l y^m z^n$. The so-called Cobb-Douglas production function is written $Q = bL^\alpha K^\beta$ where $\alpha + \beta = 1$.

Then $MP_L = \dfrac{\partial Q}{\partial L} = \alpha b L^{\alpha-1}K^\beta$. But $AP_L = (Q/L) = bL^{\alpha-1}K^\beta$.

Therefore,

(1)
$$MP_L = \frac{\partial Q}{\partial L} = \alpha\left(\frac{Q}{L}\right).$$

Similarly,

(2)
$$MP_K = \frac{\partial Q}{\partial K} = \beta\left(\frac{Q}{K}\right).$$

Labor's absolute share $= (\partial Q/\partial L)L = wL = \alpha Q$. Labor's relative share $= (\alpha Q/Q) = \alpha$. Likewise, capital's relative share $= \beta.$[2]

---

[2] α and β are also the respective elasticities of productivity. For instance, the elasticity of productivity with respect to labor—the proportionate change in output resulting from a given proportionate change in labor inputs—is defined as $[\partial(\log Q)]/[\partial(\log L)]$. But $\log Q = \alpha \log L + \beta \log K$, and $(1/Q)(\partial Q/\partial L) = (\alpha/L)$. Therefore, $[\partial(\log Q)]/[\partial(\log L)] = (L/Q)(\partial Q/\partial L) = \alpha$.

Dividing (1) by (2) we obtain the marginal rate of substitution of capital for labor

$$\frac{MP_L}{MP_K} = \frac{w}{r} = \frac{\alpha}{\beta}\frac{K}{L} \quad \text{or} \quad \frac{K}{L} = \frac{w}{r}\frac{\beta}{\alpha}.$$

With constant returns to scale, each factor receives that fraction of total output indicated by the value of its exponent and the exponents sum to unity; since factor prices are proportional to the respective productivity of each factor, the relative shares are constant and independent both of the capital-labor ratio and of total output.

Summing up, linear homogeneous production functions imply: (1) the marginal product of a factor varies only with changes in the *relative* amounts of the factor employed; (2) the participating factors are complementary such that an increase in a variable factor increases the marginal productivity of the fixed factor; and (3) if one factor increases relative to another factor, its relative price will decline but the relative shares of the two factors will not be affected.

We have already proved that factor payments in accordance with marginal productivity will exactly exhaust the total product when the production function is linear and homogeneous. But what will happen when the production function is not of this type?

Competition in factor markets will always insure that factors are rewarded their marginal value (revenue) product irrespective of the character of the production function. If the production functions are not linear, however, the total product will either exceed or fall short of the sum of the distributive shares. In the case of diminishing returns to scale, the sum of market-imputed factor payments will fall short of the value of output, leaving a residual. In the case of increasing returns, the total product is insufficient to reward all the contributing factors according to their marginal productivity. The explanation of these propositions lies in the relationship between average and marginal costs. A production function that is linearly homogeneous generates a horizontal *LRAC* curve. In the case of increasing returns or decreasing costs, the *LRMC* curve lies below the *LRAC* curve. Since payment according to the marginal product of a factor is simply a corollary of marginal cost pricing, it is hardly surprising that the firm suffers losses in this phase of its operations. This is the basis of the Hotelling-Lerner proposition that marginal cost pricing in all industries would require subsidies for any industry operating under decreasing costs. Similarly, a price that would cover long-run marginal costs when $LRMC > LRAC$ would necessarily leave a residual. But when $LRMC = LRAC$, the product will be exhausted by the sum of all factor payments.

This is nicely brought out by the Walras-Wicksell proof of the product-exhaustion theorem, which proceeds from the cost-minimization conditions combined with the long-run equilibrium condition that unit costs must equal the sales price of the product. If $Q = f(K,L,S, \ldots)$, then the equilibrium condition is that

$$(1) \qquad pQ = K \cdot p_k + L \cdot p_l + S \cdot p_s + \ldots ,$$

where p_k, p_l, and p_s are the prices of the factors and p is the price of the final product. Costs are minimized by maximizing net revenue.

$$\pi = R - C$$
$$= pQ - (Kp_k + Lp_l + \ldots) .$$

Hence

$$\frac{\partial \pi}{\partial K} = p \frac{\partial Q}{\partial K} - p_k = 0 , \qquad \frac{\partial \pi}{\partial L} = p \frac{\partial Q}{\partial L} - p_l = 0 , \ldots$$

Whence

$$(2) \qquad p \frac{\partial Q}{\partial K} = p_k , \qquad p \frac{\partial Q}{\partial L} = p_l , \ldots$$

Substituting (2) into (1) we have

$$pQ = Kp \frac{\partial Q}{\partial K} + Lp \frac{\partial Q}{\partial L} + \ldots$$

or

$$Q = K \frac{\partial Q}{\partial K} + L \frac{\partial Q}{\partial L} + \ldots$$

Generalizing this argument, output is at a maximum when the total first derivative with respect to output is zero:

$$(1) \qquad dQ = \frac{\partial Q}{\partial K} dK + \frac{\partial Q}{\partial L} dL + \ldots = 0 .$$

Minimum cost implies that

$$(2) \qquad p_k dK + p_l dL + \ldots = 0 .$$

Multiplying (2) by any real $\lambda > 0$ and subtracting from (1) we have

$$(3) \qquad dK \left(\frac{\partial Q}{\partial K} - \lambda p_k \right) + dL \left(\frac{\partial Q}{\partial L} - \lambda p_l \right) + \ldots = 0 .$$

Factoring dK, dL, dS, the coefficient of each of which is equal to zero because the sum of the several terms is zero, we have

(4)
$$\frac{\partial Q}{\partial K} = \lambda p_k \,, \qquad \frac{\partial Q}{\partial L} = \lambda p_l, \cdots$$

Therefore

(5)
$$\frac{\partial Q}{\partial K} K + \frac{\partial Q}{\partial L} L + \ldots = \lambda p_k K + \lambda p_l L + \ldots = \lambda C = Q \cdot$$

And hence

$$MC = \frac{dC}{dQ} = \frac{d(Q/\lambda)}{dQ} = \frac{C}{Q} = AC = \frac{1}{\lambda} \cdot$$

Returns are varying as $d^2Q/dC^2 \lessgtr 0$. If $d^2Q/dC^2 = 0$, then $\lambda = 1$ and substitution in (5) will show immediately that product exhaustion is satisfied.

As a final check on the argument, we can define an elasticity of total cost as a function of output as

$$\kappa = \frac{Q}{C} \frac{dC}{dQ} = \frac{MC}{AC} \cdot$$

Likewise, the elasticity of average cost can be expressed

$$\epsilon = \frac{Q}{C/Q} \frac{d(C/Q)}{dQ} = \frac{Q^2}{C} \frac{d}{dQ} \left(\frac{C}{Q}\right) = \frac{Q^2}{C} \frac{1}{Q^2} \left(Q \frac{dC}{dQ} - C\right)$$
$$= \frac{Q}{C} \frac{dC}{dQ} - 1 = \kappa - 1 = \frac{MC - AC}{AC} \cdot$$

If $\kappa = 1$, $\epsilon = 0$, and we have the case of constant returns to scale with average equal to marginal costs. If $\kappa < 1$, $\epsilon < 0$, average cost exceeds marginal cost, and we have increasing returns to scale. If $\kappa > 1$, $\epsilon > 0$, we have diminishing returns to scale with average cost increasing as output increases.

The reader who is still incredulous can try the following example: write down numbers for capital, labor, and output; increase labor by 1 per cent and allow output to rise by the marginal product of labor, or less than 1 per cent. Now increase capital by 1 per cent and consider three cases: (1) output rises by 1 per cent over the initial amount; (2) by less than 1 per cent; and (3) by more than 1 per cent. Write down the three implied marginal products of capital. Compute the corresponding factor rewards by multiplying the respective marginal products by the *original* inputs of labor and capital. When the two factor returns are added, they will $\gtreqless$ total output according as output rose by an amount $\gtreqless$ 1 per cent when both inputs were increased by 1 per cent.

3. THE OPTIMUM SIZE OF THE FIRM

When Wicksteed first discovered the product-exhaustion theorem, he argued that it was universally valid. It was not really, he said, "a law of distribution, but an analytical and synthetical law of composition and resolution of industrial factors and products, which holds equally in Robinson Crusoe's island, in an Indian village ruled by custom, and in the competitive centers of the typical modern industries." Part of the explanation for Wicksteed's curious conclusion is that, like most of his contemporaries, he considered the laws of increasing, constant, and diminishing returns to be mutually exclusive alternatives instead of their representing different phases of the long-run cost curves of a firm. But this is not the whole explanation. As Mrs. Robinson has said: "For most of the contemporaries of Wicksteed (though not, I think, for Marshall), the 'theory of marginal productivity' was a formulation of a somewhat mysterious law of nature. For the modern economist it is merely a series of self-evident propositions displaying the implications of the initial assumption that the individual employer acts in such a way as to maximize his profits. It is this fundamental difference in point of view which gives what appears to the modern reader such a perverse and fantastic character to the controversies surrounding the 'adding-up problem.' "

Wicksell's Proof of Product Exhaustion. It was Wicksell who first realized that product exhaustion is not usefully defined as holding under any and all circumstances. Exhaustion of the product must be regarded as a condition of equilibrium corresponding to a point at which the production function becomes tangent to a linear homogeneous function. Wicksell's argument is that the market will produce this condition in the long run. If a hiring agent pays all the other hired agents their marginal products, he may be left with more than the marginal product of the service he owns. If so, the hired agents are themselves induced to become the hiring agent, which tends to eliminate the residual. On the other hand, if the residual should prove to be negative, the hiring agent will cease to be a residual income recipient and rent the use of his services at the value of its marginal product. The hiring agent, of course, is the entrepreneur, but Wicksell assumes that entrepreneurship is not itself a factor of production: its function can be carried on by any factor, say, the salaried manager. Be that as it may, the result of the process just described is that, under perfect competition and the free hire of factors, the firms tend to operate at the lowest point of their *LRAC* curves, at an output level and with a combination of resources such as to yield a linear and homogeneous production function.

Wicksell's argument assumes that there is an optimum size of the firm. At this point we must raise the question, which we have so far ducked, whether there are in fact genuine economies or diseconomies of scale. If the long-run cost curves of the firms in an industry are horizontal, the size of each firm is indeterminate. If the size of each firm is indeterminate, so are the number of firms in the industry. This, in turn, casts doubt on the stability of competition in the industry. This explains why economists have been loath to abandon the notion of U-shaped *LRAC* curves, but it does not tell us whether there are any grounds for that idea.

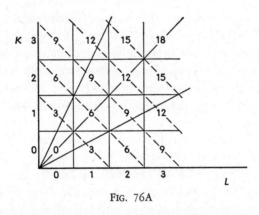

Fig. 76A

The Indivisibility Thesis. If two productive agents are perfect substitutes for each other when used in combination to produce a given output, they are necessarily infinitely divisible: the isoquants in this case are straight lines, meaning that the marginal rate of substitution of the two factors is constant. To illustrate, we construct a production table such that a given total amount of capital and labor produces the same total output irrespective of the proportions in which the two factors are combined. MP_L is defined for any given amount of K and can be read off the table as the first interval difference along any row. Similarly, ML_K can be found by looking up any column. In all cases, MP_L and MP_K are constant. Since $MRS = MP_L/MP_K$, MRS is always constant. Perfect substitutability leads not only to constancy in the marginal products but also to constancy in returns to scale: the isoquants are equidistant along any vector from the origin.

It is clear that convex isoquants reflecting diminishing marginal productivity imply that the factors are not perfect substitutes for each other. The obvious explanation of this phenomenon is that infinite divisibility of all the participating factors cannot be obtained in the short run. Some factors, such as capital equipment, for instance, are available only in discrete amounts in the short run. Similarly, if constant returns to scale do not prevail in the long run, it must be because less than perfect divisibility of all the factors prevents them from being perfect substitutes for each other. *Ergo*, varying returns to scale are explained by indivisibilities: this is the indivisibility thesis.

Let us paraphrase the argument: there is a certain optimum proportion of factors; because the factors are available only in discrete lumpy units, this optimum proportion cannot be attained unless the aggregate amount of the factors employed is large; the inefficiency of small-scale production is due to the failure to obtain the lumpy factor in fractional units having proportionate efficiency; with perfect divisibility the optimum could be achieved for any aggregate. Hence, economies of scale are due to indivisibilities. The same argument will account for diseconomies of scale by the existence of some indivisible agent, such as managerial co-ordination. It follows that all the phenomena that characterize nonconstant returns to scale are reducible to indivisibilities.

The argument that the production function must be linear and homogeneous and that, when it is not, lumpiness of some factor is the explanation, is not a proposition that could be controverted by empirical evidence. After all, a perfectly divisible perfectly homogeneous factor of production is defined as a class of units of productive service that are perfect substitutes for one another. From this it follows immediately that increments in the amounts of a factor are of the same unit-efficiency and, hence, that their efficiency is invariant with respect to scale. To say that economies of scale would be nonexistent if factors were available in infinitely divisible units is tautological because an indivisible factor is defined as one which is *not* equally efficient in all amounts. Nevertheless, the tautological character of the indivisibility thesis does not destroy its usefulness. Its purpose is the same as that of all tautologies in economic theory: to help us in thinking about the problem by providing a classificatory scheme.

Genuine Variable Returns to Scale.   No one contends that inputs are in fact fully divisible: if we follow Samuelson's advice and restrict "factors" to inputs of measurable physical goods and services, divisibility of these "factors" will not imply constant returns to scale. But over and above that consideration, it may well be that efficiency is affected by the absolute amount of the inputs combined in production.

In recent years, Chamberlin has vigorously asserted the importance of genuine economies and diseconomies of scale. Biology furnishes many examples of genuine nonproportionalities,[3] and it may be that physical production is characterized by similar properties.

Moreover, even if the factors themselves are perfectly divisible, the activities they perform may be nonproportional to output. Such activities as record keeping, credit and finance administration, and production planning, need not be proportional to output even with fully divisible factors of production. What if doubling the size of orders and sales does not double the paper work required because of the use of carbon paper? Furthermore, the existence of random variables in the production function may create economies of scale via the principle of pooled reserves. Seventy years ago Edgeworth argued that, owing to the law of large numbers, a commercial bank's holdings of cash reserves for purposes of liquidity vary less than proportionately to the volume of deposits. Since then it has been shown that optimal inventory safety margins as protection against random variations in demand vary with the square root of demand; similarly, auditing costs and quality controls tend to vary with the square root of the items to be audited or checked.

Diseconomies of Management. On the side of technical *dis*economies, however, it seems difficult to come up with any very convincing examples of genuine nonproportionality. There are no financial diseconomies of scale, and selling costs do not seem to be subject to diminishing returns. It is true that when a firm has saturated its market, selling difficulties may appear. This is a limitation on the side of demand, however, not on the side of costs. The chief factor making for diseconomies of scale appears to be diseconomies of management, reflecting the indivisibility of managerial functions. But why should it not be possible to overcome managerial diseconomies by decentralization of decision making? In the real world this is, of course, exactly what happens, but, since this amounts to a change in the quality and type of managerial services, it is ruled out in static analysis. Similarly, the assumption of a given level of technical knowledge rules out the possibility of learning to overcome administrative bottlenecks by progressive subdivision of functions. But managerial services defined to be unalterable by experience take on the character

---

[3] An oft-cited example is that of the flea, which can jump over a man if the man is scaled down to the size of a flea but which cannot jump at all if it is scaled up to the size of a man. The strength of the flea's bones and muscles is proportional to their cross-section, which is an area. His weight is proportional to volume, which is a cube. Hence, if we increase the scale of a flea by a thousand, we increase his strength by a million but his weight by a billion.

of a fixed factor. Hence, managerial diseconomies may be said with justice to be due entirely to indivisibility.

The Growth of Firms. Managerial diseconomies will insure a limit to the amount of expansion that a firm can undertake in a *given* period. But the fact that there is a size that is optimum with respect to static efficiency does not mean that growing firms are bound to become inefficient at some point. Technical and even managerial diseconomies of scale need not limit the size of the firm in contrast to the plant: processes can always be duplicated when they become inefficiently large. Even if there is an optimum output for each of the firm's plants and product lines, there may not exist an optimum output for the firm as a whole. Moreover, even if a multiplant firm is too big to maximize efficiency with given resources, it may not be able to achieve efficiency at all without some rate of growth. Once again, it is apparent how remote is the traditional theory of the firm from the actual laws that govern the growth of firms in the real world.

It is interesting to see what happens to the concept of an optimum size of the firm when the problem is viewed dynamically. Suppose that the long-run optimum size of a firm is at least as large as that of the whole industry so that long-run stable equilibrium of the industry under perfect competition is impossible from the viewpoint of static theory. Assume now that the average and marginal cost of producing a given output at a given moment of time is a decreasing function of output but an increasing function of the rate of *increase* of output at that moment. Then, given the rate of output at t, average and marginal cost will be increasing with the rate of output at $t + 1$ if the rate of growth of output has accelerated between the two periods. Each firm will now have an equilibrium output at each moment of time, equating the marginal cost of producing a given rate of output at that moment to the price of the product, and yet output will increase from one moment to the next. What we have is a moving equilibrium, and stability now consists of a tendency to approach a rate of change of output rather than a given level of output. Provided the industry's demand curve continues to shift to the right, attainment of long-run equilibrium may in this way be permanently delayed and pure if not perfect competition might exist indefinitely.

4. THE THEORY OF PROFIT

In the long run the reward of each factor, including the hiring factor, equals its marginal value product; there is no residual for the entrepreneur, and profits are zero. But what of those theories that speak of profit as the returns to a distinct fourth factor of production called "organization" or "entrepreneurship," comprising the services of ultimate co-ordination and decision making as well as risk taking or uncertainty bearing? It would seem that in this case we can simply apply standard marginal productivity theory and define "normal profits" as the marginal product of the entrepreneur. Thus, we could say with Marshall that in long-run equilibrium profits are "normal" because pure residual profits are zero. Is this a tenable point of view?

The Meaning of Pure Profit. First of all, we have to make it clear what we mean by pure profit. However confused in their terminology, economists since the days of Adam Smith have always meant to exclude all necessary cost outlays from the definition of pure profit. Pure profit is a return over and above opportunity-cost payments, the payments necessary to draw forth productive services from their most remunerative alternative employments. At the same time, pure profit is also a return in excess of "real" costs, since it is not required to maintain any productive agent in existence. Pure profits are therefore perfectly analogous to Ricardian rents *when land has no alternative uses whatever.* If land does have alternative uses, ground rent must be paid by the firm in order to secure land for the firm's use. Similarly, if the transfer cost or opportunity cost of the ultimate decision maker is positive, pure profit must be defined net of the wages of management. By definition, whatever it is that defines the contribution of the entrepreneur, pure profit cannot be a payment necessary to retain the services of the entrepreneur; this is true for each individual firm as well as for society as a whole. It may be tempting to say that the exposure to uncertainty involved in the act of investing capital is a disutility and that the person who assumed it cannot be expected to do so without a reward. But it is the prospect of gain that induces investment, and there is no reason to assume that the disutility of the expected loss always and necessarily exceeds the utility of the expected gain. There is no evidence that the bearing of uncertainty is a real cost and that uncertainty bearing would cease to exist if pure profits were zero on the average. Similarly, the fact that some businessmen earn consistently more than others might lead us to define pure profit as a "rent of ability," an intramarginal surplus accruing to superior business talent. But in the never-never land of long-run equilibrium such intramarginal rents would be imputed to costs in the form of wages of superior management. The rent-of-ability theory of profit is really a theory of differential wages traveling in disguise.

Sticking to our definition of pure profit as being neither an opportunity cost nor a real cost, we can define it as a residual left over after all contractual costs have been met, including the transfer costs of management, insurable risks, depreciation, and payments to shareholders sufficient to maintain investment at its current level. There is no inherent reason why these profits should be positive for any firm in a single year, and, although some firms may show pure profits or losses over long periods of time, the presumption is that in the economy as a whole pure profits will be zero in the long run.

The Entrepreneur as a Factor of Production. If we treat the entrepreneur as a distinct factor of production, receiving his marginal product, we cannot, without contradiction, equate this marginal product to pure profit. Pure profit is either the marginal product of some factor or it a nonimputed residual. We have just concluded that it is a residual. Hence, the marginal product of entrepreneurship cannot be pure profit.

But the concept of the entrepreneur as a factor of production, separate from and in addition to the conventional triad, is itself inconsistent, as Edgeworth never tired of pointing out. We cannot define the marginal product of a factor unless the factor is both infinitely divisible and strictly homogeneous. If it is not infinitely divisible, the *marginal* product cannot be calculated. If it is not strictly homogeneous, we are not talking about one and the same factor, because the units of a factor are always perfect substitutes for each other. In practice, the definition of a factor always represents some compromise between divisibility and homogeneity. All too frequently, if a factor is rigorously defined as being finely divisible, the resulting factor class has little economic significance. And, on the other hand, if it is defined as satisfying homogeneity in the strict sense, it turns out not to be infinitely divisible.[4] But in the case of entrepreneurship the usual requirements of compromise have to be carried to excessive lengths. For the firm, the entrepreneur does not seem to be a divisible agent, certainly not

---

[4] In the *Co-ordination of the Laws of Distribution,* Wicksteed tried to reduce constant returns to scale to a tautology by defining all inputs as being strictly homogeneous. Instead of accepting the crude productive triad of classical economics, he decided that "we must regard every kind and quality of labor that can be distinguished from other kinds and qualities as a separate factor . . . instead of speaking of so many £ worth of capital we shall speak of so many ploughs, so many tons of manure, and so many horses, or footpounds of power." It follows that a proportionate increase in all these strictly homogeneous but indivisible inputs must increase output equiproportionately. But Wicksteed failed to realize that he had tacitly banished the concept of a marginal product. If one input is indivisible, the smallest increase in output that will leave input proportions unaffected is a 100 per cent increase. In that case, however, the marginal productivity principle cannot be applied. To calculate the marginal product of an input it is necessary to define an input as being finely divisible as well as homogeneous.

very finely divisible. Moreover, entrepreneurs are too heterogeneous to permit us to talk of units of entrepreneurial inputs. Even if we could define something like an entrepreneurial man-hour as the fundamental unit of supply, there would seem to be little relationship between the quantity supplied and the amount of service rendered.[5]

Profit as a Return to Uncertainty Bearing. Suppose the production function is linear and homogeneous and a function only of physical inputs such as labor and capital equipment. Is pure profit then zero by definition? It was Knight's contribution to show that the presence of uncertainty about the future may allow entrepreneurs to earn positive profits despite product exhaustion and competitive equilibrium. Production takes place in anticipation of consumption, and, since the demand for factors is derived from the expected consumers' demand for output, the entrepreneur is forced to speculate on the price of his final product. The product price is not determined unless the rate of reward of the factors is given, but the latter is not determined unless the price of output is known. The entrepreneur

[5] If the firm maximizes profits, the supply of entrepreneurial effort to the firm is necessarily independent of the net revenue of the firm. Suppose net revenue is a bell-shaped function of the hours of entrepreneurial effort applied, with the extremum value corresponding to the level of output at which $MR = MC$. Concave indifference curves imply that the entrepreneur is willing to forgo income if it costs more effort: there is an increasing MRS between income and effort. Hence, the firm will fail to maximize profit. The conventional assumption of pecuniary profit maximization, however, implies that the indiffer-

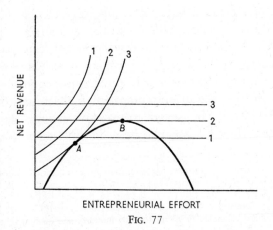

ENTREPRENEURIAL EFFORT

Fig. 77

ence curves are horizontal: the MRS between income and effort is always constant and zero; the marginal utility of leisure to the entrepreneur or the income elasticity of supply of entrepreneurial effort is zero. This assumption accords very well with the classical notion of accumulation for its own sake: "profit for profit's sake" rather than "profit for use." Thus, even if we can define a unit of supply of entrepreneurship, traditional theory denies any relationship between the quantity supplied and the end results for the firm.

resolves this dilemma by guessing the price at which output will sell, thereby translating the marginal physical products of the factors hired into anticipated marginal value products. Although the factors hired on a contractual basis must be awarded their *anticipated* marginal value product, the entrepreneur as a residual claimant may make a profit if realized total receipts prove to be greater than forecasted total receipts.

Knight's theory does not attribute profit simply to dynamic change, for, insofar as these changes are foreseen, they cannot generate a difference between selling price and cost. Nor are they due to risk, for a known risk is hedged against by taking out insurance. Profit is due to a unique kind of risk not susceptible to measurement, namely, the uncertainty generated by dynamic change. To call profit a reward for bearing the "real" cost of uncertainty or an inducement to bear uncertainty implies that there is a connection between the level of profit and the irksomeness of bearing uncertainty. But no such connection exists. If uncertainty bearing were a productive service, marginal productivity theory would apply to it and there would be no need for a special theory of profit. Profit is the difference between *ex ante* and *ex post* returns. It is not a distinct distributive share, but it is an element found in the payments to all types of productive agents. When most entrepreneurs take a bearish view of the future, the contractually hired agents will receive less than the *realized* value of their marginal product. Hence, the entrepreneur's profits are really drawn from the productive factors themselves. This is not exploitation, for, in the absence of the entrepreneur, the factors themselves would have to gamble on the future. Similarly, when most entrepreneurs are bullish in their outlook, there are losses because the hired factors are rewarded on the basis of their *anticipated* marginal products and these exceed the value of the marginal products that are ultimately realized when output is sold. Knight himself inclines to Adam Smith's view that entrepreneurs are on balance optimistic in their outlook; the very uncertainty of the prize draws a number so large that average earnings are probably negative.

Other Causes of Profits. The classical conception of profit as an income accruing to a socioeconomic class enjoying the status of employer, and combining the functions of both capitalist and manager, has given way in modern economics to the conception of profit as a noncontractual windfall gain accruing to a disembodied entrepreneur. There is no problem about where these profits come from: they constitute, as it were, a tax on the productivity of the hired agents. The traditional question whether profit is a reward for the performance of a specific service or whether it is the result of exploitation is really concerned with the nature of interest, not of profit.

So long as we retain the assumption of perfect competition and constant returns to scale leading to product exhaustion—the sum of the anticipated distributive shares equals the anticipated value of total output—profits are due solely to noninsurable uncertainty. But if we drop these assumptions, a number of new kinds of profit make their appearance. There is "monopoly profit," owing to restricted entry into the industry. Then there is "monopsony profit," owing to a divergence between average and marginal factor costs. Finally, there are "Ricardian rents," resulting from inelasticities in the supply of factors; unlike the other gains, these are not the object of entrepreneurial expectations and do not violate the assumptions of linearity and perfect competition. Nevertheless, all these do come within the purview of the uncertainty theory of profit. Any monopoly or monopsony profits that are predictable will be capitalized, and the same thing is of course true of correctly foreseen rents. As a result the market value of the firm's assets will exceed their current cost of production, and the imputed interest on these assets, including discounted monopoly returns or rents, is not "profit" proper. Thus, if all market results were predictable, contractual plus imputed costs would always tend to exhaust the receipts of firms. Profits cannot be positive unless there is noninsurable uncertainty. The theory of profit, therefore, has no place in neoclassical analysis because its fundamental theorems rest upon the assumption of perfect certainty.

READER'S GUIDE TO THE COMMON *SENSE OF POLITICAL ECONOMY*

"Never was a work of this kind more unfortunately named," writes Robbins in his introduction to the 1932 reprint of Wicksteed's *Common Sense of Political Economy* (1910). "It is not 'common sense' in the ordinary sense of the term, and it is not *political* economy. It is, on the contrary, the most exhaustive non-mathematical exposition of the technical and philosophical complications of the so-called *marginal* theory of pure Economics, which has appeared in any language."

Wicksteed's brief introduction to the book is a lucid summary of all its salient features: (1) the equimarginal principle of resource administration as the master theme of economic theory; (2) the attack upon the concept of the Economic Man as an unnecessary vestige of older analysis; (3) the rigorous demonstration that Ricardo's residual rent theory is a marginal productivity theory with the relation between the fixed and the variable factors reversed; (4) the idea of the supply curve as a reverse demand curve; (5) the attempt to revise the doctrine of the laws of return; and (6) the constant reminder, in opposition to Marshall, of the revolutionary character of marginal utility economics and its decisive break with the classical mode of economic reasoning (see also pp. 812, 819).

Consumer Behavior. The first chapter discusses the economics of household behavior, introducing the notion of a "scale of preferences," or, as we would say, a generalized utility function, after effectively disposing of the objection that "a great part of our conduct is impulsive and a great part unreflecting" (pp. 28–33). Wicksteed does not claim that transitivity or "the consistency postulate" is always satisfied, but, presumably, it is legitimate to assume transitivity (pp. 33–34; also pp. 122–24). It must be said that he dismisses this question too easily. This is followed by a long chapter that provides an exhaustive, and exhausting, explanation of the meaning of Gossen's second law: satisfaction is maximized when resources are so distributed among different uses as to secure equal want satisfactions in all uses. Few writers have ever taken such pains to explain to the nonmathematical reader why marginal significance can be expressed in terms of either increments or decrement and why discontinuities and indivisibilities do not constitute decisive obstacles to marginal analysis. The law of "diminishing psychic returns" is carefully expounded to avoid the misconception that the marginal utility of a good must decline monotomically throughout the whole range of consumption (pp. 82–83; see also pp. 435–38). As does Marshall, Wicksteed reminds us of the necessity of assuming constant tastes (pp. 84–86; see also pp. 491–92), but his illustrations of the workings of the law, charming as they are—see the parable of "the indolent young man" and the case of Caesar "that day he overcame the Nervii" (pp. 78–79)—tend to degenerate into "dinner-table demonstrations." Notice the mention of backward-bending labor supply curves (p. 77) and the Jevonian emphasis upon prospective costs (pp. 88–89).

Chapter 3 is concerned with indivisible durable goods whose services accrue over a period of time, making it impossible to "keep margins trimmed." The notion of positive time preference, as distinct from irrational underestimation of the future, is skillfully woven into the discussions (pp. 112–14). Interdependences between the individual utility functions—bandwagon and snob effects—are briefly considered (pp. 115–6). By the time we have reached the end of chapter 3, every possible objection that critics have raised against the concept of the rational calculating consumer has in one way or another been touched upon. Yet Wicksteed never raises the methodological question of the appropriate level of abstraction in the analysis of consumer behavior. Why assume that the individual can in principle bring about "the ideal coincidence between marginal significances and market prices" when this is admittedly an unrealistic assumption?

In chapter 4 we make "the momentous transition from personal to communal economies" and begin to study "the forces which regulate the terms on which alternatives are offered." Isolated exchange may not yield a determinate equilibrium (pp. 140–31), but "in an exchanging community . . . there is a perpetual tendency to establish an equilibrium," such that "the relative marginal estimates formed by all the individuals, of all the exchangeable commodities of which they severally possess a store, are identical" (p. 143). This does not mean that aggregate welfare is maximized in equilibrium, for "there is no theoretical means of constituting a comparison between the sensations and experiences of two different minds" (pp. 145–50; see also p. 170). The reader should now turn to Book II, chapters 1–4, which show how to construct curves of total and marginal utility as well as individual and market demand curves. The treatment of consumer's surplus is excellent and avoids most of the pitfalls in the concept: the marginal utility of money must be approximately constant, the individual surpluses are not additive because each marginal utility curve is drawn up on the basis of other things being equal, and consumers' surplus has no meaning whatever because "communal curves of price-and-quantity saleable cannot be interpreted psychically, though they rest on a psychic basis" (pp. 467–90). Wicksteed stresses the ubiquity of commodity interdependence (pp. 478–79); inferior goods are briefly discussed in the appendix to chapters 2 and 3 (pp. 490–91).

The Content of the Maximand. Turning back to Book I, chapter 5, we find a detailed analysis of the concept of *homo oeconomicus.* In a famous passage Wicksteed poses the conflict between the introspective and behaviorist approach to economics: "We may either ignore motives altogether, or may recognise all motives that are at work, but in no case may we pick and choose between the motives we will and the motives we will not recognise as affecting economic conditions" (p. 165). "Economic forces and relations," he points out, "have no inherent tendency to redress social wrongs or ally themselves with any ideal system of redistributive justice" (p. 169). Vulgar harmony-doctrine is dismissed with great force and eloquence (pp. 189–92), and the whole of this chapter, in its insistence upon the impossibility of isolating "economic motives" and its emphasis upon the means-end character of rational action, reads nowadays as an introduction to Robbins' *Nature and Significance of Economic Science,* in which economics is defined as the science that studies, not certain kinds of behavior, but rather one aspect of behavior in general.

Price Formation. After this digression we return to the problem of price formation in chapter 6. The individual scales of preferences have been summed to yield collective scales, market demand curves, in fact. Given the stock of goods in the market, the price depends on the market demand curve, which registers not only the intentions of buyers but also those of sellers at their "reserve prices" (pp. 229–34). Notice the brief discussion of the problem first analyzed by Walras: final equilibrium in a market is not independent of the path that the market takes toward the equilibrium point (pp. 226–27). The chapter closes with an interesting description of the whole range of possible markets from the oriental bazaar dependent upon bilateral bargaining to competitive retail trade at quoted prices to monopolized markets (pp. 248–61).

Supply as Reverse Demand. We must pause here and examine Wicksteed's concept of "reserve price." The prospective sellers have a reservation price below which they have an own-demand for the good being traded. Thus, the general demand curve in the market shows the monetary evaluation of marginal satisfactions that will be placed upon varying quantities of an existing supply by *everyone* in the market. In a moment of enthusiasm, Wicksteed even went so far as to deny the existence of supply curves: "what about the 'supply curve' that usually figures as a determinant of price, co-ordinate with the demand curve? I say it boldly and baldly: There is no such thing." But then he adds that "what is usually called the supply curve is in reality the demand curve of those who possess the commodity" (p. 785; see also pp. 506–7, 516, 823–24).

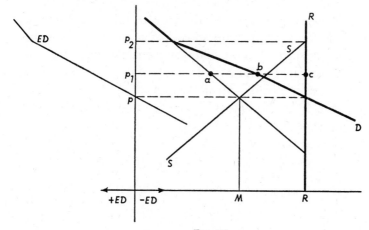

FIG. 78

Wicksteed's argument is perfectly straightforward if we think of supply as a rate sold in the market out of a given stock = OR by "producers" who are themselves "consumers" of the particular product. We are in a Marshallian market period, with this difference, that the buyers and sellers are not well defined separate groups of individuals. Wicksteed assumes that sellers have an own-demand for their own commodity if prices fall below the reservation price p_2 (see Fig. 78). A Marshallian supply curve SS could now be built up out of the quantities sellers want to dispose of at each price; the difference between the quantities offered OM and the total stock at hand OR measures their withholdings at each price. But Wicksteed suggests instead that we add to the buyers' demand curve the own-demand of sellers: this is always the lateral difference between the total stock

OR and the quantity offered by sellers. At the price p_1, for example, we add $bc(=ab)$ to the demand, and so on. Mounting the sellers' reservation demand curve on the buyers' demand curve, we obtain the total market demand curve, intersecting *RR* at p, *OM* being sold to buyers and *MR* retained by sellers. Whether we draw a supply curve or not, the equilibrium price is therefore one where new demand plus reservation demand is equal to the total stock available. Notice also that in the case of sales out of stocks, Wicksteed's total demand curve is also the excess demand curve with the axis transposed.

The Doctrine of Alternative Costs. Since Wicksteed's construction yields the same price and quantity as that of Marshall's, we may wonder why Wicksteed was so insistent on the notion of "supply as reverse demand." It is true that reversibility of supply curves is an everyday occurrence in markets where dealers sell out of stock. But in most consumer markets, producers do not themselves consume what they produce and the product in question does not change hands more than once. For agricultural commodity markets, the stock exchange, or the money market, the Wicksteed construction can be clarifying. But in most markets of continuous production for a well-defined group of consumers the Marshallian cross is more useful and less likely to be misunderstood. The source of Wicksteed's vehemence about reversible supply curves lies in the central Austrian assumption, which he made his own, namely, that the supply of all productive resources is fixed. He wanted to show that, as Robbins has put it, *"all* psychological variables can be exhibited as phenomena of demand acting on fixed stocks—either of products or factors or time—or human capacity." The concept of reversible supply curves made its first appearance in Böhm-Bawerk's famous example of a horse market in which the suppliers are themselves farmers who have a use for horses. Supply here is conditioned not by the "real cost" of calling a commodity into existence but by the cost of excluding other uses, including that of the supplier himself. Wieser had generalized Böhm-Bawerk's example into the doctrine of alternative costs: given the stock of productive agents, competition will so distribute the services of these agents as to equalize their marginal value product in all uses. The costs of producing a commodity reflect nothing but the competing offers of other producers for the services of the factors used to produce it; they represent the payments needed to attract the factors from their next most remunerative employment. In equilibrium, the marginal productivity of resources in all uses and the alternative opportunities forgone from producing an increment of any commodity will be equalized. Thus, as Wicksteed liked to say, cost of production is simply and solely "the marginal significance of something else" (p. 382).

The importance of the alternative cost doctrine, to those who espoused it, was that it demonstrated the fallacy of all "real cost" theories of value. The Austrians spoke with disdain of Marshall's two-sided theory, in which supply prices call forth the services of productive agents by overcoming physical and subjective resistance, as a concession to classical economics. Alternative cost theory made both demand and supply dependent upon utility by tracing all costs back to utilities forgone. "The only sense, then, in which cost of production can affect the value of one thing," Wicksteed remarked, "is the sense in which it is itself the value of another thing. Thus, what has been variously termed "utility," "ophelimity," or "desiredness," is the sole and ultimate determinant of all exchange values" (p. 391). And again, after showing how the pricing of a fixed stock can be analyzed without drawing a supply curve, he generalized the argument to the case of continuous production: "cost of production is merely the form in which the desiredness a thing possesses for some one else presents itself to me. When we take the collective curve of demand for any factor of production we see again that it is entirely composed of de-mands, and my adjustment of my own demands to the conditions im-posed by the demands of others is of exactly the same nature whether I am buying cabbages or factors for the production of steel plates. . . . It is not until we have perfectly grasped the truth that costs of produc-tion of one thing are nothing whatever but an *alias* of efficiencies in production of other things that we shall be finally emancipated from the ancient fallacy [of real costs] we have so often thrust out at the door, while always having the window open for its return" (p. 788). Significantly enough, he added a footnote in which he conceded that "as we recede from the market and deal with long periods . . . cases may arise in which something like a 'supply curve' seems legitimate. The terms on which nature yields increasing supplies of some raw material, for instance, cannot be legitimately regarded as the reserve prices in which she expresses her own demand!"

Alternative Costs and Factor Prices. Before resolving this con-flict between the Austrian and Marshallian approach, let us see how Wicksteed actually applies the doctrine of alternative cost to the earn-ings of productive agents. In chapter 7 he presents the capital market as "the market in advances," in which present income is exchanged against future income; the rate of interest expresses the terms on which these alternatives are available to individuals. The rate of interest is positive because claims against future income will somehow exceed claims against present income; an incisive discussion of the *raison d'être* of consumption loans (pp. 268–80) is followed by an eclectic and far-ranging discussion of the "grounds for interest" (pp. 280–310; see also pp. 748–53, in which all time-period theories of capital are rejected in favor of the concept of perpetual income streams). It is strongly suggested that saving is not a function of the rate of interest, certainly not in the long run (pp. 294–98).

Similarly, it cannot be assumed that labor is supplied according to the principles of rational cost accounting, that is, according to the discounted value of the prospective returns net of construction and maintenance charges. "The production of undifferentiated human capacity . . . must in the main be regarded as 'consumption' technically, not production . . . The whole question of the ultimate supply of human effort, therefore, carries us far beyond the limits of economic inquiry" (pp. 336–37). For nonhuman resources there is a constant tendency for allocation at equilibrium to produce an equalization of the marginal significance of all uses of each resource. As applied to labor, this doctrine had certain limitations. Owing to the division of labor, the reserve price of labor is effectively zero in the short run (p. 324). Moreover, labor is notoriously immobile between occupations, and labor-training is frequently more influenced by the financial status of parents than by prospective rates of reward (pp. 332–36). Nevertheless, every worker substitutes leisure for wage income at the margin and "remuneration for human effort, so far as it is determined by economic forces, follows the law of the market, just as the price of commodities does" (p. 338). Presumably, this means that labor will be supplied at a given wage rate so as to equate the marginal rate of substitution between leisure and effort to the wage rate (see pp. 522–26), while at the same time the supply so forthcoming will be allocated between occupations so as to equalize the marginal cost of one commodity in terms of any other.

But the limitations of alternative cost theory when applied to labor go further than Wicksteed seemed to realize. As Adam Smith had shown, competition tends to equalize, not the monetary returns, but the "net advantages" of different occupations to individuals. And if differences in the psychic costs of two occupations result in differences in total earnings of homogeneous units of labor, then the cost of labor to one industry is not equal to the alternative product that labor could have produced in another industry. What this means is that "real costs" in the form of the relative irksomeness of different occupations do have an effect on the allocation of human resources between competing lines of production. The problem goes even deeper than that. In order for the market to equalize alternative costs, however interpreted, the resource in question must be capable of variation at the margin. But labor cannot, as a rule, sell its services in varying proportions to different buyers: the choice between different occupations is essentially an either-or decision. The workers' decision to enter an occupation is not a marginal choice and for that reason there seems to be a fundamental nonparallelism between the allocation of human and nonhuman resources.

The conflict between alternative cost theory and real cost theory can be formally resolved by treating leisure and "agreeableness of work" as displaced goods. Either we say that the optimum distribution of labor services between different industries and occupations is one which equates differences in the marginal value product of the services to differences in the marginal disutility of labor, or we say that it is one which equalizes opportunity costs interpreted as including the nonpecuniary returns attached to producing a given product. The choice of an occupation with a smaller money income and a lower disutility must now be regarded as the worker's joint purchase of leisure and agreeableness. Thus, differences in monetary returns to units of homogeneous labor represent prices paid by workers for different conditions of work. By this verbal sleight-of-hand we can rescue the proposition that equilibrium prices will be equal to opportunity costs. Nevertheless, the fact remains that, unless workers are indifferent among occupations and unless the factors of production are perfectly inelastic in supply, the production-possibility curve defining all optimum feasible outputs from a given amount of productive factors is not uniquely given. We may *say* that equilibrium prices will be equal to the slope of the production-possibility curve, but we cannot draw a unique production-transformation curve on the basis of a given amount of labor, capital, and land.

Alternative cost theory has the advantage, by its very terminology, of focusing attention on the question of static allocative efficiency. But ignoring short-period variations in the supply of effort leaves us with a range of indeterminacy. One may quarrel about the empirical significance of this range—most of the arguments between Marshall and Edgeworth, on the one hand, and Wieser and Böhm-Bawerk, on the other, over Jevons' theory of the disutility of labor took this form— but it cannot be denied that it exists. Real cost theory emphasizes the variability of factor supplies even in the short run and goes beyond alternative cost theory by remaining in touch with the problem of dynamic allocative efficiency involving the growth of population and the accumulation of capital.

Distribution. Wicksteed rejects not only the classical triad but any attempt to enumerate definitively the factors of production: "We know already that the same principle determines the claims of them all so that the division, could we accomplish it, would have no theoretic importance" (p. 367). Every factor receives a share determined by its marginal product, including the entrepreneur regarded as a separate quantifiable factor (pp. 367–72). He renounces the notion of product exhaustion from marginal productivity payments (p. 373n) but does not in fact abandon the idea. "Within limits, the most apparently unlike of these factors of production can be substituted for each other at the margins, and so brought to a common measure of marginal serviceableness-in-production" (pp. 361; also pp. 779, 798); given complete substitutability between the factors, no distributive share can really be a residual (see p. 792). Interestingly enough, Wicksteed is perfectly aware of the fact that the entrepreneur is really engaged in "a series of speculative transactions based on estimates made in advance." He comes very close to saying that the presence of uncertainty creates the possibility of "profit" from a divergence between anticipated and realized marginal products (pp. 372–73; also p. 798).

The Laws of Return. We pass on to Book II, chapter 5, dealing with the laws of return. In contrast to Marshall, Wicksteed draws a clear distinction at the outset between diminishing returns from increments of one productive agent and diminishing returns from increases in the scale of the plant (pp. 527–28). The law of diminishing returns in the former sense is said to be "an axiomatic statement of a universal principle." But this is true only if the production function is linear and homogeneous, a fact that Wicksteed denies to be generally true (pp. 529, 534).[6] The classical generalization that diminishing

---

[6] If $Q = bL^a K^\beta$, then $MP_L = aQ/L = aAP_L$. If $a + \beta > 1$, so that increasing returns to scale prevail, then it need not be true that $\partial^2 Q/\partial L^2 = (\partial/\partial L)(aQ/L) < 0$.

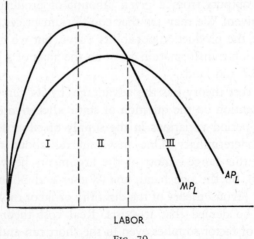

LABOR

FIG 79

returns apply to agriculture while increasing returns apply to manufacturing is soundly condemned (p. 533). Nevertheless, "whether in agriculture or manufactures, it seems to be a fairly general rule that when an increased demand causes an increased production that presses against the existing limits, at first cost of production will rise, but ultimately it will fall" (p. 534). Part of the confusion in Wicksteed's treatment of the laws of return is that he does not appear to regard increasing returns as an instance of economies of scale to a firm. When he draws a downward-sloping supply curve, it is the *LRAC* curve of an *industry* (p. 535) and it is specifically described as a nonreversible curve (p. 536). Thus, he concludes that all reversible short- and long-run industry supply curves are upward sloping but that historical cost curves fall to the right (pp. 537–39). This may explain his failure to see the incompatibility of increasing returns to scale with perfect competition (pp. 529–30). At any rate, though this chapter marks a great advance on Marshall's discussion of the laws of return, it is far from dealing adequately with the subject. Twenty years were to pass before the problem of decreasing cost industries was satisfactorily resolved.

Wicksteed's refutation of the theory that "rent does not enter into cost" fails to point out that the Ricardian assumption of a fixed amount of land does imply that rent is not a cost from a social point of view (pp. 540–42). It is odd that Wicksteed, believing as he did in land nationalization (see pp. 686–90), should fail to discuss the social implications of relative fixity in the supply of land. Here as elsewhere in the *Common Sense,* however, he reiterates his belief that land is not ultimately limited in quantity even in Great Britain (pp. 365, 533). The chapter closes with an attempt to contribute to "the gaiety of nations" by vanquishing the Malthusian specter of immanent diminishing returns to further increases in the labor supply (pp. 546–49).

The Law of Rent. Chapter 6 is the most deservedly famous chapter in the whole book. With characteristic thoroughness, Wicksteed demonstrates that rent determined as the mixtilinear area under the marginal product curve of labor and capital is identical to rent determined as the rectilinear area under the marginal product curve of land. Once again, Wicksteed fails to point out that this is true only if the production function is homogeneous and of the first degree. His numerical examples, however, clearly assume constant returns to scale (see p. 555), and indeed product exhaustion is categorically affirmed to hold universally (p. 573). The practice of labeling as "rent" any and all intramarginal surpluses is sharply condemned on the ground that it promotes the use of unscientific residual-claimant theories (pp. 568–73). In point of fact, however, there is no basis whatever for the widely shared belief that a residual-claimant explanation of a distributive share is inherently unsatisfactory. The habit of defining land à la Ricardo as a "free gift of nature," Wicksteed suggests, should be abandoned once and for all (pp. 573–74).

Applied Economics. Chapter 7, on banking, bills, and currency, contains very few surprises. The power of banks to create credit is completely

---

This follows from the fact that if $\alpha + \beta > 1$, then it is possible that $\alpha > 1$; but if $\alpha > 1$, then $MP_L > AP_L$, which is a necessary but not sufficient condition for MP_L to be increasing. It is true that rational factor-hire precludes regions I and II but that is to say that diminishing marginal productivity is not an axiom but a corollary of equilibrium.

misunderstood (pp. 586–87) but this is what we would expect in a prewar treatment of the subject. The quantity theory of money is attacked as a tautology, with the result that Wicksteed has difficulty in explaining how inconvertible paper currencies maintain their value (pp. 610–22). Book III contains some "samples of analysis" of applied economics. The discussion of gambling (pp. 628–34) is perfectly Marshallian in tone. The housing problem is touched upon but not really explored (pp. 634–36). A brief note on voluntary unemployment is followed by a discussion of "recurrent general depressions" that might have been written by J. S. Mill a half-century earlier (pp. 637–40). The problems of social accounting are mentioned: "The 'services' for which the wages of shame are paid constitute a part of the national revenue as much as any other; but if Portia is Brutus' wife and not his harlot her companionship ceases to count in the national revenue" (p. 651). The notion that current income per head affords an indication of what equal distribution would yield to everyone is effectively scotched; the point of Wicksteed's argument is to show that valuation of national income is not independent of its distribution, an obvious point that is nevertheless frequently overlooked (pp. 652–56). Wicksteed proceeds to show that redistribution would render "the realisation of the usual middle-class ideal impossible"; nevertheless, the weight of his argument comes down in favor of income equalization (pp. 656–62). Protectionist sentiments grounded upon beggar-my-neighbor policies are neatly confuted (pp. 666–75). The advantages of extending the scope of state enterprises and other forms of collective action are sympathetically considered (pp. 675–83; see also pp. 341–42). Owing to fewness on the buying side in a labor market, "workmen, taken severally, are at a disadvantage in bargaining with the employer" (p. 690). When marginal labor costs exceed average labor costs, competition among employers will fail to bid wage rates up to the marginal value product of labor (pp. 691–92). This is particularly true if entry into the industry is limited (p. 692). But "while discovering the economic justification of collective bargaining we have also unveiled the theoretical possibility of its being an economically destructive force" (p. 692). The book closes with a review of the methods that might be adopted to alleviate the economic problem of poverty.

NOTES FOR FURTHER READING

1. *The Demand for Factors of Production.* For a useful review of the history of marginal productivity theory, with special reference to labor, see Douglas, *Theory of Wages,* chap. 2, and P. A. Samuelson, "Economic Theory and Wages," chap. 15 in *The Impact of the Union,* ed. D. McCord Wright (1951). J. R. Hicks, "Marginal Productivity and the Principle of Variation," *Ec,* February, 1932, discusses Pareto's objection to variable input coefficients. D. H. Robertson, "Wage Grumbles," *Economic Fragments* (1931), reprinted in *Readings in the Theory of Income Distribution,* takes up this as well as other criticisms that have been directed against the marginal productivity theory of wages. See also a clarifying survey of "The Meaning of the Marginal Product," by F. Machlup, *Explorations in Economics* (1936), reprinted in the *Readings* just cited. G. F. Bloom, "A Reconsideration of the Theory of Exploitation,"

QJE, 1940, also reprinted in the *Readings,* subjects the Pigovian concept of exploitation to a thorough re-examination. The instructive debate between R. A. Lester and F. Machlup on the empirical content of marginal productivity theory in labor markets, conducted in the pages of *AER* in 1946–47, is reprinted in *REA,* Vol. II. For a brief but penetrating discussion see Schumpeter, *History,* pp. 939–44, and Hutchison, *Review of Economic Doctrines,* pp. 315–19. W. Fellner weighs the "Significance and Limitations of Contemporary Distribution Theory," *AER,* May, 1953, made up as it is of a marginal productivity theory on the demand side. For the concept of "induced" technical change see W. Feller, *Trends and Cycles in Economic Activity* (1956), chap. 8.

2. *Linear Homogeneous Production Functions.* The indispensable reference on the role of product exhaustion in the genesis of marginal productivity theory is Stigler, *Production and Distribution Theory,* chap. 12; see also chap. 7, on Wieser's imputation theory, and chap. 11, pp. 296–308, on Clark's marginal productivity theory. J. Robinson, "Euler's Theorem and the Problem of Distribution," *EJ,* 1934, reprinted in *Collected Economic Papers,* Vol. I, provides a brilliant analysis of the economic meaning of product exhaustion; the concept of the marginal productivity of the entrepreneur to the industry, however, is open to question. Schumpeter, *History,* pp. 1026–52, reviews the general concept of the production function, citing recent literature. See also the sharp but somewhat misleading comments by P. A. Samuelson, *Foundations of Economic Analysis* (1948), pp. 74–87, which denies that there is any tendency toward product exhaustion even under perfect competition. On linear programming see the brief exposition by R. Dorfman, "Mathematical, or 'Linear' Programming," *AER,* December, 1953, and the extended treatment by Dorfman, Samuelson, and Solow, *Linear Programming and Economic Analysis.* For a review of the mathematics of linear homogeneous production functions see R. G. D. Allen, *Mathematical Analysis for Economists* (1938), pp. 260–64, 284–89, 315–22, 340–43, and 369–74.

3. *The Optimum Firm.* The *locus classicus* for the notion of the optimum firm is E. A. G. Robinson, *The Structure of Competitive Industry* (1932), chaps. 2–7. See also an influential essay by N. Kaldor, "Equilibrium of the Firm," *EJ,* 1934, reprinted in *Essays on Value and Distribution* (1960). Chamberlin's assault on the indivisibility thesis was launched in the essay, "Proportionately, Divisibility and Economies of Scale," *QJE,* 1948, reprinted in *The Theory of Monopolistic Competition* (6th ed., 1948), Appen. B. Quite apart from its central thesis, this article is a valuable pedagogic exercise. On the basic argument see "Two Comments" by A. N. McLeod and F. H Hahn, and "Reply" by Chamberlin, *QJE,* February, 1949; T. M. Whitin and M. H. Peston, "Random Variations, Risk and Returns to Scale," *QJE,* November, 1954; D. Schwarzman, "The Methodology of the Theory of Returns to Scale," *OEP,* February, 1958. The empirical evidence is reviewed by C. A. Smith, "Survey of Empirical Evidence of Economies to Scale," *NBER, Business Concentration and Price Policy* (1955). See also E. Penrose, "Limits to the Growth and Size of Firms," *AER,* May, 1955. Some of the implications of economic dynamics for the theory of the firm are discussed by M. W. Reder, *Studies in the Theory of Welfare Economics* (1947), chaps. 9–10.

4. *The Theory of Profit.* F. H. Knight, *Risk, Uncertainty and Profit*

(1921), covers the history of profit theory up to the publication of his own landmark. J. F. Weston, "The Profit Concept of Theory: A Restatement," *JPE,* April, 1954, sketches the history of the discussion since that time and defends the uncertainty theory. M. Bronfenbrenner supplies "A Reformulation of the Naïve Profit Theory," *SEJ,* April, 1960. The naïve theory in question is the pre-Knightian Marshallian theory that profit is a return to the entrepreneurial function of ultimate decision making and uncertainty bearing, which is usually positive even in the long run and a genuine distributive share in a competitive economy.

On the various meanings that have been assigned to the term "entrepreneur" see L. M. Fraser, *Economic Thought and Language* (1937), chap. 15. Edgeworth's criticisms of received doctrine on entrepreneurship are canvassed by Stigler, *Production and Distribution Theory,* chap. 5, pp. 125–29. Schumpeter, *History,* pp. 893–98, discusses the concept of entrepreneurial functions and explains why one should avoid drawing supply curves for entrepreneurial services. The fact that profit maximization implies a definite hypothesis about businessmen's behavior was first pointed out by T. Scitovsky, "A Note on Profit Maximisation and Its Implications," *REStud,* 1943, reprinted in *Readings in Price Theory.*

5. *Wicksteed.* On Wicksteed's *Common Sense* see Stigler, *Production and Distribution Theories,* chap. 3, and Hutchison, *Review of Economic Doctrines,* chap. 5. For an interesting portrait of the Unitarian minister, classical scholar, and economist, see C. H. Herford, *Philip Henry Wicksteed; His Life and Work* (1931). The reader may gain an accurate impression of the conflict between real cost and alternative cost theory by perusing Edgeworth's reviews of some Austrian publications of the 1890's, such as W. Smart, *An Introduction to the Theory of Value on the Lines of Menger, Wieser, and Böhm-Bawerk* (1892); Wieser's *Natural Value* (1893); and Böhm-Bawerk's *Ultimate Standard of Value* (1894)—all of which are reprinted in *Papers Relating to Political Economy,* III, pp. 31–32, 50–64. In a classic essay, "On a Certain Ambiguity in the Conception of Stationary Equilibrium," *EJ,* 1930, reprinted in *REA,* Vol. I, L. Robbins showed that the battle between the English and the Austrian school stemmed from "a failure on the part of the participants to perceive that each was adopting a different assumption with regard to the conditions of equilibrium . . . Marshall and Edgeworth were assuming the fluidity of supply of capital and labor which was characteristic of the classical conception of equilibrium. Böhm-Bawerk and Wieser were assuming the fixity of supply which is the assumption of Clarkian statics." Böhm-Bawerk's concessions to the disutility theory are reviewed by Stigler, *Production and Distribution Theories,* pp. 182–92. On the shortcomings of alternative cost doctrine in dealing with the allocation of labor between employments, see F. H. Knight, "The Common Sense of Political Economy," *JPE,* October, 1934. The conflict between the Austrian and the English approach to the nature of costs flared up again in the 1930's in the theory of international trade: see Viner, *Studies in the Theory of International Trade,* pp. 489–93 and 516–26, and G. Haberler, "Real Costs and Opportunity Costs," *International Social Science Bulletin,* Spring, 1951.

Chapter 12

AUSTRIAN THEORY
OF CAPITAL
AND INTEREST

1. BÖHM-BAWERK'S THEORY OF INTEREST

LAND AND LABOR are "original" or primary factors of production whose supply is either fixed or a function of noneconomic decisions. But capital is a produced or intermediate factor whose supply is dependent on the land and labor expended in the past in producing it. This distinction between land and labor, on the one hand, and capital, on the other, is fundamental to Böhm-Bawerk's theory of interest. It leads straightway to a formulation of the problem of "the origin of interest." In long-run competitive equilibrium the value of the total product will be exhausted by factor payments in accordance with marginal productivity. Since capital goods are themselves the product of previous applications of land and labor, their value should be equal to the cost of wages and rents incurred in producing them. In other words, the entire net value added of final goods should be precisely equal to the payments made to the "original" factors. If interest exists it must be due to the fact that there are not two but three "original" factors, say land, labor, and "waiting." But this Böhm-Bawerk denied.

The role of capital in production is to permit adoption of more productive but also more time-consuming "roundabout" methods of production. Robinson Crusoe can catch fish directly by a hand-to-mouth technique or indirectly by the roundabout method of constructing a net. With the aid of the net he can catch more fish than could be caught without it, even after allowing for the cost of constructing and maintaining the net. This is what we mean when we say that capital is physically productive. But physical productivity is not the same thing as value productivity. If physical capital is to yield a net value product, something must prevent it from being produced up to the point at which its abundance reduces its value down to the cost of construction and maintenance. This "brake" on the production of capital goods,

Böhm-Bawerk proceeds to show, lies in the nature of roundabout methods themselves. It is complemented by the phenomenon of time preference. The ultimate limitation on investment is a limitation of the time we are willing to wait for a return. As a result, the value of all finished goods will not even in long-run equilibrium be completely swept back to the "original factors."

The Productivity of Greater Roundaboutness. "That roundabout methods lead to greater results than direct methods" Böhm-Bawerk declares, "is one of the most important and fundamental propositions in the whole theory of production." This is a statement few would deny. But Böhm-Bawerk goes further: roundabout methods are necessarily and always more time consuming than direct methods, and every increase in the length of time for which the "original" factors are invested in production increases the total product at a diminishing rate. This proposition, like the previous one, is defended on the basis of "the experience of practical life," but it is far from a matter of common experience. Is it never possible, even at a constant state of technical knowledge, to increase the total product by investing in less time-consuming methods of production? Is it really true that capital can be expended only in lengthening the period of production?

It is obvious, of course, that if the rate of interest in the economy is positive no one will adopt a more roundabout method, yielding its results at a later date, unless it is more productive. But this proposition cannot be reversed to prove that capital can be invested only by increasing the degree of roundaboutness. A reduction in the rate of interest does encourage the adoption of longer processes insofar as it increases the present value of a given stream of future returns, but it also renders hitherto unprofitable projects feasible by reducing initial capital costs; these projects may well require less time to complete than the range of previously adopted methods. Be that as it may, it is not really legitimate to establish Böhm-Bawerk's propositions about the nature of roundaboutness on the basis of a positive rate of interest when the purpose of these propositions is to prove that the interest rate will be positive.

Böhm-Bawerk's assumptions are very strong: it is not simply that more roundabout methods are generally more productive but that every "wisely chosen" lengthening of the period of production increases the total product at a diminishing rate to the time of the lengthening; furthermore, the production period cannot be extended without additional capital, and, conversely, capital can be invested in only one way, namely, to lengthen the production period. Böhm-

Bawerk's proof of these assumptions, gradually elaborated in reply to criticism, either takes the form of assuming that the rate of interest is positive, then ignoring the effect of a lower interest rate on installation costs as well as the possibility of investing capital in new products rather than in new methods, or else falls back on the premise that capital is previously applied labor, land being neglected for the sake of simplicity. Since capital is *vorgetane Arbeit,* the more capital there is, the older is the average age of the capital stock. The latter proof is based on the original-factors doctrine and hence carries little conviction. But it helps to shed light on the major shortcomings of Böhm-Bawerk's capital theory. Most of his reasoning makes much better sense when it is realized that his "capital" is only circulating capital, funds tied up in the form of goods-in-process. The function of working capital is not to co-operate with labor in production but, as it were, to support labor during the interval between the application of inputs and the emergence of output. Assuming the amount of labor to remain fixed, longer production periods obviously require more working capital per man, and, conversely, more working capital per man is required only when it is found that the period of production can be profitably extended. Indeed, we shall see that in the end Böhm-Bawerk produces a theory of interest that is identical to the classical wages fund doctrine, with this difference—that the length of the period of production is now a variable and not a technically given constant.

The Three Reasons for Interest. Before proceeding to the demonstration that the most profitable lengthening of the period of production is a function of the interest rate, Böhm-Bawerk raises the question of "the origin of interest." Interest arises out of a process of lending present income against the return of future income; some individuals in the community are willing to pay a premium or *agio* on present income for the privilege of disposing of it as they see fit for a period of time. The question, Why is the rate of interest positive? may be expressed in Böhm-Bawerk's language as: Why are people willing to deliver only a certain quantity of goods in the present if they receive a greater quantity of goods of the same kind and quality in the future? In modern terminology this might be translated into the question: Why is it that the price of a bond is less than the total future payments confidently expected from it? Why are people not so eager to buy bonds as to bid their prices up to the point at which net interest disappears?

Böhm-Bawerk's answer is that there are three "reasons" or "grounds" why people on the average prefer present to future goods, discounting the future by paying a premium on present goods. The first two operate to create a demand for consumption loans: (1) "different circumstances of want and provision" in the present and in the future; and (2) "under-estimation of the future." The third "reason" influences production loans: (3) "the technical superiority of present over future goods."

The First Reason. The argument here rests on people faced with present poverty and on those expecting to be better off in the future; both groups will prefer present over future goods. To make sense of this argument, we have to distinguish between a stationary and a dynamic economy. The appropriate assumption for a static theory of interest such as Böhm-Bawerk's is that the income stream is constant through time. As Wicksell pointed out, this immediately disposes of the first "reason": the young, who are acquiring their skills, have a high discount on the future, but the old, who have passed their years of maximum earnings, probably discount the present in favor of the future. A stationary economy would have a population of uniform age distribution. Hence, there is no reason to think that one class of people will predominate over the other.

On the other hand, if we assume that the income stream is rising through time and that everyone expects it with perfect certainty to continue to rise, then the law of diminishing marginal utility of income necessarily implies positive time preference. This proposition was established for the first time by Landry in *L'Intérêt du Capital* (1904): if individuals act so as to maximize the sum of utilities over all future time, they will be willing to pay a premium for present goods when income is rising through time. The reason for this is that increments of present consumption will add more utility than will have to be sacrificed in the future when the loan is repaid simply because future income will be higher. And this is true even if present consumption can be substituted for future consumption on even terms, that is, if the interest rate is zero. A rising income stream leads via the buoyant demand for consumption loans to a positive rate of interest. As soon as the rate of interest is positive, however, we no longer need the law of diminishing income-utility to account for positive time preference. Ordinary rational optimizing behavior will now produce the same result.

All we have to do is apply the equimarginal principle, for it must hold for intertemporal consumption planning as much as for the distribution of expenditure within any given time period. The rational individual will so distribute his expected future income among different years as to insure that the marginal dollar received in any year makes the same contribution to total utility as any other. He will convert the expected flow of income into a planned flow of consumption expenditures in such a way as to equalize the weighted marginal utility of the present value of planned consumption over all future periods, the weights being the interest rates ruling in the market at the appropriate times. In the discrete case of annual income payments, assuming that the individual's utility surface remains constant through time, the allocation formula reads:

$$\frac{MU_1}{(1+r)^1} = \frac{MU_2}{(1+r)^2} = \cdots = \frac{MV_t}{(1+r)^t},$$

where the MU's stand for the marginal utility of the respective annual consumption expenditures and the rate of interest r is conveniently assumed to remain constant through time.

Thus, the marginal intertemporal rate of substitution between consumption in the current year and all future years must be equal to the given discount rate.

$$\frac{MU_1}{MU_2} = \frac{MU_2}{MU_3} = \cdots = \frac{1}{(1+r)}.$$

Since $MU_1 = MU_t/(1+r)^{t-1}$, the more distant the income period—the greater the value of t—the smaller the discounted marginal utility of future consumption relative to current consumption expenditure; the more distant the income period, the more the individual must get additional units of a good today to compensate him for a unit less tomorrow. If the consumer were really indifferent between different time periods, he would have to consume more in the future than in the present to be in equilibrium at a positive rate of interest. The increase in future consumption would have to be greater, the more distant in time the prospective consumption expenditure. As t approaches infinity, future consumption would approach satiety and present saving-income ratios would rise close to unity. Casual empiricism suggests that individuals do attach a time discount to the marginal utility of the present value of future income streams. Since a positive interest rate *means* that goods are estimated as less valuable the later they are available, this observation is not very surprising. But it illustrates the difficulty of establishing the notion of intrinsic time preference on the basis of people's behavior in an economy in which interest already exists.

To avoid fatal ambiguity of language, we must define time preference in terms of a zero rate of interest. Positive time preference means that individuals prefer a present income over the same amount of future income despite the fact that these are available on the same terms. It is clear that this definition adheres to Böhm-Bawerk's meaning and intent; failure to observe it renders discussion of the three "reasons" meaningless.

We can summarize our conclusions with reference to the first ground by saying that it fails to show why a stationary economy should exhibit a definite pattern of time preference; furthermore, it must rely on a dubious law of uniformly diminishing utility of income to demonstrate that a dynamic economy will exhibit positive time preference.

The Second Reason. The second independent "reason" for positive time preference is perspective underestimation of the future, a tendency toward myopia on the part of economic agents, which Böhm-Bawerk attributes to: (*a*) deficiency of imagination, (*b*) limited will power, and (*c*) the shortness and uncertainty of life. This second "reason" was criticized by Menger and Wieser and many others because it implied irrationality of behavior. Menger had himself proposed the second ground in the *Grundsätze* but deleted it in a later edition lest it be construed as giving support to Böhm-Bawerk's theory; Wieser went out of his way in *Natural Value* to observe: "One may thus say that it is a sound maxim among all peoples of normal development to appraise alike the present and the future." Even Wicksteed thought that "ordinary prudence estimates the significance of a unit in the future just as that of a unit in the present." Indeed, it is rather peculiar that all the fundamental criticisms of this second "reason" have come from members of the Austrian School.[1]

The argument that the assumption of myopia must be rejected because it implies irrational behavior is methodologically unsound: any motives, rational or otherwise, that are shown to be significantly related to economic behavior ought to be considered by economists. This is nothing more than traditional practice. J. S. Mill was fond of pointing

---

[1] What is even more surprising is that Böhm-Bawerk himself denied that abstaining from present consumption constitutes a cost, even though it is irksome. In *Capital and Interest* (1884), he attacked the abstinence theory of interest on the grounds that interest is often paid without any corresponding "pain" and that the theory involves double counting. The first objection simply confuses average and marginal abstinence; in equilibrium the rate of interest is equal to the marginal supply price of abstinence and all intramarginal savers will earn a saver's surplus. The second objection is difficult to grasp but appears no less fallacious. What Böhm-Bawerk seems to have meant is that true abstinence involves the renunciation of present consumption to build up the capital stock: to add the pain cost of abstaining permanently from a present enjoyment to the alternative cost of choosing future in preference to present goods is to engage in double counting. This argument ignores the fact that the choice between present and future goods is not like the choice between two goods available in the present precisely because of the second "reason." Böhm-Bawerk would not have rejected the abstinence theory, which, properly speaking, is embodied in his second "reason," if it had not been for the fact that adherence to the original-factors doctrine prevented him from admitting that abstinence or waiting is an independent "real" cost of production.

out that economics studies man as a creature motivated by pecuniary self-interest, but, as Malthus had shown, sexual instincts are so strong that men rear large families despite the fact that self-interest dictates family limitation. Hence, the motive to procreate without limit, Mill concluded, is an aspect of human behavior that economics cannot afford to neglect.

However, moralizing about time preference apart, there are a number of valid arguments that have been advanced against "deficiency of the telescopic faculty" as a general assumption. Deficiency of imagination and limited will power are offset by the desire to bequeath fortune to heirs and, particularly, by the widespread social approval of "rainy day" saving, which Marshall argued was ever more the characteristic feature of industrialized countries. If we take the evangelical overtones out of Marshall's language, it comes down to the proposition that the rate of time preference declines as income per head rises: the larger the income per head, the less anxious anyone is to supplement present consumption by borrowing or drawing on accumulated savings. Certainly, the possibility of not being able to enjoy future income through death or physical incapacity suggests that individuals do frequently discount the future, but loss of earning power is feared quite as much as loss of future enjoyment and leads to a discount on the present. There is no reason, of course, to presume that individuals have uniform time-preference rates for all future periods: this would be like assuming that people are rationally irrational. It may be that individuals are indifferent between income now and income two or three years later, while incomes in the remote future are heavily discounted. On the other hand, the shortness and uncertainty of life may make for precisely the opposite effect. It is true that a bird in the hand is worth two in the bush, but the individual may expect to be unable to catch the birds in the bush.

Prodigality and improvidence, on the one hand, saving and abstemiousness, on the other—can one strike a balance? The modern view is that there is no more reason for thinking that most people discount the future than that they discount the present, always remembering that these are subjective discount rates independent of the rate of interest. As we shall see, Irving Fisher expresses Böhm-Bawerk's second "reason" by saying that the time preference of each individual depends on the size, certainty, and time shape of his income stream; it is not assumed that people are typically "patient" or "impatient." As Fisher uses it, "the impatience principle" does not denote a psychic discount of the "true" future value but simply the fact that people will not defer the enjoyment of income except for sufficient reasons. A sufficient reason in the real world, of course, is the existence of a positive rate of interest. It is perfectly possible that aggregate time preference is zero or even negative in the United States today, meaning that at a zero rate of interest personal savings would still be forthcoming.

The Third Reason. Every investment of goods in productive processes increases the resulting product, albeit at a decreasing rate. Present goods can be invested and reinvested as they accrue tomorrow, but goods available tomorrow can be invested only tomorrow. This "technical superiority of present over future goods" is not a matter merely of a larger physical product but also of a larger value product. Present goods applied today yield a physical output in the future when applied to roundabout production larger than an equal quantity of goods applied at a future date to direct production; furthermore, they yield a physical product larger than an equal quantity of goods applied at a future date to roundabout production—because of diminishing returns from lengthening the period of production. Since the larger of two quantities of the same good available to an individual at the same time is the more valuable, a quantity of present goods always has a greater value than the same quantity of future goods. This is Böhm-Bawerk's formulation of the meaning of productivity theories of interest: the net physical productivity of capital by itself creates a discount on the future, independently of the factors of needs, provisions, and perspective.

Böhm-Bawerk insisted, despite repeated attacks, that the third "reason" constitutes an independent ground for a positive rate of interest. But, as Fisher and others argued, the first two "reasons" operate both on the demand and on the supply side in the loan market, while the third "reason" affects only the demand for production loans. Without the aid of one of the two other "reasons," the admittedly greater physical productivity of more roundabout methods will not by itself create a premium on present goods. Thus, the "technical superiority of present over future goods" will make it possible to supply more goods in the future than at present with the same resources; this causes provisions in the future to exceed provisions in the present, and the first "reason" then explains why people will discount the future.

The Interaction of the Three Reasons. Fisher's argument about the interaction of the three "reasons" is fundamental. Assume that myopia is absent so that we are interested only in maximizing the product, regardless of when it is maximized. The fact that capital is productive would not cause anyone to prefer income today over tomorrow, since by definition we are indifferent about the date at which the final product emerges. The productivity of capital, however, will influence the relative abundance of goods today and tomorrow; with real income rising through time, people are willing to pay a premium for goods available today instead of tomorrow and a positive rate of interest emerges. In the absence of something like a law of diminishing utility of income, only undervaluation of the future can account for the fact that the productivity of capital leads to a positive rate of interest.

Böhm-Bawerk's three grounds together provide an exhaustive explanation of the existence of interest in a stationary as much as in a dynamic economy. In a stationary state, the presence either of the second "reason" or of the third "reason" in combination with the second constitutes a necessary condition for the interest rate to be positive. And, contrariwise, the rate of interest can be zero only (1) when the flow of income is constant through time, (2) when time preference is neutral, and (3) when the net product cannot be increased by postponing consumption to invest in production.

The interaction of the three "reasons" not only explains the existence of interest but also fixes the length of the average period of production that will yield the highest present value. Since any further roundaboutness always promises a further increase in the value of the total product, a zero rate of interest would encourage an unlimited increase in the period of production.[2] This would mean a scarcity of present goods, leading via the first or the second "reason" to the re-emergence of interest and the reversal to direct methods of production. The true function of a positive rate of interest, then, is to act as a brake on the tendency to neglect present wants by overextending the period of production. The interest rate rations the limited supply of present goods among industries in accordance with the community's estimation of the relative value of present and future goods. If an economy is highly "capitalistic," the stock of consumer goods will be large, the degree of roundaboutness great, and the increment of product yielded by further extensions of the average period of production small. Hence the

[2] This is not quite right, as Wicksell showed. The fact that increasing roundaboutness is subject to diminishing returns will make lengthening profitable to only a limited extent. If by investing $50 I can receive $100 of final product from a one-year process or $150 from a two-year process, it will pay me to choose the shorter process in both years: at the end of the first year I can then reinvest $100 at double the scale, ending up with $200 instead of $150. On the other hand, if I had to invest $75 to get $100 from a one-year process or $150 from a two-year process, the longer process would be more profitable: $100 reinvested in the second year would bring only $133.30. Thus, if indefinite lengthening is to be profitable, the final product must increase at more than a geometric rate as time increases at an arithmetic rate. Diminishing returns from lengthening the period of production precludes this possibility.

rate of interest will be low. This is Böhm-Bawerk's explanation of the tendency of the rate of interest to fall as the capital-labor ratio rises, reflecting the twofold diminution of the advantages of greater roundaboutness and the disappearance of the premium on present goods.

The Determination of Interest. In the last part of the *Positive Theory of Capital* (1889), Böhm-Bawerk finally moves beyond the question why the rate of interest should be positive, to ask how the rate is actually determined. At this point the argument shifts ground radically: no more is heard of consumption loans, personal saving, and discounting of the future. The economy consists of capitalists and workers. Capitalists are conceived in the classical manner as active entrepreneurs in possession of capital. The demand for funds emanates solely from capitalists and the supply comes primarily from retained earnings. Moreover, all capital consists, in effect, of means of subsistence advanced to workers. Hence, the determination of the rate of interest is a matter of the exchange of labor for consumer goods. Capitalists do not, but workers do, typically undervalue the future because of the good old classical reason that workers cannot afford to wait for the fruits of their labor.

With a fixed supply and composition of the subsistence fund, a datum in Böhm-Bawerk's model, the rate of interest is determined by the marginal productivity of lengthening the average period of production. The point at which greater roundaboutness ceases to yield a positive addition to the total product is outside the horizon of even the wealthiest societies. At a zero rate of interest, capitalists would have an infinite demand for present goods to advance to their workers. Thus, the rate of interest rises until the entire subsistence fund is used in lengthening the average period of production. The lower the interest rate, the longer the profitable period of production, because at a lower rate of interest the present value of a stream of future goods is greater and hence the premium on present goods is smaller. And so the equilibrium rate of interest is determined by "the productiveness of the last extension of process economically permissible," that is, by the marginal productivity of extending the period of production. The wage rate will then be equal to the marginal productivity of labor discounted to the present.

Despite Böhm-Bawerk's ceaseless criticism of productivity theories of interest, his own theory in the last section of the book clearly attributes interest to the productivity of capitalistic methods of production. Indeed, it is nothing more than a marginal productivity theory of capital so stated as to bring out the fact that capital is a two-dimensional quantity of time and physical size. It bears an obvious similarity to the wages fund doctrine: instead of assuming a given labor supply and a fixed period of production of one year to determine the wage rate as a function of the variable subsistence fund, Böhm-Bawerk assumes the supply of labor and the subsistence fund to be given and then determines the wage rate and the interest rate as a function of the variable period of production. The theory remains static: we are not examining economic behavior *through* time but the allocation of resources between different methods of production available at one *point* in time, each of which requires different periods of time for its completion.

2. THE AVERAGE PERIOD OF PRODUCTION

Most modern versions of the theory of production assume either that production is "timeless" or that the investment period is determined by technical conditions. All the inputs are applied at a single moment of time, and output emerges at some later single moment. Capital theory begins by taking this simple case and treating the investment period as an independent variable in the production function. We will adopt Ragnar Frisch's terminology and call this (1) the point input–point output case. The analyses of wines laid up for storage and trees planted for timber production, which figure so prominently in neoclassical capital theory, are examples of the point input–point output case. Then we have the situation in which the inputs are applied continuously in variable patterns over time: (2) the flow input–point output case. So far, capital is merely circulating capital or goods-in-process. Then we have investment in durable capital goods, where the input of a single date yields output at various future dates: (3) the point input–flow output case. Last, we reach full generality with the really typical case of (4) flow input–flow output.

One would imagine that capital theory was largely interested in (3) and (4) involving investment in fixed capital. However, all Böhm-Bawerk's work and most of Wicksell's was concerned with the optimum investment period of continuously applied circulating capital, that is, with (2) the flow input–point output case. Cases (3) and (4) involve insuperable difficulties resulting from the fact that there is now no way of linking particular units of input embodied in fixed equipment with particular units of ripened finished output: all the inputs embodied in durable equipment are jointly responsible for the whole stream of output. In terms of isoquants, when durable capital is used, we cannot tell how many units of capital are being combined with labor in a given short run to produce the constant product of that period.

Böhm-Bawerk's Model. Böhm-Bawerk's chapter "The Interest Rate in Market Exchange," deals with the two inputs, homogeneous output case; all output is made up of consumption goods; inputs are applied continuously at a uniform rate and consist of labor-years and consumer goods to feed and clothe workers. The amount of labor and the amount of working capital are fixed. Workers are indifferent between occupations, and uniform wage rates prevail throughout the economy; the firms all have identical production functions. Our first problem is to define a metric for capital, in this case working capital. It will not do to express capital in money values because that presumes knowledge of the rate at which to discount the future services of capital: the purpose of the model, however, is to determine the unknown rate of discount. Nor can we express capital even in this simple case simply as a physical stock of consumer goods because that could ignore the two-dimensional quality that characterizes capital as a factor of production. A given physical amount of capital need not have a homogeneous age structure; indeed, it never has except in the point input–point output case. The heterogeneous structure of the real capital stock makes it necessary to measure capital by the average "period of production" utilized in the economy: the average time that elapses between the instant a factor input is applied to production and the instant its fruits become available for consumption.

The process of investing working capital to support labor during the cycle of production may be likened to a flow of water into a reservoir. The average length of time that each drop of water remains in the reservoir obviously depends on the rate of flow of water per hour and the size of the reservoir. The bathtub theorem, as Dorfman has called it, says that in a reservoir of given volume the average number of hours of detention of water equals the stock of gallons of water in the reservoir divided by the rate of outflow = the rate of inflow in gallons per hour. Thus, when the tank holds 10 gallons and the rate of flow is 2 gallons per hour, the average period of detention of a drop of water is 5 hours. Similarly, inputs remain frozen in an enterprise for an average period of time that depends on the rate of flow of inputs and output and the total amount of capital available. If the flow of inputs equals the flow of output, the average period of production of the enterprise for a given size of plant is equal to the dollar value of the capital funds invested in the plant divided by the dollar flow of inputs per year. The quotient or average period of production is neither a pure number nor a period of clock time. Thus, this period is lengthened either when more capital is invested for the same clock time or when the same capital is "frozen" in production for a longer clock time.

The average period of production of a one-sector economy may be written as

$$p = (K/I),$$

where K stands for the amount of real capital and I for the flow of inputs or the rate of investment. In a stationary economy, however, net

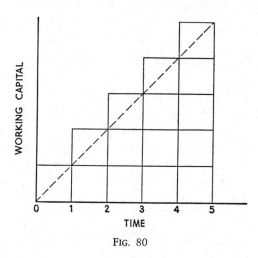

FIG. 80

investment is zero and the application of inputs corresponds to capital consumption: workers continuously consume the stock of food and clothing, which is at the same time being continually replenished. Ignoring the consumption of capitalists as negligibly small, capital consumption is going on at the rate $Nw = I$ where N stands for the given number of workers in the economy and w for the wage rate. Thus,

$$p = (K/Nw).$$

The next step is to show that the average period p for which labor is tied up, when applied continuously throughout the fabrication period of the economy, is $\frac{1}{2}t$, where $t =$ the absolute length of the period of production. This proposition goes back to Jevons and is easy to verify. Suppose one unit of labor costing \$1 is applied every day for a 5-day fabrication period. (See Fig. 80.) The total amount of working capital required to complete one cycle of production is then \$$(1 + 2 + 3 + 4 + 5) = \$15$ or $\frac{1}{2}tC + \frac{1}{2}C$, where C represents the labor costs of a unit of output and the total cost of producing 5 units of output $= \$25$. We have applied labor discretely, however. In the continuous case the working capital required $= \frac{1}{2}tC = 12\frac{1}{2}$.

Jevons presented the general case of continuous investment and consumption of capital as shown in Figure 81. To emphasize the time dimension of capital, he distinguished between AQ, "the amount of capital invested," and the area OQB, "the amount of investment of capital." The latter is the "amount of capital invested" multiplied by the average time for which it is invested. If capital is invested and disinvested continuously and uniformly through time, "the amount of investment of capital" is equal to the greatest "amount of capital invested"

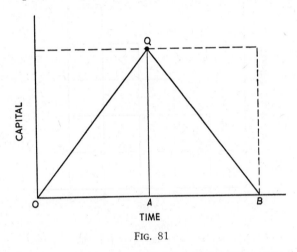

FIG. 81

multiplied by one-half the time elapsing from the beginning to the maturity date of the investment: $AQ \cdot \frac{1}{2}OB$.

To come back to Böhm-Bawerk's model, we can now write the basic equation of the model as set forth by Wicksell: $p = \frac{1}{2}t = K/Nw$ or $K/N = wt/2$. As a physical stock, capital is the accumulated result of $\frac{1}{2}Nt$ man-years of labor. The total value of labor tied up in the capital stock is precisely half the value invested in the total output of a period of production.

Now for the technical relations. Output per worker per year is $Q = f(t)$; the production function obeys diminishing returns: $f'(t) > 0$ and $f''(t) < 0$. Facing given wage rates, capitalists will maximize the annual rate of profit per worker with respect to t, the parameter under their control.

$$r = \frac{f(t) - w}{\frac{1}{2}wt}$$

and

$$\frac{dr}{dt} = 2\frac{wt[f'(t)] - w[f(t) - w]}{w^2t^2} = 0$$

$$= 2\frac{tf'(t) - f(t) + w}{wt^2} = 0$$

$$f(t) - tf'(t) = w .$$

The wage rate so determined is equal to the marginal product of labor:

$$Y = NQ = Nf(t) = Nf\left(\frac{2K}{Nw}\right),$$

$$w = \frac{\partial Y}{\partial N} = f\left(\frac{2K}{Nw}\right) + Nf'\left(\frac{2K}{Nw}\right)\left(-\frac{2K}{N^2w}\right)$$

$$= f(t) - tf'(t) ,$$

where $f'(t)$ is the marginal product of extending the period of production; $tf'(t)$ is the total imputed interest per man-year of labor estimated at simple interest: the wage rate is equal to total output per man-year minus $tf'(t)$. The rate of interest (profit) per worker:

$$r = \frac{f(t) - w}{K/N} = \frac{tf'(t)}{\frac{1}{2}wt} = 2\frac{f'(t)}{w} .$$

We could have found this directly by taking the marginal product of capital. Differentiating $Y = Nf(t)$, we obtain

$$\frac{\partial Y}{\partial K} = Nf'(t)\frac{\partial t}{\partial K} = Nf'(t)\frac{d}{dK}\frac{2K}{Nw} = 2\frac{f'(t)}{w} .$$

Each entrepreneur maximizes his annual income by investing capital in a process whose length is t, and as a result a positive rate of interest emerges reflecting the advantages of more time-consuming methods of production. The gist of Böhm-Bawerk's elaborate arithmetical argument can now be illustrated in one diagram (Fig. 82). The curve $K/N = wt/2$, a rectangular hyperbola, shows an inverse relationship between w and t when K provides full employment. If w rises, the flow of consumables provided by K will be drawn down at a greater rate and the period for which the stock of capital suffices will fall. With a given K and N, w varies inversely with t. The schedule of the marginal product of labor MP_L is traced by starting, say, at t_2 and finding the corresponding value of the production function $f(t)$, then moving along the tangent to find w_1 and marking the corresponding point on the MP_L curve for t_1, and so forth. But what determines w_1? At w_1, producers adopt t_1, but the given amount of K will provide full employment only if $t = t_2$. Since $t_2 < t$, at w_1, there is an excess supply of labor and wages fall. The same consideration will show that a wage rate that would cause producers to adopt t_2 would lead to an excess demand for labor, driving wages up. t is a length of the production period, corresponding to a wage $= w$ at which labor is fully employed. Since $r = 2\dfrac{f'(t)}{w}$, the slope of the production function $f'(t) = \dfrac{rw}{2} = OW/OR$. It is easy to see by graphic inspection that the higher the wage rate, the longer the period of production, the greater $2/r$, that is, the lower the rate of interest.[3]

Therefore, with a given size of the labor force and a given capital stock, Böhm-Bawerk's model determines the equilibrium wage rate,

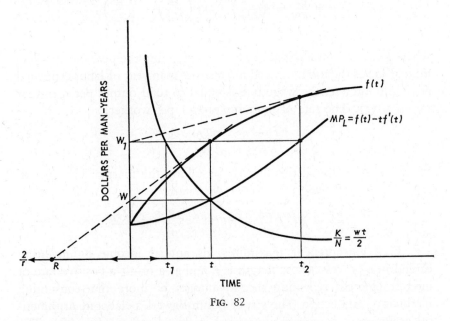

FIG. 82

the equilibrium interest rate, and the optimum period of production for the economy as a whole.

The Definition of the Average Period. By treating the whole economy as a single consumption-good sector, Böhm-Bawerk managed to reduce capital to a stock of unripened consumables on the way to

---

[3] In Böhm-Bawerk's arithmetical example $K = \$15$ m. and $N = 10{,}000$. There are 1,500 enterprises in the economy. In equilibrium, each enterprise invests its capital of $10,000 into a production period $t = 6$ years. The annual wage rate $= \$500$ or $tf'(t) = \$150$, and amount of capital per worker, or $wt/2 = \$1{,}500$. The rate of interest $= 2f'(t)/w = 10$ per cent. Each worker *now* receives the present value of his entire future marginal product, that is, $\$500(1 + 0.10)^6 =$ approximately $900: in 6 years the value of output per man $= \$3{,}900$, but the value of wages paid out $= \$3{,}000$. We say "approximately" because the wages bill is actually accumulated at compound interest: the correct formula is $w = f(t) e^{-(0.10)6}$ or $(500/e^{-0.6}) = \$900$.

completion. The model fails, however, to come to grips with many of the fundamental problems of capital theory. For example, the rate of interest cannot fall to zero for, by definition, $f'(t) > 0$ no matter how large the capital stock. As soon as we take up a two-sector economy, however, the fact that machines are used to make machines as well as consumer goods makes it possible to depress the rate of interest to zero even if $f'(t) > 0$. Although every increment of capital yields a positive increment of output, it is a diminishing increment; the cost of maintaining capital, however, remains constant. A time must come when the gross product of capital is just equal to depreciation charges. At that point, the net productivity of capital has fallen to zero and, in the absence of positive time preference, the rate of interest will be equal to zero.

The period of production, which is a simple enough concept when capital consists solely of working capital, becomes much more difficult to handle when the economy consists of two or more sectors that use each other's output as well as their own output as inputs, particularly when one or more of the sectors produce durable machines that become inputs at one instant of time but then yield their output slowly over a stretch of time. Indeed, it has been argued repeatedly, for instance, by Clark in the 1890's and by Knight in recent times, that the average period of production of fixed plus working capital cannot be calculated except under special conditions and that when it is calculated it turns out to be of infinite length. To this problem we now turn.

It must be said at the outset that the term "period of production" has been used in a bewildering variety of senses. First, there is the distinction between the absolute and the average period of production, which we have already encountered. Either of these, however, may be interpreted as applying to a single product, a single factor, or to the economy as a whole. As applied to the final product, we are "looking back" from the end result to the beginning of a process. As applied to the factors, we are "looking forward" from the application of inputs to the completion of a process.

The absolute period of production can be defined as the time interval lapsing between the first application of primary factors and the emergence of the final consumer good for which these factors were responsible. For the economy as a whole, the looking-backward version of the absolute period refers to the interval of time between the present and the application of the first "original factor" that contributed to *any* output at this moment passing into consumption. In the looking-forward version it refers to the time interval between the present and the emergence of the last product attributable to *any* factor now employed. Obviously, in either case, the absolute period is infinite in length. But the absolute period has almost always been applied, not to all output or all factor inputs, but to a particular finished product or a particular primary factor. This is true of Böhm-Bawerk, who adopted the "looking backward from the product" version, and of Wicksell and Hayek, who worked with the "looking forward from the factor" version. And the absolute period of production of particular products or particular factors is not infinite if we accept the doctrine of "original" factors.

The average, as distinct from the absolute, period can similarly be applied to a particular product or to the whole economy. It is usually expressed in the looking-forward sense and asks the question: How much time on the average will elapse between the investment of primary factors at this moment and the emergence of the output that will be imputed to their activity at this moment? In the looking-forward sense, the average period cannot refer to a particular factor applied at a moment of time or it would not be an average period. Hence, it should be understood as referring only to the economy as a whole, which is exactly how Austrian writers have always employed it.

Böhm-Bawerk's Definition. Böhm-Bawerk's practical suggestions for measuring the average period of production involve astonishing terminological and conceptual confusions. Early in the *Positive Theory* he introduces the concept of an average "time interval" (*wegdauer*) between the successive applications of primary factors and the completion of consumption goods. When these primary factors are applied from the "highest stage" up to the consumer, he calls this time interval the average period of production. But what he really means is the absolute period, for he immediately introduces yet another term, "average waiting time" (*durchschnittliche Wartezeit*), which he notes is always equal to one-half of what he has just called the average period. In other words, what *we* have called the absolute period, *he* calls the average period when the primary inputs are continuously applied through time; and what *we* have called the average period, *he* calls the "average waiting time."

Although the rigorous closing section of the *Positive Theory* deals only with working capital, earlier sections of the book suggest how to measure the average period when durable machines are used or when the primary factors are not invested at a uniform rate. In the flow input–point output case, in which all capital consists of consumer goods-in-process, the average period of production is simply the sum of the investment periods of all the labor inputs weighted by the number of inputs. Böhm-Bawerk typically assumes that the individual investment periods are "staggered," that is, applied discontinuously at the beginning of each year. Thus, if $x =$ inputs of labor-days per year and $t =$ years invested, then the average period of production

$$p = \frac{\Sigma(xt)}{\Sigma x} = \tfrac{1}{2}t + \tfrac{1}{2} .$$

If labor is applied at a nonuniform rate in the successive years, the inputs will have to be dated and weighted accordingly. Nevertheless, the average period of production remains a weighted arithmetic mean of labor-days per years, weighted by the duration of labor services up to the moment of final sale, divided by the total number of labor-days applied. If the labor inputs are of different types, so that their rates of reward are different, the investment periods must be weighted, not by the number of inputs, but by their total values. Böhm-Bawerk always assumes labor to be a homogeneous input, so this problem does not arise.

Now for the flow input–flow output case. In calculating the time elapsing between the investment of primary factors in the production of a machine of given durability and the moment when the machine-made product reaches the consumer, we have to add the following time periods: (1) the construction period of the machine; (2) half the lifetime of the machine, on the assumption that it continuously releases the value of the primary factors that have produced it; (3) the time from the instant the machine is used to the instant at which its output reaches the final consumer. We then add these time intervals and divide by the number of primary factors applied. On the other hand, the average period of investment in the consumer goods sector using machines is influenced only by (2) and (3). Böhm-Bawerk gives the following oversimplified example to bring out the nature of the calculation. Suppose the production of a consumer good requires 100 labor-days at the rate of one labor-day per year applied on the first day of nine successive years and applied in the tenth year to finish the good; the time of finishing is zero. Then the weighted average period of production

$$p = \frac{(1_x \cdot 1_t) + (1_x \cdot 2_t) + \ldots + (1_x \cdot 10_t) + (90_x \cdot 0_t)}{10_x + 90_x}$$

$$= \frac{55 \text{ labor-days per year}}{100 \text{ labor-days}} = 0.55 \text{ years} .$$

Another good also requires 100 labor-days over a ten-year period, but now the rate of applying labor is different.

$$p = \frac{(1_x \cdot 5_t) + \ldots + (8_x \cdot 5_t) + (20_x \cdot 9_t) + (20_x \cdot 10_t)}{100_x}$$

$$= \frac{560 \text{ labor-days per year}}{100 \text{ labor-davs}} = 5.6 \text{ years} .$$

Since the elements making up this average differ greatly in magnitude, the average is affected by the kind of mean selected. Why calculate the average period as an arithmetic mean? Why not a geometric or a harmonic mean? The weighted geometric mean or log mean—as its log is simply the arithmetic mean of the log of the constituent items—in the first of the two examples is

$$\sqrt[100]{10 + 9 + \ldots (\tfrac{1}{365})^{90}} = 1.3 \text{ years} .$$

We have to assume a one-day fabriation period to avoid a geometric mean of zero. If we assume the same thing for Böhm-Bawerk's example, the arithmetic mean $= 1.45$. In general, there is no reason to prefer the arithmetic to the geometric mean, and yet the two will always give different results. This is a point that Fisher brought up repeatedly against Böhm-Bawerk and that the latter never even tried to meet. The fact is, however, that it does not matter which mean we use provided we keep using the same one. The average period of production is intended to provide an ordinal index of capital intensity for purposes of comparing different equilibrium situations characterized by differences in the amount and structure of capital. This purpose is served just as well by one mean as by another so long as we do not switch means in the middle of the comparison.

But there is a more serious failing in Böhm-Bawerk's calculations. As Wicksell pointed out, Böhm-Bawerk always implies that the accumulated inputs earn simple interest, and very different results are obtained if the inputs earn compound interest. The fact that the inputs earn interest does not appear explicitly in Böhm-Bawerk's examples, but that is because the interest factor always cancels out when the inputs earn only simple interest. For instance, if one man-year is invested for two years and a second man-year is invested for one year, the average period of production by Böhm-Bawerk's formula is:

$$p = \frac{(2_t \cdot 1_x) + (1_t \cdot 1_x)}{2_x} = \frac{3_{tx}}{2_x} = 1\tfrac{1}{2} \text{ years} \cdot$$

This should really be written as:

$$\frac{1_x(1 + 2r) + 1_x(1 + r)}{2_x} = \frac{2_x(1 + pr)}{2_x} .$$

Solving for p, we get the same results as above: $p = 1\frac{1}{2}$ years. With compound interest, however, the formula becomes:

$$\frac{1_x(1 + r)^2 + 1_x(1 + r)}{2_x} = \frac{2_x(1 + r)^p}{2_x}.$$

Solving for p, we have

$$p = \frac{\log (2 + 3r + r^2) - \log 2_x}{\log (1 + r)}.$$

At $r = 0.10$, $p = 1.51$ instead of 1.5. The difference is small because the number of years involved are few. But if the absolute period were longer, the difference would become more pronounced. In Wicksell's formula the earlier inputs are more heavily weighted by the compound interest factor and, hence, the average period of production is longer. What this means is that the calculation of the average period of production is not invariant with respect to the interest rate. A lower rate of interest immediately shortens the average period of production even if production processes have not changed because it lowers the weights attached to earlier inputs.

Is the Average Period Infinitely Long? We asserted earlier that the absolute period of production of particular primary inputs and hence the average of all such absolute periods will not be infinite in length. This has been denied, however, on the grounds that it is impossible to trace back all capital to labor and land expended in the past: there was no time in the past, however distant, when the primary factors alone were combined to produce a machine. But, even if for the moment we accept the original-factors doctrine, it is still true that it may nevertheless be impossible to discover any moment of time when the primary factors alone were employed to produce "intermediate means of production." The reason lies in the whirlpool structure of production. Böhm-Bawerk always assumes that the "stages of production" form a linear hierarchy in which the output of "higher" stages are always used exclusively as inputs by "lower" stages nearer to final consumption. But this ignores the circularity that characterizes much of production: some of the output of the coal industry may be used to generate electricity in a factory that makes coal-cutting machinery, or, more pointedly, coal itself may be utilized in the coal industry to generate electricity to drive ventilating machinery. Production may take the form of linear sequences like raw cotton → yarn → grey cloth → dyed cloth, but it also embodies circular relations like iron ore → steel → mining equipment → iron ore. In input-output studies this kind of interdependence has been found to characterize a significant portion of interindustry relations in advanced economies. Hence, the absolute period of production, even when defined with reference to particular products or particular factors, may be infinite in a good many cases.

But, while the absolute period may be infinite, the average of such absolute periods can be finite. It is well known that an infinite series of successively diminishing values can converge to a finite limit under certain circumstances. This is essentially what is true of the average period of production. An economy's capital stock is, in Samuelson's words, "a perpetual stew, to which something is always being added and from which something is always being taken out. . . . Some part of what is now being added will never come out of the stew, just as some part of what is in the stew is of infinite age. But it is a simple exercise in infinite processes to show that the average age of the stew is finite, and the average expectancy of a particle staying in the stew is also finite." Whirlpool structures, while presenting difficulties for the calculation of an average period of production, do not make it impossible to define an average period of finite value. "The schoolboy's penknife may contain iron from a mine opened up in the time of Caesar," to quote Stigler's homely example, but the iron applied in the first century is so small as to have a negligible influence on the period of production of the current iron-using process. It is true that past investments are weighted by time, but this is offset by the small amount of inputs invested in earlier periods: the bulk of labor and of labor expended on producing machines has been expended in the recent past.

All this supposes, however, that there is some sense in which "original" factors can be defined. One of the arguments that the opponents of Böhm-Bawerk's concept have employed against it is that labor is really a produced factor via expenditures on labor-training and education and that even the so-called free gifts of nature need to be maintained and kept up if they are to be forthcoming. Since the average period of production is defined in terms of "original factors," any denial of that concept involves a denial of the average period of production. Now, it is perfectly true that the original-factors doctrine has been the source of much confusion and sterile metaphysical arguments. We only have to think of Marx's theory of surplus value or the endless discussion of rent as a price-determined income. Nevertheless, there is real meaning to the assertion that some resources are *economically* non-augmentable, even if this assertion is only a matter of degree and point of view. The rate at which entrepreneurs will invest working capital is clearly an economic problem. And machines do have their supply prices. But the supply of "land," meaning all permanent income-yielding goods, whether natural or man-made, is virtually fixed, and the production of labor, certainly in the long run, is not merely a matter of rational cost accounting. In this sense, and only in this sense, labor may be considered an "original factor." But this is quite enough, or almost quite enough, to give definite meaning to the average period of production.

To define the average period of production in the flow input–flow output case, we have to borrow a leaf from Cassel and admit the presence of a primary factor other than labor or land related specifically to investment in fixed capital. It was Böhm-Bawerk's failure to do this that prevented him from extending the argument to durable capital goods. Let us suppose that the economy consists of two sectors, one of which produces homogeneous consumer goods called food and another which produces homogeneous machines of a given technical durability at a steady rate. It is assumed that the machines are productive, in the sense that a given amount of resources devoted to maintaining and replacing machines will always result in a greater flow of output, though only after a lapse of time, than will the application of the same amount of resources to the immediate production of foodstuffs. There are two primary factors, labor and "waiting." Waiting represents the social cost of forgoing the option of devoting resources to the production of food in order to use them to maintain and build up the stock of machines. It is a genuine factor service, performed at a specific place and time and measured in terms of the goods in which it is embodied: one unit of food deferred for one unit of time. The owner of a machine can sell the machine at any time for its current, depreciated value and consume the proceeds in the form of food. By not doing so, he is performing the scarce service of "waiting," as measured by the current value of the machines estimated in terms of foodstuffs times the length of the waiting time. Thus, the total rate of waiting in the economy equals the total value of machines in the economy measured in terms of foodstuffs, and the "stock of waiting" equals the amount of waiting performed in the past that is congealed in the existing stock of machines.

The period of production of the economy as a whole is the appropriately weighted average of the periods of investment of all the "original factors" used in the economy. We have designated labor and waiting as the only primary factors. All we need do to get the over-all period of production is to define the period of investment of labor and of waiting and to find appropriate weights to add these together. The period of investment of labor P_L depends on the flow of labor services performed per year and the stock of unrealized labor services embodied in the stock of new and old machines in the economy. P_L, measured in man-years, is equal to the stock of embodied labor divided by the value of labor services performed in a year. The period of investment of waiting P_W is likewise a function of the flow of waiting performed per year plus the stock of waiting congealed in the existing stock of machines. But the dimensions of waiting are foodstuffs forgone per year and the quantity of waiting so defined depends on the units in which foodstuffs are measured. A period of investment, however, has the dimensions of time and must not be influenced by the choice of units of measurement other than the unit of time. It looks as if we cannot measure the quantity of waiting performed in a year in natural units. We can measure it in value or price-times-quantity units, however, for prices will cancel out in the averaging process.

Having decided to use value weights, we now derive the average period of production for the economy as a whole. The labor term of the over-all average period is equal to P_L times the flow of labor L in the economy. Since $P_L =$ the stock of embodied labor services divided by L, $P_L \cdot L$ is the value of unrealized labor services congealed in the current stock of machines. In the same way, the waiting term of the over-all period is equal to $P_W \cdot W =$ the unrealized waiting services in the stock of machines. And, since there are no other "original factors," the labor term and the waiting term add up to the total value of the stock of machines in the economy. These must now be weighted, however, by the units in which labor and waiting are measured. When value weights are used, the sum of the weights will be the value of labor performed in the economy in a year plus the value of the waiting performed. Since labor and waiting are the only primary factors in the economy, the sum of these weights will add up to national income. Thus, the weighted average period of production for the economy as a whole is the value of the stock of machines divided by the national income; in short, the capital-output ratio! But this is exactly what we might have expected from the "bathtub theorem": the average period of detention of a drop of water is equal to the content of the reservoir divided by the rate of flow of water; the average period of production in an economy employing capital is equal to the stock of capital divided by the rate of flow of the primary inputs.

We will recall that our two-sector economy produces machines of a given technical life. How, then, is the average period of production lengthened? Not by producing more durable machines but by producing more machines of the same durability. In the one-sector model that Böhm-Bawerk analyzed in detail, the period of investment is lengthened by lengthening the time period for which each consumer good remains in the pipelines. In the two-sector model, increased round-aboutness is brought about by investing more capital in machines of the same or even of lesser durability. Thus, the durability of machines in an economy is no indication of the length of the average period of production. This is corroborated by the well-known fact that an increase in the durability of machines need not raise the capital-output ratio, measured as it usually is in net terms. Choosing equipment with a longer life always raises the gross capital-output ratio because long-lived equipment is dearer relative to annual gross output than is short-lived equipment. But, since annual depreciation quotas are normally less the more durable the machine, net output may well increase. At the same time, net capital may be smaller if the reduction in depreciation quotas is not outweighed by the rise in interest charges. In consequence, the ratio of net capital to net output may decline despite an increase in the durability of machines.

Suppose we now take one further step toward the real world and permit the period of production to be lengthened by the introduction of longer-lived machines, whose higher initial cost is offset by their lower annual maintenance and depreciation charges. This brings up a new problem, which Wicksell discussed in his review of Ackerman's book: what is the optimal durability of a machine? Insofar as the average period of production is concerned, it is still possible in principle to calculate a finite period of production, but a single period of production can now reflect different capital structures corresponding to different capital-labor ratios. If, in addition, the economy produces many different kinds of final goods, the period of production will be influenced by the preference patterns of consumers for final goods. The significance of the period of production is, in this realistic case, limited to measuring the capital intensity of the economy relative to the pattern of consumer demand.

The Average Period and the Capital-Output Ratio. It has not been fashionable in recent years to talk about periods of production. "Nearly every one who comes to the study of capital falls a victim to Böhm-Bawerk's theory at some stage or other," wrote Hicks in *Value and Capital*. "The theory stands up very well to the most obvious objections which can be made against it; yet, as one goes on, difficulties mount up. The definition of the 'time taken in production' gets harder and harder; and so most people find themselves driven, in the end, to abandon the theory, even if they have nothing much to put in its place." The capital-output ratio, however, is a standard item in every modern economist's toolchest. But the fact of the matter is that the capital-output ratio comes down to the same thing as the average period of production: they both attempt to measure the average amount of "waiting" that is incurred in investing more capital to increase the flow of output. The Austrian proposition that in a static equilibrium a fall in the rate of interest lengthens the average period of production and that an increase in capital, for a given quantity of labor and a given production function, lengthens the average period has its counterpart in modern economic theory. With two inputs and a linear homogeneous production function, the rate of interest is equal to the derivative of the production function with respect to capital and every fall in the rate of interest increases the capital-output ratio; this is simply a corollary of diminishing marginal productivity of capital. (See Fig. 83.) If $Q =$

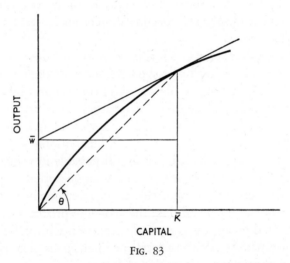

FIG. 83

$f(K,L)$, then, by definition, $\partial Q/\partial K > 0$ and $\partial^2 Q/\partial K^2 < 0$. Given the wage rate $\bar{w}(= \bar{W}/L)$, profit maximization will cause K amount of capital to be invested. Cot $\theta = K/Q$, and this will increase for every increase in the quantity of capital consequent upon a rise in wage rates and a fall in the interest rate.

Where Böhm-Bawerk went wrong was in thinking that the average period of production would lengthen even with technical change. In the first edition of the *Positive Theory* the distinction between capital accumulation along given production functions and shifts in the functions owing to technical change associated with additional capital was not clearly drawn. Subsequently, Böhm-Bawerk admitted that some innovations do reduce roundaboutness. But the capital so released, he insisted, tended to be applied to lengthening the period of production elsewhere. Only if the innovation is both capitalsaving and product-replacing will the average period of production be shortened. This he dismissed as an exceptional occurrence, citing the secular increase in physical capital per head as presumptive evidence of the greater frequency of time-increasing innovations: "industrial experience will verify two propositions . . . first, that with the larger capitalistic equipment, the product per unit of labor increases; and second, that this increase in product does not go on *pari passu* with the addition of capitalistic equipment." But "industrial experience" has not verified the belief that the capital-output ratio tends to rise through time. Although capital per man has been rising, technical change has increased output per man sufficiently to prevent the capital-output ratio from rising. On the basis of the available evidence it appears that developed economies have not experienced any appreciable increase in the average degree of roundaboutness over the last fifty to seventy years.

Nevertheless, the fact remains that, as Kaldor has said, "the 'law of roundaboutness' is merely a derivation from the general law of non-proportional returns." "Merely" is perhaps an inappropriate qualification, for "the purpose of the 'investment period' approach," adds Kaldor, "is to reduce the production function to two variables, substituting 'waiting' for the services of all produced factors with interest as the price of 'waiting.' In this way—and only in this way—can *capital as capital* be treated as a factor of production commensurate with 'labor.' "

Synchronization of Production and Consumption.   It appears that the concept of a period of production does not break down when applied to economies in which capital goods are used to make capital goods. This disposes of J. B. Clark's favorite argument against Böhm-Bawerk's theory. But this was not Clark's major objection. If we confine ourselves to stationary conditions, he argued, the length of time for which a stock of capital is embodied in production turns out to be economically irrelevant. In stationary equilibrium, with net investment equal to zero, the number of production periods that are coming to a close at any instant of time are just equal to the number of production periods just beginning. Hence, stratification of the economy into production periods of different lengths can be only an arbitrary procedure, having no economic significance. A stationary state involves automatic synchronization of inputs and outputs; capital is necessarily maintained intact, and the only demand for capital is for replacement purposes;

there is no waiting whatever for output because every application of inputs that bears their fruit some time hence is matched by the simultaneous emergence of output from past outlays of productive effort.

To reinforce his point, Clark distinguished between specific capital goods and "capital" in general. Pure "capital" he described as a permanent homogeneous fund of *value,* invested in an ever-changing series of concrete capital goods, but distinct from them in the same way in which a reservoir is distinct from the drops of water of which it is at any given moment composed; since the capitalized yield of equipment is a net yield, pure "capital" is also a fund of automatically replaceable values.

It is difficult to see just what all this means. Clark does not pretend to show that synchronization is a condition of equilibrium in the static state; on the contrary, synchronization is laid down as an axiom, and, since this is tantamount to postulating that capital is maintained intact, we are then told that capital maintains itself automatically. But there is nothing automatic about capital replacement even in stationary conditions. It is true that to maintain capital, once an equilibrium level has been reached, requires no further net investment but only reinvestment of funds regularly recovered from sales. But it is also true that when a community succeeds in maintaining a stock of machines, the members of the community have fewer goods available for consumption in the present than they would have if they failed to replace worn-out machines. By definition, in a stationary state no one can refrain from present consumption in order to augment future consumption, but they can increase present income by depleting future income. Their refusal to do so expresses the social cost of "waiting." The general principle remains the same in either a stationary or a dynamic economy: there is a time lag between the initiation of capital formation and the increased supply of consumer goods that capital formation makes possible. Even with zero net investment and perfect synchronization of production and consumption, the time structure of the capital stock is not a matter of indifference. Everything else being the same, the members of a stationary economy are always better off the longer the average period of production. Clark's definition of "capital-in-general" simply eliminates the problem of time by definition. Obviously capital as a fund of abstract purchasing power cannot possibly have a time structure.

The gist of the conflict between synchronization economics and advance economics, to use Schumpeter's terms, can be seen quite easily by resorting to that copybook example of capital theory: the planting of trees for timber production. Suppose we have a forest with fifty rows of trees from one to fifty years old, of which the oldest row will be cut every year, while a new row is simultaneously planted. In other words, production and timber consumption are perfectly synchronized. The fact that the average period of production of the forest is twenty-five years is irrelevant, according to Clark. Once the process is synchronized it does not matter whether the oldest row is fifty or ten thousand years old. But, Cassel or Hayek would argue, there is a definite limit, even in this case, to the possibility of investing available inputs in the production of timber, subsumed under the rubric of "waiting." First, we have to abstain from increasing the present supply of timber by cutting down trees less than fifty years of age. Second, more waiting would allow the trees to grow older and so lead to an increase in the future supply of timber. The last case is excluded by the assumption of stationary equilibrium and zero net productivity of "capital," but the first remains valid and expresses the social cost of waiting in a stationary state.

Clark's argument clearly implies that the rate of interest in a stationary state will be zero. Waiting-theorists have always argued that the rate of interest cannot be zero in a stationary economy. A zero interest rate would mean that there would be no reason to refrain from consuming capital. If capital has a zero net yield, why devote resources to maintain it? A positive rate of interest is needed to keep the stationary state stationary. As Cassel used to say, interest is "the price paid for waiting," and in a stationary state it is a bait to keep people from consuming their capital rather than a reward for deferring present enjoyment.

It is clear that this argument is valid only if people have positive time preference.[4] It is not necessary to prevent anyone from depleting capital if everyone regards a dollar tomorrow on the same terms as a dollar today. If everyone acts so as to maximize the sum of utilities over all future time, the law of diminishing marginal utility of income at a zero rate of interest gives us as an even distribution of income over

---

[4] Cassel produced an argument having nothing to do with time preference to show why the rate of interest must be positive in a stationary state. Sargant had argued that the supply curve of "rainy day" saving is negatively sloped. Cassel pointed out that, since rainy-day savers can save only a certain amount out of present income but contemplate a definite annual income from their capital, a fall in the rate of interest does not increase the supply of saving but increases the length of time in which savings will have to be made. Take the example of someone who saves $1,000 a year and looks forward to future annual income of $1,000. At 6 per cent it takes 12 years to accumulate the required capital fund of $16,000; at 3 per cent it takes 24 years; at 1 per cent it takes 70 years. At near zero rates, Cassel concluded, the shortness of the earning period of the average individual will alone cause people to deplete their capital and thus maintain a positive premium on present income.

time. This is really obvious: "reasons" 1 and 3 for a positive rate of interest are absent by definition under stationary conditions; if now "reason" 2 is assumed away, the rate of interest will be zero. We conclude that the average period of production in an economy *is* irrelevant if time preference is neutral and capital yields no output net of maintenance and replacement. So long as time preference is positive, however, zero net productivity of capital or synchronization of production and consumption will not reduce the rate of interest to zero. Hence, it will not deprive the time structure of production of economic significance.

The controversy reached its culmination in the first chapter of Schumpeter's *Theory of Economic Development*. Schumpeter's purpose was to construct a model of an economy in which technical change is missing and then to demonstrate that under these circumstances the rate of interest would necessarily be zero. Without technical change, he argues, the economy must settle down to a "circular flow," a stationary and synchronized economic process in which there is no uncertainty about the future. This implies that the net yield of capital has fallen to zero, and, assuming that there is no intrinsic rate of time preference, this implies that the rate of interest will be zero. Thus, interest would not exist in competitive long-run equilibrium visualized in static theory. Only innovations and dynamic change can produce a positive interest rate. There is nothing surprising about this conclusion. The whole argument proceeds by spelling out definitions but fails to establish Schumpeter's thesis that an economy without innovations must settle down to a "circular flow." A capitalist economy minus innovations does not yield a stationary state, for there is still the possibility of increasing the total product through the routine investment of land and labor in the construction of capital goods.

3. FISHER'S THEORY OF INTEREST

Fisher's book *The Rate of Interest* (1907) opened with the remark that "if the theory to be presented in this book is correct, interest is an index of the community's preference for a dollar of present over a dollar of future income"; the book consisted essentially of "Böhm-Bawerk improved by ageing minus the period of production." It addressed itself specifically, however, to the problem of investment planning and provided an elegant framework in which to study the interaction of the three "reasons" for a positive rate of interest. The book was extensively revised in 1930. The later version is now recognized to be what Schumpeter called "the peak achievement, so far as perfection within its own frame is concerned, of the literature of interest." Not least of its qualities is its superb pedagogical structure. "It teaches us, as does no other work I know, how to satisfy the requirements of both the specialist and the general reader without banishing mathematics to footnotes or appendices, and how to lead on the layman from firmly laid foundations to the most important results by judicious summaries and telling illustrations."

Willingness and Opportunity. Fisher sees no difference between explaining why there is interest and explaining how interest is determined. He is content to show that individuals in receipt of income try to alter the successive amounts of income available for consumption uses at various times through saving or borrowing. The resultant price that is paid for income now rather than for income later is the rate of interest. The determination of this rate depends on the interaction of "willingness" and "opportunity," which together exhaust the relevant subjective and objective forces. First, "the impatience principle," which might just as well have been called "the patience principle": with respect to prospective income, its time period, and its uncertainty, circumstances are easily envisioned that might cause "patience" to dominate "impatience." Individuals redistribute their consumption over time in an optimum way, but nothing is said about the forces that cause them to regard one particular kind of redistribution as most desirable. Next, there is the "investment opportunity principle"; the rate of investment opportunity is called the rate of return over cost. The rate of return over cost is defined with reference to at least two investment options: by "cost" is meant the loss of withdrawing one income stream; by "return" is meant the gain that results from substituting a new income stream; it is that hypothetical discount rate at which the present value of two investment options are equalized. Whenever this hypothetical rate exceeds the market rate of interest, an alternative option is chosen.

Rate of Return over Cost. This last point needs amplification, since Keynes has identified his own "marginal efficiency of capital" with Fisher's "rate of return over cost." Keynes's marginal efficiency of capital or "internal rate of return" refers to a single investment option. It is that rate of discount which maximizes the net present worth of an investment by equating the present value of the series of prospective receipts to the present value of the total replacement cost of the investment. In short, it is that discount rate which maximizes the present value of net revenue. The present value of net revenue available t years hence, discounted at the market rate of interest, is

$$V = \frac{\pi}{(1 + r)^t}.$$

Continuous compounding gives

$$V = \pi e^{-rt}.$$

The present value of a *stream* of net receipts over t years discounted at an internal rate of return is

$$
\begin{aligned}
V &= \int_0^t (\pi) e^{-ix} dx = \pi \int_0^t e^{-ix} dx \\
&= \pi \left[-\frac{e^{-ix}}{i} \right]_{x=t} - \pi \left[-\frac{e^{-ix}}{i} \right]_{x=0} \\
&= \left(-\frac{\pi}{i} e^{-it} \right) + \frac{\pi}{i} \\
&= \frac{\pi}{i} (1 - e^{-it}).
\end{aligned}
$$

V is maximized by setting this expression equal to zero. Thus, the marginal efficiency of capital is that discount factor which sets net present worth equal to zero. If the internal rate of return i exceeds the market rate of interest, this means that further capital outlays on this investment project will increase net present worth.

Fisher's rate of return over cost is that critical discount factor at which *two* or more investment options have the same net present worth.

$$\int_0^t (\pi_1 - \pi_2) e^{-ix} dx = 0.$$

The ranking of investment options, Fisher then showed, depends on the rate of interest. A particular option may have a higher present discounted value at one rate of interest and not at another.

Diagrammatic Exposition. By placing income today on the horizontal axis and income tomorrow on the vertical axis, we can express all possible conditions of "willingness" and "opportunity" in terms of the appropriate shapes of indifference maps and a transformation curve depicting the production possibilities of converting present income into future income. We assume, of course, that we can speak of income as if it were a composite commodity always made up of exactly the same proportion of goods. Tomorrow's income means next year's, for, if there were more than one possible period of investment, we could not depict the result on a two-dimensional graph.

The "willingness lines" are convex to the origin owing to the law of diminishing marginal utility of income. Their steepness expresses the community's time preference. Positive time preference means that the willingness line has an absolute slope greater than unity *at the constant income-stream line.* Since the rate of interest is zero along this line, this definition corresponds to our earlier usage. Neutral time preference is shown by willingness lines that are symmetrical around the 45° vector. Thus, in Figure 84, willingness line 1 reflects negative time preference, willingness line 2 reflects positive time preference and willingness line 3 depicts neutral time preference.

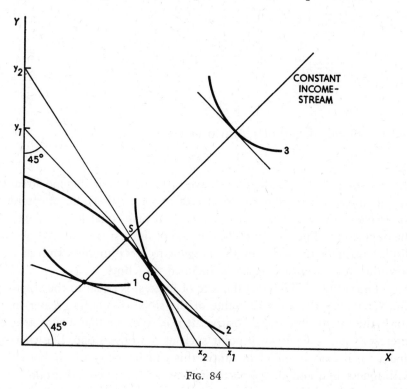

FIG. 84

The "opportunity line" or technical-transformation curve reveals the net productivity of capital. It is concave to the origin owing to diminishing returns from sacrificing present income to obtain future income. If a given amount of today's income can be transformed into a larger amount of tomorrow's income, the opportunity line will not be symmetrical around the 45° vector coming out of the origin. The greater the net productivity of capital, the steeper the opportunity line.

The rate of interest is determined by the point of tangency between a willingness line and the opportunity line. We now have a simple rule, which tells us that the rate of interest will be positive if the tangency point has an absolute slope greater than unity. This follows from the definition of the rate of return over cost. If $x =$ income this year and $y = f(x) =$ income next year, then the present value of x now and y next year:

$$V = x + \frac{y}{(1 + i)} = x + \frac{f(x)}{(1 + i)} .$$

The present value will be maximized if

$$\frac{dV}{dx} = 0 \text{ and } \frac{d^2V}{dx^2} < 0$$

$$\frac{dV}{dx} = \frac{(1 + i) + f'(x)}{(1 + i)} = 0 .$$

Thus,

$$(1 + i) = -f'(x) ,$$

and the marginal rate of return over cost

$$i = -[f'(x) + 1] .$$

If we assume that all individuals have optimized their income streams by equating the rate of return over cost to the market rate of interest, we arrive at the result that $-(1 + r)$ is always equal to the slope of the opportunity line $f'(x)$. Thus, the rate of interest is measured by the displacement of the slope of the tangent to a willingness and an opportunity line from a negatively inclined $45°$ line.

Thus at Q in Figure 84 the rate of interest is equal to the slope of line x_2y_2; since the absolute value of the slope of x_2y_2 is greater than unity, the rate of interest is positive. It is easy to see that a zero rate of interest requires a tangency point such as S whose slope, like that of line x_1y_1, is exactly equal to unity; this can happen only if both the willingness line and the opportunity line are symmetrical around the $45°$ vector, meaning that time preference is neutral and the net yield of capital is zero.

Some Uses of the Diagram. Any theory about the real rate of interest can be expressed in terms of Fisher's basic diagram. For instance, Knight has denied repeatedly that it is possible to generalize about time preference and has, therefore, espoused a pure productivity theory of interest. He agrees that in equilibrium the rate of interest will be equal to the annual yield of an investment divided by the cost of investment: that is, $(1 + r) = -f'(x)$. But the size of the capital stock at any time is so great, he contends, that new investment decisions have little effect on the rate of interest. The yield of capital goods at any moment is almost entirely determined by existing technology and the fixed supply of resources in the economy. In terms of our diagram (Fig. 84) this contention amounts to asserting that the opportunity line is linear. Obviously, time preference will in this case affect the amount invested but not the rate of interest. This is simply another illustration of the Marshallian rule that demand has no influence on price if production is carried out at constant cost. The basic question here is an empirical one: Is it true that the size of the capital stock is such that no feasible additions from annual investment could appreciably influence the rate of interest? In recent years, gross private investment in the United States has run at 4–5 per cent of the stock of reproducible wealth, including land. This hardly accords with the idea that new investment has a negligible effect on the rate of interest.

Schumpeter does not imply that the production-possibility curve in a stationary economy will be a straight line throughout its length. By definition of stationariness, however, there is no demand for production loans. He makes consumer loans depend on time preference, and he admits, of course, that these are capable of causing interest to exist even in a static world. If the willingness lines tended toward verticality, the demand for consumer loans could be brought into equality with the supply only at a positive rate of interest. This means that positive interest will also be earned in production even though the economy is stationary. Without imputed interest, depreciation accruals will be lent to consumers: positive interest is now the condition for maintaining capital intact. Schumpeter cannot even determine the level of "productive interest," as he calls it, without reference to time preference. To postulate neutral time preference as he does is really to beg the question he wants to put. It does not require innovations to produce positive time preference. A low level of income per head in a society experiencing no growth will by itself produce myopia.

The Theory of Investment Decisions. Facing a given interest rate, each person in the economy optimizes the size and time shape of his income stream by borrowing or lending, by investing or disinvesting. The sum total of these adjustments determines the rate of interest, subject to the market-clearing condition that desired lending = desired borrowing or planned saving = planned investment. This can be illustrated with the simple case of two individuals having expected claims to present and future income in amounts indicated by Q_1 and Q_2. This is only Fisher's second, not his third and final, "approximation," since future income is expected with perfect certainty.

In Figure 85 the concave opportunity lines OP denote the ability to convert present income into future income by investing in capital goods; actually, the OP curve is an envelope of the most profitable investments for the individual, dividing the feasible from the infeasible

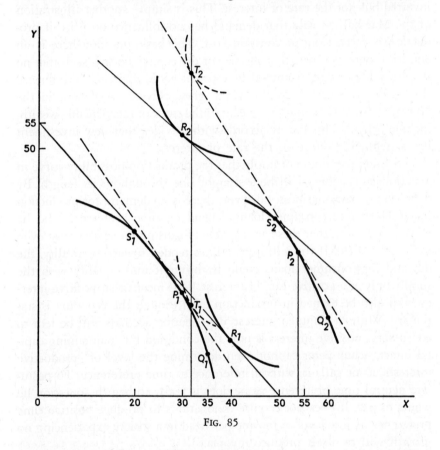

FIG. 85

distribution of income over time. Each person faces a given interest rate, shown by the slope of the parallel "market lines," and reaches an optimal position by altering the shape of their income stream until the concave OP curve is tangent to the convex W curve. Both individuals will begin by investing until they attain positions S_1 and S_2. Then they will borrow or lend until they reach their highest attainable W curve, ending up at R_1 and R_2, respectively. This chronology of action is, of course, merely an expository device.

Individual A invests $15 of income (the horizontal distance Q_1S_1), borrows $20 (the horizontal distance S_1R_1), and thus ends up with a larger present as well as future income by dissaving $5 (the horizontal distance Q_1R_1). Similarly, individual B invests $10 ($Q_2S_2$), lends $20 ($S_2R_2$), and saves $30 ($Q_2R_2$). Each individual maximizes utility subject to given tastes and income restraints, and aggregate lending equals aggregate borrowing.

We have assumed an interest rate of 10 per cent: r is equal to the negative slope of the market-line minus 1, or $[(55 - 50)/50] = 0.10$. If the rate of interest were higher, as shown by the dashed lines, then A would want to invest only $5 ($Q_1P_1$), to borrow only $3 ($P_1T_1$) but to save $2 ($Q_1T_1$). At the same time, B would want to invest only $6 ($Q_2P_2$), but to lend $21 ($P_2T_2$) and to save $27 ($Q_2T_2$). Since B wants to lend more than A wants to borrow, the rate of interest must fall back to 10 per cent.[5] In equilibrium the rate of interest must equal the marginal rate of transformation in production as well as the marginal rate of time preference in consumption. In addition, the rate of interest must equate desired lending to desired borrowing. But this is equivalent in this case to equating planned saving to planned investment. At $r = 0.10$, A's desired borrowing of $20 is equal to his desired investment of $15 plus his desired dissaving of $5; and B's desired lending is equal to his desired saving of $30 minus his desired investment of $10. Therefore:

Desired Lending		Desired Borrowing
$S_2 - I_2 = 30 - 10$	$=$	$I_1 - S_1 = 15 - (-5)$
$S_2 + S_1 = 30 + (-5)$	$=$	$I_1 + I_2 = 15 + 10$
$S = 25$	$=$	$I = 25$

The Real and the Money Rate of Interest. With a constant price level, the money rate of interest on riskless loans will equal the real rate of interest. Up to now we have tacitly assumed that the real rate of interest will not diverge from the money rate. We now introduce one of Fisher's famous propositions: the money rate of interest is equal to the real rate of interest plus the rate of change in the price level. Thus, when prices are falling at 5 per cent per annum a zero money rate of interest corresponds to a real rate of 5 per cent. This proposition

[5] Notice that individual A's supply curve of saving is positively inclined but individual B's supply curve is backward bending. The condition for a backward-bending saving-supply curve is, of course, that the income effect of a higher interest rate is negative and outweighs the substitution effect. This in turn implies that the successively higher W lines converge to the right: the rate of time preference increases with income because future income is an "inferior good." This is hardly a plausible general assumption, but it can occur for some ranges of income. The common belief in the interest inelasticity of saving must be due to a negative income effect just canceling out the substitution effect.

is not original to Fisher. We met it earlier in Marshall's *Principles,* and it goes back to Thornton's *Nature of the Paper Credit.* Nevertheless, Fisher was the first to see all its implications and to weave it into a systematic theory of the real rate.

To clarify the logic of the argument, let us suppose that a physical unit of capital sells at a price of p dollars and earns a rental of q dollars per period. To avoid an index-number problem, we will assume that there exists only one physical good, which can be either consumed or used as capital in the production of more of itself. Under competition, the stock of capital will be used as an input until its marginal value product equals its rental flow per period.

$$p \frac{\partial Q}{\partial K} = q \cdot$$

The rental per year is simply the annual expected return—of which there may be a whole series over future years—minus the annual running expenses and depreciation charges: it is the net current product of the capital good. Dividing through by the price of replacement of a unit of capital, we obtain

$$\frac{\partial Q}{\partial K} = \frac{q}{p} \cdot$$

The marginal physical product of capital is equal to the money rental of a dollar's worth of capital, or the real rental per period. The marginal physical product of capital can be called the commodity's own-rate of interest. With a constant price level and perfect arbitrage this own-rate will equal the money rate. If prices are falling, however, the real rate will have to exceed the money rate to induce people to hold the commodity. When prices are falling at 5 per cent per annum, a money rate of interest of 5 per cent gives people no incentive to hold the commodity unless the own-rate of interest is higher than 5 per cent. Conversely, if prices are rising, a given money rate will imply a lower real rate. Thus, the money rate of interest

$$r = \frac{q}{p} + \frac{1}{p} \frac{dp}{dt} \cdot$$

This proposition permits us to say something more about the economics of the stationary state. We saw that the real rate of interest in a stationary state would be zero if time preferences are neutral. But even a stationary economy contains goods, like wheat and timber, that enjoy percentage increases per unit of time in terms of themselves. At a zero rate of interest for money there would be an infinite demand for money to buy and store goods that have an own-rate of growth. To prevent this from happening, prices would have to fall at a percentage rate equal to the physical productivity of goods like wheat and timber.

A zero or negative money rate of interest is always difficult to maintain without some way of depreciating money. If money is not depreciating, the demand for money-to-hold will always drive up the rate, since the cost of storing money is neglible. In the absence of inflation, a zero or negative money rate can be achieved by a tax per period of time on currency and deposit holdings. This, by the way, is the origin of Gesell's stamped-money scheme to encourage investment. In the absence of price changes, the money rate cannot be zero or negative if the real rate is positive: who would not be an entrepreneur if his creditors were willing to pay him for it? The excess demand for money loans would soon raise the money rate to a level above zero. The real rate, in distinction from the money rate, can be zero, but it cannot be negative. While goods can be carried forward in time, they cannot be carried backward. When the real rate is positive, people are induced to convert present goods into future goods, and this can always be done, at least if the goods are not perishable. But at a negative real rate, the incentive is to convert future goods into present goods. This can be carried out only insofar as it is possible to draw down on stocks of goods. Hence, a negative real rate results in a high demand for present goods of a non-durable variety, which will tend to drive the real rate back to zero.

The Real Rate in a Dynamic Economy. We have shown that in static equilibrium the real rate of interest will equal the marginal productivity or demand price for capital and the marginal rate of time preference or supply price of capital. But this implies that both net saving and net investment are zero. It follows that in a dynamic economy the real rate of interest is necessarily greater than the social cost of providing capital and less than the social advantage of using it. The individual's marginal supply price of "waiting" is that discount rate which just causes him neither to add to nor to draw upon his accumulated savings. The marginal supply price of "waiting" to the community as a whole is that discount rate which just neutralizes the average rate of time preference in the community, causing net saving to be zero. Therefore, when the community adds to its savings, the market rate of interest must exceed the social rate of time preference. Similarly, positive net investment implies that the market rate of interest is less than the marginal productivity of capital, for otherwise the stock of capital would not be added to.

What governs the rate of investment in an economy is not the marginal productivity of capital but the "marginal efficiency of invest-ment." An individual equates the marginal value product of a capital good to the rate of interest on the money he would have to borrow to buy it. But when the economy as a whole increases its capital by invest-ment, the concept of a marginal product of capital loses its meaning: the other inputs are not held constant when the amount of capital em-ployed is increasing. The marginal product of capital is a static concept, applicable if net investment is zero. When net investment is positive, the marginal product of capital exceeds the rate of interest and invest-ment per unit of time will be such as to equate the marginal efficiency

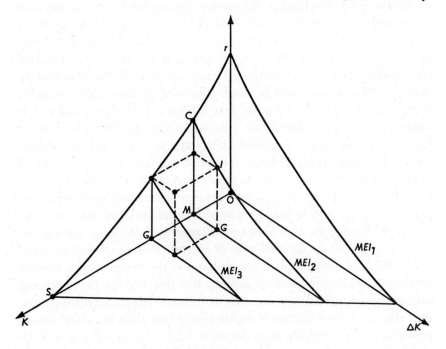

FIG. 86

of investment to the interest rate. The analogy is that of the marginal productivity theory of wages, which provides for the optimum *use* of labor. A firm is in equilibrium when $MVP_L = w$; its rate of hiring is then zero. Suppose w changes. We then have the question: how quickly will the firm alter its labor force? This is a question about the theory of the rate of hiring that is analogous to the theory of investment.

The distinction between the marginal productivity of capital and the marginal efficiency of investment is nicely brought out in one of Lerner's diagrams (Fig. 86). When the size of the capital stock $= OM$, the marginal product of capital $= CM$. If net investment $= MG$, the marginal efficiency of capital $= GI = r$. Since $CM > GI$, the rate of interest is less than the marginal product of capital. In the next period, the capital stock is larger by the amount of net investment MG and a new MEI curve will show how much investment takes place in this period, and so forth. A movement along the investment axis, therefore, always implies a movement along the capital axis. In the absence of technical change lifting all the curves, the tendency will be to approach stationary equilibrium at S where the marginal product of capital is equal to MEI and net investment has ceased.

Real versus Monetary Theories. The theories of interest that we have studied in this chapter focus their attention upon the "real" forces of productivity and thrift. The action of monetary authorities in recent decades and the presence of unemployment have seriously diluted the impact of the real forces contemplated in the neoclassical theory of interest. As a result, economists have ceased to be concerned with real theories of interest. The textbook theory of interest today is either a liquidity preference theory, in which the money rate of interest depends on the total demand for stocks of bonds acting on an exogenously determined supply, or a loanable funds theory, in which the rate of interest depends on the demand and supply of a flow of securities.

It is sometimes suggested that there is a conflict between real and monetary theories of interest. According to real theories, interest is the pure yield of capital and a reward for abstaining from present consumption. According to monetary theories, interest is the price of money and a reward for parting with liquidity. These are supposed to be inherently conflicting explanations. Keynes himself seems to have fostered this interpretation when he stated dogmatically that interest is not a reward for waiting but a reward for not hoarding money. But general equilibrium considerations must show that interest operates simultaneously, as D. H. Robertson has put it, on "the threefold margin" of consumption decisions, investment decisions, and bond versus money holding decisions. In other words, interest simultaneously rewards waiting and the forgoing of liquidity as well as expressing the pure yield of capital. The only proviso we need to add to this conclusion is that, while waiting is a private as well as a social cost, parting with liquidity is only a private cost. Society cannot choose between lending for investment and the safety of cash. From the social point of view, capital can be held in real terms only in the form of goods, and this is never safe or liquid. No choice is involved because uninvested savings are irretrievably lost to society.

Given the enormous influence of the monetary authorities on the rate of interest nowadays, how much significance should we attach to real theories of interest? Patinkin offers a way of answering this question. A real theory determines the interest rate in the commodity market, while a monetary theory determines it either in the bond market or in the money market. We can say that interest is a real phenomenon if it behaves like a relative price and a monetary phenomenon if it behaves like an absolute price. As we saw in our earlier discussion of classical theory, changes in the quantity of money and in liquidity preferences which leave relative prices invariant also leave the rate of interest invariant. On the other hand, technical change that affects the yield of capital and changes in time preference that affect saving decisions alter relative prices and also alter the rate of interest. The forces that have altered absolute prices over time have little effect on the long-run rate of interest. In that sense, we can conclude that the long rate is essentially a matter of real forces.

4. THE RICARDO EFFECT

The rise of Keynesian economics in the 1930's was marked by fierce controversy over the saving-investment identity, the nature of the consumption function, the alleged superiority of liquidity preference theory over the loanable funds approach, the efficacy of monetary and fiscal policy to induce recovery, and many other hornets' nests that Keynes had uncovered with the publication of the *General Theory*. In the background the old debate on capital theory, which had been reopened by Knight in 1933, raged on without showing any signs of being resolved. But even here the influence of Keynes made itself felt. In *Profits, Interest, Investment* (1939), Friedrich Hayek linked the Austrian theory of capital to the phenomena of the business cycle in an effort to show that, contrary to Keynes, a rising level of consumption must after a certain point reduce rather than increase the rate of investment. It is only fitting that we bring our discussion of capital and interest to a close by examining this favorite offspring of Böhm-Bawerk's last and greatest pupil.

The Concertina Effect. Hayek takes it for granted that commodity prices typically rise faster than money wages in the upswing of the business cycle: real wages fall in the boom. If entrepreneurs expect this higher price-wage ratio to persist, labor will be substituted for machinery. In Hayek's terminology, the fall in real wages leads to changes in the relative profitability of different methods of production

in favor of shorter or less roundabout methods. At some point investment demand for "capital widening" in response to expanding consumer demand for current output—the Keynesian acceleration principle—is more than offset by this type of "capital shallowing," and total
investment demand in the economy falls off. Conversely, in a depression
the rising level of real wages brings about a revival of investment as
"capital deepening" begins to offset the decline in induced investment.
The reasoning involved is familiar to any student of Böhm-Bawerk: the
length of the period of production varies directly with real wages and
inversely with the rate of interest. But, whereas Böhm-Bawerk had applied this doctrine to long-run equilibrium conditions, Hayek adapted it
to the circumstances of the business cycle. The length of the period of
production falls in the upswing and increases in the downswing according to what has been aptly called "the concertina effect."

The Demonstration of the Effect. The Ricardo Effect takes its
name from Ricardo's argument that a general rise in money wages leads
to a substitution of machinery for labor. Ricardo assumed that labor
costs in the machine goods industry were below the general average in
the economy as a whole, so that the rise in money wages did not produce
a proportionate rise in the price of machines; hence, the money rate of
interest declined. We who are no longer so confident that the machine
goods industry is especially capital intensive need firmer grounds for
Ricardo's proposition.

If an increase in the level of wages raises machine prices in the
same proportion as the price of labor, neither the real rate nor the
money rate of interest will fall at all. Suppose labor costs are 50 per
cent of total costs, on the average, then a 10 per cent increase in money
wages first of all raises the absolute price of finished goods by 5 per
cent. If the machine goods industry has the same capital structure as output in general, machine prices also rise by 5 per cent. This then raises
the price of output by 2.5 per cent, but as machines are made by machines we have not yet taken into account the effect of the 5 per cent rise
in machine prices on the price of machines. Following this through, we
see that all prices will eventually rise by 10 per cent, leaving the rate of
interest constant. But if the rate of interest remains constant, the rise in
wages will raise production costs of different methods and processes
proportionately to the share of wages in total costs. Hence, it does not
make it more profitable to invest in more capital-intensive methods.

The Ricardo Effect is really a misnomer, because Hayek tries to
show that even when Ricardo's assumption is not met, namely that the
relative prices of labor and machinery change, it will still be true that

a rise in wages will induce substitution of capital for labor and vice versa. In his initial essay on the problem, published in 1939, Hayek presented an example in which direct and indirect labor is applied at various dates to the production of a commodity. The rate of interest is 6 per cent and is equal to the rate of profit per annum on capital. Now, while money wages remain constant, the price of the product rises by 2 per cent so that real wages fall 2 per cent (see accompanying table).

	LABOR INVESTED FOR				
	2 Yrs.	1 Yr.	6 Mos.	3 Mos.	1 Mo.
Initial amount of profit per turnover at 6% p.a............12	6	3	1.5	0.5
Add 2% profit due to rise in product price.................14	8	5	3.5	2.5
Final rate of profit p.a., neglecting compound interest....... 7	8	10	14	30

The initial amount of profit earned on each turnover of any amount of labor is simply the difference between the money wage rate and the undiscounted marginal value product of labor. A rise in the product price raises the amount of profit on each turnover proportionately irrespective of the length of the period of turnover. But the time rate of profit rises more for labor invested for short than for long periods. This leads to a substitution of short-period for long-period investments—a shift toward finishing goods at the expense of constructing machines—until the time rate of profit is once again equal for each investment period. *Ergo,* a rise in the ratio of output to input prices, a decline in real wages, leads to substitution of direct for indirect labor and shortens the average period of production.

It has been argued that firms do not normally confront a range of turnover periods of capital as great as Hayek supposes. Hence, the Ricardo Effect would not account for much investment reallocation. But this criticism ignores the fact that the argument applies not only between firms but also within firms, and within firms the turnover period does range from a few months for working capital to several years for equipment and building. Hayek's subsequent restatement of the Ricardo Effect explains the mechanism more convincingly in terms of money capital. A rise in the ratio of output to input prices increases the time rate of profit on working capital more than on fixed capital. This induces the firm to invest its liquid capital funds in processes with a high rate of turnover. When the fall in real wages is general, the result is that the average period of turnover of gross investment expenditures in the economy as a whole declines; in other words, the average period of production is shortened.

Notice that the Ricardo Effect does not depend on a falling rate of interest. On the contrary, the rate of interest, as well as the relative price of labor and machines, is assumed to be constant. But what of our earlier contention that a change in real wages does not induce factor substitution when the rate of interest is constant? This conclusion still holds, and more than one critic has argued that it disposes of Hayek's argument. Let us restate the criticism: the equimarginal rule states that the optimal combination of labor and capital is one where the *MRS*, or ratio between the marginal physical products of any two factors, is equal to the ratio of their marginal factor costs for the same period of time. In this case the ratio of marginal factor costs is the ratio between the wage rate and the annual interest plus depreciation charges on machines. Since neither the relative prices of labor and machinery nor the rate of interest have altered in the case Hayek analyzes, the ratio of marginal factor costs remains the same as before. It is true that the rise in the product price increases the scale of output, but, if the production function is linear and homogeneous, so that the *MRS* of labor and machines is independent of scale, this does not induce factor substitution.

To put teeth in the Ricardo Effect, we must assume either a nonlinear production function, in which the *MRS* between the factors alters in favor of direct labor as the scale of output expands,[6] or else an upward-sloping supply curve of credit to the firm. Hayek readily conceded

6

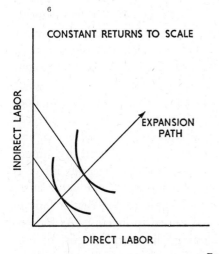

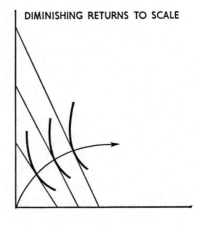

CONSTANT RETURNS TO SCALE

DIMINISHING RETURNS TO SCALE

INDIRECT LABOR

EXPANSION
PATH

DIRECT LABOR

FIG. 87

this point, arguing that the traditional assumption of competitive theory of a perfectly elastic credit-supply curve to each firm—constant marginal = average cost of borrowing—leads to absurd results. If a firm is free to borrow funds without some absolute ceiling, or expectation of a ceiling, to the amount it can borrow at a finite rate of interest, it will borrow enough to push the marginal yield down to zero, knowing it can always borrow to repay principal and interest, and so on *ad infinitum*. This is tantamount, however, to command of funds in perpetuity and, since the funds are commanded with perfect certainty, this is equivalent to ownership of them. The indefinite capacity to borrow at any finite rate of interest thus turns out paradoxically to be equivalent to a zero rate of interest. Some kind of "capital rationing," therefore, or else an explicit time lag between the inputs of this period and the output of the next, is an indispensable logical element in the theory of the firm. The presence of either of these two elements, however, validates the Ricardo Effect.

The Meaning of Capital Rationing. We have delivered a tentative verdict in favor of the Ricardo Effect in consequence of the existence of capital rationing. But "capital rationing" is a vague phrase: it does not mean that capital is available to the firm only in a definitely fixed quantity, but rather that the marginal cost of borrowing capital funds rises with every increase in indebtedness. But even this is ambiguous. Does it mean that the marginal interest cost to the firm is an increasing function of the total capital invested or that it is an increasing function of the rate of investment per unit of time, irrespective of the total amount already invested? That is, $r_m = f(K)$ or $r_m = f(\Delta K)$? In the first case, capital is a limiting factor to the firm's scale of operation but not to its rate of investment. In the second case, it would not necessarily limit the firm's scale except in the short run. If the second meaning is accepted, the Ricardo Effect falls to the ground because a fall in real wages will not reduce capital intensity if the rate of investment is not rising at the time. But presumably investment does increase in the upswing. We recall, however, that the Ricardo Effect is supposed to demonstrate that "capital shallowing" will offset "capital widening" at some stage in the boom, after which date total investment demand will decline. We have just shown that the Ricardo Effect is operative only if $\Delta K > 0$. Hence, "capital shallowing" can *never* offset investment demand for widening for the simple reason that it fails to operate when the rate of investment has ceased to increase. As soon as the Ricardo Effect offsets capital widening, the marginal cost of borrowing ceases to rise for firms that are investing and the effect upon capital intensity of the rise in product prices relative to money wages dies away.

To rescue the Ricardo Effect, we have to interpret the upward-sloping supply curve of credit to firms under capital rationing as a relationship between the marginal rate of interest and the total capital stock of the firm. Is there any evidence for such an interpretation? Yes, if the firm operates with some of its own funds. According to Kalecki's much-discussed "principle of increasing risk," the subjective risk to the firm of increased indebtedness rises with every increase in the amount of borrowed capital relative to equity capital. Since loans take precedence over the claim of owners to the gross income of the firm, the riskiness of additional credit is an increasing function of dollars borrowed. Moreover, lenders rely primarily on the value of the firm as a going concern for their security, and hence a large loan is less attractive to lenders than a small loan. Therefore, given the firm's own capital, the marginal cost of borrowing to the firm will rise with the total amount of capital invested in the firm. This vindicates the Ricardo Effect.

But is it realistic to assume a given amount of the firm's own capital during the business cycle? What of the familiar fact that as much as 50–75 per cent of corporate investment relies on internal sources in the form of retained profits and unused depreciation accruals. The firm's own capital is added to during the upswing by the ploughing-back of undistributed profits and hence the supply curve of credit as a function of the firm's capital stock is constantly shifted to the right. Thus, a fall in real wages need not reduce capital intensity because shifts in the marginal credit cost curve may be more than adequate to offset the limitation of capital.

The marginal cost of borrowing to the individual firm is therefore no simple unique function of its capital stock or, for that matter, its rate of investment. It seems to be a function of current planned investment over additions to the firm's own capital through retained profits and the new issue of shares in the preceding period. At any rate, shifts in this function will usually render the Ricardo Effect inoperative in the boom phase of the business cycle unless we introduce additional factors like monetary restrictions.

Conclusions. In hunting down the assumptions and postulates of the Ricardo Effect, we have arrived at the perhaps anticipated conclusion that it is only another instance of the vice of neoclassical economics: the hasty application of static theorems to the real world. A list of Hayek's basic assumptions will show that by relaxing any one of them we obtain a more useful explanation of the downturn than is afforded by the Ricardo Effect: (1) capital equipment is utilized to capacity—but labor need not be fully employed; (2) capital equipment is perfectly divisible; (3) there is no technical change, and constant returns to scale prevail in all industries; (4) money wage rates and machine prices are constant; (5) the market rate of interest is constant, but firms face less than perfectly elastic supply curves for borrowed funds; (6) elasticities of expectations are equal to unity, that is, everyone expects future prices to rise at the same rate as current prices. It is obvious that, if price expectations are inelastic, a rise in output prices means a relative rise in present prices as compared to expected future output prices; obviously, this leads to a relative fall in the demand for durable inputs tending to augment future output. But Hayek does not rest his case on inelastic price expectations.

Would it be possible to test "the concertina effect" statistically? A rough-and-ready index of the average period of turnover of investment expenditures in the economy is the ratio of total investment in business inventories to the net total investment in both inventories and durable equipment. If Hayek is right, this ratio should rise in the boom and fall in the slump. It has been shown that this ratio is indeed positively correlated with the level of money income, but, unfortunately, it is not positively correlated with the level of real wages.

Money and Real Wages. At the very outset of the discussion some readers may have wondered whether it is really true that real wages fall in the upswing and rise in the downswing. In the *General Theory,* Keynes threw out the idea that money wages and real wages usually move in opposite directions. This sounds very much like Hayek's basic assumption, and yet Keynes was forced in the end to accept the finding that money and real wages usually rise together, although they do not always fall together. But there is a confusion of terminology here. In neoclassical theory "real wages" do not denote the purchasing power of money wages over the cost-of-living basket of goods but, rather, money wages expressed in terms of the current output that labor produces. In Hayek's argument it is evident that "real wages" refer to the product wage rate. And, in fact, while real wages in terms of what workers buy with their money wages do not usually fall in a boom, the product wage rate—money wages deflated by an index of wholesale prices—does typically decline in the upswing.

There is nothing amiss with the a priori argument, which Keynes seems to have had in mind, that money wages vary inversely with product wages. Wage rates are determined by real demand and real supply functions. A fall in employment under perfect competition raises real wages by raising the marginal physical product of labor, by definition of diminishing marginal productivity of labor. Prices are always determined by the condition that marginal costs equal marginal revenue. Marginal costs have now fallen; hence, prices fall and so do money wages. Or, to put it the right way up, as incomes fall in a slump, money wages fall and accommodate themselves to the marginal physical product of labor, whatever it is. The level of real wages is entirely independent of the level of money wages because prices are always equated to marginal costs without any time lag. In a boom, money wages, marginal costs, and sales prices rise, while real wages decline corresponding to the lower marginal physical product of labor at higher levels of employment. Thus, on neoclassical grounds it is perfectly true that real wages properly defined fall in the upswing and rise in the downswing of the business cycle.

READER'S GUIDE TO THE *LECTURES ON POLITICAL ECONOMY*, VOL. I[7]

If Wicksteed's *Common Sense* supplies a classic exposition of the subjective theory of value, the first volume of Wicksell's *Lectures* (1901) provides a masterly statement of the neoclassical theory of production and distribution. It is not any easy book to read. Indeed, only Walras's *Elements* is more difficult. But "no student of economics has completed his training," said Schumpeter, "who has not read the whole of this volume." Wicksell reconstructed Böhm-Bawerk's capital theory and transformed his explanation of interest into an explicit marginal productivity theory in which interest as the marginal productivity of waiting becomes co-ordinate with wages and rent as the marginal productivity of labor and land. By discarding Böhm-Bawerk's one-commodity economy in favor of a multiple-commodity treatment, Wicksell went far toward bridging the gap that existed between the Austrian and Walrasian schools. The average period of production, as Böhm-Bawerk expounded it, comes near to being nonsense: whatever validity the concept may have rests on Wicksell's restatement of it. Wicksell has been justly called "the economist's economist": few writers have commented with so much penetration on the ideas of their predecessors and contemporaries as he did.

Utility and Value. The introduction constitutes a defense of abstract economics. Note in particular the incisive critical comments on the German

[7] We shall occasionally refer to Wicksell's *Value, Capital, and Rent* (1954), which was published in 1893, eight years before the first volume of the *Lectures*. On some questions the two books provide an interesting contrast in treatment.

Historical School (pp. xxii–xxiii, 11), the emphasis on the importance of population theory (p. 6), and the declaration that modern economics, grounded as it is in individual utility maximization, involves "a thoroughly revolutionary programme" (p. 4).

Chapter 1 takes up the question of value theory by resolving Smith's water-diamond paradox (pp. 18, 29–30). A money cost-of-production theory is shown to involve circular reasoning (pp. 21–22). Ricardo's theory of value is briefly but sympathetically examined (pp. 22–23; see also *Value, Capital, and Rent,* pp. 35–41). In Ricardo, cost of production depends on marginal cost, but the location of the margin depends on demand and, hence, in turn, on the whole configuration of prices. Ricardo managed to ignore this because he treated demand as given by the size of population (pp. 24–26). The case of joint supply creates independent difficulties for the classical theory of value (p. 26).

Chapter 2 introduces marginal utility as a synthesis of utility and scarcity. Wicksell stresses the variability of the marginal utility of money. An exchange equilibrium involves only intrapersonal, not interpersonal, comparisons of utility (pp. 31–33, 43).

The question of measurability of utility is considered in chapter 3. Wicksell concludes that utility is a cardinal magnitude because "we can generally say" that differences between the successive intervals on a utility scale can be compared (pp. 37–39; see also Appendix, pp. 221–22). The simple case of choice between the direct and the indirect use of a given stock of agricultural products, with a constant rate of technical transformation, is treated graphically (pp. 39–41). Possible interdependence of utility functions is emphasized at the outset (pp. 41, 42 and 45). Strong substitutability in consumption may produce the illusion of a positively sloped demand curve (pp. 44–45). The supply curve of labor may be backward sloping (pp. 45–46). The worker's marginal utility of wage income will, in equilibrium, equal his marginal disutility of effort. An increase in wages lowers the marginal utility of income and hence results in more work. But, on the other hand, his real income has risen, which tends to shift the income-utility curve upward, thus favoring less work and more leisure. This is nothing but the later distinction between a substitution and an income effect, which in this case operates in opposite directions. An increase of pay for overtime, Wicksell observes correctly, will usually increase the supply of effort: since this affects the marginal rather than the average rate of remuneration, the substitution effect is likely to outweigh the income effect (p. 46). Next, the proportionality rule for an exchange equilibrium is set out mathematically, both for additive and for generalized utility functions (pp. 47–49).

Jevons' treatment of "isolated exchange" does not yield a determinate solution because we have a single equation but two unknowns to be determined (pp. 49–51). The case of barter exchange is then treated graphically: demand and supply curves for B are drawn (reverse supply and demand curves for A), with the price of B in terms of A chosen as the abscissa (pp. 55–58). The reason the supply curve of B turns down eventually in Wicksell's diagram is that the rising price of B necessarily lowers MU_A faster than MU_B; this is a consequence of the assumption that every offer of B implies a demand for A

(p. 57; for a slightly different treatment of the same diagram see *Capital, Value and Rent,* pp. 83–92). This leads up to the problem of multiple equilibria and the possibility of an unstable equilibrium (pp. 59–60). The "admittedly artificial example" on pages 60–62 may be passed over.

Exchange of three or more commodities requires the use of a medium of exchange to facilitate arbitrage (pp. 63–65). There follows a simple but elegant statement of the Walrasian method of establishing the existence of a general equilibrium solution (pp. 65–71; for a similar but more detailed exposition see *Value, Capital, and Rent,* pp. 79–82). Money is assumed to be an abstract unit of account; hence, the Walrasian solution leaves absolute prices indeterminate (p. 67). "This is obvious," Wicksell remarks, "so long as we regard the functions of money as purely formal." In reality, he adds, the demand for money-to-hold is never a matter of indifference (p. 68). This says everything that Patinkin tried to say with respect to the indeterminacy of absolute prices in some versions of the Walrasian system (see Appen., pp. 223–25, where Cassel is criticized on this score).

Chapter 4 deals briefly with the objections to marginal utility theory based on the importance of discontinuities and habitual consumer behavior (pp. 68–72).

Welfare Economics. Does perfect competition maximize "the gains from free exchange"? Walras, like Jevons, fell into the error of generalizing from the two-persons two-goods case (p. 74). The first objection to this generalization is that competition does not preclude multiple equilibria. If each of these is a welfare optimum, the original proposition is shorn of its usual meaning (p. 75). Moreover, state intervention can clearly increase the welfare of some individuals; since interpersonal comparisons of utility are by nature imprecise, it is not obvious that the general loss from, say, a protective duty exceeds the particular gains to some parties (pp. 76–77). If we assume equal individual capacities for want satisfaction, the principle of diminishing marginal income utility leads directly to the conclusion that greater equality of income distribution increases welfare (p. 77). This assumes that total income is independent of its distribution. Wicksell is not unaware of this assumption (see pp. 78–79, 82). The equimarginal rule in exchange implies a welfare optimum if and only if the utility functions are the same for all parties and if the final equilibrium is independent of the initial quantity of goods possessed (pp. 79–81). The same argument is set out with illustrative arithmetical examples in *Value, Capital, and Rent* (pp. 64–76). This brilliant refutation of Jevonian harmony doctrine concludes with an irritable comment on Pareto's definition of a welfare optimum (pp. 82–83).

Imperfect Competition. Wicksell's treatment of imperfect competition in chapter 6 follows Marshall closely. Some discursive remarks on joint supply lead into a brief discussion of retail pricing (pp. 86–88). Because of site advantage the product may be spatially differentiated; the result is a higher price and a larger number of retailers than would be the case if the market were perfectly competitive. When total cost is constant, so that marginal cost is zero and lies along the horizontal axis, the monopolist maximizes profits by setting price at the point of which the elasticity of demand equals unity (pp. 90–91). Wicksell is curiously reluctant to use the concept of elasticity, following Cournot rather than Marshall. When total costs are variable, instantaneous profits are maximized when the first derivative of the net revenue function vanishes (pp. 92–93). Wicksell treats the case of a linear demand curve with constant marginal costs. This produces the conclusion that when $MC = 2$, profits are maximized by raising the price $\frac{1}{2}MC$. This result is generalized for nonlinear demand curves by Mrs. Robinson (*Economics of Imperfect Competition*, p. 55). She shows that the monopoly price $= \frac{1}{2}(OA + MC)$. Her OA corresponds to $p = 24$ in Wicksell's Figure 5. If Wicksell's figure is redrawn so that g as well as p falls to zero, the formula reads: $MP = \frac{1}{2}(24 + 2) = 13$.

One of Edgeworth's theorems in the field of price discrimination is discussed in terms of a rather special graphic solution (pp. 93–95). Any sharp distinction between monopoly and competition is explicitly disavowed (p. 96); shades of Chamberlin! A brief comment on Cournot's duopoly analysis closes the section. Curiously enough, Wicksell finds Cournot's symmetry assumption more "reasonable" than those of Bertrand and Edgeworth (pp. 96–97).

Production and Distribution. Chapter 7 criticizes the Walrasian assumption that the supply of productive agents and the technical input-output coefficients may be regarded as given, so that equilibrium in factor markets is simply a by-product of equilibrium in product markets (pp. 97–99; see also the comments on Wieser's imputation theory in *Value, Capital, and Rent*, pp. 24–26). Notice the brief reference to Say's Law (pp. 97–98). The problem of interest is that of allowing for the role of the time element in production (p. 99).

We have finished the elementary and derivative section of the book and are beginning to touch on Wicksell's original contributions. The introductory section to Part II is given over to a general discussion of the role of production and distribution in a stationary state; various limitations on the analysis are laid down (pp. 103–5), and a three-factor model is postulated (p. 107). Marshall's fourth factor of production, namely, organization or enterprise, which earns profit just as capital earns interest, is dismissed as lacking quantitative precision (p. 107).

Chapter 1, "Non-Capitalistic Production," asks the reader to suppose an economy so primitive that the marginal productivity of capital is negligibly small. If, furthermore, we assume that the period of production is one year, we arrive at a pure wages fund theory. Under these circumstances, how will the product be divided (pp. 108–10)? The law of diminishing returns is incorrectly defined in terms of proportional instead of incremental returns, that is, as a matter of diminishing average rather than marginal productivity (pp. 110–11). Marshall is criticized for applying one law of returns to agriculture and another to industry. The law of increasing return, so-called, is a matter of returns to scale, while the "law of diminishing return" applies universally to increases in one factor, holding the rest constant (p. 111).

The marginal productivity of labor determines the wage rate, subject to the condition that all labor is fully employed (pp. 112–13). Rent is a surplus, determined by the gap between the average and marginal product of labor (p. 113). Like Clark and Wicksteed, Wicksell does not draw an average product curve, which somewhat mitigates the error of defining diminishing returns in proportional terms.

The theory is restated in terms of a simple but misleading production function.

$P = kL + S$, where k is a constant ($=400$) and S is a fixed amount of land (pp. 114–16). $MP_L = \partial P/\partial L = k \ (1/2\sqrt{L})$; in equilibrium $w = MP_L = 400(1/8) \cdot 10s. = 500s.$ Wicksell approximates the marginal product by adding a seventeenth worker. He concludes by showing that for any production function of the form $P = kL^a + S$, labor's share depends uniquely upon the value of a (p. 116). Since only one factor is variable, the example is not very instructive.

There follows a lucid statement of the Ricardian rent theory as a special case of the general marginal productivity theory (pp. 116–18). Carey's objection to Ricardo's theory of rent is briskly refuted (p. 119). Rodbertus' rent theory is criticized (pp. 119–20). Rodbertus' argument is simply that when all prices correspond to labor values and the rate of surplus per man is everywhere the same, the rate of profit is necessarily higher in a labor-intensive industry like agriculture. The landlord pre-empts this surplus, thus equalizing the rate of profit between agriculture and industry. The trouble with this argument is that products are not sold at their labor values. Wicksell passes over this point but goes to the heart of the matter by questioning the arbitrary assumption of an equal rate of surplus value per man. The intimate connection between Rodbertus' rent and Marx's "absolute rent" should be obvious.

Wicksell recognizes that when the law of diminishing return is stated in terms of the average rather than the marginal product, we may get an apparent contradiction to the law (p. 122). His denial of any phase of increasing marginal product to a variable factor, rather obscurely formulated, is clearly wrong (p. 123; see also p. 243 n.).

Ricardian rent theory is now generalized to any variable factor (pp. 124–25). Wicksell is careful to point out that the margin in question is not Ricardo's extensive margin resulting from the application of labor and capital to inferior grades of soil, for here one of the necessary conditions of marginal analysis, namely, constancy in one of the co-operating factors, is violated: the quality of land is varied, while the quantity of labor and capital is being increased.

Is the total product exhausted when each favor is rewarded its marginal product (pp. 125–26)? In a famous passage, Wicksell argues that perfect competition will drive the firms to operate at an output at which profits are zero and constant returns to scale prevail (pp. 128–31). Wicksell notes some of the qualifications that must be made with respect to the general validity of the product-exhaustion theorem (pp. 131–33). He neglects the question of uncertainty, however.

Wicksell now turns to the influence of innovations on factor prices. The discussion lacks precision because of his failure to distinguish between labor-saving and landsaving innovations (pp. 135–36). Ricardo's analysis of technological unemployment is neatly refuted: Ricardo failed to consider the re-absorption of labor due to falling wages (p. 137), Wicksell now shows, arithmetically, graphically, and mathematically, that a laborsaving innovation must increase the total product, although it need not increase labor's absolute or relative share of income (pp. 137–40). If the marginal product of labor falls short of the subsistence wage, welfare will be maximized by paying wages below subsistence and making up the difference by subsidies (pp. 141, 143). This follows from the fact that the product is maximized when $w = MP_L$, which in turn implies full employment of labor. Wicksell concludes that there exists no "simple and intelligible criterion" for judging the effect of a factorsaving innovation upon wages (p. 143). Notice that he nowhere mentions the possibility of capitalsaving innovations.

Capital. With chapter 2 of Part II we reach the subject of capital. Wicksell begins with some comments on the definition of the term "capital" (pp. 144–45). One central difficulty is that capital, as distinct from capital goods, is itself a quantity of value. Interest is nothing but a percentage rate of growth in the value of output. The present value of a capital asset is the flow of future income derived from the use of the asset discounted by this percentage rate of growth. As Fisher would have said, in this sense capital is not on the same footing with land and labor: capital is simply any stock, while every flow of income is analogous to interest, being a rate of growth per unit of time in the value of an asset. Wicksell does not express himself in this manner, but this seems to be what he means (p. 145). He goes on to remark that capital goods, as distinct from capital, are man-made while virgin soil and unskilled labor are "original factors" (p. 145).

Wicksell digresses briefly to show why marginal productivity theory cannot be simply applied to capital, as it has been to labor and land (pp. 147–49). From the viewpoint of the individual entrepreneur the price of value of capital is taken as given, and, to that extent, marginal productivity theory is fully applicable. But for the economy as a whole every increment of capital necessarily alters wage and interest rates and, hence, changes the purchasing power of capital over goods in general: this is the so-called Wicksell Effect, of which more in a moment. This restates the point made above: capital cannot be treated on all fours with labor and land because capital cannot be measured in terms of its own technical units; particular capital goods yield quasi-rents, not interest. We can "escape from this difficulty" by resolving all capital into the constituent amounts of original factors that are embedded for a time interval in the productive process (pp. 149–51).

The assumptions of the preliminary model are that capital produced in year t is invested, fully used up, and replaced in year $t + 1$. Stationary conditions prevail (pp. 151–53). Interest is the difference between the marginal productivity of direct and indirect labor and land (p. 154). Böhm-Bawerk's three "reasons" for a premium on present goods are clearly irrelevant to investment decisions on the part of entrepreneurs, as Böhm-Bawerk himself admitted, but they are relevant to personal saving decisions, or, as Wicksell says, to the "accumulation of capital" (p. 154). But on "the fundamental simplifying assumption of stationary economic conditions" these two grounds drop out (p. 155). That leaves only the third ground, the technical superiority of present over future goods. Here Böhm-Bawerk claimed too much. All that it is necessary to assume is that "waiting" is sufficiently scarce to raise interest above zero (p. 155). It is shown that in equilibrium the rate of interest will equal the ratio of the marginal product of indirect labor $(l_1 - l)$ to its marginal cost (l) (p. 156). This is a special case of the equimarginal principle. "In given technical conditions" the increase of capital will cause the marginal product of capital to fall (p. 157).

Now the analysis broadens out to consider investments for two or more years. Capital in real terms consists of goods in transit (p. 158). A simple diagram is used to visualize the structure of capital in a stationary state (pp. 159–60). The long-term interest rate is equal to the short-term rate when allowance is made for the greater risk but lesser liquidity of long-term paper (p. 161). A fall in the rate of interest makes it profitable to use more inputs in two-year capital investments and fewer in one-year investments. This dependence of the "average period of investment" on the rate of interest, "already recognized by Ricardo," is the crux of the Austrian theory of capital (pp. 162–63).

Increased roundaboutness will produce a scarcity of present labor and hence raise its marginal product. But an increase in the "average period of investment" without a change in initial costs leaves a larger net income from a given annual outlay. For this reason currently available inputs may become more abundant, thus lowering their marginal productivity. This seems to be the sense of Wicksell's distinction between the growth in "height" as against the growth in "breadth" (p. 163). The passage is obscured by Wicksell's failure to spell out the meaning of "expansion in height" as against "expansion in width." This calls for a clarification of Wicksell's conception of capital structure or "the stratification of capital through time" (p. 151).

The Capital Structure. Wicksell speaks of the capital structure as having both a vertical and a horizontal dimension, being capable of expansion in both dimensions. The horizontal dimension or "width" refers to the proportion of primary factors annually invested in replacement of capital goods of various maturity dates. The vertical dimension or "height" refers to the length of time for which the various capital goods are invested. If goods of different maturity dates are arrayed in descending order of the length of their investment periods, the result will be a triangular capital structure diagram (Fig. 88).

If we know the investment period of all capital goods in the structure and the interest rate, as determined by the marginal productivity of capital, we can compute the weighted average investment period for this structure as the center of gravity of the capital structure triangle. The "height" of the structure is then represented by the center of gravity G. "Expansion in width" means a proportionate increase in all capital goods of different maturity dates: it would rotate the convex compound growth curve to the right and hence decrease the amount of uninvested primary factors. This would not change the "height" dimension of capital; G would move laterally to the right. But "expansion in height" would raise the center of gravity of the capital structure by increasing the proportion of capital goods invested for long periods at the expense of those invested for short periods. This kind of "forward tilting" of the capital structure will release primary factors and so shift *G* upward. The reason for this is that annual replacement requirements per unit of primary factors invested fall as the capital structure is stretched out. A mixed effect of both expansion in "height" and in "breadth" would represent net positive investment concentrated on the

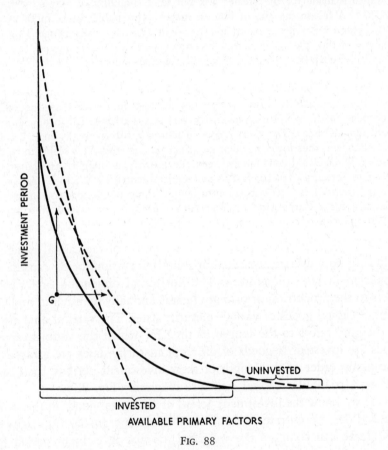

FIG. 88

more time-consuming processes; hence, *G* would shift both upward and to the right.

Growth in "height," therefore, corresponds to what Hawtrey called "capital deepening," while growth in "breadth" corresponds to Hawtrey's "capital widening." Apparently, Wicksell considers it typical for capital structures to expand initially by widening. This must before long reduce the rate of interest and bid up real wages and rent. This disturbs the equilibrium composition of the capital stock and induces deepening. Deepening, however, counteracts the decline in the interest rate and the rise in wages and rent, but it can never do so entirely for the obvious reason that the more available primary factors are "frozen" in the capital structure, the larger the triangular area under the compound growth line (pp. 163–64; see also p. 288).

As Wicksell points out, a laborsaving innovation will make deepening more profitable and may initially reduce wages. But, since it raises the average productivity of labor as well as the marginal productivity of capital, it is very likely to lead to capital widening as well as deepening: "the capitalist saver is thus, fundamentally, the friend of labor, though the technical inventor is not infrequently its enemy" (p. 164).

Having completed the foundation of "our static theory of capital," Wicksell mentions the fact that the flow input–point output case does not raise new "questions of principle" over the simple point input–point output cases so far considered (pp. 165–66).

Böhm-Bawerk's Theory of Interest. The next few pages review Böhm-Bawerk's theory of interest. Böhm-Bawerk's cavalier treatment of Ricardo draws a reproof. Ricardo laid the groundwork for the Austrian theory of capital by showing that an increase in wages will induce a substitution of capital for labor and thus lengthen the period of production (pp. 167–68). Wicksell is critical of Böhm-Bawerk's lapse into the classical wages fund doctrine and the attempt to prove that a premium on present goods would arise simply out of the process of lending and borrowing consumption goods, independently of the productivity of investment (pp. 160–70). The third "reason" for interest, which argues that the physical productivity of capital implies value productivity, is defective as an independent reason for a positive rate of interest (pp. 170–71; see also *Value, Capital, and Rent,* pp. 106–15).

These are minor criticisms at best, for "it may justly be said that the work [*The Positive Theory*] contains, albeit in a somewhat imperfect form, the real and definitive theory of capital" (p. 171). Walras and Pareto, on the contrary, abstract completely from the time element, and their theory of production is one that pertains under "essentially noncapitalistic conditions, even though the existence of durable, but apparently indestructible instruments, is taken into account" (p. 171). Wicksell apparently changed his mind about this criticism, for in a review of Cassel's *Theory of Social Economy,* published in 1919, he remarked that either we can follow Walras and define real capital as consisting of only producers' good or we can regard real capital as an aggregate of fixed and working capital having a time structure: "We can *either* adopt Walras' method of taking a *cross-section* through social production at a moment of time . . . *Or else* we can refer everything back to the original factors of production in conjunction with waiting (or preferably *time*). Here we make a *longitudinal section* instead" (pp. 236–37; see also pp. 226–27). Since Walras espoused the Clark-Knight view of capital, it is not clear whether Wicksell meant by this comment to endorse the Walrasian procedure as a perfectly satisfactory alternate explanation to the Austrian one.

The Optimum Storage Period. There follows Wicksell's classic analysis of the point input–point output case. The question is: What is the optimum storage period for wine produced in a given year at a fixed cost, the sales price W being an increasing function of time (p. 172)? We are given a definite quantity of circulating capital K, which is supposed to be sufficient for four years' storage. The price of unstored wine W_0 will vary relative to the price of inputs, that is, grape juice V_0, so as to employ the whole of K in storing wine for four years (pp. 173–74). It is now assumed that $W_3 - W_5$ is known. In order to determine the optimum selling time, we need to find the present value of new wine V_0, the equilibrium rate of interest i and the *value* of K in the community (p. 174). Given $W_3 - W_5$, the choice of a 4-year storage period implies a definite i. It is a simple matter, therefore, to calculate the discounted value V_0 (p. 175). If interest is added discretely at the beginning of each year, K_4—consisting entirely of stored wine—must equal $V_0 - V_4$ (p. 175). The amount of interest $= K_5 - K_4$, the value increment from extending the period of investment by one year. Therefore, the rate of interest is $(K_5 - K_4)/K_4$. A further increase of K is then shown to lower i and to raise V_0 (p. 176). The rate of interest is thus the marginal productivity of "waiting" (p. 177).

The whole analysis is now presented again in mathematical form, allowing for the fact that interest is added continuously over the period concerned (pp. 178–79). The final output of matured wine W is a function of the period of investment t and is equal to the initial outlay on grape juice V_0 accumulated at compound interest. The present value of W therefore $= f(t) = V_0 e^{it}$. Hence, $V_0 = W e^{-it}$. In general, entrepreneurs will estimate the present value of the gross receipts stream and the future cost stream by discounting each at the market rate of interest and maximizing the difference between these values. But in this case, as in Jevons' analysis, costs of production are constant. Hence, maximizing the net discounted money profit from wine activity is equivalent to maximizing the present value of revenue $V_0 = W e^{-it}$. Facing a given interest rate r, the only variable at the entrepreneur's disposal is t, the length of storage. Thus, differentiating $V_0 = W e^{-rt}$ with respect to t, we obtain

$$ d\,\frac{(W e^{-rt})}{dt} = W' e^{-rt} - r W e^{-rt} \cdot $$

Setting this equal to zero, we see that the implied rate of interest $r = W'/W = f'(t)/f(t)$, which is identical to Jevons' formula.

We have assumed above that r is given and that V_0 is maximized. But Wicksell, like Böhm-Bawerk, assumes that V_0 is given and that the entrepreneur maximizes i, the average internal rate of return: i is that rate of discount which, when applied to all future returns from the investment, makes their present value equal to the total cost of the investment. As Wicksell suggests, the same formula can be used. From $V_0 = W e^{-it}$

$$ i = \frac{\log W - \log V_0}{t} \, ; $$

i is at a maximum when

$$\frac{di}{dt} = t\left[\frac{W'}{W} - (\log W - \log V_0)\right]\frac{1}{t^2} = 0 \cdot$$

Hence

$$\frac{W'}{W} = \left[\log W - \log V_0\right]\frac{1}{t} = i \cdot$$

What To Maximize? The Wicksellian notion that entrepreneurs maximize an internal rate of return, rather than the present value of the net worth of an investment calculated at the going rate of interest, is based on the assumption that the firm has no access to the market for borrowed funds and that its scale of operations is effectively limited by the amount of its own capital. The reason for this assumption, apparently, was to give substance to the idea of an optimum size of the firm. Unwilling to rely on the Marshallian diseconomy-of-management argument, Wicksell chose to argue that the entrepreneur can always

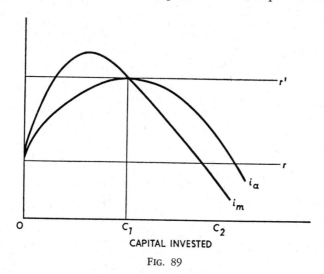

FIG. 89

reinvest his profits at a constant average = marginal internal rate of return (see, e.g., p. 244). If the firm can borrow funds, maximizing the rate of return on its capital invested will give the same result under perfect competition as equating the "marginal efficiency of capital" or marginal internal rate of return to the market rate of interest. The firm will borrow so long as the internal rate earned on additional credit exceeds the market rate of interest. But even if the firms have no access to the loan market, the market rate of interest cannot be less than the average internal rate of return without inducing an increase in the number of firms such as to drive up the rate of interest.

The investment that maximizes net present worth by making the "marginal efficiency of capital" i equal to the market rate of interest is OC_2 units of capital (Fig. 89), while that which maximizes the "average efficiency of capital" is OC_1 units. When i_a is maximized and the firm cannot borrow funds, a change in r will not affect the amount of capital invested or the optimum investment period. But if all firms are in this position, more firms will go into operation to take advantage of the fact that $r < i_a$. Hence, the rate of interest rises to r', and now all the maximization criteria coincide.

The Value of Capital. Having determined the optimum storage period, Wicksell now considers the problem of the valuation of capital. V_0 now stands for the aggregate value of the annual grape harvest and W for the total sales value of matured wine. When production is continuous, K is the value of working capital needed to keep the process running measured in terms of the product, that is, the grape juice continuously invested in production and calculated at compound interest over period t. Naturally, it is also equal to the capitalized value of total profits (p. 179).

$$K = V_0 \int_0^t e^{ix}dx = V_0\left[\frac{e^{ix}}{i}\right]_{x=t} - V_0\left[\frac{e^{ix}}{i}\right]_{x=0}$$

$$= V_0\left[\frac{e^{it}}{i}\right] - V_0\left[\frac{1}{i}\right]$$

$$= \frac{V_0}{i}(e^{it} - 1) = \frac{W - V_0}{i}.$$

"By logarithmic differentiation of (1)" (p. 179), we obtain

$$it = \log W - \log V_0$$

$$idt + tdi = \frac{dW}{W} - \frac{dV_0}{V_0},$$

"and applying (2),"

$$i = \frac{W'}{W} = \frac{1}{W}\frac{dW}{dt},$$

"we obtain"

$$\frac{dW}{W} + tdi = \frac{dW}{W} - \frac{dV_0}{V_0}$$

$$-tdi = \frac{dV_0}{V_0}.$$

But

$$-tdi = -t\frac{di}{dt} = \left(\frac{W'}{W}\right)tdt = \frac{WW'' - W'W'}{W^2}tdt,$$

which, written in determinant form, is

$$\frac{\begin{vmatrix} W & W' \\ W' & W'' \end{vmatrix}}{W^2}tdt.$$

Thus we arrive at Wicksell's equation 5 (p. 179), from which it is clear that the present value of the harvest V_0 will vary directly with the time of storage t but inversely with the rate of interest i. The storage period in turn varies inversely with i but directly with K (p. 180). This is shown by differentiating K with respect to t when V_0 is given.

$$\frac{dK}{dt} = \frac{1}{i^2}[i(W' - V_0') - i'(W - V_0)]$$

$$= \frac{1}{i^2}[i(W' + tdi) - i'(W - V_0)]$$

$$= \frac{1}{i^2}[iW' - i'W + i'V_0 - i'it]$$

$$= \frac{1}{i^2}\{iW' - i'[W - V_0(1 + it)]\} \cdot$$

Since $i' < 0$, while the expression in square brackets is always positive, the whole expression will be > 0 so long as $W' > 0$. Similarly, from

$$K = \frac{W - V_0}{i} \text{ or } W = iK + V_0 \text{ ,}$$

we get, holding V_0 constant,

$$\frac{dW}{dK} = i + K\frac{di}{dK} + \frac{dV_0}{dK} \cdot$$

From formula 5 we have

$$\frac{dV_0}{V_0} = -tdi \cdot$$

Hence

$$\frac{dW}{dK} = i + (K - V_0 t)\frac{di}{dK} \text{ (p. 180)} \cdot$$

Since i falls for every increase in K, and since K is always $> V_0$ when $i > 0$, the marginal product of capital is always less than the rate of interest. Therefore, von Thünen's formula that interest is determined by the "yield of the last increment of capital" is in error (p. 180; also p. 177 and *Capital, Value and Rent*, pp. 137–38). This is the now celebrated Wicksell Effect.

Now follows one of Wicksell's famous diagrams (p. 180). (See Fig. 90.) The curve representing the function $W = f(t)$ is drawn on semilog paper, where $y = \log W_t$ and $x = t$. The initial cost of production is incurred at $t = 0$, that is, $y = 0$ is the price of unstored wine. Since $W_t = V_0 e^{it}$, $i = (\log W_t - \log V_0)/t$. For every i there is a family of parallel discount curves represented by the equation $W_t = V_0 e^{it}$, with gradient i and cutting the vertical axis at $y = V_0$. From the tangency condition we can now read off the maximum t and the corresponding discounted value of the wine sold for any given i. As before, Wicksell instead assumes a given V_0 and reads off the maximum internal rate of return associated with the optimum t.

Up to now it has been assumed that labor and land were invested once and for all at $t = 0$ so that V_0 stood for the initial fixed cost outlay. Now it is observed that, when the inputs are invested continuously, the wage rate will equal the discounted marginal product of labor ($w = We^{-it}$), and similarly for rent (p. 181). Contradicting his previous discussion of Euler's theorem,

Wicksell now speaks of product exhaustion as an "identity" (p. 182). Of the five equations that determine the rate of interest, Wicksell observes, one is actually missing. The amount of circulating capital, which is really unknown, has been assumed as given (p. 182). That is to say, the annual grape harvest V_0 has been taken as a datum. This is a fatal admission, which points up the special character of the point input–point output case and shows in what sense it really fails to get beyond the wages fund doctrine. Notice the comments that when the inputs are invested at a uniform rate during t, the average period is just half the absolute period of investment; then, and only then, is Jevons' formula for i correct (p. 182 n.; also 191 n.).

Böhm-Bawerk's method of calculating the average period of production implies that inputs earn only simple interest. When the inputs earn compound interest, the average period of production or investment is not independent of the rate of interest. In terms of the previous analysis, this means that W is not merely a simple function of t and that the notion of an optimum t that maximizes an internal rate of return for a given cost outlay becomes virtually

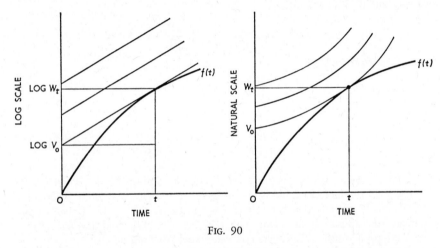

Fig. 90

unmanageable (p. 184). Wicksell's efforts to talk round this difficulty are not very convincing. He notes in addition that the same problem would arise even with simple interest if the flow-output rather than the point-output case were analyzed (p. 184). The purely notional meaning of the concept of "average waiting time" is frankly conceded (p. 184).

The Wicksell Effect. Wicksell accepted the concept of an average period of investment as an ordinal index of degree of capital intensity in the economy. He noted, however, that the length of this average period was not itself adequate to determine the ratio of capital to labor because an increase in the supply of capital altered the units in which all existing capital was measured. The Wicksell Effect has to do with the revaluation of the capital stock as a change in investment alters the rate of wages and interest. This is a little different from the usual index-number problem because it would exist even if all output were homogeneous. While the marginal private product of each capital good tends to equal the rate of interest that would have to be paid on the capital invested in it, the marginal social product of capital, Wicksell found, was usually less than the instantaneous rate of interest. The marginal social product of capital is the output increment per unit of capital resulting from an increase in net real savings. The reason the marginal social product is usually less than the interest rate is that a portion of net real saving is absorbed in rising real wages during a period of capital formation.

Suppose the supply of capital increases owing to new voluntary saving. The rate of interest falls, and costs of production decline. Existing firms now earn a capital gain on each worker employed. The

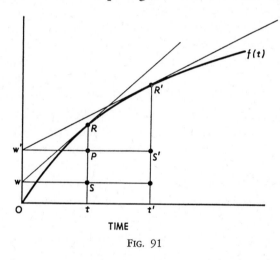

TIME

FIG. 91

fall in the rate of interest, however, induces new firms to enter the market and bids up the wage rate. This makes it profitable for everyone to substitute capital for labor. The rate of interest tends to equality with the marginal product of voluntary saving, but the marginal social product of capital equals the output increment divided by the new voluntary saving plus the involuntary capital gains. It follows that the market rate of interest, based on a smaller divisor, exceeds the marginal social product of capital. Thus, claimed Wicksell, von Thünen, Jevons, and Böhm-Bawerk are wrong: the rate of interest is not equal to the increment of output divided by the increment of capital, at least not the final increment of capital.

Take the flow input–point output case with a given amount of working capital and a single homogeneous product. (See Fig. 91.) Suppose firms maximize their net returns by choosing the average period of production t which is equal to one-half of the absolute period. The market-clearing wage rate is w. Assuming that we are dealing with simple interest, so that the discount curves are straight lines, the rate of interest is equal to the absolute interest earned by RS divided by the amount of capital invested $OwSt$, or the slope of the discount line divided by Ot. If the rate of interest falls, a higher wage will have to be paid not merely for the increase in the period of production contemplated (tt') but for the whole period. The marginal social product of capital is now $= R'S'/Ow'S't'$, but the rate of interest $= R'S'/Ow'Pt$ since $tPS't'$ is absorbed by the rise in wages. Hence, the rate of interest exceeds the marginal social product of capital.

One may well ask why a similar effect does not arise when labor and land vary, the amount of real capital being kept constant. The reason, of course, is that, whereas land and labor can each be measured in terms of their own technical units, capital can be measured only in terms of value (see p. 149). Capital cannot be measured in physical terms, not simply because it is too heterogeneous but because it is two-dimensional. The services of labor and land cannot be stored as such except in the form of real capital, and hence today's labor or land becomes fully effective in creating output without any absorption of real wages or rent into capital income. This is not true of net real saving, resulting in increased subsistence goods or in machines produced, because their production and consumption take time.

The Wicksell Effect constitutes, according to Mrs. Robinson, "the key to the whole theory of capital accumulation." As she puts it, the value of a given type of machine depends on the real wage rate: "at a higher wage rate there is a higher value of a given type of machine." As stated by Wicksell and Mrs. Robinson, the *net* effect of a rise in w and a fall in r is always to raise the value of capital in terms of the product. Indeed, Wicksell nowhere mentions the fact that the tendency of a higher wage rate to absorb money capital in the form of wages is partially offset by the fall in r, which releases some money capital hitherto used for interest payments and now available for the purchase of real capital. Obviously, whether wage absorption will outweigh the release of interest charges depends on the relative weight of labor and capital in the production of social output. In general, there is no presumption either way. When capital is just goods-in-process, as in the Wicksellian analysis, it is hardly surprising that the value of capital in terms of the product rises when w rises and r falls. But, when durable machines are employed, it is perfectly possible for an increase in wages to bring about a downward revaluation of machines in the same direction as the interest rate. In fact, when Wicksell came to deal with Ackerman's problem of investment in durable equipment, he discovered the Wicksell Effect in reverse: the marginal social product of capital may exceed the interest rate. He was puzzled and admitted that his previous discussion of wage absorption was not generally valid (pp. 268–69, 292–93).

Wicksell's criticism of the von Thünen formulation is misplaced because the latter is concerned with *real* capital and its yield to the individual firm. What the Wicksell Effect shows is that the rate of interest need not be equal to the *money* value of social capital. This does not concern the individual firm because under perfect competition the prices of factors are taken as constants. A marginal increment of accumulation involves an error in measuring the capital stock in consequence of the Wicksell Effect, but, since the change is a marginal variation around an equilibrium level, the error is of "the second order of smalls." But the economist who wants to make structural comparisons between different stationary states cannot ignore the Wicksell Effect. The purchasing power of the stock of capital over goods in general in equilibrium depends not only on the wage and interest rate but also on the way in which equilibrium is attained. The *value* of capital in two stationary states having the same real amount of capital may be different. It is difficult to see, however, how a Wicksell Effect in what must generally be regarded as an unpredictable direction can be "the key to the whole theory of capital accumulation." The problem of measuring capital remains, despite recent work, the outstanding unsettled question in economic theory.

Definitions of Capital. Now we are out of the woods and come back to the age-old dispute over "capital in the narrower sense"—intermediate products—or "capital in the wider sense"—all sources of income of any kind (pp. 185–86). Wicksell tries to justify his preoccupation with short-lived capital by arguing that most durable equipment is "virtually" nonexhaustible and therefore earns rent, not interest. He goes so far as to suggest that disinvestment of fixed capital is "usually impossible" (pp. 186–87; see also p. 237).

Böhm-Bawerk's decision to exclude the subsistence fund from "social capital" is dismissed as a purely terminological confusion (p. 187). Capitalists do not receive a discounted share of the product but, rather, an undiscounted residual after all factors have received their discounted marginal products (p. 188). This is a truism when profits are zero, since the residual as a percentage of capital invested is itself the discount factor. Böhm-Bawerk's contrary assertion, which Wicksell attacks, probably refers to the profits of the entrepreneur, not the interest of the capitalist; and, of course, profits are not advanced out of capital.

The famous dispute as to whether wages are paid out of capital or out of the final product is nicely resolved (pp. 188–90). The reader is reminded of the basic truth of the fourth of Mill's "propositions respecting capital" (p. 191). The point that rent is a discounted marginal product is brought home in an arithmetical example (p. 192). The "not yet defunct" wages fund theory is briefly discussed (pp. 193–95; see also pp. 245–46). The trouble with the theory is that it failed to treat the turnover rate of capital—the reciprocal of the average period of production—as a function of the interest rate. Senior's last-hour theory, as well as Marx's unsatisfactory criticism of it, illustrate the dangers of ignoring the implications of the fixed production period assumed in the wages fund doctrine (pp. 194–95).

Since little is heard nowadays of discounted marginal products, it is necessary to add that there is no difference in principle between an undiscounted and a discounted marginal productivity theory, provided we realize that the marginal product in question is not the same in the two theories. Productive agents receive the value of their marginal product in terms of immediate results, and this is necessarily equal to the discounted value of the finished consumer goods that their activity will eventually realize, that is, the discounted value of the future yield of their immediate product. Time theories of capital put emphasis, of course, on the fact that labor and labor alone receives a discounted share, while capital receives an undiscounted share. Followers of the Clark-Knight view of capital object to such terminology as being misleading, but no logical error is involved.

A final section on general equilibrium brings Part II to a close. Mill's theory of international values is briefly discussed (pp. 198–200). The problem of general equilibrium is first stated verbally and then mathematically (pp. 200–204). The analysis of the stationary state is incomplete without a theory of saving, despite the fact that net saving is zero under stationary conditions (pp. 202–3).

The Accumulation of Capital. The opening remarks on the motives for savings and the possibility of backward-sloping supply curves of saving are strongly suggestive of Fisher's approach, in which the rate of interest depends on the interaction of "willingness" and "opportunity" (pp. 207–9). Wicksell seems to believe that any positive rate of interest brings about net investment, which implies the anti-Austrian conclusion that $r = 0$ under stationary conditions. Wicksell hedges by a vague reference to "approximately stationary conditions" (p. 209).

He dismisses Cassel's argument designed to show that the rate of interest cannot fall to zero as having insufficient weight in the total picture. Cassel assumed that at near-zero rates those who save for old-age security will be forced to consume their capital; the shortness of the normal earning period of an individual would alone create a shortage of personal savings (pp. 209–11). The reason for the apparent failure to satiate demand for capital is the presence of uncertainty about the future (p. 211). A collectivist society could ignore uncertainty and hence would grow more rapidly than a capitalist economy (pp. 211–12). Capitalists as a class favor war because it destroys capital and hence raises the rate of interest (pp. 212–13). When the assumption of stationariness is abandoned, the problems of capital theory become "essentially different" (p. 213). Various possibilities are discussed, rather awkwardly, in terms of the principle of diminishing marginal utility of income (pp. 213–14). A "perfected capitalistic system" is one in which the marginal product of capital has fallen to zero (p. 214). But in a private property system this might lead to an undesirable rise in rents (pp. 214–15). von Thünen's "natural wage" is considered as an early example of a theorem about capital accumulation (pp. 216–17).

Cassel's Theory of Social Economy. This review article by Wicksell contains a whole series of unusually incisive comments on a book that was at one time very highly regarded: on the subjective theory of value (pp. 221–23), on the indeterminacy of absolute prices (pp. 223–25), on general equilibrium (pp. 225–27), on welfare economics (pp. 227–28), on imperfect competition (pp. 228–29), on the paradox of decreasing costs (pp. 231–32), on the theory of capital and interest (pp. 223–41), on population growth (pp. 241–42), on the theory of rent (pp. 242–45), on the wage theory (pp. 245–49), on monetary theory (pp. 249–54), and, last, on business cycles (pp. 254–57).

Durable Capital Goods. At the age of seventy-two, Wicksell wrote a review article on Ackerman's still untranslated book dealing with the point input–flow output case. The analysis is exceedingly complicated despite the fact that the problem is artifically simplified by the assumption that the efficiency of the machines in question is constant over time until, for technical reasons, the life of the machine suddenly comes to an end. There are no variable operating costs, and there is no way of lengthening the output stream by making repairs. The machine, in other words, is very much like a light bulb. The problem that Ackerman and Wicksell analyze is how the entrepreneur chooses among a variety of constant-efficiency machines, the durability of each machine being a function of how much labor is invested in their manufacture. In the real world, machines are of the diminishing efficiency type and require greater repair and maintenance charges the older they get. The economic life of such machines is usually shorter than the technical life, which can be extended almost indefinitely through adequate repairs. Here, even under static assumptions, there is the problem of how long it pays to go on extending the lifetime of a given machine, a problem that must be solved simultaneously with the problem of choosing between alternative machines of different technical durability. A cursory examination of Wicksell's article, however, will show that there is quite enough to worry about even when there are no economic problems connected with the utilization of chosen machines.

First, Wicksell presents a straightforward definition of the discounted capital value of all future income, b per year, obtained continuously from a machine (axe) during its life of n years (p. 276). In equilibrium, this expression is equal to the cost of production of the axe measured in labor (formula 4, p. 276). Costs increase, but less than proportionately to the durability of the axe; hence, the cost function 5 on p. 276. It is then shown that the optimal life of the axe depends uniquely on the particular cost function, whatever the size of income per year. The most profitable length of life of the axe varies inversely with the rate of interest (p. 279). As long as the amount of labor invested is fixed, Jevons' formula for the rate of interest still applies (pp. 279–81).

Suppose that the stock of axes is of uniform age distribution from 0 to t

years (p. 281). At any moment there are *nt* axes in use and *M* laborers out of the total labor force *A* are occupied in replacing the *n*th part of the stock worn out each year. The problem is to choose that *t* which will maximize profits. For the derivation and solution of Wicksell's equation 15 (p. 283) the reader is referred to Allen, *Mathematical Analysis for Economists*, pp. 404–5, where Allen's *n, a, r,* and *x* stand for Wicksell's *M, b, p,* and *nt.*

When the cost function is of constant elasticity—Wicksell's equation 5, on page 276—equation 15 can be simplified as a function of *M, b,* and *w* (p. 284). A new model is then presented using a linear homogeneous production function and with *M* a constant proportion of *A* (pp. 284–91). The mathematics here is not really difficult, but a good deal of patience is required to work out the results. The reader should press on, however, because the general drift of the argument is set out in words. The last section examines anew the crucial question whether a fall in the rate of interest, leading to an increase in capital, always lengthens the "height" of capital or whether it may extend its "breadth" (pp. 293–99). Wicksell's conclusion is that the Austrian result holds even for fixed capital except where the second-order conditions for profit maximization fail to obtain (p. 295 n.).

NOTES FOR FURTHER READING

1. *Böhm-Bawerk's Theory of Interest.* The bulk of Böhm-Bawerk's writings on capital and interest have recently been newly translated by G. D. Huncke and H. F. Semholz and published in a three-volume edition (1959). Volume I contains *The History and Critique of Interest Theories* (1884), together with *Recent Literature on Interest* (1914). The *History and Critique,* previously published under the title *Capital and Interest,* is one of the most extraordinary polemical productions in the whole history of economics. Over a hundred authors are fitted into a Procustean classificatory scheme of five types of interest theories. There has been much discussion not only about the way the different writers are distributed among the five categories but about the categories themselves. With surprising regularity, Böhm-Bawerk's treatment is most unfair to those authors who come closest to his own approach: Ricardo, Senior, Jevons, and Menger. *Recent Literature on Interest* contains a characteristically oversubtle attack on Marshall. Volume II of the new edition comprises *The Positive Theory of Capital* (1889), Book II, chaps. 2–5, and Book IV, chaps. 1–3, of which still repay study. Böhm-Bawerk never properly revised or finished the first edition of his work, and for fifteen years, while active as a Minister of Finance in the Austrian government, he had no opportunity to prepare a second edition. In the third edition of the book (1912) he added twelve "Exkursus" to meet the various criticisms that his ideas had received. These are reprinted in Volume III of the new edition: the first and second "excursion," dealing with the effect of innovations on the average degree of roundaboutness, and the twelfth, dealing with Fisher's critique of the alleged independence of the third "reason" for interest, contain significant clarifications of the general argument.

Schumpeter's obituary article on Böhm-Bawerk, published originally in 1914 and reprinted in *Ten Great Economists,* is perhaps the most readable general account of the theory ever given (see particularly pp. 174–90). It is an enthusiastic account, as befits an obituary notice, but it is valuable precisely because of its efforts to be wholly sympathetic. See also the brilliant account in Schumpeter, *History,* pp. 844–48, 898–909, and 924–32. For contrast see Stigler's merciless critique from the standpoint of the "perpetual income stream" and "indestructible capital fund" approach: *Production and Distribution Theories,* chap. 8.

A good introduction to Böhm-Bawerk is V. Edelberg, "The Ricardian Theory of Profits," *Ec,* February, 1933; Ricardo's insight in perceiving that the problem of capital can be reduced to "the relative time that must elapse before the results of labor can be brought to the market" supplies the key to the Austrian conception of capital. Rogin, *The Validity and Meaning of Economic Theory,* chap. 13, provides a superior textbook exposition of Böhm-Bawerk's theory, marred on occasion by some peculiar quasi-Marxian prejudices. G. Arvidsson, "Reasons for a Rate of Interest," *ET,* 1953, reprinted in *IEP,* No. 6, 1956, revives old controversies with the argument that the third "reason" does afford an independent ground for the existence of interest.

2. *The Average Period of Production.* We have leaned heavily on two articles by R. Dorfman: "A Graphic Exposition of Böhm-Bawerk's Interest Theory," *REStud,* February, 1959, and "Waiting and the Period of Production," *QJE,* August, 1959, with a "Comment" by E. Neuberger, February, 1960. Böhm-Bawerk's famous arithmetical example in the closing chapters of the *Positive Theory* is expounded graphically à la Dorfman by the editors of *EET,* pp. 542–48. Dorfman's second article is the only important contribution to the subject of production periods that has been published in recent decades: it proves that the average period of production in a two-sector economy is equal to the capital-output ratio and demonstrates the sense in which "waiting" is a genuine scarce factor on a par with labor. The present leader of the British Labor Party, H. T. N. Gaitskell, attempted to salvage the concept of an average period in an illuminating article: "Notes on the Period of Production," *ZN,* VII, No. 5, 1936; IX, No. 2, 1936.

The Knight-Hayek controversy on capital theory reached something of a climax with N. Kaldor, "The Recent Controversy on the Theory of Capital," *Ecom,* 1937, reprinted in *Essays on Value and Distribution* (1960), which defends the average period of production as "meaningful" but "irrelevant" to a dynamic economy. This article contains a complete bibliography of the debate. Out of the enormous flood of over fifty essays, the following items seem to be the most useful: J. M. Fleming, "The Period of Production and Derived Concepts," *REStud,* October, 1935; F. A. Hayek, "The Mythology of Capital," *QJE,* 1936, and F. H. Knight, "Capital and Interest," *Encyclopaedia Britannica* (1946), both of which are reprinted in *Readings in the Theory of Income Distribution;* and, for the mathematically sophisticated reader, C. P. Gifford, "The Concept of the Length of the Period of Production," *EJ,* December, 1933; J. Marschak, "A Note on the Period of Production," *EJ,* March, 1934; and C. P. Gifford, "The Period of Production under Continuous Input and Point Output in an Unprogressive Community," *Ecom,* April, 1935. For an illuminating comparison of the problem of determining the age structure of a biological population with that of an economy's capital stock see K. E. Boulding, *The*

Reconstruction of Economics (1950), chap. 11. Kaldor's bibliography is brought up to date by J. F. Weston, "Some Perspectives on Capital Theory," *AER*, May, 1951, a sketchy review, which gives an account of the present status of the controversy. The neoclassical "Essentials of Capital Theory" are reviewed and commended by F. Lutz in *The Theory of Capital*, ed. F. Lutz (1960).

On Clark's concept of "synchronization" see Stigler, *Production and Distribution Theories*, chap. 11, pp. 308–15. P. A. Samuelson, "Dynamic, Statics, and the Stationary State," *REStud*, 1943, reprinted in *REA*, Vol. I, gives a sympathetic account of Schumpeter's theory of the "circular flow" and shows that the prices of durable goods would not be infinite at a zero rate of interest. See also G. Haberler, "Schumpeter's Theory of Interest," *REStud*, 1951, reprinted in *Schumpeter, Social Scientist* (1951). W. Fellner and H. S. Ellis, "Hicks and the Time-Period Controversy," *JPE*, August, 1940, attacks Hick's revival of the production-period concept in chapter 17 of *Value and Capital;* this article closes with an excellent brief statement of the Knightian view.

For a valuable review of the history of the logomachy in capital theory see Fraser, *Economic Thought and Language,* chap. 14.

3. Fisher's Theory of Interest. For an illuminating presentation of Fisher's Theory see the recent book by J. W. Conard, *An Introduction to the Theory of Interest* (1959), chaps. 4 and 5. The best chapter in this somewhat uneven book is chapter 15, on the neoclassical theory of the interest rate. *The theory of interest in our discussion has not been specified as short or long term because the rate of interest as an effective rate of return for any given period of time will be the same on all securities regardless of term, provided net return is defined inclusive of capital gains and losses as well as interest income;* this fundamental theorem of the neoclassical theory of the rate structure is nowhere more clearly explained than in chapter 15 of this book. J. Hirschleifer, "On the Theory of Optimal Investment Decisions," *JPE*, Auugst, 1958, and "Marginal Efficiency and Capital: Comment," *EJ*, September, 1959, demonstrate the general applicability of Fisher's theory to problems of capital budgeting. W. Leontief, "Theoretical Note on Time-Preference, Productivity of Capital, Stagnation, and Economic Growth," *AER*, March, 1958, and "Comment" by F. M. Westfield, December, 1959, use the basic Fisher diagram to illustrate the process of economic growth.

On the distinction between the marginal productivity of capital and the marginal efficiency of investment see A. P. Lerner, *Economics of Control* (rev. ed., 1953), chap. 25, and T. Scitovsky, *Welfare and Competition* (1952), chap. 9, an excellent chapter, which contains much else besides. A. H. Hansen, *A Guide to Keynes* (1953), chaps. 5 and 8, are also useful. Almost every possible type of supply curve of saving has been postulated by one neoclassical economist or another; for a review of the subject see Douglas, *The Theory of Wages,* chap. 17, particularly the summary diagram on p. 457.

Finally, there is F. A. Lutz, *Zinstheorie* (1959), chaps. 1–5 and 7–9. It is a pity that this book has not been translated, for it is undoubtedly the best survey of the history of interest theory since Böhm-Bawerk; its brevity commends it to students.

4. The Ricardo Effect. See F. A. Hayek, "The Ricardo Effect," *Ec,* 1942, reprinted in *Individualism and Economic Order* (1948), chap. 2, for reference to the extensive discussion of this effect. The fundamental criticism of Hayek's thesis is given by N. Kaldor in "Capital Intensity and the Trade Cycle," *Ec,* 1939, and "Professor Hayek and the Concertina Effect," *Ec,* 1942, both reprinted in *Essays on Economic Stability and Growth* (1960). The last of these two pieces is an important contribution to *Dogmengeschichte,* attributing the Ricardo Effect to Wicksell rather than to Ricardo. S. Tsiang, *The Variations of Real Wages and Profit Margins in Relation to the Trade Cycle* (1947), chap. 7, reviews the theoretical argument with great clarity and attempts to test it statistically. See also H. Makower and W. J. Baumol, "The Analogy between Producer and Consumer Equilibrium," *Ec,* February, 1950.

5. *Wicksell.* If Marshall is the typical example of an economist who lived the life of a scholarly recluse, Wicksell is the perfect example of an economist who was always embroiled in public controversies as the passionate advocate of one unpopular cause after another. In a magnificent biography, T. Gardlund, *The Life of Knut Wicksell* (1958) reveals Wicksell's complex character and re-creates the Swedish intellectual atmosphere in the years before World War I. *Selected Papers on Economic Theory,* ed. E. Lindahl (1958), makes available for the first time some of Wicksell's many untranslated journal articles. The most interesting of these are his reviews of Pareto's *Cours* (1899), Pareto's *Manuel* (1913), and Bowley's *Mathematical Groundwork* (1925). A paper on "Böhm-Bawerk's Theory of Capital" (1911) gives a succinct summary of Wicksell's final assessment of the ideas of his mentor.

Stigler, *Production and Distribution Theories,* chap. 10, and C. G. Uhr, "Wicksell: A Centennial Evaluation," *AER,* December, 1951, reprinted in *EET,* review Wicksell's contributions to theoretical economics. Uhr's article has since become a book: *Economic Doctrines of Knut Wicksell* (1960). Chapters 5–7 treat the problems of capital and interest. Chapter 5 contains an excellent analysis of Wicksell's conception of the capital structure and the nature of the conflict between the Austrian and the Clark-Knight view. Chapter 6 examines the Wicksell Effect with great thoroughness. On the Wicksell Effect see also J. Robinson, *The Accumulation of Capital,* chap. 11, and the notes at the end of the book on "The Neo-Classical Theory of Wages and Profits," "Income from Property as the Reward of Waiting," and "Wicksell on Capital"; E. Osborn, "The Wicksell Effect," *REStud,* June, 1958.

On the mathematics of compound interest see Allen, *Mathematical Analysis for Economists,* pp. 228–37 and 401–3; on Fisher's theory of interest see pp. 376–78; on Wicksell's wine-storage problem see pp. 248–50 and 362–64 and problems 17, p. 265, and 13, p. 379; on the Wicksell-Ackerman analysis of durable machines see pp. 404–5 and problems 33–37, p. 411.

F. A. and V. Lutz, *The Theory of Investment of the Firm* (1951), chap. 2, discusses alternative criteria of profit maximization. But J. Hirschleifer, "On the Theory of Optimal Investment Decisions," *JPE,* August, 1958, criticizes Lutz's preference for the present-value rule over the internal-rate-of-return rule. Chapters 5 and 6 of the *Theory of Investment of the Firm* analyze the scale versus the deepening effect of a fall in the rate of interest; this leads up to a careful discussion of the Ricardo Effect in chapters 9–11. The reader is warned that this is a difficult book on a difficult subject. A. Smithies, "The Austrian Theory of Capital in Relation to Partial Equilibrium Theory," *QJE,*

November, 1935, may be read as an introduction to the Lutz study. The case against "The Discounted Marginal Productivity Doctrine" is stated by E. Rolph, *JPE,* 1939, reprinted in *Readings in the Theory of Income Distribution.*

The Austrian theory of capital survives today in E. Lindahl, *Studies in the Theory of Money and Capital* (1939), and F. A. Hayek, *The Pure Theory of Capital* (1941). Both authors reject the concept of an average period, however defined, and prefer to work with the concept of a multidimensional heterogeneous capital structure. Hayek's *Pure Theory* was poorly received (see A. Smithies, "Professor Hayek on *The Pure Theory of Capital,*" *AER,* December, 1941) and suffers from imprecision at critical turning points in the argument. But it contains many valuable flashes; see, in particular, chapter 4, on the characteristics of the Austrian as against the Anglo-American approach to capital; chapter 5, on the nature of the capital problem; chapters 6, 11, and 14, which reject the concept of the average period of production or investment; chapters 17, 18, and the very interesting Appendix I, on productivity versus thrift (Hayek reconsidered his conclusions on this score in *Ec,* February, 1945); chapter 13, on the distinction that Wicksell draws between the instantaneous rate of "force of interest" r and the actual compound rate (e^{r-1}); and, finally, chapters 20 and 21, on capital accumulation.

The reader who is still wondering "what it is all about" is recommended to try his teeth on M. Dobb, *Political Economy and Capitalism,* chaps. 5 and 6, a powerful Marxist critique of any and all orthodox theories of interest grounded on time preference, productivity, or any other real cost of providing capital. The reader who cannot meet the attack has failed to learn the lessons of Austrian theory.

Chapter 13

GENERAL EQUILIBRIUM AND WELFARE ECONOMICS

1. WALRAS AND GENERAL EQUILIBRIUM

WE HAVE SHOWN that each consumer with given tastes and income maximizes his utility position relative to the prices ruling in the market so as to obtain the same marginal utility per dollar from every product he purchases. At the same time, each producer maximizes his profit position relative to ruling factor prices by employing the factors of production in such proportions and quantities as to obtain the same marginal value product per dollar of factor outlays. This leads him in the long run to build a plant of optimal scale, producing the output quantities for which least average cost equals marginal cost equals the given demand price for the final product. When we sum the demand prices of the consumers in a particular product market, the market demand price must in equilibrium equal the market supply price obtained by a similar process of summing the individual supply prices of the participating firms in the market. At the same time, however, the resulting demand prices of all industries in a particular factor market must equal the supply prices of the owners of the factor services. The aggregate demand for all factors in any period must equal the incomes received by households from supplying factor services over the same period. This provides the household with the given incomes with which we started in the analysis of consumer behavior. But what reason do we have for thinking that the whole process hangs together? Business firms enter product markets as suppliers, but they enter factor markets as buyers; households, on the other hand, are buyers in product markets but suppliers in factor markets. Is equilibrium in product markets necessarily consistent with equilibrium in factor markets? Is general equilibrium possible? And, if possible, is it unique, or are there several configurations of prices that will satisfy the condition of general equilibrium? Even if a unique general equilibrium exists, we may ask whether it is stable. Does the market mechanism lead to convergence on the general equilibrium solution, and, once it is attained, does it remain there?

The Concept of General Equilibrium. These are the questions that Walras attempted to answer in the *Elements of Pure Economics* (1874). As is so often true with searching questions, no one had realized how difficult it might be to answer them precisely. Indeed, it took some time before the questions themselves sank in. Students of Austrian economics in the last quarter of the nineteenth century were still asking: Are prices first determined in the market by demand and supply and then given to consumers to permit them to reach an optimum quantity adjustment, or do consumers first decide how much to purchase and these decisions then result in market demand prices? Even if we start with given factor supplies and fixed coefficients of production, factor prices are not determined until firms have decided to produce certain outputs; but this decision implies knowledge of product prices, which, in turn, are not determined until households have received income from the sales of factor services at given prices. Obviously, product and factor prices are determined simultaneously. Many contemporaries of Walras found this proposition difficult to comprehend. They never quite overcame the suspicion that the argument involves a vicious circle. They could understand the validity of partial equilibrium analysis based on the assumption that certain variables in the analysis are treated as parameters. But they could not grasp the idea that the existence of n partial equilibria each involving n variables did not in any way guarantee a total equilibrium for the whole economy made up of n markets.

The analogy that immediately suggests itself is that of the consistency of a set of simultaneous equations. If each equation represents partial equilibrium in one market, then a set of such equations may well prove to be inconsistent, such that no values of the n variables simultaneously satisfies all n equations. For example,

$$2x + y = 10 \; ;$$
$$x - 2z = 2 \; ;$$
$$y + 3z = 9 \; .$$

For $x = 3$ we have the first two equations that $y = 4$ and $z = \frac{1}{2}$; but these values of y and z do not satisfy the third equation. Equilibrium in some markets may therefore lead directly to disequilibrium in other markets. The problem of determining the existence of a general equilibrium is thus analogous to the problem of finding a unique solution for a set of simultaneous equations.

Long before Walras, Cournot had realized that "for a complete and precise solution of the partial problems of the economic system, it is inevitable that one must consider the system as a whole." But Cournot thought that the problem of general equilibrium was beyond the resources of mathematical analysis. Walras's genius lay not only in seizing upon the problem that Cournot had recognized but in showing that it is capable of being solved, at least in principle. Oddly enough, Walras lacked the mathematical finesse of Cournot, or for that matter of Marshall or Wicksell, and his demonstrations are not only mathematically clumsy but ambiguous and unfinished. Yet there is an architectonic quality to the whole performance that has led some commentators to credit Walras with the supreme achievement of theoretical economics. According to Schumpeter, Walras's *Eléments* is nothing less than the "Magna Carta of exact economics."

The Walrasian System. In setting forth the Walrasian model, we will use Walras's own symbols to facilitate reference to the text, chiefly lesson 20 of the *Elements*. We begin with the following parameters:

1. Technical *coefficients de fabrication, nm* in number, being the fixed amounts of *n* productive services T, P, K, . . . required to produce *m* products A, B, C, . . .

$$a_t, a_p, a_k, \ldots$$
$$b_t, b_p, b_k, \ldots .$$

2. The *rareté* or marginal utility functions of each individual for *n* productive services and *m* consumer goods, *nm* in number.

$$r = \phi(q) .$$

Walras assumes that productive resources are capable of being consumed by their owners directly. Although the number of workers, machines, acres of land, and so forth are given in amount, their supply is variable even in the short run. To deny this while at the same time keeping to the assumption of fixed "coefficients of fabrication" might mean that there is no set of prices for productive services that would clear all factor markets simultaneously. This explains the logical necessity of the form given to the *rareté* functions. It leaves unanswered, however, the question of what it means to say that owners of machines have an own-demand for machines. We shall return to this problem later. For the moment, we need merely note that assumption 2 means that the supply curve of productive services must turn backward at a certain price since this supply curve is nothing but the owners' aggregate demand curve for all other resources. Walras did not neglect to notice this fact. Indeed, this is how he stumbled on the possibility of multiple equilibria.

The reader may wonder why anything should be treated as given in a system purporting to provide a truly general equilibrium solution. But this query involves a misunderstanding of the concept of an equilibrium system that must always be defined in terms of given initial conditions. The difference between partial and general equilibrium analyses is not that one does and the other does not make *ceteris paribus* assumptions but that, in general equilibrium analysis, as Samuelson has observed, "the historical discipline of theoretical economics is practically exhausted. The things which are taken as data for that system happen to be matters which economists have traditionally chosen not to consider as within their province. Among these data may be mentioned tastes, technology, the governmental and institutional framework, and many others."

Individuals are in possession of given initial quantities of productive services (q_t, q_p, q_k, . . .) at given prices (p_t, p_p, p_k, . . .). They also face given prices of consumer goods (p_a, p_b, p_c, . . .). Hence, the budget equation of each individual stipulates that the quantities of the services offered (o_t, o_p, o_k, . . .) times their prices equals the quantities demanded of consumer goods (d_a, d_b, d_c, . . .) at equilibrium prices.

$$o_t p_t + o_p p_p + o_k p_k + . . . = d_a p_a + d_b p_b + ...$$

All prices are "normalized" by being arbitrarily defined in terms of one of the goods, the *numéraire*. Hence, $p_a = 1$. The equimarginal rule for utility maximization requires that the marginal utilities of the various goods purchased and productive services retained for direct consumption be proportional to their prices. This gives n equations for productive services:

$$\phi_t(q_t - o_t) = p_t \phi_a(d_a) ;$$
$$\phi_p(q_p - o_p) = p_p \phi_a(d_a) ;$$
$$. . . . .$$

and $m - 1$ equations for goods:

$$\phi_b(d_b) = p_b \phi_a(d_a) :$$
$$\phi_c(d_c) = p_c \phi_a(d_a) ;$$
$$. . . . .$$

There are thus $n + m$ equations to solve for n unknown supply functions for productive services.

$$o_t = f_t(p_t, p_p, p_k, \ldots, p_a, p_b, p_c \ldots) ;$$
$$o_p = f_p(p_t, p_p, p_k, \ldots, p_a, p_b, p_c \ldots) .$$

and $m - 1$ unknown demand functions for consumer goods.

$$d_a = f_a(p_t, p_p, p_k, \ldots, p_a, p_b, p_c \ldots) ;$$
$$d_b = f_b(p_t, p_p, p_k, \ldots, p_a, p_b, p_c \ldots) .$$

By Walras's Law one of the equations is not an independent equation in the sense that it is automatically satisfied if the others hold. We thus have $n + m - 1$ equations to solve for $n + m - 1$ unknowns. For the moment we will assume that money does not enter the utility functions: all exchange is carried on with money, but money is not a real good and is neither wanted for its own sake nor produced like other goods. Thus, the demand and supply schedules are functions of relative prices and are homogeneous of zero degree in absolute prices. This leaves absolute prices indeterminate, but Walras himself relaxed this assumption at a later stage and included *encaisse désirée* in the utility functions.

When we sum all the individual supply and demand functions we obtain:

1. The market supply equations for productive services, n in number:

$$O_t = \Sigma o_t = F_t(p_t, p_p, p_k, \ldots, p_b, p_c, p_d, \ldots) ;$$
$$O_p = \Sigma o_p = \ldots\ldots\ldots\ldots\ldots\ldots\ldots\ldots\ldots\ldots\ldots ;$$
$$\ldots\ldots\ldots\ldots\ldots\ldots\ldots\ldots\ldots\ldots\ldots\ldots\ldots .$$

2. The market demand equations for finished goods, $m - 1$ in number:

$$D_b = \Sigma d_b = F_b(p_t, p_p, p_k, \ldots p_b, p_c, p_d, \ldots)$$
$$D_c = \Sigma d_c = \ldots\ldots\ldots\ldots\ldots\ldots\ldots\ldots\ldots\ldots$$
$$\ldots\ldots\ldots\ldots\ldots\ldots\ldots\ldots\ldots\ldots\ldots\ldots .$$

Furthermore, the quantity of factor services demanded must equal the quantity supplied and the prices of final goods must equal average costs. This gives us two further sets of equations:

3. Market-clearing conditions for n factor markets:

$$a_t D_a + b_t D_b + c_t D_c + \ldots = O_t ;$$
$$a_p D_a + \ldots\ldots\ldots\ldots\ldots = O_p ;$$
$$\ldots\ldots\ldots\ldots\ldots\ldots\ldots\ldots\ldots\ldots .$$

4. Equality of unit costs and prices for m final goods.

$$a_t p_t + a_p b_p + a_k p_k + \ldots = 1 ;$$
$$b_t p_t + \ldots\ldots\ldots\ldots\ldots = p_b ;$$
$$\ldots\ldots\ldots\ldots\ldots\ldots\ldots\ldots\ldots .$$

There are $2m + 2n - 1$ independent equations, and these are exactly equal to the number of unknowns to be determined: (1) the quantities of productive services supplied, n in number; (2) the quantities of final goods demanded, m in number; (3) the prices of productive services, n in number; and (4) the prices of final goods, $m - 1$ in number. We recall that the technical coefficients of production are fixed. In an appendix to the third edition of the *Elements* (1896), entitled "Notes on the Refutation of the English Theory of Rent by Mr. Wicksteed," Walras dropped the assumption of fixed coefficients and adopted the general marginal productivity theory. He retained the assumption of constant returns to scale, however, together with the assumption that all firms have identical cost functions. Thus, we have to take account of nm additional unknown input coefficients, but at the same time we acquire nm additional equations, namely, n equations stating the proportionality of the marginal productivities of the factor services to their prices multiplied by the m final goods in the economy. But what about the m linear homogeneous production functions? These certainly enter into the system, but they are matched by the loss of m unit cost = price equations: cost minimization under constant returns to scale already implies that prices are equated to average cost. Thus we end up with $nm + 2m + 2n - 1$ independent equations to determine $nm + 2m + 2n - 1$ unknowns. The system is "determinate," as Walras would say.

The Existence of General Equilibrium. The demonstration of the existence of a general equilibrium solution is often said to involve nothing more than the counting of equations and unknowns to insure that there are as many equations in the system as unknowns to be determined. In general, it seems obvious that this condition must be satisfied for a complete and consistent solution. Geometrically speaking, the values of, say, x and y are not determined unless we have an intersection point of at least two lines in two-dimensional space; similarly, for the values of n variables in n-dimensional space. Having two curves corresponding to two equations does not, however, guarantee the existence of a solution: the curves may fail to intersect. Nor does it preclude the existence of multiple equilibrium points: equilibrium is not unique. Moreover, it is not enough that we obtain unique solutions; we require that the system determine prices that are economically meaningful, that is, real nonnegative and finite prices. Thus the simple rule of counting equations and unknowns may easily break down.

Equality in the number of equations and unknowns is *not* a sufficient condition for the existence of a solution, let alone a unique solution. Indeed, it may not even be a necessary condition. This is a subtle point, but it can be verified very simply. It is not a sufficient condition because it is possible to find a system of two equations in two unknowns that has no solution in the domain of real numbers, the only domain that has any economic meaning. For instance,

$$x^2 + y^2 = 0,$$
$$x^2 - y^2 = 1$$

gives $x = \sqrt{\frac{1}{2}}$ and $y = i\sqrt{\frac{1}{2}}$, where the imaginary number $i^2 = -1$. On the other hand, it is not a necessary condition because $x^2 + y^2 = 0$, a single equation in two unknowns, does have a unique solution for x and y in the domain of real numbers, namely $x = 0$, $y = 0$; similarly,

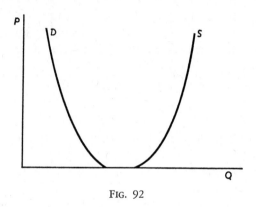

FIG. 92

the following two equations in one unknown have a unique nonnegative solution: $x = 3$.

$$x^2 - 6x + 9 = 0;$$
$$x^3 - 3x - 18 = 0.$$

The examples suggest that a unique general equilibrium solution may involve zero prices and indeed even negative prices reflecting costs of disposal. Suppose the demand and supply of some good determines a zero or negative price. It is therefore either a free good or a nuisance good. Even if it is merely a free good, it cannot be excluded from the Walrasian system. It is the market that determines which goods shall be free and which scarce. Moreover, there may be a tendency, as Menger claimed, for the range of free goods to narrow in the course of development. The Walrasian equations, therefore, must include all goods and not merely those that are normally economic goods. This is something that Walras never realized. Hence, his demonstration of the existence of a general equilibrium is unsatisfactory.

It is possible to restate the Walrasian model to allow for negative prices and quantities of goods. But negative factor prices and quantities present more serious difficulties. If the "coefficient of fabrication" is fixed and if the supply of resources is also fixed, it is easy to see that it may not be possible to satisfy the market-clearing equations for productive services at nonnegative factor prices. Obviously, they can always be satisfied at negative prices, but the notion of workers' paying firms to employ them makes no economic sense. If the supply of a factor still exceeds demand at zero prices, the factor has become "redundant." "Redundancy," not "unemployment," is the right word because the economic value of the factor in question has fallen to zero. If the factor-supply schedules are actually elastic, as Walras supposed, the possibility of this kind of structural unemployment is reduced but not eliminated. Although the supply curves are backward bending they are very likely to be positively sloped at low rates of return. Thus, as the factor returns fall to zero, the supply of productive services is reduced and the rise of "voluntary unemployment" absorbs most or all of what would become structural unemployment. The abandonment of the assumption of fixed technical coefficients likewise reduces the possibility of redundant factors. It does not guarantee its elimination, for, even at a zero wage rate, labor cannot be substituted for capital indefinitely without reducing the marginal productivity of labor below zero. But, so long as there exists any "industry" in which labor without equipment can produce a desirable commodity, it can never become redundant even at a zero wage. A standard example of such an "industry" is domestic service. In the long-run equilibrium, the marginal productivity of labor in domestic and personal service will necessarily equal the biological or cultural minimum wage; if the long-run supply of labor is not sufficiently elastic to produce this result, some institutional device of "sharing" output will spring up. The fact remains that in the context of neoclassical theory, redundancy of factors is extremely unlikely.

If the market-clearing equations for factors can be satisfied at nonnegative prices, it suggests intuitively that the other equations can also be satisfied at nonnegative prices and outputs. That this is in fact so was not rigorously proved until 1935. Wald's original proof has since been generalized and refined by Arrow and Debreu. No verbal exposition can do justice to their solution of the problem. Suffice it to say that the Walrasian system does possess an economically meaningful, though not necessarily unique, nonnegative solution, provided the "convexity" assumption is satisfied: returns to scale must be constant or diminishing, and there must be no external effects either in production or in consumption.

Stability and Determinacy. The popular view that Walras merely counted equations and unknowns to demonstrate the existence of a general market equilibrium is unjustified. Walras also tried to show how the market will solve the equations by propelling the economy toward an equilibrium. To show that an equilibrium solution exists is not enough, even when equilibrium is unique. It must also be shown that equilibrium is stable—a departure from equilibrium sets up automatic forces that bring the system back to equilibrium—and that it is determinate, meaning that the final position is independent of the path that is taken toward equilibrium.

In principle, determinacy raises problems different from those raised by stability, and, indeed, Walras's discussion of the stability conditions and the theory of *tâtonnement,* his solution to the problem of determinacy, are discussed entirely separately from each other in the *Elements.* We saw earlier that Walras's stability analysis was based on the criterion that the rate of price change varies directly with the amount of excess demand. As did Marshall, Walras always discussed unstable equilibria in the context of multiple equilibria: the unstable position is always an intermediary one between two stable positions. But Walras's instability arises from the intersection of a backward-rising supply curve of a productive service with a more steeply falling demand curve. This involves the possibility, but not the necessity, of multiple equilibria. Marshall, however, had in mind the case of instability's arising out of a forward-falling supply curve intersecting with a less steeply falling demand curve. Here multiple equilibria will necessarily be present. Neither of them realized that the two supply curves in question have different meanings. A backward-rising supply curve of a factor—it would be better to call it an offer curve—shows the maximum quantity of factor services that will be supplied at a given rate of return. A forward-falling supply curve, however, shows the maximum price at which an industry will supply a given quantity. The Marshallian criterion of positive or negative excess demand price, really positive or negative profits, which is quite plausible for the stability analysis of forward-falling supply curves, is inappropriate for the analysis of backward-rising offer curves. On the other hand, the Walrasian criterion of the sign of excess demand seems unsuitable to the analysis of Marshall's downward-sloping industry supply curves.

Walras went beyond Marshall in discussing not only stability in one market but also multimarket stability. Suppose that all prices except prices in the shoe market are in equilibrium. Applying the Walrasian rule to the shoe market, we change the price so as to eliminate positive or negative excess demand. This must upset the equilibria in other markets because their equilibrium positions are defined with reference to the initial disequilibrium price of shoes. We thus have to make further adjustments in all other markets and then again in the shoe market, and so forth. Presumably, the successive adjustments in other markets cancel each other out or diminish in significance relative to the necessary adjustments in the shoe market. In this way the whole system moves toward multimarket equilibria. This is as far as Walras carried the argument. In *Value and Capital* Hicks tried to show that multimarket stability does exist provided that strong income effects are absent. The subsequent criticism of Hicks's failure to make specific dynamic assumptions about the manner in which the system reacts to deviations from equilibrium may be said to have led to the emergence of economic dynamics as a new branch of economic theory.

The problem of determinacy as well as of stability is discussed in Marshall's *Principles*. Marshall's appendix on barter shows that equilibrium is indeterminate unless the marginal utility of one of the goods exchanged is constant. If this is not true, the final rates of exchange will not be independent of the terms on which the first exchanges were made: in the process of trial and error the respective offer curves will shift about with every exchange and a final equilibrium may not emerge. In the general case of market exchange this problem disappears in partial equilibrium analysis because the marginal utility of money of "insignificant" goods may be considered as approximately constant and hence unaffected by initial purchases at disequilibrium prices. This assumption is inadequate for general equilibrium analysis. The gains and losses of exchanging at disequilibrium prices in one market will spill over into other markets and may thus prevent attainment of multimarket equilibrium.

Walras's solution is the theory of *tâtonnement* or "groping." He assumes that buyers and sellers announce the quantities they wish to trade at prices *criés au hasard*. Reducing the price offer when there is negative excess demand and increasing it when there is positive excess demand, they continue to announce their uncommitted intentions to purchase until they hit upon a price that secures equilibrium in all parts of the market. Buyers and sellers in this way discover the true equilibrium price before they undertake to exchange any goods. In the case of the purchase and sale of productive services, it is supposed that entrepreneurs are furnished with "tickets" that are provisional contracts to buy given quantities of factor services at stated prices. The contracts are provisional in that the purchase is binding only if the stated prices turn out to be equilibrium prices for the system as a whole. This insures that the final position of equilibrium is independent of the actual path followed in reaching the equilibrium position.

Walras's theory of *tâtonnement* encompasses Edgeworth's concept of recontracting in a wider framework of stability analysis. Edgeworth assumes that buyers and sellers enter into provisional contracts in order to take advantage of the possibility of recontracting at a later date. As long as the price is in disequilibrium, someone will be willing to recontract. In the end, an equilibrium price is reached where no recontracts are to anyone's advantage, and at this point all contracts are honored and exchange takes place.

Walras's theory of *tâtonnement* has often been ridiculed; Edgeworth's theory of recontracting has by and large escaped calumny. Yet they come down to the same thing. Both theories are designed to demonstrate that in really perfect markets equilibrium is determinate because the formation of prices is not the result of acts of exchange but is already determined when exchange takes place. Walras never doubted that "value in exchange, when left to itself, arises spontaneously in the market as the result of competition. As buyers, traders make their demands by outbidding each other. As sellers, traders make their offers by underbidding each other. The coming together of buyers and sellers then results in giving commodities certain values in exchange. . . . The more perfectly competition functions, the more rigorous is the manner of arriving at value in exchange." *Tâtonnement* or recontracting is a purely analytical device to evade the problem of how equilibrium is approached by a process of trial and error in the less than perfectly competitive markets of the real world. The Walrasian theory, however, goes beyond the idea of recontracting by trying to show that equilibrium is not only determinate but also stable.

Capital Theory. To conclude our discussion of Walras, we must comment briefly on his theory of capital. Walras was the first clearly to advance the fundamental distinction between stocks of resources and the service-income flows yielded by them, a distinction that Fisher was to make famous. Walras defines resources or simply "fixed capital, i.e. capital in general" as "all forms of social wealth which are not used up at all or are used up only after a lapse of time." "Circulating capital or income" he defined as "all non-durable goods, all forms of social wealth which are used up immediately." This peculiar identification of the income yielded by resources with "circulating capital" illustrates the fact that Walras's theory of capital is solely concerned with durable producers' goods; raw materials and other goods-in-process are treated as if they are immediately consumed on the implicit hypothesis that capital goods are instantaneously constructed. Walras begins by noting that the prices of capital goods are rigidly proportional to their net yield at given interest rates. This is due to the fact that depreciation charges and risk premiums that are deducted from the annual gross revenue are said to be proportional to the price of the capital good, apparently irrespective of the magnitude of interest charges. If there are h capital goods, we thus have h present value formulas that relate the discounted value of capital goods to the known net yields via the rate of interest. We have h equations but $h + 1$ unknowns. Hence, the rate of interest is indeterminate. The situation corresponds to stationary conditions; the stationary economy, according to Walras, has no market in which the values of its capital goods are determined because no new capital goods are produced.

This argument, which drew Wicksell's objections, is clearly based on the assumption that depreciation and replacement allowances are technically given constants. As Barone pointed out, it is a simple matter to render the value of capital determinate in a stationary economy by making the reinvestment of depreciation allowances a function of the rates of interest. Walras's analysis is concentrated, however, on a growing economy, in which the cost of producing new capital goods supplies additional equations to determine the interest rate. Entrepreneurs will demand new capital goods until their yields equal the supply price of saving. With fixed coefficients of production for new capital goods, we obtain h equations stating the equality of the prices of capital goods and their current production costs. In addition, we have h further equations defining capital values as the present value of their perpetual net yields.

We now move over to the supply side. In the first three editions of *Elements* Walras simply postulated a given supply of savings. In the fourth edition (1900) he introduced a utility theory of saving by carrying over the formal analysis previously applied to consumption. To establish the direct link between utility and capital goods that have no utility, he invented a homogeneous good E which stands for a "slab of perpetual income" per unit of time. Each household has a normal demand function for E,—in effect, a normal demand function for new investment goods—whose price is the reciprocal of the rate of interest:

the greater the net yield of capital goods, the cheaper the price of E, the greater the demand for rights to perpetual net income. The unknown prices of capital goods are now replaced by the single price of E. In equilibrium, the demand for slabs of permanent income and the supply of savings must be distributed between industries according to the equimarginal rule so as to make the net yield of capital goods proportional to their values, the factor of proportionality being $1/E$ or the rate of interest. To the previous two h equations we can now add another equation, stating the equilibrium condition that the quantity of new capital goods supplied equals the quantity demanded, which in turn is equal to gross savings. In addition, we have an equation stating that the total supply of gross savings—the quantity of E demanded times its price—is a function of all prices. These $2h + 2$ equations equal the $2h + 2$ new unknowns to be determined: h prices of capital goods; h quantities of new capital goods; the interest rate as the reciprocal of the price of E; and the supply of gross savings E. With the rate of interest and the value of new capital goods thus determined, the value of old capital goods is also determined, namely, by discounting their yields by the rate of interest established in the new capital goods market.

Monetary Theory. Walras preserves the symmetry of his system by introducing circulating capital along with the demand for money-to-hold. Consumers hold two kinds of "circulating capital": stocks of consumer goods and cash balances. Entrepreneurs, likewise, hold inventories of goods and cash balances. The quantities of inventories and cash balances demanded and supplied are now derived as functions of all prices, and the usual market-clearing and zero-profit conditions are developed to show that the extended system is determinate.

In deciding how much money to hold to finance his transactions, the individual considers only the real purchasing power of money over goods and services. The total sum of the liquid real balances or *encaisse désirée* that society wishes to hold must in equilibrium equal the existing stock of money. The mechanism by which this equilibrium is achieved consists of variations in the interest rate. "The effective demand for money is a decreasing function of the rate of interest" because interest is the price of forgoing the utility derived from holding assets in liquid form. Since the marginal utility of the services of a stock of money balances must stand in the same ratio to the rate of interest as the marginal utility of any other good or service, the "price" of money must be the same in both its monetary and its nonmonetary uses; in other words, the money and the real rate of interest must be equal in equilibrium. In this way, Walras integrates the theory of money into his general equilibrium system.

Evaluation of Walras's Capital Theory. When we recall the prolix discussions of the exponents of the Austrian theory of capital over the definition of capital, the interdependence of the three "reasons," and the meaning of an average period of production, Walras's theory of capital seems extraordinarily simple and elegant. In contrast to the thousands of pages that Böhm-Bawerk and Wicksell lavished on the subject, Walras takes exactly forty pages in the *Elements* to show how the rate of interest is determined. The Walrasian theory is formally impeccable; but what is its substance? Walras went to a great deal of trouble in the fourth edition to introduce net saving as an integral part of the system, and yet he said nothing concretely about the question of the shape or character of the offer curves of saving. To treat saving simply as a demand for a special kind of consumer good, namely *E,* is unsatisfactory because saving involves a comparison between present and future utilities. Judging from one of Walras's letters to Böhm-Bawerk, he did not deny the existence of time preference. Yet he never mentioned it in the *Elements.* Furthermore, he gave no reason why new capital goods should be demanded and, if they are, whether the durability of new machines will be different from the old as a function of interest and wage rates. Indeed, he totally neglected the problem whether capital formation takes the form of widening, deepening, or shallowing. Real capital in Walras has no time structure, which raises the question: How is capital to be measured? To measure it consistently, as Walras does, in money terms is to leave unexplored the problem of the actual heterogeneity of the capital stock. No wonder Walras's theory of capital is a simple one. Despite the appearance of dealing with the problem of capital formation in a progressive economy, he really advanced a theory of how capital is to be maintained intact in a stationary state.

Here, as elsewhere, Walrasian economics is thin in substance, stressing form at the expense of content. Take the famous rule that *les entrepreneurs ne font ni bénéfice ni perte,* which underlies his unit cost = price equations. This rule is not the result of a theory of the firm or of the industry showing that zero profit is a tendency approached in stationary equilibrium. It is simply a postulate to the effect that entrepreneurship is a free service. Indeed, it is not too much to say that Walras has no theory of supply. Even the supply of productive services by households is treated only in a purely formal sense. And, although he adopted the marginal productivity theory in the third edition of the *Eelements,* he made no contribution whatever to its development. In effect he went on emphasizing the multiplication of a level of output of fixed composition involving no change in the factor proportions. His treatment of welfare economics and even his monetary theory would supply additional evidence of formalism, but the point is already sufficiently clear. Walras's contributions to substantive economics is almost solely confined to the theory of consumer behavior, where he did see much further and more clearly than his contemporaries.

"The fox knows many things, but the hedgehog knows one big thing," said a Greek poet. Walras was a "hedgehog" rather than a "fox." We may be a little charitable in overlooking the weaknesses in his works since the one big thing he did know, namely, the interdependence of all prices and quantities, was perhaps the first genuine novel idea to emerge in economics since the days of the *Wealth of Nations.*

2. PARETIAN WELFARE ECONOMICS

The work of Pareto represents a decisive watershed in the history of subjective welfare economics. Earlier writers in the utility tradition had always treated "welfare" as the sum of the cardinally measurable utilities of the individual households of the community; an optimum allocation of resources was one that maximized welfare in this sense. By the time of Marshall it was recognized that this "felicific calculus" rested on the assumption that all individuals have identical income-utility functions. In which case it followed, of course, that an optimum allocation of resources was achieved only when the distribution of income was perfectly equal.

The Benthamite postulate that the greatest total happiness is simply the arithmetic sum of the happiness of individuals evades the problem of interpersonal comparisons of utility by selecting the one case in which such comparisons raise no difficulties. Virtually all writers before Pareto in this way ignored the question of comparing different optima associated with different income distributions. Marshall worked with a concept of consumers' surplus without sufficient acknowledgment of the fact that this aggregate surplus is a function of individual variations in income. Edgeworth discarded the concept of equal capacities for want satisfaction in *Mathematical Psychics* but then defended the rule of equiproportionate sacrifice in taxation on the assumption of uniform individual income-utility functions. Wicksell criticized Jevons' and Walras's generalization of the optimum exchange conditions on the grounds that the optimum conditions of production and exchange depend on the initial factor endowments and distribution of property in the economy. Wicksell faced the problem of interpersonal comparisons of utilities more candidly than did any contemporary writer, but even he advocated specific economic policies whose effectiveness rested on the assumption that individual differences in utility could be ignored.

Pareto broke away decisively from traditional practice not so much by rejecting cardinal utility and additive utility functions as by restricting himself ruthlessly to welfare conclusions that do not depend on any interpersonal comparisons whatever. The restricted meaning of a Pareto optimum can be seen clearly by examining the marginal conditions of exchange in a perfectly competitive market. As all economists

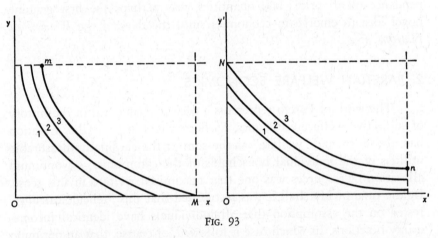

FIG. 93

since Jevons have known, the optimum conditions of exchange depend only on intrapersonal, never on interpersonal comparisons of utility.

The Optimum Exchange Conditions. Suppose two individuals are in possession of OM amounts of good x and ON amounts of good y, respectively. The indifference maps of the two individuals appear as shown in Figure 93. Following Pareto's procedure in *Manuel d'économie politique*, we now combine the indifference maps in a box diagram (Fig. 94). Every point within or on the boundaries of the shaded area represents a possible act of exchange to the mutual advantage of both parties. The slopes of the price lines MP, MP' . . . represent the ratios at which the two goods may exchange. In the case of isolated exchange, the assumption that each individual acts to maximize his satisfactions does not suffice to determine the equilibrium price at which the two goods will be traded. Trade can take place anywhere along the "contract curve" CC, being the locus of tangency points of the two sets of indifference curves.

Exchange in a competitive market, however, will always land both individuals on the same point along the contract curve, since both face the same set of given prices. If the relative price of y in terms of x is equal to the slope of the price line MP, each individual maximizes his satisfactions by acquiring additional amounts of x and y until their marginal utilities are proportional to their respective prices. Since both individuals react to the same set of prices, the ratios of marginal utilities or marginal rate of substitution for any pair of goods must be the same

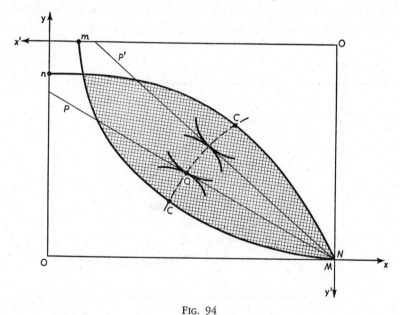

FIG. 94

for both individuals. Trade will take place at Q when the marginal rate of substitution between the two goods is the same. Q is an optimum exchange point, for neither individual can move to a higher indifference curve without pushing the other individual onto a lower indifference curve. Q is only an optimum, however, with reference to the given prices and initial quantities of x and y brought to the market. The sum of the satisfactions of the two individuals might well be higher at other points on the contract curve. Unless we are willing to make interpersonal comparisons of utility, we will have to be satisfied with the assertion that each point on the contract curve is superior only to other points within a certain limited area.

For example (Fig. 95), all points on the contract curve between

A and *B* are superior to *D* because they permit one of the individuals to move to a higher indifference curve without forcing the other individual to move to a lower indifference curve. But for that matter, *F* is also an improvement over *D*, although it is not itself an optimum point. Moreover, *F* is not comparable to either *A* or *B*, although all three are comparable to *D:* a movement from *F* to either *A* or *B* would increase the welfare of one individual, but it would necessarily decrease the welfare of the other individual. Similarly, *B* is superior to a point such as *G*, but *G* cannot be compared to *D*. An unwillingness to make interpersonal comparisons of utility means that the only changes that can be evaluated are those that make everyone better or worse off. An improvement in some people's welfare at someone else's

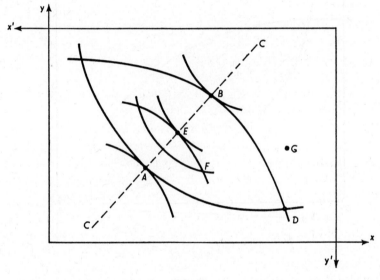

FIG. 95

expense cannot be judged. A movement *toward* the contract curve always represents an unambiguous improvement of aggregate welfare, but a movement *along* the contract curve alters the distribution of aggregate welfare among the participants in the market.

A Pareto Optimum. Pareto's formulation of a welfare maximum generalizes the results we have just achieved for the conditions of exchange. A Pareto optimum is defined as a position from which it is impossible to improve anyone's welfare, in the sense of moving him to a position that he prefers by "transforming" goods and services through production or exchange, without impairing someone else's welfare. To escape the necessity of making interpersonal comparisons of utility, Pareto refuses to evaluate "ambiguous" changes in welfare. As a result, his definition gives up the notion of a unique absolute social optimum and instead sets up an infinite number of noncomparable welfare optima. The area of comparability is extended, however, by introducing the notion of a compensating payment. This was first pointed out by Barone in a famous article on "The Ministry of Production in the Collectivist State," published in 1908 but not translated into English until 1935. Barone suggested that all changes in individual welfare can be expressed in terms of an equivalent amount of real income that the individual is willing to receive or to pay to return him to his original welfare position. The idea is a familiar one: it is nothing but a monetary measure of the consumer's surplus from a given change. A change that favors some people but harms others can now be pronounced a unanimous improvement in welfare if the gainers can compensate the losers so that they will accept the change while the gainers are still better off themselves: after the compensation payments are made, some people are better off and no one is worse off.

Barone did not insist that compensation must actually be paid, nor did Kaldor and Hicks in the 1930's. It is now realized that this is a mistake in interpretation. The fact that repeal of the Corn Laws, to select a famous example, increased the real income of consumers in general by more than it decreased the real income of landlords does not by itself prove that repeal constituted an improvement in welfare. We are tacitly assuming that a pound sterling of income yields the same utility to everybody, and that is an interpersonal comparison of utility. To avoid postulating anything about different capacities for want satisfaction, a compensation satisfactory to landlords must in fact be paid.

The insistence that compensation be paid before we pass judgment on the welfare effect of an economic change should not be construed as an argument in favor of compensation payments and, hence, the *status quo*. It is simply that, unless the losers are compensated, the proposition that free trade improves welfare involves, not only the claim that free trade improves efficiency in resource allocation, but also the alleged belief that the losses of owners in previously protected industries are outweighed by the gains to consumers in general. If we seriously believe that principles of income distribution cannot be deduced from the utility calculus by rules of logic, we must confess ourselves agnostic about situations in which compensation is only potentially feasible. It may well be that a good case can be made for failing to pay compensation, but such a case will rest on an ethical choice about income distribution, not on the "positive" grounds of allocative efficiency.

The Scitovsky Double Criterion. The effort to define a welfare optimum free from the necessity of weighing individual utilities has a respectable lineage in economics. A half-century before Pareto, John Stuart Mill distinguished between the immutable laws of production and the manipulatable laws of distribution in an effort to persuade his readers that questions about the size of the cake could be separated from questions about its division. The belief that "efficiency" and "equity" can somehow be separated represents one of the oldest dreams of economics. Virtually every economist before Pareto analyzed particular economic policies as if it were possible, first, to discuss the effects upon allocative efficiency, given the distribution of income, and then to round off the analysis by importing a value judgment about the associated changes in income distribution. The two stages of the argument were never clearly formulated, however, so it was often difficult to see just where interpersonal comparisons crept in. The value of Pareto's definition of welfare was to make the separation of efficiency from distribution crystal clear. But Pareto continued to believe that significant pronouncements about economic policy could be laid down solely on the basis of considerations of efficiency. Recent developments in the "new" welfare economics have cast doubt upon that belief.

Consider the refined double criterion of an increase in welfare introduced by Scitovsky. Before we can say that repeal of the Corn Laws increases the general welfare, we must know not only that income can be redistributed *after* repeal, so as to make everyone better off than before, but also that it is not possible to improve welfare *before* repeal simply by redistributing income. Unless this last condition is satisfied, the effect of repeal will involve more than repeal itself. It is perfectly conceivable that repeal would improve the general welfare after landlords are paid to accept the change voluntarily while at the same time it would have paid landlords to bribe consumers not to push for free trade because the required bribe is less than the contemplated loss from repeal. This produces the contradiction that free trade is inefficient from the viewpoint of the original distribution of income but efficient from the viewpoint of the final income distribution. This contradiction could not occur if free trade were a movement to utopian economic efficiency, where everyone without exception was made better off. But, normally, a change involves losses to some people, and then the double criterion must be met before we can say whether welfare has increased.

Scitovsky thus separates efficiency from equity by defining an improvement in welfare as one that, for every possible distribution of income before the change, makes everyone better off after the change, even if the compensation necessary to return to the original income distribution is actually paid. The double criterion, therefore, seems to rob us of most of the vantage ground gained by Barone's compensation principle. Once again we are barred from comparing situations with different distributions of income because these entail the weighing of individual utilities.

The double criterion for welfare is reminiscent of the index-number problem that is met in the valuation of social income when prices have changed. The question whether $\Sigma p_2 q_2 > \Sigma p_1 q_1$ has no simple meaning if both prices and quantities have changed. We can conclude only that real output has increased if a double criterion is satisfied: the value of total output must increase regardless of whether first-year or second-year prices are used as weights. In other words, we require both $\Sigma p_1 q_2 > \Sigma p_1 q_1$ and $\Sigma p_2 q_2 > \Sigma p_2 q_1$. Just as a change in prices forces us to check whether the value of output is a function of the weighting system used, so a change in the distribution of income makes it necessary to evaluate welfare in terms of the original as well as the final distribution of income. If the double criterion for an index number is satisfied, we can state unambiguously that real output has increased. This does not necessarily mean, however, that welfare has improved. Even if tastes are unchanged, each person's tastes are weighted by his total expenditure, which in turn depends on his income. Unless all goods increase equiproportionately, an increase in real output accompanied by differential price changes alters expenditure patterns and hence alters the community's valuation of social income. If the double criterion for an increase in welfare is to be satisfied, we must require that general welfare is invariant to a change in expenditure patterns and hence in the distribution of income. This calls for a particularly strong interpersonal comparison, namely, the Benthamite assertion that "each dollar vote counts the same."

Recent Welfare Economics. The "new" welfare economics descending from Pareto's work is an attempt to see how much can be said about general welfare without resort to interpersonal comparisons. The upshot of recent discussions is that very little survives once the taboo on interpersonal comparisons is imposed. This does not mean, of course, that a willingness to make interpersonal comparisons would open up an impressive range of significant theorems regarding economic policies. Nevertheless, the true function of welfare economics is to invade the discipline of applied ethics rather than to avoid it. In any working social order there is bound to be a good deal of consensus on social ends. Adopted policies, however, are almost always means toward ends that are themselves imperfectly grasped. Moreover, different ends may be in conflict with each other: consider the desirability of both full employment and price stability. The purpose of welfare economics is to influence social consensus by explicating the ends of policies and by demonstrating the consistency of particular means-ends relationships. This is no idle request for a reform of the content of welfare economics because the recent work of Arrow, Black, Downs, and others runs precisely along these lines. The future possibilities of some kind of interdisciplinary science of politics and economics largely reside in this area.

The Marginal Conditions. Once the question of income distribution has been settled by a social decision on ends, as reflected in what has come to be known as a Bergsonian welfare function, a series of marginal conditions can be set out that must be satisfied if resources are to be optimally allocated. These marginal conditions are nothing more than a set of equations that must be solved to determine the unknown amounts and prices of all goods and services allocated to each and every use. Given the Bergsonian welfare function and knowledge of the stocks of resources on hand as well as the technical constraints of production, it should be possible theoretically to solve the system of equations in terms of the unknowns. In view of Walras's contributions to the theory of general equilibrium, it comes as something of a shock to realize that the marginal conditions were never stated explicitly and in detail until very recently. Even Pareto and Barone did not go very far beyond a statement of the optimum conditions of exchange. The entire inventory of optimum conditions appeared for the first time in Lerner's articles on socialist economics in the mid-thirties, culminating in two classic articles by Bergson and Hicks in 1938 and 1939.

As a useful review of virtually the whole of neoclassical microeconomics, we will now list the more important optimum conditions. The reader can verify any of these himself by the usual equimarginal considerations.

1. *The optimum condition of exchange.* The ratio of the marginal utilities or marginal rate of substitution for each pair of consumers' goods must be the same for all households that consume both. In other words, all households must end up somewhere along a contract curve.

2. *The optimum condition of production.* Within the limits of

technical requirements the ratio of the marginal physical products or marginal technical rate of substitution for each pair of productive factors must be the same for all firms in an industry producing a homogeneous product; in other words, the marginal rate of transformation must be equal in all firms composing the industry. With the productive factors measured along the axes of a box diagram, the isoquants of any pair of firms must be tangent to each other; all firms must end up somewhere along the production contract curve. By extension, the marginal rate of transformation between any two products must be the same for any two firms that produce both.

3. *The optimum composition of output.* If conditions 1 and 2 are satisfied, the marginal value product of each factor will be the same in each industry and the prices that are used to arrive at these marginal value products will be equal to the common values for all households of the marginal rates of substitution. In the case of capital goods, the prices represent the present discounted value of their marginal value products in the consumer goods industries. Summing up, the marginal rate of substitution between any pair of products for any household consuming both must be the same as the marginal technical rate of transformation between them in production.

4. *The optimum intensity of factor use.* The marginal rate of substitution between the rate of reward for work and leisure must be equal to the marginal technical rate of transformation between hours of work and the resulting product. What this means is that it should not be possible to increase the value of output by paying a worker to shift to another occupation.

5. *The optimum intertemporal condition.* If we distinguish among inputs according to the moment of time in which they are applied and among outputs according to the moment of time they emerge, the previous marginal conditions can be applied to yield the optimum conditions for allocation of factor inputs and product outputs through time. The rate of interest on riskless securities must be equal to the marginal temporal rate of transformation between every pair of factors and products and the marginal temporal rate of substitution between every pair of factors and every pair of products. The rate of interest, that is, must equate the marginal time preferences of all individuals with the rate of return over cost. When uncertainty is present, the marginal rates of substitution between every pair of assets of different degrees of riskiness and liquidity must be equal for all households.

All these conditions may be summed up in the one grand criterion: *Between any two goods (products and factors) the subjective and technical marginal rates of substitution must be equal for all households and all production units, respectively, and these subjective and technical ratios must be equal to each other.*

Together, the five conditions constitute a necessary basis for the attainment of maximum welfare. Since they are marginal or first-order conditions, they do not suffice to guarantee a welfare *maximum*. In addition, we require second-order "diminishing returns" conditions to the effect that all indifference curves are convex and all transformation curves are concave to the origin in the neighborhood of the maximum welfare position. But, even if both first- and second-order conditions are satisfied, we cannot be sure that we have reached a *maximum maximorum:* "There is nothing in the marginal conditions," as Boulding has pointed out, "which can differentiate the top of a molehill from that of Mount Everest." For welfare to be at a maximum, the "total conditions," as Hicks calls them, must also be satisfied: it must be impossible to increase the sum of producers' and consumers' surpluses by introducing a new product or by withdrawing an old product. Provided the marginal, second-order, and total conditions are all satisfied, static welfare will be maximized. We stress again, however, that this maximum is merely one of an infinite number of Pareto optima among which we cannot choose without postulating a particular Bergsonian welfare function, that is, without postulating a scale of values for the evaluation of individual utilities. But, once we have introduced a particular method of comparing different individuals' utilities, a Pareto optimum need no longer be superior to another position that is itself suboptimal. But perhaps this is an obvious point: there always exists some weighting system that would make any position optimal.

The Optimal Characteristics of Perfect Competition. "At least from the time of the physiocrats and Adam Smith," Samuelson has observed, "there has never been absent from the main body of economic literature the feeling that in some sense perfect competition represented an optimal situation." In precisely what sense is now apparent: under *perfect* competition, all the marginal as well as the second-order conditions of a welfare maximum are automatically satisfied by the market mechanism. This is not to say, of course, that Adam Smith or any other classical economist justified a competitive economy because it achieved the static efficiency conditions of general equilibrium. We know that they defended competition largely in terms of its dynamic effects on individual incentives. But the classical argument that the flow of capital and labor levels the rate of profit and wages between industries is a disguised way of stating that the static efficiency conditions will be satisfied. The spelling-out of the marginal conditions, therefore, makes explicit one of the grounds on which competition can be and has been justified.

It is sometimes thought that the less exact requirements of *pure* competition would suffice to guarantee attainment of a social optimum: every household and firm buys or sells such a small part of the total amount of every commodity that prices cannot be influenced by individual actions; furthermore, all prices of homogeneous products and factors are uniform throughout the economy. These two conditions are necessary but not sufficient, however. In addition, all products and factors must be infinitely divisible and infinitely mobile, all economic agents must have perfect knowledge of available alternatives, and external effects in production and consumption must be absent. Obviously, these conditions, defining the characteristics of *perfect* competition, are never attained in the real world. We may ask, however, whether appropriate government intervention might not enable us to approximate the requirements of perfect competition. In particular, public operation of large-scale enterprises operating at decreasing costs would remove the chief threat to the maintenance of perfect competition. It may seem paradoxical to justify nationalization of industries on the grounds that it would buttress competition. But, as Barone was the first to realize, Paretian welfare economics demonstrates that efficient resource allocation requires perfect competition, not private ownership of the means of production. The price system is not a capitalist institution but simply a set of "coefficients of transformation," which could serve the same functions in a centrally directed economy as in a capitalist economy. The state could permit consumers and workers to maximize their own advantages while forcing the managers of enterprises to act *as if* they were private profit maximizers. After meeting the efficiency conditions, profits could then be redistributed in accordance with a value judgment about the desirable distribution of income.

Marginal-Cost Pricing. Let us look more closely at the argument for public ownership. When the optimum condition of production is restated in monetary terms, it reduces to the proposition that price must equal marginal cost. With perfect divisibility of every factor of production, perfect competition will drive all firms to minimize the average cost incurred in the production of the optimum output. What about the case of indivisibilities either in the factors employed or in the production units themselves? With bridges, railways, and utilities, overhead costs may be so heavy as to cause marginal cost to be below average cost for the entire relevant range of operations. Marginal-cost pricing will therefore lead to losses. Is it still true that even in this case the attainment of the optimum condition of production requires *marginal*-cost pricing without regard to whether or not total costs are covered by receipts from sales?

The answer is "Yes" if we are to preserve the fundamental condition that every factor will be equally productive in every use. This means that public enterprises operating at decreasing costs will have their deficits covered by public funds. This raises problems of administrative procedure because the funds themselves must be raised in such a way as not to violate the marginal conditions. On a theoretical plane, however, the more interesting question is: Should prices be set equal to short-run or to long-run marginal costs? The rule is that prices should be set so as to cover incremental costs at given factor prices. If there are any variable costs, price must equal the short-run incremental cost of producing output in order that the existing plants be used optimally. As a longer period of time is considered, more costs become variable and price must equal long-run marginal costs. For each particular period of time there is an appropriate marginal cost. In practice, it may be desirable to use a multipart price system, charging consumers one price to cover overhead costs when these can be separately imputed to each household, and another to cover marginal costs. But this is a special case, which does not invalidate the rule of marginal-cost pricing. In general, it is preferable not to attempt to make such projects as bridges and railways self-liquidating and to cover deficits by means of lump-sum taxes.

It has been argued that the need for subsidies can be avoided altogether by making prices, presumably product prices, proportional rather than equal to marginal cost. The optimum conditions will still be satisfied, it is said, even when prices are merely proportional to marginal cost. But this is clearly a mistake: if the prices of consumer goods are not equal to marginal cost, while factor payments are equal to the marginal value products of factors, the product mix will no longer be optimal and, in particular, the optimum relationship between work and leisure will be violated.

When Hotelling resurrected the concept of marginal-cost pricing for public enterprises in 1938, he advanced the general principle that subsidies to decreasing cost industries should be financed out of nonmarginal or lump-sum taxes. A lump-sum tax is by definition one that falls upon either producers' or consumers' surpluses and therefore does not violate the marginal conditions by being dependent on the activity of the individual or the enterprise taxed. He suggested that income taxes, taxes on inheritance, and taxes on the site value of land were examples of lump-sum taxes. He proposed charging a rental in addition to marginal cost in cases in which the demand for a public service at marginal cost exceeded the available supply. Using these sources of revenues, he thought that it would be possible to finance a change from average-cost to marginal-cost pricing without affecting prices, thereby increasing the general welfare. It was later pointed out that an income tax is in effect an excise tax on work. Despite the traditional presumption in favor of an income tax, an excise tax on specific commodities with low price and income elasticities may be superior in terms of welfare to an income tax that alters the marginal rate of substitution between work and leisure. With this qualification, however, the original Hotelling thesis that the adoption of marginal-cost pricing would improve the general welfare by meeting the marginal conditions has never been effectively challenged.

It will be recalled that the optimum conditions of general welfare subsumed in marginal-cost pricing do not rest on any judgment comparing the utilities of different persons. But, since the taxes required to finance marginal-cost pricing are not necessarily collected from the households that benefit from the introduction of such a scheme, it would seem that we are committed to an interpersonal comparison unless the gainers actually compensate the losers. Directly or indirectly, the introduction of a compensation payment would mean that the revenue required to subsidize a product would be derived from the consumers of the product. A tax per unit purchased would violate the marginal conditions by falling upon the margin of purchase. It would be necessary, therefore, to sell the marginal unit to each consumer at its marginal cost, the difference between marginal and average costs being recouped by charging more than average costs on the intramarginal units. But this is tantamount to abandoning marginal-cost pricing in favor of price discrimination. If this should prove impossible to adopt in practice, as is often argued, the "positive" case for marginal-cost pricing would have to be abandoned.

This objection could be dismissed if the utility of income were the same to all individuals and if factor supplies were perfectly inelastic and hence independent of the particular method of taxation adopted. But, if these conditions were satisfied, marginal-cost pricing could be defended on the basis of the "old" welfare economics. Once having admitted interpersonal comparisons of utility, however, we could easily justify the pricing of many goods at other than marginal-cost levels in terms of the existing inequalities in income distribution. Once again we see that the "new" welfare economics attempts the impossible by trying to separate efficiency from equity. It is not possible to design a price system solely on an ethically neutral criterion of efficiency and then to expect that the accompanying redistribution of income will in no way affect efficiency. The quest for an ideal pricing criterion involving no recourse to interpersonal valuation is doomed to failure.

Nonmarket Interdependence. The notion of a social optimum enshrined in the set of marginal conditions assumes that an efficient allocation of resources can be determined simply by comparing the value of output in different uses: a transfer of any factor or product from one use to another alters welfare only insofar as it results in a change in the value of output. But suppose the transfer of factors to a particular firm gives rise to external diseconomies in the form of the production of smoke as an incidental by-product of the firm's operations? Or suppose a transfer of products to some consumers diminishes the satisfaction of other consumers who are trying to "keep up with the Joneses." In all such cases, in which the various production and preference functions are interdependent, we must replace the Pareto-optimum conditions by Pigou's golden rule of welfare maximization: equalization of marginal private and marginal social costs of all resources in all uses. Direct interactions between firms and households, that is, nonmarket linkages, violate the efficiency conditions: a dollar's worth of a consumer's expenditure will no longer purchase the same value of factor units irrespective of the product acquired. We see now that perfect competition is not a sufficient condition for allocative efficiency because perfect competition is compatible with external effects in production and consumption that violate efficiency. It is also compatible with a fixed work week, which violates one of the marginal conditions, namely, the optimum intensity of factor use. And, as we saw earlier, perfect competition is not even a necessary condition for allocative efficiency because central planning could theoretically achieve the same results.

Public Goods. It is convenient to classify divergences between private and social costs or benefits under two headings. First, we have nonappropriable "real" external economies or nonchargeable diseconomies. Little more need be said on this score except to remind the reader of our earlier distinction between narrowly statical reversible economies, which alone are relevant here, and the really important irreversible dynamic economies so often associated with the activity of investment. Second, we have the case which Pigou completely ignored, namely, that of "public goods." The peculiar nature of public goods is that their consumption is necessarily joint: the more there is for one household, the *more* not the less there is for any other. This was pointed out as early as 1890 by Mazzola, an Italian writer on public finance. The joint demand for public goods has the implication, as Wicksell emphasized in his *Finanztheoretische Untersuchungen* (1896), that the market mechanism will fail to induce consumers to reveal their preferences for such goods. Each individual, if left to his own devices, will contribute nothing to public services simply because the total supply of public goods remains unaffected by his decision; everyone benefits from public goods, whether he pays or not.

Despite the fact that both nonmarket interdependence and public goods create a divergence between private and social costs, their significance for welfare economics is by no means the same.

Nonmarket interdependence can always be counteracted in principle by appropriate taxes and bounties designed to close the gap between marginal private and marginal social cost. If we can find some utopian lump-sum tax or bounty to do the job, the problem is solved in the spirit of Paretian welfare economics. For example, the marginal social product of a factory located in a residential neighborhood is much less than the marginal private product. No one household is motivated to bribe the factory to move into an industrial area, since the private cost would exceed the private benefit. Since each rational citizen is motivated to let others bear the cost while he shares in the benefit, a voluntary association of citizens is not likely to develop. But the state can levy a head tax on the residents of the area and use the funds to bribe the factory to move away. If the value of real estate rises in consequence, everyone is better off.

In the case of public goods, however, there is no question of balancing taxes collected from the beneficiaries of a change against compensating bounties paid to those harmed by the change. Public goods will not be provided at all in a purely competitive market because their benefits are indivisible: since everyone enjoys the benefits of national defense, police protection, parks, playgrounds, public roads, schools, hospitals, and the like, no matter who pays for it, everyone is motivated to evade payment, and hence the benefits are not forthcoming. But if everyone were coerced into paying his share of the cost of public goods, everyone would be made better off.

It is clear from this kind of reasoning that no market test can establish the "proper" quantity of public goods. As Wicksell realized, only a political decision through the ballot box can determine the quantity of public goods provided. It is true that there are very few examples of pure public goods: public roads really yield divisible benefits in the sense that "the more there is for you the less there is for me." Nevertheless, as long as activities have even a trace of public character, price calculations fail to drive the system to the social optimum. Irreversible external economies, previously ruled out on the grounds that dynamic changes have no place in an examination of the static optimum conditions, now come back to plague us. The divergence between private and social costs or benefits created by dynamic external effects are in reality almost always due to the "public" character of economic activity. For example, education clearly conforms to the definition of a public good. We reach the conclusion that the very distinction between static efficiency and dynamic efficiency is untenable.

Pigovian Welfare Economics. Pigou's analysis of the divergence between the marginal private and the marginal social product is confined to the problem of "real" external economies or diseconomies associated with *marginal* increments of output. But most of the cases Pigou discussed involve what Hicks has called the total rather than the marginal conditions. Examples in point are town planning and slum clearance, both of which contain degrees of "publicness." In these cases no lump-sum scheme of taxes or bounties can bring private and social cost-benefit calculations into harmony. The same thing is true of most irreversible external effects. Consider, for instance, the following list of real external *dis*economies of the dynamic type culled from the pages of the *Economics of Welfare:* industrial accidents, occupational diseases, employment of female and child labor, air and water pollution resulting from the disposal of untreated waste products, and unemployment resulting from technical change. All these cause social losses, but their removal would almost certainly violate the marginal conditions. The determination of the *physical* magnitudes of the diseconomies would itself be a difficult task, since they fall by definition outside the price system. Even if we could express them in physical terms, we could not value them subjectively without a scale of valuation, that is, without a welfare function telling us how to compare the utilities of the different victims suffering losses. Pigou's own method is to calculate social costs by adding up the direct and indirect costs associated with a given unit of investment, all valued at market prices. But if market prices reflect only private costs, not social costs, this method of valuation breaks down. It is only in partial analysis that we can employ Pigou's method. When the divergences between private and social costs are pervasive throughout the economy, we cannot use market prices as a measure of satisfactions.

Pigou used the size of the national dividend as an indicator of welfare: the national dividend is maximized only if the marginal social product or, what comes to the same thing, the marginal social cost of all resources in all alternative uses is the same. It is obvious that this definition of a welfare maximum is based on interpersonal comparisons. Moreover, the touchstone of Pigou's policy prescriptions is "the transference of wealth from the rich to the poor": if such a transfer does not diminish national income, it must improve welfare. The dependence of this kind of reasoning upon the Benthamite assumption of arithmetically additive utility functions is self-evident. But to criticize Pigou's approach because it is based on normative assumptions is to miss the point. The purpose of the book was precisely to show that a real-world imperfectly competitive dynamic economy is riddled with direct nonmarket interactions, which could be removed if we were willing to make certain "reasonable" and broadly appealing interpersonal comparisons of utilities. Pigou was not writing a theoretical treatise but a tract for the times. The "arithmetic of redistribution"—that favorite argument of Victorian conservatives against income redistribution—was the butt of his attack, and his message was that attempts to raise the income levels of the poor need not be negatived by automatic economic forces. It should be evident by now that value judgments cannot be avoided in practical welfare economics. The problem is that of making them explicit and ethically appealing. It is on the last score that Pigou's book is really open to criticism.

Conclusions. *The Economics of Welfare* seems to confirm one of the oldest of radical criticisms of the competitive system: consumers' choices as expressed in market values do not necessarily reflect the social significance of goods and services; there are utilities and not just desired ends that competition does not suitably produce. And, indeed, no one can continue to believe in the spontaneous co-ordination of private and social interests who has digested Pigou's insistence on the possible interdependence of firms and households. Even the hallowed principle of consumers' sovereignty loses its force. Suppose an excise tax on alcohol will reduce the quantity of alcohol consumed. If consumers' satisfactions are interdependent, the adoption of such an excise tax cannot be construed as a denial of the general principle that the individual himself is the best judge of his own well-being: individuals would feel themselves better off if they were simultaneously induced to drink less. The proceeds of the tax can then be used to bribe the liquor interest to acquiesce.

The existence of a "bandwagon effect" in consumption thus gives scope to government action to improve welfare. Consider now the case of the introduction of a new product. We already know that market tests fail to indicate whether a new product should be produced. Once produced, however, it may be bought by each individual because others are buying it. But if wants are interdependent, its withdrawal would leave no one worse off. Hence, consumers' sovereignty does not provide a suitable standard to weed out undesired products. The startling implications of considerations such as these in a world in which most consumer goods are differentiated are obvious.

With product differentiation, each firm is confronted with a downward-sloping demand curve. Even with zero profits—the so-called "tangency solution"—the number of firms will be larger, the average cost and price higher, and output lower than under perfect competition. But these disadvantages are counteracted by the variety of products available under monopolistic competition. If consumers' preference functions were independent, we would have to conclude that consumers were paying for the variety they desired. But, with the presence of "bandwagon" and "snob" effects, we need some criterion of the socially desirable amounts of variety, for the ordinary market test no longer has any meaning.

The trouble with Pigou's distinction between private and social costs is that it cannot be made rigorous. Paretian welfare economics, on the other hand, achieves a stringent and completely positivist definition of the social optimum. The practical relevance of this achievement for policy, however, is nil. A loose rule such as that entry into industries should be kept as free as is technically feasible has more relevance for public policy than the ideal principle of marginal-cost pricing. Pigovian welfare economics, on the other hand, is frankly normative and geared to practical applications: "it is the promise of fruit and not of light that chiefly merits our regard." It assumes a world of free competition with degrees of immobility, indivisibility, and imperfect knowledge not found in the Paretian model of perfect competition. Its shortcomings lie not so much in its dependence on normative assumptions as in its effort to depict what are really structural failures of the market mechanism as merely marginal divergences between the private and the social product.

NOTES FOR FURTHER READING

1. *Walras and General Equilibrium.* Eighty years after it was published, Walras's *Elements of Pure Economics* was finally translated into English

by William Jaffé (1954). One would have to look far and wide, even in so abstract a social science as economics, to find a book that moves so consistently on a high level of abstraction. As the translator has observed: "The argument is progressive, moving deliberately to a premeditated climax, and unless the reader moves with it in sympathy with the author's intention, the meaning is lost. The book is all the more difficult because the theory, though essentially mathematical, is expressed in primitive mathematics and then paraphrased in crabbed prose." Walras's lack of expositional clarity has led one famous economist after another to advance different interpretations of the text, only to realize later that they had misinterpreted Walras's meaning. With a book so imperfectly executed, a reader's guide would seem to be essential. Fortunately, Jaffé's sixty-page chapter-by-chapter commentary supplies this need very adequately. The reader is particularly urged to peruse the following commentaries: on the relation between Marshallian and Walrasian stability conditions, pp. 502–3; on the meanings of *rareté,* marginal utility, and *Grenznutzen,* pp. 506–7; on the maximum-satisfactions doctrine, pp. 510–11; on the *rareté* of capital goods, pp. 517–18; on the meaning of *tâtonnement,* pp. 520 and 528–29; on Gossen's utility theory, pp. 523–24; on Walras's theory of capital formation, pp. 531–32 and 536–41; on cash balances and the theory of money, pp. 542–47; and, finally, on marginal productivity theory, pp. 549–53.

A biography of Walras by Jaffé is now in preparation. For a suggestion of the rich harvest that awaits reaping see W. Jaffé, "Unpublished Papers and Letters of Léon Walras," *JPE,* April, 1935. Jaffé's translation of the *Elements* has drawn some reappraisals of Walras's work. M. Friedman, "Walras and His Economic System," *AER,* 1955, reprinted in *EET,* and R. F. Harrod, "Walras: A Re-Appraisal," *EJ,* June, 1956, express the skeptical judgment of the "literary" economist. For an enthusiastic appraisal see R. E. Kuenne, "The Architectonics of Léon Walras," *KYK,* IX, No. 2, 1956: Kuenne quarrels with some of Jaffé's commentaries.

One of the most readable discussions of Walras's system is by J. R. Hicks, "Léon Walras," *Ecom,* 1934, reprinted in *DET.* Stigler, *Production and Distribution Theories,* chap. 9, is particularly useful on Walras's capital theory. Stigler's *Theory of Price* (1952), chap. 16, provides a simplified statement of Walras's equational system in modern notation. For a laudatory nonmathematical treatment in rich detail see Schumpeter, *History,* pp. 998–1026. The student is advised, however, to leave this reading until he has developed a feeling for Walras's analytical devices. Marget, *The Theory of Prices,* Vol. II, chap. 8, part 1, defends the concept of general equilibrium against the charge of "sterility."

G. Pirou, *Les Théories de l'équilibre économique de L. Walras et V. Pareto* (1938) presents a general account of the evolution of the Lausanne School. For a brief exposition of the Walrasian system, followed by a superb review of Pareto's contributions to the theory of general equilibrium, see V. Ricci, "Pareto and Pure Economics," *REStud,* October, 1933. C. G. Phipps, "Pareto and Walras on Production," *MeEc,* April, 1954, resolves the verbal controversy between Walras and Pareto over the merits of their respective treatments of production.

The classic article on "The Determinateness of Static Equilibrium," is by

N. Kaldor, *REStud,* 1934, reprinted in *Essays on Value and Distribution.* For an excellent formulation of the problem of existence proofs see R. Dorfman *et al., Linear Programming and Economic Analysis,* chap. 13. This chapter not only discusses the famous existence-proof of Wald, but gives an elegant proof of its own. Unfortunately, the chapter can hardly be followed in every detail without a knowledge of linear programming or at least a reading of the preceding chapters 2–10. Nevertheless, even the tyro will glean many insights from this treatment; pp. 375–81, comparing the neoclassical with the linear programming model, are particularly valuable. W. J. Baumol, "Activity Analysis in One Lesson," *AER,* December, 1958, and J. R. Hicks, "Linear Theory," *EJ,* December, 1960, contain some interesting additional material on the question of existence theorems.

Patinkin, *Money, Interest, and Prices,* Note B, tries to show that the theory of *tâtonnement* is the first example of true dynamic analysis. R. G. D. Allen, *Mathematical Economics* (1956), chap. 10, and J. M. Henderson and R. E. Quandt, *Microeconomic Theory* (1958), chap. 5, discuss the Walrasian problem of multimarket equilibrium in relation to the more recent developments in dynamic stability analysis.

Walras's theory of capital formation and his monetary theory have given rise to numerous conflicting interpretations. On his theory of saving see W. Jaffé, "Léon Walras's Theory of Capital Accumulation," in *Studies in Mathematical Economics and Econometrics,* ed. O. Lange *et al.* (1942), and L. Foss, "Some Notes on Léon Walras' Theory of Capitalization and Credit," *MeEc,* April, 1957. The evolution of Walras's monetary theory in the successive editions of the *Elements* and in Walras's other writings are traced in detail in two articles by A. W. Marget: "Léon Walras and the 'Cash-Balance Approach' to the Value of Money," *JPE,* October, 1931, and "The Monetary Aspects of the Walrasian System," *JPE,* April, 1935. Despite its title, R. E. Kuenne, "Walras, Leontief, and the Interdependence of Economic Activities," *QJE,* August, 1954, with "Comment" by J. M. Henderson and R. E. Quandt, November, 1955, concentrates on the role of money in the Walrasian system and defends Walras against the charge of dichotomizing the pricing process. Patinkin, *Money, Interest, and Prices,* Note C, is a commentary on lessons 29 and 30 of the *Elements;* Patinkin insists that Walras's treatment does leave absolute prices indeterminate and that Walras cannot be described as an exponent of the cash-balance approach in the accepted sense of the term. For Kuenne's reply, see "Patinkin on Neo-Classical Monetary Theory: A Critique in Walrasian Specifics," *SEJ,* October, 1959. O. Lange, "The Rate of Interest and the Optimum Propensity to Consume," *Ec,* 1938, reprinted in *Readings in Income Distribution,* derives Keynes's theory as a special case of the Walrasian system. See also Lutz, *Zinstheorie,* chap. 6.

It may come as a surprise to many readers that Walras had a pronounced interest in applied economics. Indeed, he thought that the ultimate *raison d'être* of abstract economic theory was its potential usefulness in improving human welfare. Walras was bitterly disappointed with Pareto because the latter rejected most of Walras's cherished ideas on social reform. F. Oulès, the present holder of the chair founded by Walras, has tried to rejuvenate the emphasis on social ethics. For a systematic review of Walras's views on economic policy and the recent work at Lausanne on the concept of "social equilibrium" see M. Boson, *Léon Walras: Fondateur de la politique economique scientifique* (1950). The chapter on Walras in Hutchison, *Review of Economic Doctrines,* emphasizes Walras's views on applied economics.

2. Paretian Welfare Economics. Pareto's contributions to economics and sociology are discussed by J. A. Schumpeter, "Vilfredo Pareto, 1848–1923," *QJE,* 1948, reprinted in *Ten Great Economists,* and Hutchison, *Review of Economic Doctrines,* chap. 14. There is an interesting biography by G. H. Bousquet, *Vilfredo Pareto: sa vie et son œvre* (1928). None of Pareto's major economic works have yet been translated into English. Chapter 6 of his *Manuel* contains a statement of the concept of social optimum. In a mathematical appendix to the book, Pareto develops the marginal conditions, concluding with a demonstration that perfect competition maximizes welfare. Later, he seems to have realized that his argument provided only necessary, not sufficient, conditions for a social optimum. At any rate, the article on "Mathematical Economics" in the *Encyclopédie des Sciences mathématiques* (1911), reprinted in *IEP,* No. 5, 1955, contains nothing on the doctrine of maximum satisfaction. E. Barone, "The Ministry of Production in a Collectivist State," is available in a volume edited by F. A. Hayek, *Collectivist Economic Planning* (1935). Barone's succinct summary of the conditions of general equilibrium under atomistic competition and his suggestions of how the planning authorities might duplicate "the competitive solution" are still worth reading.

There are at least five article-length and four book-length surveys of the new welfare economics, but the most complete and concise treatment in brief is by F. M. Bator, "The Simple Analytics of Welfare Maximization," *AER,* March, 1957. This beautiful essay touches on many issues we have passed over: corner tangencies, community indifference curves, increasing returns to scale, discontinuities and kinks in the various functions, and dynamical extensions. Moreover, it provides a historical note on the literature and an almost complete bibliography. Among the items listed by Bator the following are particularly valuable for their comments on the older welfare economics: A. Bergson (Burk), "A Reformulation of Certain Aspects of Welfare Economics," *QJE,* 1938, reprinted in *REA,* Vol. I; Samuelson, *Foundations of Economic Analysis,* chap. 8; Myint, *Theories of Welfare Economics,* Part II; and W. J. Baumol, *Welfare Economics and the Theory of the State* (1952).

N. Ruggles, "The Welfare Basis of the Marginal Cost Pricing Principle" and "Recent Developments in the Theory of Marginal Cost Pricing," *REStud,* XVII, 1, No. 42, and XVII, 2, No. 43, 1949–50, are the answer to every student's prayers: a lucid critical survey of a voluminous diffuse body of literature. The first of these two articles traces the emergence of the principle of marginal cost pricing out of the Marshall-Pigou analysis of decreasing cost industries and the confusing discussion of the 1930's on socialist economics by such writers as Dickinson, Dobb, Durbin, Lerner, and Lange. The second article reviews the discussion centered on Hotelling's famous contribution, concluding that marginal cost pricing fails to satisfy the claims of its adherents. For a forgotten early contribution to the debate see J. M. Buchanan, "Knut Wicksell on Marginal Cost Pricing," *SEJ,* October, 1951. In the meantime, the debate continues: see J. Wiseman, "The Theory of Public Utility Pricing—an Empty Box," *OEP,*

February, 1957; M. J. Farrell, "In Defense of Public-Utility Price Theory," *OEP*, February, 1958; J. Wiseman, "The Theory of Public Utility Price: A Further Note," *OEP*, February, 1959. The clearest statement of the excess burden of indirect taxation is by Musgrave, *Theory of Public Finance*, chap. 7.

Bator's bibliography carries the debate down to 1957. Since then the whole field has been surveyed again by J. V. de Graaf, *Theoretical Welfare Economics* (1957), and E. J. Mishan, "A Survey of Welfare Economics, 1939–1959," *EJ*, June, 1960. de Graaf's elegant monograph pays particular attention to external effects and the less familiar difficulties of uncertainty and varying time horizons; Mishan is valuable on such problems as the construction of community indifference maps, consistent social ordering, and second-best optima. Both authors despair of the possibility of practical welfare economics. Paretian welfare economics is restated in linear programming terms in the first of T. C. Koopman's *Three Essays on the State of Economic Science* (1957). The educational value of this exercise is difficult to exaggerate: it brings the student to the frontiers of modern mathematical economics with surprisingly little pain. For a similar effort see W. J. Baumol, "Activity Analysis in One Lesson," *AER*, December, 1958.

On Pigovian welfare economics see the excellent brief discussion by Hutchison, *Review of Economic Doctrines*, chap. 18, and the critical treatment by Myint, *Theories of Welfare Economics*, chap. 10, which seems, however, to put too much stock in consumers' surplus analysis as an alternative to Pigou's marginalism. Chapter 11 of Myint's book, entitled "Towards a Broader Concept of Welfare," is one of the few places where the deeper ethical problems of welfare economics are systematically discussed. F. M. Bator, "The Anatomy of Market Failure," *QJE*, August, 1958, is the most recent treatment of the much discussed question of the actual significance of direct interaction between firms and households. See also the first chapter of Musgrave's *Theory of Public Finance* for the distinction between "social wants" for public goods and "merit wants" for goods whose social benefits diverge from private benefits.

Chapter 14

NEOCLASSICAL THEORY OF MONEY, INTEREST, AND PRICES

UNTIL THE 1930's, the quantity theory may be said with some justice to have been everybody's theory of money. This is not to say that it was universally accepted: it was attacked, vehemently and repeatedly, by a series of minor writers. But no rival theory was offered in its place, and all the leading economists adhered to some version of the quantity theory. As is well known, the quantity theory contained three main branches: the transactions approach popularized by Fisher's *Purchasing Power of Money* (1911); the cash-balance approach, developed by Marshall, Walras, and Wicksell; and the income approach associated with Wicksell and Keynes, culminating in the explicit introduction of the concept of the income velocity of money in Pigou's *Industrial Fluctuations* (1927). Fundamentally, the quantity theory drew its strength from the uniformly recurring correlation between substantial changes in the quantity of money over short periods and the price level. Not only did M and P vary in the same direction, but both the velocity of circulation and the income velocity of money exhibited impressive stability through time. The relative stability of the turnover rate of money, however, led to the tendency to treat velocity as a natural constant, thus reducing the "Equation of Exchange" to an identity rather than an equilibrium relationship. It was this oversimplication more than anything else that contributed to the downfall of the quantity theory.

Fisher and Marshall. Fisher's quantity theory, as distinct from his quantity equation, states that $P = f(M, V, 1/T)$ with M being the active variable. Popular impression notwithstanding, Fisher stopped short of anything like a rigid quantity theory. For one thing, he discussed the problem of "transition periods," which clearly indicates that the equation of exchange holds only in equilibrium. For another, he admitted the existence of a lagged relationship between the rate of interest and the price level, which allowed T to influence V and M. Finally, there is really little indication in the book that he considered V to be an institutional datum. That it was so interpreted by others, there can be no doubt. Ironically enough, his contribution to monetary theory consisted precisely in a detailed discussion of the forces determining V.

In Fisher, T is the real volume of all market transactions during a period of time and V is the number of money transfers between individuals and firms during the same period of time in connection with all purchases and financial transactions. M stands for coins, bank notes, and demand deposits, on the assumption that reserve requirements are determined by rigid conventions and that checking deposits bear a stable relationship to hand-to-hand circulation. If, instead, we define T_y as real national income per year, then V_y becomes the number of times a unit of money leaves the cash balances of ultimate income recipients during a year. The aggregate amount of money that the community may wish to hold in the form of cash balances can be expressed as a certain proportion k of real annual income. For example, a representative individual may wish to hold enough cash balances to buy one tenth of his real annual income; thus, $k = \frac{1}{10}$, $V_y = 10$, and M circulating ten times per year would be sufficient to buy T_y at the current price level. Writing $Y = T_y$, we reach the Cambridge income equation $M = PYk$. Except for the different definition of T and the associated price index, the income equation is identical to the transaction equation $M = PT/V$.

By its very formulation, the cash-balance approach focuses attention on the demand for money-to-hold. But even the transactions approach, insofar as it constitutes an explanation and is not merely the statement of an identity, embodies a theory of the demand for money. What it says is that with M autonomously determined, $D_m = 1/V = M/PT$ or $D_m = k = M/PT$. Unfortunately, these equations do not explicitly contain the rate of interest or cost of holding money, and they do not take into account the rate at which prices change as well as the level of prices. The reason for this, of course, is that the equations hold in equilibrium only when the rate of interest has returned to its previous level and the rate of price change has fallen to zero. By not writing out an explicit demand function for money, however, quantity theorists exposed themselves to a fundamental misunderstanding of their procedure. A naïve version of the theory, which gradually gained currency, held that the only motive for holding cash was that of avoiding the embarrassment of default arising out of imperfectly synchronized expenditures and receipts. Thus V or k were construed not as functions of the level of real income and the rate of interest but as institutional constants. According to the quantity theory of money, it was said, the turn-over of the money stock was interest inelastic. How much this misrepresents the best of neoclassical monetary theory, the subsequent pages will amply reveal.

Meaning of the Quantity Theory. What does it really mean to say that a writer is a quantity theorist? Friedman has recently attempted to renovate the quantity theory, and his answer to this question runs somewhat as follows: A quantity theorist believes, first of all, that the demand function for money is highly stable, at least more stable than, say, the Keynesian consumption function. This does not mean that the demand function is regarded as given: for example, the sharp rise in velocity during a hyperinflation may be consistent with the notion of a stable demand function for money if that function includes a variable referring to expected price changes. Second, a quantity theorist must assert that the factors affecting the supply of money are independent of those affecting the demand of money. This explains why quantity theorists since the days of Thorton have attacked theories, such as the real-bills doctrine, which regard the supply of bank credit as being perfectly elastic. The real-bills doctrine argues that changes in the demand for money call for corresponding changes in supply and that the supply of money cannot alter but for a change in demand because banks extend credit only on the basis of self-liquidating "real" bills. Third, quantity theorists are driven, in one way or the other, to insist on the "realness" of the rate of interest. If the rate of interest were solely determined in the money market independently of the forces of productivity and thrift, the rate of interest could be considered as being determined by the aggregate demand for money, given its supply. If interest were merely a "monetary" phenomenon, the monetary authorities could push it to any level they chose.

It is no accident that the quantity theory held sway when long-run analysis dominated economic thinking. Neoclassical writers were, of course, perfectly well aware of the problem of cyclical fluctuations. Nevertheless, the focus of analysis was always on the long-run tendencies to full employment. If, at a given price level, the public were unwilling to buy back the full capacity output—if the demand for real balances M/PT exceeded the supply PT/V—prices would fall until the existing supply of *real* balances satisfied the demand. The only thing that could cause *real* income to fall below full employment levels was inflexibility of prices. We would nowadays prefer to say that income can fall below full employment levels only if investment falls below the savings that would be forthcoming at a level of income corresponding to full employment. But with perfect price flexibility this is hardly a useful formulation of the problem. Any deflationary tendency would immediately reduce saving via the real-balance effect, thus restoring the balance between saving and investment. As long, therefore, as we can posit a fair degree of price flexibility, the quantity theory remains a useful formulation. In effect, this means that its role will be confined to analyzing inflationary phenomena and secular changes in the level of prices.

Wicksell Rehabilitation of the Indirect Mechanism. Marshall's *Evidence and Memoranda* before two Royal Commissions in the late 1880's and particularly his article on "Remedies for Fluctuations of General Prices" (1887), which presents in a short space all the essential elements of his monetary analysis, emphasize the "direct mechanism" connecting money and prices in the tradition of Cantillon and Hume. The "indirect mechanism" is by no means neglected, but it is not developed at length. Wicksell's contribution to monetary theory, on the other hand, consists of a careful restatement of the "indirect mechanism" linking money to prices via the rate of interest. In *Interest and Prices* (1898) the "direct mechanism" virtually disappears, but in the *Lectures,* Vol. II (1906) Wicksell modifies his position and combines the "direct mechanism" involving the real-balance effect with a new version of the "indirect mechanism." In view of Wicksell's writings, it is surprising that Keynes's chapter on "The Classical Theory of the Rate of Interest" in the *General Theory* was based entirely on Marshall and Pigou, both of whom paid little attention to the interrelationship between the interest rate and price movements. The Wicksellian theory is touched on by Marshall, who had learned it from J. S. Mill. Mill, in turn, derived it from Thornton. But Wicksell was the first writer after Mill systematically to develop the implications of Thornton's discovery.

The expansion of bank credit, Thorton had argued, can express itself or become effective only through a reduction in the money rate of interest. As soon as the addition of credit ceases, prices adjust themselves to the new size of the money stock and the rate of interest returns to its former equilibrium level determined by the rate of return on real capital. Following this argument, one would expect the bank rate and the general price level to move in opposite directions. But the foremost critic of Ricardian monetary theory, Thomas Tooke, author of the influential *History of Prices* (1838–57), showed that, on the contrary, the market rate of interest and the price level were positively correlated. This finding, corroborated in later days, was dubbed Gibson's Paradox by Keynes in *The Treatise on Money.* The paradox is not hard to explain when it is realized that capital accumulation and technical change tend to alter the real rate independently of monetary forces. The bank rate will therefore trail behind the real rate. What is needed to disprove the theory is not a positive correlation between prices and the absolute height of the market rate but a positive correlation between prices and interest differentials. But Tooke's primitive demonstration of Gibson's Paradox seemed to place the entire mechanism in doubt. It was Wicksell's intention to account for the paradox and at the same time to defend the quantity theory against its critics by providing a more detailed explanation of its operation. It is a striking fact that Wicksell was not aware of Thornton's *Nature of the Paper Credit* (1803) or of the echoes of Thornton's argument in Ricardo's *Principles*.

The Cumulative Process. Wicksell expounds his theory first of all on the assumption of a pure gold standard: "money" is currency only and not demand deposits; increases in demand deposits are treated as increases in the velocity of metallic bank reserves. Later, the analysis is extended to a "pure credit system," where the only form of bank reserves is central bank credit. Let us expound his theory under the former conditions.

An effective fall in the bank rate—a fall that drives the market rate downward—raises the volume of investment per unit of time and shifts up the demand function for capital goods. Under perfect competition, the prices of capital goods will rise and the prices of consumer goods will at least not fall. If the economy is fully employed, the whole wage-price level will rise. But this once again shifts up the demand functions for capital goods, and so, at a given reduction in the bank rate, the price rise becomes "cumulative." Provided reserves are held in monetary metals, however, the cumulative process does come to a halt. In the inflationary upsurge, there is an external and internal drain into hand-to-hand circulation and not only do banks run up against a legal or conventional reserve requirement, owing to the fact that the increase in deposits reduces the reserve ratio, but, what is more important, the internal and external drain depletes absolute reserves. Action will therefore be taken to protect the reserves. The bank rate will be raised to choke off the inflation. Similarly, if the price level declines through an increase in the bank rate, the progressive accumulation of excess reserves forces banks, for lack of earnings, to reduce the bank rate to stimulate borrowing. This serves to restore equilibrium.

In a "pure credit" system the reining-in effect of limited bank reserves does not exist. Here the process is truly self-generating. Although forced saving and the real-balance effect might moderate the price rise, the fact is that the monetary authorities can now determine the price level at will by appropriate variations in the discount rate. The other extreme of a "pure credit" system is a "pure cash" system in which banks are forced to hold 100 per cent of their deposits in the form of metal reserves. In this case, the "cumulative process" cannot get started. In the real world, the elasticity of bank credit is neither infinite, as in the case of a pure "credit system," nor zero, as in a "pure cash" system. The monetary authorities can start a cumulative movement, but sooner or later they are forced to bring the process to a halt.

Monetary Equilibrium. In *Interest and Prices* Wicksell spoke of the market and the "natural" rate of interest. The natural rate of interest seems to refer to the rate of interest that would exist if capital goods were lent *in natura*. This is a confusing concept because there is no single *rate* of interest in a barter economy: in the absence of money, the physical yields of heterogeneous capital goods cannot be reduced to a common denominator. It could be taken to refer, however, to a statistical average of the own-rates of commodities. But no such clumsy device is really necessary. There is evidence that Wicksell came to regret his own terminology: on the one occasion when he chose to express his theory in English, he used such phrases as "the ordinary rate," "the normal rate," and "average profits on capital" as synonyms for the "natural" rate.

Let us define the "natural" rate in Wicksell's words as "the expected yield of newly created capital." A cumulative process is said to be created by a discrepancy between the market rate of interest and this expected yield on investment. But now we run into a difficulty. Expected profits at any given moment represent a schedule of magnitudes expressing different future streams of income. The bank rate or market rate is not a schedule but a given numerical value. To it there corresponds a certain point on the schedule of expected profits. It pays to invest if the percentage yield of capital goods exceeds the going rate of interest on loans, due account being taken of risk. Since investment is always pursued to the point at which the expected stream of future returns capitalized at the prevailing market rate of interest equals the cost of capital goods, anticipated profits from marginal investment always coincide with the rate of interest, no matter what it is. In other words, there cannot be a discrepancy between the market rate and the expected yield of investment.

This difficulty may well be the explanation of Wicksell's initial preference for speaking of a rate on capital lent in kind instead of speaking directly of the anticipated money rate of profit. But the resolution of the difficulty lies in some averaging procedure. We must think of the yield of investment as an average over the long run of rates ruling at the moment. Moreover, although the marginal efficiency of investment is brought into equality with the rate of interest in every time period, net investment will continue from period to period so long as the marginal productivity of capital exceeds the marginal efficiency of investment. In a stationary economy this distinction disappears, but in a growing economy the bank rate will necessarily exceed the real yield of *capital*. If the economy is operating at full employment levels, a bank rate that preserves price stability will have to be set so as to insure that net investment does not exceed net voluntary savings.

With a stable price level, the market rate of interest will be a direct expression of the expected yield on investment. At the same time, this rate of return on investment will be equal to the bank rate. We thus have to keep in mind three, not two, different rates: the average rate of return on investment, the money rate of interest, and the bank rate. If the bank rate diverges from the going money rate of interest, the price level will begin to move, and this will create an additional divergence, as Marshall and Fisher had shown, between the money rate and the effective real rate of return on investment. With a bank rate of 5 per cent, a 1 per cent rise in prices makes the effective loan rate equal to 4 per cent, that is, equal to a 4 per cent nominal bank rate at constant prices. Thus, once prices have begun to rise, inflation is aggravated by the fact that debtors can pay back less than the real value of the funds they have borrowed. This also means that the banks are now induced to raise loan rates lest they suffer capital losses on their loans because of depreciation. In this way we arrive at Wicksell's three criteria of monetary equilibrium: the loan rate of interest is at equilibrium if it is equal to the rate: (1) "which more or less corresponds to the expected yield of newly created capital," (2) "at which the demand for loan capital and the supply of savings exactly agree," and (3) "at which the general level of commodity prices has no tendency to move upward or downward." Together, these three criteria constitute the prerequisites of "neutral money," a monetary system so managed that all disturbances from equilibrium are eliminated.

Saving-Investment Concepts. Saving and investment in Wicksell's system are not equal by definition as they are in the Keynesian system: $Y \equiv C + I$, $S \equiv Y - C$, and, therefore, $S \equiv I$. With Keynes of the *General Theory*, but not Keynes of the *Treatise*, saving and investment refer to the same period of time. On the other hand, when Wicksell speaks of an excess of investment over saving as creating inflation, he means an increase in the money value of output that is not translated into disposable income in the time period under consideration. Likewise, when he refers to saving's exceeding investment, he is thinking of the attempt to postpone consumption, which produces a cumulative fall in prices and in the money value of output. Perhaps Robertson's schema comes closest to systematizing Wicksell's conception of saving and investment. If we let the superscripts e and d refer to earned and disposable income and the subscripts refer to the appropriate time periods, we have

(1) $$Y_t^e \equiv C_t + I_t .$$
(2) $$S_t \equiv Y_t^d - C_t \equiv Y_{t-1}^e - C_t$$

Equation (1) states that today's earned income is spent today. Equation (2) states that today's saving is equal either to today's disposable income minus today's consumption or to yesterday's earned income not consumed today.

From (2), we have

(3) $$Y_{t-1}^e \equiv S_t + C_t .$$

Subtracting (3) from (1), we therefore have

(4) $$Y_t^e - Y_{t-1}^e \equiv I_t - S_t .$$

Thus, when $I_t > S_t$, income is rising, and vice versa when $S_t > I_t$.

The now familiar neo-Keynesian distinction between planned and realized saving and investment, with realized saving and investment always equal by definition but planned saving and investment equal only in equilibrium, is derived from Myrdal and Lindahl, the Swedish heirs of Wicksell's monetary theory.

In this setup, planned consumption is always realized, but *ex ante* saving and investment need not equal *ex post* magnitudes. Writing subscripts p and r for planned and realized variables, the strategic definitional identities are as follows:

(1) $$S_p \equiv Y_p - C .$$
(2) $$Y_r \equiv I_r + C .$$
(3) $$C \equiv Y_r - I_r .$$

Subtracting I_p from (1) we have

(4) $$S_p - I_p = (Y_p - C) - I_p .$$

Substituting (3) into (4), we obtain

(5) $$S_p - I_p = [Y_p - (Y_r - I_r)] - I_p$$
$$= (Y_p - Y_r) + (I_r - I_p) .$$

Thus, an excess of planned saving over planned investment implies either a deficiency of realized as compared with expected income or, since investors' capital equipment spending plans are assumed to be carried out, an unintended increase in inventories, or both.

Price Stabilization. To return to Wicksell's argument: the three criteria of monetary equilibrium must be satisfied simultaneously. The market rate of interest is determined by the demand and supply of loanable funds. The demand for loanable funds consists of investment demand *plus* demand for inactive cash balances. The supply of loanable funds consists of personal and business savings *plus* bank credit. If investment demand and intended savings are in equilibrium, a stable price level implies that net credit creation is absorbed into inactive balances.[1] This can mean only that the bank rate is equal to the market rate and the latter, in turn, is equal to the real rate. No matter where we begin,

[1] Lerner's graphic treatment (Fig. 96) of the loanable funds theory of interest brings this out. $S + M$ is the total supply of loanable funds: S is the supply out of planned private and business savings, and M is the supply through net credit creation. $I + H$ is the total demand for loanable funds: I is the investment demand and H is the demand for purposes of "hoarding." All functions are defined for a given income.

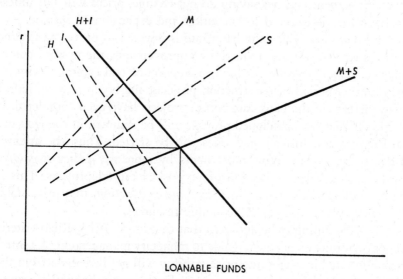

LOANABLE FUNDS

FIG. 96

The distinction between this theory and Keynes's liquidity preference theory is analogous to the distinction between investment theory and capital theory. Liquidity preference theory is concerned with an asset-holding equilibrium in which the demand and the supply of the money stock are equal. Loanable funds theory considers hoarding and dishoarding as a flow of funds that are nonzero in value when the stocks are in disequilibrium. In equilibrium the two theories yield identical results.

we always end up having to satisfy all three criteria before we can conclude that the money market is in equilibrium.

A new difficulty now presents itself. As Wicksell's friend Davidson pointed out, economic growth involves continuous increases in productivity. If prices are to be kept stable, the money supply will have to
increase with the rate of increase of productivity. Thus, the bank rate
will have to be low enough to induce a net inflow of money into circulation through loans or open-market operations. But then the bank rate
that will stabilize prices will be below the rate at which the demand
for investment funds will equal the supply of savings. Or, to state it in
another way, in order to preserve monetary equilibrium, banks should
always tailor their lending to liquidity preferences by furnishing no
more than demands for inactive balances. But, if they obey this rule,
prices will fall with every reduction in inputs per unit of output, thus
disturbing the established equilibrium. It is not even necessary to assume
technical change, Davidson might have added. The fact that investment
is capacity-creating will produce the same difficulty. In every period, net
investment will increase the potential output of subsequent periods.
If net investment and net saving do not change, prices will fall unless
the bank rate is lowered to encourage the expansion of income.

Furthermore, when the bank rate is lowered to prevent a decline
in prices resulting from productivity improvements, the upward cumulative movement encourages the construction of real capital. Owing to
the gestation period of construction projects, the boom may be halted
by an increase in the bank rate before projects have been completed. It
is unlikely that the abandoned projects will be resumed in the next upward movement. Instead, new ones will be started. Thus, the attempt
to damp down cumulative movements by monetary policy may give
rise to an increasing collection of unfinished capital projects. This is
the basis of Hayek's charge, in *Prices and Production*, that price stabilization involves a waste of economic resources.

It is beginning to be apparent that the simple Wicksellian criteria
do not constitute an adequate guide to monetary management. A central
bank interested in preserving price stability will get little help from the
maxim that they ought to maintain equality between the market rate of
interest and the average rate of profit on capital. In fairness to Wicksell, however, we should note that he himself pointed out the difficulties of averaging the net yields of investment, the inadequacy of most
existing price indexes, and the impossibility of stipulating anything but
a gross divorce between the two rates. Moreover, he used his own theory primarily to explain secular changes, such as the deflationary move-

ment of the Great Depression of 1873–1897. Such secular swings in
the price level, he argued, were fundamentally due to the failure of
monetary policy to adjust to the decline in the "natural" rate caused
by capital accumulation.

By defining the prerequisites of "neutral" money, Wicksell recognized that money need not be neutral. Unless banking policy under-
takes positive action, "spontaneous" changes in the "natural" rate will
lead to oversaving. It is one of the peculiarities of Wicksell's theory that
it starts out by picturing the banking system as a passive agent tailoring
its loan rate to the yield of investment and ends up by advocating active monetary policy to achieve price stability. The technical shortcomings of the theory are largely due to its starting point. By the time
we reach the conclusion, we have developed all the pieces which, when
fitted together, supply a complete rationale for monetary management.
The value of the exercise is that here, for the first time, monetary forces
are clearly brought into play to explain the level of aggregate economic
activity.

Expectations. We noted earlier that Wicksell brings the "cumulative process" to a halt by the actions of banks to protect their reserves.
He ignored the stabilizing tendencies of forced saving and the real-
balance effect. Furthermore, he paid no attention to changing expectations. We must now ask whether the idea of a cumulative movement is
not in fact dependent on certain assumptions about the state of expectations.

Wicksell starts from a situation of static equilibrium and then de-
duces the effects of a lowering of the bank rate. In the static state, expectations are determined by the results of previous periods. Wicksell
assumes that this is also the case during the cumulative process. Given
the background of static equilibrium, it is reasonable to assume that
producers regard the rise in the price level as temporary. This means
that, while the current prices of capital goods are above normal levels,
the prices of output accruing in the future are expected to fall back to
normal levels. Hence, the calculated net yield of current investment
must fall, causing investment to sink below normal. To be sure, the cost
of borrowing has declined, but, since producers also expect the price of
capital goods to fall back in the future, they will postpone investment.
In fine, when expectations are governed by normal price situations, we
will get alternative swings of investment and prices around the normal
level, instead of a cumulative process.

Wicksell's analysis implicitly assumes that expectations are not
governed in the way described above. Indeed, his system is entirely de-

pendent on what Hicks has called an "elasticity of expectations of un-ity," meaning that a change in current prices changes expected future prices in the same direction and in the same proportion. The argument really has nothing to do with a peculiarity of monetary equilibrium. Whenever future prices are expected to move just as spot prices do, any disturbance from equilibrium sets off cumulative instability. If, every time we demanded more bread, not only the spot price but also the price expected in the future were to rise, equilibrium in the bread market would never be established. Wicksell did at one point admit that producers may begin to anticipate price increases—the case of elastic expectations—in which case the cumulative process "creates its own draft." But he did not realize that the very notion of cumulative instability rests on the assumption that people expect future prices to rise as fast as current prices.

Keynes and Wicksell. The contrast between Wicksell's mone-tary theory and Keynes's income-employment theory rests fundamen-tally on the Keynesian divorce between saving-investment equilibrium and employment equilibrium via the notion of rigid wages, interest-inelastic investment demand and "the liquidity trap." Insofar as there is underemployment equilibrium, this throws the emphasis of remedial action on fiscal policy rather than on monetary policy. As long as the full employment ceiling has not been reached, changes in the price level are regarded as purely adaptive in nature and subordinated to fluctuations in real output. The Keynesian model of income determi-nation, with its building bricks of the consumption function and the multiplier, have, of course, no counterpart in Wicksell. Government expenditures, a neglected source of income and price variations in Wicksell, now enter the picture on the same footing as private expendi-tures. Once we pass the full employment ceiling, however, it looks al-most as if we are back in the Wicksellian world. As long as inflation is a phenomenon of aggregate excess demand, Keynesian analysis agrees with Wicksellian theory in holding that the process is "cumula-tive." There are automatic checks to the inflationary process, but it is agreed that these will rarely suffice to eliminate an inflationary gap. First of all, there is the Pigou Effect, or what we have called the real-balance effect: people decrease their flow of spending because they feel that the real value of the stock of money is too small for their needs. Next, there is the diversion of resources from consumers to investors through forced savings, with the new proviso that, if fixed income groups have a higher than average propensity to consume, the aggregate consumption function will shift downward. Third, there is the dim possibility of inelastic price expectations: people postpone their spending because they do not expect prices to continue to rise. Fourth, there are lags in wage adjustments that can slow down inflation but can never eliminate it. This does not carry the argument very far beyond Wicksell. But now come the really new elements. The Keynes Effect states that a rise in prices lagging behind an increase in the money supply will raise the rate of interest by raising the transactions demand for cash, thus discouraging investment. This will not entirely stop inflation because the rise in interest rates is moderated by the fact that it frees speculative balances to meet some of the new transaction needs—the notion that people hold speculative balances is missing in Wicksell. Finally, there are "automatic stabilizers": for example, tax collections will rise faster than prices as a result of the progressive income tax, thus curtailing consumption spending.

A modern banking system is very nearly a Wicksellian "pure credit" system, not in the sense of 100 per cent reserves but in the sense that the banks hold large amounts of perfectly liquid government bonds. It would seem that this should strengthen the significance of Wicksell's analysis. But, in fact, monetary policy has not come into its own in the recent inflationary period. One reason is the belief in the increasing significance of cost-push inflation created by a declared government policy of "full employment at whatever cost": if unions impose a higher money wage rate at full employment, the government is committed to ratify the inflation by deficit spending to prevent unemployment. This makes the supply of money a dependent variable in the analysis. A hard-money policy to fight inflation seems to conflict with the objectives of a high rate of growth. Monetary policy nowadays appears to be permanently subordinated to the exigencies of the international power struggle. The widespread acceptance of the doctrine of "creeping inflation" shows how far we have traveled from the neoclassical belief in the virtues of price stability.

READER'S GUIDE TO WICKSELL'S *LECTURES*, VOL. II

The presentation of Wicksell's own monetary theory is squeezed in between long sections on earlier monetary theory, monetary history, and various currency systems. This is true both of the presentation in *Interest and Prices* and in the *Lectures*. The latter, however, took into account some of the criticisms that the earlier volume had received. In the last year of his life, Wicksell made further concessions in an article with the title "The Monetary Problem of Scandinavian Countries," appended to the English edition of *Interest and Prices.*

Velocity. The second volume of the *Lectures* opens with an excellent introduction on the functions of money. Wicksell assumes here that the money system is a "properly functioning one": savings are immediately converted into investment via the intermediary activity of banks, and there is no hoarding of coins or bank notes. The second chapter, containing historical material, may be passed over without much loss. Chapter 3 takes up the crucial problem of the demand for cash balances as reflected in the magnitude of V. Given the quantity of money, "the average period of idleness" k is the reciprocal of V, the transactions velocity of money. The determination of V presents profound problems, Wicksell notes, because it varies with the payment habits and degrees of vertical integration in an economy. The motives for holding cash consist of transactions and precautionary motives (p. 71). The use of credit amounts to a "virtual" transfer of currency; credit increases the transactions velocity of a given stock of money (p. 67). In a "pure cash" economy V would be an institutional constant and the rigid quantity theory of money would hold without qualification. But with the introduction of credit, V becomes a function of economic variables governing the degree of liquidity preference.

The evolution of banking institutions is pictured in terms of the progressive substitution of credit for metallic currency (pp. 71–87). Ultimately, this leads to the "ideal bank," the case of a "pure credit" system: all money is in the form of demand deposits and bank notes (pp. 84–87). There is no longer any danger of an internal drain from credit expansion, and the banks can bring about any specified price level by discount policy. One difficulty of the pure credit system is the need for gold in international settlements. This leads Wicksell to a discussion of banking policy under gold standard conditions (pp. 91–122). The statement of the "characteristic features" of the modern banking system (p. 80) does not mention the power to "create" deposits, but Wicksell nevertheless seems to be aware of the phenomenon (see pp. 86–87). Wicksell fails to distinguish between one bank, which cannot "create" deposits unless they are backed by excess reserves because of the possibility of withdrawals, and all banks, which can together "create" unbacked deposits. This crucial distinction appears in some of the older literature but was not forcefully brought home to the profession until the publication of Phillips' *Bank Credit* (1920).

The Demand Curve for Money. The traditional problems of index-number theory are discussed in the opening pages of chapter 4. Next, Wicksell proceeds to a masterful defense of the quantity theory of money. In holding that the exchange value of money varies inversely with its quantity, quantity theorists assume that the market-equilibrium curve is a rectangular hyperbola (p. 142). Wicksell does not assume, as did Marshall and Pigou, that the demand curve for paper money or for gold in its monetary use is a rectangular hyperbola. Wicksell's curve varies both the amount of money and the level of prices; it is a locus of intersections of demand and supply curves of money.

This point requires explanation (see Fig. 97). Let D_1 and S_1 represent the market demand for and supply of *nominal* money balances. The intersection at A determines the equilibrium price level P. Each individual demand curve for nominal balances is downward sloping because at higher prices the typical individual will want to hold more money balances. The precise shape of the curve depends on how the desire to hold *real* balances competes with the desire to hold commodities. In the normal case, when neither real balances nor commodities are "inferior goods," the individual, and therefore the market demand

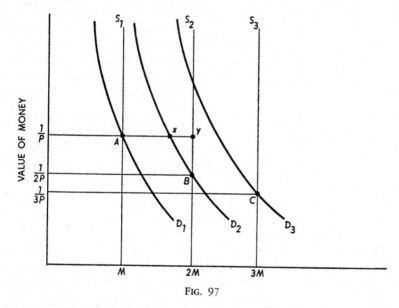

FIG. 97

curves, will slope downward at an elasticity less than unity. A demand curve of unitary elasticity would mean that an individual would want to hold the same amount of real balances when prices fall despite the fact that he is better off. But the typical individual will reduce his nominal balances to buy more goods when prices fall at given levels of real income. This is the real-balance effect that Wicksell states in so many words (pp. 142–43).

Suppose now that M is doubled and distributed equiproportionately to the initial money endowments of individuals. The demand curve for money will shift to the right because, with more money but the same absolute prices, people will want to buy more commodities and therefore will want to hold more nominal balances to finance their increased transactions. There is now an excess supply of money xy, which is identically equal to the excess demand for commodities. The excess demand for commodities drives up P until prices have doubled at $1/2P$. Prices must rise in the same proportion as money, for otherwise there will be idle balances that someone does not want to hold. These would act to drive prices up further. Irrespective of the shape of the demand curve, point B must lie on D_2 corresponding to $2M$ and, of course, it must lie on S_2. Likewise, C must lie on D_3 and S_3 corresponding to $3M$.

Consider now a curve connecting ABC, being a locus of the intersection points of the demand and supply curves. This curve will be a rectangular hyperbola connecting M with the corresponding equilibrium levels of money prices. Being a rectangular hyperbola, the product of the abscissa and the ordinate values of every point of the curve remain constant. But since the ordinate values show the relative price of money—the amount of real income that must be surrendered to acquire one unit of money—the area of the subtended rectangle shows the *real* value of the amount of cash balances demanded. In other words, the market-equilibrium curve ABC shows the demand of all individuals for nominal balances at alternative price levels when the real supply of cash balance stays the same. Individuals have no incentive to change their demand for real balances if both the money supply and the price level vary in the same proportion. In equilibrium, money is "neutral" because all "real" magnitudes, including the rate of interest, do not change.

Walras, Marshall, Pigou, and many other writers in this period were fond of the theorem that the demand schedule for money has unitary elasticity throughout its range. They regarded this as a deduction from the theorem that a doubling of the money stock doubles absolute prices. But just as an increase in M with P constant leads to a less than proportionate increase in the amount of *nominal* balances demanded, an increase in P with M constant also leads to a less than proportionate increase in *nominal* balances demanded. In the absence of a "money-illusion," the demand curve for money will have an elasticity less than unity. Marshall and Pigou confused the curve along which money balances and prices are always in equilibrium with the true demand schedule for cash balances. This confusion may well be due to the fact that Marshall always placed price on the vertical axis irrespective of whether it was the dependent or the independent variable in the argument. Wicksell, who always followed the traditional mathematical practice of measuring the independent variable on the horizontal axis, was less likely to become confused between individual and market demand schedules, price being an independent variable in the first case and a dependent variable in the second.

The proposition that market demand curves for money are necessarily rectangular hyperbolas is tantamount to postulating the rigid quantity theory. It amounts to saying that T/V is always a constant and hence sets up the identity $MV \equiv PT$. The point of the real-balance effect is to show that the public's desire to "hoard" at a given money supply is not the same regardless of the level of prices and the rate of interest. As Wicksell justly observes: "It will be readily seen that the whole dispute [about the quantity theory] turns ultimately on this last point: whether the velocity of circulation of money is of an autonomous or merely subordinate significance for the currency system" (pp. 143–44).

The Direct and Indirect Mechanism. The difficulties of verifying the quantity theory empirically are briefly discussed (pp. 144–45). There is a brief mention of Cassel's "Law of 3 per cent": using 1850–1910 data, Cassel argued that the annual increase in the stock of gold must be in the order of 3 per cent to keep prices stable (p. 145). Cassel's method of analysis has been much criticized: it was shown subsequently that there was little if any correlation between the rate of increase in the supply of gold and the rate of expansion in bank notes and deposits over the period 1850–1910. But this objection may rest on defective statistical data. It appears that the growth of total media of payments from 1870–1914 did vary directly with the gold supply (*QJE*, August, 1957).

The relative cost of producing the monetary metal determines the supply of money under a gold standard. International price levels are governed by the comparative "cost of obtaining gold" (pp. 146–48). Contrary to Marx's belief, a commodity theory of money is perfectly compatible with the quantity theory (p. 149). But the dangers of the commodity theory are the tendency to overlook V or to regard it as a purely passive variable (pp. 149–51) and the failure to explain the value of an inconvertible currency (pp. 151–52). Absolute prices cannot be explained by propositions about relative prices (pp. 154–55). Ricardo showed that a rise of wages in all industries, including the gold industry, cannot raise absolute prices but merely alters relative shares (pp. 156–57). The classical proposition that a "higher standard of living" implies higher absolute prices, inasmuch as the higher standard suggests a greater efficiency in "obtaining gold," must be qualified by the nature of imports and exports and by transport costs (pp. 157–58). A general rise in prices implies excess demand for money or excess supply of commodities. "This may sound paradoxical," Wicksell comments, in the light of Say's Law. But Say's Law refers only to the "ultimate" state of equilibrium (p. 159). "Any theory of money worthy of the name must be able to show how and why the monetary or pecuniary demand for goods exceeds or falls short of the supply of goods in given conditions" (p. 160). Notice the recognition of the real-balance effect in the reference to Hume's exposition of the "direct mechanism" (pp. 160–61).

The effect of the discovery of new gold fields is brilliantly analyzed (pp. 161–64). The gold-mining country will incur an import surplus through an upswing in activity, which will tend to distribute gold to the rest of the world. Prices will rise in the gold-receiving countries, and in consequence the demand for investable funds as well as the real rate of return on investment will rise in these countries. If the banks are "fully loaned up" before the gold discoveries, they will now find it necessary to raise the bank rate. Not only will the rise in prices precede the rise in the rate of interest, it may even precede the increase in the money supply. Since the gold producers import on credit, the increased demand for imports may raise prices everywhere before gold has actually started to flow between countries. Once prices and interest rates have risen, the subsequent arrival of gold merely serves to keep prices up (pp. 164–65; see also pp. 197–98 and p. 215). For such transitional periods, Tooke's objection that periods of rising prices are periods of rising, not falling, interest rates and that the rise in prices generally precedes the increase in the money supply is sustained. Nevertheless, in the long run, the increase in the money stock is accompanied by a secular decline in interest rates. Notice the passing comment on the distinction between the nominal and the effective real rate of interest (p. 168).

The reliance on convertibility as a check to excessive note issue constitutes the essence of the "currency principle" (p. 171). As has been so often pointed out, this ignores the possibility of expanding credit through checking deposits (p. 172). The "banking principle," on the other hand, leans heavily on the discredited real-bills doctrine (p. 173). Tooke's contraquantity theory, with its distinction between note issue against government bonds and note issue against commercial loans, is disputed (pp. 173–74). J. S. Mill argued correctly that restriction of discounts to "real" bills would not insure stability either in the quantity of money or the volume of credit (pp. 174–75).

The Two Rates. The concept of divergence between the market and the "natural" rate of interest is now introduced by way of a discussion of Ricardo's and Tooke's monetary doctrines. Wicksell shows how Ricardo's preoccupation with the causes of the premium of bullion over paper, as well as the existence of the Usury Laws, stood in his way in analyzing the relationship between the interest rate and the price level (pp. 172–82). Tooke's stress on the cost aspects of interest at the expense of every other consideration led him to absurdities: the money market turns out always to be in unstable equilibrium (pp. 182–87). Notice the assumption that the elasticity of expectations is "normally" unity (p. 185). Now we are ready for the "positive solution." The money rate of interest is at its "normal" or "natural" rate if it corresponds to the rate of return on real capital, equates the supply of and demand for real savings, and is neutral in its effect on the price level (pp. 192–93). All this assumes full employment of resources (p. 195). As long as bank credit is perfectly elastic, any divergence of the market rate from the real rate brings about a cumulative process (pp. 196–97). The only limit to the process is an internal, and perhaps also an external, drain (pp. 198, 200–201). If the banks lower the market rate, the rise in prices may be arrested by forced saving; but forced saving will have to outweigh the decrease in voluntary saving caused by the decline in the market rate (p. 199). Davidson's objection that price stabilization may throttle growth is obscurely contested (p. 199).

Now, finally, Wicksell resolves Gibson's Paradox. All variations in the level of prices not brought about by changes in gold production have their origin in a passive bank rate trailing behind the active real rate. Statistics about prices and interest rates fail to reveal the dynamics of the process (pp. 202–8).

Business Cycles. A theory of the trade cycle involving overinvestment in the boom is sketched very tersely (pp. 209–14). Wicksell's article referred to on page 209 has now been translated under the title of "The Enigma of the Business Cycle," reprinted in *IEP*, No. 3, 1953. It is noteworthy that Wicksell repudiates a monetary theory of the business cycle (p. 209). These pages and a reading of Wicksell's article will dispel the idea that he was one of those so-called "classical" economists who argued that price and wage flexibility would automatically banish the problem of cyclical unemployment.

Currency Reform. In the last pages of the book Wicksell tries to reconcile his previous argument for internal price stabilization with the international gold standard mechanism. As long as a country is on the gold standard, its central bank is not free to stabilize internal prices irrespective of the relationship between domestic and world prices. His way out of this dilemma is the concept of an international clearings union to divorce the value of money from that of gold: the central banks of different countries must agree to redeem each other's currencies at par in their respective national currencies. Moreover, they must agree to follow a common discount policy with reference to an index of international prices (pp. 119–26, 216–17, 221, and 223). Significant changes in gold production under gold standard conditions are not the only causes of price movements beyond the control of banks. Countries on an inconvertible paper standard may inflate by fiat issues of paper notes or by large-scale government borrowing from the central bank (pp. 166–68). The latter, as well as rapid changes in productivity, constitutes the most important causes of changes in the price level in recent decades. And it is precisely on these points that Wicksell's theory of monetary equilibrium as a guide to banking policy broke down.

NOTES FOR FURTHER READING

The fundamental content of the quantity theory is admirably expressed by Hegeland, *The Quantity Theory of Money,* chap. 10; chaps. 5 and 7, on the Cambridge School and on the Swedish literature, are also helpful. Schumpeter's treatment covers a broader front and is particularly useful in correcting misconceptions about Fisher's version of the theory: *History,* chap. 8, pp. 1074–1122. For a brief description of the income approach to monetary theory see A. H. Hansen, *Monetary Theory and Fiscal Policy* (1949), chaps. 3 and 6, or Hutchison, *Review of Economic Doctrines,* chap. 21. The history of the income approach is discussed in great detail by Marget, *Theory of Prices,* Vol. I, chaps.

12–13. The present status of the theory of the demand of money is canvassed by J. C. Gilbert, "The Demand for Money: The Development of an Economic Concept," *JPE*, April, 1953; it emphasizes the necessity of paying attention to the role of uncertainty. The "Chicago" tradition in monetary theory, established by H. C. Simon and L. W. Mints, has been carried on in recent years by M. Friedman: see his essay, "The Quantity Theory of Money—a Restatement," in *Studies in the Quantity Theory of Money*, ed. M. Friedman (1956).

A summary of Wicksell's ideas in his own words is to be found in "The Influence of the Rate of Interest on Prices," *EJ*, 1907, reprinted in *Source Readings in Economic Thought*, ed. P. C. Newman *et al.* (1954). Keynes pays tribute to Wicksell in a famous chapter of the *Treatise on Money* (1930), entitled "The 'Modus Operandi' of the Bank Rate." For a typical example of the development of Wicksell's ideas into a monetary over-investment theory of business cycles see G. Cassel, "The Rate of Interest, the Bank Rate, and the Stabilization of Prices," *QJE*, 1928, reprinted in *Readings in Monetary Theory*, ed. F. A. Lutz and L. W. Mints (1951). Marget, *Theory of Prices*, Vol. I, chaps. 7–9, provides *inter alia* a detailed analysis of the various meanings assignable to the concept of the "natural" rate of interest. The publication of Myrdal's *Monetary Equilibrium* (1939) gave rise to a re-examination of Wicksell's criteria of monetary equilibrium. See H. Neisser, "Monetary Equilibrium and the Natural Rate of Interest," *SR*, November, 1941; J. Marschak, "Wicksell's Two Interest Rates," *SR*, November, 1941; T. Palander, "On the Concepts and Methods of the Stockholm School," *ET*, 1941, reprinted in *IEP*, No. 3, 1953. The last of these three articles is a brilliant critique of the operational significance of Wicksell's theory for practical monetary policy. R. Frisch offers a rigorous synthesis of Wicksell's "real" and "monetary" theory of interest in a hitherto unpublished essay "Wicksell," *DET*. The reader is warned that this is a very difficult and at times somewhat obscure article. See also Hicks's marvellously succinct statement of the indeterminacy of absolute prices in Wicksell's model of the cumulative process: *Value and Capital*, pp. 251–54.

For a critique of neoclassical monetary theory and the contrast between neoclassical and Keynesian interest theories see D. Patinkin, *Money, Interest and Prices*, chaps. 8 and 15. The book also contains several valuable historical notes. Note D deals with the bogey of "circularity," which has prevented one writer after another from applying marginal utility analysis to money. Note E discusses Wicksell's monetary theory. Note F quotes Fisher on the real-balance effect. Note G deals with the Marshallian notion that the demand curve for money has unitary elasticity. Note H dissects the third book of Cassel's *Theory of Social Economy* (1918), a notorious example of the "invalid dichotomization" of the pricing process. Note J shows the recognition of both classical and neoclassical economists of the permanent influence of a monetary change on the rate of interest in case of forced saving. For a discussion of the forced-saving doctrine, in its various guises old and modern, see F. Machlup, "Forced or Induced Saving: An Exploration into its Synonyms and Homonyms" *REStat*, February, 1943. For an excellent review of the analytical issues in the long debate over "the indeterminacy of absolute prices" in neoclassical monetary theory see S. Valavanis, "A Denial of Patinkin's Contradiction," *KYK.*, VIII, No. 4, 1955.

The evolution of Wicksell's ideas on monetary policy in the course of the debate with Davidson are traced in great detail in Uhr, *Economic Doctrines of Knut Wicksell,* chaps. 10–11. "Explanations of the Great Depression," by such leading economists as Marshall, Wicksell, Fisher, and Cassel, are canvassed by W. W. Rostow, *British Economy of the Nineteenth Century* (1948).

Chapter 15 : KEYNES VERSUS THE CLASSICS

THE MODERN neo-Keynesian theory of income determination can be represented by five equations:

(1) The income function: $Y = C(Y, r) + I(Y, r)$.

(2) The demand for money balances: $\dfrac{M}{P} = L(Y, r)$

(3) The aggregate production function: $Y = f(N)$
  with $f'(N) > 0$ and $f''(N) < 0$.

(4) The demand for labor: $f'(N) = \dfrac{w}{P}$

(5) The supply of labor: $N = f\dfrac{(w)}{P}$

Y refers to the gross national product at constant prices. C and I refer to consumption and investment as functions of Y and the rate of interest r. M is the money supply in current dollars, and P is a price index of the goods and services entering into GNP. Labor is the only variable factor of production, and the labor demand schedule is derived by taking the first derivative of the aggregate production function. The demand and the supply of labor are functions of the *real* wage rate.

The entire model is depicted in Figure 98. Beginning with equation (3), the aggregate production function reflecting diminishing returns appears in quadrant IV. Quadrant III depicts equations (4) and (5), which together determine the level of employment and the real wage rate at full employment levels. The figure in quadrant I is the Hicks-Hansen diagram of monetary equilibrium in the Keynesian system. The IS curve represents equation (1) and shows the relationship between the rate of interest and the equilibrium level of income as determined by the equality of planned saving and investment. Given the money supply, an exogenous variable determined by the monetary authorities, equation (2) is represented by the LM curve and depicts the equilibrium relationship between the demand and supply of money at the prevailing price level. The heart of the Keynesian system is tucked away behind these last two schedules. Before we can make use of our diagrammatic construction, therefore, we must be certain that we grasp why the *IS* and *LM* curves have the shapes and slopes that they have.

The IS *Curve.* According to our original income function, saving as well as investment is a function of both Y and r. Keynes himself, however, viewed saving solely as a function of income and invest-

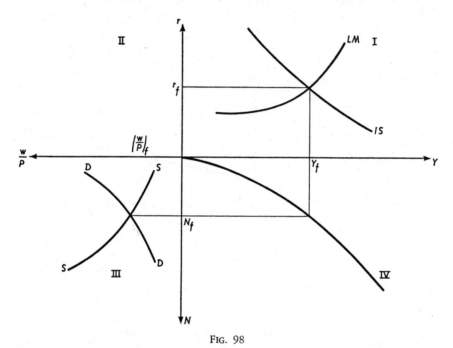

Fig. 98

ment solely as a function of the rate of interest. The saving function is derived from the consumption function in the familiar post-Keynesian 45° diagram (Fig. 99). For convenience, the consumption function is drawn as a straight line, taking the form $C = (a + b)Y$ in which a, the intercept value, and b, the marginal propensity to consume, are constants. The investment demand schedule is separately depicted as a function of the rate of interest. Given the rate of interest, there is a level of income that will equate planned saving to planned investment. Ignoring the public sector, the Hicks-Hansen *IS* curve is simply the locus of all possible combinations of r and Y that are consistent with the equality of planned private saving and investment.

The argument is not affected by making both saving and investment functions of Y and r. We can then derive the IS curve by combining a crude "Keynesian" diagram, in which saving and investment are functions of income, and a crude "Classical" diagram, in which

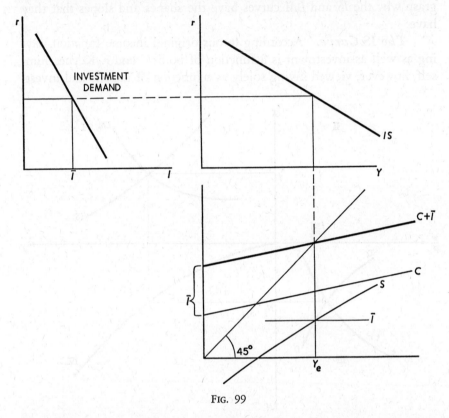

FIG. 99

they vary as a function of the interest rate (Fig. 100). I_1 and S_1 in the "Keynesian" diagram assume $r = r_1$, I_2 and S_2 assume $r = r_2$, and so forth: the higher the rate of interest, the less is invested and the more is saved at every level of income. If $r = r_1$, then $S_1 = I_1$ at E_1, yielding the equilibrium level of income Y_3. At higher interest rates, the corresponding intersection points yield lower equilibrium income levels Y_2 and Y_1. In the "Classical" diagram we have a separate saving and investment function for each level of income: S_3 and I_3 correspond to Y_1, S_2 and I_2 to Y_2, and so forth. Again we obtain a family of intersection points combining successively lower interest rates with successively higher incomes.

Points A and B in the "Classical" diagram show different amounts of investment corresponding to r_2 and r_1, given the level of income Y_1. At that income level, the same points can be found in the "Keynesian" diagram. Similarly, F and G show the various levels of saving at $r = r_1$ for different levels of income; they can be located in either diagram.

The locus of intersections E_1, E_2, E_3 yields the IS curve (Fig. 101). The verbal explanation of the negative slope of the IS curve is that

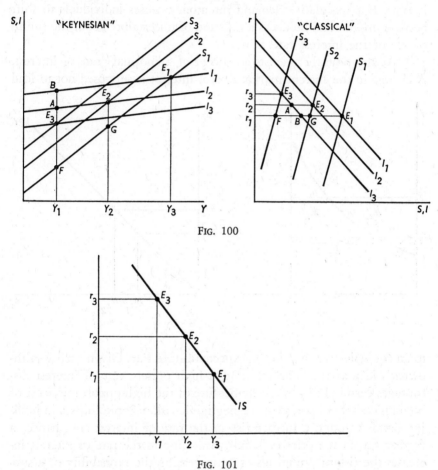

Fig. 100

Fig. 101

when the rate of interest is high, investment is low; if investment is low, so is income in consequence of the multiplier; with income low, saving is low. On the other hand, high income levels yield high saving levels; the interest rate must then be low to produce an equivalent amount of planned investment.

The **LM** *Curve.* Keynes decomposed the demand curve for money into $L_1(Y) + L_2(r)$, where $L_1(Y)$ represents the demand for transactions and precautionary balances and $L_2(r)$ represents the demand for speculative balances. Speculation with respect to the future course of the interest rate is alleged to be the only source of the interest-elasticity of the demand for money. Active balances to finance transactions and to provide a reserve against possible discrepancies between the inflow and the outflow of money vary solely with the level of money income. But speculative demand for money causes individuals to shift between money and bonds as a function of uncertainty about the future course of the interest rate.

At any time there exists a concept of a "normal" rate of interest. A change in the current market rate of interest is supposed not to lead

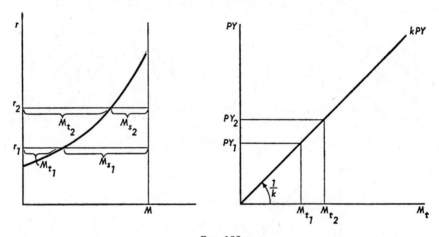

FIG. 102

to an equivalent change in the expected future rate. Given each wealth-owner's idea of the "normal" rate, a high present rate of interest discourages cash-holding, not only because of the high opportunity cost of holding cash, but because of the negligible risk of capital losses in holding bonds through a further rise in the rate of interest and, hence, a further fall in the price of bonds. A decline in the rate of interest increases the risk of capital losses by increasing the probability of a subsequent rise, and therefore encourages the shift out of bonds into money. At very low interest rates and high bond prices, almost everyone will expect a rise in the rate of interest and will therefore prefer to hold cash.

The total demand for money may be conveniently rewritten as $D_m = kPY + L(r)$, that is, the sum of the transactions demand M_t and the speculative demand M_s. (See Fig. 102.) At r_1, speculative demand is M_{s1} and transactions demand is M_{t1}, and so on. In order for the desired amount of money ($M_t + M_s$) to be equal to the actual stock of money M, money income must be at the level PY_1 to call forth M_{t1}. Combining both diagrams in Figure 103, we obtain a family of negatively sloped demand curves for money, each curve corresponding to a given level of income. Given the money stock and the price level, we can now derive the LM curve, showing all the possible combinations of r and Y that make the public willing to hold the stock of money in existence. (See Fig. 103.) Rising income levels are associated with higher interest rates for each price level because, as income rises, the transactions demand for money increases, leaving less of the fixed real money supply to satisfy the speculative demand for idle bal-

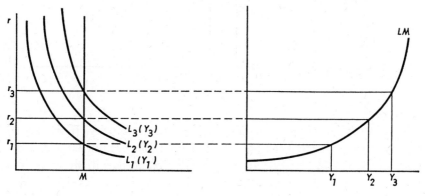

FIG. 103

ances. Hence the rate of interest must rise to choke off speculative demand.

The Hicks-Hansen Diagram. The intersection point of the IS and LM curves (Fig. 104) satisfies the double condition of monetary equilibrium: actual saving and investment equal desired saving and investment and, in addition, the desired amount of money is equal to the actual supply of money. As long as the IS curve cuts the LM curve from above, this equilibrium point is a stable one. A rightward shift of the LM curve is due either to an increase in the money supply or to a decrease in the underlying liquidity preference schedule. Owing to the nature of the speculative demand for money, the LM curve becomes increasingly inelastic at higher rates of interest. Thus, equal increases in the money stock will lead to successively smaller reductions in r and successively smaller increases in Y.

It should be noted that a shift in the liquidity preference schedule is not quite the same thing as a change in the "velocity of circulation." A decrease in "the propensity to hoard" L_2 may simply mean a lower rate of interest, not a decrease in the actual amount of hoarded money

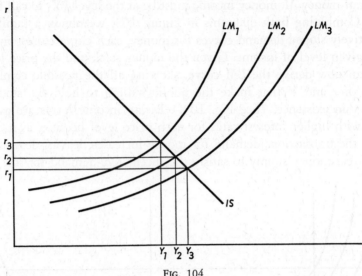

FIG. 104

drawn into idle balances, that is, an increase in velocity. If the actual money supply and transactions demand for money is unchanged, a decline in the speculative demand for inactive balances will show up in a fall in the rate of interest rather than in a rise in the level of prices.

A rightward shift in the *IS* curve reflects either an upward shift in the underlying investment demand function or a downward shift in the saving function. (See Fig. 105.) A reduced propensity to save raises

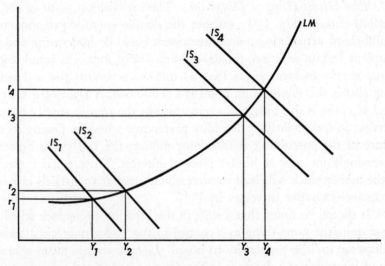

FIG. 105

the *IS* curve by a uniform amount along its whole length. This will raise Y moderately and r substantially if the *LM* curve is inelastic; if the *LM* curve is elastic, it will, on the contrary, raise Y substantially and r slightly. In verbal terms: a reduced propensity to save raises income through an increased demand for consumer goods, leading to further increases in consumption and investment via the multiplier. A larger amount of money is now tied up in transactions balances, diverting funds from speculative balances through a rise in the rate of interest. How far the rate of interest will have to rise to bring the demand for money into equality with the unchanged supply of money depends on the elasticity of the L_2 curve.

Full Employment Equilibrium. We come back now to our original Keynesian model. With flexible wages and prices, full employment will be automatically maintained. If real wages exceed $(w/P)_f$, money wages will fall due to the excess supply of labor. This reduces costs and lowers prices, thus increasing the real value of cash balances M/P. This in turn shifts the *LM* curve upward and to the right, lowering r and expanding investment demand until the output corresponding to full employment has been absorbed. Abstracting entirely from the dynamic effects of falling prices, it follows that income is established at the full employment level in the labor market, the interest rate then equates saving and investment on the *IS* curve at this income level, and, finally, the price level adjusts so as to satisfy liquidity requirements at this rate of interest.

This argument is entirely in the neoclassical tradition. The rate of interest is determined solely by the saving-investment process, independently of monetary forces. Monetary forces serve to determine not the rate of interest but the level of prices, and an increase in the quantity of money has no lasting effect on real income and employment. We now introduce the three Keynesian specifics that make possible an underemployment equilibrium: (1) the "liquidity trap," (2) the low interest-elasticity of investment, and (3) the stickiness of money wages.

The Liquidity Trap. Keynes suggests that liquidity preferences may become satiated in a severe depression when shrinking income has reduced the transactions demand and monetary policy has increased the money supply. The liquidity preference schedule becomes infinitely elastic owing to the unanimous expectation of investors that the rate of interest cannot fall any further; bond prices are so high that no one expects them to rise still higher. Consequently, everyone prefers to hold idle cash, and monetary policy is put out of commission. It is not neces-

sary to assume that the liquidity preference schedule is perfectly vertical. The "liquidity trap" may take the form of a very low interest elasticity of the LM schedule. Open-market purchases of government bonds
can push down the interest rate, but the effect is so slight that it may be
necessary to absorb all bonds in private hands in exchange for cash before a full employment income level is reached. Unless the monetary
authorities are willing to become the sole debt holders and, therefore,
the sole lenders in the economy, which is not politically feasible, an
easy money policy is ineffective in inducing recovery.

Suppose that at $(w/P)_a$ there is an excess supply of labor,

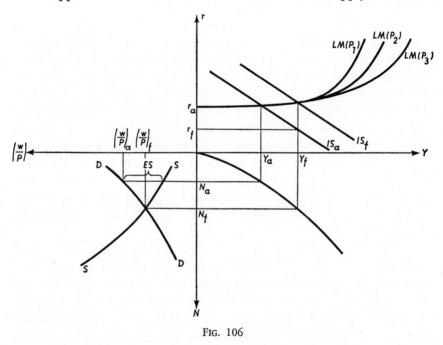

Fig. 106

exerting a downward pressure on money wages and prices. The fall in
prices would expand aggregate demand by shifting the LM curve to the
right, thus lowering the rate of interest, which in turn would cause an
upward shift in the IS curve. If the IS curve were at the level IS_a, the
rate of interest required to equate planned saving and investment at
income Y_f would be r_f. But the infinite elasticity of the LM schedule prevents r from falling below r_a. The result is that Y and N are
prevented from rising above the level N_a and Y_a by inadequate effective demand. The real wage will stay put at level $(w/P)_a > (w/P)_f$.
Competition for employment will reduce money wages, costs, and
prices, but the falling price level, while increasing the quantity of

money in real terms, has no influence on the rate of interest and hence cannot stimulate investment demand. The system is in equilibrium at less than full employment.

Interest-Inelastic Investment Demand. We have drawn the *IS* curve as a straight line. It is reasonable to assume, however, that investment demand becomes increasingly unresponsive to a falling rate of interest. Hence, despite the elasticity of the *LM* curve, full employment may not be achievable. (See Fig. 107.) If the *IS* curve became per-

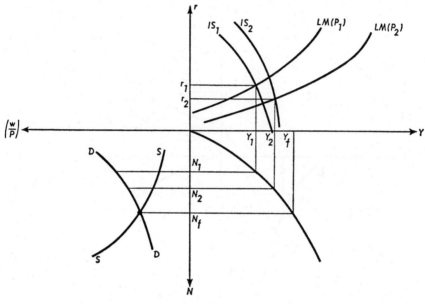

Fig. 107

fectly inelastic, falling wages and prices would merely reduce the rate of interest and would fail to expand income. Another possibility is that a negative rate of interest is required to equate investment to full employment savings. The *IS* curve will therefore cut the income-axis and lie to the left of an income level corresponding to full employment. As long as it costs nothing to hold money, the money rate of interest cannot be negative. Hence, the *LM* schedule has a floor at a zero rate of interest. In consequence, the *IS* and *LM* curves can never intersect at a full employment income level. Once again, the only kind of equilibrium possible is underemployment equilibrium.

Wage Rigidities. Keynes assumed that wages are rigid downward because workers are subject to a "money illusion": they are not willing to work at reduced money wages, but they are willing to work at lower real wages brought about by a rise in prices. The supply of labor thus depends upon nominal and not upon real wages. Powerful trade unions or minimum wage laws, however, will do just as well to account for downward rigidity in money wages.

Assume that w is fixed at $\bar{w}$. In order to have full employment, the price level must be at P_f and the interest rate at r_f. However, the money supply is such that at P_f, $LM(P_f)$ intersects with the IS curve at $Y_1 < Y_f$ and $r_1 > r_f$. (See Fig. 108.) Hence, full employment can-

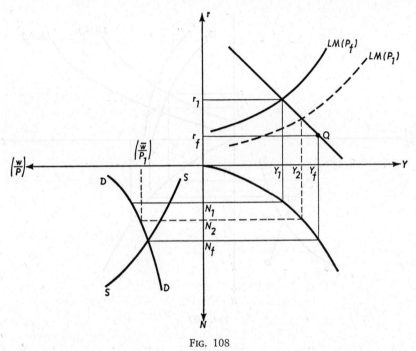

FIG. 108

not be achieved. If output and employment are at Y_1 and N_1 with a price level P_1 to establish the real wage rate appropriate to N_1, the LM curve will be at the level $LM(P_1) > LM(P_f)$. This is because P_1 must be less than P_f in order to make $(\bar{w}/P_1)$ higher than (w/P_f). Income and employment will tend to rise because aggregate demand exceeds current output. Therefore, income must lie between Y_1 and Y_f, and so forth for N, r, and P. Equilibrium will be reached somewhere above Y_1 but below the full employment level.

An increase in the quantity of money sufficient to shift $LM(P_f)$ to a position where it intersects IS at Q would establish full employment. This is the Keynesian case against the neoclassical quantity theory of money: changes in M alter not only the level of prices, but also the level of output, employment, and the interest rate. In effect, we have added a new equation $w = \bar{w}$ to our original model, giving us six equations to determine five unknowns. The quantity of money now becomes our sixth equation, rendering the model determinate once again.

The Pigou Effect. The essence of the Keynesian argument is that there is no automatic mechanism that will tend to eliminate unemployment. The liquidity preference schedule is too interest elastic and the investment schedule is too interest inelastic for a fall in the rate of interest to generate full employment. The demand for labor is determined by real wages. Since reductions in money wages will be followed by equivalent reductions in prices—in the short run, all marginal prime costs consist of wages—workers cannot increase employment by accepting wage cuts. The only hope is that wage cuts might indirectly affect aggregate demand through the interest rate. But, owing to the liquidity trap or the low interest elasticity of investment demand, the interest mechanism has no chance to act. Hence, wage cuts merely lead to a fall in effective demand.

Falling wages and prices, however, raise the real value of liquid assets. Private debts will increase in real value, but the increased wealth of creditors will be offset by the decreased wealth of debtors. But public bonds and fiat paper money also increase in aggregate real value, and the government, alone of all economic units, does not tailor its expenditure to the real value of its assets and liabilities. If a rising real value of consumers' wealth stimulates consumption—people's "tastes" for real wealth being given—then there is always some fall in prices that will be adequate to satiate the desire to save and to stimulate consumption sufficiently to produce full employment. This is the real-balance or so-called Pigou Effect, in honor of the first economist clearly to state the hypothesis. On the comparative static level at which Keynes conducted his argument, no reply can be made to this "classical" argument. In other words, the *General Theory* fails to prove the possibility of a competitive underemployment equilibrium.

We can modify our original model to allow for the real-balance effect by including the real value of the stock of liquid assets in equation (1). Equation (1) now becomes

$$Y = C\left(Y, r, \frac{M}{P}\right) + I\left(Y, r, \frac{M}{P}\right),$$

where M is the money value of currency, deposits and government securities held by the nonbank public minus the public's indebtedness to the banks. Keynes himself admitted that falling prices may stimulate effective demand via the effect of reducing the transactions demand for cash; at a given money supply, this increases the supply of money available to satisfy the speculative motive and hence works to reduce the interest rate. In other words, the Keynes Effect states that falling prices will shift the *LM* curve to the right, lowering *r* and increasing *Y*. Nevertheless, the liquidity trap or the low interest elasticity of investment deprives this effect of practical significance. The point of the real-balance effect is that falling prices shift not only the *LM* curve but also the *IS* curve to the right. As the demand for consumption goods rises, the level of saving out of any given level of income will fall, requiring a higher rate of interest to bring saving into equality with investment at that income level. Even with the liquidity trap or the low interest elasticity of investment, full employment equilibrium is in principle attainable.

The real-balance effect provides the cornerstone for the modern neoclassical affirmation of the self-regulating character of a market economy. Its significance, however, is often misunderstood. It does not imply that monetary or fiscal policies are unnecessary to induce recovery. Admitting the stimulating influence of an increase in liquidity does not imply indifference toward the amount or rate of price fall necessary to achieve full employment equilibrium. The real-balance effect is, after all, a comparative static argument. It says nothing about the dynamics of a slow adjustment to gradual deflation with its undesirable distributional effects—the bulk of liquid assets are held by the well-to-do—and its possibly perverse repercussions on expectations. Pigou himself conceded that the real-balance effect was of little practical importance. The purpose of spelling it out was to undermine the Keynesian paradox of equilibrium at less than full employment. The heart of the Keynesian Revolution is now seen to be, not the concept of underemployment equilibrium, but the notion of unemployment *disequilibrium*. In Patinkin's words: "the main message of Keynesian economics becomes that the automatic adjustment process of the market (even with the real-balance effect—and even when supplemented by monetary policy) is too unreliable to serve as a practical basis of full employment policy. In other words, though the real-balance effect must be taken account of in our *theoretical* analysis, it is too weak—and in some cases (due to adverse expectations) too perverse—to fulfill a significant role in our *policy* considerations."

Keynes versus the Classics. We are now in a position to raise the question with which this chapter is fundamentally concerned. What is the exact nature of the innovations that led Keynes to results different from those obtained by what he called "classical" economics? For purposes of comparison, we set down the "classical" and "Keynesian" models of income determination in their simplest forms.

	Classical	Keynesian
(1)	$M = kPY$	$M = kPY + L_2(r)$
(2)	$Y = f(N)$	$Y = f(N)$
(3)	$f'(N) = w/P$	$f'(N) = w/P$
(4)	$N = f(w/P)$	$w = \bar{w}$
(5)	$S = f(r)$	$S = f(Y)$
(6)	$I = f(r)$	$I = f(r)$
(7)	$S = I$	$S = I$

The novel features of the Keynesian model are, first of all, the addition of the speculative demand for money to the "classical" transactions and precautionary demands; second, the suppression of a supply of labor function and its replacement by the assumption of rigid wages; third, the notion that consumption, and therefore saving, depend on income rather than on the rate of interest. Even now there is no agreement among economists as to which of these constitutes the crucial difference between Keynesian and "classical" analysis. Perhaps the majority vote has come down on wage rigidities as the crucial Keynesian innovation. But this would seem to deny the novelty of the Keynesian argument. Every economist before Keynes recognized that rigid wages could cause unemployment. Keynes himself anticipated this objection by insisting that the essential element in the case for underemployment equilibrium is the liquidity trap, based on the speculative demand for money. This is what prevents the interest rate from stabilizing aggregate demand and dispenses with the "classical" quantity theory.

In reply to this, it has been said that speculative demand can be added to the classical model without changing its basic conclusion, provided wages are flexible. This is true, however, only if by adding speculative demand we mean that the demand for money becomes interest elastic. The distinguishing characteristic of Keynes's treatment is the presence of a money illusion in the speculative demand for money. In Keynes's book, doubling both the stock of money and the prices decreases the demand for real speculative balances. For that reason $2M \neq 2P$. Some proportion of the increased money supply will seek an outlet in the purchase of bonds, and these purchases will depress the rate of interest until the resulting increase in M_s, together with the increase in M_t brought about by the price rise, has absorbed all the extra money. It is the absence of a money illusion that justifies the familiar theorems of the quantity theory of money, not merely the demand for speculative balances.

There is nothing surprising about this assertion. The notion that equation (1) accurately depicts the neoclassical theory of money is a doctrinal travesty. It implies that the *LM* curve is perfectly inelastic, and, since equations (5), (6), and (7) imply a perfectly elastic *IS* curve, this kind of "classical" model rigidly dichotomizes the pricing process: monetary forces cannot affect the interest rate, and the saving-investment process cannot affect real income. But, even with perfect certainty and hence the disappearance of a speculative demand for money, it will still be true that the greater cost in earnings forgone of holding cash balances will cause the amount of balances demanded to fall when the interest rate rises. The precautionary motive emerges clearly in Walras and then in Wicksell and Fisher—there are hints of it in Marshall—and it suffices to make the demand for money interest elastic. Indeed, Keynes himself said as much.

Moreover, the idea that Keynes's predecessors held that saving and investment determine the interest rate is belied by the ancient lineage of the loanable funds theory. It is true that few writers before Keynes distinguished explicitly and emphatically between saving and lending, on the one hand, and investing and borrowing, on the other. But it is not true that the leading pre-Keynesian writers assumed Say's Identity with its implication that the money market is always in equilibrium. The loanable funds theory is implicit in Thornton and Ricardo, it is admirably expounded in Book III, chapter 23, of Mill's *Principles,* and it is contained not only in Wicksell and Fisher but also in Pigou. The history of the forced-saving doctrine alone shows that the classical and neoclassical writers did not entirely neglect monetary influences on the rate of interest.

The "neutrality" of money postulated by the quantity theory can be destroyed just as well by money illusion in the labor market as by money illusion in the money market. If the labor supply depends on nominal and not on real wages, doubling the money stock will cause a less than proportionate increase in prices. The presence of money illusion, therefore, would seem to be the factor responsible for Keynes's novel conclusions. It is difficult to see, however, that money illusion could persist in the face of flexible wages and prices. Sooner or later, the real-balance effect must break through the money illusion and re-establish behavior in terms of real balances and real wages. This throws us back on rigid wages as the *differentia specifica* of the Keynesian case for underemployment equilibrium.

It has been argued that it is the consumption function that is really at the heart of the Keynesian analysis. The basic cause of unemployment lies in the insufficiency of planned investment relative to planned saving and the inability of a lower rate of interest to depress saving or to stimulate investment. If saving is not affected by changes in r and the interest elasticity of investment is low, equations (5), (6), and (7) may not have a solution at $r > 0$. With such an "inconsistency" between saving and investment, wages and prices will fall without limits unless wages are sticky. The rate of interest will fall to zero except to the extent that speculative demand will cushion its fall. But wage rigidity and speculative demand are not themselves fundamental. The rate of interest and wage-price level adjustment cannot equate saving and investment at full employment owing to the nature of the saving and investment functions. The burden of bringing planned saving into line with planned investment falls on income, and the extent to which income must fall below full employment levels to perform this task depends on the magnitude of the multiplier, which in turn depends on the slope of the consumption function. In this view, the fundamental Keynesian ideas are really contained in the simple 3-equation model (5), (6), and (7); the rest is mere excess baggage.

Whatever the ultimate decision on Keynes's fundamental contribution, the important question is whether the policy implications of Keynesian economics differ from those of "classical" economics. In so far as the economy has reached or exceeded full employment, neoclassical economics would seem to gain little by a Keynesian revision. If there is no unemployment problem, there is nothing to prevent monetary policy from driving up the rate of interest to the point at which the speculative demand for money disappears. Once the LM schedule has become interest inelastic, any increase in aggregate demand will be choked off by a rise in the rate of interest, and the attempt to acquire additional active balances by selling bonds or by retaining current saving in cash will prove abortive. The multiplier is zero, and the results of the Keynesian model, with its neglect of the effects of price level changes, become irrelevant.

The real question, however, centers on remedial action to eliminate unemployment. The traditional "classical" weapons are said to be (1) monetary policy and (2) wage cutting. What impact Keynes has had on economics lies in casting doubt on the efficacy of such policy measures, suggesting instead that the government practise deficit financing by spending on public works. That Keynes's predecessors placed much faith in monetary policy is not open to question. But it is not true that they ignored the need for compensatory public works expenditures. Nor is it true that they invariably advocated wage cutting as a practical cure for unemployment. The influence of Keynes on the analysis of these questions was one of degree, not of kind: the upshot of Keynesian economics was to strengthen the case for public works and to place the burden of proof on anyone who would propose to remedy unemployment by manipulating the wage rate.

The Traditional Case for Public Works. The last three decades of the nineteenth century saw a remarkable diminution of interest on the part of English economists in the problem of unemployment and business cycles. It is only around the turn of the century that systematic work on business cycles begins to appear, first in Germany with the works of Tugan-Baranovsky, Spiethoff, Aftalion, and Juglar, then in the Anglo-Saxon world with the writings of Mitchell, Hawtrey, Robertson, and Pigou. The case for countercyclical public works was stated for the first time in the *Minority Report of the Poor Law Commission* (1909). The *Minority Report,* which was largely due to the Webbs, with a statistical supplement by A. L. Bowley, recommended public works expenditures when unemployment reached 4 per cent of the labor force. This idea was endorsed, with qualifications, by Beveridge in *Unemployment, A Problem of Industry* (1909), and elaborated by the Webbs in their book, *The Prevention of Destitution* (1911). Public works to relieve the unemployed is an idea as old as the Bible; what made the *Minority Report* a milestone in the history of the public works doctrine was that it advocated public spending to smooth out cyclical fluctuations and to stabilize total economic activity.

In *Wealth and Welfare* (1912) Pigou attacked the doctrine that the state, by increasing public construction, was only "diminishing employment with one hand, while it increased it with the other." The proceeds for public spending, he pointed out, would draw down on "funds which would normally have been stored" or "which would normally have been consumed by the relatively well-to-do." He had used the same argument to show that public spending can increase aggregate employment as early as 1908 in his inaugural lecture as successor to Marshall at Cambridge. The so-called Treasury View, which he was attacking, had not been heard of since Ricardo's time—although there are faint echoes of it in Mill's *Principles*—but it was apparently being appealed to once again. Hawtrey in *Good and Bad Trade* (1913) used it to dismiss the policy proposals of the *Minority Report.* Pigou returned to the theme in *Unemployment* (1913). In considering the case of an increase in public spending matched by an increase in taxes, he said that "it is probable that only a part of the extra taxes people pay would be taken from funds they would otherwise have devoted at that time directly or indirectly to wage-payments. Hence, the true result of relief works and so on is not to leave the aggregate amount of unemployment in the country unaltered, but to diminish that amount." In other words, an increase in taxes reduces spending by (a multiple of) a *fraction* of that increase, while the disbursement of tax receipts on public works construction increases spending by (a multiple of) the *full* amount spent; the net effect is expansionary.

It is evident that Pigou's argument rests on what has come to be known as the balanced budget multiplier. Provided taxpayers and unemployed workers have the same marginal propensity to consume and provided private investment is not sensitive to the level of public spending, the balanced budget multiplier is unity. For example, if $MPC = 0.9$, the multiplier or reciprocal of the marginal propensity to save is 10; raising taxes by $10 reduces aggregate demand by $90, but increasing public spending by $10 increases aggregate demand by $100. The net effect is to raise aggregate demand by the amount of the increase in the balanced budget. It is true that Pigou speaks, not of a fraction of income spent on consumption, but of a fraction of income devoted to wage payments. This is hardly surprising considering the negligible importance of income taxation in 1913. The failure to make any reference to the concept of a multiplier deprives his argument of any quantitative precision but does not affect its essential validity.

The significance of Pigou's attack on the Treasury View is that it demonstrates the case for countercyclical public works spending without resorting to the notion of deficit finance. Economists before Keynes generally disapproved of unbalanced budgets. But the idea that this prevented them from advocating fiscal policy to eliminate unemployment is not supported by the evidence.

Pigou qualified the argument for public works in *Unemployment* by noting that the successful application of a compensatory policy requires that labor be highly mobile between private industry and public construction. Despite these qualifications, however, he left no doubt that public works spending could be expected under normal circumstances to lessen unemployment. This became the standard view of economists after the first World War. Hawtrey alone of all British economists in the 1920's opposed the case for public works on theoretical grounds. He never tired of insisting that the business cycle is purely a "monetary phenomenon": "additional public expenditures can give additional employment . . . only if it increases the rapidity of circulation of money"; hence, "the true remedy for unemployment is to be found in a direct regulation of credit on sound lines." Nevertheless, despite the consensus of economic opinion, the Treasury followed Hawtrey and remained hostile to the idea of planned countercyclical public works, with or without budgetary deficits. Churchill's budget speech of 1929, attacking "the orthodox Treasury dogma that public works spending is ineffective," fell entirely on deaf ears. As late as 1939 Sweden was still the only country that had made any serious attempt to put a compensatory public works policy into practice.

The Economics of Wage Cutting.   According to neoclassical theory, it is the relationship of wages to prices, not the absolute level of either one, that determines employment and output. Suppose there is an excess supply of labor at a given money wage rate and a given level of prices. If there is free competition, the unemployed will offer their services at lower money wage rates rather than remain idle. Whether this results in additional employment depends on whether prices fall in a lesser proportion than do money wages. The usual assumption of marginal productivity theory is that the money wage rate is independent of the final demand for the product, so that prices are unaffected by the fall in money wages. But this assumption, while appropriate to the single firm or industry, cannot be applied to the economy as a whole. Keynes complained in the *General Theory* that "classical" writers provided no satisfactory explanation of what would happen to sales prices in the event of a general decline in money wages. The logic of the "classical" position, Keynes thought, called for prices to fall in the same proportion as wages, providing no incentive for employers to hire additional labor; with labor as the only variable cost in the short run and no money illusion in the labor demand or supply functions, wage cutting could not increase employment. Keynes's reconstruction of the "classical" formulation ignored the real-balance effect of a general deflation of wages and prices. Real spending would necessarily increase as prices fell, thus causing money wages to fall proportionately more than prices, with a consequent tendency to expand output and employment.

The way in which money wage rate adjustments would restore full employment was so carelessly stated by most "classical" writers that we would do well to spend a moment in reviewing the argument. The object lesson of "classical" analysis is to deny the "philosophy of high wages" which has long formed an essential element in the creed of labor. The proposition in question is that money wage cuts are undesirable because wages are incomes; as wages fall, so does the demand for final goods. But this crude underconsumptionist argument ignores the fact that the demand for labor as well as the demand for consumer goods depends on real, not on money, incomes. Since wages are costs as well as incomes, prices will fall when money wages are reduced. If prices fall as fast as wages, consumption is in no way stimulated.

Once we ignore the fact that it is the relationship of wages to other prices that is relevant to the employment problem, the labor creed can be turned upside down to justify wage cuts. On the assumption that

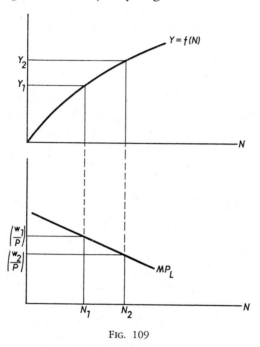

FIG. 109

the elasticity of demand for labor is greater than unity, a wage cut would raise the total money wage bill. If prices do not fall, this means an increase in labor's real income and therefore an increase in the demand for consumer goods. But what is ignored in both arguments is that wage income is not the only source of demand for consumer goods.

Suppose the labor demand curve of a "representative" firm producing consumer goods is highly elastic, so that

$$N_2\left(\frac{w_2}{P}\right) > N_1\left(\frac{w_1}{P}\right).$$

The money wage is cut from w_1 to w_2 (Fig. 109). Employment expands and output increases by the amount Y_1Y_2. Will the increase in the demand for goods on the part of workers be sufficient to absorb the extra output? The answer is "No," even when the *MPC* of workers is unity, for the simple reason that the entire increment of output does not go to workers. On the assumption of profit-maximizing behavior, output Y_2 would not be chosen if it did not yield larger profits than Y_1; employers do, after all, have the option of producing the previous output Y_1 with the lower wage rate w_2, yielding larger profits than before. If they prefer to produce Y_2 it must offer greater profits than Y_1. Thus, some part of the increased income associated with the larger output goes to nonwage earners and, unless their *MPC* is also equal to unity, the increase in consumers' demand is less than the increase in supply. Hence, prices fall. If all firms in the economy are practising wage cutting, prices must fall in the same proportion as wages, regardless of the elasticity of the demand for labor.

In its more sophisticated versions, the labor creed relies on the probable fact that the *MPC* of wage earners exceeds that of profit receivers. Therefore, a rise in money wages will redistribute income in favor of workers, leading to a net increase in consumers' demand. But this effect takes place only if prices rise less than money wages. If they rise in equal proportions, everything is as before in real terms. The implication of profit-maximizing behavior is that employers will require an equal percentage increase in prices when money wages rise, unless there is some indirect repercussion through the rate of interest or the real-balance effect. For, if real wages did rise, output and employment would fall, but, owing to the fact that the average *MPC* of the community is necessarily less than unity, the reduction in real income reduces supply more than it reduces demand. Hence, prices must rise until the initial wage-price ratio is restored.

Reasoning in terms of a static model, we may conclude that general wage changes cannot *directly* affect aggregate consumption demand as long as: (1) employers maximize profits under competitive conditions, (2) the real consumption of all individuals is a function of real income, and (3) the average *MPC* of the community is less than unity. Any argument in favor of wage manipulation to cure unemployment must rest either on the *indirect* effects via liquidity, the rate of interest, foreign trade, and taxation, or on the *dynamic* effects connected with the state of investors' expectations.

With respect to the indirect effects, the weight of argument clearly comes down in favor of wage cutting. First, there is the Pigou Effect and the Keynes Effect of wage-price deflation. Second, in an open economy deflation is likely to stimulate the demand for exports. Third, since the bulk of taxes in a modern economy take the form of progressive income taxes and since transfer payments (negative taxes) are fixed in money terms, a decline in prices and in money incomes stimulates demand by lessening the burden of real taxes. When it comes to the dynamic effects, however, the argument may go either way. If the labor demand and supply curves have the normal shape, involuntary unemployment *means* a real wage rate in excess of the equilibrium wage. If wages are truly flexible, then by definition equilibrium can be reached only by reducing money wages and/or prices. But this is a tautological argument. What we want to know is: Will a decline in fully flexible wages lead to the achievement of full employment equilibrium?

We must assume, first of all, that wage flexibility is theoretically compatible with full employment. The *SI* and *LM* curves may intersect at a zero or negative rate of interest at which no wealth holder would willingly hold a security in preference to cash. But, even if wage cutting is a theoretically possible solution to unemployment, it may not be a meaningful or practicable solution. The flatter the liquidity preference schedule and the steeper the investment schedule, the greater the required fall in wages and prices to achieve full employment equilibrium. A sharp decline in prices may be impossible to accomplish in any reasonable period of time. It is perfectly true that wage cuts and the associated expectation of increased sales may engender investment in inventories or plant and equipment, justifying the original expectation. If investment depends heavily on the state of business confidence, a rise, once in process, may easily cumulate. But, if prices fall without limit over a considerable period of time, expectations may become price elastic. Businessmen now postpone investment in expectation of lower prices in the future, in consequence of which aggregate demand falls instead of rises. Thus, no simple generalization about the dynamic effects of wage changes will suffice: it all depends on the rate at which wages and prices are changing.

We sum up by noting that however fallacious the idea that unemployment can be cured by raising money wages, it is not possible to recommend wage cutting as a remedy simply on the basis of the beneficial "indirect" effects of wage-price deflation.

What Economists Said. We turn now to what economists really said about wage cutting before the publication of the *General Theory*. The impression that Keynes conveys is that the "classical" economists favored wage cutting on the basis of static microeconomic reasoning, illegitimately generalized to the economy as a whole. For evidence of this characterization of orthodox theory he pointed to Pigou's *Theory of Unemployment* (1933), "the only detailed account of the classical theory which exists." Pigou's book does argue, in great detail and with considerable care, that all-round reductions in money wages in the real world may be expected to stimulate employment. But some reviewers of Pigou's book praised it for its "novel contributions," and others found its reasoning at best unclear and at worst questionable.

And, indeed, Pigou's argument was new, for instead of relying on the "indirect" effects, he appealed to the "direct" stimulus afforded by wage cutting. A general decline in money wage rates, he argued, will involve a less than proportionate decline in real wage rates, despite the fact that costs fall as fast as money wages. The reduction in money wages does not *in the first instance* alter the income of nonwage earners; therefore, purchasing power does not fall as fast as money wages, causing an expansion of output. Presumably, this initial stimulus is more than sufficient to offset the depressing effect of the decline in the level of money wages, so that real wages and employment increase permanently. On comparative static grounds, this argument does not hang together. It seems, in fact, to depend on quasi-dynamic considerations introduced *ad hoc* in an otherwise static context.

Pigou had been more cautious about wage cutting in earlier writings. In *Industrial Fluctuations* (1927) he argued not only that unemployment was due to real wages being "too high"—which is true by definition—but also that "high" real wages were an active cause of unemployment. But he was not sanguine about the possibility of altering real wages per medium of money wages and pointed out that money wages might have to fall to zero in a deep depression to eliminate unemployment.

Turning to other prominent economists writing in the 1920's, we find a mass of conflicting evidence. In *Industrial Fluctuations* (1915) D. H. Robertson dismissed wage reductions in a slump and supported the public works proposals of the *Minority Report;* he did not revise his views in later years. Keynes and Hawtrey favored monetary management as a cure for unemployment, and Henry Clay, in reply to Pigou, denied that unemployment could be causally attributed to real wages being "too high." Everyone agreed that wage cuts would *in principle* lessen unemployment via the "indirect" effects on the rate of interest and the balance of payments, but the general tenor of informed judgment was that such a remedy was both impractical and inequitable. A certain amount of unemployment was accepted as the price of the deflationary policy of restoring the gold standard at prewar parity. Wage cutting was sometimes defended, not so much as a method for curing unemployment as a device to stimulate exports. The decline of certain basic export industries led to the demand for structural rather than general wage flexibility, emphasizing the need to cut wages in "sheltered" industries. In general, the striking characteristic of British economics in the 1920's was the lack of concern over unemployment and the failure to realize its extent. All through the decade, unemployment hovered around 10 per cent of the labor force, but comprehensive statistics were not available before the revised edition of Beveridge's *Unemployment* (1931). Still, as late as 1932 we find Edwin Cannan suggesting that general unemployment is due to labor "asking too much," but at the same time another "classical" economist, P. H. Douglas, was arguing that the best way of *Controlling Depressions* (1935) was through compensatory public works rather than through the policy of wage cutting.

Conclusion. It appears that the body of ideas discussed under the name of "classical" economics represents a convenient strawman of Keynes's invention to represent the thinking of his predecessors. For Keynes, a "classical" economist is any writer who defends Say's Law. By Say's Law Keynes meant the proposition that any increment in output will automatically generate an equivalent increase in spending and income such as to maintain the economy at full employment. Since, in Keynes's view, the main stream of economic thought had never abandoned Say's Law, any orthodox economist, from Ricardo to Pigou, was guilty of the sins he attributed to "classical" economists. To hit a target so broadly conceived, it was necessary to simplify. And simplify Keynes did, virtually implying that all previous discussions of business cycles were inconsistent with the corpus of received doctrine.

The difficulty with Keynes's characterization of orthodox theory is not simply that no single economist ever held all the ideas Keynes attributed to the "Classics" but that almost no economist after 1870 considered the type of macroeconomic problems with which Keynes was concerned. The strength of neoclassical theory lay in microeconomic analysis, which was ill suited to the discussion of remedies for general unemployment. Even the valid case for Say's Law as a long-run proposition had never been stated correctly or with sufficient care to bring out its limited practical significance. What Keynes brought to economics was not so much a new set of tools, or even a new type of analysis, as a strong reminder of the danger of committing the fallacy of composition in deriving policy conclusions from an analysis that was wholly static and microeconomic: propositions about parts do not necessarily apply to the whole. His great substantive achievement was to convert the loose macroeconomic reasoning of neoclassical monetary theory into a testable, easily manipulatable, aggregative model of the economy that could be applied straightway to significant contemporary problems.

Now that the Keynesian revolution has been assimilated, the contrast between the *nouveau* and the *ancien régime* seems much smaller than Keynes himself could ever have anticipated. But this is the fate that time visits on all theoretical innovations. It is doubtful whether Keynes would have made as much of an impression if he had not over-sold his wares. The process of discovering where the older writers really went wrong inevitably leads to a deflation of the innovator's claims. Nevertheless, very little work in economics since 1936 has not reflected, in one way or another, the unmistakable stamp of Keynes's contribution.

NOTES FOR FURTHER READING

So much has been written on Keynesian economics that only a few choice items can be mentioned here. Every student will presumably want to read Keynes's *General Theory of Employment, Interest and Money;* a first reading might omit chapters 4, 6, 14, 16, 22, and 23, all of which digress from the main argument. A. H. Hansen, *Guide to Keynes* (1953), now available in paperback, is undoubtedly the most useful single book to have on hand while studying Keynes. R. F. Harrod, *The Life of John Maynard Keynes* (1951) creates a vivid if somewhat idolatrous portrait; a book as fascinating for the general reader as it is for economists.

On the conflict between the Keynesian and the neoclassical theory of employment see J. R. Hicks, "Mr. Keynes and the 'Classics'" *Ecom,* 1937, reprinted in *Readings in Income Distribution;* D. H. Robertson, "A Survey of Modern Monetary Controversy," *MS,* 1938, reprinted in *Readings in Business Cycle Theory,* ed. G. Haberler (1944); and Hansen, *Guide,* chap. 7. G. Haberler, "*The General Theory,*" and W. Leontief, "Keynes and the 'Classicists,'" in *The New Economics,* ed. S. E. Harris (1944), contain acute comments on the nature of "classical" economics. The most recent discussion of the problem is by Patinkin in *Money, Interest, and Prices,* chap. 14 and Note K. See also the very useful review by W. L. Smith, "A Graphical Exposition of the Complete Keynesian System," *SEJ,* October, 1956.

How accurate was Keynes's indictment of received doctrine? Strangely enough, this question has not yet been systematically answered. But see Hutchison, *Review of Economic Doctrines,* chap. 24; Hansen, *Guide,* chap. 1; J. R. Schlesinger, "After Twenty Years: The General Theory," *QJE,* November, 1956; K. Hancock, "Unemployment and the Economists in the 1920s," *Ec,* November, 1960. A. Paquet, *Le conflit historique entre la loi des débouchés et le principe de la demande effective* (1953), is full of interesting material bearing on this issue. The reviews of Pigou's *Theory of Unemployment* (1933) provide interesting reading in the light of Keynes's attack on the book: see R. F. Harrod,

EJ, March, 1934; R. G. Hawtrey, *Ec*, May, 1934; and P. M. Sweezy, *JPE*, December, 1934.

On the pre-Keynesian history of "The Compensatory Theory of Public Works Expenditures" in England and America see the article by C. J. Anderson, *JPE*, September, 1945. The significance of the concept of the multiplier, as a quantitative relationship between a net increase in spending and the consequent expansion of income, seems not to have been clearly grasped until Kahn's famous article in *EJ*, 1931: see A. L. Wright, "The Genesis of the Multiplier Theory," *OEP*, June, 1956. Writers who are sometimes regarded as precursors of Keynes, such as Hobson or Foster and Catchings, prove upon examination to be forerunners, not of Keynes, but of modern growth economics. See D. J. Coppock, "A Reconsideration of Hobson's Theory of Unemployment," *MS*, January, 1953, and A. H. Gleason, "Foster and Catchings: A Reappraisal," *JPE*, April, 1959. For a discussion of a writer who synthesized saving-investment analysis with ideas rooted in the quantity theory of money almost a decade before *The General Theory* see W. Fellner, "The Robertsonian Revolution," *AER*, June, 1952.

The twentieth anniversary of the publication of Keynes's opus gave rise to a paper on "What Is Surviving?" by W. Fellner, *AER*, May, 1957, with its useful distinction between "cyclical Keynesianism," "stagnationist Keynesianism," and "fundamental-theoretical Keynesianism," the first two being self-explanatory and the latter denoting a theoretical position that denies the existence of the Pigou Effect. It is the first, Fellner concludes, that alone has survived. On "fundamental-theoretical Keynesianism" see the recent exchange between J. R. Hicks, "A Rehabilitation of 'Classical' Economics?" *EJ*, June, 1957, and D. Patinkin, "Keynesian Economics Rehabilitated: A Rejoinder to Professor Hicks," *EJ*, September, 1959. See also the acute appraisal of H. G. Johnson, "The *General Theory* after Twenty-five Years," *AER*, May, 1961.

Chapter 16

A METHODOLOGICAL
POSTSCRIPT

WHAT DO economists know? How much does economics explain? What are the principles upon which economic theories have been accepted or rejected? What features have characterized endurable economic ideas? These are some of the questions posed in the Introduction to this book. In one way or another they have all been answered in the course of the argument. But they deserve separate comment now that our review of the evolution of economic theory has been brought down to the present.

Economic theory, since the days of Adam Smith, has stood for a mating of a priori assumptions and empirical generalizations in the production of "theories" or hypotheses that yield predictions about events in the real world. However much the assumptions have involved nonobservable variables, the deductions have been ultimately related to observable variables because economists have always wanted to "explain" in the sense of predict, economic phenomena as they actually occur. In other words, economists have always regarded the core of their subject as a "science," in the modern sense of the word. Their goal was to produce accurate and interesting predictions that were, in principle at least, capable of being empirically verified. In practice, they may have lost sight of these considerations, but no economist writing on methodology has ever denied the well-known criterion of verifiability. Such writers as Cairnes, Sidgwick, Jevons, Marshall, Böhm-Bawerk, Pareto, Harrod, and Robbins frequently emphasized other matters, but nothing they wrote would suggest outright denial of the prediction-producing purpose of economics and the necessity ultimately to compare every prediction with experience.

The difficulty, however, is that the criterion of verifiability can be interpreted with different degrees of stringency. If predictions are not contradicted by events, the theory yielding these predictions is accepted with a degree of confidence varying uniquely with the magnitude of the supporting evidence. But what if it is contradicted? If no alternative "simple" and "fruitful" hypothesis "explaining" the same events is available, frequent contradiction will be demanded. But what degree of frequency will prove persuasive? Economists abhor a theoretical vacuum as much as nature abhors a physical one, and in economics, as in the other sciences, it is true that theories are overthrown by better theories, never merely by contradictory facts. But, since opportunities for crucial controlled experiments to verify theories do not appear very often in the social sciences, economists are bound to be more demanding of falsifying evidence than are physicists. In the nature of the case, it is more difficult to weed out poor theory in economics. Hence, economists are frequently forced to resort to indirect methods of testing hypotheses, such as examining the assumptions for their degree of approximation to reality or testing the implications of the theory for phenomena other than those regarded as directly relevant to the hypothesis. This opens the door to the easy criticism that economics is a failure because its assumptions—such as consistent preference ordering, profit maximization at equal risk levels, and the like—do not conform to reality. Unfortunately, scientific methodology offers no rules for the appropriate simplification of reality for purposes of constructing fundamental assumptions other than the verifiable predictions that can be deduced from them. If economics could conclusively verify its theorems, no more would be heard about the lack of realism of its assumptions. In the meantime, economists will have to live with this kind of criticism and to meet it on its own ground. The knowledge that every natural science is full of untestable fundamental assumptions and that there is, after all, no such thing as a "realistic" assumption is always of some comfort.

It has been claimed that experience has verified the predictions of orthodox price theory. The evidence, it is said, is difficult to present because it is embedded in a host of empirical monographs concerned with questions other than the validation of basic price theory. Be that as it may, it would seem that most economists who have had doubts about the value of received doctrines have stilled these doubts, not by searching for tangible evidence of the predictive power of economic theory, but by reading the substantive contributions of the leading critics of orthodox analysis. Bad theory is still better than no theory at all.

The presence of "disturbing" influences surrounding every economic event, inhibiting the possibility of conducting "crucial" experiments, makes for further and more serious differences between a social science such as economics and a natural science such as physics. Many economic phenomena have not yet lent themselves to systematic theorizing, and yet economists do not wish to remain silent because of some methodological fiat that real science should consist only of verifiable theorems. A "theory" is not to be condemned merely because it is as yet untestable; not even if it is so framed as to preclude testing, provided it draws attention to a significant problem and provides a framework for its discussion from which a testable implication may some day emerge. It cannot be denied that many so-called "theories" in economics have no substantive content and serve merely as filing systems for organizing empirical information. To demand the removal of all heuristic postulates and theorems in the desire to press the principle of verifiability to the limit is to proscribe further research in many branches of economics. It is perfectly true that economists have often deceived themselves—and their readers—by engaging in what Leontief once called "implicit theorizing," presenting tautologies in the guise of substantive contributions to economic knowledge. But the remedy for this practice is clarification of purpose, not radical and possibly premature surgery.

Furthermore, the line between tautologies and verifiable propositions is not always easy to draw. A "theory" that is obstensibly a mere collection of deductions from "convenient" assumptions and that is so framed as to be nonverifiable under any conceivable circumstance may be reinterpretable as a verifiable proposition. After a hundred years of discussion, economists are still not quite agreed as to whether the Malthusian theory of population is nothing but a very complicated tautology, so stated as to "explain" any and all demographic events, or a verifiable prediction about per capita income in the event of population growth. Whatever Malthus' own intention, the theory can be so stated as to meet the criterion of verifiability. The concept of a negatively inclined demand curve in conjunction with an inclusive *ceteris paribus* clause is a nonoperational concept because, if quantity and price are both observed to decline together in the absence of changes in other prices, incomes, and expectations, it is always possible to save the original proposition by the contention that tastes have changed. But the concept can be rendered verifiable if we hypothesize that tastes are stable over a relevant period of time or change in a predictable fashion. The assumption of stable tastes is a genuine empirical hypothesis, and, in one sense, all work on statistical demand curves has been concerned with testing this hypothesis.

The same comments apply to the supply side. The notion of a

production function—the spectrum of all known techniques of production—is by itself a metaphysical concept. Businessmen have not experienced all known techniques, and the cost of obtaining more experience with techniques already known to others is not negligible; for the firm, the vital difference is not between known and unknown techniques but between tried and untried methods. Nevertheless, economists have found it convenient to put all available technological knowledge in one box called a "production function" and all advances in technique in another box called "innovations." But again, the concept of a production function can be given an operational interpretation if we hypothesize that production functions are stable. This may well be very difficult to verify in practice, but in principle there is no reason why it could not be verified. And so the two fundamental propositions of neoclassical price theory, to wit, positive excess demand leads to a rise in price, and an excess of price over cost leads to a rise in output, are both capable of being falsified, despite the fact that they have frequently been laid down as immutable laws of nature.

To drive these comments home, let the reader ask himself whether the following familiar propositions—the list is merely suggestive—constitute verifiable or heuristic statements; if the former, whether they are verifiable in principle or in practice and, if the latter, whether and in what sense they represent fruitful points of analytical departure.

1. A specific tax on an article will raise its price by less than the tax if the elasticity of demand is greater than zero and the elasticity of supply is less than infinity.

2. The elasticity of demand for a commodity is governed by the degree of substitutability of that commodity in consumption.

3. The impact effect of a rise of wages in a competitive industry, everything else being the same, is to reduce employment.

4. In the absence of technical change, a rise in the capital-labor ratio results in diminishing returns to capital.

5. An innovation is any change in technique that reduces input requirements per unit of given output.

6. An "industry" is a group of firms whose products are perfect or near-perfect substitutes for one another.

7. Perfect competition is incompatible with increasing returns to scale.

8. Profit maximization is a plausible assumption because the competitive race insures that only profit maximizers survive.

9. An equal rise in government expenditures and receipts will

raise national income by the amount of that rise if the community's marginal propensity to consume is positive.

10. Inflations are either demand-pull or cost-push in origin.

Even if agreement could be obtained on how to test the *validity* of economic theories, we would still have to assess their *significance*. This introduces the problem of normative, as distinct from positive, economics. After a series of attacks on utilitarian welfare economics, a "new" welfare economics was erected in the 1930's by eschewing the bugbear of traditional welfare economics, interpersonal comparisons of utility. "Scientific" welfare economics has lately come in for its share of destructive criticism, and some economists have echoed once again the old Seniorian cry that economics should be wholly "positive" in character. But, whatever we may think of modern welfare economics, there can be no doubt that the desire to evaluate the performance of economic systems has been the great driving force behind the development of economic thought; certainly it has been the source of inspiration of almost every great economist.

Indeed, it would be difficult to imagine what economics would be like if we succeeded in eliminating all vestiges of welfare economics. We should, of course, never be able to discuss *efficient* allocation of scarce means among competing ends, for the question of efficiency cannot even be raised without a standard of evaluation. Even means and ends cannot be distinguished without specific value premises. Are productive resources means or ends? Why strive to maximize output if work is pleasurable and uncultivated land has a value in its own right? The separation of means and ends is more than an expository device. By presenting the price system as a neutral mechanism for allocating some things called "means" among other things called "ends," economics is inevitably biased to minimize the personal non-measurable forces acting on the market. In other words, it is constantly engaged in making the fundamental value judgment that only certain types of individual preferences are to count. We all know, of course, why economics has confined its attention to those motives for action that can be evaluated with "the measuring rod of money," but the fact remains that value judgments are involved at the very foundation of the procedure. Moreover, neutrality of means, desirability and rationality of free individual choice, neglect of personal interaction, not only are normative assumptions commonly made in welfare economics but are also necessary to give significance to the theorems of positive economics. For predictive purposes it may be sufficient to say that people act *as if* they maximized utility. For normative purposes, however, we have to assume that they ought to do so or else we have to know in fact that they do so. Thus, introspection must be admitted as a method of research in welfare economics although it has no place in positive economics.

Casting a backward glance at the history of economics in the light of these comments, we can hardly fail to notice how often economists have violated their own and later methodological prescriptions. The classical economists emphasized the fact that the conclusions of economics rest ultimately on postulates derived from experience and introspection. Methodological disputes in the classical period took the form of disagreement over the significance and sufficiency of the underlying assumptions on which the whole deductive structure was built. Despite J. S. Mill's pronouncement that "we cannot too carefully endeavour to verify our theory, by comparing . . . the results which it would have led us to predict, with the most trustworthy accounts we can obtain of those which have actually been realized," no real effort was made to test classical doctrines against the body of statistical material that had been accumulated by the middle of the nineteenth century. The debatable issues in Ricardian economics all hinged on the relative weight of forces making for historically diminishing and increasing returns in the production of wage goods. This question was capable of being resolved along empirical lines, given the fact that some information on money wages and the composition of working-class budgets had been made available by the 1840's and that the concept of a price index had passed by this time into general currency. Yet, despite the knowledge that population was not "pressing" upon the food supply, that "agricultural improvements" were winning the race against numbers, that the rise of productivity in agriculture was steadily reducing the real cost of producing wage goods, the classical writers clung to the belief in the imminent danger of natural-resource scarcities.

The standard defense was to attribute every contradiction to the strength of "counteracting tendencies." In effect, the classical economists treated certain variables that entered into their analysis as exogenously determined, such as the rate of technical improvement in agriculture, the disposition of the working class to practice family limitation, and the supply of entrepreneurship. But, instead of confessing their ignorance about the exogenous variables, they advanced bold generalizations about their probable variations through time. For the most part, they did not raise the question whether the exogenous variables were really independently determined constants. In addition, they failed to inquire whether the phenomena labeled "counteracting tendencies" entered as additional parameters to the original equations of the model or whether they in fact altered the structure of the equations themselves. It was because the motives for family limitation were not in fact independent of the conditions of the race between population and "subsistence" that the Malthusian theory of population predicted so poorly. It was because Ricardian economics failed to deal with the problems of technical change in agriculture—falling back upon the belief, denied by historical experience, that English landlords were not "improvers"—that the Corn Laws did not entail the harmful effects that Ricardo had predicted. Had the classical economists acted on Mill's urging to "carefully endeavour to verify our theory," such weaknesses in the structure would have come to light and led to analytical improvements. As it was, the absence of any alternative theory to that of Ricardo, of equal scope and practical significance, discouraged revisions and promoted a defensive methodological attitude.

The model of perfect competition that evolved after the marginal breakthrough of the 1870's owed much to the older welfare propositions of the loosely stated "invisible hand" sort. By limiting the scope of the analysis, however, greater rigor in model construction became possible. The argument was typically related to a few continuous variables and confined to explaining the direction of small changes in these variables. All the growth-producing factors, such as dynamic expansion of wants, population growth, technical change, even "time" itself, were placed in the pound of *ceteris paribus.* The system of endogenous variables was then shown to have a unique steady-state solution. The problem of the existence of equilibrium was passed over by the method of comparative statics, which begins with an equilibrium situation and then traces out the adjustment process to a new stable equilibrium when the value of one or more of the parameters is altered. Indeterminacy was eliminated by excluding all interdependence among utility and production functions, and stability was insured by restricting the functions as to shape and by abstracting from ignorance and uncertainty. The entire procedure was justified by the short-run purpose of the analysis, although this did not prevent excursions into welfare economics involving long-run considerations.

The endogenous variables manipulated in neoclassical models were frequently incapable of being observed, even in principle. But this was perfectly defensible in view of the heuristic function of "as if" theorizing. Unfortunately most of the theorems that emerged from the analysis likewise failed to be empirically meaningful. For one thing, these were nonstochastic models, which are notoriously useless for predictive purposes; that is, the relationships among the variables were deemed to be exact and the parameters did not contain terms for random errors. Furthermore, the microeconomic character of the analysis made testing difficult in view of the fact that most available statistical data were of an aggregative nature: the problem of deducing macronomic theorems from microeconomic propositions was not faced until Keynes's work showed that there was a problem. In addition, the rules for legitimately treating certain variables as exogenous—that they be independent of the endogenous variables in the model, or related to them in an undirectional manner, and that they be independent of each other—were constantly violated. It is obvious that tastes, population, and technology not only affect and are affected by the typical endogenous variables of neoclassical models but in turn affect each other.

The standard excuse for treating variables as exogenous that clearly are not exogenous is analytical tractability and expository convenience. For a whole range of practical problems it is in fact a very good excuse. But the temptation to read more significance into the analysis than is inherent in the procedure is irresistible, and most neoclassical writers succumbed to it. Ambitious propositions about the desirability of perfect competition were laid down with insufficient scruple. Of course, it was recognized that competition was a regulatory device of limited applicability. Important differences between private and social costs and benefits, monopoly through increasing returns to scale, or an ethically undesirable distribution of income gave scope to government action. But these qualifications were grafted upon, rather than incorporated within, the competitive model. Furthermore, the growth-producing factors that were now regarded as noneconomic in character ceased to receive systematic analysis. Having marked the boundaries of economics, neoclassical writers openly confessed noncompetence outside that boundary and were satisfied to throw out a few common-sense conclusions and occasionally a suggestive insight. It takes no effort of historical perspective to realize that the second half of the nineteenth century indeed invited a complacent attitude to economic growth: it is only natural that an author like Marshall should think that growth would take care of itself, provided that "free" competition, surrounded by supporting state controls, would furnish an appropriate sociopolitical environment. Nevertheless, the result was to leave economics without a theory of growth or development other than the discouraging one that the long-period evolution of an economy depends largely on the long-neglected noneconomic factors.

Contemporary economics still lacks a systematic demographic theory, a satisfactory theory of innovations, or a rigorous explanation of the source and nature of entrepreneurial supply. It may well be that the neoclassical distinction between economic and noneconomic factors is itself a hindrance in the study of long-run development. It may not be feasible to isolate the process of economic growth, as that phrase has come to be understood, from the general context of social evolution. And yet the weight of tradition is such that economics has resisted and may well continue to resist the blurring of a distinction that has long given economics a status as a separate field of study.

SUGGESTIONS FOR FURTHER READING

Reading in methodology should begin with J. N. Keynes's masterly volume, *The Scope and Method of Political Economy* (1891). This book not only touches upon all the traditional issues of *Methodenstreit* in economics but faithfully reflects the methodological attitude of leading neoclassical writers. In more recent times, the *locus classicus* from which all discussion begins is L. Robbins, *An Essay on the Nature and Significance of Economic Science* (1932). But, whereas J. N. Keynes sought to rationalize existing practice, Robbins appealed to the profession to follow new ones: economics was to be freed from value judgments. It is not clear whether Robbins really wanted economists to abandon welfare economics altogether or whether he meant merely forcefully to separate "positive" from "normative" economics so as to deny scientific status to the latter. Nor is it clear, even after repeated reading, whether he really meant to commit himself to *radical apriorism,* despite the fact that many passages in the book invite that interpretation.

Radical apriorism holds that economic theory is simply a system of pure deductions from a series of assumptions not themselves open to empirical verification or general appeal to objective experience. In opposition to this point of view is *ultra-empiricism,* which refuses to admit any postulates that cannot be independently verified; ultra-empiricism, in other words, asks us to begin with facts, not assumptions. But even an apriorist may agree that the predicted results deduced from assumptions, if not the fundamental assumptions themselves, should be subject to empirical testing. And few ultra-empiricists, no matter how much they insist that all scientifically meaningful statements must be conceivably falsifiable by observation, go so far as to deny any role whatever to tautology in scientific theorizing. The controversy is over matters of emphasis, and economists since the days of J. S. Mill have always occupied the middle ground between extreme apriorism and empiricism.

In Robbins' book the question of how economic propositions are to be verified is passed over all too lightly. The merit of introducing the verifiability criterion of logical positivism into economic discussion, albeit in an extreme form, belongs to T. W. Hutchison, *The Significance and Basic Postulates of Economic Theory* (1938). Hutchison, like Robbins, permits his argument **to** develop by innuendo and implication. He seems at times to suggest that economics should be purged of all tautologies and that the completion of this task would leave little standing. But a sympathetic reading of the book might produce a more charitable interpretation: see F. Machlup, "The Problem of Verification in Economics," *SEJ*, July, 1955, and T. W. Hutchison, "Professor Machlup on Verification in Economics," *SEJ*, April, 1956. M. Friedman, "The Methodology of Positive Economics," *Essays in Positive Economics* (1953), argues that much criticism of economic theory has missed the target by scrutinizing assumptions instead of testing implications; the validity of economic theory is to be tested, not by the descriptive "realism" of its assumptions, but by the accuracy of its predictions with respect to the phenomena with which it is concerned. Friedman's position is unassailable until it is realized that he is insisting on empirical testing of predictions as the *sole* criterion of validity; he seems to be saying that it makes no difference whatever to what extent the assumptions falsify reality. This is indeed a dubious thesis and one that he himself qualifies in a section of the article entitled "The Use of Assumptions as an Indirect Test of a Theory." T. Koopman, "The Construction of Economic Knowledge," *Three Essays on the State of Economic Science* (1957), suggests that, in view of the difficulty of testing implications in economic theory, "realism" of assumptions—conformity to observed behavior—is a desirable check on the validity of theory. See also E. Rotwein, "On 'The Methodology of Positive Economics,'" *QJE*, November, 1959.

D. F. Gordon clarifies the meaning of "Operational Propositions in Economic Theory," *JPE*, April, 1955. K. Klappholz and J. Agassi, "Methodological Prescriptions in Economics," *Ec*, February, 1959, attack *the* "methodological fallacy," the notion that the progress of economics can be hastened by laying down methodological rules for the pursuit of economic research. They also pass in review a recent book by S. Schoeffler, *The Failures of Economics: A Diagnostic Study* (1955), which takes the somewhat novel position that economics by its very nature is not and never can be a science. For an illuminating discussion of neoclassical methodology see J. Buttrick, "Towards a Theory of Economic Growth: The Neoclassical Contribution," in *Theories of Economic Growth*, ed. B. F. Hoselitz *et al.* (1960). The student who needs to be provoked into thinking deeply about the value of traditional economic theory should immerse himself in the writings of the American Institutionalist School. Embracing such diverse writers as Veblen, Mitchell, Commons, J. M. Clark, Tugwell, and Means, the movement was united alone in the negation of orthodox economic theory and the view that the economic system cannot be fruitfully analyzed in terms of the quasi-mechanistic terminology of equilibrium theory. For a thorough but pretentious study of the leading Institutionalists see A. G. Gruchy, *American Economic Thought* (1947). On Veblen in particular see W. C. Mitchell, Introduction to *What Veblen Taught: Selected Writings* (1936), reprinted in *DET*, and the uneven *Thorstein Veblen: A Critical Reappraisal*, ed. D. F. Dowd (1958). See also K. E. Boulding, "A New Look at Institutionalism," *AER*, May, 1957, with some very revealing comments by the discussants.

INDEX OF NAMES

INDEX OF SUBJECTS

This book has been set on the Linotype in 10 and 12 point Garamond #3, leaded 1 point. Chapter numbers and titles are in 18 point Spartan Medium. The size of the type page is 27 by 46½ picas.